MW01014153

In the Court of King Crimson

Panegyric Publishing, Littlecote House, Lower Road, Hardwick, Buckinghamshire

First published by Helter Skelter in 2001

Revised and expanded edition published by Panegyric, 2019

A catalogue record for this book is available from the British Library ISBN 9781916153004

Copyediting and proofreading by RefineCatch Limited, www.refinecatch.com
Design and typesetting by www.ianrossdesigner.com

Printed and bound in Great Britain by Clays Ltd, Elcograf S.p.A.

Sid Smith

In the Court of King Crimson

An Observation over Fifty Years

If a man does not keep pace with his companions,
perhaps it is because he hears a different drum.
Let him step to the music which he hears,
however measured or far away.
Henry David Thoreau

This book is dedicated to my sister Lesley and my wife Debra,
the two women in my life without whom I doubt I'd be able to tie my shoelaces.

Contents

Acknowledgements

I'd like to Thank Dept:
My thanks first and foremost go to my publisher, Declan Colgan, whose immersive reservoir of patience I was in danger of drinking dry over the years since he asked me for a revised edition of this book. The kindness and support both he and Denice have shown me during this time has been remarkable and I cannot thank them enough. He won't thank me for saying this, and will probably want it taken out, but without Declan's tireless advocacy, care and attention on behalf of King Crimson, the numerous boxed sets, vinyl editions and related items would simply not have been possible. Every King Crimson fan on the planet owes him a massive debt to go alongside the massive debt they've probably incurred having bought all the stuff he's manufactured over the years.

Back in the '90s, I met John Kimber at the *Epitaph* playback. It was like we'd known each other all our lives. When I was writing the first edition of the King Crimson biography, on my many visits to London, Kimber would put me up in his house in leafy Highgate. I doubt I could ever have finished the book back then without his physical and, at times, financial support. His words of encouragement and insight, then and in the twenty-first century, have been immensely helpful. Over the past few years I'd attempted to get the revised edition out but in my fits of indolence, attacks of imposter syndrome and (too) numerous crises of confidence, Kimber gently talked me back off the ledge and, without blowing smoke up my arse, managed to persuade me that there was some value in doing what I do.

A huge debt of gratitude to Sean Hewitt. For getting on for nearly 20 years I've had a near-weekly telephone conversation with Sean, usually on a Saturday afternoon. I've frequently nearly blacked out from laughing so much during these calls. I can honestly say that, every time I've come off that phone, my understanding of the world has been improved. Without Sean's wit and insight on music, and much else besides, I'd be a poorer person. Sean's ability to be able to quote verbatim something somebody once said 40 years ago frequently leaves me speechless in admiration. In addition to being something of a raconteur, and a sweary one at that, he's also a writer of admirable clarity so it made sense to ask Sean to take on the unenviable task of turning my meagre sentences into something that's readable, illuminating and even entertaining every now and then. I really can't thank him enough. It goes without saying any mistakes in this book are mine and mine alone.

I'd also like to thank the good people at DGM; namely David Singleton for his boundless enthusiasm, vision and belief; Alex 'Stormy' Mundy whose dogged exploration of the tape archive has unearthed some real gems of previously hidden Crimhistory - without his persistence the Crimverse would be a whole lot poorer and Hugh O'Donnell for his patience when dealing with my tardy responses to his requests for KCCC copy or the essays for the big boxed sets over the years. Alex and Hugh have always been kindness itself when responding to my frequent requests for help and for this I'm grateful.

In the 2001 edition of the book, I thanked "all the Crims past, present and future". While that remains the case I'd like to give especial thanks to the following: Ian McDonald for support and the openness with which he shared his knowledge, insights, and hospitality in 2012 in New York; John Wetton for the many, many hours he gave to me on the blower and in person. It was an honour and a privilege to know him; Ian Wallace, who with his wife, Margie, used to ring me from Nashville, radiating warmth, wisdom, and goodwill; Trey Gunn and Pat Mastelotto have been exceptionally generous with their time since 1998. I'd also like to put on record the many kindnesses Jakko Jakszyk has shown me since we met back in 1999 and take some satisfaction at the ways in which our chess games turned out in the end.

Finally, I'm indebted to Robert Fripp for his candour, assistance, encouragement, and gentle and sometimes not so gentle prodding. Most of all I want to thank him for helping to bring into being some of the most extraordinary music that has moved me in ways that I can't really put into words.

When the original edition of the KC biography was published in 2001, I thanked lots of other folks for their varying degrees of advice and information. Since 2001 as I've worked on different things of a Crimson hue, there are many others who've made similar heroic efforts to provide me with information, gossip, tidbits and all manner of nerdy facts. Just as with the first edition of the book, not everything they contributed will have made these pages but I'm incredibly grateful for their efforts and interest in my work.

In no particular order, thank you to:

R. Chris Murphy, Trevor Lever, Scott Steele, Michael Peters, Darren Woolsey, Keith Tippett, Tony Gassett, Neil Talbot, Tony Maddern, Antoine Caron, Travis Hartnet, Steve Hackett, Mike Champagne, Campbell Laird, Ian Parry, Reed Urie, Dave Salt, Rob Ayling, Sean Body, Jonathan Brainin, Andrew Keeling, John Smallwood, Chris Wilson, Bill Munyon, Tobin Buttram, John Bungey, Jason Birnie, Ian Bond,

Biff Blumfumgagnge, Andy Leff, Steven Wilson, Bill Munyon, Adrian Holmes, Bill MacCormick, Robert Wyatt, Rhett Davies, David Bottrill, Machine, Thomas Olsson, Markus Reuter, Brent Keefe, Steve Dinsdale, Graham Field, Mike Barnes, David Enthoven, John Gaydon, Willie Christie, Tim Young, Dave Stewart, Andy Zax, Tony Lowe, Neil Murray, Theo Travis, Brian Godding, Roy Babbington, Wilf Gibson, Patricia Fripp, Chris Mills, James Wills, Andrew Williams, Julie Tippetts, Robert Frazza, Bryan Helm, Markus Reuter, Al Okada, John Stevens, Jacob Herringman, David Cunningham, Judy Dyble, John Relph, Toby Howard, Brian Thompson, John Young, Toby Howard, Dan Kirkdorffer, Tom Redmond, David Symes, Peter Giles, Charlotte Bates, Phil Miller, Tony Gebelle, Paddy Spinks, Barrie Sillars, Andrew Burke, Chris Taberham, Andy Howarth, Dik Fraser, Chris Smith, Paul David, Maurizio Comandini, Rick Whitehurst, Rob Murphy, Bruce Pilato, Steve Sthole, Kade Graves, Jon Green, Martin Morris, Chris Burrows, Gered Mankowitz, Gary Weisel, Tim Bowness, Yuka Fuji, Hikaru Sasaki, Pete Woods, PJ Crook, Richard Maughan, Alan Cowdery, Robin Miller, Stan Lee, Tino Licinio, Stephanie Poe McCook, Jonathan Dann, Mike Dickson, Gert-Jan Blom, Diana Maio, Mark Newstrom, George Chkiantz, Chris Raven, Mark Charig, Jeffery Duke Jr, Nick Evans, Richard Chadwick, Julie O'Hanlon, Fred Challenor, David Jackson, Patrick Schuleit, Jeff Fayman, Neil Sadler, Remco Helbers, Matt Seattle, Dave Gregory, Jerry Ewing, Peter Grenader, Alessandro Pizzin, Jo Kendall, Paul Richards, Barry Andrews, Richard Williams, Hernan Nunez, and anyone else who I've inadvertently omitted.

All quotes come from interviews I've conducted unless otherwise indicated.

Preface

I first saw King Crimson on 8 December 1972 at Newcastle Odeon. The Islands-era band had been to Newcastle City Hall twice before, but in May 1971 they simply weren't on my radar. By their second appearance in October that year they very much were but, for reasons I now cannot understand, I missed out on going to see them.

When *Earthbound* was released in the summer of 1972, I was a huge fan, eagerly soaking up every note the band recorded in a non-chronological sequence. I didn't have all the albums so sometimes had to walk a couple of miles to a pal's house just to hear *The Devil's Triangle* or *Prince Rupert's Lament*. Because Earthbound was so cheap, released on Island's budget label, HELP (a privileged status it shared with ELP's *Pictures At An Exhibition*), everyone had a copy. Despite the rough sound quality, I recall lots of my friends loving the record. Then came the news that there was a new King Crimson and that they were going to be touring.

There was no way I was going to miss out this time around. A couple of us wondered if the new Crimson would be performing Peoria, a number we liked so much we'd perform Boz's scatting with backing a cappella in unison to bemused and probably deeply irritated passers-by.

It's no exaggeration to say that this concert changed my life. That phrase is often bandied about. You'll read or hear impassioned testimonials about how this song or that album was a life-changing experience. Often it's just a rush of well-meaning enthusiasm and one we can all empathise with. But the evidence as to exactly how the encounter brought about a truly significant change can be very hard to quantify.

In my case, it's pretty easy to demonstrate the impact this concert had upon me. First of all, if I hadn't gone to see King Crimson and instead handed over my 60p at the Mayfair Ballroom to see The Velvet Underground (also in town that night), it's very likely you wouldn't be reading this book and I wouldn't have had a small professional relationship with King Crimson since 1997.

Less obviously perhaps, my adolescent brain wouldn't have been scrambled by the huge amounts of non-rock data that flew directly off the stage at substantial velocity and volume directly into my long-haired head. This was where the real change occurred. King Crimson's music opened up my ears to all sorts of other possibilities. You might think Jamie Muir's theatrical presence would have distracted from the music. In fact, it had the opposite effect, focusing attention, or mine at least, on the drama within the playing. One moment there was a bone-crunching rock riff, then a beguiling pastoral interlude, then a bitter-sweet song, then a collection of strange unfamiliar musical shapes and textural angularities as perplexing as they were intriguing. Simply put, I'd not seen a band that played anything remotely like this before.

In 1972, in the run-up to the Crimson gig, I'd clocked up many concert hours with Mountain, Jethro Tull, Rory Gallagher, Captain Beefheart, John Mayall supported by Matching Mole, Stone The Crows, Deep Purple, Curved Air, Mott The Hoople, Ten Years After, Roxy Music, Free, Groundhogs and two consecutive shows by Led Zeppelin. You could argue that Matching Mole's discursive jazz-rock and Roxy Music's idiosyncratic refraction of post-war pop culture are the most obvious exceptions to what looks like a pretty steady, albeit classic, diet of blues-based rock. However, as much as I loved all of those bands, King Crimson's gathering of eclectic strands of avant-garde sound daubs, fiery extemporisation and vibrant experimentalism opened up my head to other sounds, other approaches to what constituted music, what music might be. I didn't rationalise it like that at the time, of course, but how I know that this was what I was processing internally is because, after that King Crimson concert, nothing sounded the same again. It wasn't so much that I stopped liking those other groups but rather that their impact and influence had been significantly lessened by David Cross, Robert Fripp, John Wetton, Bill Bruford and Jamie Muir who had, in the course of an hour and a half, extended my musical horizons. The axis of my world had been tilted. Everything had changed and nothing was like it had been before.

There were still three months or so until the release of *Larks' Tongues In Aspic* in March 1973. As I waited expectantly for the album, I had only a flash memory of certain motifs and moments which I constantly replayed in my head: the terse violin figure at the head of *LTIA1*; the pounding riff and jolting cross picking section; Wetton's melancholic voice singing "We lay cards upon the table, the backs of our hands"; strange drones; disembodied voices; end-of-the-pier laughter; ominous winds; the demented slash and thrash of *LTIA2*. In keeping this "tangle of night and daylight sounds" alive and running in a constant loop, I was desperately trying to keep a hold of the heat that had been generated that night.

I've been chasing after the trail of that heat ever since, attempting to make contact with what felt like a magical force then and even now, all these years later, still holds an emotional and intellectual charge that feels utterly transformative. This book does not aim to provide an insight into the mind or motivations of Robert Fripp or indeed any of those who've been members of King Crimson. Nor is it a philosophical or musicological discourse that dissects the architecture or the meaning of the music. It will, however, tell you about the surface noise that gets produced when certain combinations of musicians bring their talent and their instruments to record on to tape or play to a crowded hall. It can't replicate that elusive heat I was talking about, but it will shine a light upon some of the interactions resulting from all these players' times in the court of King Crimson.

Sid Smith
March 2019, Whitley Bay

Moore Theatre, Seattle – 6 October 2014

The last date of any tour is always special and tonight there's a palpable sense of celebration, not only audible among the capacity crowd's whoops and throaty cheers, but also clearly visible on the faces of each member of the band as they walk out on stage.

There are plenty of reasons for fans to be happy. After an absence from the live stage of six years, the announcement in 2013 that King Crimson would be returning took everyone – including some asked to be part of the ensemble – by surprise.

This was the return nobody expected after Fripp's public declaration that his days as a touring player were behind him. But here he was with Tony Levin, Jakko Jakszyk, Mel Collins, Pat Mastelotto, Bill Rieflin and Gavin Harrison and a setlist including numbers that had not been played live in over 40 years – and, in some cases, ever.

And if the audience are enjoying it then they are not the only ones. Evidence of the band's enthusiasm is peppered throughout: the wry smiles between Fripp and Jakszyk during The ConstruKction Of Light*; Collins' thumbs-up signs to his bandmates; Levin throwing his head back and laughing out loud in response to the solos unfolding around him; indulgent grins from the entire group as they nod their heads and tap their toes while watching Harrison's virtuoso drum break during a blistering* 21st Century Schizoid Man.

That singular spotlight on one player is a rare moment within the decades-spanning playlist because this King Crimson feels like the most collectively integrated line-up since the 1960s. There is no room for a front man. Indeed the front of the stage is taken up with the three drummers whose presence extends far beyond a headline-catching gimmick into something essential to the whole enterprise. As they share out beats, grooves and percussive expression in much the same manner as Fripp's pioneering interlocking guitars concept from the 1980s, the music isn't so much played as simultaneously circulated through the body electric of all seven players.

The cheering and shouting continues long after the band have left the stage. Tucked away in a large dressing room in the bowels of the Moore Theatre, the band assemble, hot but happy. Fripp is pouring them each a glass of champagne. A toast is raised and they commit themselves to more Crimsonising in 2015.

Lobby call: Noon – 7 October 2014

Fripp, Jakszyk, Collins and Harrison are gathering outside the hotel, towing their baggage, minus Levin, whose plane leaves for New York later in the day, and Mastelotto, who is staying over for a day before returning home to Texas. Bill Rieflin arrives to say goodbye. As a Seattle resident, he's just a short car ride away from the resumption of his home life.

There are hugs and fond farewells with crew members and management. Smiles, quips and affectionate barbs. It's the lingua franca of men saying goodbye to other men, the common bond of about as intense a shared experience as it's possible to imagine.

A black cruiser van rolls into the hotel forecourt. The last load-out on American turf gets under way as a black van with mirror-tinted windows rolls into the hotel forecourt exactly on time. The jigsaw of bags and cases is precariously stacked in the too-small boot space behind the passenger seat. After a little fussing over what goes where, all climb aboard to notch up the last few miles to SeaTac.

The van's interior black leather and too-bright-chrome trimmings exudes a trashy glamour and the seating eschews the usual regimented seating in favour of an executive conversational aesthetic. Appropriately for a van trying to be too cool for its own good, the air con is set to "severe arctic blast". A shout up front to the driver asking him to turn it down gets a welcome thaw going.

"It's too warm now!" Gavin Harrison is holding court. As the mileage counter ticks ever closer to "mission accomplished", he's entertaining the troops with acid comments about industry people as he has done for the entire tour. Band and crew chuckle. Jakko makes a crack at Gav's expense – they've been doing this double act for over 30 years. Even convicted felons get time off for good behaviour. Not these two.

Jakko's intervention has everyone on board pissing themselves. Harrison dives into a mock moan tailspin. He doles it out, pained, hurt, the slings and arrows of outrageous etc. The more he moans, the more laughter circulates.

In the front seat behind the driver, his preferred and usual spot, Robert Fripp can be seen talking into his phone. He's been locked in some kind of conference for several minutes. Amid the laughter, Fripp suddenly cranes around, his stern visage considering the rowdies behind him.

"Please, sir, it wasn't me! Please, sir!" shouts Jakko, pointing wildly at Harrison. More laughter, more heads shaking from side to side. Fripp raises an eyebrow, holds up his mobile phone, presses a button and out of the tiny tinny speaker comes a Hi-NRG dance track. Then, after the introduction has sparked bemused looks, come the vocals: Robert Fripp's autotuned robotised voice singing and skipping over the beats: "Gavin is a whinging git … Gavin is a whinging git."

The whole van erupts into laughter. Actual tears in eyes for some. People doubled-up, almost falling off the pimped up black leather seats, rolling in the aisles as the van takes a tight corner. It definitely feels like the party on the last day of term.

Under the pale and wintry afternoon sun, the van rolls past the goods yards and industrial parks and their lengthening shadows. Beyond the cement fields, greenery beckons and SeaTac soon looms into view.

Check-in complete, the Crims take off to the corners of the airport counting down to the gate call. In the departure lounge various strands of the tour party are slouched in seats in varying states of ennui, with only the banter between Jakszyk and Harrison providing anything in the way of entertainment. When Jakko goes to the toilet, Gavin starts again.

"'ere, did I tell you about the time when I was looking after Jakko's flat back in the '80s when he was living in Los Angeles? I paid some of the bills on the place when he was away. When he came back he owed me a few hundred quid but he never had any money. Then, he was on Top of the Pops with Level 42. He came 'round my place and asked if he could use the phone. He rang the wardrobe department at the BBC and asked if the jacket he was wearing when he was on telly was available to buy. It was, but for something like 400 quid. 'I'll have it,' he says, even though he'd told me he couldn't afford to pay me back the money he owed me for looking after his place. And, worse, he uses my phone to make the call!"

More mock pain, more laughter from those in earshot. Gavin rides the laugh. The secret of comedy, like drumming, is timing. There's a pause as things settle down. "Mind, don't tell him I told you," and once again those around crack up.

Over the course of the past eight weeks, since they established base camp in upstate New York before the tour, there have been many very similar moments. It was perhaps a subtle barometer of how the musicians were dealing with the inevitable frustrations and difficulties of being part of a touring band. Over its history King Crimson has had more than its fair share of those issues.

What feels different here, though, is that the group members appear very relaxed and comfortable in each other's company, notwithstanding the ribbing Rieflin receives whenever he deliberates over a menu in a restaurant or requests that his room is changed upon checking into every hotel along the way.

It feels as though this group embodies the first of the King Crimson principle that accompanied the return of the group – let's enjoy what we're doing. Though that dictum referred primarily to the playing, it also applies to the different personalities and their respective interactions.

Eventually the gate is called. The queue lines up and boards. As people peel off to take their respective seats, figuring out who you're going to be sharing the next nine hours with, Fripp and Jakszyk bump into each other outside the toilets on the border between first and cattle class. The older guitarist mentions to the younger guitarist that this has been one of the most enjoyable touring experiences he's had for a very long time.

It's definitely the beginning of something new.

I

It's mid-August 1969. The apocalyptic blast of *21st Century Schizoid Man* is abruptly cut off in mid-flow as recording engineer Robin Thompson mutes the speakers. Below, in the cavernous performance area of Wessex Studios, Robert Fripp, Michael Giles, Ian McDonald, Peter Sinfield and Greg Lake stop work to welcome the arrival of artist Barry Godber, carrying a large rectangular package wrapped in brown paper.

A few weeks previously, Sinfield had commissioned his friend Godber to come up with something for the cover for King Crimson's debut album. "I used to hang around with all these painters and artists from Chelsea Art School," says Sinfield. "I'd known Barry for a couple of years … he'd been to a few rehearsals and spent a bit of time with us. I told him to see what he could come up with. I think I probably said to him that the one thing the cover had to do was stand out in record shops."

Godber tore off the brown paper and laid the painting on the floor as the band gathered around to see. Greg Lake vividly remembered the moment. "We all stood around it and it was like something out of *Treasure Island* where you're all standing around a box of jewels and treasure … this fucking face screamed up from the floor and what it said to us was *Schizoid Man* – the very track we'd been working on. It was as if there was something magic going on."

Magic and King Crimson never seemed to be far apart in 1969. Even before they'd played a proper gig in London there was an expectant buzz about the monstrous sounds emanating from the band's rehearsal room in the cellar of a café on the Fulham Palace Road. Exactly one month after their first proper rehearsal on 13 January, Decca's A&R man Hugh Mendl had been persuaded by Crimson's managers David Enthoven and John Gaydon to sample the band. Mendl, who had previously signed Giles, Giles & Fripp to Decca, brought with him Moody Blues producer Tony Clarke, with a view to having Crimson sign up to the Moody's own still-nascent Threshold label.

"We had taken various people down to see them and everybody who saw them was blown away by them apart from Muff Winwood, who was then A&R at Island," remembers Enthoven. "I'll never forget he turned to me and said 'They're a bit like the Tremeloes, aren't they?' I thought to myself 'What the fuck are you listening to?'"

While many bands were cranking up the volume as the burgeoning underground scene demanded, what distinguished King Crimson from most of its peers was their lethal combination of claw-hammer brutality and surgical precision. They were summoning up musical forces not only capable of immense subtlety but also the ability to knock punters into the ground like so many tent pegs. This impressive combination had the word-of-mouth bush telegraph working overtime.

Almost every band starting out has a wish list of hopes and dreams – getting good; getting in print; getting on John Peel; getting big; getting signed; getting an album in the Top Ten. In 1969 King Crimson got the lot. Even seen from fifty years later, the rapidity of their progress remains breathtaking.

In April they played their first London gig at The Speakeasy to great acclaim. In May they recorded a session for John Peel. That same month, Jimi Hendrix saw them play at another London watering hole, Revolution. Shaking Fripp's hand, Hendrix declared excitedly to anyone who would listen that Crimson were the best group in the world. With that endorsement still ringing in their ears, in June they sat down at Morgan Studios with best-selling producer Tony Clarke to start recording their first album.

Counter-culture house magazine *International Times* interviewed the group and it was evident that the mood in the Crimson camp was (understandably) upbeat. Fripp talked about recording a double album with one side per track, while Sinfield wanted to ensure that music and album cover comprised a total package.

They'd gone from zeroes to would-be heroes with an audacious masterplan to be the best band in the world, a growing reputation for killer concerts and an album in the works. Not bad going in just six months.

Yet the 12–18 June sessions didn't go quite as smoothly as expected. Something about the sound at Morgan wasn't working for them. As they swapped to the more spacious Wessex Studios, the band prepared for the gig that would seriously accelerate an already fast-track career – supporting the Rolling Stones at Hyde Park on 5 July.

David Enthoven and John Gaydon immediately understood how important it was for King Crimson to be on that bill. "It was going to be a huge gathering of people and a great opportunity for the band to play to that kind of crowd … and we were trying every means possible to bribe and corrupt dear Pete Jenner from Blackhill Enterprises who was organising the whole thing. I was happy to give him quite a lot of money. They wouldn't take the money but they put us on the bill because of the sheer brazenness of us! I would've done anything to get on that bill."

King Crimson stepped on to the Hyde Park stage before an estimated audience of 650,000 – a nerve-racking experience, as Greg Lake vividly remembered. "I'd never seen that many people in my life for any reason. I mean, you'd need a war to see that many people …! They weren't there to see me or King Crimson, they were there to see the Rolling Stones, so in a way it wasn't that bad … All of a sudden we play *Schizoid Man* at blinding speed and unbearable intensity. Suddenly everyone starts to take notice and stand up. Then we started playing the beautiful stuff like *The Court Of The Crimson King* and *Epitaph*. Well, by then it was game, set and match. It worked very well. I realised it was a turning point the moment I walked off stage because you can't go down that well at an event that big and it not be significant."

Returning to Wessex Studios on 7 July, Crimson and Tony Clarke had a second attempt to record the album. Almost immediately more doubts about the results resurfaced. Maybe it wasn't the studio that was the problem. Maybe it was the producer? Clarke's preferred way of working – slowly building up big backing tracks as he'd done with the Moody Blues – wasn't suiting Crimson's dash for dynamics and cocky live-take bravura. Drummer Michael Giles felt Clarke was trying to tame Crimson's energies and shape the band into something they were not. Lake agrees. "The general sense we had was that his main motivation was to make us another version of the Moody Blues and we didn't want that."

On 16 July, they decided to walk away from Clarke and the prospect of a Threshold release that came with him. It seems almost inconceivable that a young band who'd only been together just over six months would take this kind of risk. Another example of Crimson's so-called "Good Fairy" that they talked about, or testosterone-fuelled balls of steel?

Greg Lake: "You've got to remember that all the people in King Crimson were very strong personalities. They were very intelligent, very good musicians and all opinionated – not in a nasty way but everyone was passionate about what they were doing. There wasn't anyone along for the ride. All very dedicated and all of us out to change the world in one way or another. The fact of the matter is that when it came to music making and the music *we* were making, really Tony didn't know enough about it. We felt that we could make a better job of producing the record because we knew more about it than he did."

In order to finance the self-produced album, Enthoven and Gaydon swung a deal with the Thompson family who owned Wessex Studios that guaranteed the £15,000 recording costs. To do this, Enthoven remortgaged his house in Petersham Place and a further loan of £4.5k was taken out from Barclays Bank in the Gloucester Road. "A bit of a punt really," Enthoven smiles. "It was either a test of commitment or bloody madness on my part! We knew it was going to be successful so at the end of the day – it was just down to money and we had to find the money to do it."

As Neil Armstrong and Buzz Aldrin walked about on the Moon, on Monday, 21 July, King Crimson walked into Wessex Studios, took control of their own fate and began work on their debut album for the third time. Over the next fortnight, in between gigs, the band spent three days laying down backing tracks for *In The Court Of The Crimson King*; a day a piece on *I Talk To The Wind* and *Epitaph*; a day on *Moonchild* and its improvised instrumental work-out and, finally, Crimson's magnum opus, *21st Century Schizoid Man*, completed in just one devastating live take.

August was spent mixing the original eight track tapes down to two tracks to carry out extensive overdubs. Pete Sinfield recalls their no-nonsense approach. "We weren't one of those bands who rolled a couple of joints and had a scotch before we started work at midnight. We used to get up there at lunchtime and work through until we were exhausted at around nine or ten and not push it ... we worked fairly hard and we did it very quickly. We could do it very quickly because everyone knew their parts very well because we'd rehearsed it and played it, which helped a lot."

The album's final overdub – Robert Fripp's one-take guitar solo for *Schizoid Man* – was completed on 20 August 1969, with plans already under way for the finished album to be released on Chris Blackwell's Island label. If the band and their fans, including The Who's Pete Townshend (who famously dubbed the album "an uncanny masterpiece") thought things had been moving fast already, the whole adventure went into hyperspeed when the album was released in the UK in early October.

Going straight into the top five of the album charts, the potent, ground-breaking music and its iconic album sleeve, one of the first without band name or record company logo on its gatefold front, demanded to be heard.

Pete Sinfield: "Not having the name on the front cover meant that if you were fingering through the racks in the record shop and you came across it, you had to open it up to see who it was. You were being led further into our world. Hopefully then you'd want to hear it and then buy it. It was exactly done that way. I remember being in Oxford Street just after it was released and seeing a whole shop window full of them and I stood there thinking "struth, what have we done?""

They'd been together less than nine months!

Running like the soundtrack to some epic, unreleased movie, the album was a decisive break with the blues-rock motifs still dominating much of the underground scene's output. There's no lengthy solos anywhere on the album. Instead, the group's collective firepower is directed into beautifully crafted and detailed arrangements, symphonic allusions and precocious ambition.

The unrelenting pace of Crimson's life on the road began to take its toll once the band arrived in the USA as the album – released in America on Atlantic – entered the Top 30. In the midst of a kaleidoscopic American travelogue that crossed vast coast-to-coast distances, Michael Giles and Ian McDonald, homesick, lovesick and beginning to find the hurly-burly pace more than they could handle, decided to quit at the end of the tour.

When Crimson left the stage of San Francisco's Fillmore West on Sunday, 14 December, it was over. The whirlwind of 1969 had seen them play over 70 gigs and get an album out in a mere 335 days.

Though King Crimson would continue with different line-ups, the only album by the original, short-lived group became a defining moment in rock's development.

Greg Lake had no doubts about its significance: "It fired the starting pistol on progressive rock. I think that there were other bands that you could also credit with bringing about a new attitude in music: Pink Floyd were one band that brought new stuff along. So I wouldn't say Crimson were the only band to bring new things along but we were certainly fundamental and important in the progressive movement. The album provoked a lot of changes."

Peter Sinfield admits to a certain amount of pride in the album's achievements. "You don't think about the legacy of an album as you're doing it but I have learned, just by being around long enough, that it's the greatest feeling in the world to have done something like that. To have written something that lasts and has a bit of a timeless feel to it … we didn't philosophise about it at the time because we didn't have time all those years ago."

II

In 1967, a tired and frustrated Michael Giles sat in the garage of his home in Bournemouth wondering about the future and thinking about the past. He and his brother Peter had just left the group Trendsetters Ltd, the band which had provided a ticket out of Bournemouth and on to the touring circuit of provincial England and Europe. Along the way, they had backed stars of the day, recorded several singles and made innumerable TV and radio appearances but, after three years of hard slog, there didn't seem to be any mileage left in the band. Bored with its diet of bright and bouncy R'n'B covers, Michael and his bass-playing brother, Peter, jumped off the treadmill and came home to think about the next step.

Winton, in Bournemouth's suburbs, was where he and Peter grew up. Their father, a violinist, spent his childhood in Herefordshire where he knew composer Ralph Vaughan Williams and later played in orchestras and small groups around the Bournemouth area. Also a talented portrait painter, he encouraged his children to appreciate music, exposing them to classical and jazz, as well as popular songs.

Born 1 March 1942, Michael started playing first, taking up the washboard during the skiffle craze and later moving on to drums, for which he discovered a natural aptitude, using pots, pans and cardboard boxes before acquiring a basic kit containing a bass drum and snare with a cymbal attachment.

He was soon settled into his first proper band, Johnny King And The Raiders, and, like thousands of other youngsters swept up in the music craze of the 1950s, was playing live. "Bournemouth was not like the other industrial cities, you know, people living a tough, hard working-class life, looking for a way out by being a footballer or a musician or something else," recalls the drummer. "The only reason I've been able to come up with as to why we became musicians, was because there wasn't anything to rebel or fight against. So it was the frustration of not having enough challenge. But we weren't doing it with another agenda as a means to escape. If we were seeking to escape then it would have been from a kind of nothingness. We weren't driven by angst or terrible conditions."

The group had a regular gig in a local hall and attracted quite a following, including Michael's younger brother Peter (born 17 June 1944). It became obvious, though, that the lead singer couldn't sing and play bass at the same time, as Peter recalls. "I just happened to be there and I played a little guitar – I was just fifteen-and-a-half – so they said 'Do you want a try?' So I just started playing this thing and it was just magical – I loved that sound! It was so exciting to play. From then on I was in the band and before I left Bournemouth Grammar School in 1960 I'd played 34 gigs!"

Ultimately, The Raiders went on to play more than 100 gigs in and around Bournemouth from January 1960 to August 1961, experience that paid off with a victory in a "Battle Of The Bands" show in Bournemouth's Westover Cinema. This did not go unnoticed by The Dowland Brothers – the semi-professional big fish in Bournemouth's small pool. They lost no time in asking the Giles brothers to join their group and the two sets of brothers played their first combined gig that November.

Peter immediately noticed the increased level of musicianship in the group, placing new challenges upon his technique and level of performance. "The Dowlands were very pro and their standard was very high. The chords were right, the vocal harmonies were good – no hit or miss stuff, very slick for that time. They both stood there with the guitars and one was right-handed and one was left-handed and they sang very well. They had a three-piece band behind them consisting of Mike, me and a guitarist, Alan Bowery. Roy Phillips also played in the band for a while and he later played keyboards in The Peddlers."

The band gigged within a 100-mile radius of Bournemouth but the favourite venue for many was the Downstairs Club in the centre of the town, where there were often after-hours sessions at which musicians from different bands could get together to socialise, make deals and check out the opposition. Zoot Money, Andy Summers and future member of The Shadows, John Rostill, were all regulars.

Peter remembers the slightly down-at-heel image of the place was just what they were looking for, after a hard night's gigging. "The Downstairs Club along Holdenhurst Road was pretty seedy, flaky paintwork, no effort had been made, and the guy that ran it, Jerry Stukes, was a hell of a character. We were talking with him once and he'd dropped his cigarette butt-end in his coffee and he just stirred it up and drank it!"

But the drab reality of their day jobs – Michael worked for a company providing fêtes and had spent a spell in a gents' outfitters; Peter was a fitter for a soft furnishing firm – ensured that such socialising was for weekends only.

As good as The Dowlands were on the local scene, Giles remembers that he and his brother were growing in confidence and ambition. "Mike and I just always knew where we were in the music and would be the ones who would notice when the keyboard player was rushing it or whatever. Mike was always a better player than I was but I had that feeling for the music which compensated. The gear I used to have was a Leak valve amp and a home-made speaker – it was so incredibly crude and it wasn't that loud! I dare say the sound was dreadful by today's standards but you learn as you go along."

The music scene in Bournemouth was vibrant and, on any night of the week, the prospective punter was spoiled for choice. Dave Anthony and The Moods were wowing the crowds as was the Jal Rafini Band featuring the unlikely talents of Zoot Money, future bedsit hero Al Stewart and nascent Radio One DJ Tony Blackburn. Yet The Dowland Brothers still held their pre-eminent position in the semi-professional pecking order and for several years both Peter and Michael were more than happy, totting up over 220 gigs with them. Eventually though, the ambitious brothers began to look for an opportunity which would allow them to turn professional.

Michael and Peter's chance came in January 1964. Businessman Roy Simon, eager for a slice of the growing music scene, commissioned market research to find out what young people looked for in a band. Then he went about constructing a group, placing ads in *Melody Maker.* With nothing to lose, the Giles's auditioned and joined their first pro band: Trendsetters Ltd.

Making it down to London in 1964, Trendsetters landed a deal with Parlophone and recorded several singles, none of which set the charts alight. The band, also including Allan Azern on piano and vocals, Michael Blakesley on trombone and Bruce Turner on guitar, was even hired to back American vocal harmony group The Drifters on tour around the UK.

Playing twice nightly in cinemas and halls, Peter enjoyed the camaraderie of life on the road and the humour which sustained them. "We had so much fun. At the Manchester Hilton we were in the lift and there were five of us and four of them all singing – in as many harmonies as we could find – *What A Friend I Have In Jesus* at the top of our voices and the doors open! Lots of fun and nonsense!"

"Life on the road is after all a pretty ludicrous way of earning a living. You spend three hours driving up the motorway in the back of a cold and draughty van to play a one-and-a-half hour set to a possibly indifferent crowd. One of the time-honoured methods of surviving the experience has been the development of a collective humour. An emotional short-cut where words can be truncated to a single sound or a raised finger will become the object of hysterical laughter."

He further recalls the lengthy stints in the bierkellers of Germany – ten weeks at a time, playing seven nights a week, from 9.00 pm until 4.00 am with one 20-minute break. The comedy routines were a practical necessity as trombone player Michael Blakesley's lip went in no time. "We had to develop a cabaret act to get us through it and we did that by pissing around. Ten weeks – it was gruelling but that's where the bonding came from. We came back with this fully-fledged stage act where the keyboard player and I used to do a Peter Cook and Dudley Moore routine which used to go down a storm everywhere, and we'd finish off singing their theme song *Goodbyee* and it got very wacky. I remember we did a James Brown number and I used to start it off with a firing pistol; a really loud blank and at the end of the intro when I fired this thing, the place would jump out of its skin."

Despite the very best efforts of the group and its management, and appearances on the BBC's *Juke Box Jury*, Radio Caroline and their own show on Radio Luxembourg, The Trendsetters seemed unable to make the transition from programme fillers to first division stars. Eventually a combination of relentless touring and lack of chart success sapped the spirits.

By 1967, Peter was writing his own material, much darker compositions with appropriately sombre titles like *Murder* and *Nightmares In Red*. They tried releasing singles under names such as The Trend and The Brain and over the years rumours have persisted that the latter track featured Robert Fripp on guitar. However, both Peter and Robert flatly deny this as the brothers had yet to meet their future partner. Faced with industrial scales of indifference and apathy, they eventually decided to call it a day.

As far as Michael recollects, there was no deep conversation about breaking up but more taking stock of the way the music scene was leaving the Trendsetters' courteous beat music behind. "There's the Beatles, there's The Nice, there's The Rolling Stones, there's Bob Dylan – there's all these other people who are doing something. 'Why aren't we doing something?' We felt as though we were adequately equipped to do something. So why not? That's about as far as the discussion went. The decision to stop the Trendsetters thing was really as simple as that. It wasn't that it was acrimonious – it was just time to change." For Peter the moment was especially significant. "When Trendsetters died, Mike and I sat down and thought 'What are we going to do?' And then it became serious."

III

Ten miles outside Bournemouth is Wimborne, the picture-postcard town where Robert Fripp emerged from a solidly working-class background.

His father, Arthur, was the eldest son of a family of six who was told to leave school at 16 to become a farm worker at Longham – 2½ miles outside Wimborne – to help feed his brothers and sisters. Eventually, he took night classes and found work at auctioneers and estate agents Welch & Lock. During the Second World War ("when money was no use but an egg was!", according to his son) he was paid in chicken, eggs and corn for auctioneering at Verwood Market. Eventually, he bought the firm by taking on its debts to prevent its bankruptcy.

Edith Green, from the mining community of Abertillery in South Wales, settled in Bournemouth – where signs in windows read: "No Welsh. No Irish" – and met Arthur, marrying him on Christmas Day, 1939, at a Nonconformist Chapel in Chapel Lane, East Borough, Wimborne. During the war, she secured relatively well-paid employment in the Bournemouth Records Office, earning enough to help her husband buy his own business in Leigh Road, Wimborne.

Gradually, after the war, the Fripps prospered and, in 1945, Edie gave birth to their first child, Patricia. One year, one month, two days and twelve-and-a-half hours later, in the Bear Cross Nursing Home midway between Wimborne Minster and Bournemouth, Robert followed her into the world on 16 May 1946.

Five years later, he started at Broadstone Primary School. In the UK at that time, education was streamed from the age of 11, with only the brightest creamed off to grammar school. Robert duly earned a place at Queen Elizabeth's Grammar School in Wimborne.

Talking to *Disc*'s David Hughes in 1970, Fripp said: "There were only ever a few people in the whole school I got on with. Ever since the age of ten I've been very much on my own – and of course at that age I was aware of it and upset. I suppose when you're young you think it's a fault not having friends."

His lack of respect for the school regime and some of the lessons goaded Fripp into precocious displays of protest, such as eating his lunch in class, and quick-fire one-liners such as: "If you had half the intelligence of a pea, you'd be twice what you are now."

Such behaviour was outrageously hilarious to his classmates and endeared him most notably to Gordon Haskell. Haskell was illegitimate, so perhaps a shared sense of outsiderdom drew the pair together. Haskell visited the Fripp household on occasion but found it unusual. "I spent a lot of time with him and it was a strange life.

His mother and father didn't seem to share their life with him and so he was left to his own devices, studying and left in his own little cocoon."

If Fripp found little in the way of stimulation at school, the music of the day *did* capture his attention. He was swept along in the trad jazz phenomena, queuing to see Acker Bilk, Monty Sunshine and Chris Barber. The first two records Fripp ever bought were *Hound Dog* by Elvis Presley and *Singing The Blues* by the UK's slightly tamer rebel-rouser Tommy Steele in April 1957. By Christmas Eve that year, his infatuation with music was so intense that his mother, despite having already obtained all his Christmas presents, swept into Bournemouth and bought Fripp his first guitar. This last-minute gift was to change Fripp's life.

Though his mother sang and his father played the violin, Fripp judges that he did not come from a musical background. Although naturally left-handed, he opted to play the instrument right-handed and set about applying himself to mastering the guitar. His progress was swift ("rock at 11, trad at 13, modern jazz at 15", he says today). Fripp took guitar lessons from piano teacher Kathleen Gartell at the Corfe Mullen School of Music a few months after getting his guitar. Through her, he had a stint in the Corfe Mullen Youth Orchestra playing first violin, and guitar solos, as well as a little teaching of fellow pupils, at 13. In 20 lessons with Mrs Gartell, Fripp had gone through both of her guitar books. So she sent him to guitar teacher Don Strike.

Strike was steeped in 1930s jazz and here players like Django Reinhardt came to Fripp's attention. This interest would later widen to include modern jazz players and composers like Charlie Parker and Charlie Mingus, in particular his piece *Abstraction*.

Fripp's father paid for the lessons, which lasted two years, but it was Edie who got Fripp there and back from each lesson at the Strike music shop in Westbourne Arcade (it's still there), come rain or shine. Now Fripp's diligence and disciplined approach found a new focus. Haskell remembers, with some admiration, the tenacity with which Fripp followed the lessons. "To me, he was like a paraplegic that had learned to walk. He'd overcome tremendous odds. He had music lessons and overcame his inability to be a natural musician by inventing something of his own which nobody could question," he says.

After Strike, Fripp had ten lessons in "modern" styles – Latin, substitute chords – with Tony Alton in Winton.

By 1961, having just turned 15, Fripp had evolved to the point where getting a band together was the next natural step. "I was encouraged to play with others by Don Strike, who told me it was time for me to play with other people! After one or two connections I met with Graham Wale from Stapehill, near Wimborne, a hope-to-be singer who was forming a group."

Another recruit was classmate Gordon Haskell. Fripp remembers: "Gordon asked me while throwing discus on the school playing field, 'Here mush, if I buy a bass, can I join your group?'" Fripp gave Haskell a few lessons. "He taught me a 12-bar or something. He didn't teach me much but it was enough to get me going," says Haskell.

Fripp himself was playing a Hofner President though a Watkins six-watt amplifier and the pair got down to the finger-wilting business of learning a set and recruiting other band members. These included Tino Licinio on vocals and guitar, with the drums supplied initially by Graham Wale and subsequently Chris "Fergy" Ferguson. Thus The Ravens were formed.

They lasted a year or so. However, as his O-Level exams loomed, Fripp concentrated on his studies and dropped out, effectively splitting the band. In 1962, Fripp left Queen Elizabeth's with seven O-Levels and joined his father's firm of auctioneers and estate agents as a junior negotiator. By the time he was 17, he already knew that he wanted to become a professional musician. Returning from a holiday in Jersey with his sister Patricia, he broke the news to his mother. But her tearful reaction to his announcement meant that he had to put his aspirations on hold.

In 1964, as the Giles Brothers turned professional with Trendsetters, Fripp was playing guitar in the Chewton Glen Hotel with The Douglas Ward Trio, plus a few other local hotel/dance band gigs. He also was teaching guitar for the Eddie Moors music shop in Boscombe. One of his pupils was Al Stewart, who would later find success as a singer-songwriter. Talking to writer James Ellis in 2001, Stewart remembered being impressed with his tutor. "I did take a dozen lessons from Robert. He lived down the road in Wimborne and he was an astonishing guitar player, even in our late teens. He tried to teach me jazz chords. It was like learning algebra in school. They're the two things I have never had any use for in the subsequent 40 years of my life."

But Fripp was soon in a new band at Gordon's suggestion, with Haskell on bass and Licino on guitar and vocals, joined by Stan Levy on drums and Reg Mathews on vocals. Their makeshift rehearsal room was at the end of the garden of Reg's parents' house at the Tatnam Hotel in Poole. After rehearsals, the band would decamp to the hotel bar and discuss what name they might adopt. Fripp recalls the issue was settled as they enjoyed a pint next to the toilets. Haskell "looked up from drinking a beer, saw the name over the male conveniences and, with a characteristic gurgle of laughter, announced: 'The League of Gentlemen!'" The name was soon playfully corrupted to become The Plague Of Gentlemen by members of local rivals The Meddyevils with whom they shared the circuit of church halls and youth clubs a couple of times a week.

Haskell had a growing interest in black music from America, which he preferred to any of the LofG's material. "I've always felt black music rather than white music.

I was brought up with a churchy background and I came back and learnt the tunes, you testified and so on. And the rhythm of the Stax and Motown music was so in tune with me that I should have been black. I wasn't very white. The League Of Gentlemen were a vocal harmony group, so Tino was the leader and he liked four-part harmony such as *Yakety Yak*. We were quite popular playing white pop, weird instrumentals and some of The Shadows. The Coasters was the only black thing we did."

After a year or so with the LofG, the academic demands on Fripp meant that he had to leave and, in 1965, he went to Bournemouth College to study for A-levels. Not long after the League Of Gentlemen split up, the band was socialising in the Library Hall in Poole when a local lad by the name of Johnny Johnson picked a fight with Tino. As Fripp recalls: "Gordon and Stan Lee came running to tell me that 'Tino's in a fight'. I ran over to see my friend on the ground having his head kicked. My response was immediate."

Fripp weighed in, rescuing Licino from a more severe beating. However, both Fripp and Licino required hospitalisation and Fripp's mouth was seriously damaged – "Pulled off my face, and torn. Ten stitches. Tino's face was an unrecognisable puffy mass," he recalls. Haskell still feels some guilt. "Robert weighed in and they both ended up going to hospital and I didn't go to the rescue. So I was a coward. We were 18 years old. I don't really have a defence except that I was on the other side of a crowded room and I saw a scuffle but I didn't go in. I guess it's on my conscience." The case made the local Press and the villain of the piece was jailed for two years.

At Bournemouth College, Fripp met John Wetton and his friend Richard Palmer-James. During the same year, he started taking an interest in the career of Greg Lake, another local guitarist creating a stir on the scene. By now Fripp was supporting himself playing guitar at Bournemouth's Majestic Hotel – a job left vacant when Andy Summers (later Police guitarist and Fripp collaborator) went off to London with Zoot Money. The Majestic Dance Orchestra's youngest and least experienced member stayed on for three years, backing Bob Monkhouse, Norman Vaughn, Joe Baker, Lita Roza, Julie Rogers, Salena Jones and other established cabaret acts.

Having passed his A-levels in Economics and Economic History early, Fripp was scheduled to go to London as a student at the College of Estate Management. By now he was playing in a short-lived trio called Cremation, which he describes as "appalling", but before leaving for college, he knew he could play the role of the dutiful son no longer. On his 21st birthday in May 1967, he told his family he intended to become a professional musician. What else was there to do but answer an ad for a singing organist?

IV

The Giles brothers understood that if they were going to get anywhere they needed to be living in London, at the heart of the music industry. They also knew they needed a band and their preference was a trio fronted by a singing organist. Hence the advert.

Peter Giles recalls the long search for the right combination. "We scoured the Bournemouth area for two or three months and auditioned loads of players, all of whom were completely useless. We absolutely despaired and somebody told us that there was this guitarist called Bob Fripp who was supposed to be pretty good but he didn't sing. But we thought 'What the hell ...'

"We'd paid our dues, we'd done a full apprenticeship whereas Fripp had just played in a few local bands that I'd never heard of. But he certainly could play and he had his chops down, there's no question about that. So we thought, 'Why not?'" However, their motivations in wanting to team up were not entirely honourable, as the bass player admitted: "The other thing about Fripp was that he had a friend who was an accordion player who had a gig in London so that was very useful. So he had this ready-made gig to go up to in London, so it looked as though it could be promising and Fripp seemed nutty enough that we could get on with him."

After a whole month of playing and recording together, Fripp asked Michael Giles whether he had the job. "He rolled a cigarette, looked down and put the cigarette in his mouth, lit it, puffed on it and said 'Let's not be in a hurry to commit ourselves to each other.' The question was asked as a joke: obviously, we were working together. Michael's difficulty in making a commitment was subsequently a recurrent leitmotif."

In September, the trio left for London with a tenuous prospect of backing chart-topping vocal harmony group The Flowerpot Men. "When we came to London for the first time in July '68, Mike and Peter Giles had got a gig, through their previous connections as members of Trendsetters, backing the Flowerpot Men. So we all moved from Dorset to London. They turned up for me at my parents' house on Leigh Road in Wimborne at 6.00 am, and there we were moving to London. We parked and went to the agent at 10 o'clock in the morning and he said the job had fallen through. I'd never understood why he couldn't have picked up the phone the evening before and told us. What he did do was sign a cheque for £5 for petrol which he gave to Peter Giles. But there was no explanation. Even today I don't understand why he hadn't told us at least before 10 the preceding night. So we went to the Giaconda café in Denmark Street and there we heard that The Flowerpot Men had another backing band. I think it was Ten Years After. I didn't mind looking for work. I minded being screwed over by a character in a position of authority and responsibility who had no interest in acting rightly or decently. So we drove back to Wimborne at midnight that night. 'Hello Mum.' She didn't seem surprised."

But London still beckoned and, within a couple of weeks, the trio were back in the capital. It was Michael Giles who found 93a Brondesbury Road, off the Queen's Road near Kilburn Park. The move was borne out of necessity after Fripp and Michael Giles spent three days sharing an "awful" room belonging to a doctor in Coldharbour Lane, Brixton. "It was probably the bloodstains on his bedding that helped Michael come to a clear decision," offers Fripp.

Of their new accommodation, Michael recalls: "It was eminently suitable for the three of us. Robert used to spend all day practising, writing a few things. Peter was writing, I was practising just with sticks and drum pads and working in palais bands in the evening to support my wife and children back in Bournemouth."

Fripp utilised a contact with an accordion player and, for one week, they backed an Italian crooner dubbed 'Hot Lips' Moreno at the La Dolce Notte restaurant in Jermyn Street. Fripp recalls that this gig was so short-lived because of a pay dispute between the band, who received £35 weekly wages, and their agent. "The restaurant was paying £45, but we didn't know that. We went on strike on the Thursday, went back on Friday and were fired on Saturday."

They returned to the comfort of Brondesbury Road. The large living room was immediately converted into a makeshift studio, essentially consisting of one large wooden frame covered with discarded carpet underlay and felt dragged from skips. Even though they only had a Revox tape machine – purchased from The Dowland Brothers – and one overhead mike, Peter Giles was seasoned enough to know how to get the best from this basic set-up. "We never wrote anything together. We all wrote separately and they'd be knocked into shape very quickly. We spent a lot of time in the home studio and I'd just go in there and switch the gear on and tell people when to play and when to stop, and I just took over the whole recording process.

"The first track would be drums, bass and guitar – so three things would go down on to one track and we'd keep the level reasonably safe. Then we'd go and add two vocals on top of that and maybe one or two guitars or something on top of that. Maybe four bounces and then on the last, I'd wang everything up, not bothering about the meters but listening for distortion."

For light relief, Peter and Robert would collect discarded sheet music from publishers and see who best could sight-read the tunes. With the music on the stand, one of them would count in and then they would both play the piece. This bit of fun was not without its repercussions, however, as Peter was to discover. "Fripp, the poor bastard, had to play lead line and the tune straight off and I only had the bass line to worry about. So at some stage during this I had said something to him that he took to mean that I was better at sight-reading than he was. But my intention was a bit of ribbing, as a joke. About three or four months later he came up with this venomous thing that I had said that I was a better sight-reader than he was. He'd held this grudge against me for all that time."

From time to time, the Giles brothers met up with faces from the past, though this could be a source of anguish, as Michael recalls: "Peter and I bumped into Noel Redding. He was in another band in Germany and we knew him from there and we got talking. He told us he was rehearsing with a black American guitarist and a drummer called Mitch Mitchell and of course it turned out to be Jimi Hendrix. We thought, 'How come they're doing it and we're not?'"

A relative new boy in London, Fripp looked up Gordon Haskell who had made the move a year or two earlier. Haskell knew there was little or nothing in the way of authentic black music in and around Bournemouth and settled for the next best thing: The Dowland Brothers. He played with them until 1966 when he joined the Southampton underground R'n'B band Fleur De Lys who eventually established themselves in London, for a while being the house band in clubs like The Speakeasy.

At this time, Jimi Hendrix was the talk of the town and was no stranger to Haskell. The pair had met when Fleur De Lys shared the house owned by The Animals, whose bass player, Chas Chandler, had returned from the States with the guitarist in tow. Soon after that, The Animals lead guitarist Hilton Valentine set up a studio date with Fleur De Lys backing Hendrix on three tracks. The band's proficiency meant that, for producer/manager Frank Fenter, it was far more profitable to pay the group to record rather than tour.

What they didn't realise at the time was that the group were able to earn Fenter £1,000 in the studio while they were on £15 per week. "We all were in the studio all day – sometimes 12 hours or all night. Then we'd go to The Marquee to see all the bands – Eric Clapton, Jeff Beck, Gary Moore, Jimmy Page. And then you'd go to The Speakeasy and go and do a gig yourself for this in-crowd and there'd be guest singers like Sharon Tandy, and that was when Hendrix got up with us on two occasions. I was wet behind the ears and Hendrix said to me 'sing a blues!' and I'd never sung a blues in my life. I put that right soon enough but I was just a bass player. I was writing a couple of sweet tunes which happened to get covered and happened to get to number one in South Africa and Australia. But I was naïve, although I had a good feel for the bass. But I wasn't a singer!"

The rising trend toward psychedelia saw the band coerced into writing songs which reflected the multi-coloured "liberated" feel splashing the music scene with day-glo colours. Haskell saw Pink Floyd's first gig at The Marquee and knew that something was most definitely in the air when Zoot Money proved an old dog could learn new tricks after all. "First of all, he was doing The Flamingo Jazz Club in Soho with his big band and horns and stuff. Then they became Dantalion's Chariot

– Zoot was always right on the button with his timing. He was the first guy to go up to London from Bournemouth and he was like a godfather to me in terms of how it could be done."

With the advent of the Floyd and the groundbreaking work of The Beatles, musical experimentation was more acceptable and Fleur De Lys managed to persuade Frank Fenter to put up the money for a jam session with Vanilla Fudge. They entered Mayfair Studios and recorded for 12 hours non-stop. "It was phenomenally exciting and then we went to the office the following day with the results and Frank almost hit us because he said it was the biggest load of shit he'd ever heard," recalls a chastened Haskell.

Though responsible for providing the backing tracks to numerous singles and relishing their role as bespoke backing band to the rock-pop cognoscenti of the day, Fleur De Lys seemed unable to break through in their own right. "We wished we were better. We had it in us to do it but there were a lot of distractions," believes Haskell. "We weren't sitting down writing songs enough. We were working for Frank – backing other people perhaps more than we should have done. We'd kind of gotten lazy and there was a bit of indulgence in the old funny baccy department and things did go a bit haywire."

Fripp went to the offices of Polydor Records to get in touch with Haskell, who knew that Fripp was likely to be moving to London via his mother. "He went 'round to where my mother worked and she said 'Gordon is doing really well, he's got a number one in South Africa and Australia'. He'd had his hair done and he arrived in the middle of the night where my mom worked as a night nurse and scared the hell out of her because he had this Hendrix-type hair. Peered through the window and nearly scared her to death!"

Haskell helped out by listing Fripp as his favourite guitarist on his Fleur De Lys band biography, figuring that it was a way of getting his old schoolfriend's name about. Fripp saw the potential of teaming up with Haskell again when he heard that the moderately successful Cupid's Inspiration needed a bassist and guitarist. Haskell was impressed with Fripp's resourcefulness. "He'd obviously done a bit of networking because he came up with the Cupid's Inspiration for him and me because he clearly wanted to retain our schoolboy friendship and link. Perhaps because he was lost in London? I guess he'd just heard of a job and shared it with me."

In the end Haskell got the job and Fripp was left behind. But the irony for Haskell was that the job was short-lived and, after backing Scott Walker on tour, came to a bad end. Not for the last time in his career as a musician, a dispute over money was the cause of his departure. Haskell had understood that the wage in the band was to be raised. "We did the Scott Walker tour, a four-nights-a-week package show, record in the Top 20 and £10 pounds per week. I stuck it for 12 weeks waiting for the money to be corrected but it never was, so I quit. Meanwhile, Robert is messing around with the boys but the tragedy is he tempted me away from my happiness in the Fleur-De-Lys."

Back in Brondesbury Road, Giles, Giles and Fripp were struggling. Without any live work, the trio relied on state benefits and by December a tired and despondent Fripp returned to Wimborne to see his family and to take up the guitar stool for the Christmas season back at the Majestic Hotel.

Returning to London in 1968, GG&F were largely unaware of the huge social and political movements radicalising the young generation in the capital and, to a lesser extent, the provinces. Peter Giles: "We weren't sixties. We never took part in any trends in terms of clothing or teenage philosophy – we bought none of that and we went our own sweet way at all times. We never partook of all that. It went over our heads. I mean you either had to be a mod or a rocker and we were neither. We were ourselves." Fripp's take on this was to identify the bass player as the conceptual centre of the trio. "Peter had no interest in fashion, nor in Marshall stacks on 11. I followed his lead, as the more experienced player, for around a year. You also had to have some money to be involved in the sixties scene and we didn't."

If GG&F were socially and sartorially out of step, so was their music. As they beavered away in their home studio, the material slowly came together but it was quirky and at times almost anachronistic, neither quite rock, folk, jazz or classical but a perhaps ungainly hybrid, shot through with their own skew-whiff sense of humour.

GG&F relied on this humour to inveigle their way into record company foyers and beyond, as Peter remembers: "We went to the top guy in Decca, Hugh Mendl. We used to go in all dressed up and cause a stir in the building. Fripp used to go around in an evening suit with one motorcycle gauntlet and we used to steal some flowers from a garden on the way and stick them in the gauntlet. I had a trenchcoat which was two sizes too big for me and my brother wore some ridiculous things. It used to focus people's attention."

Having passed on the Beatles, Decca were now extremely acquisitive in the hope of discovering another Fab Four or their equivalent. It was the quality of GG&F's demos which helped get them a record deal. But their delight at being signed was tempered by realism. Most bands would have been overjoyed, but the Giles brothers' experience told them a record contract didn't guarantee anything. Fripp knew enough to recognise a liability when he saw one and sat up most of the night at the kitchen table re-writing the onerous Decca contract in GG&F's favour before sending it back to Mendl – a memory which still brings a smile to Michael's face. The band was duly signed for two singles and an album and each received £250 as an advance.

Decca producer Wayne Bickerton had come up through the ranks, having played with ex-Beatle Pete Best (who, not surprisingly, Decca had signed). But his pairing with GG&F was not a success. The trio began recording their debut album in Decca's studios at Broadhurst Gardens, initially with engineer Bill Price and with Bickerton supervising.

Having Bickerton forcing suggestions on them merely increased tension and resentment within GG&F. Peter remembers: "There are innumerable stories about bands who've got record deals on the basis of having produced these brilliant demos. They go into a big studio and of course they're shit, they completely lose the spirit, because of the imposing natures of the studio and the inhibitions that this causes."

Fripp recalls that, as the session unfolded, Bickerton would question the band about the material they were playing. "Wayne would always ask, in broad Scouse accent, 'But is it commairceeal?'. Peter would always reply: 'Fucking sure it's commercial!' He lied."

It was not until near the end of the sessions, and specifically the recording of Fripp's *Erudite Eyes*, that GG&F started to find themselves. The song, written only a month before, allowed them to move up to another level. For Peter, as for the others, it was a turning point. "Until then we just thought it was a load of fucking shit. We were praying that something would happen in the studio where we could feel that we were part of the bloody album."

But the fatal flaws in the line-up were becoming more obvious to Fripp. "It was very clear to me that there were a trio of very good players who had almost nothing to play that would galvanise them. Songwriting was not their greatest forte. *Erudite Eyes* was a vehicle, a platform, to get the team up and running, and prepared to take a leap. In this sense, it's a forerunner to *Schizoid Man*, which served the same function, but in a more sophisticated and satisfactory way.

"A profound disagreement in principle between Peter and myself, which continues to this day, is that Peter believes himself to own the copyright of the Brondesbury Road recordings, as if he were the record company which hired the players to make those recordings. So, in his view, he is producer, record company and owner of the phonographic copyrights. I don't hold this view. We were a collective, each supporting each other by mutually contributing."

On its release in September 1968, the album only notched up 600 sales ("Worldwide!" says Fripp). To be fair, it must have been difficult for the average punter to connect with its curious mixture of vaudeville, the Goon-ish humour of *The Elephant Song*, plaintive ballads like *Little Children* and the earnest poetics of *The Crukster*. It's not that *The Cheerful Insanity Of Giles, Giles And Fripp* is a bad album by any means but its lack of any clear direction lends it a listless finishing coat.

The title and Gered Mankowitz's portraiture reflected the humour but obscured any serious intentions. As one of the album's big influences, the Bonzo Dog Doo-Dah Band's 1967 album Gorilla, demonstrated, musical jokes – like any other form of comedy – are a serious business. The skill is in going beyond in-jokes which leave an audience baffled.

The wordplay of Fripp's *Rodney Toady* saga and Michael Giles' *Just George* creates the impression of a thematic unity which, for the most part, remains illusory. Poring over the juvenilia of any artist for signs and indicators of the future isn't always a good thing and perhaps it's best to accept the album for what it is – the product of three musicians in search of material.

Peter Giles invested his time at the kitchen table in Brondesbury Road inventing droll press releases which acknowledged the hopelessness of their situation in an ironic and self-deprecating fashion, as the first June edition of *Disc and Music Echo* recognised in its pop gossip column. "Incredible press release for Giles, Giles and Fripp group which says 'one of countless groups who have come to London with the vain hope of making good'. It's a hard business." Similarly, *Record Mirror*'s The Face passed on his or her anonymous congratulations to GG&F for the best press release of the month.

Decca took out banner adverts mentioning the single *One In A Million* alongside The Moody Blues' *Voices In The Sky*. In *Melody Maker*, Keith Moon of The Who faintly praised the Moodies but dismissed GG&F's attempts, saying: "There are hundreds of these songs with the same backing and slightly altered words. The violins are in the bathroom. Good riddance to that."

Yet *Record Mirror* positively brimmed with enthusiasm. "This really is a splendid album. Beautifully arranged with The Breakaways here and there among the star musicians, and the main trio on some well-above-average material. Performed with a stack of personality too. One has to listen carefully for the lyrical nuances, but it's well worth the effort ... a sort of fairytale fantasy, with continuity and mood-switching."

But, despite Peter's legwork, the record went nowhere fast. As far back as June, the trio had decided to start playing with other musicians. Peter scoured the classified section of *Melody Maker* and came across an ad which caught his eye: "Judy Dyble requires brilliant and creative bass guitarist/vocalist and lead guitarist/vocalist. Musicians only."

Peter made the call and arrangements were made to meet up the following week at Brondesbury Road. The phone call was to have profound consequences on all their subsequent lives and careers.

V

Epiphany comes in all shapes and sizes and for a young Ian McDonald, growing up in Osterly in London's sprawling suburbs, it arrived one Sunday afternoon in the gawky shape of Hollywood actor James Stewart.

A bored McDonald had turned on the TV to see Stewart in *The Glenn Miller Story*. "I still remember vividly the scene in which James Stewart (as Miller) is in a rehearsal and the trumpet player cuts his lip or something so that the trumpet can't play the top line. So Miller re-arranges everything for the clarinet to take the top line, which is where he discovers the Glenn Miller sound. That moment and scene has always struck a chord with me, as it were, and I've had a personal identification with wanting to find my own sound, I guess. As a result of that I think I probably wanted to play trombone at one point."

McDonald was born on 25 June 1946, the son of middle-class parents whose house was often filled with the sounds of Les Paul, Guy Mitchell, Frank Sinatra, Ella Fitzgerald and well-known classics such as Rimsky-Korsakov's *Scheherazade*. Despite the presence of a piano in the house and the fact that his father also played a little guitar, McDonald's first musical memory was of playing drums. "I loved drums from a very early age and there was a track called *Skin Deep* by a drummer called Louie Bellson which was two sides of a 78. In fact, the drums were my first instrument in a way. I used to have a couple of drumsticks and set up piles of magazines and bang on them."

When he was 12, the family moved to Teddington near Twickenham, and he started attending the fee-paying Emanuel School in Clapham Junction. Also at the school in the year above him was Elton Dean, later a member of the Keith Tippett Sextet and Soft Machine, with whom McDonald would play in Tippett's Centipede.

His father taught him three or four chords on the acoustic guitar. "My father had a guitar, though not a very good one. It was a Spanish-type guitar but with metal strings – it was very difficult to play. So we rented a guitar and I played it at a school concert, putting two or three tunes together, and then I put a rock band together for a school concert when I was about 14 or 15 and did a couple of local gigs."

By 1961, McDonald's behaviour and lack of interest in school had become a cause for concern. "There was a short time where my parents were going crazy because they didn't know what to do with me. I'd been asked to leave school and I was only about 15-and-a-half."

Deciding that he needed a sense of discipline, they packed him off to join the Army and, though less than happy at the prospect, McDonald made the best of it by ensuring that he would take up music during his service. "I joined as a junior bandsman. You can join when you're 15-and-a-half and then join a regiment when you're 17 or so. During this time you have lessons on the instrument of your choice. Mine was clarinet, although I had actually wanted to learn saxophone, but the recruiting officer suggested I play clarinet first and go on to learn sax if I wanted to. I didn't want to go but I more or less had my arm twisted into going."

McDonald lost no time in forming a band with members of the Army and RAF doing R'n'B covers and playing gigs in the evenings and at weekends. In 1963/1964, he attended the Royal Military School of Music and, after a posting in Northern Ireland, was despatched to British Guiana in South America for six months. By this time The Beatles had become a worldwide phenomenon. "I remember when I was in Boys' Service hearing *Please, Please Me* and *Love Me Do* and songs like that. I remember as soon as I heard them, I recognised immediately that there was something special about the sound and the songs. In British Guiana, things like *Day Tripper* and *We Can Work It Out* were out at the time and I just thought they were great. I was going crazy because of all this music stuff that was happening in England – Swinging London – and I was stuck in a jungle in British Guiana just dying to be part of what was going on, hearing Beatles records on the jukebox in the canteen at the Army barracks and just wanting to be out of there and wanting to do something so badly."

Despite his isolation from the exciting musical developments, Ian's Army career did give him a broad-based musical education involving playing in cocktail jazz groups, wind quartets, male voice choirs, swing groups and big bands.

He also developed his compositional skills, writing and arranging several pieces in the big band/swing idiom. Though not quite as revelatory as the moment in *The Glenn Miller Story*, it nevertheless was thrilling to have his work performed and played. He wrote a big band swing piece called *Three Score and Four* which was never performed but, a few years later, would turn up in an altogether new and dynamic setting.

Back in Belfast, McDonald set about persuading his father to help buy him out of the Army. He was a popular soldier and, after a huge send-off party, flew out of Belfast bound for London. It was 1967 and he was 21.

Back in Teddington, McDonald took a while to re-adjust. "When I came out I still felt emotionally like a 16-year-old because it's not a real environment and you don't have a normal kind of teenage social life. Decision-making and creative thought is not encouraged in the Army. You have to conform and you are told what to do and it's a terrible thing for a teenager to do, especially if you're forced into it and you have creative abilities."

McDonald spent a lot of time listening to the new music on the radio, particularly DJ John Peel's seminal radio show. He got a job in a local record shop, providing himself with a ready supply of what was new and happening. He was also able to borrow his mother's car and make regular visits to the expanding London club scene. The Middle Earth in King Street, Covent Garden, was widely regarded as one the best venues and McDonald recalls seeing the first line-up of Fairport Convention there. The band featured vocalist Judy Dyble. The pair became friends and worked together trying to write material although, sadly for Judy, her time in Fairport was short and she was unceremoniously sacked in favour of Sandy Denny.

In the meantime, he also auditioned for a band led by an itinerant hippy computer programmer called Pete Sinfield.

Sinfield was born on Fulham Palace Road near Putney Bridge on 27 December 1943, as bombs dropped on London during the Second World War. In the sleevenotes for the 1993 re-issue of his solo album *Still*, Sinfield recalled his unconventional early life. "In many ways I had the ideal upbringing for a songwriter. My part-Irish mother who owned and lost various hairdressing shops was, as were her many 'bona' friends, a born non-conformist. Between the ages of four and eight as she went from venture to venture, I was left much of the time in the capable hands of our delightful German housekeeper Maria who was formerly a highwire walker with the famous Flying Wallendas."

Sinfield attended Danes Hill preparatory school in Oxshott in Surrey and, for one year only ("because my wonderful, bohemian, bisexual mother ran out of money!"), the City of London public school.

Danes Hill gave Sinfield his hunger for books and literature. He speculates he would have become a lawyer or joined some other respectable profession had it not been for English master John Mawson. His school report offered this assessment of the 11-year-old's capacity for English: "We have seldom seen such an old head on such young shoulders … ideas beyond his age … but careless and untidy … He must practise his handwriting during the holidays because examiners will not bother to decipher his often very interesting work."

From here, Sinfield attended Ranelagh Grammar School in Bracknell. In 1959, at 16, he left school and drifted through a variety of jobs and travelled around Europe before eventually going to work for Lyon's Electric Office on the Bayswater Road as a programmer in the mid-sixties. The cultural explosion galvanised Sinfield back into writing. "If you listen to *Fairytale* by Donovan – 'Yellow is the colour of my true love's hair', I thought I could do that … it doesn't sound hard. I'd written things way back in school magazines and so on and I then stopped. When I started again, whilst hanging out with my artistic friends, instead of saying 'come and see my etchings' I could say 'Oh I've written this new poem'. I was influenced by all the things I read and all that was going on. Books like *The Prophet* by Kahlil Gibran and Alan Watts (author of *On the Taboo against Knowing Who You Are*, published in 1966) – he was one of the first Zen philosophers writing in magazines like IT and *Oz* – *Gormenghast* and whatever else."

By 1968 Sinfield was setting poems to music and had formed a band with friends Dik Fraser on bass and Mike Nicols on drums and, with Ian McDonald briefly in tow, they bravely grappled with material which was, by Sinfield's own admission, not quite up to the mark. In their set at the time was the original version of *In The Court Of The Crimson King*, before McDonald came up with a completely different melody. Sinfield suggests that this was the real genesis of Crimson. "Robert claims with some fondness that King Crimson was born below George's (café) in January 1969. I beg to differ. In my opinion, King Crimson was born in 1968 a few seconds after Ian, having played the original version of *ITCOTCK* with my band Creation, turned to me with the immortal aside, 'Look Peter, someone has to tell you. Your band is absolutely hopeless … still, erm, you write some interesting words. Why don't we write a couple of songs together?'"

McDonald remembers the name of the group changed quite a bit. "First of all it was WDIES which stands for World Domination In Easy Stages and then we became Infinity." Sadly, Infinity was positively finite and quickly broke up, but it brought together McDonald and Sinfield as a songwriting team.

While working with Sinfield, McDonald maintained his sessions with Dyble and the pair placed the advert under Judy's name in *Melody Maker* which led them to Brondesbury Road and Giles, Giles and Fripp.

Peter Giles immediately recognised in McDonald a gifted writer with a strong harmonic sense and the chops to match. Although the Gileses were happy to work with Dyble, their main interest was McDonald. The five met in June 1967 just before the single *One In A Million* was released. Joining forces with McDonald in this way, GG&F's career had effectively ended before it had really even begun.

Brondesbury Road was once again a hive of activity. *Murder*, written by Peter Giles around the time of *Nightmares In Red*, contained some interesting harmonies which were orchestrated by McDonald. Another Peter Giles song, *She Is Loaded*, benefited from a three-part harmony arrangement. *Under The Sky*, *Make It Today* and *I Talk To The Wind* were McDonald/Sinfield tunes on which the versatile McDonald played acoustic guitar as well as flute and keyboards.

Dyble found GG&F much more structured and tightly disciplined in their approach than the relatively laid-back Fairport. "I think we used to turn up at about two-ish and then Robert would take me into the kitchen and teach me something that he thought I should be able to sing. My range was not that high and I'd not had any formal training and nobody had ever rehearsed me in that way so that was something new and unusual. I was grateful because it did make me feel I could sing differently and I could reach stuff I'd not been able to before."

She recalls with a shudder the conditions in which she and McDonald would have to record. "Peter Giles had set up a vocal booth with carpet underfelt over a kind of cage and Ian and I were cramped in, sweating like little piggies with bits of fluff over us, singing our little hearts out in this dead-sounding area in the middle of the room. It was the fluff up the nose that got to me. How Ian managed to play I don't know. He used to come out dead!"

McDonald and Dyble's relationship broke up during the sessions at Brondesbury Road. Fripp invited her to spend the weekend at his parents' place in Wimborne, although nothing happened between them. "He always left you guessing as to why you were doing something, so I don't know why I was there. I didn't know whether it was a boyfriend/girlfriend thing or whether it was a friendship thing and I was so naïve and innocent then I couldn't guess. It totally freaked me out and I said 'I've got to go home', and I felt so stupid because I went home. His mother said, 'Why do you want to go home? You've only just arrived,' and I felt really guilty about that because she was really sweet, but Robert was so strange."

In July 1968, Dyble decided to leave. She recalls: "There was a lot of free music trying to get out but it was trapped inside. Some of the tunes were hard to get to grips with – you'd think they were going in one direction and suddenly they'd leap off and you'd think 'What am I supposed to do there?'"

In a remarkable demonstration of faith triumphing over common sense, Decca invited the group, now with McDonald on board, to re-cut *Thursday Morning* on Saturday, 6 July. The new arrangement featured additional flute and clarinet as well as extra harmony from the new member but, despite these refinements, the single (coupled with *Elephant Song*) failed to do anything on its release later in the year. Still interested, Decca invited the group back into the studio to lay down some more of the new material.

Over two days at the end of July, the group recorded Fripp's *Drop In*, *She Is Loaded* and *Under The Sky*. *Drop In* would resurface in King Crimson but the last two languished in Decca's vaults until the CD re-issue of the GG&F album in 1992. *She Is Loaded* is a solid, punchy performance with a much rockier aspect than anything the original trio had managed. "Ian has got an amazing sense of harmony. The three-piece harmonies, he just did in seconds. He said: 'Peter, you sing that. Mike, you sing that.' We just sang it. And he sang the middle eight section," recalls an impressed Peter Giles.

The track tells the tale of a cuckold whose wife wins a fortune on the football pools and thus is condemned by his own craven nature to a loveless but luxurious life. It's rare in rock or pop music to have lyrics as satirical or as waggish as these. Once again, Giles implanted an old in-joke into the song which had listeners scratching their heads. "When we were in cover bands we'd have to sit and listen to the lyrics and some you just couldn't make out. You'd come across a line and, for the life of you, you could not imagine what it could possibly be and you'd sit 'round in a group and normally with four of you someone would get it. But other guys would say 'What the fuck is that?.' So I wrote this line, 'There was a time she did rain me gone ted' and I love the idea of people trying to work out what the line could possibly be without the lyric sheet. It's absolutely meaningless but it sounds as though it might mean something."

Under The Sky, erroneously credited to Fripp rather than McDonald and Sinfield, was a ballad of its time. Featuring an able performance by McDonald on flute and vocals, it sounds far more accomplished than anything on the album. It was clear that McDonald was a real asset to the trio – but what did he make of them? "I thought Robert was a very interesting player. He used to show me these guitar techniques such as cross-picking and these exercises he wrote. I guess I sensed that these were professional people and I wanted to work with them. I tend not to go through big thought processes about things like this. I'm intuitive about these things and once I was there, I stayed and didn't have to go through any questioning —I knew that these guys were good."

McDonald was also vital in providing the connection which would enable them to give up worrying about the daily grind of the Labour Exchange and dead-end day jobs. His father's sister, Phyllis, had married an industrialist from the North called Angus Hunking. Although the Hunkings knew nothing about music, they were impressed by their nephew's proposal that they provide the group with a loan as a way of investing in the entertainment industry. The four band members all piled into the Mini car Ian had borrowed from his mother and set out to visit the Hunkings' home in Cookham Dean, Berkshire. By 5 September, a legal contract had been drawn up by Hunking's solicitor and was duly read and signed by the band.

The document was extremely generous in the band's favour. The loan of £7,000 would not have to be repaid until no later than three years later. Even allowing for the 10% annual interest, it gave the group the resources it needed to really make a go of things. Fripp, Peter Giles and McDonald were all to be paid £30 per week for eight consecutive weeks while Michael was paid £40 because of his married status.

Things appeared to be looking up for GGF&McD as the band auditioned and got the starring role in a television commercial for Dunlop tyres. The script required a suitable 'groovy'-looking bunch of guys and their female singer to get to and from gigs and become stars. Naturally their success was assured by the safety and reliability of Dunlop tyres, which helped them speed from one gig to another. Filming in Ross-on-Wye took a day or so and the group were augmented by a young model playing the group's singer. She was Mary Land who would later become the drummer's second wife and grace the cover of the *McDonald And Giles* album in 1970.

On Thursday, 11 September, Giles, Giles, Fripp and Ian McDonald entered Studio 2, in a sub-basement at the BBC's Broadcasting House, to provide the backing for Al Stewart's appearance on the *My Kind of Folk* series. Of the five songs performed, only three featured GG&F – *You Should Have Listened To Al*, *Old Compton Street Blues* and *In Brooklyn*. All three tunes would later appear on *Love Chronicles*, Stewart's second album, in 1969. A grainy off-air recording, previously thought to have been lost, began circulating among collectors in 2018 and it's fascinating to hear the quartet at work. Fripp's lead embellishments are an early example of his sustain technique complete with some uncharacteristic bluesy note-bending. The session was broadcast on 18 September, the week that saw the release of *The Cheerful Insanity of Giles, Giles & Fripp*. Back in Dorset local papers ran one or two "local boys make good" stories. The 11 September edition of the *Bournemouth Echo* carried a short story along with a moody Gered Mankowitz publicity portrait. The article also carried the news that the group was soon to make an appearance on BBC2's *Colour Me Pop* show. This came about thanks to Peter pushing his contacts, another occasion when all the hard work during his time with Trendsetters paid off. "I chatted up a producer to get that programme. We did a whole half-hour programme when people like The Hollies were doing half a programme with somebody else."

On Wednesday, 13 November, GGF&McD were filmed doing silly things in a field for the show. But beneath the jollity all was not well. Clear tensions were opening up between Peter and Robert Fripp. Evidence of this can be clearly heard in their different approaches to composition. Whereas Giles favoured smartly observed scenarios housed in a light, slightly wry, pop style, Fripp, never overly interested in lyrical content, veered more toward a demonstrative, harsher sound built around his considerable technique and pronounced taste for minor keys. His approach, with which Michael Giles ultimately agreed, was more rock-orientated.

The day after the filming, between midnight and 4.00 am, Fripp and Michael Giles discussed the future. Specifically Fripp suggested that what the band needed was a strong front man and vocalist, suggesting Greg Lake, whom he had known in Bournemouth.

On Saturday, 16 November, the group were in Studio B at the BBC Television Centre in Shepherd's Bush to record their performance for the show using tapes recorded at Brondesbury Road by Peter Giles. As the tapes were transferred up to 15-ips masters, the BBC engineers were extremely complimentary, comparing them favourably to a professional studio recording.

The show was transmitted on Saturday, 30 November. It featured GGF&McD miming *Drop In*, *Digging My Lawn*, *Make It Today*, *She Is Loaded* and another Fripp composition called *Tremelo Study* (Fripp recalls that this provided the musical basis for the chamber piece *Prelude: Song Of The Gulls on Islands*). Outdoor footage showed *Thursday Morning* and there was a specially animated sequence for *Elephant Song*.

After the recording, Fripp suggested that Lake should replace either him on guitar or Peter Giles on bass and vocals. Fripp's forcing of the issue coincided with the review period determining whether Angus and Phyllis Hunking would continue to provide funds, possibly an additional factor in his timing. But, looking back, both McDonald and Peter Giles feel that his actions were unnecessary and confrontational.

"I don't remember any clandestine discussions. Maybe there was or maybe there wasn't. That thing of Fripp offering to leave is just a ploy basically and totally unnecessary because it would have happened quite naturally," says Peter Giles. "Fripp is very cute with political moves. I don't remember any of that. As far as I'm concerned I was just getting pissed off. We'd always dreamt about making our music. We'd had everything on our side and nothing was happening so where was it going to go from there?"

Fripp disagrees with this perception. "My offer to leave GG&F was genuine, as was my offer to leave Crimson in December 1969 rather than Ian and Michael. And the discussions weren't clandestine, they were open. The matter was not 'forced': it was timely. To have continued at the review period, knowing that the band was not going to continue, was not quite straightforward and not quite honest. I had come to a personal decision and, rather than let matters drift, better to act clearly and openly. If the instrumental breaks of *Schizoid Man* are beginning to whisper in one ear, while the other is hearing *Digging My Lawn*, what do you do? This illustrates the purely musical gulf."

In Michael Giles' heart, he knew that Fripp's musical route was the one he preferred. "You must remember that Peter and I were never as thick as thieves. We were always individuals. As much as I love him, we were never some kind of inseparable brotherhood that had a design on the world which had to be carried out. Fripp and I just sat down and decided we had to do something. What did we have to lose? For some reason completely unknown to me to this day, Peter didn't feel that way."

With a conviction that remains undiminished more than 30 years after the event, Peter Giles reflects: "When something is in your heart and you've followed your heart and you've given your very best shot – like when you're in love with somebody (it's no different) – you live with them for a bit and you try your damnedest but it just keeps getting into this muddy water all the time, terrible rows and whatever. Then sooner or later you say that I can't go on with this. It just doesn't work, for whatever reason.

The year that we were together seemed a very short space of time. Bearing in mind the context that Mike and I were very suited musicians, we'd been around in studios, gigs, playing with stars and so on.

"A year of wholehearted devotion to this thing was a lot of effort, I tell you. I did everything in that band to make it work. I did all the press releases, every bloody thing. I was the prime mover. It was me that had the contacts and did all the chatting up. I was quite good at it and it was probably right that I did do it. I'd given it my very best shot and nothing had come of it – same old thing; every single goes down the tubes, the album didn't budge. What could you do? I put my hand on my heart and just gave up."

The *Colour Me Pop* transmission should have been a career highpoint but, by the time of its broadcast, Peter Giles had left and Greg Lake was installed in Brondesbury Road.

VI

By 1968 Greg Lake was playing seven nights a week in The Gods. Born on 10 November 1948, Lake was brought up in Oakdale, a working-class housing estate outside Poole. In 1960, his mother bought the 12-year-old Lake his first guitar and lessons from Don Strike, the same tutor who had coached Fripp two years earlier. Lake had good cause to remember his time with Strike. "He was a good teacher but a bit of a disciplinarian. On my guitar, I had to do these violin exercises by Paganini, which were a weird concoction of music. You were required to read the music, but I always tended to play them by ear. Whenever my eyes would stray from the music score, he'd hit my fingers with a ruler."

Lake formed his own group, Unit Four, in which he played lead guitar and sang, in 1965. He remembers: "Fripp used to come along and check me out. He used to jump over the wall at clubs because he couldn't afford to get in and he would come along and watch me, and at the end of the gigs he would come up and talk and we'd start to chat about guitar and play a bit and so on. We discovered that we'd both had the same guitar teacher and we both had similar guitar techniques and we struck up a friendship. I used to go 'round to Robert's house and we used to play guitar duets in his bedroom and that kind of thing."

By 1967, Lake had developed something of a reputation as a local hotshot, as Fripp recalls: "It was obvious to those in the playing pool that some of us would go to the professional route and leave Bournemouth, where semi-professional and professional life were virtually the same. It also seemed likely that some of our team would become successful, and some famous. In my circle, Greg Lake was considered one of the front-runners for fame."

Following a brief stint in The Time Checks, Lake helped form The Shame who eventually secured the interest of MGM and in September 1967 released their first single. A cover version of a little-known Janis Ian song, *Too Old To Go 'Way Little Girl*, features Lake on surprisingly assertive vocals and piercing lead guitar. Even on this early outing Lake's voice is completely recognisable and the addition of Traffic-like sitar locates the disc firmly within the home-grown UK psychedelic movement.

Fripp roadied for The Shame for a week in Penzance while waiting for his place in university, recalling: "Greg and I spent many late nights and early mornings with guitars, trying to make teenage sense of our lives, discussing and planning the future of the world. At the time Greg was one of my closest friends, and we enjoyed the kind and degree of intimacy which young men with guitars will easily understand."

Fripp moved up from roadying to actually playing lead when he guested on *Love* by Lake's next band, Shy Limbs. The track was the B-side to *Reputation* recorded in late 1968 but not released until 1969, and also included drummer Andy McCulloch in the line-up. There's a cheery Beatles-like optimism about the track but Fripp's lead lines offer a decisive break from the comping chord work that typified the constraints when recording GG&F's debut.

Lake went on to join The Gods, an established band which featured future Uriah Heep members keyboardist Ken Hensley, drummer Lee Kerslake and bassist/ guitarist John Konas. In The Gods, Lake was gigging on a nightly basis. But in November 1968 he received a call from his old friend Fripp offering him a job.

The call was quickly followed up by a personal visit from Michael Giles, who drove in his old Ford Anglia from London to Lake's house. "Robert stayed in London and I went down to have a talk to Greg. I was very impressed with his physical presence and the sound of his voice. I never saw him play or anything, we just had a meeting."

In December, Lake moved to London although accommodation still had to be sorted out – he and Fripp had to share a bed at Brondesbury Road for three days. Michael Giles soon heard the difference Lake made. "I couldn't sing like that, Robert couldn't sing at all, Peter couldn't sing like that. None of us had that sound or power."

Under McDonald's auspices, the as-yet-unnamed band negotiated a further loan from Hunking. Aside from the wages, administered by Fripp, the band now started buying equipment and, as 1969 came around and the lease on Brondesbury Road expired, they desperately needed a place to rehearse and store the recently acquired but hernia-inducing Mellotron. On 9 January, Fripp rang 'round with exciting news: the band's first booking. To be more accurate, it was GG&F's first booking, ironically their first and only – after they had broken up!

It was a week-long residency at a Newcastle nightclub. No doubt spurred on by this, that same day the band tried to conjure up a suitable name and it was agreed that Pete Sinfield and Dik Fraser would become road managers. By the next day Sinfield had found a suitable rehearsal room in the basement of the Fulham Palace Café, owned by Peter and George Calatychos, at 193 Fulham Palace Road. On Monday, 13 January, the band moved the Mellotron there from McDonald's parents' home and had a blow until 10.15 pm, after which McDonald ended up at Sinfield's writing tunes to two new riffs.

The regime at the café was disciplined, with rehearsals, usually starting around 6.00 pm, including weekends. Material included *Michael From Mountains* by Joni Mitchell, *Lucy In The Sky With Diamonds* by The Beatles, *Drop In* by Fripp, *Tomorrow's People* by Michael Giles and a ballad called *Lucky Man*, which Greg Lake had been kicking around for a few years. As Lake reveals, this could be quite an intimidating environment. "It was better not to make mistakes in that band 'cos it could be very ugly. Well, there was a sort of 'death look' that would go about. It was if you played anything that wasn't tasteful you'd get a quizzical look. It could be anybody. You might get a dirty look from Michael or Fripp or me. There was a sort of code for musical behaviour. You just didn't play the wrong thing at the wrong time but you were expected to play calibre music – that was the general expectation of everybody." Sinfield started to construct a basic light show in the basement, adding considerably to the atmosphere. Lake still regards the creative use of lights as vitally important. "It's something to this day that I still tell people doing lighting productions. I say 'Do we need all these fucking lights up there?', and they say 'Oh yeah' because of this reason or that reason and I tell the KC story; one light bulb in the right place is worth 100 varilights going off at the wrong time. Pete was great – he's a great artist."

Speaking to *Rolling Stone*'s Mark Williams, Fripp was unequivocal about the importance of Sinfield's visual flair. "With the lights he's had an opportunity to affect the music. He's developed the flashing sequences to such an extent now that he knows exactly what we're going to play before we play it and is ready to hit exactly the right colour at the right time. He can use this understanding to create or extend the mood of a passage too. If, for instance during a quiet musical passage lit with blues and green, I begin to start laying down some heavy rock chords before the rest of the group are ready for them, the fact that Pete isn't giving me some harsh red and yellow light deters me from taking it any further until the band are ready." The infernal impression was strengthened on Wednesday, 22 January, when the name "King Crimson" was adopted. A poetic device designed to represent Beelzebub in Sinfield's lyrics, the name was audacious and brimming with confidence, encapsulating something of the determination, self-possession and intention surrounding the band.

By the end of January, David Enthoven and John Gaydon were on board as managers, leaving their jobs at the offices of the music and theatrical agency Noel Gay. "I'd been there with Richard Armitage, who was Noel Gay's son, as his personal assistant on the road looking after David Frost and Manfred Mann," says Gaydon. Having eked out a low-level pop career as vocalist and guitarist with Band Of Angels, his step into management seemed a logical step given the failure of a solo career including a cover version of country and western song *Almost Persuaded*, released in 1967. Educated at Harrow, he joined Noel Gay and promptly got his old school friend Enthoven, who had roadied for Band Of Angels, a job at the agency. "I had made a decision to quit accountancy for the second time because I couldn't get my head around it," says Enthoven, who was given the agency's catalogues to look through for potential exploitation. "I remember being given all of the Bell catalogue and was asked to go through these songs and see if anything could be a hit single. I must have gone through 60 or 70 of these things and pulling out *The Letter* by The Boxtops and thought it was fantastic. John and I were sharing together at Petersham Place and we were listening at this time to Blood, Sweat And Tears, John Sebastian, *Bookends*, *Satanic Majesties*, *Sgt Pepper* and we were smoking a lot of dope. In the Noel

Gay catalogues there languished GG&F who I always thought were The Scaffold. I had no idea who they were, the name sounded like a comedy act to me. It was just literally by chance when I was down in the country at my mother's house that I saw Colour Me Pop and GG&F came up with Ian McDonald. 'Fuck me,' I thought, '*that's* GG&F.' I had no fucking idea. Not a clue. That's how ignorant I was about what they were doing. I immediately saw that and thought we've got to talk to them."

John Gaydon recalls that the duo thought that GG&F had something they might be able to work with. "It was Fripp who got in touch with us and invited us to that basement in the New Year. Of course they were not remotely like GG&F. We were so blown away when they performed in the café. In those days bands would play a number, stop and have a cigarette or what have you but they played an entire set all the way, a lot of which turned up on *In The Court Of The Crimson King*. Our mouths were just hanging open. Music like that didn't exist really. They did the whole thing, Mellotron, strobe lighting and everything downstairs in that tiny café. David and I looked at each and said this is our ticket out of Noel Gay."

When they left the agency they brokered a deal where they would continue to look after Strawbs and folk singer Julie Felix, whose guitar Fripp would later borrow to use on the recording of Crimson's debut. Given their wealthy backgrounds, the pair had no qualms about leaving their positions – but the inciting incident was encountering King Crimson. "We'd never heard anything like it," said Gaydon. "We knew we had to do something to get this band out into the world and we gave in our notice at Noel Gay the next day." Enthoven agrees. "Walking in and seeing that first rehearsal was honestly the most mind-blowing thing I've ever seen."

With the zeal of the recently converted, Enthoven and Gaydon used their connections to begin talking to record companies, beginning with Decca, an obvious choice given Hugh Mendl's signing of GG&F. Moody Blues producer Tony Clarke was dispatched to check out the band. Suitably impressed, Clarke declared his desire to take them into the studio. Promoter Brian Hutch wanted to take the band to America. To say that things were happening quickly is something of an understatement. In that air of excitement, the band piled into David Enthoven's blue VW on Saturday, 22 February, at 2.00 pm to travel to Newcastle for their residency at Change Is, a nightclub owned by comedian and TV personality Bob Monkhouse in the city's west end. The band stayed in digs ten miles outside the city centre, across the Tyne and right in the firing line of the ice-cold gales whipping in from the North Sea.

Change Is was a three-storey fun palace and Newcastle's trendiest nightspot. Each week the theme of the venue changed. The first week was "Love". The second week was "Fun". The week Crimson played the theme happened to be "Horror". As Sinfield and Fraser drove up the frozen motorways with the gear, the band went over to the club. Fripp recalled that the urge to get to the venue wasn't entirely musically inspired. "Greg said we should go into the club and line up the birds for the coming week. He looked on me, somewhat rightly, as an inept puller. Once in action I was assured, but to get to that point was a problem. Greg for his part had all the lines down and could charm nearly everyone he wanted, and he took it on himself to give me some help in strategy and manoeuvres." Under Lake's expert tutelage, Fripp picked up two girls that week but sadly for him that wasn't the only thing the hapless guitarist acquired, as a visit to the clap clinic in London's Gower Street and a diagnosis of gonorrhoea would later reveal. McDonald remembers that the band went down well, although the material was hardly likely to be what the Geordie crowd would have been expecting. At the start of the group's second set, by way of explanation to punters more used to the chintzy club acts, bemused club manager Romark (stage hypnotist Ron Markham) announced: "Ladies and gentlemen, Giles, Giles and Fripp, who for reasons best known to themselves have changed their name to King Crimson, will have a freak-out without the aid of pot, LSD or any other drugs."

One of the bands working at Change Is that week was The Georgia Quartet. "I never liked that name," laughs sax player Neil Perry. "It made us sound like a trad jazz outfit." They would later change their name to Quincy which, Perry says, was "still not quite right but better than the previous one". Working as many semi-pro nights as they could in the vibrant club scene, Perry and his colleagues held down day jobs. "The band lived all over the region and I was always last to get dropped off. It could sometimes be five in the morning before I'd get to bed, and then I had to be at work by 9.00 am. Some days I was dead on my feet." He recalls watching Crimson at Change Is and, although the music wasn't quite to his taste, being impressed by the standard of the musicianship. As a result, Perry remembers that his bandmates decided they should change direction, opting for a less poppy sound in favour of something heavier. That experience would be typical of other bands around the country encountering King Crimson's brutal precision and eclectic brand of rock and improvisation. McDonald also recalls Fripp taking a radio mic into the club toilets, adding a distinctly earthy ambient mix to the band's sound. At another point, during an improvisation, Lake and McDonald engaged in a mock fight. On the last night a girl in the audience fainted, although whether this was due to sheer excitement or poor air conditioning is unknown.

A week later, having earned a return booking, the band were on their way back to London and their first appearance in print as King Crimson. This was in the pages of the underground's standard bearer, *International Times*. Columnist Simon Stable predicted great things of the band who were also regular customers at his record shop, Simon's Stable, on the Portobello Road. A month later, Stable was again prompted to wax lyrical about the band in *IT*. "A café in the Fulham Palace Road is keeping within its bowels an incredible sound. The sound is made by a group called King Crimson and if you can imagine a combination of The Family, The Pretty Things and The Moody Blues all rolled into one you'll have a pretty good idea what they sound like."

VII

The trip to Newcastle had helped the band focus on what aspects of the show needed work and by the time the booker for the prestigious Speakeasy Club came to see them they were firing on all cylinders. Sinfield was working unpaid as roadie, lighting man and sound engineer. However, his role was increasing and he sought to make his position more formal. "I'm driving the van and then eventually we do some gigs and Dik Fraser is there – I brought Dik into it because, believe me, you cannot lift a Mellotron by yourself. There came a point where I was doing all these things – the lights, the sound and writing. We were down in Bristol or Plymouth and they nearly dropped the Mellotron on me and they are big bastards. So I had to say in a band meeting that I can't do all of this. And it was a moment in time that if I became part of the band because of my lights, sound, writing and various art-directing activities, if you like, then I didn't have to do the humping equipment which I'm definitely not built for. We had this Volkswagen and the van, which meant one of the band members would have to go in the van so we'd take it in turn. So it was quite a crucial moment for me, but they agreed and so from there on you see me in pictures sitting on the grass or whatever. Rather like Keith Reid of Procol Harum. I was a member of the ensemble although I didn't appear on stage."

But there was much work to be done on the band's image. If Lake was unimpressed with Fripp's chat-up technique, he was even less thrilled with the guitarist's dress sense. "When I got to the band I seem to remember that Robert was dressed in a red maroon pullover, grey flannel trousers, black Oxford shoes – he was dressed to go to grammar school! So I took him to Portobello Road and we walked along the road and I noticed there was a shop there which had a top hat and a cloak. And I remembered that Fripp was intrigued by Paganini and he used to play a lot of his exercises. It occurred to me that this top hat 'Jack The Ripper' style – the black magic of Paganini – all of that might suit him as an image. We got him kitted out in this gear but it got toned down and became a hippie kind of thing."

Not counting the trial run in Newcastle, King Crimson made its official live debut on Wednesday, 9 April, at The Speakeasy. The club in Margaret Road was a favourite haunt of record company people, musicians and journalists. The gig was powerful and went down well. Afterwards, the band was ecstatic. McDonald dropped Fripp and Lake off at their flat in Leinster Square and Fripp recorded in his diary: "Massive success. The word starts to creep about in the business." McDonald drove to his parents' house in Teddington, arriving after 5.30 am to write up the day's momentous events, noting that The Moody Blues were there as was Ginger Baker and Manfred Mann. McDonald reported that Crimson "blew their minds". Two days later the band supported Marc Bolan's Tyrannosaurus Rex at the Midnight Court at the Lyceum Theatre in the Strand, but didn't play until 4.15 am. Bill Bruford was at this gig and recalls the professional way Crimson took the stage, with no tuning up or superfluous announcements, before launching into the strobe-driven *Schizoid Man*. As he walked home, Bruford began to regard Crimson as a kind of benchmark by which everything else would be judged.

To help get the buzz going, the band had 100 posters printed, designed by their friend Barry Godber. They featured a stylised eye surrounded by a flame silkscreened on to reflective foil-style paper and boasted the enigmatic slogan 'King Crimson is …'. McDonald and Sinfield flyposted along the King's Road and other strategic locations. Those burning eyes of the outsider looking into the city would quickly adorn Michael Giles' double bass drum heads and of course obliquely hinted at Godber's later cover artwork for their debut album.

In April, discussions moved rapidly between EG Management and the Moodies' camp regarding the recording of the album with the Moody Blues, clearly seeing King Crimson as an important addition to their emerging business plan. The band met producer Tony Clarke and Graeme Edge and Mike Pinder of The Moody Blues to discuss recording and possibly supporting the Moodies on tour. Clarke suggested Morgan Studios in London, and the following month the band went along to Chaplin Road to check it out, bumping into Jethro Tull who were there recording *Stand Up*. Decca Studios was also considered, but the memory of working there was still fresh for Giles and Fripp. McDonald spent a lot of time listening to the style and production of the Moody Blues, in particular their latest album *On The Threshold Of A Dream*, perhaps trying to imagine how the proposed collaboration with Clarke would work out. Giles, however, was suspicious of the interest coming from the group whose album had just gone to number one in the UK's charts and into the Top 20 in America. He wondered if they were trying to discover, and perhaps appropriate, whatever it was that made Crimson tick. "I think they were terrified. There was a power and an energy coming off Crimson that couldn't be denied." On 19 April, *Melody Maker* reported that The Moody Blues were to launch their own record label, then called Circle. "The label will release records produced by the group and their own producer Tony Clarke. Their first release has not been scheduled but will be a group called King Crimson. The launch of the new company will not affect the group's contract with Decca Records."

On 14 May, the band played three well-received sets at Revolution, a nightclub in London's Bruton Place. McDonald records this gig as the best to date. It was also the first time Fripp played sitting on a stool. Speaking to Richard Williams in *Melody Maker* a year later, Fripp outlined his objections to the stereotypical guitar heroics then expected. "The difficulty of playing live is fighting off the showbiz thing. I can see the beauty of (Keith) Emerson, ligging about the organ, but I could never do that and make it work satisfactorily. It'd look false because that's not the kind of bloke I am. In the early days of Crimson we sat down and discussed the presentation of the band. The idea we thought we'd work to is that each man could be himself as far as possible on stage, and, for me, I said I'd be most happy sitting down behind an amplifier, and that all I'd have to worry about would be the playing and let everyone else jump about if they wanted to. I said I can't play the guitar standing up – completely different technique required – so the management bought me a tall stool instead." Not everyone was impressed by the decision. Fripp remembers Greg Lake commenting: "You can't sit down, you'd look like a mushroom!"

Crimson's avalanche of plaudits from more senior members of the industry continued at Revolution, with Jimi Hendrix expressing his admiration when he came backstage to congratulate Fripp. "Hendrix, dressed in white with his right arm in a sling, approached me afterwards and said 'Shake my left hand, man, it's nearer to my heart.' He was jumping up and down at his table, saying 'This is the best group in the world!'."

Two days later, on Fripp's 23rd birthday, Crimson were at The Marquee supporting Steppenwolf. Located at 90 Wardour Street in London's Soho, the club was a key component in Crimson's story. A vital stepping stone for any band wishing to make a reputation for themselves, the cramped surroundings played host to countless bands hoping to use it to take a great leap into the unknown, it launched many rock legends. At the Steppenwolf gig, members of Yes were in the audience. Having headlined the club several times, most recently just two days previously, Yes were there to check out the new kids on the block. Although this was only Crimson's ninth gig in London, the buzz was accelerating. Bruford, who'd already seen them, watched agog impressed by Crimson's startling control of dynamics, while guitarist Pete Banks' drink never left the bar for the duration of the set. Both players realised that Yes really had to up their game.

Neil Murray, respected bass player with Gilgamesh, National Health and, later, Whitesnake, Black Sabbath and Brian May, was an 18-year-old studying design at the London College of Printing when he first saw King Crimson at The Marquee. "I was really bowled over by them. This was before their first album came out and the thing that sticks in my memory, apart from the intricacies of the guitar playing, was their version of *Mars*. That was about the first time I'd been in a closed environment with really bright strobe lighting going on and it made me feel pretty strange. Nowadays I can't stand that sort of thing but at the time I thought 'Wow this is incredible'. It was a kind of multi-media experience. It wasn't just the sound and looking at the band. It was real intense visual stimulation going on as well. I think the reaction generally was standing there a bit stunned saying 'wow'. The whole thing was slightly odd anyway with Robert Fripp sitting down and looking very much the professor. For me, the thing about KC was the whole unit and the overall effect of it."

Mel Collins, then saxophonist with Circus, was well aware of Crimson's growing reputation and caught them several times in the New Paths slot playing with saxophonist John Surman's Octet at The Marquee. "New Paths was the idea of Marquee's manager, John Gee. He had the idea to promote the new young jazz players along with what he considered were new young jazz/rock bands. To introduce a young audience to this new generation of music and hopefully create a cross-over, before there was a cross-over in fact. It was quite a brave thing to do, really, at that time. So, he put John Surman and his band on the Sunday night with King Crimson and the Keith Tippett Band on Wednesday night with my band, Circus. Consequently, we would go and see King Crimson and John Surman. Crimson were the band at the time. They had this light show and clever time signatures, which was all very innovative and new. I liked them very much and nobody had done what Crimson were doing really. We saw them at a much higher level compared to what we were doing in Circus. Everything about Crimson was fantastically organised, management, equipment, it was all very impressive. They had it all in one bag. They were commercial as well and it was a good package looking at it in a business sense."

Guitarist Tony Lowe, who would later go on to be a member of the band Waves which also featured future Crim David Cross, attended several Marquee gigs. "The club itself was one of my favourites back in the day. It was always hot and stuffy but that didn't seem to matter. The bar was unusual at the time because it was partly soundproofed and it was actually possible to talk if there was music on in the main area. If my memory serves me right, there were mirrors along the end wall in the main room. Those gigs with Crimson were packed. The queue got longer every week as the word went 'round. Crimson at The Marquee became such a regular thing that one night Robert Fripp started the show by saying with a slight grin, 'Welcome to the King Crimson Show …' Their performances there were indeed legendary. I've never experienced anything like it since. I'm not sure if I can put my finger on exactly what struck me so hard about the band but I was well and truly hooked. I first realised how lights could be used at these gigs, and watching Pete Sinfield at the side of the stage, controlling them on such a little set-up was always entertaining. The lighting was changing exactly with the dramatic changes in the arrangements. I also remember Robert Fripp coating his hands with talcum powder just before playing. Most of the shows opened with *Schizoid Man* LOUD! I think if they'd had decibel level rules in those days, those guys would have definitely broken them. Before breaking into *Court Of The Crimson King* they would wander around their instruments going from improvised jazz into strange and often haunting areas of music. They were a force to be reckoned with …"

Another young guitarist, Steve Hackett, then 19 and a member of a band called Quiet World, remembers seeing Crimson there. A friend had told him that if he went he wouldn't be disappointed. He wasn't. "It was a kind of double header with John Surman's Octet, full of extremely competent jazzers but it struck me that it was very much pure jazz, acoustic instruments, playing into mics. Then Crimson came on and what was different was the power. It was very loud in that small club and it was very precise. At first it was difficult to tell if I was hearing guitar or sax and of course they were using strobe. It was difficult to tell quite what was what but it was being played very precisely and came across with a ferocious energy."

The pairing of Surman's Octet and King Crimson was indicative of the prevailing feeling that arbitrary barriers could be broken down. Writing in The Marquee's May newsletter, John Surman observed: "As far as working with King Crimson is concerned, I think it's a gas. I'm not interested in compartmentalising music. I just hope we'll spark them off and they'll spark us off. I think the kind of people who are going to come and hear us will be young people not worried about names. I just hope they dig it."

Crimson made 13 appearances at The Marquee in 1969 and each one added fuel to the word-of-mouth publicity machine. In June they were back at The Speakeasy, this time jamming with Donovan for an hour. According to *Rolling Stone*: "To See Donovan amongst the hierarchy of the pop world, everybody trying viciously to out tight-trouser each other, down in the dark depths of the London's Speakeasy, was rather incongruous. He had forsaken the comparative solitude of his country home to see King Crimson, a group who are clearly going to become a formidable force in rock music and who are already causing the aforementioned pop hierarchy to gasp in collective awe."

"It is obvious that Donovan's presence at the club was quite deliberate and though he is, judging by his past history, an inveterate avoider of publicity and a shy performer to boot, he was clearly out to have a good time. Not content with having his senses caressed and flattened in quick succession by the quite astounding King Crimson, he got up and requested a jam with them. Eventually the whole scene developed into something like a 'Donovan and King Crimson play the great rock'n'roll hits of the fifties' session, with Don shouting the lyrics of such numbers as *Kansas City*."

Simon Stable wrote in *Top Pops* magazine that Donovan reckoned King Crimson were the best band since The Beatles and that Pink Floyd's Rick Wright had also made it along to the Speakeasy gig.

IT's Mark Williams would also enthuse: "In case you weren't aware, King Crimson are the most beautiful, tight, original group to emerge on the British scene in at least two years. I seriously advise you to see them while you can because I strongly believe that in six months' time their appearances will be few and admission prices high."

VIII

On Thursday, 12 June, the day after McDonald left his parents' house and moved into Nevern Mansions in Earls Court, Crimson started work with Tony Clarke at Morgan. Clarke was an ambitious, likable character who cut his teeth playing bass in the pop boom of the late '50s and early '60s, when picking up an instrument was like being issued with a passport to the island of Cool. He soaked up skiffle and goatee-stroking sophisticated modern jazz in his art college days. With the winning smile of a true believer, he met the touring stars backstage, pressed the flesh, shared the buzz and knew without a shadow of a doubt his life had to go from semi-pro to the real deal.

Yet the appeal of life as a working player waned somewhat as he entertained thoughts about life on the other side of the counter. Poacher turned gamekeeper, he grabbed a job in the promotions department at Decca in 1963 and got into plugging for a while. His ambitious streak propelled him to talk to Dick Rowe, the head honcho of Decca A&R whose musical instincts had famously deserted him when it came to passing on The Beatles.

Rowe had Clarke start at the very bottom of the A&R food chain, gathering up the scores and charts after recording sessions, filing in the sheet music library. He'd traded a bass guitar for a clipboard and a stopwatch as he noted down titles, times, details. Clarke epitomised the kid who makes his own luck. When a colleague couldn't make a recording session, Clarke took over the controls and faders. Toward the end of 1965 he oversaw a pleasant toe-tapper called *Mirror Mirror* by Pinkerton's Assorted Colours. A glistening autoharp-driven piece of pop whose lyrics contrived to transform the murderous vanity of the wicked queen in the Brothers Grimm's Snow White into sunny, wide-eyed love song, it was something of a fairytale ending for Clarke when the single got to number nine in the charts in January 1966, gaining him a job as a full-time producer.

Eager to learn, for the next year Clarke absorbed everything around him in Decca; he got friendly with the engineers, the boys in the cutting rooms, talked to them, paid attention to where the mics were placed in a session, asked all the questions and ate up all answers with the gusto of a man on the edge of starvation. He sat in on the Monday morning A&R meetings, heard the yaying and naying on all kinds of pop, including Dick Rowe giving Jimi Hendrix the thumbs-down. Clarke was 27, a dapper figure in a corporate suit and tie, when Decca and Dick Rowe decided to give The Moody Blues one last chance and told Clarke to make something out of their demo tapes.

The band hadn't really done much since their big hit, *Go Now,* back in 1965. The demo Rowe played Clarke in truth wasn't really the same band. The line-up had undergone some crucial changes in the shape of Justin Hayward and John Lodge. They were still trading off the back of their hit when The Beatles changed the game with *Sgt Pepper's Lonely Hearts Club Band*. Realising that their long-term survival meant coming up with original material, they sojourned to a small town in Belgium, far away from the pop crowd. Emerging anew to reflect the psychedelic colours of the summer of '67, Justin Hayward's *Nights In White Satin* caught Decca's attention.

The arrival of the Moodies' demos coincided with the development of Decca's Deramic Sound System. At a time when the vast majority of households in the UK listened to their music on mono record players, stereo and hi-fidelity reproduction was still seen as something rather aspirational, a bit of an extravagance; nice if you could afford it – a bit like the new colour TVs introduced in the UK that same year.

To have what was at that stage a group fading to has-been status recast as the flagship for their new stereo system was a brave decision on Decca's part and *Days Of Future Passed* represented a triumphant regeneration. Though initially intended by Decca to be a pop-meets-classical match with the band augmented by an orchestra to play Dvorak's *New World Symphony*, the Moodies gently ignored the suggestion and inveigled their own material into the project, wrapping a set of disparate songs inside an elaborately packaged concept album chronicling a day in the life. Peter Knight's arrangements are relaxed and decidedly light-touch. Performed by the London Festival Orchestra, a floating agglomeration of classical players who coalesced into a house band for Decca, Knight's contribution is so important not because of the content of his rather literal easy-on-the-ear orchestrations but for an intention going beyond the usually subservient ornamentation traditionally ascribed to the orchestra in pop songs. Rather, the presence of the LFO was intended as a string-driven Midas touch that would transform base material into something precious. Hoisting the humble pop song to critical respectability was the name of the game. In case anyone missed this point, Decca boss Hugh Mendl breathlessly described the view from the newly-conquered artistic Everest: "... The Moody Blues have at last done what many others have dreamed of and talked about: they have extended the range of pop music, and found the point where it becomes one with the world of the classics."

Mendl's delight at the opportunities this album opened up wasn't simply musical: "For such a fusion of pop composition and classical writing, it seemed obvious that the Deramic Sound System would be the ideal recording technique. And here in DSS's deep, wide spectrum of 'all-around sound' it has, we believe, become more possible than in other way to be totally submerged – and hence totally committed to such a deeply emotional statement of the human condition today."

In the music papers, Decca's copywriters wasted no time proclaiming the message: "... modern day's music unbounded influence excitingly realised in symphonic terms makes this imaginative LP unique." Another spread offered the high-concept tagline

"When beat and classics meet" beneath a shot of the band looking earnestly out from the page below a packshot of another Deramic Sound System release, *Gypsy Romance* by Laszlo Tabor and his Orchestra. The music, much like the band itself, was nicely turned out. Despite a few concessions to fashion – foppish neckerchiefs, overly generous lapels, capes and frills et al. – this was a group that wouldn't scare your granny. Swooning strings with sweeping motifs amidst earnest poetics, it proffered an innocuous psychedelic day trip.

Perhaps more than any other moment on the album, *Nights In White Satin* is the point at which the different agendas, hopes and aspirations of the songwriter, the performers, the arranger, the producer and the record company executive converge. The undoubted climax of *Days Of Future Passed*, it's unlike anything else on the album. Hayward's gently existentialist folk song was augmented by a beautifully-judged amalgam of real and ersatz strings whose differing tonalities welled up into a beguiling simmer. When Hayward emotively sings "I love her" atop Mike Pinder's growling brass Mellotron and the sudden clamour of tremulous, massed voices in the distance, it's remarkably powerful. *Record Mirror*'s four-star review dubbed it "a very ambitious record. Since *Sgt Pepper*, groups have realised what CAN be done and the Moodies have been lucky enough to be involved in an LP which could give them the reputation for which they have long been searching."

The title of their follow-up, 1968's *In Search Of The Lost Chord*, encapsulated the quest most forward-looking groups identified with, that sense of looking for something more meaningful or profound in their work as the underground scene emerged and pop consciously transformed into rock. Though they approached this question from very different points of the compass, King Crimson and The Moody Blues at least had that in common and the initial association made some sense. However, the alliance was short-lived. Fripp remembers a couple of the band going down and hearing two or three songs in the basement. "A few days later the entire band came to see Crimson play at The Speakeasy. They hadn't heard the heavy stuff such as *Schizoid Man* or *Court* at that point. We were meant to be going out on tour with them but they came and saw us live and after that Crimson were dropped from the support slot. They knew we'd blow them off stage," concludes the guitarist.

The first track to be recorded was their set opener, *21st Century Schizoid Man*. Although McDonald was impressed with the recording of the backing track, inspiration deserted him when it came to laying down his solo the following day. It may well have been something in the air as engineer Andy Johns complained of feeling unwell and promptly collapsed. The group then laid down *I Talk To The Wind* with vocals completed on Saturday, 14 June. Over the next three days, the group concentrated on *Epitaph* but became increasingly unhappy. By 19 June, after a long discussion with Clarke in McDonald and Sinfield's new flat, they agreed to abandon the sessions. One of the reasons given was that that Morgan wasn't quite big enough and that the band needed more space. *IT* reported in early July that: "King Crimson have been thru a week of changes. After spending a 'four-figure sum' recording several tracks at Morgan, they found that they were dissatisfied with the sound they'd been getting. They're now looking for another studio … This week also meant a change from Marquee-Martin to Chrysalis for their agency. The group had been with Marquee-Martin for only about six weeks. One of their first gigs under the new arrangement is an appearance at the Hyde Park free concert on 5 July."

The heart of the matter was a difference in approach between the band and Clarke which Crimson saw as Clarke wanting to dilute the band's power through a softer production. This difference was not openly acknowledged at the time and the band's forthcoming appearance at the Hyde Park free concert supporting The Rolling Stones provided a useful shift in attention and priorities.

IX

As Willie Christie parked his BSA Thunderbolt just outside of The Beatles' Apple building in Savile Row he was feeling a little nervous. At the age of 18 he was about to have a close encounter with rock aristocracy. Earlier in the morning he'd received a phone call from his pal, writer BP Fallon, telling him to meet him at The Beatles' HQ that day. Fallon was doing a piece for the *Melody Maker* and the editor wanted some pictures. Having got his gear ready, Christie met Fallon in reception and together, made their way into the basement to rendezvous with The Rolling Stones. "It was just a couple of days before the big free concert in Hyde Park in July 1969," recalls Christie. "I was really just a kid at the time and I didn't really have much of a clue. I'd been working as an assistant to the photographer David Anthony in Australia the year before. Although I'd taken a few shots here and there since returning to London earlier in the year, this really was something of a different order."

Their Satanic Majesties were encamped in less than palatial conditions, easing in new recruit Mick Taylor. Christie recalls Taylor kept his back to the photographer for most of the session, and Jagger was also less than happy at his presence as they worked through material that would make up the setlist for the event originally intended to launch the new line-up but, following the death of Brian Jones on 3 July, would now act as a commemoration of their recently sacked colleague. Relieved when the job was done, Christie ascended to the pavement, making his way past the ever-present group of star-struck young girls languishing at the doorway in the hope of sighting their idols. "I'd just packed away my gear and BP was making his way to Jagger's Bentley because they still had an interview to do. Just then I looked up and saw Cliff Richard driving his rather sporty Jensen into Savile Row, passing by Jagger as he did so. I wish I'd had the camera out to grab what would've been a fantastic image. The old guard and the new there in one shot. You couldn't make it up."

With Cliff making his way towards his slot in the light entertainment gulags of the BBC and ITV, the Stones were headed to their coronation in Hyde Park on 5 July, kings of a youth culture that had undergone a radical transformation. Although estimates vary, somewhere in the region of 650,000 young people filled one of London's largest parks to hear the Stones.

Sharing the bill were half a dozen bands representing an eclectic smattering of the nascent underground scene: Screw, Roy Harper, Family, Battered Ornaments, Alex Korner's New Church and the Third Ear Band and King Crimson. All were looking for the kind of leg-up such exposure could give them. It was only Crimson's 18th gig but managers David Enthoven and John Gaydon knew how important this concert would for the progress of what they regarded as the best band in the world. Enthoven, who later guided Robbie Williams to solo stardom, regarded it as a pivotal moment. "I knew we had to get on the bill come what may. I went to see Peter Jenner of Blackhill Enterprises, who was organising the bill, and I offered him a cash bribe," he laughs. "I'd taken a bag with some money in and I'd put it on the table, telling him he could have the lot if he would put Crimson on the bill. Jenner was embarrassed by Enthoven's guileless bribery attempt and refused to accept the cash. "Bless him, he put them on the bill anyway."

The first of these large-scale concerts had been staged on 29 June in 1968 and was organised by Blackhill Enterprises primarily as a showcase for Pink Floyd. The popular location and good attendance ensured that a further three were staged that year, with a broad-based bill of folk, blues and rock. The following year, Eric Clapton used the area in the park known as the Cockpit to unveil the short-lived Blind Faith supergroup on 7 June. The next concert was the debut of new guitarist Taylor with the Stones.

The Stones had been rehearsing just two days earlier when the media reported that recently sacked guitarist Brian Jones had died. For a few hours the Stones' participation, and the concert as a whole, was in doubt as Blackhill and the band's management anxiously repackaged it as a tribute to the late musician.

On Saturday, Crimson assembled backstage waiting to go on. The still-fledgling band was, incredibly, about to perform to a crowd of hundreds of thousands.

When they took to the stage they restricted themselves to a truncated set: *21st Century Schizoid Man*, *The Court Of The Crimson King*, *Get Thy Bearings*, *Epitaph*, *Mantra*, *Travel Weary Capricorn*, an improvisation and, to close, Gustav Holst's *Mars*. Dik Fraser recalls that during the opening number a large framed photograph of Brian Jones fell, almost catching Greg Lake. The bass player shrugged off the mishap, but several people backstage thought it was some kind of augury or supernatural manifestation.

But it was a good day for Crimson. The newest member of the road crew, Richard Vickers (better known as Vick), recalled in his memoir of that period: "The high point of that gig was the whole audience rising to their feet as one and cheering Ian McDonald's solo during *Schizoid* – I remember the hairs on the back of my spine rising in unison as the roar from this huge crowd went up."

In the crowd stood Jamie Muir. Having only recently moved down from Edinburgh, the future Crimson percussionist was then playing with free improvisers such as John Stevens and Derek Bailey. He was impressed by the force Crimson created. "What was incredible was that they just exploded on to the scene fully matured. Most bands come along and then develop but Crimson just came on and exploded with this very adult, intelligent, cutting-edge music. It was just this whole package that went wallop!"

Fourteen-year-old Trevor Lever, attending his first concert, found Crimson perplexing. "At one point I thought an orchestra was playing but through my binoculars saw only four blokes on the stage. 'Where's the orchestra?' I asked a mate. 'Dunno,' was the informed reply. 'Who is this playing?' I said to no-one in particular. 'King something,' I was told. I made a mental note to check this band out at a later stage." It was the start of a love affair with the band which Lever, who has seen shows by every incarnation of the band between 1969 and 2018, continues to this day. Another audience member, Chris Hill, was just 16. He climbed a tree to better see the band, perhaps little realising that, by 2001 he would, as head of the Royal Bank of Scotland's commercial division in the south, be working as bank manager to Fripp and his Discipline Global Mobile company.

Dik Fraser looks back with a cool professionalism. "The thing is you have to figure that when you're taking part in a 'monumental event' it's not so bloody monumental. It's just worrying and scary or exciting or whatever. You don't think 'Oh this is going to go down in history'. It's only when people come along 30 years later still asking about it that you get a feel for how big it was."

Enthoven, celebrating his 25th birthday, was underneath the stage cranking up an old air-raid siren as the band above him churned through the closing moments of the thunderous Mars. For him, it was a defining moment in the Crimson story. "It was wonderful seeing what appeared to be hundreds of thousands of people standing up in awe and ecstasy at the song's finale. It was the best birthday present I could have had. They all stood up. The whole fucking bowl just stood up. Everybody. It was rammed and they all stood up and cheered. It was mind-blowing. The stage manager, I've forgotten his name, was trying to get us off and trying to pull the plug and everything and we just said let it run. We went over by about five minutes. He'd been really rude but at the end he gave us a nod as if to say 'Yes, OK, it was worth it'. We just knew we'd pulled it off. I didn't even bother to stay and watch The Stones. I just got on my bike and fucked off."

McDonald agrees that it was the point at which Crimson arrived, but adds: "It would sound blasé to say that this was just another gig for us, though in a sense it was; we were having a great time discovering and enjoying our music, but we were also experienced enough individually not to be too greatly affected by any particular venue."

Their 30-plus minutes over, some of the band went backstage and watched the headliners from the side. The event was filmed by Granada TV but Crimson were not featured. If you freeze-frame the early parts of *The Stones In The Park*, released on DVD in 2006, you can see, albeit momentarily, Fripp watching the band from the wings. For years it was assumed that there was no moving footage of the Crims in action. In *Mojo* magazine's article documenting the event, Fripp asserts: "There is no film of us playing at Hyde Park. All you can see of anything to do with King Crimson is my face between the palm fronds for one second. Then we were thrown offstage. Yes, we were thrown offstage. 'Get off,' they said. They didn't explain why, they just said 'Get off'." In fact some silent footage of the band performing *21st Century Schizoid Man* later surfaced. With audio dubbed from the audience bootleg recorded that day those few minutes provide a tantalising glimpse of the first line-up in action.

Sinfield was less than impressed with the gig, feeling that the band was below par, but Lake disagrees: "It was the first open-air gig that Crimson played and to that extent it wasn't as sonically controlled as the ones indoors. Pete didn't have his lights to play with but it was an extraordinary show." In his diary, Fripp noted: "Standing ovation. Mammoth success, of importance which will take time to appreciate. We'll look back to see this day in years to come and fully realise its significance."

Lake observes: "I think that even if that Hyde Park thing hadn't have happened, I don't think it would have affected the popularity of King Crimson. The band had spread like wildfire." Certainly the next night when Crimson played their regular slot at The Marquee, the club was packed. Sinfield regards that gig as infinitely superior to Hyde Park. "The Marquee the next night. NOW that was a humdinger! Oh yes indeedy!" McDonald noted in his diary note that the band certainly picked up a few new admirers: "Went to The Marquee. Did gig. Came back with nine chicks(!)."

John Gaydon agrees with Sinfield. For him the real buzz came from the run of gigs at The Marquee. "Oh, those shows were fantastic. Obviously Hyde Park was a big deal but for me the smaller shows really had something else going on." Such personal preferences aside, the outdoor gig undoubtedly put Crimson on the national map. The *NME* had reservations regarding certain aspects of the day but was full of praise for "the excellent four-man King Crimson who sang *20th Century Schizoid Man* and did a Donovan song urging everyone to get stoned, taking great flights into jazz and getting the crowd on their feet." Chris Welch in *Melody Maker* was also enthused. "King Crimson brought the first wave of excitement with their heavily arranged and powerful performance, culminating with a dramatic interpretation of Holst's *Mars* from *The Planets* suite."

Elsewhere in the same edition, BP Fallon's feature on the band breathlessly reported: "They haven't been playing together long. In fact they've only done 15 gigs. And already Island Records in Britain and Atlantic in America in a joint deal are waving an advance at them of over £100,000; Mercury have gone even further, with a tempting enticement of £150,000. Being beckoned by these staggering figures is no group of past-acknowledged musical heroes with a price on their individual names. No. It seems as if Ian McDonald, Greg Lake, Fripp, Mike Giles and Peter Sinfield have bounded over from nowhere to become King Crimson." Fallon ended his piece with a bold prediction: "King Crimson are going to be giants. Perhaps I'm wrong.

Perhaps. Give it a year and we'll know. No, dammit. Six months will do. Really ..."

Also in the crowd, having dropped some acid but sadly minus his camera, Willie Christie marvelled at the sheer spectacle of it all. If the accidental crossing of Mick Jagger and Cliff Richard's paths that Christie had witnessed back in Savile Row represented the passing of the baton from one musical generation to the next, then King Crimson supporting The Rolling Stones at Hyde Park undoubtedly signalled another.

Fripp has had plenty of time to ponder the repercussions of that day and the extraordinary events of 1969 which catapulted King Crimson to the record-buying public's attention. "Any group working together has to have a common aim. The '69 band's common aim was to be the best band in the world, whatever we understand by that, but that was the shared aim. Not the most successful band in the world, not the most famous band in the world – the best band in the world. And while you share that aim, and that is your primary focus together, things might happen."

X

Now ensconced in Wessex Studios, King Crimson and Tony Clarke resumed work. It wasn't going well. Crimson found themselves increasingly dissatisfied with the results, eventually opting to produce themselves. Given that they still had only a handful of gigs under their collective belt, one can't help but think that this band must have had balls of steel to tell one of the country's best-selling producers his services were no longer required. Fripp: "It wasn't balls of steel. It was just this wasn't right. Look at it a different way; this has to be right. It wasn't right. I believe we had a meeting in the EG Volkswagen Beetle and the decision was taken: if we produce ourselves we'll make mistakes but they'll be our mistakes and not someone else's. Tony Clarke would get me strumming rhythm chords to *I Talk To The Wind* for hours through the night. Well, through the night is not my best time for working. Strumming lots of chords is not the best use of me as a guitar player. In other words, he didn't see these artists; he didn't see this band. Not really. He saw what he obviously thought was a good band at the very least and it would be good for him as a producer and he probably gave it his best shot, but it wasn't the production for us. That's not a criticism of him as a producer. It was just a mismatch between producer and artist. I saw him a few years after that at Heathrow. I can't remember exactly what was said but there was an edge there. There was something not resolved for him. He seemed to have a bit of attitude about it. For me it was clear he wasn't the producer for this band. It doesn't mean the band's bad or wrong or the producer; it's just not the match."

Overcoming this setback, the group worked solidly on the material. Having found out how they didn't want their debut album to sound they set about fashioning the material they had into something that reflected their aspirations. It wasn't plain sailing. In his diary, on the tenth day of recording, Fripp dryly noted: "If you talk to the wind much longer, we might develop an advanced stage of boredom." After 22 days in Wessex with gigs between sessions, Fripp noted on 21 August: "At 8.30 am the album is put together."

Although several labels were keen on signing King Crimson, there was really only ever one contender. Island Records was the label. Initially promoting reggae acts, co-founder Chris Blackwell had been keen to get into the rock scene. "Guy Stevens was the one who told Chris Blackwell about Crimson," says Enthoven. "It was Guy who said that Island had to sign Crimson. It wasn't a difficult decision for us because the only records we really bought were either Atlantic or Sue Records label or Island Records. I bought anything that came out on Island. Chris Blackwell, to his credit, came to the mews and did the deal with us on the back of an envelope. He offered us a paltry amount which I think was £3,000 but he only really wanted the rights for the album in the UK at that time. Later on, we did bring the rights for Europe back into Island but then it was just the UK he was interested in."

The usual record deal of the day would have been the company giving the band and management an advance on sales, i.e. the standard business model. This of course meant that the record company owned the recording outright. With Crimson it was different. The loan from Angus Hunking had given the group a significant degree of independence and the financing of their debut was underwritten by Enthoven's bank loan. In light of this, Blackwell suggested that EG license the record to Island, meaning that the ownership of the record resided with the group and its management. It was a far-sighted deal and an indicator of the more altruistic impulses at work in at least that particular corner of the music industry.

There can't have been many label bosses even back then who, after signing the deal, would then have celebrated by going out to buy motorbikes. "The three of us shook hands and then went straight out and bought a BSA Thunderbolt each," laughs John Gaydon. "We then drove out to Henley to William Piggott-Brown's farm and drove through the cornfields. I hadn't even passed my test at that point and we smoked a lot of dope that night. I remember Chris's bike sat in the Island Studios in Basing Street off Portobello Road in the foyer for years."

If you ever wanted proof that King Crimson was a band in a hurry, consider this: by the time *In The Court Of The Crimson King* was released in October 1969, the band had been together less than nine months. The dynamic contents of the record, and its equally arresting cover art by Barry Godber, assured the album entered the Top 10 on both sides of the Atlantic. It was Fripp's idea to subtitle the album *An Observation By King Crimson*, lending the five pieces an implicit concept while retaining a slightly mysterious edge. It was also Fripp's suggestion that there be no print anywhere on the exterior artwork. Gaydon recalls Island Records being worried about objections from retailers. "Fripp said, 'Well, it'll be the only record in the shop without anything down the spine on it, so they'll know which one it is.' Which was brilliant when you think about it."

The album and the band would become regarded as standard bearers in the progressive rock movement of the 1970s. In 1969 progressive was a term applied to folk, blues, jazz and other forms of music and generally taken to mean it was moving forward or making a break with accepted traditions. It was not until the end of the '70s that the term became a generic pigeonhole. In 1997, writing liner notes for the Epitaph boxed set, Fripp's distaste for the term 'prog' and being lumped in with a raft of other bands was evident. "At the beginning of 1969 Crimson were 'Underground' and by the end of 1969 had become 'progressive'. After 1972, and into the 1980s, Crimson became part of 'Art Rock' and in the 1990s seems to be considered part of a 'Prog Rock' revival ... The only part of this to which I take exception is to have Crimson since 1970 regularly placed alongside Yes and Genesis, and frequently ELP. We may have shared the same part of the planet and space in time, even a musician or two, but our aims, way of doing things, history and (even) music, are very different … One simple reason Crimson is a bad example of mainstream Progressive Rock is that Crimson changed its direction and/or personnel whenever a particular musical approach had run its course. A primary rule of commercial success is to repeat yourself. Clearly commercial success was not the priority for Crimson and in this we succeeded, which is the second simple reason that Crimson is a bad example of mainstream Progressive Rock."

King Crimson's debut is interesting in that it directly influenced bands such as Yes and Genesis and countless other acts, and in many commentaries is often referred to as the first "proper" progressive rock album. There's surely no simpler way of starting a heated debate between fans of progressive music than to pose the question: what was the first prog rock album? There is no shortage of candidates. The Nice are certainly deserving of consideration with the ambitious fusion of rock and classical music on 1968's *Ars Longa Vita Brevis*. Similarly, it could be argued that the long-form exposition of Procol Harum's *In Held 'Twas In I*, also from 1968, stretched the usual boundaries that had once corralled artists aspiring towards something more expressive than the three-minute pop song.

On the other side of the Atlantic, recording just one LP in the summer of 1968, Touch were the brainchild of keyboard player Don Gallucci, previously with seminal garage band The Kingsmen. Inspired by The Beatles' *Sgt Pepper's Lonely Hearts Club Band*, and with a little help from his LSD, the resulting eponymous album, released in 1969, was about as far removed from the frat-rock chug of The Kingsmen's *Louie Louie* as it's possible to get. Jazzy, twiddly arrangements, expansive solos, obscure lyrics and time signatures that would flummox a tap-dancing millipede certainly make it an intriguing and often compelling missing link between psychedelia and prog rock. As previously noted, The Moody Blues' *Days Of Future Passed* will be mentioned as the progenitor of them all. Though there may never be a definitive answer, Crimson's debut is perhaps the first mature expression of the progressive movement rather than Prog with a capital 'P', ossifying into a style and positing legions of historical re-enactment societies posing as bands.

Writing in 2018, King Crimson manager David Singleton was asked to approve a TV advert which described King Crimson as "The Forefathers of Progressive Rock". David notes: "The label seems ill-fitting. It is very possible that *In The Court Of The Crimson King* (both song and album) may have been the birth of a genre. And I well understand those (such as Steven Wilson) who think that *Starless* is the defining prog rock song. But such a large amount of their work sits outside this … Let us start at the very beginning: *21st Century Schizoid Man*, which led to the dismissive comment: 'A poor man's Black Sabbath. Nothing more. Nothing less.' Are Black Sabbath prog rock? If not, how can this be? Is not *Schizoid Man* just a great rock song? Or, running through recent setlists, *Cadence And Cascade*, *Bolero*, *Islands*. Or, from the 1980s, *Discipline*, *Indiscipline*, *Neurotica*? What of the 'Adrian Belew' songs –

Matte Kudesai, Heartbeat, Sleepless, Walking On Air, Dinosaur, Eyes Wide Open …? I am not sure that all these are necessarily 'rock', let alone 'prog' – unless the term is so loose as to be utterly meaningless?

"I have loved *Red* from the first moment I heard it. And if 'progressive rock' means taking rock into new places, then this certainly progresses. But if it is of a genre, I find no similar pieces with the same compositional power elsewhere. Or *The ConstruKction Of Light.* This speaks in a language that hardly exists elsewhere in the Crimson repertoire, let alone outside it. Or the Wagnerian majesty of *Level Five.* The only use of a 'genre' is that if I play music by someone else of the same genre, I find a similarity. This is a punk band. That is a punk band. I do not hear *Red, The ConstruKction Of Light* or *Level Five* elsewhere. In fact, I do not find King Crimson elsewhere. Duh! They are unique. That is the attraction. Calling King Crimson 'The Forefathers of Progressive Rock' strikes me as pointless as calling The Beatles 'The Forefathers of Heavy Metal'. Is it not time that we stopped insulting this band with lazy epithets, and accepted that they are simply 'King Crimson'?"

The power of the album (and its cover) was tangible. The band's ability in *21st Century Schizoid Man* to wield such aggression with a scalpel-like precision is one of the obvious points of impact. However, as David Singleton suggests, if all this album had at its disposal was a heavy riff, it wouldn't be revered in quite the same way. The band's capacity to temper the aggression with a soaring melodicism and harmonic detail that left contemporaries marvelling at its richness is a crucial component of its longevity. The dreamy lyricism of *I Talk To The Wind* maintained a vein of darkness that neatly avoided it becoming a pie-eyed hippy trip. *Epitaph* and the title track's combination of instrumental grandeur and Greg Lake's astonishingly confident vocal possessed subtlety and an ambition that bordered on the symphonic. Even the oblique improvisation within *Moonchild*, commonly viewed as the album's weakest point, marks out a vision that is distinct from any of the other rock albums released that year.

Forty years after *In The Court Of The Crimson King* was originally released, Porcupine Tree founder and KC enthusiast Steven Wilson found himself working on new stereo and 5.1 mixes of an album he revered as a teenager. "The whole remixing process has been a window into something slightly surreal for me, that's for sure. One of the funniest things was when I got the master tapes for *Court* and listening through to *Schizoid Man* … And you realise that this was basically cut live, this historic burning piece is basically the birth of progressive rock right there in front of you and you get to the end of the take and you hear Michael Giles say 'How did you feel about that?'. The irony of hearing that at the end of what you know to be a piece of history just made me laugh! Of course at the time they were just guys in the studio cutting a take but now it's part of history and the idea that it could've possibly been bettered seems ridiculous in a way."

As on the other albums in the Crimson catalogue which were given the remix treatment, Wilson worked closely with Robert Fripp. The guitarist was a regular visitor to Wilson's home. "We spent about three days just doing a new stereo mix and were able to go back, in some cases, two generations of tape because of course what they were doing in those days was always doing sub-mixes and bouncing down. If you're working on an eight-track multi-track tape you start off by tracking the drums across two tracks, the bass and the acoustic guitar. Then if you want to carry on filling up the tape you're very limited. So what you then do is reduce that to a stereo bounce down on to a second tape machine – on a second reel of eight-track tape which then frees up six tracks on that tape for you to fill up with Mellotron overdubs. So then you do another reduction to a third reel of tape.

"Every time you do that of course two things are happening. First, you're committing yourself to the balance between those instruments you're bouncing down. So if you're doing the final mix and the acoustic guitar is too quiet in a section, there's nothing you can do about that because you've already done the reduction of the bass, drums and guitar: the relationship between those instruments is already set in stone. So a lot of the time what we were doing was picking things out of the mix. For example, Robert always felt that the acoustic guitar at the start of *Epitaph* was swamped by the Mellotron. So we were able to pick that out by going back to the slave reels and synching them with the original tracking reels so we were going back to the very first generation. So number one: that gave Robert more flexibility with what he wanted to hear in the final mix; and number two: we actually got better quality because we weren't using any second or third generation bounce-downs. That makes it closer than even the original band were at the time of the recording. When they were mixing it they weren't able to go into the mix in that kind of detail; they weren't able to say 'I'd like to pull out that one guitar phrase' and pull it out of the mix. They were very much committed to that what they'd already bounced down. We were able to go into the music in a way that no-one's been into it before."

Several decades removed from the events of 1969, Fripp offers this perspective on the group and the times in which it came into being. "One of the prime principles of King Crimson's *raison d'être* was progress – moving forward. What was important was to honour the spirit but not the form – you honour the spirit of the law not the letter of the law. Would we have sat in 1969 and articulated that a core principle is we continue to progress? Well, Michael Giles was probably the closest to it in articulating it, and in him it would have been attitude. That's the word he would've used; whether you had the right attitude; you had to keep moving."

XI

With the album finished, the explosion of success that would embroil the players was still some way off when, at the end of August, Crimson and a circle of friends assembled at journalist Simon Stable's house to hear the results of their work. Stephanie Ruben used to help Stable write his music column and had seen Crimson at Hyde Park. She was impressed with the music and the personalities. "Simon was a friend I came across and he used to write columns for *The International Times*, *Melody Maker* and so on. He was always waving the flag for these bands, not just Crimson, and he was such an enthusiast from the classics, to opera, to everything. He had a record shop in Portobello Road where he lived. He used to hang out with John Peel, Jeff Dexter, Andy Dunkley and all those guys. Crimson had just finished recording the first album and they would come and visit Simon. I went there once and he said he'd got a couple of the band coming 'round to play their tapes and Peter Sinfield and Ian McDonald turned up." Not long after, Ruben and Sinfield became partners and the pair started living together at the flat in Earl's Court along with McDonald. McDonald had recently fallen head over heels in love with Charlotte Bates whom he'd met during the abortive sessions with Tony Clarke. Michael Giles was seeing Mary Land whom he'd met on the Dunlop shoot the previous year. Both of these women would feature on the cover of McDonald and Giles' sole post-Crimson release in 1970.

Ruben remembers being almost intimidated by Fripp. "My first experience of Robert was that he was this enigmatic and evasive personality. I'd already heard all the stories about Robert – you know, he was difficult to work with but he played like an angel with melodies to make you weep. I think I imagined that he'd be quite tall but he's not. But I would say it was a presence that he had. I found him intimidating because I wanted his recognition. I had just turned 20 and he was unlike anybody else that I had hung out with. He was not approachable and he was certainly not open to soppy talk. He was never a giggler and he didn't let you in on the usual behavioural cues."

Even in 1969 Fripp had developed a reputation for being fastidious, a facet of his character which did not endear him to 17-year-old Charlotte Bates. "Well, I found Fripp extremely annoying and irritating. We went to his flat one day and it was like there was a line painted on the floor, an invisible line but it was definitely there. And one side was his half of the room and the other side was his girlfriend's and all his books were fanatically placed and I think they had plastic covers on them. He was just so meticulous it would drive me nuts! I just found him like an old man. He would just practise for 29 hours a day and I always thought he was a robot rather than a musician. He was determined to be technically good but he never played with any soul, I don't think – it never touched my soul, put it that way. It wasn't his age, it was his mannerisms and the way he was. I suppose some people are born at 40 aren't they, you know what I mean?"

The band were out on the road and the standard policy was that girlfriends were not allowed to accompany them. However, as Bates recalls, this did not prevent Lake availing himself of any opportunities which came his way. "I can remember one gig at the London College of Printing and I was sitting somewhere at the back or the side of the stage. There was all this anticipation that there is before a band comes on, and then there was this 20-minute gap with all of the band except Greg on stage. We had to go and get him in the end and he was bonking in the changing room. Greg was a great big ego, a big penis on legs. He put it about and he was proud of it. He was very into his image and chicks."

Notwithstanding Lake's method of pre-show preparation, Crimson continued to excite audiences. Mogul Thrash bass player John Wetton saw them at London College. "There wasn't a weak link in that band. Usually there's one or two dominant players and a couple who are prepared to take the back seat such as in The Beatles, Pink Floyd, The Rolling Stones and so on. I'm not saying they're weak links but they're guys who don't come forward but are prepared to do the legwork and there are usually one or two who dominate. But with Crimson that was not the case at all. Mike Giles was phenomenal and there really wasn't anyone on the stage who didn't have the ability. There weren't really many bands at the time who were all as consistently good as that line-up."

Gordon Haskell went to The Marquee and was also struck by the force of the music. But for him there were slightly more sinister aspects. "The timing of King Crimson was absolutely perfect because it was the antithesis of that optimism and beauty of the times and it was a dramatic prediction of where we are now. Bearing in mind where I'm coming from, which was love, beauty, happiness and spirit, I saw them as Satan!" If Haskell thought he could smell a whiff of brimstone in Crimson's music then the cover of the album released in October probably confirmed his worst fears. The screaming face on the sleeve was painted by Barry Godber.

Born in 1946, Godber attended Chelsea Art College, where Sinfield would often hang out on his days off. "He was one of the most charming, beautiful, in face and spirit, mischievous souls I have ever met. A comparison – well a sort of Nick Drake … but not as 'obviously' profound and moody. He was a darlin' man … He got all the girls … I used to watch and follow him around with a mixture of admiration and envy." Future Crimson roadie and tour manager Dik Fraser recalls they would all spend a lot of time getting drunk in the Six Bells pub in Chelsea. At the time Fraser was picking up work with Andy Dunkley and also took on more unusual driving jobs, sometimes accompanied by Godber. "I'd known Barry for a while. There was a group of people who hung out and he was one of them. I had a job in 1967 which involved delivering tacky reproduction furniture in Europe in a Transit Cube van. I'd drive to various places and I had one trip that I had to make to the South of France, so I took Barry with me. I mean, who's going to turn down a free ride to Monte Carlo?"

Disenchanted with painting, Godber got a job at the same computer firm as Sinfield and Fraser and settled down to programming the large mainframe machines. Godber became a regular visitor to the basement rehearsal room, designing a poster for the group, consulting with them about the design of a folder for band biographies and adorning Michael Giles' double bass drums with its distinctive flaming eyes artwork. When it came to producing a cover, Godber listened to tapes of the album and produced two startling paintings. Using watercolours, Godber looked into a shaving mirror and constructed one of the most fearful self-portraits ever to grace an album sleeve. Known by fans as 'the schizoid man', the painting was extremely powerful and received an overwhelming endorsement from the band and its supporters.

The inside cover was more benign. Some have interpreted this face as that of the Crimson King himself but, whatever its meaning, it conveys an inner peace and calm to counterbalance the fury of the outer cover. Only by delving inside did you find out that *In The Court Of The Crimson King* was "an observation by King Crimson".

Godber died the following year of a heart attack at the tragically early age of 24. Lake has no doubts about the qualities of the sleeve. "I'll tell you what makes it a great cover. First of all, it's a great cover because it's a great record. Second, it's a kind of appropriate picture, certainly for *Schizoid Man*, but third, the guy died after doing it – it's a kind of primal scream before the guy died. It's the stuff legends are made of. How many more properties can an album cover have going for it than that?"

In October, the album was released with an endorsement from no less a shaker and mover than The Who's Pete Townshend, who was asked to endorse the album by EG. Famously calling it "an uncanny masterpiece", Townshend noted: "A friend listening to the album from a room below says, 'Is that a new WHO album?'. Deeply I'm ashamed it isn't but I'm also glad somehow. That kind of intensity is music, not Rock."

The appearance of the cover glaring out of record shop window proved irresistible for many shoppers. Rhett Davies, who would later produce King Crimson's *Discipline*, worked in a branch of Harlequin Records in 1969 and remembers its impact. "I did a window display when that record came out. I phoned up the label and asked them to send me over 20 album sleeves so I could do a big window display. The entire window at the Liverpool Street branch was given over to it and I stuck a joint in one of the mouths."

With just a handful of gigs, and their groundbreaking appearance on the stage at Hyde Park, the band was seen by many as The Next Big Thing. But, now that the album was soon to be public property, there was a sense of anti-climax in some reviews. The *NME* spotted an apparent lack of drive in the material compared to their live performances and in doing so coined a recurring leitmotif of many subsequent Crimson album reviews over the next 30 years. Less measured was a short piece in *The International Times*, which described it as "the ultimate album", while Disc lauded the brilliant mixture of "melody and freak-out, fast and slow, atmospheric and electric". *Melody Maker* dependably intoned: "This is one you should try to hear."

Rolling Stone, which weeks earlier had gushed about Crimson, seemed a bit confused itself as it lamented "confusion" and a lack of musical consistency. "'Confusion is my epitaph' they sing on *Moonchild* and confusion certainly sums up this album ... The confusion comes in the mixture of styles on the LP ... The difficulties come through the lack of positive force on the whole LP. The title track in particular is a weak parody of the same number when delivered to a live audience . . . In judging this LP, one must discriminate between their live performance and the result of their time in the studios . . . Bob Fripp, lead guitarist, admits willingly that the group play for themselves. Hearing this album, they may well be bored."

Thus began the media's long love/hate relationship with Crimson.

XII

The hype surrounding King Crimson, deserved and otherwise, had already made its way across the Atlantic. "After the first Marquee Club gig everybody was coming up to us and chasing us," says Enthoven. "Dee Anthony from New York was saying he wanted to represent Crimson as management in America. We needed a management office there and Dee was an experienced person. He'd worked with Tony Bennett and Dee got us involved with Frank Barsalona at Premier Talent Agency so we went there." After Enthoven and Gaydon had partied in Ibiza at a friend's wedding they flew on to the States with just £50 between them. Arriving in New York was exciting, Gaydon recalls. "There was a beauty parade of interested parties. Apart from Ahmet Ertegun at Atlanta, Jac Holzman from Elektra came to see us and Mo Ostin from Warner Brothers as well as some others I can't remember now. They all wanted to sign us." Enthoven and Gaydon sat in the various offices with a very simple sales pitch: They played the album from start to finish. "It really sold itself," laughs Enthoven. After listening to it all the way through, Ertegun's reaction was immediate. "He offered us a deal right there and then," recalls Gaydon. He offered us $100,000 and I think a 12% royalty on retail. He said the only other artist offered those terms at Atlantic was Aretha Franklin but he added, 'don't tell anyone else'."

Jubilant at having signed with Atlantic, the pair celebrated by going to Central Park. "We got the cheque and we must have gone off and got pissed because when we were in Central Park we just jumped in the lake there. A policeman came up and said we'd better get out. We told him we were celebrating and he said, 'Well, you're not going to live too long if you don't get out because that lake is full of poison!' We were just two happy lads. We'd gone down to the wire with nothing and come up with this cheque for a huge amount of money." On his subsequent visits to England, Ertegun always hooked up with E&G. "We'd go out on the razzle with Ahmet whenever he came over to London because he liked young girls and we'd take him 'round places we knew."

Back in the UK, the press continued to monitor Crimson's progress. The *NME*'s Nick Logan presciently acknowledged that Crimson's very success also contained the makings of its downfall. "Fashions are pleasant but can be dangerously short-lived. In roaring out from nowhere in a matter of half a dozen months to become the fashionable underground attraction of the day, King Crimson have a problem. 'It's very worrying,' agreed drummer Mike Giles, speaking from their manager's Kensington mews house before the group left for its debut tour of America. 'But I cannot see what on Earth we can do about it.'"

EG's desk was starting to groan under the weight of offers and the following year was set to make the bustling pace of 1969 look tame. And yet there was, for some of the band, a sense that things were slipping from their control. Talking to David

Hughes in *Disc*, Fripp understood the pitfalls of having acquired a celebrity status in such a short space of time. "We're already suffering from very unkind remarks and also from too kind remarks. People seem to be either violently pro or anti us. And if there's one thing we have not learned to do properly yet, that's how to balance our life correctly and work hard yet still remain healthy . . . Three of us have been ill during the past month."

The last major gig for King Crimson in the UK was supporting The Nice at Croydon's Fairfield Hall on 17 October. Featuring the London debut of Keith Emerson's *Five Bridges Suite* with a full orchestra conducted by Joseph Eger (who had studied with Leopold Stokowski), it was another facet of the rock-meets-classical experiment which had seen Deep Purple's *Concerto For Group And Orchestra* performed the previous month at the Royal Albert Hall. Bassist and vocalist with The Nice, Lee Jackson recalls that although they were keen on such artistic collaborations there was never really enough time to get it exactly how they wanted it. "We'd played it earlier in Newcastle where it had been commissioned for the Arts Festival there, but the budget didn't run to an orchestra so we played it at the City Hall there as a trio. In London we had three hours' rehearsal in the afternoon of the gig. Joseph Eger and the orchestra had the music for it and that was the first time I'd ever heard the introduction that Keith had written. I was sitting in the audience and there were tears going down my face as I looked at Keith on stage, standing by the conductor. I'd heard him play bits of it on the keyboard but to hear the orchestra playing it was unbelievable. He orchestrated it all himself, writing out the charts over two long picnic tables in this rehearsal room we had. When he was finished, he'd say to me, 'first violins', and I'd take them over to the other side of the room out of the way, and then he'd get on with the cello, and so on. When I first heard it all come together I was blown away." Jackson recalls watching King Crimson at this and other gigs where they shared the bill, especially in America. "I thought they were great. I used to go out drinking with Greg Lake. Little did I know that him and Keith had a chat at the San Francisco Fillmore about forming what would become ELP which put an end to The Nice. Mike Giles was a fantastic drummer and later on I got him to play on a couple of Jackson Heights albums I made after The Nice fell apart."

Writing in the *Croydon Advertiser*, reviewer Barry Shinfield offered this perspective on Crimson's contribution to the evening. "King Crimson, who have a growing following, opened the concert. They were dramatic, not only musically but visually, with imaginative and effective use of stroboscope and lights. They also had a sense of humour: recreating, for the first few bars, some vintage Victor Sylvester. Predictably, the highlight of their appearance was *Court Of The Crimson King*, the best number they have written so far, which is on the second side of their recently-released LP, *In The Court Of The Crimson King*. Other numbers from the LP included *21st Century Schizoid Man*, a black view of our times if there was one, and *Epitaph*. There was also, with apologies, an unfinished instrumental with the prospective title of *Trees*, which began with an uncharacteristic, soothing harmonising and degenerated into a monotonous series of improvisations, but then caught the attention again with a brilliantly restrained ending."

Melody Maker thought Crimson stole the show. "A horde of hairy idiot dancers freaking out to the music of a sober-faced and dinner-jacketed symphony orchestra must rate as one of the more bizarre scenes of the year. But it was a fitting finale to an astonishing show with The Nice and King Crimson at Fairfield Hall, Croydon, on Friday. This was another ambitious attempt by The Nice to combine electronic rock with the rich acoustical sound of a full orchestra. It was exciting and entertaining – but musically it must be rated as only partial success.

"Musical honours went to King Crimson, who played a near faultless set and confirmed their reputation as a really important new group. They thundered into the cataclysmic *21st Century Schizoid Man*, followed by the beautiful *Epitaph*, and a new work, *Trees*, and the incredibly heavy *Court Of The Crimson King*. All their songs were impeccably arranged and executed and Robert Fripp's guitar work was excellent throughout: sometimes lyrical, sometimes jagged and always working in tight partnership with drummer Michael Giles. They closed with Mars from Holst's *Planets* suite hammering out the menacing riff over an eerie wail from Ian McDonald's Mellotron. Together with Peter Sinfield's brilliant lights, they created an almost overpowering atmosphere of power and evil."

In a short but sweet mention, *Record Mirror* said that Crimson "showed themselves to be the best band in Britain for many years. A still incomplete work, called *Trees*, worked out many fresh ideas of rhythms and harmonies. Crimson are off to America next week and, on this showing, they could be magnificent."

Trees featured three-part harmonies provided by Lake, McDonald and Giles and certainly had the potential to be a major new piece with sections written by McDonald which would later be reused on McDonald and Giles' *Birdman Suite*. Fripp had also contributed more awe-inspiring fast running lines that mirrored those he had brought into *Schizoid Man*.

Crimson arrived in New York on 27 October, and the following day there was important business to tackle, as Ian McDonald's diary indicated. "Spent all afternoon cutting LP at Atlantic. Went to Central Park with David and Pete. Group had dinner with Dee Anthony at his place. Went to see group audition with Dee. Back to Dee's then hotel." David Enthoven recalled the dinner at Anthony's house. "Dee Anthony got us really drunk. I just remember Robert and I going off and being really sick in Dee's loo, and Robert looking up at me, his glasses all covered in puke and groaning to me, 'We're not doing that again!' When Robert went for it, he went for it!"

As the tour got under way, Fripp noted in his journal: "King Crimson's first US gig to an audience with a high proportion tripping and expecting a happy soul band. We began with *Schizoid Man*. The audience never recovered from the first shock, their condition being delicate anyway. I had the impression of the crowd being squashed." Roadie Vick recalled the night with some amusement in the 1997 *Epitaph* booklet. "The audience were completely out of their head on synthetic mescaline and every time the strobes went off during *Schizoid Man* this very audible 'Aaaaah' ran 'round the room – it was hilarious."

Speaking to *Record Mirror* about the tour, Fripp said of the Vermont show: "It was a trial gig to see how things would go. As things turned out it wasn't bad. We had some initial troubles with the power supplies. We had to have one for the Mellotron, one for the amplifiers and one for the lights. Eventually we sorted the lot out."

"Then we had a very favourable reception at Boston – at The Tea Party. The audiences in Boston are very cool – not given to going wild, but we went down rather well. We played with one of Bill Graham's groups called Aum and with Al Kooper who's got this nine-piece band together – with Otis Redding's son as drummer."

Regarding the steady sales of the album back home, the guitarist commented: "It's very nice to see the album so high in Britain. Speaking for myself, when I hear how well it's doing I feel it's not me in some way. It's as though it's another band – I have this objective feeling toward it." The interview moved to an interesting insight into the band's plans for the year ahead. "Before King Crimson left for the States they premiered a new composition, provisionally called *Trees*, at the Fairfield Hall, Croydon. I asked him how the composing was coming along?"

"'The number's going to be renamed. We've written quite a lot for our second album which we should be recording in February for release in April or May. We're doing a lot of writing in our hotel rooms.'"

By the time the band arrived in New York, the piece had been significantly reconstructed to form *A Man, A City*, retitled *Pictures Of A City* in 1970 during the sessions for *In The Wake Of Poseidon*.

After flying to Boston, the band spent the next three days playing at The Boston Tea Party with Al Kooper. Crimson had some trouble settling down and gelling as a unit, a matter not helped by the erratic behaviour of the Mellotron. (Fripp: "When the band hit treble forte the American power supply dipped in voltage. The effect of that was to change the speed at which the Mellotron turned its tapes. The effect of that was to change their pitch. The effect of that was to put the Mellotron roughly within a quarter tone of the rest of the band.") Back in New York on Monday, 3 November, the band approved the pressing of the album and hung out for a meal with singer Joe Cocker with whom they shared the bill later in the month.

In Chicago the following Friday, the band played at the Kinetic Playground with Iron Butterfly. They had meant to stay on and play with The Who but the venue was torched by the local Mafia over an insurance dispute. Vick explained the drastic measures needed to keep the Crimson roadshow running. "The fire department had got it under control in time but the water used to douse the fire had completely waterlogged the equipment. Amplifiers were dried overnight with hairdryers, oven-baked for three hours each and then thoroughly checked by a local techie. Water had swollen the wooden keys of the Mellotron. Molly in the English office found and shipped another one out making us, I believe, the only band to carry three full-size Mellotrons."

Such was the interest in Crimson back home, Giles had been asked to provide dispatches for *Melody Maker.* One headline – "Good day from a very homesick scribe" – perfectly summed up the drummer's feelings. McDonald was sending off missives of a different kind. By the time Crimson got to Chicago, after just ten days in America, McDonald had written 12 letters to Charlotte Bates back in London and had received eight from her. With lots of free time on their hands, some of the band and crew hung out, got smashed on dope (excluding Fripp and Giles) and watched TV.

On Monday, 10 November, as the 300 miles of freeway rolled out between Chicago and Detroit, McDonald and Sinfield wrote the bulk of *Cat Food.* By Sunday, 16 November, back in New York, a combination of too much speed (and the consequent lack of sleep), marijuana and homesickness was beginning to take its toll on McDonald. Desperately missing Bates, he was writing several letters to her every day.

By now McDonald was phoning John Gaydon in London and insisting that Bates be flown out, despite the band rule about girlfriends on tour. Sensing that McDonald would not be put off, Gaydon acquiesced. As Stephanie Ruben recalls: "Charlotte had just met Ian and we were desperate that they had just left us behind but Robert said 'no women, no girls'. Although Charlotte did go out to New York at Ian's insistence but otherwise it was no women. Of course, it was 'ladies of the road' but not us!"

Knowing that Bates was flying out, McDonald's spirits lifted and the entire afternoon of Thursday, 20 November, was spent with the band rehearsing *A Man, A City.* On the following Saturday, on the other side of the Atlantic, there was a huge send-off party at the EG offices with champagne and a dope cake baked for the occasion. "I remember feeling incredibly sick on the plane after all the champagne and dope cake," explains Bates. "I was only in New York for four days but it was good to see Ian because he'd been away for a couple of months." McDonald's diary for Sunday, 23 November, is passionately direct: "To Kennedy Airport to meet Charlotte. T.F.Much! Ate at Haymarket with her. Hotel. Bed. Together." Four days later, Bates flew back to England. Yet almost before the plane cleared the airport, McDonald once again felt lost and adrift. Worse still, the creeping unease and sense of confused isolation wasn't just confined to him.

XIII

On the surface, all of Michael Giles' musical ambitions were finally in his grasp. In practice, the strange unreality of life on the road was taking its toll on him, too. "I was the oldest hand at being on the road although not in such a mega way, although being on the road is the same whether you're staying in the best hotels or the worst . . . I suppose it makes it a bit easier but not much. You just live for those two hours and the rest of it's crap."

"It's all that hanging about in hotels and airports, backstage . . . it's a strange place. I used to think of it and still do like it's the lions coming into the circus through those cages and then let loose and they've got to perform and then they're taken away again. Bands are penned up in small places, aircraft, hotel lobbies, hotel rooms, dressing rooms . . . it's all this containment. No wonder they go mad when they go on stage. It's a spectacle with caged-up human animals living in a transitory environment and then they're let loose for a couple of hours in a public circus."

Giles was looking for some meaning to it all and spoke to a bandmate. "On an American internal flight during the US tour, *circa* November 1969, Michael and I were sitting together," remembers Fripp. "He turned to me and said 'Do you know/want to know the secret of life?'. I don't recall whether I asked for the answer or simply listened. 'Life is love,' said Michael. He gave me a copy of *The Prophet* by Lebanese mystic Kahlil Gibran around the same time."

Unlike McDonald, Giles wasn't taking any drugs but he too was lovesick. He'd being going out with actress Mary Land and in September a British national newspaper, the *Daily Express*, ran a small article about Land's "rock star" beau.

> *Mary Waits for the Likely Man*
>
> The man most likely to marry Mary Land, 21, currently appearing at the Vaudeville Theatre in *The Man Most Likely To*, is pop drummer Michael Giles, 28, of the King Crimson group.
>
> They were walking the peace of Hyde Park yesterday far, far away from the relative turmoil of the Isle of Wight where Michael's group would, but for illness, have performed at the Dylan folk festival. "We hope to marry next year," says Mary. There is meanwhile, the problem of Michael's marriage to overcome. He has two children and the divorce proceedings are in progress.
>
> "We'll marry when he's free," says Mary. "But I wouldn't dream of going off on honeymoon if the play was still running. That's not done any more in theatre, you know."

Giles' love life, family issues and his growing disenchantment with life on the road soon came to a head. At end of November, the band flew from New York to Miami for the Palm Beach Festival. The release of the album meant that the group picked up some airplay but word of mouth and the hype machine all played their part as the correspondent for the *Palm Beach Post-Times* eagerly reported: "Around the lobby of the Colonnades Beach Hotel, here the word is spreading that the King Crimson musical group are the one to keep your eyes on."

This was the serious rock'n'roll circus, being ferried by helicopter to and from the gigs to share the bill with The Rolling Stones, Johnny Winter, Sly And The Family Stone, Janis Joplin et al. McDonald recalls hanging out with members of Spooky Tooth, meeting up with Jagger and Janis Joplin and some very un-Crimson photo calls by hotel swimming pools. Fripp also recalls the hotel but for very different reasons. "By the pool at the Sunset Marquis, off Sunset Boulevard in LA, I remember a discussion/conversation with Michael where he was saying that KC should become a studio band, rather than a touring outfit. There was no 'outcome' from this conversation, but I was concerned."

At the start of December, Crimson opened in Los Angeles at the Whisky A Go Go and, although they played well and stunned the crowd, weren't to everyone's liking. The *LA Times*' John Mendelsohn decried the band's efforts. "No, these boys are neither guitar-smashing rowdies nor pelvis-wriggling trouble-makers, but rather, artists, shrewd manipulators of myriad rock and other techniques. And they are boring beyond description."

Eric Burdon, lead singer with The Animals, wasn't impressed with Crimson, shouting and heckling their second show on opening night. Anne Moses, who reported on Burdon's interjections in her column for *NME*, talked to Lake about his impressions of the States so far and their ideas for gaining a foothold in the pop charts. "Like so many British groups, King Crimson seem hesitant about releasing singles on the American market. 'If we find a single which we think is valid as a single, not one released purely for the purpose of promotion, we'll release a single. Otherwise, no. We won't create a single. Most of our album tracks are eight or nine minutes and that's how they will stay. We won't cut them down for singles because they are total works. Chop a piece out of it and it's like chopping a corner out of a painting.'"

As the band left LA, McDonald and Giles decided to quit. The decision was both liberating and daunting but now at least the pair could see some light at the end of the tunnel. Dik Fraser picked up McDonald, Giles and Fripp from the hotel and he remembers the moment when the news broke. "I was driving the car from LA up to San Francisco (we stopped off at Big Sur for the night) and, on the way up from LA to Big Sur, Ian and Mike were in the back, Fripp was in the passenger seat and they laid it on him in the car, so I was the first to hear it. 'We can't take it anymore'. . . Fripp was pretty much unhappy and he got very quiet."

McDonald still feels uncomfortable about the way he left and his failure to properly discuss the issues and problems. "I was 23 years old. Things might have been different had I been in groups beforehand, but this was the first experience of being in a significant rock group. I think the main thing was that I wasn't ready for all that happening. Things were happening very quickly and in a big way. We were blowing audiences' minds and the thing was turning into this monster that was growing and maybe at the time I wasn't equipped to deal with it. Fripp was stunned, I know – he was heartbroken about it and I'm sure he still is, deep down. He probably hasn't forgiven me for doing that . . . everyone was stunned."

In the front seat, Fripp felt sheer incomprehension that McDonald and Giles did not place a greater value on Crimson. "My stomach disappeared. King Crimson was everything to me. To keep the band together, I offered to leave instead but Ian said that the band was more me than them." Reflecting on the event, the guitarist says: "I am no longer heartbroken, and haven't been for many years; probably, since 1972. I have long since forgiven Ian, so long that I can't remember when. Since we recognise in others what we know most deeply in ourselves, perhaps Ian is still heartbroken, deep down? My difficulty at the time was to understand why. Surely, the group was more important than the individuals? It was to me. Ian told me that my feel wasn't right for his music. I offered to leave, if that would keep the group going."

There could be no doubt that King Crimson comprised some truly gifted and original talents, yet its members were spectacularly inept at talking to each other about their basic concerns and problems. Band meetings were almost always taken up with the practicalities of getting from A to B rather than any discussion about the things in between. This aspect of the band's personality was just as important as the musical side but, to all intents and purposes, remained largely ignored.

Stephanie Ruben saw a fragile alliance of five young men all at different stages of personal and social development. "Put all these five guys together and they all seemed to have part of the puzzle in the making of this band, which made it untenable but glorious too." As Fripp wrote in the booklet to the *Epitaph* boxed set of live recordings by the band, released 18 years later: "Everyone was involved. This is how a group works – if one person thinks of an idea, sooner or later someone will play it. The committed energy of each member of the band generated some spectacular and audacious leaps into the unknown. Crimson didn't know what they couldn't do and went for it with gusto. Often."

The received wisdom tells us that King Crimson was and remains Robert Fripp's band. To be fair, the guitarist has spent much of the past 50 years denying and seeking to disprove this assertion. What Fripp brought to the band was an unimpeachable determination to connect with the music, subsuming in the process the extended soloing featured by many of his contemporaries in 1969 and the early 1970s. Of his own contribution, Fripp says that he brought a *raison d'être*. Though the single-minded intensity of his pursuit would frequently alienate him from others, Fripp's incisive playing was probably the band's secret weapon – always keeping things together but using intelligence and technique to devastating effect when unleashed.

What McDonald may have lacked in band and touring experience, he more than made up with his astonishing versatility. He gave Crimson a breadth and scope which made it the template for the progressive era. His broad-based musical training provided the band with a first-class arranger, accompanist and soloist. Equally at home in jazzy extemporisation, folk-tinged elegant ballads or the Gothic splendour of the band's classical flirtations, McDonald gave Crimson the necessary reach to realise its ambitions. Moreover, he was a gifted, prolific writer with an effusive rock sensibility, unafraid of superlative harmonies, with an ear for truly royal hooks. In 2001, Robert Fripp described McDonald's contribution as "sheer musicality".

Fripp's suggestion that Greg Lake replace either himself or Peter Giles was both desperate and inspirational. In one sense the acquisition of Lake was the last chance for a group of musicians going nowhere fast. Lake's majestic voice was more than equal to all the instrumental blood and thunder and powerfully capable of soaring over it with impressive ease. More than this, he was a seasoned front man of raw confidence stemming from his years of playing to crowds. Blessed with a copper-bottomed playing style, albeit not always suited to the improvisatory side, he was essential in giving Crimson much of its onstage drive and impact.

Numerous witnesses who saw the band have spoken of the extraordinary control and precision of Michael Giles. Arguably one of music's most lyrical drummers, he avoided cliché and formula to stay witty, loquacious and unswervingly ambitious. Fripp says: "Giles was the only player of the period who stood at the same level as Hendrix. It is impossible to exaggerate how good Giles was – he never, ever, played badly." Giles didn't contribute tunes but rather added a presence or, as Fripp puts it, authority. Giles regarded himself as a bridge between the different facets of the group's musical personality.

For any band, objective feedback is crucial and here Peter Sinfield understood the signs and symbols resonating within the music. What Sinfield didn't understand, his visionary imagination and quick wit would simply create. Perhaps more than anyone, Sinfield had an innate sense of the group in terms which transcended the music and bled into the worlds of art, poetry and contemporary culture.

All of these strands contributed to the band's meteoritic celebrity and reputation. However, Fripp in particular has often talked about the esoteric factors he believed accounted for Crimson's achievements. More than that, Fripp has argued that the music created the band rather than the other way around. "I think one would have to say that a musician acknowledges that music is a power. You don't have to believe in God but a musician believes in music as if it were a God and one would have to say with that band that something took place outside of the band and the words I'd use would be that music leant over and took us into its confidence.

"Music played that band for a short period of time. In King Crimson, we called this our Good Fairy. We knew it had nothing to do with us. And yet, despite the foibles, weaknesses, animosities and limitations of the members of that remarkable group, something exceptional occurred. Despite the people. I attribute this to the promptings of our Good Fairy, however (as adults) we might interpret the utter benevolence of that impulse which came into the lives of particular young men in a specific time and place."

This is not a view widely shared in the team. Taking the release of GG&F's only album and its rapid dissolution as his starting point, Sinfield writes: "Within a year of its release and demission, somebody had stirred a cauldron, pointed a bone, painted a throne and crowned a king. You'll work it out." More explicitly, in response to an account of the period posted on Fripp's online diary in August 1999, Sinfield retorted: "Elf/Good fairy? What difference? If you ever dare to really look . . . OPEN EYES – Boo!!"

Lake saw it as a combination of the right people in the right place at the right time. "King Crimson had this strange blend of personalities and the net result of it was music that was dangerous and passionate. These elements in combination I think are probably the most fascinating in music. Where there's a passion the music is always living on the edge, where there aren't any rules and certainly not rules which are obeyed. It was a very special band." Dik Fraser is equally doubtful about the "Good Fairy". "What good fairy? I certainly say they were lucky. Do I think there was a guardian angel? Naw, c'mon, give me a fuckin' break, Robert. It makes good copy. I certainly don't believe it and I don't believe Robert really believes it."

Fripp does believe it, though. If you talk to him in person, it's possible – despite the passage of time – to see his eyes tear up or his voice crack with emotion when he discusses this aspect of his experience. He remains deeply moved when he recounts his exposure to what he firmly believes was a force that was distinct and independent of the players. The attribution of their success to the "Good Fairy" was simply code for something deeper and more far-reaching; no matter how unfashionable or esoteric it sounds, Fripp is unshakable in his view that the power he experienced as a young man was not the result of the musicians but something ineffable and timeless. Crudely put, the album came about not because of the five individuals involved but through what Fripp calls the Creative Impulse reaching back from a point in the future, pulling those players towards it. He accepts that stating this is likely to be greeted with cynicism and suspicion. "What most people write about is the visible history of King Crimson, fact and function, who did what and who said what and to whom. The invisible history is not the world of facts but the world of value. It's the qualitative world over the creative process. You can't prove anything. All you can do is bring forward a witness who said I was moved by this, were you? So how on Earth do you explain the invisible without appearing to be a looney? For the '69 Crimson the creative explosion was utterly remarkable and anyone that got near the band came into a world where that creative power was present. This includes the people in the band, the management, the record company, BP Fallon, The Moody Blues, and all these characters. This was a remarkable creative explosion which happened despite the people involved and not because of them. Now, it's very difficult to argue for the notion of a benevolent creative impulse that so wishes to give itself away in the world that it sometimes calls upon unlikely characters to give it voice, and unlikely characters to give it ears. Nevertheless I suggest that it is true. The difficulty after the event, when the juice seems to be in abeyance, or the Good Fairy no longer seems to bend over and whisper in the ear is, what do I do now? At the time, the explosion was such that it carried everything before it. It changed not long after Hyde Park. To begin with, the focus and commitment of all the players was completely on this. Then the success and the explosion, and for those who were more interested in women, the attention moved a little and the focus in King Crimson began to disperse within the band perhaps immediately after Hyde Park. But the moment was so strong that it kept everything moving until the band fell apart in December."

Whether one attributes Crimson's staggering success to some external benevolent force, Peter Sinfield's guidance, hard graft or plain luck, the extraordinary popular appeal enjoyed by this line-up has never been equalled in Crimson's 50-year career and the velocity of that popularity would shake it apart. Giles believes that the inability to talk to each other about their real concerns was exacerbated by the breakneck momentum of their success. "People gave themselves to the music rather than even trying to verbalise animosities and I think, if the band hadn't have been so successful so quickly, then those animosities would have had the time to be discussed and sorted out whilst there was still a joint endeavour. But because success was so meteoric there was no time for anything."

While McDonald accepts that he was desperate to be reunited with Bates, he is quick to point out that to blame his departure on his girlfriend would be to simplify the situation. "I was probably not emotionally mature enough to handle it and I just made rather a rash decision to leave without consulting anyone. There wasn't a strong management support and had there been someone I could have perhaps talked to in the management, I might have been talked out of leaving before I made the announcement. Nobody from management said, 'Look, I understand how you feel. We've only got a couple of gigs, we'll be back in England soon, cool out and then we'll talk.'"

Enthoven accepts that as managers he and John Gaydon should have done more to keep the band together. "There *was* a bit of a power struggle within the band, I think. Robert was very motivated. Ian was clearly creatively more song-driven than Robert. That was the relationship that we should've recognised and tried to hold that together. We probably weren't mature enough to deal with it but actually we never saw it as our job. Nowadays, I would have fought tooth and nail, being older and wiser. But back then we were all the same age, and we were kind of all mates in a funny sort of way and you probably shouldn't be mates with the people you work with."

Gaydon also accepts that EG's hands-off approach wasn't helpful. "I guess we should've tried harder to keep them together and spoken to them like we were the grown-ups and they were the children. We should have told them to keep it together and not be spoilt brats. We should have done all that but we didn't think like that then. We were too laid back, too hippy, 'yeah man' and all that hippy shit."

McDonald, however, totally accepts his role in the situation. "I'm entirely responsible for my actions and I'm not blaming EG. I'm just saying that that was what the situation was at that time. The band itself didn't really interact socially. Peter was my friend because we wrote together but I didn't even tell him and I just made the announcement."

Word about McDonald and Giles' departure spread through the band and crew and inevitably robbed the shows in San Francisco of some of their potency. But relationships remained good, if somewhat out of kilter. Just as the departing pair were filled with a euphoric sense of freedom, Lake, Sinfield and Fripp were faced with the challenge of how to carry on.

Their first priority was to honour the remaining performances at the Fillmore West and this they did with a set of exemplary, though tired, performances. Thankfully these were taped by Vick using the Fillmore's in-house eight-track direct from the mixing desk and became the basis of the 1997 *Epitaph* set, which graphically exposed the terrifying clout of the band in concert. Lake initially lacked Fripp and Sinfield's belief that something could be rescued, and meeting Keith Emerson at the Fillmore in San Francisco and discussing the possibilities of working together provided him with an escape route if needed. But for the time being he kept his powder dry, determining to see how things might work out.

As Sinfield trekked around the shops, cafés and boutiques of Sausalito (where he first came upon a painting called *The Big Friend* by Sulamith Wülfing on a calendar he would later use for the cover of his solo album *Still*), he had much to think about. McDonald had brought the lyricist into contact with GG&F but Sinfield had carved for himself a distinctive role as an all-purpose vibe guide, musical guinea pig and stylistic barometer. In just a year he had gone from anonymous wordsmith, unpaid roadie, style guru, light and sound operator to one of the last remnants of the original band. Now, with the departure of McDonald, a potential future for which he had worked so hard was in danger of becoming last year's headlines.

When King Crimson left the stage of San Francisco's Fillmore West on Sunday, 14 December, it was over. The following day, the band boarded a plane for Heathrow and an uncertain future. Somewhere in the wintering sky, a series of new balances, alliances and ownerships began to materialise.

LEVEL 2: *And reels of dreams unrolled …*

Tuesday, 23 September 2014, and Mel Collins is on the bus provided by the local promoter travelling from a hotel out near the interstate down to Madison, Wisconsin, and the Barrymore Theatre where King Crimson will play later in the evening. As the spacious lanes of the freeway shorten into streets clogged with traffic, lined with houses, shops, and bustling with people, free time contracts into show time. Stepping out of the van in the car park near the stage door, Mel is greeted by a clutch of autograph hunters who've been waiting in the baking sun for a couple of hours. Met with fistfuls of Sharpies, Collins suddenly resembles a politician surrounded by a scrum of reporters. Unfailingly polite, Collins agrees to the numerous requests to sign the album sleeves presented to him. There is a special kind of excitement evident in the collectors wishing Mel to sign their vintage copies of In The Wake Of Poseidon, Lizard, Islands *and* Earthbound*; a giddy wonderment that the albums they've cherished for decades are being signed by one of the players. Ten minutes or more passes as Collins signs, smiles, and repeatedly says "thank you" to the numerous compliments: "I love your solo on* Cadence *And* Cascade*"; "Hey, man.* Lizard *changed my life, y'know …";* "Sailor's Tale *blew my mind …"*

As the testimonials keep coming, it's clear that this music is deeply felt, as though the signature now fresh on the sleeves connects the then and now. Collins is momentarily taken aback when one collector hands over a copy of Collins' pre-Crimson band, Circus's self-titled album to be signed. "Christ, you don't often see that one!" He laughs as his younger self is catapulted into the present. Conscious of the time, Collins gradually pulls himself away, apologetically explaining he has to go inside for the sound-check and promising that he'll sign more at the end of the show. It's a scene repeated at each of the 19 gigs King Crimson play during September and October that year. It was a special tour in every respect; King Crimson's return to live performance after a six-year hiatus and the first tour with Mel Collins since 1972. As they watch Collins disappear into the theatre, the fans gazing at their newly-signed albums look like they can hardly believe it. Mel knew how they felt. It's not something he could have predicted either. "What strikes me the most about revisiting these songs after all this time is how complex and demanding they can be. There's such a lot going on in them. Back then, though, we didn't think about any of that, at least not consciously. There was a lot of energy and a lot of exploration going on that we could try with Crimson. I can't imagine any other situation where I would have had that freedom."

But, as Collins recalls, that freedom came at a price. Between 1970 and the early months of

1972, King Crimson was a challenging place to be and in order to fully appreciate the achievements of the music it's instructive to recognise the adversity from which it came.

I

When, in a 1969 PR handout, Fripp wrote: "The fundamental aim of King Crimson is to organise anarchy, to utilise the latent power of chaos, and to allow the varying influences to interact and find their own equilibrium," he couldn't have known he was describing the circumstances that would surround the making of *In The Wake Of Poseidon.*

In the immediate aftermath of McDonald and Giles' announcing their departure, Greg Lake, who at that point had not yet committed to ELP, remembered discussing the possibility of carrying on with Fripp and Sinfield. "Robert had asked me if I wanted to continue the group under the name of King Crimson and I think I would have done had it just been one of the two of Ian and Mike who had left. It may have been possible, although very difficult, to replace one of those guys, but, for anyone who's familiar with the music of King Crimson, you would know how important Ian McDonald and Michael Giles were to the actual creative energy of the band. And of course, with both of them missing, I just did not feel it was the same band and should not have the same name. Nowadays it probably doesn't matter as much, but then there was this thing of integrity and I just felt that it wasn't a totally honest way forward to call the band King Crimson."

With Lake on the way out, the search began for a new vocalist. Astonishingly, through a mutual management connection and without recourse to the band, EG's Mark Fenwick booked the then largely unknown Elton John to sing on the second King Crimson album. After listening to John's 1969 debut album, *Empty Sky*, Fripp decided that he wasn't right for Crimson. Despite the cancellation, John received a fee without ever having sung a note or entered a studio with Crimson. It still seems an odd incident to Fripp, who says: "Oprah Winfrey introduced Elton on her show as one who has overcome personal difficulties, such as rejection by the group King Crimson! And I didn't know that Elton got paid. This was never told to me at the time."

Singer Peter Straker was approached. An intriguing contender, Straker had been in the original cast of the hippie exploitation musical *Hair* and was regarded as a powerful singer and performer. Though Crimson were keen to secure his services, Straker's management wanted more than EG were prepared to pay and the deal came to nothing. "It was more the manager's attitude that scuppered it for me. This was a career move on his behalf, rather than a conviction move," remembers Fripp. After a minor flirtation with rock music, Straker returned to a successful career in the theatre.

Sinfield remembers pressure from EG and Island for the remnants of Crimson to get back into the studio and get on with the business of recording the follow-up to *Court* to maintain the band's momentum. So, with the group having drawn a blank trying to finding a suitable replacement, Lake was persuaded to come back and record the vocals for the bulk of what became *In The Wake Of Poseidon*. In return for his work, he negotiated payment in the form of Crimson's PA system. "The actual phrase used by Greg was 'for my art'. So, there you are. Greg was being paid with the WEM PA for his art," comments Fripp.

That still left a rhythm section to be found.

There was nothing sentimental at play in Fripp's decision to call the Giles brothers. Rather it was a pragmatic impulse borne from his desire to keep Crimson alive. Although they hadn't parted on the easiest of terms, Fripp had no hesitation in bringing Peter Giles into Wessex. "I didn't consider Greg as a bass player for *Poseidon*. He was not a natural bass player, and his parts had only developed within rehearsals. Peter Giles could walk in and play bass, Greg could not," says Fripp. Peter was by now working for the same computer firm which had also employed Sinfield, Barry Godber and Dik Fraser, having put his musical aspirations on hold since the dissolution of GG&F. He was both pleased and surprised to get a call inviting him to the sessions and speculates that there might have been a pang of conscience over his ousting from the nascent Crimson by Fripp. "I think that there was some guilt on their part because I'd been the donkey, the ox of the band, and I was the one who'd got absolutely nothing from it, whereas they'd gone on … I didn't feel that, but I can understand if they felt that. It's a decent thing to feel. So I think that's one of the things about the configuration of *Poseidon*. They thought: 'Why not have Pete playing bass and Greg singing, Pete's a better bass player anyway, let him have a bash,' and I think that was very nice of them to do that."

It's easy to forget that even by the spring of 1970 the continuation of King Crimson wasn't a foregone conclusion. "Things looked bloody wobbly for a while," says Enthoven, recalling the ripples of concern sweeping through the EG offices on the King's Road. While the band, who'd helped establish EG as one of the most creative music management teams in the industry, had come to such an abrupt halt, the revenue from its success carried on regardless. Faced with the enormous task that would be required to keep the show on the road, stepping away from the wreckage of what used to be King Crimson would have undoubtedly been the easier of the two options. Yet this wasn't ever under serious consideration by Fripp or Sinfield. In the course of the previous year, the guitarist had experienced the sense that music wasn't something that simply sprang from the fingers or the head but was in itself a spiritual, sentient force capable of reaching down and transforming the lives of those open to its presence. The decision to carry on came from the hope that it would once again be possible to be exposed to the power of music through this vehicle. If we accept Fripp's assertion that, in 1969, it was music that played the band, then this phase of Crimson had none of the mythical grace or near-mystical convergences of fate that had informed its predecessor. This was more make-do-and-mend and a resolve strengthened perhaps not so much by any so-called "Good Fairy" but more by an instinct for survival. EG's press releases talked up the game by spinning that unnamed replacements for McDonald and Giles had already been found and that the new group planned to spend three months rehearsing before touring again. Another hopeful press source mentioned King Crimson as being part of the line-up of a peace festival planned by John Lennon to be held in Toronto later that year. That sanguine "business as usual" bravado and the speed with which the recording of *Poseidon* was undertaken indicated a heightened sense of urgency. It also speaks to the character of those left in the wheelhouse and the extent to which they could keep their nerve. Having endured years of struggle prior to Crimson, and now having a more than respectable toehold within the industry, neither Fripp nor Sinfield had any desire to return to artistic obscurity. Sat in their basement HQ, Fripp and Sinfield rummaged through their notebooks to see what might be salvaged for a new Crimson album. *Pictures Of A City*, with its roots in *Trees*, had been shorn of the haunting three-part harmony vocal introduction and other sections composed by Ian McDonald before Crimson performed it as *A Man, A City* on the final leg of their US tour. Here was a piece intended to rival the punch packed by *21st Century Schizoid Man* but which outgunned its predecessor in terms of technical dexterity and dynamic control. Fripp also dusted off *Peace*, a delicate, lyrical guitar theme dating back to 1968 and the Giles, Giles & Fripp track *Passages Of Time*. *Cat Food*, Ian McDonald and Pete Sinfield's satirical take on consumerist society, tried out in late 1969, was pulled in with musical adjustments by Fripp. There was also *Mars*. A strobe-lit favourite from their gigs, the Mellotron-heavy epic had been considered for inclusion on *In The Court Of The Crimson King* but rejected as a result of licensing difficulties from Gustav Holst's estate. Perhaps with some adjustments, however, it might just be repurposed. When it came to material specifically written for the new album, there was just *Cadence And Cascade* and the title track assembled from one of Fripp's more yearning, melodic motifs.

The tracks for *Poseidon* were learned in rehearsal in the Fulham Palace Road Café basement and then played through live by Giles, Giles and Fripp at Wessex. Peter recalls: "I didn't have a problem because they'd played some of the stuff in on stage so it was just a question of me fitting in. It wasn't difficult learning the things even though I didn't have much of an input into the arrangements whereas normally I would do. We played it live, everybody in. Do a take and if it worked, move on, and if it didn't, try it again. I think it was done without too much fuss. We'd rehearsed it all. That's the way to go into a studio; rehearse it, know what you're doing and try and get a good performance. And I think we did. The first side was great."

II

With Peter Sinfield watching on, the three players were set up in a small corner of Wessex's cavernous main studio. As they waited for levels to be set, Giles, Giles and Fripp slipped back into their old jokey personae last heard at Brondesbury Road, dipping into their dance-band past with a sprightly, impromptu rendition of Ary Barroso's *Brazil* with Michael Giles singing along off-mic. On another occasion, after tinkering with Fripp's long-running party piece, Eric Coates' *By The Sleepy Lagoon*, better known as the theme music to the long-running radio series *Desert Island Discs*, amid the laughter prior to a take, Fripp can be heard saying: "OK, let's play jazz, boys."

As Peter Giles puts on one of his Goons-inspired voices, his brother, tongue firmly in cheek, says: "I think King Crimson's a bit like the Moody Blues. Especially that *Pictures Of A City*." Fripp replies: "We could do a mock jazz number by The Crimson Stompers." And off they fly into a country and western pastiche. On another break in, they indulge in a brief spot of Elmore James-style 12-bar blues. Within what is clearly a relaxed atmosphere, the trio eventually knuckle down and record multiple takes of *Groon* with a feel that undoubtedly pays homage to Tony Williams' Lifetime whose 1969 double album *Emergency*, featuring John McLaughlin, was a particular favourite of Fripp's. The track's intriguing title was coined by Sinfield as his synapses fired somewhere between "groove" and "groan" while writing *Cat Food*. Peter Giles wasn't especially keen on the piece, feeling there was little in it beyond its initially galloping riff, echoing the antipathy he felt towards *Erudite Eyes*, an earlier "springboard" composition of Fripp's. However, as Fripp points out: "It was up to the three players to improvise!"

Also exercising their attention in early sessions was *Cat Food*. By take four they nailed the basic song with Fripp adding two more sets of overdubbed embellishments. What's interesting is how quickly they worked and how some of the extra harmonic elements are clearly already in place having either been mapped out in advance or on the fly. While some of these would be re-recorded and refined, other items present on this early run-through were preserved all the way to the final mix almost like an audio documentary, capturing the fun they had during the making of the album. Aside from Greg Lake's burst of surprised laughter, caused by Fripp dropping his trousers and showing his bare behind to the singer as he recorded his vocals, for example, the fluffed guitar line heard halfway through take four is obviously cut but Fripp's frustrated yelp was kept, adding to the anarchic character of the piece.

Another crucial aspect that gave *Cat Food* its strange charm was pianist Keith Tippett, a young player Fripp and Sinfield had met the previous year and about whom they were wildly enthusiastic.

Tippett grew up in Bristol, steeped in the music of the church choir of which he and his father were both members. Self-taught on the household piano, he came to London in 1967. "I was so romantic, I just thought I'd get off the train in London, bump into Ronnie Scott or someone like that and start playing in jazz groups. Of course it wasn't like that," recalls Tippett. For over five decades Tippett has been rightly regarded as one of the most significant pianists and composers in European jazz. Open-minded, adventurous and never inclined to play it safe, Tippett has flourished as a remarkable soloist as well as a composer for a remarkable range of ensembles both large and small. Back in 1967, the young pianist found himself on his own in a bedsit and without a piano. Tippett didn't let that get in the way of his practice however, carving out a set of piano keys on the table in his room. "When I first moved to London I didn't know anybody and I didn't make any music for quite a long time. I think marking out the keyboard was more psychological because I had no response because it was just a table but I cut out an octave or two with a pen knife. The landlady stopped my deposit because I'd damaged her table but it served its purpose – it quite literally kept my hand in!" In order to finance his enrolment at the Barry summer school for jazz players in South Wales, Tippett took on a job shredding cardboard boxes in a warehouse. "It was just around the corner from Ronnie Scott's in Frith Street, and during lunchtimes I'd go with a sandwich and a cup of tea and sit and listen outside. Sometimes I'd hear bands that were rehearsing for that night. I was gradually getting closer and closer to working there!" While at Barry, he met Elton Dean, Nick Evans and Mark Charig, all of whom would join his group – and, in the case of Evans and Charig, add their distinctive contributions to King Crimson's *Lizard* with Charig also making memorable appearances on *Islands* and *Red*. At just 20, Tippett became one of the youngest recipients of an Arts Council of Great Britain grant which enabling him to finish a suite of pieces which would appear on *You Are Here … I Am There*, recorded in a couple of days in 1968 with engineer Eddie Offord. It was set to appear on Giorgio Gomelsky's Marmalade label, which had released John McLaughlin's solo debut *Extrapolation*, but Tippett had to wait a year to see it appear on Polydor. "I think Marmalade hit money problems and there was something going on with him and Polydor. So therefore my first record suffered because of those politics. When you're young, if you're working hard you're improving rapidly and when your first record takes over a year to come out it's a pain, because by the time it's out, the band has moved on." Notwithstanding Tippett's understandable disappointment, the record nevertheless captures some of the urgency and incisive, biting skill of the young musicians. As a calling card for some of the great figures in European jazz, *You Are Here … I Am There* remains an exhilarating and frequently beautiful debut. Tippett remembers the period as being incredibly fertile. "In those days there was a lot of moving from scene to scene. At that time you had so-called progressive rock music such as Pink Floyd and Soft Machine and you had Crimson and a few other bands which didn't quite have the profile. But there was a genuine meeting at that time coming out of soul and blues and rock'n'roll."

While any pianist could have been contracted in to play on *Cat Food*, it's unlikely that any of them would have come up with the fiercely inventive approach Tippett brings to the piece. With its mixture of scattergun notes and propulsive accents, Tippett's gleefully subversive work pushes a quirky pop song into an off-kilter dimension that's much more appropriate to the Crimson universe. Tippett was pleased with his session and even more pleased to be paid promptly. A crudely edited version of the recording was knitted together and released as a single, backed with *Groon*, on Friday, 13 March, at an extremely delicate point in Crimson's career. Sporting a picture sleeve featuring a Pete Sinfield collage that included his girlfriend Stephanie Ruben's cat Cinderella, the single let an interested world know that the band was still open for business. EG Management worked their industry connections to secure an appearance on *Top of the Pops*, the BBC's flagship pop show, watched by millions every week. Taking a break from the *Poseidon* sessions on 25 March, the day before the programme's transmission, Fripp, Lake, Tippett and the Giles brothers tagged along to BBC Television Centre in Shepherd's Bush to pose for publicity shots taken by photographer Harry Hammond. Each musician received £25 for their appearance, although Michael Giles had negotiated a separate fee of £50 from Crimson managers Enthoven and Gaydon, refusing to take part unless his fee was doubled.

Smiling at the memory, Peter Giles recalls no qualms or nerves at the prospect of appearing on national TV but being rather more concerned about not having the right outfit. "I didn't have much in the way of clothing at the time and I borrowed a lovely green jacket from this guy at work. So it started off with me on bass in my friend's green jacket which he was very proud to have seen on television. It was fine apart from Fripp and Greg Lake preening themselves endlessly before we went on." The episode also included Simon and Garfunkel, Joe Dolan, Marsha Hunt, Juicy Lucy, The Four Tops, Kenny Rogers and The First Edition, Norman Greenbaum and The Who. Even by this eclectic mix's standards, Crimson's take-down of consumer culture is bizarre and remarkable. Hosted by DJ Jimmy Savile, who would be exposed as a serial sex offender after his death in 2001, in accordance with BBC practice in the '60s and '70s the show was wiped in order so the expensive video tape could be re-used. For several years the only evidence of the band's appearance were still photos of the players on stage. However, in early January 2015, social media became highly agitated when rumours that a copy of the tape had been found. In fact, what had happened was *Top of the Pops* sold the show to foreign TV stations who would insert their own presenters. In this instance, Joe Berger did the honours for the Swiss-German show *Hits À Gogo* with a cringeworthy introduction. The previously unseen footage, in which we get a tantalising glimpse of the Barry Godber-designed "flaming eyes" bass drum artwork, reveals a slightly stiff and self-conscious outfit. Michael Giles is seen wryly smiling as he pretends to keep time on his ride cymbals; Fripp drapes his arm over the top of the neck simulating the descending glissando; Keith Tippett flails his fingers in a game but fruitless attempt to approximate the audio-track. Only Greg Lake looks truly comfortable making his first appearance in front of an audience since the previous December, giving it his all. In 2011 this unlikely convergence was referenced in British newspaper the *Guardian* as No. 37 of what it called the 50 key events in the history of dance music. The musician and critic John L Walters noted: "When King Crimson appeared on *Top of the Pops*, they looked like the rock gods they almost were, with long hair, loon pants and expensive gear. Side-whiskered guest pianist Keith Tippett, however, seemed to have stepped out of Doctor Who's Tardis from a parallel Brit-jazz universe. Reading from a crumpled sheet of manuscript propped on the upright acoustic piano, Tippett added thrilling cascades of spiky dissonance to Fripp, McDonald and Sinfield's cynical, asymmetric art-rock." Although *Cat Food* was largely well-received in the music press, Peter Giles recalls hearing the song being introduced on the radio as "the worst record in the world" and felt Tippett's piano undermined what might have been a commercially viable song. "Without the piano it might have actually done something. Fair enough, though, Fripp stuck to his guns, even though the guns were pointing in the wrong direction." Tippett returned to Wessex and laid down some beautiful embellishments to *Cadence And Cascade* and then, in stark contrast, the violent excursions of *The Devil's Triangle*. After Crimson were told by EG that any request to the estate of Gustav Holst to quote directly from *Mars* would likely be refused, some slight re-writing was required and the track was re-titled. In concert the piece had always been a theatrical *coup de grâce*, its malevolent chaos animated by Sinfield's flashing strobe light. In the studio an unnerving deluge of assonant Mellotron, elements of *musique concrète* and tempestuous percussion necessarily replaced the visual impact. Describing the recording process to the *NME*'s Nick Logan at the time, Fripp noted: "This one took a long time to record. You have three basic things going on. The basic rhythms of guitar and drums. On top of that you have piano and drums fighting and above that there are various pieces making a commentary on what's going on underneath. Keith is playing bits of nursery rhymes on harpsichord and there are snatches of reggae and *The Court Of The Crimson King* in there as well." Proto-sampling efforts aside, *The Devil's Triangle* might be viewed as a bold attempt to transform what had been a live favourite into an experimental sonic adventure. While such unorthodox exploration was consistent with Crimson's reputation for upending expectations, it's more likely that its appearance was as much to do with a shortage of formally written material as any desire to nail their collective colours to the avant-garde mast.

III

While the album was still taking shape, in March Mel Collins' name began appearing in print as a new member of the band. While such bulletins were premature and caused the young sax player no end of problems with his management and fellow members of his band Circus, Fripp knew that Collins' free-flowing playing made him the candidate for the job. The sax on *Pictures Of A City* added a volatile accelerant to an already incendiary track, while the shining filigree of his flute brought a lyrical intimacy to *Cadence And Cascade*, one of the last tracks to be completed. Previous accounts of the making of *In The Wake Of Poseidon* have always claimed that, with Greg Lake having moved on to ELP, Fripp's old schoolfriend and ex-bandmate from The League Of Gentlemen, Gordon Haskell, had to be drafted in for a session fee of £50 to complete the vocal. However, the conventional wisdom of 37 years was overturned in 2007 when DGM audio engineer Alex 'Stormy' Mundy discovered a quarter-inch reel-to-reel tape of the track with Lake singing. Nobody, including those present at Wessex, had any memory of him singing the song so this came as a complete revelation to all concerned. On this one-off take, Greg's vocal is a touch tentative and the intention was probably to come back and finish it at a later session which never materialised. An apparently straightforward ballad, Lake wasn't the only one who had problems with it and it's interesting to note that the final version by Haskell was recorded a semi-tone lower and then sped up to the correct pitch.

With the album all but in the can, the tracks were strategically unveiled to friends and colleagues. Ian McDonald recalls Fripp and Sinfield calling around to his flat with a copy of the work in progress. "They played me the tracks and it seemed like they wanted my input. My feeling at the time was that they were trying to get free ideas and I just kept my mouth shut. So that was a bit weird." Fripp's recollection was different. "Probably the visit was more like a courtesy call – there was clearly a connection, recently severed, and history. Possibly we were hoping for Ian's blessing or approval." Denying that they were after "free ideas", Fripp does admit that some forces in the Crimson camp may have been hoping for a reunion of at least some of the original line-up. "Peter clearly had an ongoing relationship with Ian. And I think that Ian was moving towards a point where he was beginning to admit to himself that he had made a mistake in leaving. On a long, circuitous telephone conversation with Michael around this time, when Michael couldn't quite end the conversation and hadn't said what he clearly wanted to say, I asked Michael if he regretted leaving. For the first time, Michael said: 'Yes.'"

Having cited the darkness of the music as one of the reasons he left, it might have seemed odd that Michael Giles was back behind the drum kit only a month after quitting. "I'd already decided to be a session musician which gave me another kind of freedom where I didn't have to be associated with demonic music. So *Poseidon* was a kind of aftershock, coming down. Already being in the habit of doing dark music, it wasn't difficult to go in and do a bit more. I was a contributor, not a designer." Fripp believes that McDonald and Giles would have been prepared to rejoin Crimson later in 1970. "Peter would probably have preferred that to the situation that emerged. I recall discussing this briefly with Peter, but that possibility was not a goer for me: I felt the same impossible situation would inevitably return, given the personalities of Ian and Michael. Possibly, my refusal to countenance a 'return' was part of Peter's increasing resentment after July 1970. He preferred writing with Ian, and Ian was a friend. But, that is only speculation." Expanding on his reluctance to work in a reunited line-up, Fripp adds: "If half of the most exciting band of the year leave as it takes off, which they later acknowledge as a mistake, how could they be trusted/ relied upon again?"

With *Pictures/Cadence/Poseidon* sequenced to closely mirror the dynamic structure of *Schizoid Man/Wind/Epitaph*, Fripp and Sinfield clearly hoped to emulate the impact of Crimson's debut. Such was the momentum of *Court*, when the highly anticipated follow-up was released, the UK record-buying public put *In The Wake Of Poseidon* into the album chart at number four, where it rubbed shoulders with *Bridge Over Troubled Water, Let It Be* and *McCartney*. Over the years the way in which *Poseidon*'s track listing apes the first album has come to be seen as a mistake, but in May 1970 it wasn't seen as a problem. *Disc* conferred four stars upon the album, an honour it shared with Crosby, Stills, Nash and Young's *Déjà Vu*, while the *NME* reckoned the group hadn't lost any of its appeal. But, for Martin Wilcox in the July edition of *Rolling Stone* offshoot *Friendz*, it was all too much. "There is no doubt that King Crimson are very fine musicians and that Bob Fripp is a very imaginative writer and guitarist but why they have to waste their talents on such doomy depressing music of which there was enough on their first album is a mystery to me." At the other end of the critical scale, Richard Williams declared in his exclusive preview for *Melody Maker* that "If Wagner Were Alive He'd Work with Crimson".

While Williams liked the music, he was less than impressed by the cover, a series of individual paintings by Tammo De Jongh collaged by Peter Sinfield. "*Poseidon* was a terrible cover. It may be the worst album cover of all time," says Williams, looking back on the period. "I remember Robert showing it to me in his flat in Notting Hill. He showed me the artwork. 'They're archetypes,' he said. It just looked like a bad painting to me. You could see the first cover expressed the record very well but the *Poseidon* cover didn't. The people who bought that first album, the *Poseidon* cover wouldn't have spoken to them. When I got sent the Steven Wilson remix and re-issue in 2010, I was impressed by a lot of what was there musically and how daring that was even at a time when lots of people were experimenting; to slap those people in the studio was amazing. It can't have been what EG were expecting after *In The Court Of The Crimson King*."

Though *Poseidon*'s music and sequencing attempted to replicate the flow of the first album, Sinfield shifted the visual language to a more oblique and mysterious level. Printed on an opulent canvas-like board, the rich semiotics of Tammo De Jongh's *12 Archetypes*, though lacking the clout of Barry Godber's image, resonated at a deeper level with Sinfield's writing. De Jongh was the founder of an all-male order of self-styled monks, living communally in Lady Somerset Road near Tufnell Park, dedicated to exploring alternative styles of living from a politically Green perspective. Their work and viewpoint impressed Sinfield enough for a contact address to be included in the album credits. There it was printed in a light-catching silver typeface against the swirling clouds of one of Sinfield's own paintings, created from dropping food dye on to blotting paper. Sinfield produced several of these paintings although only one, which was owned by Greg Lake, is known to have survived. Back in January 1970, optimistic press releases indicated that the band would be back on tour by 5 April. By March, a tour which would have seen Crimson and Traffic sharing the bill was also put on hold and a less-than-convinced BP Fallon heroically said: "We are 95% confident of getting the road band together."

At that time a live Crimson seemed a distant possibility. Peter Giles had been asked if he would like to continue playing in the group on tour. Had he stayed, it is open to speculation how long he would have lasted, given his disposition. When they first worked together Fripp was very much regarded as the junior partner. Now Crimson belonged to Fripp. "I'm not sure I would have accepted Fripp on his terms … it would have been quite a battle of wills," says Peter. "I think I'm extremely easy-going and able to put in huge amounts of work for little or no reward but at the same time nobody is going to tell me what to do or have any bigger say than me. I regard my say as equal to anyone else's and maybe if I'd been in King Crimson that wouldn't have been the case. I think Fripp sensed that somewhere, that he and I wouldn't have made it over time."

Fripp says his relationship with Peter played no part in his thinking. "Peter had come to see KC at the Fairfield Hall in 1969 and afterwards, in my view, acknowledged the alternative musical vision or concept of KC. I was not asking Peter to place his conceptual vision on to Crimson: I was asking him to play bass in a live version of Crimson." Regardless of his reservations, Giles received permission from his day job at Lyons Electric Office computer firm to take a leave of absence for six months to cover a prospective tour of France and America. Unfortunately, Giles and EG could not agree upon a fee and the bass player went back to his work in computers. With Lake gone and Peter Giles out of the picture, the stage was set for one of the worst periods in Crimson's history as Fripp and Sinfield struggled to keep the project afloat.

Just after the recording *of Poseidon* and the abortive attempts to put together a touring version of Crimson, McDonald and Giles began to record their own album. For their part, the duo had left Crimson wanting to create a gentler, greener music. This was deferred for a while as Michael Giles returned to Crimson for the recording of *Poseidon*. Looking back, McDonald wishes he had done the same, having worked on a substantial portion of the music during his tenure with Crimson.

Charlotte Bates, McDonald's partner during this period, recalls that McDonald was quite low after returning to England. "I think Ian got pretty depressed really after the split. Suddenly after having most of his days organised for him he now had long gaps where he had to get on with something himself. It was a difficult patch really."

McDonald started work on constructing what would become the *Birdman Suite* on his two-track recorder at home and the couple spent some time in the country with Steve Winwood, inviting the Traffic supremo to play on the imminent sessions. Given that McDonald was one of the principal writers in the original Crimson, it would not be unreasonable to suppose that EG Management, who were looking after McDonald and Giles by default, would have expected a commercially successful album. Thus, Island Records were easily persuaded to finance the venture and, in April 1970, a small rehearsal studio in Vauxhall was hired for McDonald and Giles, along with Peter Giles, to prepare material.

In May they entered Island's studios in Basing Street and began work. The basic sessions proceeded well enough but work on overdubs, performed mainly by McDonald, was both painstaking and arduous; it was not until July that work was finished. Even then huge amounts of time were spent trying to get the right mix and the appropriate sound for the music. Looking on from the sidelines, Peter Giles questions the duo's capacity to produce their own material, sensing a lack of objectivity. "I think they just fiddled and farted and pondered endlessly about things and I think they just got bogged down. It's a wood-for-the-trees thing – they should have used broader brushstrokes because their writing was excellent. It just wasn't very well executed in terms of production."

McDonald cites time and money as the problems that undermined the album. "We spent too much time recording and not enough mixing. The mixes are just taken from the monitor mixes because we were so pushed for time and we'd spent so much money. I actually didn't want to put it out and wanted to throw the thing in the Thames but we had to put it out because of all the money we'd spent on it."

With an album whose costs had come in at around £15,000, it should have been crucial to get a band on the road to promote the finished product. Yet remarkably there was no discussion about this. "I don't think it ever arose," recalls a perplexed Michael Giles. "As much as Ian and I enjoyed working together the question just didn't arise. Probably for two reasons. I wanted to stay in London to consolidate and get through the post-traumatic syndrome of Crimson and I think he wanted to get through it his way by going to New York. I don't remember any pressure from the record company for us to promote or tour although I suppose we could have done."

A cover shoot was commissioned and, along with Charlotte Bates and Mary Giles, the duo walked through London's Richmond Park for the photos. The cover suggests two confident young men strolling through the woods with beautiful women and brilliant careers ahead of them.

Recalling that stroll, Bates points out that appearances can be deceptive. "It was Mike and Ian who wanted that picture. The actual photo is genuine and we hadn't been told to smile or anything. But it had been a rocky ride after they left Crimson and getting that album out. Things hadn't gone as smoothly as the Crimson album so things were harder for Mike and Ian. Plus they were doing that double-take thing of 'Have we done the right thing?'"

IV

The commercial success of *In The Wake Of Poseidon* ensured EG's viability as a management company who were now also looking after the newly-formed ELP and helping maintain a sense of momentum around King Crimson. There'd been talk about Crimson operating with an affiliate line-up, an ever-changing number of guests contributing around the creative core of Fripp and Sinfield. Yet, without a live band to consolidate the substantial press and public interest in the band, the whole project was still in danger of stalling. Unless King Crimson began to tour again, things would soon start to look bleak for a band for which the good luck appeared to be running out.

Mel Collins was perhaps more aware of the on/off potential for Crimson than most. As a member of the then up-and-coming Circus, he'd been spotted by Fripp playing at The Marquee, where they'd been signed up to take part in club owner John Gee's ambitious New Paths sessions. Sharing the bill on Wednesday nights with Keith Tippett's group, Collins remembers the pairing being a challenge for the fledgling group, feeling somewhat intimidated by the audience. "We were young rock and rollers trying to play jazz and we were terrified thinking that the audience were all serious intellectual jazz fans and we doubted that we were good enough. We were described in the press as jazz-rock-folk but we didn't think of what we were doing as 'jazz-rock'. It was just music we were into and that we loved." His perception of the audience altered somewhat when Stan Webb, from blues-rockers Chicken Shack, joined them on stage at The Marquee. "We were trying to avoid him because he was well gone by then," says Mel of the guitarist well-known for his serious partying. "Anyway he came down and there we are in front of what we thought was a serious jazz audience and Stan grabbed a guitar, all out of tune, and got to the mic shouting 'I'm as drunk as a fuckin' Lord' and the audience went wild with delight! All this time we were scared stiff thinking we weren't good enough and Stan Webb, bless his heart, went down a storm and the audience loved it. So I didn't take it quite so seriously after that."

It's quite possible that Collins' career was kick-started partly because of his choice of trousers when he auditioned for Guildford band The Stormsville Shakers in 1966. "I saw an advert in the *Melody Maker* for 'TV & Radio – Second tenor needed', which is a bit of a joke really. It doesn't mean anything really other than you're not the first tenor!" laughs Mel. "I went along and got the job largely because I had checked hipster pants on. I looked better than most of the other guys who'd applied for the job. They even told me!"

The Stormsville Shakers were formed in 1960 and led by songwriter Phillip Goodhand-Tait. By the time Collins joined, they'd made the transition from rock'n'roll to playing a mixture of Goodhand-Tait's original numbers and soul covers. "In 1966 the Mod thing came in. Peter Stringfellow, the celebrated nightclub owner who died in 2018, had a club in Sheffield back then and we were up there as the Stormsville

Shakers. The scene had all suddenly gone Mod with the short hair, etc. I remember Stringfellow coming into the dressing room and because I had long hair he had a go at me, telling me I couldn't be going on stage with my long hair and I should be putting it under a hat or something. He actually destroyed me completely that night. Peter Green, from Fleetwood Mac, was in the band room and he consoled me, telling me not to take any notice. Of course, about a year later in 1967, we returned and there Stringfellow was all flower power and long hair!"

This return visit coincided with the name change from The Stormsville Shakers to Circus. "Well it was the time of flower power and a name like Phillip Goodhand-Tait and the Stormsville Shakers was just too old fashioned. Zoot Money's Band became Dantalian's Chariot with them wearing flowing robes on stage. A lot of bands did that back then, changing their image to keep up with the trends."

The band – Goodhand-Tait, Kirk Riddle on bass, Alan Bunn on drums, David Sherrington on tenor sax, Ian Jelfs on guitar and Collins – maintained a gruelling schedule of dates around the UK live circuit as well as jaunts to continental Europe. In September the group released their first single featuring *Gone Are The Songs Of Yesterday* (which would later be covered as the B-side of Love Affair's *Everlasting Love*) and *Sink Or Swim*, both produced by Manfred Mann vocalist Mike D'Abo. Despite the record having no impact on the charts, Circus were reconvened by D'Abo in October 1967 to record another Goodhand-Tait tune, *Do You Dream*, and its B-side, *House Of Wood*. Released in March 1968, it sank without trace just before an appearance on BBC Radio 1's *Night Ride* programme. The group failed to impress the audition panel, who described them as "outdated, square, rubbish, badly played, out of tune". Goodhand-Tait's success as writer for Love Affair probably spared the group from further attempts to get past the BBC's radio audition panel as he began contemplating a solo career.

Collins: "I think the band was changing and to some extent it was leaving Phillip behind. Guitarist Ian Jelfs and I were stretching out as players and he saw that happening. Of course, Phillip suddenly had a lot of success with the Love Affair covering his songs and he didn't need a band anymore." When Goodhand-Tait launched his solo career in January 1969, Circus had little doubt about their ability to carry on without him. "We were pretty confident then and we knew what we wanted to do, and it was to get as far away from the pop singles and stuff as we could get. I'd started writing, Ian was taking over the vocals, we were into jazz and experimenting. It was an exciting, liberating time."

By the time of the New Paths residency at the Marquee in April 1969, there was a considerable degree of interest in the band. "It was a very creative time where you were allowed to experiment; there wasn't a formula you had to stick to. It was a fantastic time and very progressive. There was a buzz going 'round about the group and that's when Transatlantic Records signed us." Just two weeks before the recording was due to take place, original drummer Alan Bunn was replaced by Chris Burrows. Sadly for Burrows, the album sleeve features a photograph of the group taken before he joined. "I think that picture was taken specifically for the album cover before we recorded the album, which is a weird way to do it," observes Mel. "It was shot at dawn at Hayling Island on the South Coast. The photographer wanted to catch the sun coming up. But he'd set up these arc lights and so we ended up with the sun coming up behind us and the arc lights were throwing shadows the opposite way. So it looks like we were shot in a photographer's studio!"

Circus entered Morgan Studios with producer Ray Singer, whose previous credits included playing guitar in Patrick Campbell-Lyons' group Nirvana and producing Peter Sarstedt's hit single *Where Do You Go To (My Lovely)?* "Transatlantic arranged for Ray to come in. It was just a job for him, I suppose. There was no real connection between us really. Basically we went through our live set and just transferred that on to tape. The whole album was done in two days – backing tracks one day, vocals and overdubs the next and then another to mix it. During the recording of our version of a Charlie Mingus number, *II BS*, I had a mouthpiece that was squeaking like hell. I wanted to go back and re-record it but, because Ray said we were short on time, he wouldn't let me. Because we were pressed for time we were going with first takes."

Collins contributed original songs, one of which, *The Pleasures Of A Lifetime*, features an uncredited appearance by his father, Derek Collins, on alto flute. "He'd just finished a session with the *Top of the Pops* orchestra at the BBC when he came in. I wanted him to be on my first album and because I knew I couldn't play it at the time he would be the one to do it." Looking back at this song and his other original, *Father Of My Daughter*, Collins is struck by their introspective nature. "They're a bit melancholic, really. I wrote them both on the guitar and I was obviously feeling a bit sad or something. I was about 22 years old and looking back over my life in a way."

The band was well known for extensive improvisations, borrowing heavily from jazz phrasing and vocabulary, around rock-based cover material. It was not uncommon for their version of The Beatles' *Norwegian Wood* to last 20 minutes or more. This mix of jazz and pop attracted plaudits from some heavyweight makers and shakers in the arts world, notably *The Sunday Times*' respected critic Derek Jewell. In a review of the band in concert subsequently lifted for the album's original sleeve-notes, Jewell observed that "Circus were revealed as musicians of poise and imagination, especially their flautist, Mel Collins, whose range – from cool neo-classicism to a wild Herbie Mann sound – bore the imprint of his years of professional study".

Mel remembers his surprise at hearing Circus' version of *Monday Monday* used as theme music to a Dutch chat show when they were touring Europe. "The album did quite well when it was first released. It certainly made its money back," he says, although he ruefully notes that he never received a penny in royalties. After its release, Circus began work on a follow-up. "It was towards the end of 1969. We did the classic 'cottage in the countryside' where Ian and myself, we went off for a while to write the material for the second album. I think, though, we were a bit out of our depth, to be honest. We'd made one album with a lot of cover versions on it and a couple of my songs and suddenly we were supposed to come up with an entire album of original material but it just didn't happen. We went in the studio and did one or two days but it was a bit of a disaster. We didn't have the experience or writing ability to pull it off. We probably needed another year on the road as Circus to develop and then write that follow-up album."

The fact that original vinyl editions of the album command large sums of money is a source of bemusement for Collins, as was its re-issue in the CD age. "It was fresh at the time of course but I couldn't tell you why it's become so sought after these days. Perhaps it's because there's a few interesting cover versions on it? There's things I don't like about it, of course, but I suppose it's of its time. We were so enthusiastic and there were some great ideas in there but I'm amazed it keeps coming back. Very strange."

Collins' defection to King Crimson ultimately put paid to Circus. In January 1970, Collins received a telephone call asking him to come along to Wessex to help in the recording of the new King Crimson album. Despite some initial nerves, he found the session for *Pictures Of A City* and *Cadence And Cascade* relaxing and fairly easy. His capacity to work quickly and efficiently meant he was quickly sounded out about joining the band when it looked as though the Giles, Giles and Fripp configuration of Crimson was ready to tour after the completion of *Poseidon*. "Robert came down and asked me if I wanted to join and of course I said yes. It was great for me 'cos it was moving up a notch, climbing the ladder and I was very excited." Collins was also taken in hand by the recently departed Greg Lake, who offered Collins some practical help about how to look the part. "I had a meeting with Greg and he took me down Carnaby Street and the King's Road to buy me a wardrobe full of clothes. Now, I was living at home with my parents and to actually even think of having money to spend on stage clothes was untrue but I was enough of a performer to want to be a part of that world."

Joining King Crimson was his way into the first division of successful albums, prestige reputations and American tours. Yet these ambitions were cruelly cut short, as the band seemingly evaporated before his eyes. Having only recently handed in his notice with Circus, Collins now went cap in hand and asked to rejoin. Circus drummer Chris Burrows sensed the band's days were numbered, despite Collins' assurances that he would not leave again: "You knew that if the opportunity were to come up again he was going to go."

Collins didn't have long to wait. In August 1970, a month into the recording of *Lizard*, he was summoned back to King Crimson. This time Transatlantic were not so accommodating and wanted compensation for the loss of what it regarded as one of its stars in the making. Label boss Matt Joseph demanded £2,000 to buy Collins out of his contract. As a result Collins nearly lost the job. "To come up with that kind of money in 1970 was beyond me but John Gaydon and David Enthoven negotiated the price down to £500, of which they paid £250 and I paid £250. I was out of the contract and able to join Crimson full-time. They were fantastic, John and David, and I had a lot a respect for them."

V

In casting the net for new members, Fripp opted for people he knew from his past. Drummer Andy McCulloch had previously played with Bournemouth band The Shy Limbs, of which Greg Lake had been a member. "We were a duet with drums and Hammond organ with John Dickerson who wrote most of the music and I helped arrange it," says McCulloch. "We used to do gigs like The Revolution Club in London. We were ticking over, just trying to get better. Greg came in for a little but he was in and out, trying to find his feet, figuring out what he wanted to do. Then later Bob Fripp and Greg Lake got together. They were two opposites really, but it made the whole," he says.

Born in Bournemouth on 19 November 1945, McCulloch was well-travelled as a youngster. "I grew up abroad. At the age of six I went over to Canada and my father was building ships for the Canadians and then we spent seven years in Japan. I came back to England as a teenager about 17 or 18, around 1961 or 1962. Then I went to art college and my big thing then was my love of drums and music." McCulloch recalls haunting the record shops of his youth seeking out albums by Jimmy Smith and Kenny Burrell. "You couldn't just have that music any time you wanted like you can now. You had to go to the record shop and listen to it if they'd let you. It was so exciting. I remember standing in the record shops in Bournemouth with the headphones on in a booth and the staff would be banging on the door to get me out and me saying, 'Can I have it again please?' I was pottering around on drums when I was in Japan but there was no outlet for it. Once I got to Bournemouth, however, I started playing in local bands and then you get a shot at London and so on." Initially inspired by drummer Sandy Nelson, he immersed himself in the American jazz scene. "Then things like Tony Williams' Lifetime came out. It was like 'Wow listen to that!'. I couldn't get into the Miles Davis stuff but Tony Williams came along and that was it for me. I could follow everything he played. He was amazing." McCulloch was also an admirer of Michael Giles. "He was brilliant. We knew Crimson in '69 and were very pleased for their success. We'd see Bob every now and again because he was Ringwood way and we were Ferndown, which was just down the road."

In the summer of 1970, Fripp came down to Ringwood, McCulloch recalls. "Robert sat in and did some playing with John Dickerson and me. He would often come 'round as friends talking and doing that sort of thing. We weren't having any long jam sessions or anything like that. The offer to join King Crimson came out of one of those occasions where he obviously heard what I could do. Then I moved up from Bournemouth." In February 1970 McCulloch was in the audience when The Nice came to Bournemouth on what would prove to be their final UK tour. "I really enjoyed what they did. It was jazz, rock, classical music; it was everything put together and they made a very exciting evening. It was different and exciting and the drumming was terrific. You don't see Brian Davison written about but it was really funny because I remember going to see him and then there was some concert where I was playing at they told me that Blinky was in the audience to watch me (*laughs*). Likewise with Jon Hiseman, we'd go and have a look at each other's stuff." McCulloch had no inkling as he watched Keith Emerson strutting and toting a Hammond organ about the stage of Bournemouth's Winter Gardens that six months later he'd be renting a room in the keyboard player's house in London. "At the time Keith Emerson was also with EG Management and they fixed me up with a place in Keith Emerson's house. He was a real gentleman, a very nice man. They were forming ELP at the time and all the Moog stuff arrived and Keith was always up day and night tinkering away with these Moogs going all day long."

The Bournemouth connection was further strengthened when Fripp asked Gordon Haskell to join.

A month or two after his brief reunion with Fripp to record *Cadence And Cascade*, Haskell found himself on the horns of a dilemma. Fripp's invitation came at the same time as an offer to join the more commercially orientated pop vocal group White Plains. That group was put together by respected session vocalist Tony Burrows who, along with Robin Shaw and Pete Nelson, graced innumerable hits during the late '60s with bright, mellifluous three-way harmony. Perhaps the most notable was the weekend hippie anthem *Let's Go To San Francisco*, when Burrows and co. traded as The Flowerpot Men. Haskell had played with The Flowerpot Men on the cabaret circuit in late 1969 and early 1970.

His initial reaction was to decline Fripp's offer on the grounds that Crimson's music was too cold for his personal taste. Fripp, however, was not put off and drove out to Haskell's cottage near Guildford to persuade the reluctant bass player in person. "I said I would only do it if I was allowed to be me and he said: 'I want you, you've got very good timing as a bass player and I want somebody with that Motown kind of thing and you'll be able to do what you want.'"

Haskell's budding career as a solo artist had stalled. He felt distanced from, and disappointed by, his 1969 debut album *Sail In My Boat*, swaddled as it was in soft-focus strings by producer Jimmy Duncan. But, in his heart, he knew the bland pop of White Plains wasn't going to be of any great interest. So, despite misgivings about the music, Haskell agreed to join Crimson. Along with Andy McCulloch, he set about preparing for the recording of the next album in the basement on Fulham Palace Road. "I liked Gordon. He was a really nice guy and we often used to practice some of the stuff together but we'd end up going funky and rock'n'roll which we were told *wasn't what was required*," laughs McCulloch, affecting a stern schoolmasterly voice.

As they intensively worked on a clutch of new Fripp compositions, the parts were allocated to them rather than developed by the players themselves as had been the case in the run-up to *Court*. It was a regime that involved long hours of the duo playing on their own with Fripp providing an outline guitar track to indicate the broad melodic or rhythmic arrangement. "I remember the recording of *Lizard* was very hard," says McCulloch. "Bob Fripp had a lot of the music in his head as to what it was going to sound like, so you'd be working blind in the sense that we'd go and play the bass and drums with a very excited guitar track that wasn't kept. I suppose it was a guide track. So you'd play around doing stuff and then after you'd done your bit then all the stuff would come out of Bob's mind as to what he was going to put on top of it all. It was new and it was different. You're not playing the usual thing a drummer would play or you're trying not to. You're trying to take it to new heights, as it were. Not everybody was comfortable in doing something that different. Gordon and I were both struggling sometimes because it was really different to what we were used to playing."

Haskell recalls McCulloch struggled to grasp what was required. "At one point, Robert caught me saying to Andy, 'Look, Andy, this is the groove and all he's done is remove the groove. You've got to keep the groove in your head and play a load of bollocks instead.' He also caught me doing a funky version of *Cirkus*, putting in Average White Band licks, and he was fucking furious – but it was the only way I could get through to Andy that it wasn't a mystery at all."

An increasingly unhappy McCulloch would express his uncertainty to his flatmate, fellow drummer Ian Wallace, by now also living in Keith Emerson's house in Drayton Gardens. Haskell, meanwhile, would drive back to his cottage in Surrey each night and express his growing misgivings to his partner. After several sessions of being schooled, coached and tweaked, the rhythm section was finally joined by Mel Collins and not long afterwards the band, with Peter Sinfield, entered Wessex Studios to spend the next month recording King Crimson's third studio album, the band's second that year.

The first day did not get off to a particularly auspicious start. Michael Giles had never been particularly enamoured of the studio's drum sound and neither were Fripp and Sinfield. So they worked with resident engineer Robin Thompson to try and find a better one. Costly studio time ticked by as a steadily exasperated McCulloch was required to repeatedly hit various drums as microphones and positions were moved and altered. Haskell puts this entire process down to Fripp and Sinfield's relative inexperience in the studio. A seasoned session veteran used to churning out songs with the minimum of fuss, he was dumbfounded. "It was ludicrous. I'd never seen anything so stupid. They took 12 hours to get a drum sound … and it was still shite." Scathing about Fripp and Sinfield's quest, he contrasts their labours with the speed at which his musical heroes worked: "You know, Otis Redding's band took two minutes to get a drum sound and that was perfect. Fripp and Sinfield didn't know what they were looking for. That's the funny thing because when they came back the following day it was completely different. Their drum can't sound like *(Sittin' On) The*

Dock Of The Bay because that's too much like a drum … it's got to sound 'innovative'. They shouldn't have used drums – they should have used my dick. That would have pleased Richard Williams!"

When it came to providing the *Melody Maker* journalist with an update on the recording of the new album and the new band, Fripp was extremely positive and optimistic. Responding to Williams' assertion that Haskell and McCulloch had seen their own musical personalities subordinated in order to emulate the previous incumbents, Fripp replied: "It's paradoxical because the idea behind Crimson is that each man should be able to get involved and establish their own personalities in the music. But, in practical terms, when you've got new men and you know what you want, in other words, you can't allow free development beyond a certain point, then you do have to make suggestions," Fripp explained. "Andy and Gord were used to thinking of rhythm sections in a slightly different way, and I think that will come out when we go live, but we just didn't have the time to blow together for long enough to establish something that was completely ourselves. As it was, a predetermined idea had to be implemented. But I've learned more and more from this album not to expect a man to be something he isn't but to be increasingly what he is. The new rhythm section grooves and funks which none of the others did." Fripp accepted that *Lizard* was being written and directed by himself and Sinfield for pragmatic, rather than artistic, reasons but acknowledged his desire to see a return to a band-style democracy. "One of the most important points is that the men can find complete satisfaction within the unit: for example, Gord is very interested in writing and I think Mel would like to get into writing too. But since I'm interested in writing for King Crimson, they have to be allowed outlets as well, or else they get bottled up. As things are going, I think they'll be able to … they'll have to be able to."

McCulloch remembers that Fripp and Sinfield opted to bypass the usual method of listening to the material in playbacks as they evaluated their progress. "We set up two very small speakers and we didn't use the studio speakers at all. These were really small speakers. The idea was that we had to make the music in those speakers. Very often you record an album on JBLs and it all sounds wonderful but when you hear the final product three months later on smaller speakers you think what's happened to the sound? All that bigness is gone. You hear the music through these big speakers in a perfect room but you try and record it so it comes out of a pair of poxy speakers. Now and again we'd have a big speaker evening where we'd listen to stuff properly and that would give you a huge lift, you know? You'd been working so hard to make it sound good on the small ones, it was great to hear it on those big ones."

As each section was built up around Haskell and McCulloch's basic rhythm tracks, the bassist remained unconvinced. With each successive journey to and from his cottage, he would reflect on his increasingly isolated position from the rest of the band. The extent of his own sense of exclusion from the mainstream of opinion as to what constituted a good sound or take was obvious to all involved. “I remember commenting to Robert in the rehearsal room after Keith Tippett left, ‘That just sounds like a cat walking across a piano’ and he said ‘Yeah but Keith knows what he’s doing. A cat doesn’t,’ and I said ‘Yes, but it sounds the same!’” On another occasion when Haskell questioned a point of production with Fripp, the guitarist spikily retorted: “And how many hits have you had then?” Observing such exchanges from the sidelines, Mel Collins was surprised to discover that the two had once been schoolfriends, detecting little warmth between them. However, even compared to that, the bassist’s dealings with Sinfield were positively Arctic. Disdainful of the lyricist’s experiments with the VCS3 synthesiser, he reserved most of his ire for Sinfield’s lyrics, feeling them to be pretentious, inept and a case of the Emperor’s new clothes. “I always liked Peter and thought his lyrics were brilliant,” says McCulloch, going on to observe that Sinfield’s advocacy of alternative lifestyles was way ahead of his time. “Peter was into juicing vegetables and eating healthy, and all that stuff we’re all doing now. Back then though you didn’t come across it that much.” When it came to the deteriorating relationship between Fripp and Sinfield, McCulloch says he wasn’t aware of any problems at the time. “Peter’s main work was done beforehand or outside of the recording sessions and working with Bob on the lyrics at a different time to us. We were working more on getting the backing tracks and the rhythm going and learning the other songs and so on to notice anything really.”

VI

Fripp and Sinfield drafted in some more gifted young turks from the UK jazz scene in the shape of Tippett band stalwarts Mark Charig on cornet and Nick Evans on trombone. "The jazzers who I was working with also participated in pop sessions and I believe they saw them as an opportunity to cover the rent for the week," recalls Evans. "These other pop sessions were generally organised by pop groups who had a knowledge and interest in jazz. I had no formal 'session fixer' and consequently I seldom worked for pop groups without having some form of personal contact with a member from the group. Generally pop sessions were never a major source of musical income for me but were always gratefully accepted when they arose. I had an idea that standard session fees were about 30 or 35 quid. That would be for three hours in the studio." Evans and Charig played together on two evenings in a booth in the centre of the studio while the track was fed to them on headphones. Evans recalls that the method in which they laid down the written themes on *Lizard* went against his instincts as a jazz player. "Our parts were added in small sections, maybe four or eight bars at a time and after each snippet was recorded it was checked carefully in the producer's box to make sure it was exactly what Bob Fripp wanted. It took quite a time to get all my sections down on tape. I guess I remember that because during that period of my life I was working with jazz musicians who were very keen on accepting the first take of any recording. You know, capture the moment and maintain its spontaneity as much as possible. This is NOT the way pop bands operate and I found the stop-start method of working a little unnerving." Collins was present for all the sessions with the brass players but did not lay his own parts down until much nearer the end of the process. This had the effect of quelling any real improvisational sparks and Collins found it especially challenging to dig into the tracks in search of inspiration.

Haskell struggled to get any true feeling or emotion into his vocals for *Lizard*, which may have been part of the reasoning behind recruiting Yes singer Jon Anderson as guest vocalist for *Prince Rupert Awakes*. In a remarkable piece of cross-pollination between the two bands, Anderson was very happy to go over to Wessex Studios, having been a fan of Crimson from the beginning. "Well I actually went to King Crimson's first show with Chris Squire and Bill Bruford. And I said to the guys, 'We've got to start rehearsing, guys. This is not good.' The only other time that happened was when we saw John McLaughlin and the Mahavishnu Orchestra for the first time in 1972 or 1973." The vocalist was approached by Greg Lake, who relayed Fripp's interest. "I said OK and gave him my number and then about three months later Bob rang me up and said I'm going to record next month," Anderson remembers. He had no idea what he was going to sing until he turned up at Wessex, and then couldn't help but smile when he saw the title. "Prince Rupert was the name of a train that would go past our school every Wednesday and I thought it's so bizarre that he wrote this song which I sang and it had that kind of connection. Afterwards I told Bob that story, and you know Bob Fripp, he just said 'Oh. Thank you, Jon. Bye.'" laughs Anderson.

In September, the music press were invited to Wessex as the new line-up posed for publicity shots. By the end of the month, *Lizard* was all but finished. The entire band attended a playback with management and friends to listen to the new album. Like being sober at a party where everyone else is drunk, Haskell found himself feeling isolated in his dislike of the record, while everyone around him was buoyant. Well, almost everybody. "When I heard *Lizard* I wasn't keen on the drum sound," says McCulloch. "That wasn't my drum sound. I'm more Billy Cobham or John Bonham – big sound. *Lizard* was all crushed up. It's hard to make things exciting when they are all squashed. That wasn't just particular to Crimson. It would often happen to bands. You'd walk into a studio and the assistant engineers would come out with the blankets and the phone books and slam them into your bass drum and they'd put something over the snare and it'd sound like shit to me; all the life had gone from it. In later years I used to ask if I could put the drums where the grand piano is because I wanted to keep the ambience of the sound. But back then I was in no position and didn't have the knowledge to say how I thought it should be. It was only later on that I did that. For me it was struggling with the concept that was in Bob's mind and the engineer struggling to get a sound that suited Bob and what I wanted. It was very difficult. I remember going out and buying a different tom-tom because things were sounding a bit flat and we wanted a higher note."

After a little over three months of writing, rehearsing and recording, it finally appeared that King Crimson's good luck had returned. As the band took a few days out before rehearsals for live work, there was every reason to suppose that the group could work its way back to something like its previous success and acclaim. It wasn't to last. Having spent months on *Lizard*, Haskell now faced another two months learning the band's back catalogue. Fripp's promise that Haskell's songwriting would find a route into the group now seemed highly unlikely – he realised that tackling *In The Court Of The Crimson King*, *Pictures Of A City* and *21st Century Schizoid Man* would take precedence.

Unhappy with both his own performance on the album and the music as a whole, Haskell was very much a man alone. A rift was opening between Fripp and Haskell that would cause personal resentment and hostility for years to come. The only person in the band with whom Haskell felt any sense of connection and kinship was Collins. Three days into rehearsals, on Monday, 2 November, Haskell requested that the band alter the key of *Schizoid Man* to suit his lower vocal range. Fripp's response that the vocals would be processed cut little ice with Haskell and a heated argument ensued, resulting in the singer downing tools. "So I said, 'I'm not going on stage and making a cunt of myself.' So he said, 'Do you want to leave?' and I said, 'I do. I'm not going to go onstage and sing something I don't believe in. It's bullshit.' Simple as that. So I packed my gear up and, as I got to the door of the basement café, Pete Sinfield was on the left, Mel was to the right, Robert was there and he said 'You'll still get your royalties' and that was that."

A stunned Crimson was stopped in its tracks. That night Richard Williams was given the news and once again the band made the papers but this time for all the wrong reasons. "HASKELL QUITS CRIMSON" screamed the banner headlines from *Melody Maker*, with Fripp quoted as saying: "I suppose Crimson is a way of life. It's a very intense thing and I think Gordon realised that."

Haskell was livid when he read the headline and remains convinced that the band's desire for publicity had taken precedence over attempting to solve internal problems. "The *Melody Maker* came out Thursday and I left on the Monday night. Don't you think it's incredibly sharp practice to get that headline in? That was the first thing they thought of. First thing I would have thought of would've been 'Let's sort this out'. But no, it was 'Let's get some Press'. They're clever and they never miss a trick. It's pure, 100% business with these guys." But Collins recalls that the atmosphere was far removed from either the calm of Fripp's quote or the febrile plotting alleged by Haskell. The sense of despair and shock at the setback hit everyone hard. The prospective tour in January would now almost certainly have to be cancelled as the search for a new singer and bassist got under way. This was all too much for Andy McCulloch, who handed in his notice as well.

By the time the album was released in December, any hope that Crimson might return to the stage had receded. In the general air of discontent, tensions between Fripp and Sinfield started to come to the surface. A cooling-off period was created when Fripp accepted Keith Tippett's invitation to play with his large-scale jazz orchestra Centipede in France, leaving Sinfield to supervise the pressing of the album and commissioning artist Gini Barris to produce the artwork. Barris, Julie Felix's housekeeper at the time, had a Crimson connection through the folk singer's managers, David Enthoven and John Gaydon. Commissioned by Sinfield, and with only a set of lyrics to work with, over three months Barris seeded her beautiful illuminated lettering design with commentaries and allusions upon the world suggested by the lyrics.

There was also a realignment of professional arrangements which Sinfield argued should reflect the new position in which they found themselves. The original performance and record royalties split for Crimson in 1969 had been 22.5% for Fripp, Lake, McDonald and Giles with 10% for Sinfield, although there were equal shares on publishing. After the original line-up's break-up this was re-negotiated to 60/40% in Fripp's favour, with the publishing (even on instrumentals) shared equally.

Sinfield came to feel that such a settlement failed to adequately recognise the true value of his contribution. In less than a year he had moved up through the ranks from unpaid roadie to co-author of some incredibly successful and ambitious songs. He had coined the group's name and acted as a pair of trusted ears that provided a constant stream of advice, feedback and suggestions as to how improvements and additions might be made.

He was responsible for the Crimson's distinctive visual identity which had received so much acclaim from crowds and critics alike via his striking use of lights and securing one of the most recognisable record covers in history. Added to which he ensured that in a live context the FOH sound was in the hands of somebody intimately associated with the music's construction and dynamics.

By the time they came to rehearse *Lizard*, Sinfield was convinced that his contribution was equal to that of Fripp's and demanded things be split 50/50. While this was agreed, it is doubtful that Fripp was convinced by the argument that Sinfield's words held as much potency or immediacy as his music. By agreeing to the deal, Fripp may have headed off immediate conflict but added to a train of mutual resentments and grievances which would ultimately kill the trust and respect necessary to sustain the longevity of the partnership.

In the months following the release of *Lizard*, Sinfield seemed almost surprised by the novelty of his current status. To Richard Williams in *Melody Maker*, he said: "In fact, I carved and hustled my way to where I am now. Bob says he uses me as a barometer, and I also thought up the name of the band. Actually, I don't know what I do – obviously the lyrics are the most important thing, but it's got to the stage where nothing on *Lizard* was passed without my approval."

As writing and rehearsals for *Lizard* got under way, Sinfield increasingly felt that his views were beginning to be undervalued by Fripp. Stephanie Ruben remembers that Sinfield would work through the night on a particular lyric only for Fripp to give the words merely a perfunctory examination.

Sinfield's writing was always symbolically laden, operating at many levels. Yet this richness and fondness for layering his work with multiple meanings also became an Achilles heel for Crimson, with the words being frequently lambasted in the Press at the time and often regarded with derision in subsequent retrospectives. On this point, Sinfield wasn't so much hurt by the criticism as disappointed that the Press were unprepared to take the time and effort to engage with the messages and content of his words – though finding some compensation in a burgeoning postbag from admiring fans.

Dubbed the "Elfin" Sinfield by the band in 1969, he cut an enigmatic, waif-like figure. This aspect to his personality and his penchant for tiptoeing about the studio or rehearsal room in moccasin sneakers was a source of irritation to bemused newcomers like Haskell and McCulloch.

Ruben contends that this was merely a persona behind which the real Sinfield hid. "The whole image of Peter, what he gave off and what he allowed others to see, actually wasn't him. He was much more real and less elfin-like, probably the least elfin-like person, with hindsight, that I can think of. He was quite dark. He had a quiet determination and a fixation about things. Equally, his lyrics, being so flowery, were all full of hidden meanings, a lot of allegory, and were full of down-to-earth, ugly, everyday things, be it political, psychological or whatever."

"So whatever the Press picked up on, usually this flowery image or this hippie stuff, they were quick to jump on it and call it pretentious, and it would have been, if that's all it had been to it. It's odd because they allowed someone like Marc Bolan to get away with it, so to speak, and he used to chart with all that stuff. But for Peter, because he'd perhaps only so often show this darker, deeper side and yet come out with all this psychedelic lyricism, it didn't seem to sit at all. Robert didn't seem to get it."

VII

Fripp found Sinfield's work less convincing than anything the lyricist had produced on the first album but also acknowledges that the music probably offered little in the way of inspiration. *Lizard* is perhaps Fripp's first full-scale offering since emerging from the shadow of the old group. While the energies on *Poseidon* were largely concerned with consolidating the position of the group, *Lizard* attempted a more ambitious account of what might be possible if jazz and rock were commingled. But this was emphatically not "jazz-rock" in the sense of fusion proffered by the likes of Ian Carr's Nucleus, Soft Machine or American pioneers such as Miles Davis, Weather Report or Return To Forever, where the music was usually riff-based and orientated toward extended virtuoso soloing.

For the most part, *Lizard* operated within the rock tradition but drew heavily upon the jazz and classical idioms for its tonal and structural expression – hence the invitation to Keith Tippett and members of his sextet.

In fact, Fripp went as far as formally asking Tippett if he would be interested in becoming the joint musical director. Indeed Fripp was keen on whole elements of the pianist's sextet – and his partner, vocalist Julie Tippetts (Julie Driscoll) – becoming full-time Crimson members. "He rang me up in Buckingham, where I was living with Julie at the time, and said 'Here's an offer' and I said thank you! The terms would have been that I would have had musical input. He knew that I was a strong musical personality and I would have gone in and possibly taken it all in another way with his blessing because we would have been joint bandleaders," recalls a flattered Tippett.

Another effect would have been the re-writing of the royalty agreement with Sinfield – though this never became an issue as Tippett declined the offer. "I hadn't long been in London and I'd left Bristol realising that I had to go to London to play with musicians who were more experienced than myself to learn quickly – apart from that I had too much love for the sextet and it would have taken me away from the jazz scene. There were lots of musicians I wanted to learn from and play with on the jazz scene and I'd have only been joining Crimson for the money and I had too much respect for the band and Robert to do that. My music never just become another way of making money. So, I've no regrets whatsoever."

In 2001, Fripp viewed the album as "lots of ideas, mostly presented simultaneously and very few of which work. Various bits are unsure whether to try and make connection with a unified central theme or maintain their independence. Mostly, the search for a unified central theme escapes satisfaction and the constituent elements adopt a semblance of neutrality, so as not to attract culpability for their involvement. Labour and labouring, mostly joyless, strive effortfully to present the appearance of cohesion,"

Given the torment and difficulties surrounding the creation of the album, Sinfield demonstrated that his sense of humour was undiminished by using the text of *Desiderata* to advertise its release. "Go placidly amid the noise and the haste, and remember what peace there may be in silence," ran the press releases. Attributed to an anonymous 15th-century text found in a Baltimore church, the words were in fact written in 1948 by Max Ehrmann, but they nevertheless seemed to have an application to Crimson's current state of affairs and to the recently departed Haskell. "Keep interested in your own career, however humble; it is a real possession in the changing fortunes of time. Exercise caution in your business affairs; for the world is full of trickery."

The true source of the antipathy between them is hard to pinpoint but it's likely that Fripp's profound dislike of Sinfield's lyrics for much of the album poisoned the water. In his dealings with some of the players, Fripp had been seen to act in a high-handed, autocratic way to keep the project moving. "At the beginning of 1970 I felt that everything to be done for the next two years would be wrong, but had to be done anyway," says Fripp. Long after its release, the guitarist famously argued that *Lizard* was essentially unlistenable, a conclusion he'd arrived at due to a dislike of the original mix and the growing personal enmity directed at him from both Haskell and Sinfield during the recording. *Lizard* represents a radically different re-imagining of what King Crimson could be with Fripp the composer finally emerging out from under the shadows cast by the 1969 incarnation. *Melody Maker*'s Richard Williams praised Crimson for grasping "the concept that rock can be built on scale to rival classical music", while *Sounds*' Steve Peacock declared: "I am convinced that *Lizard* is by far the best thing to come from the fertile brain of Robert Fripp and Peter Sinfield so far … the music, the words and, of course, the excellent cover, make this something quite extraordinary …" And *NME*'s Nick Logan stated: "*Lizard* reflects Fripp's progression towards a welding of rock and jazz, drawing from the most exciting regions of both."

After Crimson, McCulloch wasn't sure what to do next but it was through Fripp he got his next job. Keyboard player Graham Field, who originally hailed from Dorset and knew Fripp socially, had formed Rare Bird in 1969 with the band scoring a worldwide best-seller with *Sympathy*. Signed to CBS, who looked to Field for another hit, he found himself in a quandary. "Their attitude was that as I'd written one hit, I might well write another so let's sign him up!" laughs Field. With a major label and finance behind him, he sought advice from someone well versed in the difficult art of forming groups. "If memory serves me, I'd rung Bob Fripp up and mentioned I was getting a new band together. We talked about the hell of having to start all over again, something he'd had to do with King Crimson, and he said, 'Well for what it's worth. I know a good drummer,' and he gave me Andy's number." McCulloch in turn provided the next step in forming the new group, now called Fields. "He told me about his friend, a guitarist called Alan Barry, and said that he was bloody good and on my wavelength." The group recorded one self-titled album, released in 1971, and were popular on the touring circuit in Europe. However, despite critical success and lots of radio play abroad, things came to an abrupt end when boardroom changes at CBS in London saw many acts culled from the label.

McCulloch found himself working with another keyboard player, Dave Greenslade, after the ex-Colosseum member got in touch to suggest he try out for a new band, Greenslade, with whom he made four albums for Warner Brothers before the band's demise in 1976.

Described at the time by one critic as "the abyss where modern jazz and rock meet", with its clashing styles, whirling improvisations, soaring classically tinged themes and dramatic showcases, *Lizard* remains a remarkable album. Given the ambitious ground it attempted to cover, it is perhaps no surprise that it still has the capacity to polarise opinion. When remastering the album in 2000, Fripp commented on *Cirkus*: "Gordon Haskell is struggling heroically to be a singer in a context where such endeavour is a functional impossibility: an accompaniment which declines to accompany and lyrics sufficient to set the psyches of strong men flapping. No wonder Gordon prefers Motown to Crimson as an example of good songwriting. Gordon was out of place in Crimson, and has suffered distress for nearly 30 years as a result of his (relatively minor) involvement."

Looking back, Haskell firmly believes that he was cheated out of royalties from *Lizard* because of a cynical interpretation of his status by Fripp or EG Management. The bass player rejects the suggestion that he recorded *Lizard* as a session musician, maintaining that he was a full member of the band. His view of things seems to be backed up by the credits on the album sleeve, which make a clear distinction between a core group and guests. Additionally, the press release of the time cites Collins, McCulloch and Haskell as being the new members of Crimson, rather than merely guests such as Tippett or Jon Anderson. And, given his considerable experience as a session musician, it seems unlikely that Haskell would have misunderstood his status.

The position officially adopted at the time and in subsequent years was that Haskell's full membership would have only started once the group had gone on the road. As Haskell chose to walk out before the tour, he was therefore technically in breach of contract and not entitled to any performance royalties from the sales of *Lizard*. Haskell speculates on why he did not receive such royalties. "One – it may have cost a lot of money for them to set up a tour and I screwed that up. That's one justification for me not being paid. Two – it was just a simple management thing; 'pay him off, give him his bass and £275 and call it a session. He's not going to sue us'."

In the following years, Haskell continued to harbour this grievance and his last legal attempt to redress the situation was in 1989. Haskell had lost none of his diplomatic flair when he addressed one of the letters to EG (by now Mark Fenwick and Sam Alder) "Dear Tory Swine". His case faltered when it became clear that EG's refusal to accept liability would lead to a costly court case for which Haskell lacked any financial backing. "When Sting was promoting the rain forests, I knew he knew Robert so I wrote to Sting, saying I would donate all my royalties to the rain forest and it amounts to £100,000 and you can get it from Robert. I didn't get a reply," laughs Haskell. For him *Lizard*, which has overshadowed his entire career, is a source of embarrassment and chagrin. "You may not believe this but somebody every week says 'What was it like working with Robert?' Can you imagine that? Can you imagine the strength of character that I've built up over the years? I was in Norway once in a latrine with holes in my shoes and someone comes up to me and says 'Didn't you used to be in King Crimson?' I've had to face a lot of humiliation and I've had to sing covers. I've had to do a lot to survive and I've had to work non-stop ever since, so I can honestly say I'm an honest working musician/singer/writer. It's just that it hasn't been easy. The only people who sneer at poverty are the people you wouldn't want to eat with anyway."

After recording two albums and keeping the name and concept of Crimson alive, Fripp was on the verge of admitting defeat and Collins was left to conduct auditions for new members largely on his own.

"All I can remember was Robert giving up completely, saying there's no hope. It was so traumatic that at one point Robert couldn't handle it anymore and he told me that if I wanted to carry on with Crimson and I wanted to get the band together that I should do the auditioning," remembers an incredulous Collins. "So there I am in this little rehearsal room auditioning bass players and drummers on my own, as green as I was back then – a saxophone player who didn't really know the tunes that well."

"But I was hungry to do it and when I think about it now, I can't imagine how I did it. They were coming in and we'd talk and we'd have a jam. It was crazy, really. You get all sorts of complete no-hopers who'd blag their way in and Robert was using me to filter all these people out. He wasn't daft! Eventually Robert got a new wave of energy and got involved. If I then found anybody I'd have to re-audition them with Peter and Robert, which was bizarre."

Drummer Ian Wallace had been a fan of King Crimson since seeing them at Hyde Park with The Stones and at the Marquee. The latter performance really impressed him. "*Schizoid Man* stood out above everything else and that was the one. First of all it really rocked. Second, it had a kind of jazzy 6/8 feel to it and the syncopated 4/4 solo in the middle was just unbelievable. It was so strong. I was absolutely blown away by them and I thought 'God if I could just be in that band I could do all my Tony Williams stuff.'"

Two years later he got the chance when Keith Emerson recommended that Fripp check out Wallace, another of his lodgers at Drayton Gardens. Fripp saw the drummer when he played as a member of ex-Bonzo Neil Innes' group The World.

Ian Wallace was born on 29 September 1946, in the Northern town of Bury. The son of working-class parents, his first real entry into music was when his mother bought him an acoustic guitar and he set about picking tunes out from the radio. However, it was not until he saw Acker Bilk and His Paramount Jazz Band at Bury's Royal Cinema that his true musical interests were revealed. As he stood queuing for an ice cream near the front of the stage, Wallace looked up and saw the stage lights reflecting off the coloured shells of the drums. It was an almost religious experience. "The heavens opened up with a choir of angels and something said 'That's what you're supposed to do.'"

The next day, Wallace gathered up everything he had to trade for a basic drum kit and began to practise by playing along to his favourite trad jazz records. It wasn't long before rock'n'roll diverted him and in 1962 he joined his first group The Jaguars, in which he also sang from the drum stool.

Occupying the support slot for visiting groups in concerts at the Bury Palais was a good way of meeting other musicians. One group was The Warriors from nearby Accrington. Having just been signed to Decca by Dick Rowe, The Warriors were about to turn professional but this was not an ambition shared by their drummer. Wallace recalls how, for him, opportunity literally knocked at his door. "They used to play a lot of clubs in the Manchester area and they used to drive from Accrington in a Bedford van with buffalo horns on the front. Now to get there they had to drive through Bury along the Manchester Road, where I lived at 107. The doorbell rings and it's Johnny Anderson, as he was known then, asking if I wanted to audition and I said yes."

Wallace did the audition. "A few days later Johnny was at the door and he said that they wanted me to join the band. I said I'd love to but my mum won't let me." Wallace's mother wanted him to concentrate on his career as a National Health Service clerk, though there were plans for him to study at Bolton Art College with a view to becoming an art teacher.

However, a delegation of The Warriors' parents called to the house to persuade her to reconsider. Though reluctant, his mother finally acceded, and in April 1964, Wallace handed in his notice. A week later he was driving down to London to record a single at Decca's studios. He was 17. Like so many of its day, the record didn't do anything but the band appeared on hit UK TV programme *Thank Your Lucky Stars* and even got a spot in teen exploitation film *Just For You*, along with several other groups including, in a moment of Crimson synchronicity, A Band Of Angels, featuring a young John Gaydon.

A tough apprenticeship in German clubs led The Warriors to the Storyville Club in Frankfurt. Many American GIs frequented the Storyville and through them Wallace was given jazz albums on the Impulse label, featuring players such as John Coltrane. These kindled an interest in jazz that continued for the rest of his life. In 1967, Ian heard drummer Tony Williams in the Miles Davis group and the experience changed his life. "A pivotal album for me. If I could only take one album to a desert island then it would have to be the *Four And More* album. It just completely blew me away."

When The Warriors split, Wallace returned to Bury and for a time joined a group called Big Sound. Eventually the band ended up in London with £10 between them. Wallace picked up work backing singers such as Lou Christie and Sandie Shaw and played drums on the last tour by the Bonzo Dog Band, going on to work with singer Viv Stanshall in his Bonzo offshoot Big Grunt. "I did a single with Viv on which Keith Moon played percussion and on the B-side we swapped. I think John Entwistle played trombone on it as well. It was a version of the Elvis song *Suspicion*."

Wallace was well up for the anarchic humour of the period and remembers working on a TV special with the comedian Marty Feldman which necessitated playing the drums dressed as a duck. Perhaps unsurprisingly, Wallace immediately accepted the offer of playing in Crimson.

"Fripp took me out to Doc Hunt's in Archer Street in London and we bought a double bass drum kit which Neil Innes painted for me – a lovely looking kit with English pastoral scenes on it," recalls Wallace. "I'd never played a double bass drum kit before but I think Fripp needed me to emulate what Michael Giles had been playing. But I quickly changed back to one bass drum to put more of my own identity into the playing and interpret things a little differently."

Wallace recalls the search for a suitable bassist as long and tedious. "It was me, Fripp and Mel auditioning bass players and singers and it came very close to not existing. We auditioned so many people, dozens and dozens, and we despaired of finding the right combination." On one occasion a young man auditioned and fainted through nerves, an event still preserved in DGM's tape archive. "I'd love to hear that one again," said Wallace. "We used to sit around listening to the tape of him fainting and laugh uproariously, which was very cruel, but it was so funny."

VIII

Another one of the singers auditioned was a young Bryan Ferry. Although unsuitable for Crimson, Fripp recommended that the vocalist contact David Enthoven, giving the singer a telephone number that would change his life forever. Another hopeful to descend the stairs into King Crimson's rehearsal room was session bassist Rick Kemp. He was responding to a call that Fripp had made to the Ambassador Music management agency. Kemp, originally from Little Hanford, just a few miles away from Wimborne, had been working with Michael Chapman as well as on numerous records, adverts and other jobs. He admits that he counted himself as largely retired from bass playing but the notion of working with King Crimson was intriguing. "I was aware of the albums and their fame. There was a whole mystique about them. Even getting in the room with the lads in the rehearsal room, they still seemed full of mystery to me (*laughs*). I'd never seen them live before and I wasn't even aware of the fact that they were a band that played live but I was a big fan and this was a big moment for me."

The discovery of a set of tapes in DGM's archives shed some light on how King Crimson auditions and rehearsals developed. Though it's now not possible to conclusively identify the bassist appearing on tape, those blows highlight the extent to which Crimson could swing deeper into jazz territory. Driven by Wallace's unerring ride cymbal and whip-cracking snare work, the ideas that initially emerged from *Groon* are pursued with a fiery tenacity. Some sure-footed walking bass dovetails seamlessly with Wallace. On various occasions, the busy pace subsides, dropping to near silence, waiting for the next direction to emerge. There are stop-start games, uneven skirmishing into funk-ish regions that bring to mind Miles Davis' experiments at the time. Frantic ostinatos become rallying points with Fripp at one point beating the body of the guitar to produce a highly personalised counterpoint. Here and there, fragments of the nagging chords that would later be properly developed into *Larks' Tongues In Aspic, Part II* briefly shudder into being, while a fleeting guitar theme closely resembling John McLaughlin's composition *Extrapolation* flickers into life. Throughout, the bass is alert and nimble, quick to respond to the shifts in tempo or the tonal colours advanced by Fripp or Collins. At one point, a jagged rock groove and comping chords have them wandering into something almost freeform but with a funky undertow, almost presaging the blows on the *Earthbound* tour. "I just remember playing on G minor for some considerable time and thinking I'm not making a very good job of this," says Kemp. Despite Kemp's reservations, Fripp immediately offered him the job. But the celebrations that night were short-lived as, over the next few days, Kemp got cold feet. "Fripp himself was very friendly and very helpful and enthusiastic about what I was doing but I was not all that pleased with what I was doing myself. I don't think I felt that I was that kind of player to join in with people like Ian Wallace and Mel Collins. These people were serious. I was a little intimidated by the Crimson thing, to be honest, and I'm not sure that I was the right person for them. Of course, when I called Bob I thought he'd be relieved to hear that I wasn't going to pursue it, but he wasn't. He was really quite upset. I remember him saying, 'Please don't leave,' and I thought, 'Oh my God, I'm really not sure I'm up to this.' I'd just gone through a breakup with my wife and I'd really made up my mind that I'd retired from music and I didn't want to play again." However, Kemp's retirement was itself brief. Finding himself in constant demand for studio work, several months later, in 1972, he became a full-time member of UK folk-rock outfit Steeleye Span. "I remember Fripp saying later, 'You won't be happy. It's not your sort of band.' I'm still with them of course," laughs Kemp. Ian Wallace remembered: "Everybody loved Rick and thought he was the ideal guy and he accepted the gig, but then a couple of days later he called up and decided he didn't want to do it. That was the lowest point. When we got that message we were all sitting in the basement and it was pretty much that Crimson wasn't going to happen."

By now, Boz Burrell was already on board as a vocalist and his vocals had a power which Fripp believed could be harnessed well in a new line-up. Mel Collins recalls another contender had been Dave Ambrose, who'd previously worked with Brian Auger and others, and who would go on to become a successful A&R man with EMI Records and Publishing in later years. "It didn't work out with Dave but, for some reason, he'd left his bass guitar behind and that's the one that Robert picked up when he decided to teach Boz to play the songs."

That moment of inspired connection saved the band from oblivion. It still seems astonishing that, after auditioning countless bass players, Crimson should finally settle on someone who couldn't play at all. But it was agreed that Burrell should be given a week to see how things worked out. "We had had plenty of competent professional musicians come along to audition but they didn't have the feel. Boz felt the bass parts while he was singing, whereas the musicians could play it but couldn't feel it. And if he could feel it, it could only be a matter of time before it crept down from his head through his hand and into his fingers," Fripp told *NME*'s Nick Logan. "I was really happy," said Wallace. "It had gone from being so miserable because we were right on the edge of breaking up before I'd even played a gig with Crimson. Then it went to 'Hey this could work!' and it changed the whole complexion. It was like coming back to life." Fripp taught Burrell the parts, as well as scales and tips around intonation, by rote and at the same time Wallace took him through the requirements of the rhythm section, the pair often working on their own. "It's a bit frustrating, because I don't think like a bass player yet … I've been a singer, so all I know is feeling, and when Bob tells me that I was playing a third of a beat behind, I don't even know what a third of a beat is," Boz told *Melody Maker*. In just 11 weeks Burrell was playing sufficiently well to go out on a short UK tour.

Born Raymond Burrell in Holbeach on 1 August 1946, he turned pro after leaving college in Norfolk, playing with Lombard And The Tea Time Four, which included vocalist and guitarist Mike Patto. The line-up later evolved to include Ian

McLagan, later of Small Faces on organ, and became known as Boz People. Dabbling in jazz, the group's career came to an abrupt end after their gear was stolen and debts crippled any chance of a reunion. In 1964 the pop press and public relations people went to town in marketing Boz as a doe-eyed pop idol. "Time to meet the most exciting new sound in the country – the sound of Boz. Boz is a refreshing new face on the music scene. He is at the moment creating quite a stir on the London scene, taking the world-famous Marquee Club by storm. In fact Boz is a sensation-creator wherever he goes but he doesn't have to scream to get his message across (he's very 'anti' this sort of thing!). Boz does it by putting across his numbers with a quality that you can't forget in a style that is bringing him praise from some of the most professional musicians and singers around. Boz has personality to go with his voice, completely natural, unaffected by anyone or anything, Boz is young, only 18, his musical abilities exceed those of many twice his age."

Burrell drifted into The Sidewinders, a soul-orientated band which counted Mark Charig and future Soft Machine drummer John Marshall as members. However, as he recounted to Richard Williams in *Melody Maker*, the regime was somewhat slack and eventually ground to a halt. "That band really turned me on to music because it was so full of musicians. But it was so disorganised – I mean, three months after the band packed up, the drummer rang to ask when the next gig was." In 1966 he released a 12-string driven ballad, *The Baby Song*, backed with a lively version of the theme song for the film *Carry On Screaming*. In 1968 he found more suitable material to cover. First, The Doors' *Light My Fire* and then another change in tack with his second single for Columbia, Bob Dylan's *I Shall Be Released*, with a punchy version of *Dove In The Flood* on the B-side. Backed in the studio by members of Deep Purple, the record showed off Burrell's gutsy vocals but wasn't enough to move his career forward. By the early '70s he'd renewed his acquaintance with Mike Patto, by then fronting his own band, Patto, who in turn had put him in touch with Keith Tippett's Centipede with whom Patto was singing in concert when the 60-plus strong ensemble, including Fripp, played in France in November 1970. It was through this connection that eventually Burrell had heard about the King Crimson auditions.

With nothing to lose, Boz went along to the Fulham Palace Road and gave it his best shot. As he would later tell journalist Steven Rosen: "I'd been in the business for about ten years, earning a regular wage of about £4 a week and I'd decided I've got to get myself a gig and earn some money – or I'm gonna swallow it. I've always been a bit of a jazz freak and they played some nice, up-tempo 6/8 things. It was a good experience for me."

"They couldn't find a bass player because at that stage Bob Fripp wrote songs and he heard them in his head and didn't give any other members in the band any leeway for their own expression. He wanted to hear them exactly as he heard them in his head. So I really learned the bass parrot-fashion, if you know what I mean."

The band's UK tour was wisely preceded by four warm-up gigs at Frankfurt's Zoom Club, a very familiar place to Wallace, who knew it under its original name of The Storyville. "It was great, it was my old stomping ground and it felt like Caesar being carried in on the back of his legionnaires in triumph. Wow – local boy makes good!"

But Burrell's first night went so badly wrong he nearly quit. The following day he wandered around the city, wondering whether he should stay in the band. Bizarrely enough, he came upon a game of cricket in the middle of Frankfurt and, after bowling a few overs and hearing the calming sounds of leather on willow, his confidence was restored. Collins recalls that the difficulties Boz encountered weren't just to do with his own performance. "Robert wasn't being very kind at the time and he had in his mind John Wetton to come in and play bass. They were friends from Bournemouth. It was causing a problem for Boz because he knew about this. Ian and I stuck together and said, 'This isn't fair. We've got to give Boz more space to get his stuff together; he was a good enough musician and he should have that time.' We managed to persuade Robert to keep Boz in the band but it was a tough time for him. When you think about it, he did unbelievably well to be singing Pete Sinfield's lyrics, which were really difficult. He had them written down on great big sheets of paper on the stage floor by the mic. So he's trying to sing these lyrics and play the basslines at the same time and not being a bass player. That's really hard, really difficult." The soundboard tapes that exist from the run of gigs show the band to be incredibly animated, clearly delighted to be away from their basement rehearsal room and obviously enjoying the liberation of being onstage. The shouts of encouragement and approval exchanged between members, often in mid-song, convey both warmth and intimacy. Apart from miming to a backing track for *Cat Food* on *Top of the Pops* the previous year, this was Fripp's first outing on stage with a band calling itself King Crimson since December 1969. Understandably, much of the material draws upon music that originated from that period but *Cirkus* and *Lady Of The Dancing Water* suggest that, whatever tensions resulted in their creation, the effort was worthwhile. This incarnation could also be heard establishing its own distinctive voice through a still open-ended *Sailor's Tale*. Of particular interest to long-term Crimson fans is the appearance in the improvisation of elements of what would later become *Larks' Tongues In Aspic, Part I.*

IX

Back home, the dates for King Crimson's first UK concerts since October 1969 were announced. The band gave a series of interviews where tapes of Frankfurt were coyly unveiled to largely supportive journalists. The set for the 15-date tour spanned Crimson's career and included some new material.

The first gig was at Plymouth's Guildhall on 11 May 1971. The set was released 30 years later as part of the King Crimson Collectors' Club series and provides a compelling glimpse of the group at the start of its live career. It's not until the third number, *Sailor's Tale,* that the band noticeably relax. Substantially different from the finished studio version, this early version of the piece has a looser feel with none of the brisk urgency or solemnity of its studio counterpart. In place of the abrasive guitar solo, Collins slowly unveils a flute solo briefly borrowing some eastern motifs and winding up in a dervish-like euphoria. Not without humour, the solo contains a fleeting reference to *St. Thomas* by sax hero Sonny Rollins, a tune which had been a regular feature for Collins in Circus.

Burrell announces another new tune. "It's so new in fact, that I'm squinting out of the corner of me eye to get the words together" – a reference to his practice at the time of using large cue cards. As a result, Burrell takes some interesting liberties with the words. *The Letters* was a significant re-working of *Drop In* from the 1969 setlist and in concert Fripp somewhat perversely provides the last verse with a wildly inappropriate "happy ending".

Ladies Of The Road was the only other new song and it presented the most radical departure from the Crimson repertoire, combining a blues-based sequence and a distinctly earthy, unambiguous lyric. *Get Thy Bearings* provided Ian Wallace with a launch pad for a remarkable, and remarkably funny, drum solo. "It was Peter's idea to put the drums through the ring modulator of the VCS3 and so he had control of the sound and when I hit the drum it would go through all these weird sounds and whistles. We worked on it in rehearsals. Later on I got the idea of incorporating a bit of humour into the piece and at that time Carl Palmer was in ELP and during his drum solo he'd do these very fast notes on the kick drum whilst taking off his shirt. So I parodied this by doing very fast notes on the kick drum and taking off my shirt but, halfway through taking it off, I'd get it all tangled up and fall off the stool. I'd fall off behind the drums so nobody could see me and I'd grab a big huge wad of sticks and climb up the highest point above the drums and then throw the sticks like Keith Emerson would throw daggers at his Hammond. So they'd hit the toms and ricochet off into the audience and that's when Peter would put them through the VCS3. Then I'd jump down and finish the solo with the VCS3 on, but it was quite funny. It became a nightly routine. I heard Carl Palmer was not amused and I think I stopped doing it by the first American tour."

The sell-out concert was a great testing ground for the band and, as Fripp told *Disc* reporter David Harris: "The people were marvellous. We deliberately chose Plymouth to make our debut because the audience would put up with us if anything goes wrong!" Harris goes on to report that the band had no encore prepared and so it fell to Burrell to perform a warmly received tap dance routine to popular show tune *Me And My Shadow*.

In June, Fripp was at Wessex Studios overseeing the recording of Keith Tippet's magnum opus *Septober Energy*, performed by Centipede. Tippett had wowed critics and the public not only with his lightning-fast technique but also his qualities as a composer with two highly-rated albums recorded for Polydor and Vertigo. When he came up with the idea of writing a large-scale piece that would bring together 50 musicians from jazz, rock and classical music, RCA's progressive boutique label, Neon, jumped at the chance to sign him up. During 1970, the massed ranks of Centipede played several high-profile gigs at home and abroad with RCA chartering a jetliner to ferry the musicians, gear and crew to Europe. A young Mike Oldfield saw them perform and cited them as an influence in his thinking for *Tubular Bells*. Centipede boasted four vocalists, including Tippett's wife, Julie Driscoll, three drummers and legions of brass and string players drawn from the very best contemporary music circles of the day. Featuring members of Nucleus, Soft Machine, King Crimson, Blossom Toes and Patto, Tippett's piece was informed by a utopian impulse that, regardless of genre, music was a unifying force for good. With Fripp at the controls, players were ushered in groups to overdub their parts. The combination of a complex score coupled with improvised passages added up to not only a high-pressure environment but an expensive one that allowed just four days in which to get everything done. Everything, that is, apart from Fripp's own guitar solo, for which time simply ran out. Beginning with ambiguous percussive sounds, ominous drones and ethereal vocal harmonies unfurl, until the air is filled with skittering notes and fleeting encounters between brass and strings. Spread across four side-long movements, Tippett's tone poem breaks into strident themes that march firmly along to rock grooves which form springboards into jazzy excursions. The pianist's writing focuses attention on the unconventional dynamics of the line-up but never loses sight of melodic and harmonic opportunities. Singalong chants, gothic strings, turbulent arrangements and acerbic soloing makes for a formidable and sometimes challenging listen. Guitarist Brian Godding, who'd played with Blossom Toes, took on the parts an overworked Fripp had no time to perform. The big room at Wessex was like an aircraft hangar, says Godding. "They were usually sticking in radio and TV orchestras and those kinds of bands and big ensembles in there. I remember we were all spread out all over the place which made it quite hard to record. It was very hard to hear anybody so you had to assume that what people were doing was the right thing (*laughs*). In the big room it was set up like we were all in different corners looking at each other. From our point of view, we had to keep the rhythm section together in the rocky stuff." Roy Babbington played bass. "It was such a gigantic occasion to have that number of people involved in a recording, but of course the piece of music itself didn't demand that all the people needed to present at any one time. So, it was done on a kind of shift principal. If your part came up then you were required to be at the studio. Conversely, if there were things you weren't involved in you were expressly requested not to be at the studio. This was obviously for reasons of efficiency and economics. That was policed by Ronnie Scott's guys. There were two or three of them and they were making sure the right people were in the right place at the right time. So we'd slide in to do our bit and we were then asked to vanish (*laughs*). You'd get your call which was all worked out in advance. Fripp was pretty efficient when it came to doing things like this. You'd get a timetable and everybody had one of those and needed to conform. You really weren't wanted other than at those times on your sheet. They couldn't have a bunch of people having a coffee and a chinwag for instance because there were too many people involved. It was not a party affair."

Babbington was put in the section with Godding. "Keith wanted me separate and he had a little rhythm section half in there and because I play bass guitar as well, I was a little bit more involved than the upright bass players. When it came to the straightforward driving rhythm section that was me, and the bass section was more or less part of a string section for most of the time."

Burrell was a member of the chorus and ex-Crim Ian McDonald made an appearance playing alto sax. After the release of *McDonald And Giles* the previous year, McDonald was in turmoil, having broken up with girlfriend Charlotte Bates. He started producing sessions for folk artists Gay and Terry Woods at Island's studios, but these were abruptly abandoned when he decided to go to California and enter therapy. A few months later, he was back in London and undertaking sessions for Marc Bolan and T.Rex (for the *Electric Warrior* album) and, at the other end of the musical spectrum, Centipede. McDonald had no contact with Fripp during the sessions. "It would have been too close to my leaving Crimson and I was just one of the horn players," he explains.

The critical acclaim the album received upon its release didn't translate to sales and RCA dropped Tippett after his next, more introspective, improv albums *Blueprint* and *Ovary Lodge*. Nevertheless, *Septober Energy* remains a magnificent testament to his ambitious and visionary enterprise.

In July 1971, Crimson fan Martin Morris saw the band at a one-off appearance at Watford Town Hall. As good as he felt the music was, the visual aspects to Crimson's performance are seared into his memory. "It made a huge impression on my 14-year-old psyche. I had never before experienced the light show, and the overall atmosphere in the hall made for a multi-media/multi-sensory experience which left me tingling for several days. The support band, Hookfoot, had used the Watford Town Hall 'houselight' – a single, wide angle spot which covered the whole stage. The comparison from that to the Crimson set-up was a bit like the sequence in *The Wizard Of Oz* where the film suddenly goes from black-and-white to colour! 'Breathtaking' doesn't adequately describe it."

Another Crimson fan present at that same gig in Watford was the 13-year-old Jakko Jakszyk, who was so profoundly affected by what he heard and saw that it put him on course to want to become a professional musician.

In August, the band returned to the Marquee after an absence of two years. The return attracted many who'd seen them there in 1969. Fripp recalls talking to Fleetwood Mac guitarist Peter Green at the bar. "It's good to see you making a comeback," said Green. "I've never been away," Fripp retorted. "That's what I like to hear," smiled Green in return. Crimson's stint at the legendary London club was described as a thank-you to fans, offering them an opportunity to see the band in intimate surroundings. Originally scheduled for two nights, the demand was such that Marquee manager Jack Barrie cancelled Wednesday's usual disco and added a third evening with Crimson. Only four months out from its live debut in April and with just 20 gigs under its belt, this version of King Crimson was still in the process of maturing and developing. On soundboard recordings, the band sound very relaxed indeed. Perhaps more than anything, this concert captures Crimson at an interesting point in its development, caught between the weight of its past and attempting to find its own musical identity. After a powerful *Pictures Of A City*, Boz, clearly suffering from a bad cold, announces: "This next one's a new one. It's called *Formentera Lady*." It's interesting to hear that the piece originally featured loosely-styled three-part harmonising by Boz, Mel and Ian, an idea that would be dropped in the recording of *Islands* and when the band resumed formal touring in September. Though we can't experience the light show, we do get to hear Peter Sinfield's treatments of the band using the VCS3 synthesiser. Aside from the crazed processing on Ian Wallace's solo, there's the more subtle hazing of Mel Collins' flute introduction to *The Letters*. This, again, was an element dropped by the time the song was recorded at Command on 1 September. Fripp introduces an as-yet-unnamed number which the band had recorded just a few days earlier, revealing that it had been written as a reaction to different cities. Combining elements of *LTIA1* and *Lament*, it's interesting to speculate how different in character *Islands* might have been had this piece got to the final running order.

The band played several one-off dates in the provinces and a chronically delayed appearance at the Weeley Festival on 28 August. A few days later, on Saturday, 4 September, Crimson returned to London for the 12th festival at Hyde Park, supporting Jack Bruce and leaving an estimated crowd of 60,000 roaring for more. After one or two exploratory forays in Command Studios the previous month, it was now time to start laying down a new album. After the studio-bound *Poseidon* and *Lizard*, the recording of *Islands* set the pattern for future Crimson albums in that the material was tried and tested out on the road. Cost was a factor, something Sinfield acknowledged when talking to *Disc*'s Caroline Boucher. "The albums have cost us far too much. Also, the sales figures didn't justify such expenditure. In this country, the first album sold 93,000; the second 68,000 and *Lizard* 35,000, which is sad because I preferred the last album to all the others."

On the grounds of expense and convenience, Crimson left Wessex for Command in the centre of London. A former BBC studio beneath which London Underground trains would rumble, it was both cheap and available as Crimson fitted recording between sporadic shows, requiring gruelling get-ins, set-ups and get-outs for the road crew.

For example, on Monday, 27 September, the musicians arrived at noon and recorded until midnight. The equipment was then packed in the van and driven to Leeds, where the band appeared at the Town Hall. After the gig, the band retired to a local hotel. The road crew drove back to London, having the gear set back up in the studio in readiness for 2.00 pm and the re-appearance of the group. The bulk of *Islands* was recorded in this way during September, although marathon 12-hour sessions saw most of the overdubbing and mixing completed in the first week of October when there were no gigs. Sinfield says that the album was randomly constructed as a reaction to what he calls "the intellectualism of *Lizard*".

Violinist Wilf Gibson had been part of the string ensemble for *Septober Energy* and got on well with Fripp. "Bob was great. Terribly affable. Nice bloke with a strong Dorset accent. He was always very amenable. He pretty much had his feet on the ground." Fripp asked Gibson to organise a small string orchestra for *Islands* and he assembled Tim Cramer, Colin Kitching, Steve Rolandson, Phil Saudek, Louise Jopling, Channa, John Trussler, Garth Morton and Rod Skeaping. It's this group of players Fripp can be heard addressing in the run-out track at the end of the album. Gibson's violin can also be heard in the final vamping section of *Formentera Lady* as it begins to merge with *Sailor's Tale.* There are many standout moments on this musically diverse album: *Formentera Lady*'s sunny dreamscapes with a lyric inspired by Sinfield's recent holidays in the Balearic islands; the free-jazz tussle within *The Letters*' chilling melodrama incorporating the heavy chorus from the 1969 band's *Drop In*; the skewed, mutant blues guitar licks and raucous sax of *Ladies Of The Road*; the genteel classical music climes of *Song Of The Gulls*; the emotional reverie of the title track. Arguably, the most stylistically diverse KC release to date, it features fine vocals from Boz, who heroically sang into a fire bucket for *Ladies Of The Road* while suffering from a raging hangover. There are superb jazzy flourishes as well as understated and detailed playing throughout from Ian Wallace. Mel Collins also displays both sides of his musical personality with moments both tender and brutal. If *Lizard* represented a wild party between the progressive strand of rock music and the UK jazz scene, *Islands* was, broadly speaking, a gentler kind of communion. Though his talents are under-used on *Formentera Lady*, Harry Miller was one of the most gifted bassists of his generation who, at the time of this recording, was founding independent record label Ogun. Along with Keith Tippett's delicate additions on the title track comes his cornet player, Mark Charig, whose free-flowing and impassioned blasts, over Fripp's folksy harmonium, add poignant warmth to the stirring coda of one of Fripp's most beautiful melodies. However, it's *Sailor's Tale* which overshadows everything here. The solo makes a break with the symphonic and jazz-inspired leanings of previous albums, clawing its way into spikier, fractious territory. It's the sound of Fripp hammering out new territory.

X

Upon its release, the album netted a good reaction from critics, but there were some notes of caution. *Sounds*' Steve Peacock lauded the album for its "rare sense of ease and grace" and hailed it as a "Great Leap Forward". Richard Williams also regarded the album as something of a departure, congratulating Crimson on the summery warmth of *Formentera Lady*. "At this point," Williams warned the potential buyer, "you may even be wondering if the shop assistant gave you the right album. But you'll be enjoying it." One unnamed critic was enthusiastic in the extreme. "Despite the shoddy packaging, this is one of the most extraordinary albums ever to emerge out of the general idiom of rock. It's impossible to describe the warm, lambent feeling obtained by a juxtaposition of Mark Charig's cornet over a pedal harmonium on the title track's long, gradual climax, or the breathtaking rightness of Fripp's splintery chorded solo on *Sailor's Tale*. And it's not pretentious and it's not self-indulgent." However, *Melody Maker* was less certain. "*Islands* is altogether different from their former work. Where their preceding albums had a dominant strain of almost overbearing intensity, which matched the dark imagery of the lyrics, this is more muted and soft," it declared, concluding: "This isn't the master album that Fripp threatens to produce, but the day can't be far off." For his part, self-confessed Crimso aficionado Nick Logan, writing in *NME*, observed: "*Islands* confirms a growing belief that Crimso have evolved into a skilful but somehow cold and dispassionate band. Warmth is what is lacking."

Having previously been responsible for commissioning other artists to produce album covers, *Islands* saw Sinfield step into the spotlight, as he had done with the cover of the *Cat Food* single in March 1970. In the UK, *Islands* came in an unmarked sleeve bearing a photograph of the Trifid Nebula nestling in the constellation of Sagittarius. The inner sleeve was a fragile cream-coloured gatefold with delicate islands on the outside, created by Sinfield's method of dripping food dye on to blotting paper. Inside, a collage of five individual portraits and three group shots of the band in concert marked the first time the faces of King Crimson had ever appeared on an album sleeve. On its release in the USA, the inner gatefold was used as the outer cover. "The change of cover for the US was because the UK cover was considered so feeble," explained Fripp. "The cover artist for the UK cover was Peter. Peter's 'move on stage' through the use of the VCS3 now expanded to include designing the cover as well. If this works, fine. But Peter's cover wasn't striking and wasn't in the same league as the other Crimson covers. The nebula really wasn't much of a cover either, because it hadn't been chosen as a cover."

Listening back to the album 30 years after its making, Fripp made the following observations about *Islands* and its two predecessors: "Ever been in a group? Ever been in a group rehearsing? Ever been in a group recording? Ever been in a group which did all these things but the members didn't get on? The circus of dumb living: make an album, tour; make another album, tour; make another album, tour; make another album, tour. Q: Is this all there is, dear manager, dear record company, dear agent, dear tour manager? A: Let's talk about this after the next album and tour."

With the *Islands* sessions barely finished, Crimson were indeed off on tour again, though the atmosphere was markedly different to the boisterous optimism of May. There can be few partnerships in music which have not at some point or other suffered the ravages of toxic jealousy or insidious doubt. And, although Sinfield's 50/50 split deal had initially seemed to settle Crimson's co-writers arguments over money, Fripp increasingly came to resent it.

The guitarist began to withdraw from the normal social interaction of the band. Stoic tour manager Dik Fraser remembers the period well. "It sort of degenerated because Robert decided he was never going to talk to anyone again or something. I used to drive through the great silence and I'd be driving the passenger van with Robert next to me and the boys in the back and it was like 'What time's the soundcheck? What time do we get to the airport?' That was it. That was the entire conversation with Robert for the whole tour. It was an epic little shit fit, you know? I think what we saw then was a very unhappy man making other people unhappy. He was extremely miserable and I'm sure it just spread."

Indeed it did. Wallace: "We were on the road and for two weeks Fripp wouldn't speak to anyone and he'd just sit in the dressing room playing scales over and over and over. In the van driving somewhere he just wouldn't speak to anyone and it got very frustrating and it cast a cloud over everything."

The emotional impact manifested itself in various ways. When Crimson played Edinburgh on 23 October, the drummer shared a room with Mel Collins. "I'd gone out and Mel had gone to bed and I came back in and was sat up in bed with the light on reading and Mel was asleep but suddenly he let out this unholy fucking noise, sat up in bed looking wildly at this tea tray on the stand in between the two beds and then knocked it flying. I was covered in milk and tea and sugar and he just went back to sleep. My bed was soaked and Mel was fast asleep. So I stripped the bed and got to sleep and in the morning Mel didn't remember anything about it."

Talking to *Sounds*' Steve Peacock, Collins hinted at the problems. "I can't work at battle stations, as it were. I have to be in sympathy with the other people on the stand to play my best. I can see where there are occasions when you can be productive when you're uptight but it doesn't work for long." Elsewhere in the interview, Fripp admitted responsibility for a lot of the tension. "Word was laid on me … that I wasn't aware of the effect I was having on the rest of the band … and Ian said that at several gigs he wanted to come over and lay one on me, and I was ready to throw the electric piano back if that happened."

Looking back from his own perspective, Fripp comments: "The tour was awful for me: I found myself in a position where I felt dishonest. I lost faith in the band, but not in Crimson. We were on tour and walking onstage every night, where nothing can be hidden. The performer is an open book. How to handle this sense of what I experienced as transparent dishonesty? That young man imploded and the effect on the others was clearly very hard."

"Today, an older man with an established practice, on tour I keep my focus very close. Externally, I might appear to have withdrawn. But the internal currents are different."

It had been nearly two years since Crimson had played in America and, whereas marijuana and acid had previously been the main drugs on offer, times had changed and cocaine was now omnipresent in the dressing rooms, hotel rooms and company offices of the music industry. Drug use within Crimson was a significant factor in distancing Fripp from those who indulged.

Wallace remembers: "The first American tour was the first time me, Mel and Boz had been to the States and we were like kids in a candy store … everybody was doing cocaine and we all thought it was pretty harmless, non-addictive and so on. Robert didn't do it but he was the only one. In those days everybody was doing it. Of course we found out it was very evil and very insidious but at the time everyone thought it was fine."

On the tour, Crimson opened for bands including Procol Harum and Humble Pie and were often supported themselves by Black Oak Arkansas and Sweat Hog. There was quite a lot of after-show socialising with all the bands hanging out together.

Burrell's fondness for imbibing at such get-togethers had some beneficial results. "We had to get up very early and we were all pretty hung over," explained Ian Wallace. "We hit a really bad storm and the plane, which was a small two-prop thing, was going side to side and up and down and everybody on the plane threw up, including the stewardesses – except for Boz who was sprawled in the seat next to me completely unconscious, snoring through the entire thing."

A macrobiotic Sinfield was exhausted by the tour. *Disc*'s Andrew Taylor reported: "Peter Sinfield, King Crimson's compulsive poet and one-man environment, almost wishes he hadn't joined the group on the recent six-week US tour. 'It's not that we actually failed anywhere,' he says. 'We went down reasonably-to-very well but it's just not the same as on our English tours. I think I'd be happy to stay at home and write poetry.' The problems were manifold … similar hazards re-occurred again and again and the resulting pressure on the group created much 'internal turmoil'. Sinfield returned a wreck."

As Stephanie Ruben recalls: "He got exhausted in the end and, to be fair, our home life wasn't the peaceful haven it should have been because I was a bit wild … and I think Peter was just exhausted with people he loved letting him down."

Fripp had confided his difficulties in continuing to work with Sinfield to Wallace, Burrell and Collins. "Basically he gave us an ultimatum that it was him or Peter," Wallace remembers. "We saw that Crimson wouldn't have continued without Fripp and, although he gave us a choice, there really was no choice." Once back in England, Fripp decided to phone Sinfield to tell him that he could no longer work with him.

It was an important call for the guitarist in more ways than one. "This was a personal turning point, where I accepted responsibility for myself in a particular kind of way: accepting responsibility for what I saw to be right, and accepting the consequences of acting accordingly. Even though this would cause grief. This was the first time I called myself 'Robert'. Listening to myself speak, I heard myself say: 'Hello, Peter, this is Robert.' Then: 'I can't work with you anymore.'"

"We were in the sitting room in our little cottage," Ruben remembers. "I think what made it even more poignant was that Pete had spent the day working on lyrics or the artwork for a sleeve or something. Anyway, Robert was on the line and I could see Pete's face and I knew this wasn't right … So when he put the phone down I think he said something like 'He doesn't want to work with me anymore' and, knowing Pete, he would be pragmatic and say 'Oh well it doesn't matter anymore' or 'I was ready for this' – but he wasn't. I'm not saying he wasn't expecting it but I think he thought they should work it out because it should have meant more. It meant such a lot to Pete.

"When you love something and want it to work you don't see all the problems and I think Pete missed the signs, although the signs weren't very obvious, as they wouldn't be with Robert. Pete was also highly intuitive and sensitive and I think, at the time, even if it was only for a day, it would have been too horrible a thought to think about the demise. Like a love affair, you think 'Oh we'll work this out' but Robert didn't want to bother to work it out."

Fripp's call wasn't entirely out of the blue. Ruben recalls that there had been conversations where Fripp had argued that Sinfield's role in the band didn't carry the same weight as his own. "He didn't want Peter to do lights anymore or have flying horses in the lyrics anymore, he'd moved on. To be fair, Pete's work had also moved on though, but it was different and Robert had the louder voice. If there was a choice at all as to who would leave, well of course it would have been Peter who would leave."

Fripp saw the split as the inevitable climax to "eighteen months of managing increasing personal criticism and hostility, quite apart from the specific professional context which was disintegrating".

"I was quite happy to continue writing, particularly with the other members of the band. In fact Mel and I nearly had a song on *Islands* – maybe Bob didn't like that and I was pushing for it," explained Sinfield to Richard Williams.

Collins agrees with Sinfield's analysis recalling the tentative writing partnership. While making no claims to be a great writer, the sax player was interested in developing this aspect and was grateful for Sinfield's encouragement. But the prospective partnership was short-lived as Collins felt that Fripp somehow disapproved. "I always remember him saying: 'Mel, you could be a guvnor player but you'll never be a writer.' That hurt you know, and I still have that statement with me to this day, as silly as that sounds. But Robert was a little bit older than me and much more experienced in the music business and playing and I did look up to him a hell of a lot."

Sinfield acknowledged the increasing distance between Fripp and himself. "Bob and I had been drifting apart in our writing over the past year. He'd play something for me, and I'd say 'No, I don't like it very much ... it wasn't getting through and I wasn't laying anything on him in return," he told *Melody Maker.*

Sinfield also cited an unhappiness with some of the settings of his lyrics within Crimson and indicated that he would start work on recording a solo album. "It might not be very good but at least it would be mine," he confided to Williams.

On hearing of the split, Greg Lake got in touch and encouraged Sinfield to work with him. Lake would reciprocate by lending a hand with the production of Sinfield's album *Still*, released on ELP's Manticore label in 1973.

Sinfield saw the tensions in the relationship as essentially a way of keeping creative sparks flying but views the root of the problem as being caused by Fripp resenting his interventions and suggestions. "Robert likes, nay thrives on, a bit of tension as do many in relationships ... I hold to the theory that much good work is a result of overcoming a challenge ... trading an 'I'll show you mine if ...' – in a word FRICTION. Which causes heat ... But mainly Robert and I just let each other get on and do what we did best ... with of course a mutual END in mind. I think the famous BIG problems really occurred leading up to Islands ... where I musically wanted to find a softer Miles Davis-with-vocals sexy package. Mel, Boz, and Ian were not averse to that but Robert (not indulgent of their US retro spirit of blue-cool) drank a lot of coffee and as the phrase has it – 'Asked politely for his ball back'. So, without recourse to Roger, Waters overrides and percentages on everything Crimson forever, I said, 'Sure go with it.'"

Before returning to the UK, Fripp, Wallace, Collins and Burrell discussed the future. Once Sinfield was no longer part of the operation the money, Fripp assured them, would be split equally. Furthermore, writing and composition would no longer be Fripp's exclusive domain.

Collins put the recent past out of his head and began to work on ideas for consideration. Collins and Wallace both recall that optimism was high when the band reconvened in January 1972 in Ferndown, five miles outside Bournemouth in a motel owned by Greg Lake's old friend, John Dickinson, organist and songwriter in The Shame.

On the first day, Collins duly presented a piece to the seated Fripp. "I wasn't brimming with confidence anyway, but I put it down in front of Robert. It certainly wasn't finished and it was just a couple of ideas but Robert would not play the music I'd put down in front of him. Wouldn't even attempt it. Obviously he didn't think it was good enough and he wasn't going to give it a go and so I fled from those rehearsals in tears. I was absolutely destroyed and that was how I knew I couldn't really work with Robert because he was too controlling and wasn't willing to give me a chance."

"It's true: I hoped for writing input from other members. I remember Mel's contribution, and it wasn't Crimson," Fripp explained. "I'm not suggesting it was 'bad', only that it wasn't Crimson. However much time we would have put into it, it would never have been Crimson."

Fripp accepts that he was indeed exerting control but more in the sense of what Adrian Belew would later describe as "quality control" within Crimson. "Crim has a particular flavour, scent, way of walking and doing things," Fripp continues. "If a great taste, aroma, walk and notion isn't Crim, it isn't Crim. This then moves into how to operate that quality control, and how far to go with particular individuals. With Mel, who is a sensitive character and a lovely, talented guy, a much better player than I have ever been, my 'no' was clearly a brutal experience."

As Collins fled, Wallace and Burrell were outraged at what they saw as Fripp's high-handed attitude and accused the guitarist of being hypocritical. A furious Wallace put down his sticks, told Fripp he'd had enough and quit on the spot, followed by Burrell. Fripp packed up his guitar and left without a word.

It had been quite a day; a new incarnation of King Crimson had come together and folded before even completing its first rehearsal.

XI

Even accepting Fripp's position as "quality control", his handling of Collins does appear autocratic. Tour manager Fraser is forthright in his assessment of Fripp's people skills. "Crimson has always been very hot musically with very good players – Robert does pick good players. The problem is Robert's pathetic interaction with people that brings them down, rather than the fact that the music's no good. His attitude is that 'I can get good guys and they can do what they want' and then it doesn't work. He doesn't want to be the bandleader and tell people what to do but then he can't stand it when they don't do what he wants. I don't think it's that strange. I think it's a problem a lot of people have. He's in love with the idea but the practice pisses him off."

Fripp simply thinks that it is sometimes difficult for some musicians to grasp the special nature of Crimson. He says: "In practice, Crimson goes against the grain. For about a year, players are prepared to put their default settings on hold and try different approaches. After that, there has been a tendency to get stuck. Then, conventionally, Robert acts to unfix the situation."

When he heard the news from Fripp, a highly agitated David Enthoven persuaded him that Crimson were contractually obliged to return to the States in February. Enthoven phoned a fuming Wallace the next day and managed to cajole the others into returning. Against all their better judgements, the band reunited and continued to prepare for another trek to America.

Fripp believes the band were deceived. "David told us that the tour had been booked and we were contractually liable; so, we had to go ahead with the tour. But a group that breaks up isn't able to tour. The same situation was repeated in 1974 following the break-up after *Red*."

On tour, the atmosphere lifted considerably and they became looser both socially and musically. With Sinfield no longer around, Burrell felt able to refuse to perform songs (such as *Formentera Lady* and *The Letters*) which had lyrics he felt to be unsingable, and the band began to stretch out into a bluesy funk territory.

This caused some raised eyebrows, as Wallace recalls with relish. "I remember that Alexis Korner was opening up, we were in the middle and Humble Pie were closing and for our encore I got up on stage, looked up and shouted to Mel and Boz '12-bar blues in G' and I remember Boz looking at me saying 'You can't do that!' and I said 'Watch me' and I started up and everybody joined in. Fripp on the other hand sat on his stool with his guitar 'round his neck with his hands on his lap looking down, tight-lipped and never played a note. Alexis Korner and Humble Pie and everybody backstage freaked out."

In his sleevenotes to the *Live At Jacksonville 1972* KCCC release, Fripp writes: "Improvisation has played an important, even critical role, in all Crims. This live Crimson was more a jamming than improvising outfit." Wallace takes umbrage at this description, which implicitly downgrades the band. Responding to the criticism in *his* notes for the KCCC release *Live At Summit Studios*, Wallace argues: "I think we improvised rather well, improvisation being the creation of a fresh vocabulary of notes and tones over a previously constructed format. Just like jazz musicians would play the 'head' of a standard and then solo around the chord sequence."

Listening to the relevant Club releases and the mainstream live album *Earthbound*, one is struck by the force of the performances. The rendition of *Schizoid Man* on *Earthbound* has a seething, blistering quality which is at least equal to anything which the previous incarnation managed and indeed compares well to the version that followed it. The principal differences can be measured in the improvised tracks such as *Peoria*, *Earthbound*, *Summit Going On* and on the *Earthbound* version of *Groon* which, at around 5 minutes 30 seconds into the track, sounds like another band trying to rip its way out of the shell of Crimson. These tracks and *The Creator Has A Master Plan* (a cover version from Pharoah Saunders' album *Karma*) are more of an unguarded peek into the leanings and preferences of Wallace, Collins and Burrell than of Fripp, whose contribution is somewhat reserved and lukewarm.

These pieces clearly demonstrate the conflicting forces which would have inevitably pulled the band apart (Fripp already had Yes drummer Bill Bruford in his sights as a possible band member; he had also approached Jon Hiseman, although nothing came of that). Yet, as the tour progressed, most of the band were enjoying themselves immensely and Wallace recalls talking to Fripp about the possibilities of carrying something on after the tour. "Everybody started getting along well and the Summit gig is toward the end of the tour and I do remember that Boz and I went to Fripp and said to him that we'd like to carry on but he was already making his plans and was already talking to Bill (Bruford) and so it was over. It could have gone on and we were all up for that and maybe that's where some of Boz's bitterness lies because, at that time and at that moment, Boz really wanted to carry on. We had so much fun on that tour and I know Robert did. The three of us didn't want to break up."

But Fripp had made up his mind. Today, he says: "Could it have gone on? The question is: could this band have played *Larks' Tongues In Aspic*? Not in terms of, did they have the technical ability to play it? But, was this a music they would have picked up and run with?"

"The growing difficulty for me was that I had ceased to believe in the band, but not in Crimson. That is, I ceased to believe that this particular formation could 'give voice' to Crimson (with or without Peter). Clearly, the musicianship is always at least excellent, and frequently outstanding. For all of Boz's technical limitations, purely because of his little time on the instrument, his musicianship and sheer love of music is never in doubt."

"The *Larks'* ideas had been appearing in mid-1971 and was the direction which Crimson was waiting to move towards. This in contrast with, for example, Peter's sense of Crimson moving towards a Miles area. Note, with Peter Sinfield in the band this made the American-leaning members 4 to 1. *Larks'* cannot be understood structurally (i.e. as a musical construct) as American in any way. Certainly it draws on the power of rock, but is characteristically (in hindsight, perhaps definitively) a European rock."

"The musical question is, was my sense of the next Crimson step validated by the music which the next Crimson produced, played and recorded? Probably, the answer today would be 'yes'."

"The personal question might be, could the personal interactions with the *Earthbound* band have been sweeter? Probably the answer today would also be a resounding 'yes'. But I doubt that the outcome in terms of Crimson personnel, either Peter or the three players, would have been any different."

"I accept that Fripp was an exceptionally difficult man to deal with at this period: he was focused, intense, driven and committed to the Crimson process, and had a clear sense of where he felt Crimson should be moving. He was also working in the face of growing animosity from his closest working partner, Peter, and without much overt support from the three players. Increasingly, the personal balance of the band became unbalanced: this as a statement, without attributing blame."

Collins also had his doubts about the line-up's viability and his relationship with Fripp. "I think I'd got to the point where I knew I could be destroyed by him because he was so heavy in the controlling aspect of it and I had to do it my own way. It was like being at school and I wanted to leave school as quickly as I could. There was the relationship with my father and my need to develop on my own thing and it was a similar thing with Robert. I had so much more to learn. We'd been doing the tricky time signatures and all the clever stuff and that was great but that was why I joined up with Alexis Korner along with Ian and Boz – it was exactly the opposite of Crimson and playing blues, which I'd never really done before." When Fripp returned to England, Burrell, Wallace and Collins stayed on in America to play with Korner and, along with singer and guitarist Peter Thorup, formed Snape, who released two albums: *Accidentally Born In New Orleans* in 1973 and *Live In Germany* in 1974.

Back in the UK, Fripp began sifting through tapes of the tour for what was then provisionally titled *Live In The USA*. Recorded onto cassette directly from the mixing desk, the tapes allowed no post-production overdubbing and were only subjected to basic editing and a minimal cleaning-up. Released in June 1972 on Island's budget HELP label, *Earthbound* appeared to be an austere postscript to an otherwise glittering career. Crimson's first live album, with its bleak cover and dubious lo-fi character. Long-time Crimso champion Richard Williams could find only measured praise in *Melody Maker*, saying the band were pulling in different directions and coining the phrase about this version of Crimson being essentially a blowing band. *Record Mirror* said the album represented a fall from form and grace. And Crimson's American label, Atlantic, declined to release it, judging that the questionable sound quality would result in numerous customer returns and a financial loss. But, while undoubtedly appearing brutish and crude in comparison to its studio-based predecessors, *Earthbound* does contain inspirational performances. Fripp's solo in *21CSM* is among his best of the period and the incomparable roar of Collins' sax work on *Groon* is nothing short of rapturous. Indeed, the cathartic nature of *Groon* is further evidenced by Wallace's ferociously splenetic drum solo. The track closes in an astonishing and blistering display of barely-controlled feedback, as though Fripp was somehow attempting to close the lid on this particular Pandora's box of sonic terror.

In the years after its release, Fripp actively lobbied to have the album deleted, which suggests he regarded *Earthbound* as a lapse of judgement. Ironically, demand from fans for a re-release steadily grew. Fripp wryly observed: "Once anything is released it never goes away. And if it does, it will return." In 2010, when Nick Cave's Grinderman project was working on a special version of a single from their second album, they drafted in Robert Fripp as a guest player. "I wanted to work with Robert Fripp because he has done some of the most uniquely unsettling guitar work I have ever heard along with some of the most delicate and finessed," explained Cave. "I grew up listening to a lot of the King Crimson stuff. The vinyl copy of the phenomenal live album *Earthbound* is one of my most treasured possessions."

The release of archive material has done much to rehabilitate the reputation of the 1971 band which, until the creation of the King Crimson Collectors' Club, had left behind two albums too contrasting and incongruous for posterity to judge. Wallace wishes that *Summit Studios* could receive a wider mainstream release to provide a better representation of what the band could achieve.

For many years, open hostility existed between Fripp and the members of the *Earthbound* band. There are still sore points. Burrell – who later went on to international success as the bass player in Bad Company – shunned any reference to his time with Crimson right up until his death, aged 60, in 2006. Collins has some regard and warmth for his first period with Crimson but still flinches when recalling some episodes, both musical and social.

Wallace – who died, also aged 60, in 2007 – travelled through resentment and active dislike of the band to rebuild his relationship with Fripp. "He called me up in 1992 because he was going into litigation with Fenwick and Alder and we patched it up. I got that feeling that the nice Robert was back. The next time I saw him after that was during a Frippertronics instore at Tower Records and I went up and said hello while he was setting up and he was really pleased to see me and we got our friendship back together. Robert is the one constant throughout the entire Crimson history and he owns the name. It's like Henry V or something with different advisors and generals – they all change but the King remains constant."

After all the success and struggles of Crimson's first three years, Fripp was now in sole charge of the good ship Crimson. Marked by the stomach-churning disappearance of the original line-up and dropped into struggle and uncertainty, of personal enmities whose repercussions have had their negative effect across decades, it's perhaps not entirely surprising that in the years that followed, Fripp actively shunned all but the most occasional reference to this section of his past. Yet within these albums there are inspirational episodes, brutal excursions into dark places and points of transcendent light. Despite the traumatic personal relationships informing those times, the music itself speaks with an energetic presence that set Crimson apart from their contemporaries and which remains startlingly distinct.

It's interesting to note that nearly all of those who appear on these albums went on to make significant and substantial contributions in their chosen field, with several going to commercial success that greatly eclipsed anything managed while in King Crimson. Greg Lake conquered the world with ELP; Andy McCulloch went on to Greenslade and a business life away from the stage; stadium-sized success awaited for Boz as a founder member of Bad Company; Peter Sinfield carving out a niche first as a producer, and then prospered further as an award-winning songwriter; Mel Collins became the sax player of choice across several hundred albums by some of the biggest-selling artists of the 20th century, only to end up back in a re-imagined King Crimson in 2014; Ian Wallace similarly enjoyed being in demand with Bob Dylan and other industry greats, and eventually reconciled himself with his Crimson past by joining the 21st Century Schizoid Band in 2003 alongside Mel Collins, Peter Giles, Ian McDonald and current King Crimson guitarist and vocalist Jakko Jakszyk, and established his beloved Crimson Jazz Trio in 2005. Even Gordon Haskell, after spending many years in honourable near-obscurity as a travelling troubadour, found recognition and fame in the UK singles and album charts in 2001.

The common factor that these temperamentally and musically different players share is that for the period in which they sailed aboard the good ship Crimson, they were stretched, some would say "bent out of shape" even, beyond their default settings as musicians. Perhaps this also goes some way to explaining why, whatever misgivings they may have had at the time, their period in King Crimson is often pointed to as one of the most adventurous aspects of their respective careers. The passing of Boz in 2006, Ian in 2007 and Greg in 2016 lends the music of 1969 to 1972 a certain poignancy and whatever personal enmities marked their time in Crimson, they were eventually reconciled to the fact that the music they helped to create was bold, audacious and, on reflection, worth the struggle and effort.

Musing upon the task of trying to stay true to the ideals that brought King Crimson into the world, Fripp describes the time between *Court* and *Larks' Tongues* as an interim period, remarking that it was "something I wouldn't want to undergo again". It would take the passing of many years before Fripp himself was able to make his peace with these albums and come to terms with the stormy seas he and the rest of the crew traversed. The late '60s and '70s were a time of unprecedented creativity in rock music and although there were artists who sold in much bigger numbers, King Crimson's output during this era has rightly come to be regarded as standing out for its boldness and innovation. Not one of the records from this period, with the brief exception of *Earthbound*, has ever gone out of print. These records were well-received in the press upon their release and loved to varying degrees ranging from admiration to adulation by the fans who bought them then and still continue to do so. Unlike those involved in its making, listeners have only ever known the music.

And that is surely the real story here: the music. Who could have predicted that in 2017 pieces from this era would form part of a King Crimson setlist, or be so warmly and enthusiastically received by old and new fans alike? It seems more than likely that, as Mel Collins steps out of the van at venues around the world, he'll be signing even more copies of *In The Wake Of Poseidon*, *Lizard* and *Islands* in the tours to come.

LEVEL 3: A tangle of night and daylight sounds …

It's 1973 and Jakko Jakszyk has just returned home from a school trip to Somerset and is about to listen to Larks' Tongues In Aspic *for the first time. Knowing the album would be coming out while he was away, and knowing he'd want to hear it the minute he got back, Jakko had asked his mum to buy it for him. "I remember having a bath and going into my bedroom. I'd rearranged my stereo and I'd put the pillow from my bed on the floor with one speaker either side and then put the record on."*

A committed King Crimson fan since seeing them at Watford Town Hall in 1971 and again in 1972 with an entirely different line-up, Jakko put on the album. "Of course, I thought, 'Gosh, this is really quiet.' So I turned it up! When the fuzz guitar came in it was so exciting. It got louder and louder and then, when it really kicked in, it nearly blew my fucking ears off!"

Though the precise details varied, that scenario was played out in households around the globe as fans got to grips with the perilous dynamics of a new Crimson standard. If 21st Century Schizoid Man *posited an end-of-sixties brutalist musical architecture, the arrival of* Larks' Tongues In Aspic, Parts I *and* II *in the early '70s articulated a leaner construction whose ability to shock and awe had devastating power. The cross-picked motif in* Part I *and the jagged riffing of* Part II *were a well-honed, one-two punch to the head and the body. "It was just riveting. I was a Crimson fan already and this was a whole other version of it. It was completely different and yet it sounded like King Crimson," says Jakszyk.*

In early 2014, Robert Fripp and Jakko Jakszyk were running through material for King Crimson's return to the stage. "Robert said, 'I thought we might do LTIA, Pt I,*'" recalls Jakko who, upon hearing the suggestion, was momentarily catapulted back to his 14-year-old self having his ears blown off. "As we were talking about it, Robert says 'you know these parts?' alluding to the cross-picked section. He said 'these are ergonomically difficult to play in New Standard Tuning.' I felt immediately disappointed, thinking that we weren't going to play it or maybe that we'd just play the opening riff or something. But then he said, 'You're playing in standard tuning so you can play those parts.' I remember there's that moment of silence where I'm looking around the room and realising he's not joking. So I said, 'OK. Sure.' Then, when he left, I thought, 'I can't play that!' Robert didn't tell me what the part was. I had to work that out myself, accessing the* LTIA *multi-track. I just had to keep practising it until, miraculously, I did appear to be able to play it."*

When Crimson returned in 2014, the re-appearance of LTIAI *in a live set for the first time in 40 years made for one of the most thrilling moments in a setlist already brimming with surprises. In every venue, whenever Gavin Harrison's opening percussion led into the dazzling glockenspiel/thumb piano cycles, there was always a gasp and cheer as audiences realised what was unfolding.*

I

With hindsight it's easy to mark 1972 out as a momentous year for Fripp, which saw him not only stepping out of the wreckage of yet another broken incarnation of the band he'd co-founded in 1969 but it also saw his work as a producer and collaborator blossom. They say that, if you want something done, ask a busy person and in 1972 Fripp was a very busy man indeed. In January, after the Crimson rehearsals in Ferndown fell apart, he adjourned to Command Studios to produce an album by guitarist Ollie Halsall. It was the first of a number of production jobs that Fripp would undertake that year arising, in part, from a connection with Ronnie Scott Productions created by his work on Centipede's *Septober Energy* in 1971. Halsall cut his teeth with Timebox, a popular act on the live circuit with their dance-orientated mix of R&B numbers and a minor hit with a cover of The Four Seasons' *Beggin* in 1968. A talented multi-instrumentalist, Halsall had originally played vibraphone in the band but took over as guitarist after a shift in personnel. When Timebox, in search of a heavier rock direction, morphed into Patto, Halsall's innovative legato technique came to the fore winning him many admirers – including Ten Years After's Alvin Lee and Fripp, who had been known to refer to Halsall as "The Guv'nor". His hammer on/pull off mode of playing had been previously explored by guitarists like Lee but in Patto Halsall really began to throttle up. Perhaps the nearest exponent of this style was Allan Holdsworth, whose nascent flashes of brilliance were first heard in 'Igginbottom's Wrench and their eponymous 1969 Deram album. Interestingly, the pair would briefly work together in Jon Hiseman's post-Colosseum band Tempest before Holdsworth's departure for Soft Machine.

For the Command sessions, Halsall was joined by Patto drummer John Halsey, Max Von Schmacks on violin, bassist Harry Miller, who had appeared on Crimson's *Islands*, and sax player Gary Windo, a member of Centipede. Plus guitar from Fripp. "It's music to laugh at," Halsall told *Melody Maker* in 1972. "It made me laugh, anyway; I went in there to have a loon." In the interview, Halsall revealed the track titles: *The Russian Medical Fan Dance*, *Peter Abraham*, *And He Summoned Up On The Tidal Wave* and an instrumental prosaically called *Number 3*. A fan of jazz pianist Cecil Taylor, Halsall mainly confined his contributions in the sessions to piano. By the time Halsall spoke to the *New Haven Rock Press* in 1973, the album, provisionally titled *Ollie And The Blue Traffs*, remained unreleased. Halsall explained: "I don't know what Fripp is going to do with that. He had a bunch of albums, but he's been more involved in other things now."

Several decades later, Fripp recalled the sessions as being "fairly chaotic, mainly I suspect because of drug use. Instead of arriving at the studios with rehearsed material, the players just turned up without any preparations that I could detect. Jamie Muir related this story to me; he had been told of a quote from Producer Fripp in the Command studio, dealing with the mess: 'I can handle anything, but not musicians who don't rehearse!' The examples of various collapsing things that Fripp could handle is not included in this quote!" By the time of Halsall's drug-related death in 1992, the tapes for the album had still not surfaced and have long passed into legend among Halsall fans. Fripp doesn't believe a copy of the session tapes exists in DGM's archives, although it's possible that audio engineer Alex Mundy may unearth them as he continues to document the many hours of unmarked audio the archive contains.

Fripp was still in Command Studios the same month to produce Keith Tippett's *Blueprint*. Although credited to Tippett alone, it was in fact the first album by Ovary Lodge, a trio formed with bassist Roy Babbington and percussionist Frank Perry towards the end of 1971. If RCA expected Tippett to come up with another large-scale piece like *Septober Energy*, they would have been profoundly disappointed. Keen to get away from the "three-ring-circus" hype stoked up by the label, Tippett went in quite another direction, into a more circumspect inner space that explored silence as much as the sounding of any notes. "Soundscapes was more the concept we were aiming for," says Babbington. "Very often we would stand at our instruments at the beginning and nobody would make a sound until we heard a sound somewhere. It could be in the hall, it could be traffic going past; any extraneous sound would start the process. We used to manage to time it within a few seconds of 60 minutes. Quite amazing really."

Babbington knew of Fripp's work with King Crimson prior to being at Wessex for Centipede and was also a friend of Michael Giles. "He lived near Clapham Common and we used to bump into each other sometimes on sessions or meet up for a cup of tea or something." Augmented in the studio by Julie Tippetts on voice, guitar, bamboo flute and earrings – you can hear them intentionally jangling in an especially tranquil interlude – and percussionist Keith Bailey, who had previously jammed with Fripp at the Fulham Palace Road Café basement, the collective improvisations possess a quiet intensity.

Despite the difficulties of parking around Command, which was on busy Piccadilly Circus, the atmosphere was very relaxed, Babbington says. "Fripp had candles all 'round the control room. Something to do with his karma as I recall (*laughs*) although we didn't really talk. You can't really prepare for this kind of music. You *are* prepared. There's no preamble. We find out where it goes once we've laid something down then we look for contrasts. As far as I can remember that's the way we used to work, sweeping things up and down the piano strings and working my rosin box on the strings. I used to venture into the realms of arco bass in those days and I remember working my rosin box on the strings and we got some quite remarkable sounds out of the piano. Robert Fripp's job was to capture it and produce it, which he did."

Released later in 1972, *Blueprint* may have been an artistic success but it was a commercial failure – hardly surprisingly given the nature of the content. The same fate awaited 1973's *Ovary Lodge*, also produced by Fripp, which marked the end of Tippett's association with major labels. *Blueprint* may appear to be a minor footnote in the Crimson story, but that would overlook the impact which Frank Perry and his expansive percussion rig had upon Fripp as he put together ideas for his new line-up. Filled with an array of drums, bells and devices, Perry's "kit" would have been known to Jamie Muir, another operator in the same field. While Muir's set-up lacked the same impact from a visual point of view, it seems likely that the notion of augmenting a rock act with something like Perry's set-up resonated with Fripp.

Fripp was back in Command just a few days before embarking on Crimson's final American tour in early February 1972. As with the Ollie Halsall album, this was again at the behest of Ronnie Scott Productions for their prospective progressive jazz label. In the studio were bassist Harry Miller, trombonist Nick Evans, cornet player Mark Charig and pianist Keith Tippett, along with Blue Notes bassist Johnny Dyani, drummer Keith Bailey, who had done some blowing with Fripp before Ian Wallace's recruitment, and trombonist Paul Nieman. "Three full days in a studio was a rare luxury that provided the opportunity to book a pool of musicians and record various combinations," recalled Nick Evans in 2008. This double quartet, as Fripp might have dubbed them in later years, worked both as a large ensemble and in smaller combinations with Miller and Dyani as the only constants. Evans continues: "Many hours of totally improvised music had been recorded from which we had to select enough for the double album."

However, as Fripp recalls, Ronnie Scott's company declined to release the results. "Ronnie's expected jazz/written and improvised albums, not free blowing. Keith could do it because he was disciplined. The other boys were great players but, for whatever reasons, passion, promptings of the Muse, no leadership abilities/proclivities, drugs, didn't pull focus. Simply, the results were too much of a mess to organise into an album or albums." Once again the tapes were thought lost. However, 36 years later, Nick Evans stumbled upon a rough stereo mix of what would have been sides 2 and 4 of *Guilty But Insane*. Although sides 1 and 3 remain missing, a partial account – retitled *Curiosities 1972* and credited to the Command All Stars – was released in 2008 by Reel Recordings.

Taken on their own merits, the surviving five pieces contain fine free-form experimentation. *Roots And Wings* thrashes with the collective brilliance expected of players of this calibre. Elton Dean on sopranino sax sounds uncannily like some of Evan Parker's shriller excursions as Charig's muted cornet buzzes and darts around Miller's flailing bass work. It's Tippett, Miller and Dyani who drive the piece towards an abrupt climax and it's that trio who combine on *African Sunrise*. Here, Tippett plays electric piano moving from FX-pedal abstractions into Zawinulesque pools of light. The bassists work between Tippett's clusters to provide a heady rush of racing ideas and rhythmic exchanges. Inevitably, there are points where these spontaneous collective improvisations fail to connect but there are more hits than misses. Particularly impressive throughout is Bailey's drumming, often catapulting the mood into different directions and generally egging his colleagues on into fiery invention. "The fact that so much music was made without the assistance of any pre-arranged material only goes to show the immense creative talents of all involved. I am honoured to have worked with such people," said Evans in his sleevenotes.

In June 1972, Fripp finished an album with Wiccan journalist Walli Elmlark. Very little is known about Elmlark – known as the White Witch of New York – who taught at the New York School of Occult Arts and Sciences and wrote for *Circus* magazine. She was also the co-author of the book *Rock Raps Of The 70s* with occultist Timothy Green Beckley. Published in 1972, it featured collages, poems, writings and interviews. Copies are hard to come by and very expensive. In a piece about Elmlark, website Dangerous Minds featured these words from Beckley: "Walli was known widely as the White Witch of New York. Because of her contacts in the music industry, she had established quite an eclectic clientele for whom she would offer spiritual guidance, and occasional good luck or love spells, but always of a positive nature. She didn't dabble in black magick or even gris gris (a New Orleans form of 'gray magick' that incorporates poppets and the use of talismans kept in a personal mojo bag). Walli was lively, imaginative, energetic, well spoken, and quite attractive in her flowing white garments complete with fashionable silver moon adornments. Oh, did I forget to mention long black hair, complete with dyed green streak highlights? Indeed, Walli made a very bold fashion and occult statement wherever she went."

Photographs of Fripp from the period often show him weighed down by crosses, charms and amulets and his interest in occult matters attracted considerable press attention. In a full-page article in *NME*, Fripp details the history of psychic powers existing in various members of the Fripp family and his growing use of lighting coloured candles as part of his practice of low magic. "I can tell you the significance of the colours … blue is protection. White is inspiration … pink is pure love. Orange is love and lust. Red is the lusty one … Possibly your readers will be reading this and think it's all of load of garbage – spells don't possibly work. But I can tell you, they do. I've had a couple done for me and I can tell you they work."

The album with Elmlark was called *The Cosmic Children*. Side one consisted of Fripp and Elmlark in conversation, Elmlark outlining her experiences and commitment to Wicca. On side two, she talks to DJ Jeff Dexter about cosmic children – spirits from other places who take physical forms such as Hendrix, Bolan, Bowie and Mike Gibbons, drummer with Badfinger. Talking to *NME*'s Simon Stable, Fripp said: "The function of the album is to reach out to the children like the drummer from Badfinger, I want to say: 'You're not nutty, you're not a freak because you can't relate to what's around you.'" Tales of Elmlark's magical presence extended to other members of the rock fraternity, including David Bowie, for whom, according to Angie Bowie, she performed an exorcism during Bowie's Thin White Duke period around 1975 or 1976. Rumours swirl around Elmlark who may or may not have been a Playmate at the New York Playboy Club in the early '60s or an uncredited extra in the 1960 Elizabeth Taylor film *Butterfield 8*. Her death is also the subject of speculation which variously places it as being drug-related in the late '70s or the '90s. To date, not only does *The Cosmic Children* remain unreleased but, in his extensive rummaging through the boxes of tapes at DGM, Alex Mundy has yet to turn up anything remotely resembling the album.

In August, after finishing work on *Earthbound*, Fripp returned to the producer's chair for the last time that year to work with Matching Mole at CBS' London studios in Whitfield Street. Having been invited by drummer Robert Wyatt to produce what would be Matching Mole's final album, it was evident to Fripp that there were tensions within the group. Wyatt's increasing dependency on alcohol, and his growing unwillingness to accept the role of band leader, would result in the group splitting up by the time *Matching Mole's Little Red Record* was released in October. Bassist Bill MacCormick recalls that initially things went smoothly. As was Fripp's habit, the tracking sessions were dispatched quite quickly. But when it came to overdubbing solos, things began to falter with guitarist Phil Miller. "Unfortunately it was on something I'd written and we'd played it and rehearsed it and there'd never been a problem," recalls MacCormick. "On the live take, Phil fluffed a few notes so basically he got left to try and put his guitar parts on as an overdub. There were two studios at Whitfield Street. The one we used the most was an intimate one, nice size. Then across the corridor was the orchestral studio, which was huge. The abiding image I have of this was poor old Phil, who of course was rather in awe of Fripp, which I suppose most guitarists in those days would've been, on his own in the middle of this enormous studio while we all stared at him from the control room as he tried to play his part. Of course it just got to him. That's why the track *Flora Fidgit* has no guitar part on it because eventually it got to the point where we just couldn't put him through it anymore. As I recall it, I think we just decided things were getting too unhappy for words and it was about the one point in the process where it really didn't work having Fripp in the studio because, whether he meant to or not, he intimidated Phil. It didn't make any difference to me because I never liked King Crimson anyway, but if you were a guitar player of any ilk you knew Fripp was probably capable of doing things with a guitar that nobody else in the country could do."

Brian Eno, then still in Roxy Music, was invited by MacCormick to add VCS3 synthesiser. "We'd played a gig with Roxy at Liverpool where they'd supported us so I had met Brian Eno and we got on, and so I thought it might be interesting to see what Brian might come up with. I told him what we were looking for, he came into Studio 2, did a few things which Fripp loved and it seemed to work." Not everyone in the band was pleased, with keyboard player Dave MacRae slightly put out that he hadn't been asked to play the part. Hailing from New Zealand, MacRae was Wyatt's first choice to replace original keyboard player Dave Sinclair after Wyatt saw him playing with the Buddy Rich Band and with Ian Carr's Nucleus. The album wasn't the first time MacRae's and Fripp's paths had crossed. The pianist had done a stint backing singer Annie Ross and can be heard providing distinctive Fender Rhodes on a surprising cover of KC's *Cat Food* on Ross's 1971 album *You And Me Baby*. What impression did Fripp make upon MacRae? "There wasn't a huge amount of contact between us but I think there was a mutual respect. I was beginning to form the opinion that all the musicians I was coming into contact within the UK were all total eccentrics (*laughs*) and Fripp was no exception," says MacRae. "By that I mean about where they were coming from. Their musical direction was very different to my own. I heard some of Robert Fripp's music after the event, as it were, and he was certainly an adventurous man."

Importantly, the album spawned a significant new friendship between Fripp and Eno. Although they had previously met at the EG offices, the album put them together in a working context for the first time. Just ten days after Eno completed his overdubs on *Gloria Gloom*, Fripp entered the living room of Eno's Maida Vale flat and plugged his Les Paul into Eno's Revox tape machine to record layers of inspired rhapsodic guitar that would later become the first side of Fripp and Eno's groundbreaking *No Pussyfooting*.

II

Even before Fripp returned to London after the *Earthbound* tour, there was speculation about what he would do next. "Fripp & Hiseman May Form Band" ran a headline in *New Musical Express*. That possible partnership went no further than an exploratory discussion as Fripp busied himself with production work and sounding out other potential collaborators.

In July 1972, the music press heralded a new chapter in the Crimson saga. Wearied by the frequency of such pronouncements, some journalists were growing cynical. But the surprise inclusion of two names from established bands wrong-footed industry observers. *Melody Maker*'s front page carried the sly headline "YES MAN TO JOIN CRIMSON".

Given Yes's success, drummer Bill Bruford's involvement was a shock. Yet there were clues the previous April in an interview with *Sounds*' Steve Peacock in which the drummer warms to being more of a roving musician. Of course, Bruford was diplomatic with Peacock, but the seeds of his departure were sown a month or so earlier when Yes shared the bill with Crimson at the Orpheum Theatre in Boston. It was at this show that Bruford made it crystal clear to an interested Fripp that he wanted to join King Crimson.

The son of a veterinary surgeon, Bruford was born in Sevenoaks in Kent on 17 May 1949. Educated at the private Tonbridge School, he was a bright and confident pupil who discovered his aptitude for music when he started playing drums at 13. While many of his friends were into the pop and emergent rock music of the day, Bruford was heavily into jazz – a passion garnered from numerous records and watching concerts broadcast on the legendary BBC TV series *Jazz 625,* on which he first saw the likes of Bill Evans, Max Roach, Thelonious Monk and other stellar performers.

In 1968, Bruford went to Leeds University to study sociology and economics but his studies were cut short to turn professional – not as a jazz player but as a rock musician, first and briefly, with the Savoy Brown Blues Band before he joined Yes, including remnants from Mabel Greer's Toyshop, The Syn and ex-Warriors singer Jon Anderson.

The band secured the prestigious support slot at Cream's farewell concerts at London's Royal Albert Hall in November 1968. In the audience was Michael Giles, who thought the best music of the night belonged to Yes. A combination of strategic changes in line-up and hard touring paid off and, after recording two undistinguished albums, Yes began to achieve commercial success with *The Yes Album* and *Fragile*, both released in 1971.

A long-standing fan of Crimson since seeing them in 1969, Bruford attests to the significant influence they exerted over Yes. Fripp recalls Yes bassist Chris Squire and

Bruford calling at his flat in Westbourne Park Road in March 1970, where they were treated to a preview of the just-recorded *Cat Food* and *Groon.* Fripp had the impression that the job of guitarist with Yes was on offer. "At that time, I had a very strong sense of the musical direction waiting for me; that were I to join Yes I would move the band in that direction; and that setting Yes' musical direction was not the job on offer. So we remained friends but I didn't take any action to move the relationship closer."

Bruford confirms that Yes regarded Crimson as a kind of benchmark, using *In The Wake Of Poseidon* as a yardstick to measure their progress during the recording *of The Yes Album*. In May 1972, a little over two months after their conversation in Boston, Fripp invited himself around to Bruford's flat for a meal and a chat. The drummer remembers that Fripp regarded him almost like a tomato that had ripened on the vine with Yes and was now ready to be plucked. "We went into my music room and he said: 'If I played this, what would you play?' Apparently I must have done the right thing because eventually he suggested that we do some more!"

Yes were riding on the crest of a wave with an album in the top ten on both sides of the Atlantic. Bruford had qualms about leaving but argues that Yes's success was a peripheral consideration with his overriding priority being learning and extending his craft.

He subscribed to the ethos of the jazz world, where musicians moved from group to group, ensuring a significant cross-pollination of skills, ideas and experience. "I really wanted to be a good drummer and I didn't care about the subtext of the day, which was hippy-trippy psychedelia, lysergic acid, bell-bottom trousers and so on. I didn't care about any of that. All I wanted to do was get better at the drums and the way you did that was by hearing yourself in a different context and Crimson was that different context. I'd done four years with Yes but it seemed like forever. It was a lifetime!"

Stunned at the news of his departure, Yes wished him well, though he recalls Squire harboured suspicions that Bruford was simply a pawn in some nefarious Fripp plot entailing Wicca and other dubious practices.

Yes's management was much more hard-nosed and Bruford had to sign a get-out deal that saw substantial portions of his future royalties going to the incoming Alan White. Looking back, Bruford puts this down to experience, citing that his desire was simply to get moving on to the next stage of his musical education. *Melody Maker*'s non-plussed Raver gossip column sourly noted: "All that hard work down the drain and for what? Gigs with King Crimson don't exactly last, at least on present form."

III

Bucharest, Romania: It's August 1968 and British popsters Helen Shapiro and Tony Bolton are in town with their UK backing group. With the Soviet Union glowering disapprovingly on its satellite states opening up to the West, the singing stars are unlikely cultural ambassadors to Eastern Europe. Pathé News has a newsreel showing the principals posing for press photos and walking in the park with all the usual grinning and gurning required of obliging pop stars. Then the action cuts to a performance in a concert hall. The brief footage reveals John Wetton, still a teenager, comping away behind Helen Shapiro's blue-eyed soul singing and adding high-end harmonies to Tony Bolton's full-throated cabaret rendition of Tom Jones' *Delilah*. Wetton remembered performing in a football stadium filled with pop music-starved young people on the tour. Before Shapiro came onstage, the band covered The Beatles' *Lady Madonna,* only just released in the West. "About 60,000 people in Bucharest just went mental. Absolutely fucking mental. I realised at that moment what you could do with music, about the power of music. It was just incredible. It taught me a huge lesson."

It's amazing to think that only a couple of months earlier Wetton had been kicking his heels. Desperate for a career in music, something actively discouraged by his parents, he'd been expelled from school while studying for his A-Levels and began attending Bournemouth Technical College – where he continued to neglect his studies in favour of playing bass in local bands. "The day that term ended in June 1968, I came back from college and I walked through my parents' front door as the phone rang. It was a guy asking me if I wanted to go to Romania for six weeks to play with Helen Shapiro. I bit his arm off!"

Wetton's tour with Shapiro earned him enough to buy his beloved Fender bass and, though his parents were unhappy at his choice of career, there was now no holding him back. George Martin took the young bassist under his wing around 1970, with Wetton regularly working at Martin's AIR Studios on TV commercials, backing sessions and anything else The Beatles' producer threw his way. "George Martin was very good to me. It was a bit like having the Duke of Edinburgh for an uncle," Wetton laughed.

How did a young lad from Bournemouth get on so quickly? Obviously he was a good player but that he got on in the fiercely competitive London music scene also came down to the fact that people liked him, his broad smile and his sharp humour. People enjoyed his company, something Wetton innately understood. With a combination of warmth, confidence and an eye for a good schmooze and hustle, there was no way he wasn't going to be a success.

John Wetton made the pilgrimage to London at the tail end of the late '60s. Making a fleeting connection with Fripp at Bournemouth Technical College, Wetton and schoolfriend Richard Palmer-James realised, like so many before them, that the best way to make a living as a professional musician was to move to the capital.

Wetton was born 12 June 1949, in Derby. His love of music came from a number of directions. Influenced by his older brother playing organ in church and a love of classical music that only intensified the older he got, he received the usual American rock'n'roll epiphanies. Moving to Bournemouth, Wetton became involved in the local music scene, meeting up with Richard Palmer-James along the way, playing in R'n'B outfits such as Palmer-James and Jack Knife.

Palmer-James, a couple of years older than Wetton, recalls something special about him. "As soon as he turned up at Bournemouth School for Boys he immediately became known as a musical phenomenon. I can't remember exactly why but there was a buzz about him being very musical. He was unbelievably dextrous. We'd never seen a bass player like that. Then it turned out he could play piano and guitar, sing harmonies and he was only 13 or 14. He was the youngest in the band."

In 1969, the pair went their separate ways with Palmer-James – who would later write lyrics for Crimson in Wetton's era – joining Supertramp and Wetton teaming up with ex-Coliseum guitarist James Litherland to form Mogul Thrash. In the summer of 1970, the band recorded an album produced by Brian Auger and engineered by Eddie Offord, but their blend of lengthy prog-ish stylings and brass-heavy riffing was met with public indifference, despite a surprise hit single in Belgium, and the band imploded.

1971 was a crucial year for Wetton, as he extricated himself from the contractual mire of Mogul Thrash and joined Family. Wetton had to take up the violin to be able to duplicate the parts bequeathed to him by departing bassist/violinist John Weider. But it was Wetton's confident bass work, rippling with bite and muscle, which got him noticed.

A busy Wetton also crossed paths with Bournemouth and Crim escapee Gordon Haskell, finding time to provide bass, keyboards and backing vocals on Haskell's second solo album *It Is And It Isn't.* That summer, Wetton renewed his acquaintance with Fripp, dropping in at his recently acquired cottage in Dorset. Though they made no plans to work together, Wetton regards the encounter as a pivotal stepping stone towards joining Crimson.

A little later, Fripp in fact offered his old Bournemouth College friend a job in the band. The bassist declined. "Two or three days after we had decided on Boz, John called me and offered himself for the gig," recalls Fripp. In the Press, Wetton has said that he declined the offer on the grounds that he felt that Fripp was looking for allies to even things up in the guitarist's favour. Wetton judged that joining the band on this basis would not have been a good way to proceed.

Fripp's account differs. "At the time John was first offered the gig, it was before

Boz had picked up the bass, so there were no sides to balance. And Boz wasn't playing bass then anyway. When John called, just after we'd made the decision, it was a surprise and in a way a disappointment to have to say no. But we had moved ahead and it was with Boz."

Whatever the sequence of events, Wetton was intrigued and didn't have long to wait before Fripp was back in touch. While he worked on Family's *Bandstand* album, Wetton was invited to meet Fripp and Bruford, ending up in a conversation about what each musician was looking for. For Fripp, it was travelling across the other side of the musical divide begun with the break-up of the '69 line-up. For Bruford, there was the notion of using the band to extend his creative vocabulary. For Wetton, Crimson represented an unparalleled opportunity to explore his prodigious instrumental capacity. Moreover, there would finally be an opportunity to develop himself as a singer and composer. In Family, there would be little or no chance of realising these ambitions.

By the time the meeting ended, it was agreed that the new band would abandon all previous Crimson repertoire and that the three core members would start working together as soon as their commitments would allow.

Telling their respective groups required some co-ordination, Wetton recalls. "Family was very aptly named because there was a tremendous camaraderie in the band and I felt terrible leaving it, but I knew it was the right thing to do. So we had to keep it under wraps until it was the right time. And we'd kind of arranged that we'd tell each of our bands on the same day so that there wasn't any chance of a phone call going astray and anyone getting the wrong end of the stick."

"London was like a village then and everyone knew everyone else, and if something happened in a recording studio, like in Olympic where I was recording, it would very quickly get to Advision, where Bill was recording. So we had to do things at the same time."

Wetton recalls feeling a tremendous jumble of freedom, fear, excitement and expectation as he walked back into the recording studio later that day to lay down a signature bass part for the surprise Family hit *Burlesque*.

The addition of these two well-respected players from established wings of the music scene provided a riposte of sorts to critics who had begun to wonder whether Crimson was a spent force. The first the public knew about the new line-up was when it was splashed over the front page of *Melody Maker* in mid-July.

Wetton and Bruford were recognised players but, to the vast majority of the public, the other two new members were completely unknown quantities. Jamie Muir's contribution to Crimson's re-emergence was critical on at least two fronts.

Given that the band was now playing without a Sinfield-based light show, his overtly theatrical and unrestrained stage persona provided a focus for concertgoers. Second, and more significantly, Muir opened up the Crimson landscape to a more exotic and seditious musicality. The well-regarded and confident Bruford says his exposure to Muir's influence was nothing short of revelatory.

Muir's career really began after his expulsion from Edinburgh Art School in 1966. "I'd been playing in local jazz bands where I started off playing trombone. I remember one night somebody called a tune and I didn't know what it was and I had to ask the bass player or somebody how many accidentals or something with five sharps. I remember that night I thought 'Sod this, this is just far too much studying', and I put my trombone away and just started playing drums. I used to turn away from the audience and try and work out a scale with five sharps in it and then be expected to take a solo and I thought 'this is ludicrous'. I would have had to do too much studying."

The arrival of the ESP label albums, featuring players such as Pharaoh Saunders, inspired Muir and his colleagues to make a cautious stab into the world of free jazz and, by the mid-'60s, he was part of an Edinburgh-based multi-media group called The Assassination Weapon in which he not only played percussion but also looked after the swirling, psychedelic light show.

Two years later Muir was in London playing with the exploratory Music Improvisation Company alongside John Stevens, Evan Parker, Derek Bailey, Gavin Bryars, Hugh Davies and John Tilbury – all well-respected figures of the avant-garde. By then his kit consisted of an abundance of found and unusual objects. Muir continued to listen to developments in rock and was impressed by Crimson's early albums. He'd already managed a stint in Pete Brown's Battered Ornaments and, while doing a day job in Bentall's department store in Richmond, he helped form Boris, a short-lived experimental group. Richard Williams recalls the impact they had on him. "I'd seen Boris at The Marquee with Don Weller on sax. I remember Jamie bursting a blood capsule playing around with a length of chain he was rattling and crashing about. I thought he was interesting. I thought they were a good band, a bit weird. It was just wild. You couldn't bottle it. You couldn't have got it on a record in any kind of sensible way." Although the band were championed by Williams in *Melody Maker*, there was little in the way of work and the band fell apart. It was Williams who urged Fripp to check out Muir, passing on his telephone number. "Jamie was such an interesting man," says Williams. "He was a funny combination of intensity and craziness. There was a looning side to him obviously. That Dadaist thing was interesting. He was obviously very serious but serious in a way that most musicians wouldn't have understood, which is why Robert, even with his meticulous viewpoint, did respond to him. There was one funny incident when Robert was putting the band together with Ian Wallace and Mel Collins and Boz. Robert said to me, 'Why don't you come down early, just you and me. There'll be a drumkit there and we can have a play.' He knew I'd been a drummer although I hadn't played for five or six years. It was an amusing idea, so just the two of us sat down and had a blow, just playing free. Later on, when he hired Jamie it occurred to me I wonder if he just wanted to see how it would feel playing with somebody who wasn't a rock drummer, just playing a sort of free jazz kind of thing. Anyway that was the last time I played anywhere. If Robert could get Keith Tippett on to *Top of the Pops*, why couldn't he get Jamie Muir?"

Ironically, by the time Muir got the call from Fripp, his stamina for hardcore improvisation was at a low. He was playing drums in the more conventional jazz-rock setting of Sunship with ex-Soft's sax player Lyn Dobson, future Gilgamesh/National Health keyboards player Alan Gowen, with whom Muir had also played in the Afro-rock combo Assegai in 1971, and guitarist Allan Holdsworth.

Muir remembers their first meeting. "Fripp came 'round and we played for a couple of hours, upstairs in my little rehearsal room with mattresses plugged up against the windows. All I remember was playing some really fast and furious blowouts, which from a drummer's perspective was the Tony Williams/Billy Cobham type of thing. It was fairly energetic stuff and I think we enjoyed ourselves. My feeling about getting the call was: 'Terrific.' King Crimson was the ideal for me because it was a rock band that had more than three brain cells. I was very much more an instrumental style of musician rather than being song-based and there weren't many other bands that I would have been any good in. I was extremely pleased and I felt completely at home with Crimson."

Around this time, Fripp received an invitation to hear a group called Waves, who had been in touch with EG Management and were rehearsing in the café basement recently vacated by Crimson. The band featured David Cross, a violinist from Plymouth who studied music at a teacher training college in Exeter, taking flute as a second instrument. In 1969, he was part of a folk-rock trio called The Ring, followed by a string of commercially unsuccessful semi-pro outfits, even backing the likes of '60s crooner P.J. Proby. Listening to the work of Jean-Luc Ponty, Papa John Creach and Jerry Goodman, the young player supported his musical ventures with cleaning jobs and working in a travel agency.

Highly impressed with the 23-year-old Cross, Fripp invited him to a rehearsal in Covent Garden. Cross, who had to make the choice between attending that first rehearsal or his grandfather's funeral, made the decision to play with difficulty. But his participation was extremely fertile, resulting in one poignant melody line that developed into a Crimson classic.

Muir remembers some early discussion about getting a stand-alone vocalist, an option vehemently opposed by Wetton, whose display of assertive self-confidence greatly impressed him. Fripp's recollection is different. "My memory is of asking John if he'd be prepared to be the singer, as well as bass player. This was obviously a challenge, but one he accepted enthusiastically. It's also possible that we discussed a 'singer' singer, but the level of reflection on the subject wasn't overly considerable, and not a lot of serious consideration went into it."

With Fripp's commitment to the Matching Mole sessions ending on 31 August, the guitarist only had the weekend to prepare for the Crimson rehearsals which started on 4 September in Richmond. To Bruford, the rehearsals lacked any of the compositional direction he knew from Yes, setting a pattern that would recur throughout his subsequent years in Crimson. "Richmond was the first of some dozen rehearsal rooms around the world that I've spent excruciating weeks with Robert where, on the whole, nobody appeared to know how to find the music, which continued up to my last day rehearsing with Robert in Nashville, Tennessee, in 1997. There were a lot of people sitting staring at their feet trying hard to find something that somebody else would like. On the whole, a wretched and expensive way to make music and, because I'd always found music easy to make, I've always found rehearsals incredibly slow and irritating. And no doubt I've irritated others because of that."

Some of that irritation may well have resulted from the steep learning curve all the musicians were facing, Bruford in particular having to cope with Jamie Muir's anarchic approach. Bruford was at the time something of a precocious, hot-headed musician and having to work with Muir was like taking a cold shower. Finding Muir's approach far outside his experience, Bruford quickly realised that he was now operating in a new world of serious music-making.

For Muir, this meant widening Bruford's musical horizons, partly by exposing him to records by Nigerian drummers and sessions in Muir's maisonette, with the pair crawling around on hands and knees, "playing" household appliances and domestic furniture. Talking to Richard Williams, Bruford outlined the modus operandi that the two adopted. "We define the various areas in which we play – for instance, a lot of the time he's playing non-kit instruments. I can be playing in half tempo, while he's playing twice that. There's lots of different ways we can employ it; we can even phrase together which gets very heavy. Basically, Jamie skims along the top of the music most of the time, while John and I anchor it down." Despite the confident tone, however, this transformation was not achieved without some personal pain and soul-searching, reducing Bruford to tears on one occasion.

As the weeks progressed, a bracing mixture of new and recycled material emerged. Although the band had a sense of where the music might go, this did not extend to the lyrics.

With his usual blend of the idealistic and practical, Fripp was certain that no new lyricist would enjoy the same position of close collaboration Peter Sinfield had occupied. Muir was of the view that, as intelligent creative people, they should be able to come up with the words themselves. After all, he argued, if they farmed out one of the most potent forms of communication to someone outside, why not get somebody else to write the drum parts and so on? Given this, Fripp not unreasonably asked if the percussionist had any lyrics that might be suitable. "Of course, I didn't," recalls a slightly chastened Muir. "Actually I tried, but it was absolute rubbish. It was some awful Gothic thing and I was intensely embarrassed about it and it was quite rightly politely declined."

But Muir did coin a phrase with a significance belying the off-the-wall nature of its creation. When asked to describe the music they were making, Muir came up with "Larks' tongues in aspic". Fripp not only appropriated this as the title for two compositions but recognised it instantly as the title of the album, as it graphically represented for him the descent of spirit into form, encapsulating the notion of something very precious and delicate held within matter.

IV

As the singer, responsibility for finding lyrics fell to Wetton. Setting up a tape recorder in Bruford's house, Wetton recorded a set of sketchy demos at the piano and sent them to his old friend Palmer-James, now living in Germany after leaving Supertramp in 1971. Unlike Sinfield, who had been actively involved in rehearsals and musical collaboration, Palmer-James had no direct contact with the band. "They sent a demo tape to me in Germany, accompanied by a note from John describing the structure of the songs and hinting at their final instrumentation ('swirling Mellotrons'); I sent the words back to London; and that was it."

Though their final forms were still to be determined, all the pieces for *Larks' Tongues In Aspic* were now identified and catalogued. *Larks' Tongues In Aspic, Part One*, though somewhat fragmentary, had the benefit of providing a highly visible showcase for the new group's dexterity and intentions. Fripp had been experimenting with the fast, flat-picking arpeggio parts as far back as August 1971 but it had never sounded better than combined with this band's new rugged funky punch.

It was still missing the "Chinese duet" or "water section", as it became known, between Cross and Muir on autoharp, as well as its shattering finale. Instead it petered out just after the initial solo violin figure, moving without a break into a ballad called *Daily Games* which contained an arrangement for flute played by David Cross. However, when the song was later re-christened *Book Of Saturday*, the solo was replaced by the haunting violin solo. The yearning melody conjured out of the air by Cross at that first session Covent Garden rehearsal became *Exiles* when fused with a new middle-eight and Fripp's *Mantra* theme, first performed by the '69 line-up.

At an earlier rehearsal, Fripp had presented the main themes of *Larks' Tongues In Aspic, Part Two* but they hadn't been picked up by the band. Somewhere around the middle of the Richmond rehearsals, he tried again. Though the first few sweeps were ungainly and cumbersome, titanic sparks began to fly as the complex metres unfolded and ground against each other like vast continental plates. With more than a passing nod to Stravinsky's *The Rite Of Spring*, the ferociously biting 5/4 stab of the introduction combined the intellectual rigour of 20th-century composers with the primal thrust of rock. The group immediately recognised that this was a profoundly convincing piece, though daunting in its scale and energy. Fripp had often wondered what Hendrix might sound like playing Bartok – well, this was as good an answer as he might expect.

If *Schizoid Man* was emblematic of the original Crimson's musical ability and character, then *Larks' Tongues In Aspic, Part Two* amounted to a signature tune of equal stature, ambition and authenticity. And it rocked like the clappers, drawing some of the most frenetic and galvanised performances from each member of the group. The rehearsals entailed much collective writing and collaboration. Not since 1969 had music bearing the Crimson imprint emerged in such a democratic fashion. By the time the band left England in mid-October for warm-up shows at the Zoom Club in Frankfurt, the stage was set for classic Crimsonising.

At the Zoom Club, the band tried out many disparate ideas. *Easy Money*, for example, opened with a *Strawberry Fields Forever*-style introduction on the Mellotron, took in a light and breezy straight-four soft-rock jig and then found itself addressing a darkly descending guitar arpeggio which would later surface as *Fallen Angel*.

A feature of these early gigs was extended instrumentals garnered from the months of rehearsal. These were by no means all of the experimental atonal variety, as is so often assumed. A version of the introductory chords of what was to become *Doctor Diamond* acted as a chorus and climax to a Cream-like blues-based piece with Wetton singing in unison with some extraordinarily choppy bass soloing. Alongside this were a few vigorous rock-based epics with driving, slicing Mahavishnu-esque themes locating the band in pseudo-fusion territory, all underpinned by Wetton/Bruford funk work-outs. Occasionally, Cross and Wetton would perform folky violin duets, an aspect dropped after Wetton received some criticism from former colleagues in Family.

On Monday, 17 October, the band entered the Bremen Beat Club studios at 10.00 am for their first formal appearance as King Crimson. Looking tense, slightly ill at ease and understandably tired, the band performed three pieces – a lengthy improvisation, *Exiles* and *Larks' Tongues In Aspic, Part One*.

The full performance was eventually unearthed and released on the 2012 boxed set *Larks' Tongues In Aspic: The Complete Recordings*. It's fascinating to see the band in full flight with a conscious decision to break away from the old Crimson repertoire. Whereas Boz, Mel and Ian had to a certain extent been hobbled by the necessity of playing material fashioned by previous line-ups, this version of the band carried no such baggage. Although groups such as The Mahavishnu Orchestra and Can integrated improvisation into their setlists these tended to be across the chords of the piece in the case of the former and often in the form of modal jams in the case of the latter. It's hard to think of any other rock band operating at the time who took that blistering mixture of calculated risk and blind faith as far as it could go. "There were long stretches where anything could happen and frequently did," laughed Wetton. "A lot of the time, the audience couldn't really tell the difference between what was formal and what wasn't because the improvising was of a fairly high standard. It was almost telepathic at times. You'd automatically know what the other person was going to do and when they were going to do it. Extraordinary. Those kinds of things don't happen very often."

On the video, we see Muir skulking within his exotic percussion rig, an avant-garde court jester ferrying the sounds and sensibilities of free jazz to the world of the rock band. Both playful and intense, he gives no real hint of the antics which would soon attract so much attention from the music press. "I always remember I had an urge to get Robert to let his hair down because he was very controlled in the way he played" says Muir. "At the TV gig, I really tried and tried to provoke him."

It's interesting watching the complete video how much eye contact plays a part in determining the force and direction of the music. "I was an absolute nervous wreck during that TV recording," admits Cross. "I can remember thinking 'Well, I'm going to be found out now'. Looking somebody in the eye means you're furiously sending messages out and receiving them back. It can be quite terrifying for some people to do that kind of improvising, and you need a certain degree of mutually shared experience and be quite comfortable with the people in order to be able to do that. Somehow it was safer to look John Wetton in the eye than it was to ignore him and be out on your own." Returning to the UK, the band announced a huge tour that would span most of the remaining two months of 1972, taking in 27 towns and cities, with only five days off. This Crimson was certainly a radical departure and it's easy to believe Fripp's assertion that this was the music he had been striving for since the break-up of the original line-up. Shedding much of the jazzy vocabulary of the *Islands* era in favour of a more spiky, harsher metallic aspect, it turned a cold shoulder on the past. With *Earthbound*, released in June on Island's budget label HELP, being the most recent but hardly the most representative album, none of the tour audiences could have been prepared for what they saw and heard. With nearly half of the set given over to extended exploratory workouts, this new King Crimson was undoubtedly the most challenging and uncompromising line-up to date.

When the tour began on a cold Saturday night in Hull, the only familiar touchstone was *Schizoid Man*, delivered as an encore, almost to reward the audience's patience and trust. With a good 40% of the set improvised and often featuring large clumps of atonal exploration, there were few signposts for fans, forcing them to trust the musicians, wherever the music might lead. Opening with the ethereal strains of the then-unreleased track *The Heavenly Music Corporation,* recorded in Brian Eno's front room just two months previously, playing over the PA, the five-piece Crimson took the audience on a dramatic tour of some of rock music's most extreme environments. Blasted with slabs of skull-crunching riffs, raked with hybrid polyrhythms, taunted by abrasive bouts of atonality and occasionally calmed by soothing ballads, audiences were frequently stunned. This was a radical risk-taking Crimson.

Given the difficult nature of some of the music, the overwhelmingly supportive response was surprising. Of course, challenging music and Crimson were to some degree synonymous. What might have been more of a surprise for the audience were Muir's anarchic extra-musical antics. On top of the musical assault, his visual theatrics compounded the wonderment so many experienced. It wasn't just the punters who were shocked by Muir's performance art-antics of throwing chains and spitting blood while glowering at the audience. "Jamie's onstage persona never manifested itself in rehearsals," recalls Cross. "I could have died when I first saw him start his antics on stage for the first time. I thought it was wonderful but we had no idea he was going to do it – it was completely out of the blue."

A focal point of unbelievable energy and humour in his fur-trimmed boiler suit, Muir and his arsenal of "allsorts" added an eclectic and downright eccentric sheen to the rock stage. In addition to what Muir calls "some rubbishy drums", his kit consisted of a glut of gongs and cymbals, an autoharp, bicycle horns, various whistles, lamb calls, shells, nightingale calls, tuned plastic bottles, a double banded saw (and bow), balloons, a bag of leaves and a bowl of pistachio nut shells as well as assorted domestic baking trays and kitchen utensils. This, of course, presented the sound crew with an unenviable challenge. Muir balefully recalls being swamped in the mix and having to continually press the engineer to ensure that his contribution wasn't lost.

Wetton and Bruford were completely taken aback when they saw Jamie on stage. With obvious affection, Bruford recalls: "He was a remarkable guy and a performance artist as well. I didn't really understand that the percussion was only part of it. The performance art was another side to him and he would cheerfully scale the PA stacks while the band was playing, with blood pouring out of his mouth and a little caveman fur jacket on, looking like a complete wild man. This was exciting stuff and none of us knew what was going to happen particularly. Jamie was decorative on top and visually very strong, prowling about picking up things on top of my basic beat. He had things like a prepared drum kit with baking trays in the bass drum, which went very well. Whatever I did, he had something fantastic to go on the top. It was very exciting – edgy and overheated at times."

Muir's propensity to flail his rig with chains was not without hazard, as Fripp comments. "At one point I heard a whistling sound and leaned forward attentively as a heavy chain flew through the space where my head had just occupied. It had been spun around Jamie and then released with vigour." Muir recalls: "I think it was probably just my enthusiasm and pleasure that led me in that direction. I had racks of steel plates at the back and the problem with percussion is that it has a fixed dynamic range and you can't just turn the volume and so a lot of the sound is lost if you happen to be standing 100 feet away from it. So the thing with the chains and stuff was a way of trying to generate the same degree of emotional intensity on a larger scale."

EG expressed interest in a more designed look for Muir and went as far as suggesting that he have stage costumes especially made. "They were going to put me on to some woman who was going to design me something like platform boots and a glittery God-knows-what and so I said 'No thank you, I'll sort it out myself'." When Muir played, the tight fur jacket split, and the resultant vent up the back gave birth to the trademark "fur wings". Plaudits flooded in. Reviewing the band's third gig at Guilford's Civic Hall, *NME*'s Tony Tyler described the "spiritual impact" of the group as being comparable to the first Crimson, predicting that this time the potential which Crimson had always had within its reach would be grasped. Ian MacDonald (journalist brother of Matching Mole bassist Bill MacCormick) wrote in the same paper in December that Crimson produced at least half an hour of the most miraculous rock he'd ever heard. In *Melody Maker*, Richard Williams extolled the virtues of their "90-minute barrage of phenomenal creativity".

For Fripp, this Crimson came closer than any other since 1969 to delivering. Close, but still no cigar. His judgement in 2000 was that "the material was still too ambitious for these young players to have absorbed and mastered. Alternatively expressed, it was too soon for the music to have absorbed and mastered these young players. The conception exceeded the execution." As 1972 drew to a close, there was every reason for spirits to be high in the Crimson camp. A few months before it would have been a far-sighted person who would have bet on the chances of King Crimson once again becoming one of the truly innovative and ground-breaking groups of the day. In five short months, a fresh Crimson had created a brand new repertoire with the act of collective improvisation as its *raison d'*être, rather than as a by-product of the music making. Moreover, it had persuaded huge swathes of its traditional audience to break with the past and buy into the future. Dates were set for the recording of the album early in the new year and plans for America were discussed.

It was a remarkable transformation. Muir observes that Fripp then as now had a fondness for distilling concepts into a few pithy phrases. "I remember one was not so much a saying but his approach and attitude to music, which was that you had to have people with different approaches and different personalities in a band in order to make the music interesting." Muir also remembers that another favourite Fripp aphorism, heard numerous times in Richmond back in September, was: "We can change the world."

Possibilities of change were very much in the air. Interviewed during the mixing of *Larks' Tongues In Aspic*, Bruford offered his thoughts on the band's frenetic activity. "We specifically wanted to tour before making an album, having only just met. For example, I knew of Jamie Muir's position in contemporary music but I'd never met him … it was Robert's idea to have Jamie and myself play together, and representing percussion through the ages … We're all still getting to know each other. We've learnt to play together on stage, now we are learning to play in the studio." Looking towards the future, Bruford offered: "There's a Crimson way of doing things, you know. And it's a fairly intense emotional relationship in the band … It's exhilarating to be part of and could produce magical music that will change people."

The band entered Command Studios in London's Piccadilly Circus on Wednesday, 1 January 1973, faced with the task of somehow capturing the raw energy it summoned on stage during the previous two months. The band's old stamping ground of Wessex had been tried first. Fripp recalls: "We went into Wessex to record, but fairly quickly it became obvious that it wouldn't work, particularly for a double-drummer configuration: Wessex couldn't find a drum sound whatever they did. And Command was always available at short notice!" John Wetton rolled his eyes at the memory of Command Studios: "In command is one thing you definitely were not in that studio! Things were constantly blowing up, or they were losing bits. We had the engineer, God bless him, who'd never done an edit before. We were talking away over a cup of tea and he had instructions to take a certain amount of footage out of the front of *Easy Money* so we could move the first beat of the bass drum up. So we were sitting there and every now and then would ask how the edit was going. There he was with a razor blade in his hand and then after a while he told us he'd never done an edit before. We were like 'Fuck! Put that razor blade down!' (*laughs*). Every day there was something going wrong like that."

With the title of the album assured, there was some discussion about what the cover might be. Wetton suggested commissioning Barry Godber to create something as stunning and distinctive as the first Crimson cover, not realising that Godber had died. Photographer Willie Christie mocked-up a gatefold design that included a wooded landscape and an expansive wintry, bleached-out sky. In the end it was Fripp, who had now taken control of Crimson's visual language, who sourced the sun and moon design. Neatly expressing Fripp's belief in the value of opposites working together, the simple image suggests an alchemical unity which was both exotic and magical.

Communication of one sort or another seems to be the theme at the heart of the album, whether it is the dialogue between specific instruments, the autobiographical ruminations of *Exiles*, the compositional voice Fripp had been striving to develop, the talking drum itself, the metaphorical *Larks' Tongue* of the title or the disembodied etheric voices which manifest at various intervals. With the benefit of hindsight, most of the participants feel ambivalent about the album, concluding that it lacks the focus or punch of their later work. But *Larks' Tongues In Aspic* remains a vitally important album, marking the introduction of a musical leitmotif runs right through to the present day. In this sense, it stands between the stirring origins of *In The Court Of The Crimson King* and the startling departure of *Discipline* eight years later.

Steven Wilson, who would undertake new stereo and surround sound mixes in 2012, recalls the first time he heard the album. "I was in my mid-teens and I'd borrowed it from a friend. My first reaction was that it was one of the most dynamic records you could ever hear. Within the first five minutes you've been through every extreme of volume." When it came to remixing the album, Wilson was mindful of the criticism by the band that the original recording never quite captured what they were capable of in concert. "Although the music itself is extraordinary, I approached things slightly differently than say the way I've done with previous Crimson records. I was a little bit less faithful to the original recording in the sense that I knew there were some things we could do to toughen the sound up a bit, to give the album a bit more balls if you like."

Perhaps because of their general dissatisfaction with the original sound achieved at Command, none of the musicians who recorded *Larks' Tongues In Aspic* were especially comfortable about the finished results. "I look upon it as part of the journey to *Red* if you like," said Wetton. "It didn't really capture what we could do live. As I see it, there's a very natural progression from *Larks' Tongues* to *Starless And Bible Black*, which stretches out a bit sonically. By the time you get to *Red* it's all in full flight."

Echoing the meteoric trajectory charted by the 1969 incarnation, in just five short months five musicians from different backgrounds and influences distilled their collective experience to create a rock band that, largely, stood alone in the musical landscape. "I think the music that came out of Crimson was purely a result of people being prepared to listen to each other even though they didn't come necessarily from the same branch of the tree," says David Cross. Jamie Muir puts it like this: "The essence of it was that we were still five musicians carrying with them their qualities and gifts and still trying to find a way of welding it all together into one distinct personality."

With work on *LTIA* finished, the band played two nights at London's Marquee Club. After the first live performance of 1973, on 10 February, Jamie Muir unexpectedly quit. Faced with the band's gruelling tour schedule for the months ahead, Muir concluded a path to spiritual enlightenment was preferable. Leaving the group to follow his interests in Buddhism (something he'd nurtured prior to Crimson), he informed EG of his decision. Despite offering to serve a period of notice he was urged to leave immediately. It marked the end of one brief but intensely fertile period and forced the birth of another.

Muir is certain that the other members of the band do not know or understand the circumstances surrounding his departure. At the beginning of the '70s, he had acquired a copy of Paramhansa Yogananda's book *Autobiography Of A Yogi*. Published in 1946, it documented the life and spiritual journey of this influential Indian mystic. For Muir, the book provoked a profound reaction. "I feel embarrassed even talking about it but after reading about two pages of this book, the tears just started pouring down my face and they just wouldn't stop. I didn't really know what was going on. I read a bit of that book each night before I went to bed and every time I started reading it I just started crying and crying. It was extremely bizarre and it went on for months. It felt like it was a flood just going through and washing my personality, my past and everything away."

The book also had an impact on Yes's Jon Anderson after a chance meeting with Muir at Bill Bruford's wedding. Muir enthusiastically recommended *Autobiography Of A Yogi* to the vocalist. In its pages Anderson would find the structural framing for the conceptual approach for the double album *Tales From Topographic Oceans*. Anderson said: "Jamie was like a messenger … and came to me at the perfect time in my life … he changed my life."

Muir took up meditation and adopted celibacy, gave up alcohol, cigarettes and sugar, and had a dramatic out-of-body experience. By the time he joined Crimson, he was experiencing a bewildering range of psychic and spiritual experiences on a regular basis. By the end of the first Marquee gig, he knew he had to leave, certain that if he did not follow his sense of spiritual awakening he would regret it for the rest of his life.

He met EG's David Enthoven and Sam Alder, who initially suspected Muir was on his way to join another band and tried to talk him out of leaving. Perhaps prudently, Muir chose not to go into the detail of his recent experiences but explained that he'd become totally engrossed in Buddhism. His decision was accepted.

The percussionist recalls wanting to ring Fripp and the rest of the band to have a meeting to discuss the situation properly. "But EG said, 'Don't talk to anybody, just leave and we'll handle it.' I thought that this didn't sound the right way to go about it at all, because I owed everyone an explanation. But I was also fully aware that I was causing a considerable amount of disruption and that EG would have to handle it, so I just went along with it and I never got in touch with anybody."

Muir later regretted not talking to the rest of Crimson and laughs at the story put out at the time saying his absence was due to an injury sustained on stage. "That was nonsense about my having injured myself. I think I slightly sprained my ankle but then I did that nearly every night when I played. When I heard about what they'd said, I wondered why would anybody do that – what advantage could there be in not saying what actually happened? It didn't seem to make any sense to me at all but then there were a number of things which that management did which didn't make any sense except perhaps to themselves."

Now fully conversant with the reasons for Muir leaving, Fripp is confounded by the spin EG put on Muir's departure. "It astonishes me that EG would see any need to mislead the band, or keep secret the prompting of Jamie's conscience. So much for management. EG's economy with the actualite was part of the company's Standard Operating Procedure – control. Control of information was as fundamental as control of the income supply. Clearly, EG were prepared to lie where it served their perceived interests. I am unable now, as then, to find any possible threat to Crimson's position, work and reputation, in one of the members wishing to follow the prompting of their interior life."

V

While work was continuing on *Larks' Tongues In Aspic* in the early days and weeks of 1973, elsewhere in the same building Peter Sinfield was breathing life into his debut solo album. The previous year, Sinfield had become something of a fixture at Command. As Mel, Boz, Ian and Robert worked their way around America on the *Earthbound* tour in 1972, their ex-lyricist was hunkered down for three weeks of pre-production rehearsals with Roxy Music, EG's latest signing, prior to spending ten days attempting to capture on tape the ephemeral and mercurial magic of Roxy's sound and songs. "They were very clever but they had ideas which really they had some problems playing even though they weren't the most complicated ideas. I thought they were very unusual in the mixture of kitsch and burlesque, and so clever," says Sinfield. "The first time I saw Roxy performing I thought 'Jesus!' because Bryan Ferry was worse than Joe Cocker for contorting himself but you couldn't stop watching him, wondering where he was going to contort to next. The quoting of the whole of rock'n'roll at that stage, to the best of their abilities, was fun. All of those things, the combination of novelty that they brought to the pot was terrific. It was primitive really. They really could only play three and a half chords at that point, but they played them terribly cleverly. They were also very nice people."

In the years since its release, it's been frequently said, not least by some members of Roxy Music themselves, that Sinfield's production wasn't really up to the standard of its 1973 follow-up, *For Your Pleasure*, produced by Chris Thomas, or subsequent albums. Accepting that there were limitations on time, budget – and Sinfield's overall production skills, which were more intuitive than technical – the album nevertheless is a raw, documentary snapshot of a group in the process of finding itself. There are several points where Sinfield shifts between foreground and background within the songs, a quality which keeps the ear roving between details rather than sedentary or passive. "These were just Crimson tricks. You'll find this all over *Lizard* and *Islands* where I bring vocals up, take them back, move things to the side. The other thing because it was done in Command, which I happened to love as a studio although Robert was a little bit disparaging, it had the best echo chamber that I've ever used. A real echo chamber and tiled. Sometimes I'd record in the echo chamber, the woodwinds and flute in Crimson and on my own record for effect because you can't get that sound off a plate echo. It had a particular warmth. Also there were valves in this place. Some of the equipment was really old but it had almost a Nashville sound to it, very real; big red Tannoy speakers, with a very warm ambience, and rather shoddy, which went rather well with the band. Underneath the floor, because it was an ex-BBC studio, beneath the brown carpet, there was a concrete pathway and it's where they used to record the footsteps for the long-running radio soap opera *Mrs Dale's Diary*. A nice bit of English recording history. For some reason that goes well with Roxy, doesn't it?"

Recording Roxy Music and seeing what he regarded as their relative inexperience gave Sinfield the confidence to record his own album. "What's important here isn't the Roxy Music album so much but what I did afterwards," he says. "It was the single, *Virginia Plain*, which I'm very proud of. I didn't write it of course but I encouraged it from scratch. It was an exciting time and I used to facetiously say that 'if they can make an album then so can I'. I was all excited, and although tired from making the Roxy album, I was on a roll."

The bulk of *Still* was conceived and written in the rural idyll of his home in West Cranmore in Somerset. "That was the first house that Stephanie and I had. It was certainly gloomy but it had a magical quality to it. It's very near Worthy Farm and Glastonbury. It definitely had an air to it. I was surrounded by a bunch of macrobiotic, veggie, nice hippies who happened to be good players as well who all just lived down the road. Very nice people and good players. There was a spirit about the place which was enthusing. It was very nice, having been pulverised and coping with all the Roxy stuff, including having to cope with their bass player's nervous breakdown, to get down there and have a bowl of brown rice and sit around and strum was very pleasant. It was almost as though I'd arranged it. Of course I hadn't. It was all coincidental but I had arranged to get out of London and into my first house in the country. So I thought, well I'm here with all these nice people so I might as well carry on writing. I was carrying on writing the sort of stuff I left off with from Crimson."

The relaxed atmosphere in which ideas for songs were gradually shaped came from a core group of neighbours that included drummer Alan Mennie (credited as Min), guitarist Richard Brunton, bassist Steve Dolan and Phil Jump on keyboards, both previously members of Hard Meat. Out in the country it all seemed so easy, yet once the troop of players entered the studio things became harder. "There's a danger in using your friends. It starts off really well but then you say, 'that's not quite good enough', and you do it for the eighth time and they're saying 'we can't play it any better', and I'm saying, 'yes you can', but that's because my standards are so high because I'd been playing with some amazing musicians in the past. So when your friends don't get it right 12 hours later, it gets very, very difficult. You have to be very patient and in the studio patience wears out very quickly. It's a bit like getting your friends to paint a wall or something and then they do it all wrong. What are you going to say?"

By this point in October 1972, as the *Larks*' quintet embarked on working live, work on *Still* slowed and faltered as the budget kept climbing. This wasn't especially troubling for Sinfield as the bill was being picked up by ELP's Manticore label for whom Sinfield now operated as a kind of peripatetic A&R man, producer, designer and adviser. Was he nervous about stepping out from behind the mixing desk and operating in the back room to take the spotlight as a solo performer? "No, not really. In my naïve way, I was very keen to do that. One thing I noticed is that, if you make a solo album, in the press you stop being referred to as 'ex-King Crimson' and you become 'Peter Sinfield'. So that was quite good. I had a belief in myself. It was worth a go and nobody told me to stop. I was encouraged all the way by Greg Lake and all the others at Manticore to do it."

However, he needed help getting his songs into shape. So he called Mel Collins. "Mel was happy to come over and get involved. One of Mel's frustrations of course was the terrible thing that Fripp did to him, unnerving him by saying 'you're a great player but I'm not sure about your writing'. Mel was fairly determined to have a go and show off that he could have written some stuff if he'd had a chance. So there's a little axe to grind there, I suppose."

Sinfield knew how a track should sound or feel or what elements would enhance it. Small things like lifting the sound of owls hooting at midnight from a BBC effects record, or telling your players to give it a bit more "oomph" were straightforward. But when it came to bringing in session players such as oboist Robin Miller, Sinfield lacked the specific musical skills necessary to tell him what to play. That's where Collins would come in. "I'd say, 'Mel, I need some brass here' and he'd say, 'don't worry, I'll sort that out'. For *The Night People* you'd just say, 'Mel get me the best guys' and that's what you get because he's one of them. I wanted to make sure he got a credit as associate producer because I didn't want anyone to think I'd done it all myself. I mean, how could I?"

The sequencing of *Still* has a beautiful symmetry. Each side opens and closes with the strongest material. The classical stateliness of *The Song Of The Sea Goat* and its ethereal counterpart *Still* on side one are matched by the brooding *Envelopes Of Yesterday* and the clamouring cityscape of *The Night People* which open and close the second side. The four tracks represent an autobiographical journey. "I started off with heavy tracks like *Sea Goat*, *Still*, *Envelopes* and *Night People* and filled it in from there. Because we were making albums which were 20 minutes a side, it had to have a beginning, middle and end. The structure of these things has always been important to me. It's not a concept album per se, but something that went along and was a complete thing within itself."

While fans of his work with King Crimson would easily recognise a commonality of elements between *Still* and his previous group, some aspects were markedly different. Sinfield laughs ruefully when he recalls *Wholefood Boogie*. "The album had a very English lightness of touch to it. I'd become macrobiotic, I was living in the country. I've no idea how close I was to the Earth, but I'd become closer than being in the city. I should never have tried to express all that in *Wholefood Boogie* but at least I did it tongue-in-cheek. I like a bowl of miso soup as much as the next bloke but the macrobiotic people were so sincere, the song was a kind of gentle piss-take. The problem with it is that there are things I just shouldn't sing, and rock'n'roll songs are one of them!"

While accepting his limitations as a vocalist, Sinfield admits he was naïve in thinking he could carry off the songs. "One of the problems with the album is that nobody had ever taught me about keys. Nobody was really producing the album and so Greg wasn't saying 'Take that down to B flat' or even take it up! Of course, I know now but I didn't know then. I was trying to sing in keys which were really not comfortable for me. I don't know if the musicians were either too kind or too stoned to tell me, but that's why some of the vocals on the songs are awkward in places as I was learning how to deliver. With the title track I'd managed to write a song and I couldn't even sing the top end of it. How stupid is that?" laughs Sinfield. "However, in terms of making a mistake and taking advantage of it, I got Greg to do the bit on the end of each verse. It's a great moment when he comes bursting in – it's brilliant."

It's interesting to note that the evocative use of plucked zither in the spoken sections of the title track bear a strong resemblance to the percussion/violin duet, or "water section" as Jamie Muir called it, on *LTIA1*. That's not the only Crimson connection on the record. *Envelopes Of Yesterday* chronicles the break between Sinfield and Fripp, albeit poetically and obliquely, and comes with the added presence of the fuzz bass of John Wetton – in Command at the same time working on his first King Crimson recording. "John's bass on that was really heavy. He was a mate and that's why I wanted him," explains Sinfield. "From *Still* and all my preachy cosmic stuff you get a bit of angry, because I do a bit of angry every so often. I get a few shots in at Robert. Like all these things, I nicked it from Lennon who wrote *How Do You Sleep* about McCartney. I thought I'd do one of those."

The sessions also reunited Peter and Mel with Boz and Ian Wallace for *The Night People*. Its howling brass evokes the spirit of *Lizard* but driven more directly by the rhythm section into a strange hybrid of freeform R'n'B. Sinfield's lyrics and their portrait of a decadent, bustling London by night are especially sharp and insightful. Here, Sinfield's role as vocalist is that of a tour guide in the teeming metropolis, all performed in a leery but effective sprechgesang. "My vocal on *The Night People* does have something of a Berlin-1930s feel to it, I think. If you can't sing then act it if you can. I can do a bit of 'To be or not to be' and it's a bit of an old trick. You can get away with a lot doing things like that. There are places on the album where I should have perhaps done more than that."

The appearance of *Under The Sky*, a song dating back to the sessions with Ian McDonald before he joined GG&F, is interesting. When *Still* was released in 1973 most fans didn't know that this tune had previously been recorded by GG&F in the final stages of their sessions with Decca. While that had a charm, the definitive reading of the tune is found on *Still* with Mel Collins' gorgeous, summery flute well to the fore.

Aside from Sinfield's voice, the other defining feature of the record is the use of the Freeman Symphonizer which had just come on to the market. "I think Ken Freeman brought it to us and I consciously used it because I was a bit wary of the sound of Mellotrons on the album. It was much more thin, ethereal and lighter in its sound than a Mellotron although you had to overdub it a lot of times. But in using it I was trying to get another step away from Crimson, really."

Sinfield acknowledges that the making of *Still* taught him a lot about himself and his limitations. "I should never have mixed down and put on echo on some of the vocals the way I did but I wanted to hide them, as you do. You hide them in the mix and you think that'll make it better. I do like a bit of texture going on but unless you're a brilliant arranger as well, you tend to end up with too much of this or that. That's because you haven't arranged it very well so that when you come to the mix you've got a really hard job and have to make decisions about making things disappear that shouldn't have been there in the first place perhaps." An axiom Sinfield is fond of using in respect of writing lyrics is: "When you've said, remember to edit." However, he admits that in his role of both artist and producer he should have been far more disciplined in his choices and decisions, accepting that things had gotten away from him during *Still*'s sessions. "I think perhaps somebody should have controlled me. I suppose if they had it would have been a different album. If it wasn't Greg Lake then it should have been someone else. But who else?" When it comes to bridging the gap between what you'd hoped for and what you actually ended up with, *The Song Of The Sea Goat* is the closest to what he wanted the album to be, he says. "I like the lyrics on *Sea Goat* and I don't hate the vocals too much."

If the making of the album was not an easy process, at the end of it Sinfield recalls being thrilled when the first boxes of finished records arrived at the Manticore offices. Housed in a sumptuous textured sleeve, it was adorned with a print by the German artist Sulamith Wülfing. "I love that cover. We went to Sausalito and this was when we thought we were getting our limos for free. This is how naïve we were on that tour. I'd heard about this restaurant called The Trident out there and Sausalito was so pretty. There was a shop full of Sulamith Wülfing calendars and postcards. I loved them all but I particularly loved that picture, *The Big Friend*. Some of her stuff can be a little bit fairy-gothic-twee but not that one. I'd previously asked a painter, Kit Williams, and he said he didn't want to see his pictures in WH Smith which is a bit ironic because his book *Masquerade* (1979) was certainly all over WH Smith's a few years later. So then I asked Wülfing for permission to use *The Big Friend* but she said no. I sent her a handwritten version of the lyrics and the album in a bit of desperation and she wrote back to say how wonderful she thought the words were and she was happy to let me use it for a fee of £60. Sometime later, after I'd sent her a copy of the finished album, I got in touch and said I'd be interested in buying the original. She loved the album she told me, and said I could buy it for £600. This was in 1973 and that was quite a lot of money then but I bought it and have it on the wall now."

Not unlike the cover of *Larks' Tongues In Aspic*, which contained a combination of male and female elements, *The Big Friend* also plays with notions of duality; male/female, innocence/experience, light/dark and so on. "What spoke to me about that painting I suppose was the beauty and the beast thing really. I liked the idea that within the monster there was something that liked preserving innocence."

On release in May 1973, the album was heavily promoted across the music press with full-page adverts: "Lyricist and co-producer of King Crimson and midwife to the birth of Roxy Music, Peter Sinfield has been one of the most astonishing background contributors in today's music. With *Still*, his first album, he puts his talent out front. Where it belongs." There were also TV and radio appearances for Sinfield, including *The Song Of The Sea Goat* and *A House Of Hopes And Dreams* on *The Old Grey Whistle Test*. In the BBC studio, Sinfield is backed by John Wetton, Mel Collins, Richard Brunton and Alan Mennie. Audibly nervous, Sinfield misses his cue on *Sea Goat* but does well with the second song which features a spirited tenor sax solo from Collins. At the mere mention of the *Whistle Test*, Sinfield cringes. "Oh, I hated that. What do I look like? Flouncing about, oh dear me."

In print he was far more confident. Talking to Chris Welch in *Melody Maker*, Sinfield said: "The LP is a step forward for me and it may prove to people that perhaps a bit more of King Crimson was me and that it wasn't all Bob Fripp's vibes." Clearly there was still a degree of heat between the two, with Sinfield feeling aggrieved that his contribution to Crimson was underestimated. At some point Still's salmon pink cover was replaced by a blue coloured board. When asked about the reasoning behind this change, Sinfield guffaws: "You have to remember that in the early days of the record business you weren't allowed to have any input into the design of the thing. 'What do you mean you want to have a look at the fonts?', the corporation would say. So when we actually had some power it was fun driving the blokes in the factory mad. So we did. Because we were so full of ourselves at Manticore and we had such fun annoying the guys who did the covers. For PFM's second album I did, *The World Became The World* (1974), and I said, 'What if we had a cut-out?'. So that means some poor soul in the factory has to do a die cut. For my album the prints on the cover had to be stuck on by hand. They loathed it but it was just those times when things were allowed to be indulgent. I just went off the pink. Wouldn't it be fun to change it to blue? I was a bit like a naughty boy seeing if I could get away with it. The record company just said OK but God knows what they were saying privately," he laughs.

The album was reissued on CD in 1993, but retitled *Stillusion*, containing two extra tracks, *Hanging Fire*, recorded in the same sessions as *Still* but unused, and *Can You Forgive A Fool*, co-written with *Still* collaborator Richard Brunton from a later period when Sinfield was working with ELP orchestrator and conductor Godfrey Salmon. "Took me 11 hours to sing *Can You Forgive A Fool*," says Sinfield ruefully. "It had great writing by Godfrey but that was a song I shouldn't have sung, or at least I should have taken the orchestra off." While these two tracks were welcomed by fans, they were inserted into the original running order in a way that was both awkward and disrupted the carefully constructed flow of music. Worse still was the harsh and brittle remastering, rendering the original warm production thin and vapid. Happily, the 2009 re-issue by Esoteric Recordings had a more sympathetic remastering and, importantly, restored the original track listing. The package housed a second disc which contained the two "new" tracks and several alternate mixes. While pleased to see the album properly re-issued, Sinfield says working on *Still* was stressful and exhausting. "I can't stress just how difficult recording the album was, and although there was some joy in it, overwhelmingly everything was hard work. I couldn't listen to *Still* for years. The same for Crimson and ELP. When you've been in there for hours making it, or when you've spent 50 gigs mixing it, you don't want to go near it. All I hear is the hard work and the mistakes." He contrasts this with his time working as producer with PFM, which overlapped with *Still*. "The joy of that is that I was working with wonderful musicians, the best musicians I've ever heard. So you have wonderful people, Italian food and great music and I can write anything I want on it. The only downside was the state of the vocals and trying to get them to sing in English. We just about got away with it. Now that was a happy time. It was work but they were such nice people and it was a joy to be with them. With PFM I didn't have total responsibility. I just had to do my words and make a few suggestions and then go off and make spaghetti. Lovely. Whereas after 12 hours in Command Studio doing *Still*, phew, it was hard. I was dying by that point with *Still* because there were so many decisions to make about the tracks, the writing, the mixing. It's a good job I was fairly fit at the time. It's one of the reasons I was quite pleased to not rush into another album and instead get seduced by ELP and the life of decadence to go and sit in Switzerland and write about pirates. *Still* was the hardest I think I've ever worked in my life really. There comes a point where you think 'Thank God that's finished!'. Afterwards it wasn't too hard to step away from being a solo artist."

VI

Informed by the management that Muir had injured himself and wouldn't be available for that night's concert, the remaining members of the band decided to carry on. Overnight, King Crimson became a quartet. Bruford was initially uncertain that the band would be able to continue without Muir, although his doubts were quickly dispelled as Crimson began a punishing tour of the UK, Europe and the States.

At home the press reaction to *Larks' Tongues* was mixed but generally favourable. The normally supportive Richard Williams was cool, feeling that Crimson had played safe: "Instead of a reflection of the power and sheer audacity they displayed on stage, we have something akin to 'the book of the film' – a rather wan, two-dimensional memento, which rarely kindles accurate memories of what they can achieve." *NME*'s Ian MacDonald was more impressed, declaring the record "a classic of its kind" and congratulating Crimson for the natural production.

Now minus Jamie Muir's mercurial presence, the quartet went back on the road. Joining them as support act was singer-songwriter Claire Hamill. Braving rows of fans eager to see the main attraction could be daunting for opening acts but Hamill, then still 18, was sanguine. "To be perfectly honest I was so young and so enchanted with the whole idea of performing and loving every second of it I didn't really mind whether people were indifferent or not because I had no experience of them being any other way. Starting out as I was, I hadn't done that many gigs really and the whole thing was just a blast. I didn't mind being a support act. I was just thrilled to be there and I just got on with what I saw as my job and having an enjoyable time. I liked being the support act for King Crimson. They had a very strong male following and they were very trendy. I liked their music as well so I was quite chuffed to be there. The band were very sweet. I didn't see a lot of them because usually what happens is they would do their soundcheck and when they've finished and shuffled off, you'd get about ten minutes at the end and then, half an hour later, you'd be on when the room was filling up."

Nevertheless Hamill reveals that she and Fripp were romantically linked during this period. "He used to watch my performance although probably not the whole thing, and then while I was on stage he'd leave me a little note in my dressing room. I've still got some of them. We were together for about six months. I couldn't completely give my heart to Robert. He never wanted children and it would never have worked for us because I come from a big Catholic family. I certainly didn't want a baby then but I saw that having children was going to be part of my future. Robert said he didn't want any children at the time. He was quite a young man when he was saying he didn't want to have any children but he's an old soul. He was 27 but he was like an older man in so many ways. Very deep, very serious … but he's also very light-hearted and very mushy and romantic. He probably wasn't that much older than anyone else in the band but he seemed very paternal at times, which I found lovely."

Signed to Island, her second album, *October*, came out as she toured with Crimson. "I was on the Island agency books and so were King Crimson and they were promoting both artists and that was how I got on the tour. It wasn't always easy. I supported KC at the Concertgebouw in Holland and a few days before I'd trapped my thumb in a car door in Sweden so my thumb was completely swollen and I nearly cancelled the gig. I went ahead with it but couldn't play the guitar very well and was in a lot of pain. The whole room started whistling and it was just terrible. That was a very miserable gig for me (*laughs*), I was too young to be able to handle it really. I stuck it out and did my set and didn't leave the stage until I was finished. I came off stage and was crying on my manager's shoulder saying 'Don't ever book me here again'," laughs Hamill. Despite some awkward gigs Hamill – who went on to sign with Ray Davies' Konk label and enjoy a stint as a member of Wishbone Ash – has very fond memories of the period. "It was great. Robert was an absolute darling. The rest of the boys in Crimson were all wonderful. It was a wonderful time in my life, definitely."

Had you wandered into the King's Road offices of EG Management in the early months of 1973 and looked across Dik Fraser's desk at the tour schedules coming back from Chrysalis' booking agency, you'd have noticed a distinct lack of UK gigs. This wasn't a result of any reluctance on the part of the domestic promoter. After all, as Crimson had demonstrated in the winter of 1972, their new line-up was a band easily capable of filling the 2,000-plus seater municipal venues and theatres that dotted England and Scotland and garnering near-universal acclaim from press and punters. The relative paucity of King Crimson's British and European dates had come about as a direct consequence of EG Management's policy to break Crimson in the USA. Just nine days after coming offstage in Paris, they went on at Ohio's Packard Music Hall, the start of a three-month slog around North America. After notching up 60 gigs between mid-March and the completion of the North American tour, a degree of irritability and impatience crept in. According to Bruford, Crimson's writing processes were exercises in "excruciating, teeth-pullingly difficult music-making". By the time they returned to the UK they were absolutely exhausted. During three weeks of the band holiday in July 1973, Fripp's time was taken up with the writing of *Lament*, *The Night Watch* and *Fracture*; in August, a weary and depressed band reconvened in a boathouse in Kingston to try to put together a new set.

It was now almost a year since the *LTIA* sessions. Since then *Doctor Diamond* had been the only new tune to emerge. The development of new material had always been a problem for King Crimson, with Fripp likening it to re-inventing the wheel "with other wheels running in different directions, and my own wheel working against gravity". Finding the balance between live work and writing time was always a source of tension. For his part, while pleased that Fripp had turned up to rehearsals with new pieces, Bruford would have preferred more pre-written material to be presented in full, rather than trying to write things from scratch in the rehearsal rooms. "The tunes that Robert has written all the way through, such as *Fracture*, these are good and, had there been greater output from Robert, we'd have got on quicker and faster. Robert's always done this. He's started off these bands with one-and-a-half tunes that point the general direction, and *Fracture* would have been one of them."

"I was never given the time to write," counters Fripp. "The band had a three-and-a-half-week holiday. I had three days. I recall on another occasion saying to the band that I needed time to write, rather than just continuing to rehearse. Bill, in a schoolmasterly and rather grudging fashion, would only agree if I really would do the writing as opposed to what he implied was goofing off."

In the same three weeks, Wetton headed off to Munich to spend time with Richard Palmer-James, who'd lived in Germany since 1972. "During that period I was seeing John quite a lot because he loved Munich so much. He always got laid when he came over. We'd also take an hour or two and mess around with these songs, trying this and that. He'd play a potential candidate for the next album, which at the time would have been *Starless And Bible Black.* John would work through the idea on piano or guitar or whatever was around basically. It was a different process from when I worked on *Book Of Saturday*, *Exiles* and *Easy Money* for *Larks' Tongues In Aspic*. Then it was just me on my own working with a cassette of demo ideas supplied to me by John or Robert, but with *Starless* and later with *Red* we were working on the songs whenever John was over, trying different ideas out."

Rehearsals in the unlikely surroundings of Richmond Athletic Ground's clubhouse began in the usual fashion. "I didn't see it as my job to tell everyone what to play," says Fripp. "If you're looking for an analogous template it would be more like Miles Davis or an even better one is Charles Mingus. Mingus wouldn't give the men in the band a part, and I didn't write out parts but bearing in mind that the ideas as formally composed were written for these people playing them not for any person playing. This is Crimson music written for Crimson and this specific incarnation of King Crimson."

Tired and drained, the group dragged themselves through ideas and sketches for material, including *The Great Deceiver*. "Energy reached such a low point that we were surprised we began again," noted Fripp but begin again they did. In September, they were off again on a tour that took in 19 dates in the USA and 24 in Europe. Though parts of the set were fixed, the running order was juggled around to maintain a freshness of approach. The concert stage was a place of aspiration and experimentation, where familiar tunes were strategically placed to offer the listener a point of respite or reference, in between the often turbulent journeys of discovery. By the time the band played Amsterdam's Concertgebouw on 23 November, they were tired but hitting a high point in their playing and capacity for improvisation.

The performance was recorded by sound engineer George Chkiantz and clearly demonstrates the fluidity with which the group were able to navigate the boundaries between composition and improvisation. The clarity and focus exemplified in this concert marks it out as a watershed for Crimson.

Supported by Colin Scot, Crimson had been meant to be on stage at midnight. In fact because of technical trouble it was well after 2.00 am when they kicked off. Wetton recalled: "We had a party with a few guys from Roxy Music because they were in town that night. It was a very late gig. We probably went out with the Roxy people before the concert. Mind, it could have been after because it was Amsterdam. My diary says: 'Late gig. Standout audience.' You're playing after midnight in a town that's renowned for its smoking habits. It was slow-tempo audience wise. It was quite lugubrious, I remember, but it gets a good rating here in the diary. It's a beautiful place to play. Stunning place. Red velvet seats and the name of the composers all around the balcony. You see a lot of classical concerts advertised there. It's a great place to record and we got quite a lot of good stuff from that gig."

Despite being the fourth gig from the end of the tour, with the band "long-term and deep down tired", as David Cross puts it, Crimson were tapping into something quite remarkable that evening as evidenced by the amount of music from the show used on their next album.

Aside from the magical *Trio*, the Concertgebouw furnished Crimson with the introduction to *The Night Watch*, an astonishingly forceful rendition of *Fracture* and an other-worldly improvisation they would later title *Starless And Bible Black.* Wetton regarded it as one of their finest improvisations. It highlights David Cross's other role in King Crimson as a keyboardist. Primarily a texturalist, he skilfully utilises the Mellotron and electric piano to offer a palette of rich tones in a style far removed from that of better-known keyboard exponents of the era with dark timbral blotches bleeding and seeping underneath the radiant, swirling guitar lines.

Not only did the tour feature the official debut of three new compositions, it also saw the use of an old Crimson song which had never been performed live. Wetton remembers the decision to include *Cat Food* in the set was a deliberate surprise for the audiences. They didn't play it every night but when they did there was a good albeit slightly astonished reaction.

Wetton had a soft spot for some older material. "I think our version of *Cat Food* blew the original out of the water and that bass riff just sounded fantastic. I would quite like to have played *Cadence And Cascade*, which I always thought was a great song." In soundchecks, Bruford and Wetton would sometimes play riffs based on Herbie Hancock's 1972 album *Crossings.* This brand of vibrant post-*Bitches Brew* funk had a notable impact on the rhythm section, as Wetton explains. "We were very impressed with American jazz-funk. What Herbie was doing and what Miles Davis was doing was using incredibly good players who could riff and that was a big influence on me and Bill. We brought that into the improvisations in a big way."

Everyone dealt with life on the road in different ways. Unlike Fripp, who would spend long sessions in his hotel room working on scales, Wetton almost never practised with the bass, preferring instead to work on new ideas with an acoustic guitar. Often he and Bruford would go and see other bands playing in town and, when Crimson were in Kansas City in May 1973, they were pleased to find Hancock in town, playing with the legendary Headhunters line-up. Backstage, introductions were made and, a month later, Hancock returned the compliment by coming to see Crimson at Florida's West Palm Beach, reportedly enjoying the show.

Wetton recalls that Crimson were often in town at the same time as other UK groups, often sharing the bill. Small colonies of expatriate musicians – including The Strawbs, Procol Harum, Robin Trower, Yes and Genesis – would often form in hotel lobbies and rooms where the latest news and gossip would be exchanged. Wetton recalls staying at the Holiday Inn, Lakewood Drive, overlooking Lake Michigan in Chicago in 1973. "There was a knock at the door at 2.00 pm and I'd just got out of the shower and there's Phil Collins standing there. He said: 'John do you know which room Bill's in, 'cos the front desk won't tell me?' So I gave him the number and off he went." The influence of Crimson upon the early Genesis is well known and the band allegedly kept the sleeve of *Court* up on their rehearsal room wall to remind the group what they were aspiring to. Perhaps it is no surprise that Collins asked Bruford to join Genesis on the road a few years later. Wetton revealed that Collins might have been even more influenced by Crimson. "My ex-wife lived with Phil Collins before we met and I didn't find out until years later when she told me that he would addictively listen to *LTIA*, playing it back to back, over and over. I just thought at the time he was a great drummer and a nice bloke but I had no idea that he was a fan of *LTIA* whatsoever."

As with all touring, there were high and lows. Where shows like those at the Concertgebouw seemed to encapsulate the best of the band, the performance in Rome ten days earlier demonstrated the ludicrous and potentially dangerous end of the spectrum.

At the Palazzetto dello Sport, Crimson had just finished soundchecking. John Wetton: "I gave my bass to our roadie, Tex, and was just about to leave the stage when this 15-year-old girl came up to me. 'My name is Lorena,' she says. 'My brother's here because I need a chaperone. I'd like to marry you.' What the fuck?" Back then, at home and abroad, there were legions of girls charging about from venue to venue hurling declarations of undying love and more besides in the direction of their favourite pop idols – but King Crimson? Really? Wetton admits to being taken aback not necessarily by the demand so much as the potential danger of the situation. "I laughed a bit nervously but she told me that she was serious and her brother would attest to that. 'I have a formal request from my family that you marry me.' I managed to placate the brother who looked like he would've murdered me on the spot if I'd said no and for a few moments I played along with it. It was extraordinary, there was no security because the gig wasn't anywhere near starting. Then I went and got somebody from the management to tell the girl and her brother that we would consider her request. She was deadly serious. Amazing really. Italy in 1973 didn't have a progressive feminist atmosphere. Guys were still lying on the pavement trying to look up mini-skirts at that time. For this girl to get it together, get her brother down to the gig and with her dad's permission, make a formal request that I marry her – I mean it's quite extraordinary. Took me completely by surprise! Stuff like that would happen to Crimson all the time."

Fripp recalls routine corruption in concert promotion in Italy with promoters attempting to rip off the band by lying about the true size of the audience. "The Palais was sold out; I think it held about 15,000. Anyway, it was a full house and Crimson's percentage of the gate was better than a poke in the eye with a pointed stick. Our manager, Sam Alder of EG, was out front with the promoter, viewing the crowd. 'A good crowd tonight,' said the promoter. '9,000 people.' Sam replied: 'King Crimson are not playing tonight.'"

"'Err, perhaps there are 12,000?' said the promoter. 'King Crimson will not play tonight.' '14,000?' '15,000,' said Sam. Now how the scam worked was like this: the staff collecting tickets from the concert-goers put a proportion of the tickets in their back pocket, which were shared out between the promoter and them. And then the promoter could quite justifiably say that ticket receipts were low. But any promoter in Italy, even with good political connections, accepted liability for damage at venues. If King Crimson didn't play that night in Rome, it was a reasonable guess that 15,000 rock fans would re-arrange the architecture." In fact, the performance went well, speaking volumes for the performers' ability to shut out this kind of distraction. But when the crowd demanded a second encore, the police and the promoter pleaded with Crimson to go back on, anticipating ugly scenes if they didn't.

The band tried to oblige but first had to contend with the disconnection of the PA's power cables. Additionally, the band and crowd witnessed a member of the promoter's staff beat up a hapless hippie who had managed to stray into a restricted area. "So we stopped in front of 15,000 angry people, a bleeding hippie, nervous police with machine guns, distressed ticket takers, a furious but mellow promoter … Of course the road team managed to run down the cables and eventually the power came on and we played *Cat Food*." Wetton believes fatalities were only just avoided. Of the impromptu proposal of marriage, John later found a ticket stub with the girl in question's telephone number on it. "She'd be about 55 years old now," he laughs.

For all their cerebral image, King Crimson were no strangers to the occupational hazards of a band on tour. Although they never quite got as far as throwing TV sets into swimming pools, or trashing hotel rooms, they certainly indulged in boisterous behaviour. "Like the time we were in Avignon," remembered Wetton years later.

"Crimson stayed in the same hotel that I'd stayed in as a member of Family when there'd been a food fight there. A food fight for Family was an every-night occurrence but not for King Crimson. After checking in, Wetton and company went down for dinner. "I just happened to mention about Family's food fight and the whole thing broke out again with Crimson! Everyone in the band and crew flinging food at each other – ice cream, pâté de foie gras, you name it. The poor maître d' was standing there utterly bemused. He wasn't angry, he was just thinking 'What the fuck is it with these guys? We had another English band do the same.' Thankfully he didn't twig that I was the common denominator!"

King Crimson never had much of a reputation for bad behaviour. "We get very bad press in that respect. We're not rock'n'roll, we're too studious or something. That's not quite accurate. We just did it in a different way and we did it where there weren't any journalists, like in Avignon. Crimson were actually very rock'n'roll in fact. There was plenty going on, I can assure you of that. We had our fair share of sex, drugs and rock'n'roll but not quite in the same way that Black Sabbath might have done and we weren't tarred with the same brush. Because of the technicalities of our music, people probably expected Crimson to be more studious or more monkish. We were more monkfish than monkish, I would say," said Wetton.

Alongside such cavorting, the consumption of cocaine would eventually become commonplace – though not, it should be noted, by everyone in the group. "What plays on the road stays on the road" might well have been the golden rule for many groups of the day, though it seems nobody had passed that particular memo on to Robert Fripp. Just weeks before Wetton's marriage proposal in Rome, the guitarist went on record in both *Melody Maker* and *New Musical Express* to declare his availability to as many young ladies as might be interested in meeting him. This despite admitting the numbers he'd already had congress with as being in his own words, somewhat excessive. "Sexuality pervades my work," he told bemused and slightly wrong-footed journalists at the time. You might not think of *Larks' Tongues In Aspic, Part Two* as a latter-day equivalent of *Songs For Swingin' Lovers!* or the ideal music to improve your seduction technique, but the makers of the soft porn movie *Emmanuelle* evidently thought it couldn't hurt, ripping off the track's thrusting themes as an ideal accompaniment to the on-screen action. They ended up in court and lost their case. Even today, Fripp still receives a trickle of royalties from the movie's soundtrack.

VII

On 7 January 1974, the band entered George Martin's AIR Studios in London's Oxford Street to begin putting together the seventh King Crimson album. The sessions consisted of recording *The Great Deceiver*, which initially bore the working title *No. 5 McLaughlin*, referring to the Mahavishnu-esque Wetton-composed riff, the main body of *The Night Watch* (initially referred to back in August as *Rembrandt*) and *Lament.* Richard Palmer-James recalls that *Lament* was a lyric that existed prior to John's visit to Munich in August. "It was a demo I'd already made, a country and western-style song, a sort of pastiche of Nashville. If you think of the lyric you can still do it as a country song. John took it and it was turned into a Crimson thing and where they made a couple of adjustments, but 90% of the lyric was already there."

George Chkiantz was in the studio for the duration. Chkiantz had worked at Olympic Studios and was a tape operator on the 1967 sessions for The Beatles' *Baby, You're A Rich Man* and *All You Need Is Love* and in January 1969 for the recording of George Martin's orchestral score for the *Yellow Submarine* soundtrack.

Wetton was instrumental in bringing the engineer on tour with Crimson in 1973 after the pair became friends during the recording of Family's *Fearless* album. Using Chkiantz at AIR was not without problems, as the studio preferred to use in-house staff. As an argument broke out at the faders on the first day, George Martin himself settled the issue. Passing by, Martin saw Chkiantz and commented: "Oh George, yes I know him. He's all right. It's fine." Chkiantz recalls being surprised at this endorsement from such a legendary figure.

Chkiantz recalls the challenges associated with recording Bruford's drums and percussion. "We had a splendid time trying to prepare for all the serendipity that would be created by Bill Bruford with his confabulation of tin cans and scaffolding. He looked like a spider in the middle of this metal web. Once we got everything in place we'd start bashing things and of course the drum sound would take forever to set up. It was problematic because you'd have to have a lot of open microphones to capture what he was doing, which led to leakage and so on."

At AIR, Wetton was much happier with the sound on the voice, achieved by Chkiantz by placing the active microphone just above the bridge of Wetton's nose but giving the singer a dummy mic to perform to. Wetton's confidence as a performer grew all the time, although he could be forgiven for doubting his abilities when the team flatly rejected one plaintive ballad.

He'd started writing the song at his parents' house in Bournemouth, inspired by a line – "Starless and bible-black" – from Dylan Thomas's poem *Under Milk Wood*. If the song itself failed to ignite interest, its title was applied to one of the improvisations recorded at the Concertgebouw and eventually became the name of the album.

Remembering their failure to adequately capture their improvisatory spirit on *Larks' Tongues In Aspic*, the group's policy of recording shows paid dividends. At AIR they sifted through spools of live tapes, selecting extracts not only from Amsterdam but also from Glasgow and Zurich. With the applause edited out, it became impossible to distinguish between what is live and the three studio tracks. The dividing line was further blurred when vocals and other overdubs were grafted on to *The Mincer*, originally an improv from Zurich, now transformed into an experimental attempt at songwriting.

"What I felt at the time was that almost anything you conceived of, provided you believed in it and went for it, could work; things could be as simple as you liked or as complex as you liked and it was perfectly OK to hold those different positions within the course of one performance," explains David Cross. "We don't always have to be all complexity or depth. We can have fun, it can be chaotic, it can be very simple and moving. Actually *The Mincer* is a good example of combining all those things together. I love the vocals and of course the bass and drums are working in a sneaky groove, but Robert and I were on a much more disturbed journey to what John and Bill are on; Robert and I are all over the place – it's quite bizarre, and then when the vocals come in they are so beautiful … the track brings together all these different perspectives into one place."

By 18 January, the bulk of sessions were over, with around 13 minutes of studio material in the can and live material sorted and graded for potential inclusion. There were still some overdubs needed to clean up parts of *Fracture* as well as the task of carefully removing any hint of the audience from the live tracks.

Despite having performed the song on numerous occasions in the previous year, they did not attempt to record *Doctor Diamond*. Throughout the European and American dates its structure was continually tinkered with during soundchecks. "Virtually every night it seemed like we were trying a different arrangement of that tune or slightly different lyrics," explained Wetton. "Musically it actually came from about three different tunes and it kept transmogrifying along the way. We kept trying different versions of it and couldn't settle on any one particular working arrangement. If anyone in the band was going to champion the song and tell the others that we should have a go at it that would be me, because I saw us moving more in that direction anyway. But if it didn't happen, it didn't happen for a reason, but I can't for the life of me think what that would be now. There was a reluctance to record it but to this day I have no idea why we didn't do it when we were in AIR."

When he was mastering the new stereo and surround-sound 5.1 mixes in 2011, Fripp noted: "It strikes me, listening over the past three days and dealing with the KC re-presentations and Anniversary Editions, that the KC music of the classic period, 1969–74, is quite extraordinary; and its nature has not yet been fully revealed/discussed/explained. Careless comments, even from good writers, *such as bands like Emerson, Lake & Palmer and King Crimson; or Yes, Genesis and King Crimson* – King Crimson were nothing like the other bands of its generation. More accurately: the other bands, all more popular, liked and commercially successful, with their own triumphs and failures, were nothing like King Crimson.

"The surround mixes make this clearer to me: there is a distinction and clarity, sitting in the middle of – exactly what? This isn't quite rock music, yet it's nearer rock than other forms. Crim's music changes yet is always Crim. Something astonishing is at the heart of it all, and whatever that *astonishing* is, it has not yet been fully articulated. And, were it to be, would likely attract the dopey commentary we associate with *Progressive Rock*. KC was the first group of distinct new-generation players in the music that became known as progressive. So, perhaps KC is *the* Progressive band. But, as the movement is generally regarded today, the KC music I have been listening to recently is nothing like *Progressive Rock*, while also defining it. A contradiction, certainly."

Several photographs of the group were taken inside AIR for promotional purposes and there was a suggestion that they might be used for the album sleeve. Instead the band opted to use the talents of Tom Phillips, who was suggested to Fripp by Brian Eno, one of Phillips' former students. At a time when elaborate or startling album sleeves were in vogue – a trend significantly boosted by Crimson's 1969 debut – the glacial simplicity of Phillips' black-on-white stencilled text, in stark and telling contrast to the title, nevertheless was not without impact or minimalist beauty. The austerity of the cover gave way on the gatefold to a dizzying blur, based on an earlier painting from 1970 by Phillips called *Here We Exemplify*. The panel on the reverse of the cover is taken from Phillips' adaptation of a page from a novel entitled *A Human Document* by W.H. Mallock, originally published in 1892. Since finding the book in a second-hand pile in 1966, Phillips had been revising, editing and over-painting each page and in 1970 published the first edition of *A Humument – A Treated Victorian Novel*. Departing from his original design for page 222 of *A Humument*, which contains the phrase "This Night Wounds Time", Phillips produced an image unique to the record bearing the phrase. *Starless And Bible Black* was Phillips' first album sleeve. In 1975 he would provide the same service for Eno's *Another Green World*.

Wetton held *Starless And Bible Black* in high esteem. "We were getting more experimental, trying different recording techniques, really screwing with the system; removing applause from live tracks so they sound like studio tracks – the exact opposite of what people do today where they add applause to a studio track and pretend it's live. We'd decided to remove the audience so that it sounded like a studio recording because that was the only way we could get the atmosphere. Before *Red* we could never re-create that power in the studio – it just wouldn't happen. You're in a sterile environment whereas on stage you'd got all that air and people and you'd got energy but by the time we got to *Red* we did it." The true nature of the extent of the album's live content was only revealed in the scrapbook of *The Young Person's Guide To King Crimson* in 1976, two years after the band had ceased to exist.

When looking for a title for their follow-up to *Larks' Tongues In Aspic*, they opted for Bill Bruford's suggestion of the Dylan Thomas phrase "starless and bible-black", which had also attracted Wetton.

With post-production under way on *Starless And Bible Black* (or *Braless And Slightly Slack*, as Bruford re-christened it), the various Crims went their separate ways, Wetton decamping to his parents' house in Bournemouth. At the end of January, Palmer-James and Wetton once again addressed the nascent ballad, with Wetton recording a demo cassette on his parents' piano on 1 February. Not long after that, Wetton was dispatched to Europe to talk about the forthcoming album to foreign journalists. "Dik Fraser and I used to do the press tours because nobody else could be arsed to do them. In about five days you do about ten capitals and cover as much press as you can, otherwise nobody is going to know about the album."

King Crimson reconvened at Richmond for four days' rehearsal on 7, 8, 11 and 12 March, and it was here that Wetton presented his tune. After playing it on an acoustic guitar, he looked expectantly at his colleagues but there was no reaction. "I mean: nothing. Everyone just staring at their shoes," he laughs, assuming the song to have been firmly and brutally rejected. "Nothing more was said of it and so we moved on to the next thing."

However, just a couple of days later, he was asked to present the tune once again. The ballad was now joined by chords and melodies originated separately by Fripp and Cross, and Bruford wondered whether an eight-note bass motif he'd come up with on the piano at home might be of any use. In the space of two or three days, the song which would become one of their most revered was consigned to oblivion then rescued in the nick of time.

On 15 March, at a full rehearsal at Ealing's Liveware sound stage facility, Crimson ran their proposed set boasting not just *Starless* but another new piece, *Guts On My Side*. Sections and motifs of the jazz-rock tinged piece had been appearing off and on since 1972 but, like *Starless*, it was only now finally assembled. Four days later in Udine, Italy, both songs were publicly unveiled for the first time. While *Starless* would become a highlight of the rest of the tour and, of course, take its place on *Red*, *Guts On My Side* was immediately dropped. As far as can be ascertained, the song was only played a handful of times in rehearsal and once in public. There was complete bafflement from the band when, in 2005, they were asked to identify a mystery track sent into DGM. Notwithstanding the execrable bootleg recording, there was considerable excitement over the discovery of a King Crimson track nobody knew existed.

The file was sent to Fripp, who replied: "No idea what this is. It sounds Crim influenced, and I might even be convinced it's RF on guitar – but I have no memory of this at all." Bruford was appalled. "God! What a racket!" When pressed further, with characteristic directness he said: "Sorry to be hopeless, but I don't remember anything at all about writing it or playing it." Wryly, he added: "PLEASE don't loop it and put it out as the new King Crimson album!" Fripp forwarded the track to Wetton who came straight back. "It's definitely us, no doubt about it. It sounds more *Starless And Bible Black* period, and there are burgeoning ideas from that era, plus a vocal/bass idea which surfaced in the UK in *Caesar's Palace Blues*. The linear Fratt/Crisp solo passage is unmistakable, as are the bass, drums and vocal. The song structure is wedged firmly between *Starless And Bible Black* and *Red*."

It was finally Richard Palmer-James who was able to confirm the name of the song, recalling that he had written the extraordinary lyric on 13 March while the band rehearsed at Richmond, dictating the words down the phone from Munich to a bemused secretary at EG's offices in the King's Road in London.

After two dates in Italy, the Crimson roadshow wound up in France including a rare TV appearance. From France the band began a run of dates in Germany. Wetton confirmed the strategy of playing abroad was all part of a long-term plan for Crimson. "I remember having a chat with David Enthoven in the office sometime in 1972 and he said we had to go all out for these markets; America being the prime one and Germany being the next. We did loads of provincial gigs in Germany and although the band were quite stumped as to why we were doing them, it was all part of a plan. France was already converted, as was Italy. They didn't really need the spade work; we could swan in and do a couple of major gigs, no problem. Germany, though, hadn't quite bought the package Crimson offered, and so we were told that we had to do the groundwork there and so that's what we did. Whichever way you look at it, Germany is the powerhouse of whatever economy you happen to take. Get Germany on board and the rest will follow. If the band had stuck around at the end of the recording of *Red* it would have paid off big time. The band at this stage tended to wear its rock hat in sports arenas, where it could hold its own with any of the heavyweights, using Occam's Razor to slash through protocol and kill at will but, given a velveteen concert-hall, we'd be Mahler before you could drop that aforesaid hat."

Richard Palmer-James joined Crimson for a couple of dates on that leg of the tour. "The first was in Augsburg, where I was struggling with an appalling hangover – the result of indulgences in the company of John and David Enthoven in Munich the night before – and I don't remember much about it. I then had to return to Munich for a couple of days and consequently missed the show in Heidelberg."

On the day Crimson were setting up at Heidelberg's Stadthalle, *Starless And Bible Black* was released in the UK. In a somewhat grudging review, *NME*'s Tony Tyler (who'd been a fan of KC69) perceptively observed: "Despite the overall quality and real outstanding moments on *Starless And Bible Black*, I can't help feeling it will all go largely unnoticed in the UK. In Europe it'll sell, no doubt. That's success of a kind." He'd perhaps taken his cue from the accompanying press release which ominously noted: "In April and May 1974, King Crimson make a European tour and throughout the summer will work in the US. No British concerts are planned for this year."

On Saturday, 30 March, Palmer-James took the train to Mainz to spend the afternoon in Fripp's room at the Hilton. This wasn't an entirely social visit. "We made cassette recordings of a couple of ideas which he played on his unamplified Les Paul, melodic fragments which I never in fact lyricised as far as I can remember. Robert spoke of the difficulties involved in composing, arranging and staging what he called 'epic ballads', which he saw as an important part of the Crimson experience (perhaps implying that others in his working environment didn't), and of his growing aversion to the rock circus in general. I remember being surprised at the high entertainment factor provided by the band on stage – never a dull moment, you know. I had been expecting a more introverted performance. The music was powerful and dramatic, full of technical intricacies, but still definitely a rock and roll show. At the hotel bar afterwards, Bill was full of ideas about lyrical themes for songs, which may have been a little disingenuous as John told me later that there was considerable pressure from Bill's corner at that time to increase the proportion of spontaneous improvisation on stage and on record. David Cross was subdued and devoted himself unhappily to his whisky glass. His performance, however, had been impressive."

The band then headed to the Jahnhalle at Pforzheim, traditional centre of Germany's gold trade. Palmer-James remembers the show as being intense, brooding, uneasy but brilliant. "What had seemed robust in the music the night before now became threatening. Chris Kettle gave me the cassette tape made at the mixing desk as a souvenir; the tape is defective, but the unsettling power of the performance comes through. In the dressing room afterwards, John sprawled naked on a bench, looking like he'd been shipwrecked; he didn't really recover before he went to bed. Even Robert had a few beers later in the pub. There was a quiet euphoria in the air, as if they'd survived a potentially lethal accident."

VIII

The next day, as the band went on to Kassel, Richard returned to Munich. It would be another 23 years before the five of them would be reunited in London at the playback of *The Night Watch,* held in September 1997 to celebrate the release of the live album documenting their remarkable gig at Amsterdam's Concertgebouw.

Listening to the Kassell gig, David Cross said: "I'm really impressed by the playing and the confidence with each other that is so apparent. It's the sheer joy of playing which comes across to me when I listen to this music now; it's kind of right on the edge all the time, taking tremendous risks with material that we really understood very well. It's our playing *with* the material that's so exciting for me."

"What I mean by that is if you're learning to play something, basically you go through a number of stages. You learn to play the notes, play it in time and in tune and all the things like that. Then you learn to perform it and learn to perform it quite well. Often bands only get as far as that, you know, that's the professional bit. However, beyond that is playing with the music, actually knowing the material and each other so well, that you can start doing different things on the night."

Improvisation was always a central component for this version of Crimson and though Cross regrets that, as the more sensitive ideas were often squeezed as a result of inclining toward rockier modes, he remains impressed by what they were capable of.

"In the second improvisation there's a lot of duetting that surprised me: there's Bill and I, and then the bass and violin really doing some quite subtle stuff together. It's a shame the violin is mixed down at this point but I can hear things going on in there beyond the usual stuff between the guitar and violin. It's quite nice to hear these other combinations. And really noticeable to me is the detail. Fripp's always been fantastic at the loud and soft stuff but it's the way he'll change a note that'll suddenly leap out and then it would be incredibly quiet, and it just sucks you in all the time, and then you get smashed back into your seat when everybody else comes in … It's sort of like throwing the ball up in the air, knowing 'yes, we can catch it' and then – BANG!"

The third improvisation was a beautiful duet between Cross and Fripp which flowered briefly and then gracefully disappeared. They'd tried something like this five days previously in Augsburg but then it was curtailed by Fripp, almost as if his concentration had slipped and he lost his nerve. "It's when you come out of one state of mind and into another, the left-brain taking over and making a judgement about what's going on rather than just being in what's going on. Of course, that's always death to any improvisation when you start thinking about it."

With Crimson playing at this level, a tour became an opportunity to converse, to consolidate and move forward to the remarkable moments when band and audience arrived at the same point in perfect unison. That two-way process has the potential to move both parties beyond the confines of mere geography. The odds are so stacked against it that, when that communion occurs, it's nothing short of miraculous. Such an experience cannot be contained in CDs or DVDs or photographs or words. It was there and now it's gone. Yet for those who had the good fortune to be in the right place at the right time, it's forever.

"I often get asked what my favourite venue is and I always say: 'It's not the venue but the people in it'," said Wetton. "The room is just a room really. It doesn't take on a personality until you put the punters in it; 20% is the venue, 10% is the effect and the atmosphere but the rest of it is all the people. That's the memory of a gig for me – the people."

With the UK increasingly omitted from the touring schedule – only 17 from 108 gigs in 1973 taking place in Britain and there were no UK gigs at all the following year – perhaps it is no coincidence that, as Crimson's relationship with the Press appeared to deteriorate, the band's disenchantment with the UK grew.

One reason for this antipathy was Crimson's perception that the British were not sympathetic to their music. This despite the fact that audiences of 2,000-plus enthusiastic supporters would turn out whenever the band came to town, not to mention that many fans, then as now, were prepared to travel substantial distances. But, in strict commercial terms, the American market yielded the greatest rewards.

At the time, Pink Floyd's *The Dark Side Of The Moon* had showed it was possible to reach out to huge audiences without compromising the artistic vision of a group. Of course, the nature of Crimson's music would prevent the huge FM radio play Floyd enjoyed. In an interview with *Sounds*' Pete Erskine, Fripp muses on the prospect of EG trying to promote the unmarketable, namely a new Crimson album. "We know it's going to be incredibly popular. We're very successful in Europe – even, it is said, tipped to take over from Pink Floyd. And in America this is the year we're going to do it. I therefore find it amusing that EG on the one hand have something that is overwhelmingly successful and at the same time completely unmarketable."

With their European tour completed, nine days later King Crimson took the stage in America, on 11 April 1974, to set off on the road to *Red*.

Had you spent any time with managers, musicians, promoters, record labels, Press, and even punters in 1974, at some point in a discussion about a given band's career the phrase "breaking America" would enter the conversation. The words represented an alluring, highly intoxicating cocktail whose ingredients included ambition, hope, risk, recklessness, fulfilment, status, delusion, dreams and greed.

For legions of British bands criss-crossing the state lines, America was central to any definition of "making it". Back home in the UK you might get your album reviewed in the weekly music papers, or played on the radio; you might trek to packed houses in the provinces and even sell out high-profile concerts in the capital; you might get your face on TV in continental Europe and see pretty decent sales. Yet, until you'd broken through in the States, you'd still not be regarded as a serious contender. There was the idea of America as a prize to be won, the "big country" of even bigger sales that sang its siren song to bands and bean-counters alike. But there was another America that excited the imagination of players, a hallowed, mythical place where even the names of towns and cities crackled and sparked deep in the cultural subconscious of musicians who'd grown up in staid suburbs of England. "It was a movie come to life. Fantastically stimulating, vibrant, competitive; the place where rock was invented," notes David Cross.

For all of the commercial and romantic allure, there were also inherent dangers. The fearsome resources, commitment and stamina required for the task inevitably came with a price tag which sapped morale, integrity and judgement. If you weren't careful, instead of you breaking America, that mighty country could break you, as Crimson found out to its cost late in 1969 and early 1972.

Cross, Fripp, Wetton and Bruford seemed to be having better luck as Crimson gained an undeniable momentum in the States in May–July and September–October 1973. The quartet were back in the USA from April through to July, clocking up 38 gigs, with more planned immediately after the recording of *Red*.

Despite the frequency with which the band were now touring America, Bruford recalls the organisation sometimes left a lot to be desired. "There was a nice and a very old-fashioned idea that our management at EG often sent us a telegram at the beginning of a tour saying 'good luck', 'It's going to be terrific', and that sort of morale-boosting thing. This time it was the opening of the tour where we'd probably come in on separate planes to the States and we were gathered in a miserable coffee shop in the Holiday Inn somewhere. We sat there facing an itinerary of six or eight weeks ahead of us in some ghastly places, not knowing what was going on and feeling completely abandoned, wondering if anybody knows if there's a car been rented or a van anywhere. So sitting there in the coffee shop, Robert composed a telegram to EG which said 'Help. Abandoned'. There didn't seem to be a strategy other than we went out there and everyone else was sat around at home. So in some respects it was quite amateurish. This was just four guys, three guitars and half a drum kit in the back of a van, maybe, barely knowing where we were going the next day, let alone having any kind of world-conquering plan."

The received wisdom dictated that by sheer hard slog you'd climb the ladder on the back of endless touring. A cursory glance at Crimson's itinerary as the band embarked on a tour supporting the newly released *Starless And Bible Black* certainly suggests that this was the plan. Looking back, however, Bill Bruford injects a note of caution. "Careful with this use of the word 'endlessly'. We were seen as effete Englishmen who came in for four weeks, scuttled back to England for a two-month rest and then came out and did it again. So to outsiders looking back at these times, it may seem like being on the road forever but to an American band that's more like a vacation. Those bands who got on a bus for 259 days a year, and then went home for three weeks, and then got back on the bus and did it all again – that is, our competitors, such as Black Oak Arkansas, The J Geils Band, and all the other people we were playing with – *that* was what they called touring. We weren't really competing at that level. We didn't really tour endlessly but we toured quite as much as any of us could really take, I think."

Members of the group coped with the pressures of touring in different ways and with varying degrees of success. Fripp, very much feeling burdened by doubts about King Crimson and his responsibilities in it, spent time practising the guitar, reading and scrupulously maintaining his journal. Cross candidly admits he drank more than was probably good for him. "I don't think I was that unhappy with touring but rather I was getting frustrated with the stage show and my performance, which I wasn't happy with. I found a note I'd written in the gap between these two tours that I'd contacted somebody to try and get some violin lessons. I knew I needed some help with that. I was realising that I had to take some kind of action to improve things."

As the band's profile grew in America, Wetton and Bruford fused into an invincible wall of sound which, though wonderful for audiences, had the effect of sidelining others in the band. Bruford recalls Fripp describing the experience akin to "playing with a flying brick wall" and going on to advise that any player coming into contact with it should "go with it or duck".

If it was becoming difficult for Fripp, the problems experienced by Cross were also mounting. As the players became louder, he began to find even the effort to compete dispiriting. The volume in concert, coupled with the vagaries of on-stage monitoring, blunted his hearing and tone and, ultimately, his appetite for punishment. The more he tried to move into the musical space towards which the rhythm section gravitated, the more he had to turn up. The more he turned up, the less he heard. The less he heard, the more marginalised he felt. The more marginalised he felt, the more the others would sense this and resent it. And so on.

Worse than that for Cross was a sense that there was little room for him within improvisations he felt were becoming increasingly rock-driven, demonic and, correspondingly, one-dimensional. For him the situation seemed unremittingly bleak as he describes in his notes in *The Great Deceiver* boxed set. "After gigs I would drink and drown my anger. All the time I was making progress within the group but my confidence was seriously undermined and I often felt lonely, even in the midst of 10,000 people."

Looking back, Bruford acknowledges that their impatience with Cross effectively shut out the violinist. "I don't think John and I were in any mood to wait and see if anybody could keep up with us. Robert could and so that was OK, but David didn't. I have a lot of sympathy with David now. I feel that I wasn't in a place at the time to be able to understand his 'white flag' held up as a truce, saying to us 'Hold on … could I be included in this?' I was too strong and too disinclined to wait for any passengers. It was too much success, too much exuberance, too much coffee, too much tiredness. It was being egged on by a very loud bass player. I'd do it differently now and, as I now know, musical talent is not all about muscles."

Fripp also accepts that Cross was placed in an increasingly impossible position, which saw a musical and personal distance develop between the violinist and the rest of the group as he failed to meet the strength and volume of the rhythm section.

For his part, Wetton says it was difficult to step away from the surging excitement their playing incited. "We'd generally have a rule that if it wasn't going anywhere then we could stop and go into a formal piece. The trouble was that once Bill and I were going it was difficult to stop. Robert and David might be bored out of their minds, you know, but it was very difficult to stop."

It wasn't just Cross experiencing a sense of dislocation. As the tour ground on, crevices of animosity and resentment opened. Bruford cites Wetton's on-stage volume as being a symptom of the distrust that had begun to subtly gnaw away at old alliances. "John's onstage sound got unnecessarily loud and that became a huge source of irritation. It's a way of saying 'I don't really want to hear you so I'll turn myself up'. John got louder and louder and decided he couldn't trust the sound mixer and he was going to make sure that the guy sitting at the back of a 4,000-seat room was going to hear him play. Of course, it's a chicken-and-egg thing because the more you play louder, so the sound mixer does turn you down and so on."

Wetton, himself no stranger to alcohol and other chemical substances, often found solace in the company of several different girlfriends. "I was footloose and fancy-free and we were a popular band touring the US in the '70s," he smiled, recollecting his not-so monkish existence at the time. "It was just after the late-'60s free love thing, you know. It was a lovely time to be on the road with a rock band, really." Bruford laughs at the suggestion that he also might have taken up the life of an on-road Lothario. "I wasn't much good at sex, drugs and rock'n'roll. I was too bloody knackered." Aside from thinking, practising and learning to stand on his head, Bruford reveals he took up alto saxophone, learning to play it in his hotel room. "Did he?" said Wetton, taken aback. "That's a new one on me. I don't remember that. Several times I had a room next to his and I never heard a toot!"

Seeing Crimson in concert often meant taking in at least two other bands on the same night. With tours organised through Frank Barsalona's Premier Talent Agency, the pairings could at times be incongruous. "We had some wonderful mismatches," laughed Wetton ruefully. "Although '70s audiences were very tolerant because often their edges were smoothed out somewhat by the haze that engulfed them, when you put a rock'n'roll band like Ten Years After, Black Oak Arkansas or ZZ Top with King Crimson, those kinds of pairings didn't really work. Groups such as The Mahavishnu Orchestra and Procol Harum did work well because there was some degree of crossover between fans."

Sharing the bill on numerous occasions were The Robin Trower Band. Fripp, a fan of Trower's playing, tried to catch the first few numbers of the ex-Procol Harum guitarist in concert before going backstage to prepare for his own performance. After gigs, the pair would discuss the challenges they faced with their bands, swap guitar exercises and looked into the practicalities of working together the following year.

"Robin Trower – that was a nice bill," Wetton remembered. "They had an album that was really doing well and was in the charts. I think, in fact, when it was Crimson, Robin Trower and Golden Earring, the album chart positions were in reverse order of the billing of the bands. You had Golden Earring had an album at No. 6, Robin Trower had one at 22 and Crimson had one at 67! (*laughs*). But the applause was inversely proportional. Robin used to go down really well but it was always difficult for anyone to follow Crimson. We would end with *LTIA2* or *Schizoid Man* and it'd be difficult for people to top that, really. The sound was so brutal coming from all of us it didn't actually matter what we played because when we came on, even if we were improvising from the word go, people would just stand and say 'fucking arseholes – what is this!' It had such force and presence you couldn't argue with it really." One of the many bands who ended up on the receiving end of that force was the UK band Slade. Wetton recalls his incredulity when he was told that the glam-rockers were headlining in Detroit, something of a Crimson stronghold. "We played our set, then Slade came on and they had to survive the boos and jeers. Noddy Holder, their lead singer, came up to the microphone and he said in a broad Wolverhampton accent, 'If you don't like it you can all go and have a shit!' It was superb!"

Wetton recalled the profound impact of singing in front of 18,000 people in Phoenix's Feyline Fields, between Strawbs and Trower. The same gig also lodged in David Cross's memory. "It was lovely and for me in such an alien environment, out in the desert. So different, so strange. You can't buy experiences like that. It was such a privilege to be able to take part in that event, to go on at that time was just perfect as the sun was going down."

For Cross, where Crimson appeared on the bill wasn't a particularly big deal. "It was just all part of the job. The good thing about headlining is you got to play longer, suppose. One of the things that did help us as an improvising band was that, because we did do supports, we had to tailor our set to wherever we were. Sometimes we were doing a 45-minute set, sometimes less, and you had to fit into that slot and deliver what was appropriate for that time, while at the same time give people the flavour of what you were up to. That could be quite challenging but I think that's what kept us focused."

IX

Regardless of where they were on the bill, the sound Crimson made, on what turned out to be this line-up's final, tour, was committed and forceful. It wasn't just down to volume although, as several eye-witnesses attest, the band was undoubtedly loud. Often audiences had no idea that the piece they were hearing was improvised, a forgivable misunderstanding considering the way such blows could sometimes be introduced. For example at the Palace Theatre, Providence, an audibly amused Fripp pronounces ahead of the first blow of the evening: "This is a new piece we've been working on for a considerable amount of time. This is a cosmic voyage which seeks to depict musically, seven states of altered consciousness. This is called *A Voyage To The Centre Of The Cosmos*, subtitled *My Mate Atman*."

On some occasions, such as the memorable performance at Asbury Park, there was no time for such jollity. Straight after Exiles, an ever-eager Bruford performs a typically crisp snare roll, laying down a wonderful groove. Six seconds in, Fripp can be heard shouting "F!" across the stage. A couple of beats later the bass grunts, the guitar growls and the band take a collective leap into the unknown. Years later, those who saw the performance, and the many more who heard it on *USA*, marvel at what is widely regarded as one of the finest moments of Crimson in any incarnation.

"Improvisation and extemporisation; what's the difference? Extemporisation is what the musicians do and improvisation is what happens when it comes to life," says Fripp. "Spontaneous composition? Trio is an example of that. It was improv but it sounded written. The Sheltering Sky, another example."

Listening to the improvisations from 1974, one becomes aware of distinct areas the improvisations fall into, not exactly a map but there are recurring motifs and moods. Were these consciously worked at or allowed to develop on their own?

"You work with these musicians and you have some sense of how they might respond in a certain situation," offers Fripp. "Then you have Asbury Park – 'F!'. All right, what are you anticipating might happen after that? Where is that going to go? Well, all you know is it's going to begin somewhere around F and then, who knows? So you're working with these characters; you know the areas they are likely to move to, and then sometimes it goes somewhere else. That's what it is, and sometimes it moves towards a formal structure that can be formalised in a piece – or not."

In those moments, Cross believes they were operating around the rawer edges of how music is constructed. "If you throw the rules out of the window then you do start to come up with ways of talking about music in the way that we used to; starting with big bangs, steady climb-outs, fade-outs or cross-fades. We were talking about music in rather general terms because we didn't have any specifics mapped out. When I've endeavoured to walk down anything like a similar road with musicians since, they're terrified of doing that, or if they do, they can't play a tune. Somehow we could see the value in playing tunes, singing songs and, at the same time, exploring anything else that was around or came to mind. It's dead lucky that we were able to do that. Considering how young we were, it was quite extraordinary really."

"There was an undeniable force with that band. It was not any one individual. It was the whole band," suggested Wetton. "I can't tell you because I was on stage, but I think if you were standing in the audience you would feel this raw wave of power. It was just a kind of attitude really, a big attitude coming off stage at you. What people forget is that when they think of King Crimson they tend to think of balladic, Mellotron-led stuff. Actually by the time we were doing *Red* and on the road, it's fucking metal – sheet metal coming off the stage at you."

But conflict remained, particularly for the increasingly marginalised Cross. As early as April, at Columbus, Ohio, tensions between Cross and Bruford spilled over on stage, despite the fact that Fripp judged the gig to be a good one, noting it was the "first time we're as big as we can be". By the time the band played their historic gig in New York's Central Park, the decision had already been taken that Cross and Crimson would part company. "Over my life I've come to realise that playing the violin is a core activity for my existence. It's not really something I can pick up and put down. If I don't do it, I don't feel right and I don't feel like me. So I guess if I wasn't playing as well as I wanted to, then I wasn't feeling right about me and that needed to be addressed somehow, and I guess that meant I just had to get out of the situation which I found myself in. Leaving King Crimson was not a decision made in any particular moment and was based on instinct rather than reason. Although I enjoyed so much of being part of KC, touring was increasing my levels of anxiety to an untenable degree and I didn't have the psychological resources to keep coping. The avoidance of that particular pressure grew into a more pleasant vision of the future than continuing. On stage in Central Park I loved being, there but offstage the balance was shifting fast in favour of self-preservation."

Cross's position in the band was the subject of ongoing discussion in those final weeks before Central Park. There was talk about replacing Cross in the middle of the tour with ELO violinist Wilf Gibson. Fripp had previously worked with Gibson on Keith Tippett's *Centipede* album and on King Crimson's *Islands* where he had been responsible for fixing up the small string ensemble for *Prelude: Song Of The Gulls*. Gibson, who died in 2014, remembered receiving a call about possibly joining Crimson while he was on tour with ELO in the USA. "The schedule we had with ELO made you feel like some product, like a packet of cornflakes or something rather than a musician. The criss-crossing of America on the first ELO tour was suicidal. Florida one day, Boston the next, Los Angeles the day after. We sometimes shared the bill with Crimson. There was a place we crossed paths somewhere like Fresno or Sacramento, somewhere on the West Coast," said Gibson. "You got to a stage where your brain was absolutely scrambled. It took me weeks to get over that. I went up to Norway to my in-laws and just sat in a boat fishing for about six weeks." Back at home in London, he attended a meeting at EG's offices where a firm offer was made and terms were discussed although no members of Crimson were present. "At the time my son was three years old and my daughter was one year old. The reason I turned it down was what the management put to me would have meant spending the next two years touring the States. I could see the prospect of having to bring my kids up in America which I didn't want at all. I had a house in Wimbledon that I had to keep up and it would have been a huge upheaval. I was a bit brutal about it at the time. It was a very good offer. The money they offered me was really good payment for the gigs and a retainer, but I was a bit uneasy about replacing their violinist – dead man's shoes and all that. Eventually I said 'No, it's not for me'."

Despite these difficulties, the band was still capable of magnificent improvisations. Wetton recalled: "Usually we'd start with an atmosphere, hit in with a riff and reach a climax, then fizzle out. Maybe one night in every five it would be brilliant and for us – that was enough because we'd got a result. You can't do it every night but that was a risk we were always prepared to take."

The intensity could vary tremendously, even during the same show. At Toronto's Massey Hall, on 24 June 1974 (documented on the fourth disc of *The Great Deceiver* boxed set), they launched into a blistering groove reminiscent of The Mahavishnu Orchestra's *The Noonward Race*. Yet somewhere in between *The Night Watch* and *Fracture*, the spark haemorrhages away to produce, in the aptly titled *Clueless And Slightly Slack*, an indeterminate, unfocused prodding which hangs Cross out to dry. For Fripp, there are many reasons for such an occurrence. "A performance can be violated and damaged, often in ways which are not immediately apparent or obvious. Surreptitious recording, photography, drugs kicking in, even violence on the premises, all disturb the performance. Sometimes this is connected to the group. Mostly, it is not."

The band always tried to avoid giving obvious cues to each other in improvisations which led many to miss the fact that what they were hearing was not the debut of a forthcoming composition. Wetton takes some pride in this. "We knew what was going on most of the time but nobody else did and it looks like we are performing miracles. We were very much against signals or cues which were obvious to anyone other than ourselves. There was a rule whereby, if one of the guys led off somewhere, there was an absolute commitment to follow in that direction, no matter where it might lead. It was very supportive. There had to be that understanding."

Wetton took the view that a more demonstrative player than Cross was needed. Fripp agreed, at least in part, recording that the thinking behind this was to do with Cross's widening disconnection from Crimson's musical direction. It was also agreed that problems of confidence and self-esteem had rendered Cross's personality too insecure for him to remain.

Fripp says: "The balance of the group, conceived as a quintet, had been lost. Part of this was that Jamie balanced Bill and without Jamie's counterbalance, ordering and direction, Bill's energies become increasingly unrestrained. The rhythm section got stronger, and essentially became the front line. The degree to which the guitarist held his own with them is debatable: even if considered as strong a player, he was outweighed two to one. As an individual, David Cross was probably a gentler character than Bill and John, and not as likely to move into the clinches. But, as an instrument, the violin could not hold its own in an electric power context alongside (at least) the mighty Bass Beast Of Terror."

With one eye looking out for the person and one eye on business, tour manager Dik Fraser argued that Cross might be inclined to do something stupid – and the music might suffer as well – if told that he was out. Only Bruford felt that the violinist should stay on. He was outvoted. It was agreed that Cross should be told by EG when he returned to the UK, with Fripp insisting that his objection to not telling Cross in person had been over-ruled.

Looking back, the guitarist says: "I was infuriated that, even when we began recording *Red*, David Cross had not been told by EG. This was in direct violation of the undertaking I had been given. EG's Standard Operating Procedure was clearly not one of transparency."

1974's final gig, in New York's Central Park on 1 July was always going to be an important one though, as the players left Rhode Island that morning, they could hardly have envisaged it would be King Crimson's last for more than seven years. "There was enough testosterone onstage that night to drive an F-14," Wetton recalled. For Fripp the gig had a power he'd not felt since 1969 – "the bottom of my spine registered 'out of this world'."

It was the expressed hope of Wetton and others in the team that Central Park, like Hyde Park in 1969, might thrust the band into wider recognition. "Everybody at Island and Atlantic believed in the band and gave us a lot of support, a great management team and, for my money, I thought we were the best in the game. We had the plot," says the bassist.

But the gig nearly didn't happen due to a terrible mains hum which threatened to swamp the PA sound. Fripp's inclination was to cancel unless the technical difficulties could be overcome. A vote was taken and it was agreed to go ahead. At a little after 8.30 pm, as the mellifluous strains of *No Pussyfooting* – still unreleased in the USA at that point – gently massaged the atmosphere, Crimson took the stage with a highly flammable *21st Century Schizoid Man.*

Towards the end of the set, the band played their epic new number *Starless*. Fripp recalls: "As the sun went down and we moved into the ominous bass riff emerging from the *Starless* vocal, red stage lights faded up from behind the band. For me, a stunning theatrical moment highlighting the tension within the piece and the group; a moment of resonance."

Wetton: "I don't think you get that level of energy in bands that often. I don't think there were that many bands around at the time, doing that kind of stuff, who could touch us."

Wetton later enjoyed a far more lucrative career in Asia, who at one point sold 800,000 units a day. Yet he was in no doubt which part of his career meant the most to him. "If I shuffle off this mortal coil tomorrow, that gig would be the one for me. All the stuff with Asia and everything else is just icing on the cake. That was the one … it was almost tearful it was so emotional. It should have been the beginning of something rather than an ending."

X

On Monday, 8 July – just a week after Central Park – the band entered Olympic Studios in Barnes to record the eighth King Crimson album. For Wetton, it would be the last.

Engineer George Chkiantz was back on his old stomping ground in Olympic's Studio Two and, because Wetton had a preference for injecting the bass directly into the mixing desk, the bassist spent most of the time in the control room with his old friend.

Chkiantz remembers that Bruford's kit sans percussion occupied the right-hand side of the room while Fripp and his amplifier nestled in the drum booth itself. "My recollection is Fripp sitting on a stool with the light off, quite possibly with the door pulled to, basically playing when the stuff was counted in. I'd have been happy to have had Fripp in the main room but I think he put himself in there." Fripp's recollection is that he did spend time in the main room particularly during the recording of the track *Red*, retiring to the booth only to play Mellotron parts.

As the sessions started, Fripp dropped a bombshell. "He said that he had decided to withhold the passage of his opinion. I remember this because I wondered at the time if he meant 'passing' instead of 'passage'?" recalls an exasperated Bruford. "He'd decided that his opinion didn't matter anymore."

But Bruford and Wetton had become inured to what they regarded as Fripp "pulling another moody" and did not suspect anything more ominous lay behind the remark. Both recall working with Fripp on the sessions as tortuous. What Bruford and Wetton couldn't have known was that, four days prior to the sessions, Fripp had encountered the work of English mystic JG Bennett and undergone a spiritual awakening comparable to that experienced by Jamie Muir two years earlier. "There were things going on during the recording process that I don't believe John and Bill were aware of," he says.

With Fripp having largely withdrawn into himself, it was often left to Bruford and Wetton to make big decisions about the final content. "It's a wonder that the album ever got made," recalls Bruford ruefully. Despite this, the band pulled together three new compositions in a very short time. At the end of the day, Bruford would get on his bicycle and head off home, content to leave the recording of the vocals to Wetton and Chkiantz, who would work into the evening. "I almost never asked about the meaning of a song. John could've sung the phone book for all I cared. What singers sang about was almost wholly immaterial to me. The sound of the voice I care about but, primarily, my interest was in the rhythmic machinery, in the engine room – the rhythmic counterpoint and drive of the piece. Is there any way in which what I do on the drums can make this piece better?"

Bruford's drumming and playing never sounded more potent and articulate than it did on *Red*. Indeed, it soon became obvious that this was going to be the heaviest Crimson album to date. But it was also evident that further instrumentation was needed to counter-balance the primordial crunch.

Wetton had been thinking about asking Crimson founder Ian McDonald to do some playing. "For me, Ian McDonald was the right person to come into the band. I did a lot of schmoozing with Ian and I told him that it was the ideal time for him to come back into Crimson. I wanted commercial success for Crimson at the time and my thinking was that Ian in the band would have possibly pushed us into Pink Floyd territory, out of the cult status that we were just beginning to move out of."

But Fripp was suspicious of Wetton's desire for "commercial success". "It exerted a pressure within the band which, subtly, upset the balance of energies," says Fripp. "John looks back on Crimson, but UK and Asia represent the musical direction that John helped forge, with commercial success in mind. If *Red* were to be 'the beginning rather than an ending' please consider that Fripp would have had to counterbalance the ferocious energies of the singer-bass player that would write UK and Asia hits, and a drummer who was more concerned with his own playing than the group process. If you put into this cauldron a fair amount of cocaine and alcohol on one side, and a lack of subtlety/taste on the other, you get a small snapshot of the concerns that I was dealing with to keep Crimson on track. To add another ingredient to make the pot boil a little more, how about adding a member of the first King Crimson, one who left in December 1969, giving me as a main reason that he didn't like me playing his music?"

With the backing tracks completed, McDonald laid down blistering solos on *One More Red Nightmare* and *Starless*. Wetton also drafted another player from the past in Mel Collins, while Fripp drew on the services of cornet player Marc Charig and oboist Robin Miller, both veterans of previous Crimson sessions.

A fifth guest player, who provided the cello parts on *Red* and *Fallen Angel*, was never credited. Despite rumours suggesting that Wetton, or even Charig, provided the parts, it was in fact a musician recruited from the pool of classical players who frequented Olympic's Studio One, although their name continues to elude posterity. Fripp: "I can't remember his name either. He arrived early, coming from a muzak session. Because there were MU limitations on how much running time could be recorded at one session, and they recorded their quota in two hours rather than three, he arrived an hour ahead of time!"

The appearances of such guests linked *Red* to all the previous Crimsons, acknowledging the past and bringing things full circle. The sense of lineage and linkage was not lost on members of the band, or by the fans who greeted the album's release.

During the mixing, the group discussed ideas for potential covers. As the music was playing back, the needles in the VU meters on the mixing desk bounced and crashed sharply into the red. For Wetton it seemed to symbolise where they were going with the music, and for a while this image was thought to be a strong idea for a front cover. Yet confidence was so high that EG thought it would be good to "put a face to the name" with a group portrait, the first ever to grace a Crimson sleeve. The thinking was that this would offer American retailers a more directly marketable image.

Designer John Kosh commissioned Gered Mankowitz, whose previous clients included Jimi Hendrix, The Rolling Stones and Giles, Giles & Fripp, to execute the shots of the VU meters and the portrait. Mankowitz recalls that the band seemed very ill at ease with each other. His solution was to take individual shots and then produce a composite giving the impression of the three standing together. With the pensive lighting, Mankowitz clearly alludes to Robert Freeman's classic *With The Beatles* cover, which captures four fresh but vulnerable faces at the early stages of their career. With *Red*, though, the shadow is more severely drawn, suggesting a sombre, ruminant introspection.

Not everyone liked the cover concept – or the photo session. Fripp: "I loathed the session and was ill at ease with all of it. One of the pictures had me with an acoustic guitar. Ouch."

"The idea of using John Kosh came from Mark Fenwick of EG. I disliked the idea, but had no alternative suggestion. Mark's 'creative' ideas were reliable: he was always wrong for King Crimson and Robert Fripp."

Red embraces an altogether darker, more unsettling world view than either of its immediate predecessors. There is no equivalent of *Book Of Saturday* or *The Night Watch* to provide a warmly intimate perspective. Even the vocal section of *Starless* has an anguished reproach at its core. This is not a comfortable place to be. The lack of rounded edges and incisive thorniness clearly anticipate the shock of the coming new wave. *Red* remains the only studio album to convincingly capture the strength King Crimson tapped into on stage. The fact the band had the maturity to translate this raw energy into the studio, arguably for the first time since its formation, makes the finality of *Red* all the more poignant.

Cross, however, wasn't the only person in the camp who was unhappy at the way Crimson had evolved since Jamie Muir's departure the previous year. Despite citing their final show in Central Park as the best gig since Crimson '69, Fripp's increasing disenchantment with a life spent on the treadmill of touring and recording gradually led to the conclusion that something had to change. "So why in 1974, returning from life on the road since 1969, did I wish to leave it behind?" Fripp explains, "Because it was utterly mad. Utterly mad. You can say to the other members of the band, 'Come on, this is mad.' And they say, 'But we're going to be as successful as Pink Floyd in

Europe next year,' which is also true. My concern was that the creative impulse is acting through KC. The actual behaviour, the actual life of the band was going to go off course. It hadn't gone off course but it was being set up to do that."

"The confidence level after Central Park was phenomenal both from band and public. When I came back and we started recording *Red* I was full of optimism," says Wetton. He believes that the looming prospect of success at the next level affected the individuals in the band in different ways. "I think some people are as wary of success as they are of failure. There were two of us champing at the bit to make the band as successful as possible because we could see what was possible, what we could do. What was on the horizon for us was really close and tangible. And one third of the band was going 'hang on a minute'. The more popular the band is, the less control there is. There you have a fairly big factor in the demise of the band. It's a pity because the chemistry was incredible. Ian McDonald was tantalisingly close to rejoining or at least touring with the band and that would have been the icing on the cake for me."

Fripp's idea of re-introducing Ian McDonald as his replacement was a bona fide "transmission", as he saw it, from the original King Crimson to keep a post-Fripp incarnation authentic. "I suggested this to David Enthoven, whose comment was 'We're not interested in King Crimson without you'. So at that point I let go of it. I called up Bill and John and said it's over. This is not a discussion. For me there was nothing to discuss: I was going and I'd done what I could to keep it going. If at that point Bill and John had, of their own initiative, gone to Ian and asked him if he was in and then gone to EG and they said 'We have Robert's blessing and suggestion that he would be very happy for us to run with this and we would like to run with it', then maybe it would have kept going. Where they might go with that would not be my concern or responsibility. The transmission would've been handed on to those characters, wherever they might take it."

"John tended to say that after Central Park and making *Red* we were on the way up and the next thing would've been fantastic," offers Bruford. "Me? I have no idea. I wasn't looking that far ahead. I was just trying to get through *Red*, which was hard work. I think we were all exhausted. None of us had any idea how tiring all this was. Now, of course, people know better how to preserve the lives of groups. The Beatles were the template for everything, and being toured off the road with exhaustion and bad facilities put an end to their live performances and I think Robert had spotted this; that Crimson was not the kind of band that should go on and on. We would've inevitably blown up had it carried on."

"The point is a band comes together when it had music to play. When it's played that music it moves on," says Fripp. "It might move on in the same place or not. It has to do with the nature of the creative current and creative work. As soon as you say 'Look, this really works. Let's keep doing it', you have a successful professional undertaking which is entirely honourable but the creative necessity for the band may not be there. There are different approaches for that; one is to exist for a period of time and say when the beast of Crim returns then we shall come together to serve that beast. That's one approach. Crimson was a very rare animal in that it acted in a world mediated by commerce but not limited by the world of commerce. Constrained by it, yes, but not serving it."

Whatever untoward edge or occasional resentment may have been part of life in King Crimson in 1974, it's clear that the players regarded this brief period in their respective careers as a time filled with tremendous possibilities, excitement and achievement, and perhaps, a sense of wonder that it happened at all. "It's interesting some of the difficulties we had and I'm not pretending that it wasn't hard work, particularly in the personnel/people skills department. We played that game at very high stakes so it was permanently exhausting. The playing of the instrument and engaging with music was bloody great and I was thrilled to be there," Bruford says emphatically. "I look back on it now with a great deal of fondness. It's very easy with this distance and all this scholarly enquiry to nit-pick but we should not forget that it was a blast! It was, excuse the language, fucking great!"

All those miles, all those experiences, good and bad, were distilled into the recording of *Red*, the final studio statement from King Crimson in the 1970s. Crimson was tapping into something powerful, something that was, and perhaps still is, capable of speaking to listeners in a way that can be both challenging, rewarding and, if we're lucky, transformative. Jack Kerouac wrote "Behind us lay the whole of America … and life on the road. We had finally found the magic land at the end of the road and we never dreamed the extent of the magic."

Paraphrasing Jack Kerouac, in the accumulated days, weeks and months that went into the making of *Red*, King Crimson did indeed find the magic land at the end of the road.

Forty-five years later, the extent of that magic is something that players and listeners alike are still coming to terms with. Its influence shows in unexpected places. There was a tale that spread in the '90s that *Red* was Kurt Cobain's favourite album. It's been repeated so often, though it was always hard to find the source of the tale. "I know the band were fans of King Crimson, but that comment came from me," explains Nirvana producer Butch Vig. "While on our first tour with Garbage back in '96 I kept getting bugged by journalists with questions about Nirvana. After one too many times of being asked 'What band had the biggest influence on Nirvana?', and tired of answering the obvious 'The Pixies, etc.' I calmly responded, 'King Crimson's *Red*'. I do know Dave Grohl is a fan, as is Taylor Hawkins. I'm also a big fan, I went to see them on tour in Milwaukee on the *Red* tour, and they were incredible! I've always admired Robert Fripp for following the artistic path less chosen throughout his career and creating some brilliant music!"

XI

Despite the artistic peak *Red* represented, there would be no tour, no reunion with Ian McDonald and, for John Wetton, no more King Crimson. Fripp had finally had enough.

The origins of his decision to end Crimson were complex. Looking back, it's perhaps possible to make sense of seemingly random events leading up to it. Fripp himself cites the fiasco at the Palazzetto dello Sport in Rome as a turning point. From there, the absurdities and threats of life on the rock treadmill became increasingly hard to reconcile with his growing philosophical and spiritual requirements.

It can surely be no coincidence that Fripp's decision to remove himself from the music industry was taken at a point where he had had less than six months' break in three years. However, the most important factor was his encounter with the writings of J.G. Bennett, an English writer and devotee of Russian mystic G.I. Gurdjieff. Bennett's work had a profound and immediate impact. "When I found Bennett in July 1974, the top of my head blew off. I knew that I had to go to the International Academy for Continuing Education at Sherborne, and abandoned my career – as Crimson was about to be hugely successful in Europe – to do so. This was not a product of considered reflection: it was an immediate and instantaneous recognition of personal necessity."

In an oft-quoted exchange with *Rolling Stone*'s Cameron Crowe in 1973, Fripp unambiguously described his belief that King Crimson was a magical act or a way of being, in which one could address the basic questions of identity and purpose – the who and why of life.

Fripp wanted something new and to be part of the world at what he called a macro-sociological level. "The old world was dead. How could I be part of the new one? That was my problem. It was a very fast flash that kept on reverberating for three days and put me out of phase for nearly three months. Recording *Red* was very painful for me." King Crimson as his principal means of education was now at an end. He needed to find another route.

For Bruford and Wetton, Fripp's decision – of which neither had any warning – was devastating. The making of *Red* had been difficult but the outcome was arguably the strongest Crimson release since the first album. Long-term success seemed assured. In August 1974, the final outcome of discussions about the group's next step had not been fully determined. But, as support grew for the inclusion of Ian McDonald as a permanent replacement for David Cross, the likelihood of any time out receded.

So they were stung by the suddenness of Fripp's decision – as was Ian McDonald, who had just agreed to rejoin. "I can't remember how he phrased it … 'Would you like to join the band?' or 'Would you like to come on tour with the band?', which are slightly different things, and I said 'Sure why not?' and then the next thing is, he's broken up the band. This is why from my point of view it seems as though all he wanted me to say was that I would come back and now he's going to get his revenge and break it up because he was in a position to do that."

"I was not 'offering Ian the gig'," says Fripp. "I was enquiring whether, if offered the gig, he would have accepted it. If he had said 'no' then that was an end. Saying 'yes' there were two discussions: one within the band and one with EG."

Fripp had a meeting with EG's David Enthoven and presented them with the picture of an ongoing Crimson: Wetton and Bruford with a lineage from the first band. "I felt it was credible and would have worked. David said 'We're not interested in a Crimson without you.' Presenting EG with a model for a viable, ongoing Crimson was a considerable personal freedom. It was a letting go of the responsibility which I had accepted (or abrogated, depending upon the point of view) following the departure of the original members."

In September, to the disbelief of fans, the music papers reported that Crimson had, in Fripp's words, "ceased to exist" just before the release of *Red*.

Wetton felt that the break was premature but says the possibility of carrying on with McDonald as Fripp's replacement was never discussed. "It's no secret that I wanted to be in the band for 20 years. If Robert was indeed opting out rather than breaking up the band, that option might have been considered. Robert was holding all the strings and it felt like being fired and I think Bill felt the same. McDonald, Wetton and Bruford might have been a great band had the idea been floated."

Wetton's comments about the potential of the untried line-up clearly exasperated Fripp, who asked: "Then why didn't they take the initiative?"

He also remembers an earlier conversation with Wetton which may have played a part in his decision. "While sunbathing on the roof of the Holiday Inn, Houston, Texas, just before the beginning of the final US tour in 1974, John and myself had a discussion on the future of the band. During that discussion I voiced my difficulties working with Bill. John told me that he planned to give the band another year to see where it went."

"The implication of this, to me at the time, was that John was ambitious and, if Crimson didn't get bigger, he would consider moving on. This was part of the overall equation which was in my thinking during the 'ceasing to exist' period."

Still, the bass player had been working with Palmer-James on material he considered worthy of consideration for the next step. The demos of these songs surfaced in 1998 on the duo's *Monkey Business* CD. *Magazines* and *The Good Ship Enterprise* clearly show the direction in which Wetton was interested. "*Enterprise* would have been for me on the next album after *Red*. I recorded it with Bill a couple of years after and I think it would have been great – pure Crimson. I wasn't thinking about doing a solo album or anything. I was always thinking about Crimson and what I'd present at the next batch of rehearsals."

"With *Enterprise*, the lyric already existed and I wrote the music to fit. I think it's a great lyric, the atmosphere being of a guy sitting in a lifeboat whilst everyone else is dead and he's floating away from a sinking ship. That track was right up Crimson's alley because at that time of *Red* we'd discovered an energy or focus or direction and I was completely in tune with that. I think if we'd done those tracks they would have worked really well in Crimson."

Wetton contended that Fripp was frightened of success and the subsequent loss of control that this might entail – a fact Fripp has acknowledged, arguing that his experience has taught him that nothing comes without a price.

Though he felt the break-up as acutely as anyone else, Bruford is philosophical. "My memory of the split is that I was pissed off as I felt we'd just got started. I don't know where we would have gone next. Robert probably did the right thing in retrospect. Splitting the band up was probably the right thing to do although not for quite so long – seven years? You know, you can get old waiting for King Crimson to come along."

Fripp outlined the various dynamics and aspirations at play in the group: "Conventionally in Crimson, the players are prepared to put their riffs and licks on hold for a year, while a new vocabulary and style is discovered. After a year, it's back to the old habits: the concern with working beyond the conventional and/or established falls away. The greater the success, the greater the pressure to repeat yourself. Not many performers are prepared to go against this pressure, internally and externally."

"The music, style and character of ELP – did this in any way reflect what Greg liked and wanted to achieve? How might this have shaped King Crimson had he stayed? Uriah Heep, UK and Asia – did this in any way reflect what John wanted to achieve? How might this have impacted on KC had he stayed? Greg and John look back after seven years of major commercial success and see one or two years in Crimson as their finest hour. Yet all their instincts, taste and drive went into creating constructs and music which they, as older men, consider inferior to Crimson."

"Imagine how difficult it was for a character within Crimson, with their sense of right direction for Crimson, to have to counterbalance and offset these natural (ELP and Asia) inclinations. Imagine how 'moody' the guitarist might have seemed when faced with little or no possibility of discussing this with the characters involved, characters who may well have been as difficult in their ways as the guitarist was in his.

But the guitarist wasn't fuelled by drugs, and his personal ambition was perhaps less subject to the temptation of acclaim; and more subject to a responsibility towards the Crimson project."

Red was released in October to mixed reviews, with *Sounds*' Steve Peacock ludicrously suggesting the abdication of King Crimson was a marketing ploy designed to boost record sales.

The following year, as Fripp prepared for Sherborne, with Wetton on the road with Roxy Music and Bruford touring and recording with folk legend Roy Harper, EG sounded out Wetton about working with Fripp on a live album. "David (Enthoven) said we'd have to do something about a live album from the last tour. So I said I don't have a problem with that, just tell what time the studio is booked and I'll turn up."

Less than a week of studio time was booked at Olympic. Wetton and Fripp worked from 2.00 pm to 8.00 pm each day. After a day listening to tapes, the musicians settled on the gig at the Casino, Asbury Park, on 28 June 1974, for the bulk of the album with the gig at Providence two days later providing *21st Century Schizoid Man.*

Roxy Music's Eddie Jobson was drafted in for "repair work" on the electric piano and violin parts. The session was completed in a couple of hours and Wetton recalled Fripp and the violinist getting off to a bad start. "Robert made the mistake of saying something like, 'So, young Edward, you've come to give us a hand,' to which a none-too-pleased Eddie replied 'My name isn't Edward – it's Edwin'."

USA, the second live King Crimson album, was released in April 1975. The cover – based on an idea by John Wetton – featured an eerie visual echo of the Statue of Liberty, the burning torch replaced by a piece of metal with the crudely punched legend *King Crimson USA*. The strikingly simple image also contained an Arthurian suggestion of the lady of the lake, holding the metal aloft. The striking photo of an outstretched hand on the back cover came about while on tour in the States.

The band received an invitation from Lamar University in Beaumont, Texas, to submit their hands and faces to an experimental photographic technique developed in the Soviet Union by Semyon and Valentina Kirlian in 1949. Kirlian photography purportedly reveals the aura or field of energy surrounding all living material. The glowing hand seems emblematic of the unseen energies and musical ESP of which the band was capable. Some consideration was given to using all the Kirlian portraits, but in the end only Wetton's hand was used.

But critics weren't impressed. The main gripe was that the album consisted of old material, save for the electrifying *Asbury Park*, an improvisation of such power it became a lifelong favourite of Fripp, Wetton and Bruford. Undoubtedly the high point of the album, its energy belies the fact that the band was playing on a cold, rain-sodden evening to a half-empty house.

Easy Money contains a sublimely meditative guitar solo, which Fripp contends was indicative of his growing sense of dislocation from the band and its career. "The guitarist unexpectedly launches sideways from the onward-going rock motion into a place of reflection and deep longing, it seemed to me. What was this young player trying to access/express? At the time the guitarist was approaching a radical shift in his life. Everything seemed to be going the way that made for happiness in managers, agents, record companies, road and tour managers, and the majority of young players in rock: success. For that particular young guitarist and aspirant musician that somehow missed the point. How could it? But how could it not? When music reached out and embraced the 20-year-old, returning from gigging in the Majestic Dance Orchestra, Bournemouth, and changed the course and direction of his life, it was clear music had a capacity and power that the size of record sales, cheering audiences and the smiles of management failed to reflect."

In 1975 Fripp also found the time to compile the double album *The Young Persons' Guide To King Crimson*, offering a personal overview of Crim history. It was released in 1976 in an impressive gatefold sleeve featuring the work of Scottish artist Fergus Hall with a deluxe booklet containing the cut and thrust of critical reaction to Crimson's career. Somewhat perversely, *21st Century Schizoid Man* – the band's best-known tune – was omitted, replaced in the running order by *Red*. For the collector, however, the rarities – such as 1970's *Groon* from the B-side of the *Cat Food* single and a demo version of *I Talk To The Wind* featuring Judy Dyble – made it an essential purchase. The appearance of *I Talk To The Wind* was a surprise to Peter Giles, who kept a close watch on the demos he had recorded at Brondesbury Road in 1968. "He didn't ask whether it could be used or not, though I can't imagine why not. When I confronted him about this and asked why, he just apologised sincerely but never gave a reason why he did it or even where he got the recording from."

Fripp says: "The recording was in my personal tape collection at home. I had/have several songs from GG&F and the tape of the *Colour Me Pop* show which stayed with me after the break-up of GG&F. And I loved the performance."

Looking back on this period, Fripp could sense a tide of change which would transform more than just his own career. He says: "Crimson was the only band to end at the right time. As with any English band which increasingly looks to America, it forfeits the loyalty of much of its Anglo fan base. Personally, I gave up on England in 1973. The next generation of English audiences were already looking for performers that reflected their own interests, were closer to home, who they could identify with. What connection would a young person feel to rock stars on large stages in expensive and silly clothes, who clearly enjoyed extravagance, high living and self-regard?"

"John and Bill were not inclined to the spirit of punk/new wave. I was: I had no difficulty working with Eno or Blondie, for example. An ongoing Crimson, quite apart from any other considerations, would have become increasingly out of step with developing musical currents. John worked with Ferry and Roxy, but musically that wasn't what I'd call spiky. And John didn't 'get' *No Pussyfooting*, even in 1975 when I played it to him."

The UK's press consensus was that, despite flashes of brilliance, the band never quite lived up to its potential. Five years which had produced some of rock's most ambitious and powerful moments seemed destined to figure as little more than a footnote.

LEVEL 4: *It remains consistent*

It's 2014 and King Crimson are busy rehearsing for their first American tour since 2008. Tony Levin is getting to grips with one of his favourite songs, Starless. *When Crimson hit the stage it will be exactly 40 years since that particular tune was last heard at a King Crimson concert. His enormous love and respect comes through loud and clear as he talks about what makes the piece so special for him. "John Wetton's bass part, especially when it breaks down to the quirky sparse bass part in the middle – it's not just classic, it's so him that I just kind of smile when I play it. I'm a visitor. I can't change a note of that and I can't do it the way he did it just 'cos I'm technically not able to do it. It just makes me smile. We're talking about visiting the most classic of the most classic great prog bass parts and there I am doing it and hopefully people won't be walking out* (laughs). *I only played that piece once before this band and that was when I was guesting with Eddie Jobson's UKZ when they did a short tour of Holland. I was holding the Stick and I didn't particularly play in that part. What I learned then about John – this is kind of bass stuff that only bass players care about – but there's a very particular sound that he has on those old records and it's most obvious on that section because he starts playing quietly with a nice sound and then very gradually it becomes more growly and more powerful. Most of us cannot do that on our basses. I don't know if it's our basses or our fingers. I can play a whole bunch with different amounts of strength on my bass but it pretty much sounds either soft or big or loud. There's no gradation between. So I always thought John was using some amazing pedal or the bass he had. That's not true at all. I learned when I played live with him that he sounded exactly the same playing a different bass and playing with a pick gaffa-taped to his finger instead of playing with his fingers. It doesn't matter. That sound actually comes from John Wetton and to me that's extraordinary. So what fun for me to be playing it even though I know that nothing I can do with my fingers and my basses will do it the way he did it. It's not about what I'm doing it's a tribute to what he did."*

I

Between the abdication of King Crimson in 1974 and its restoration in 1981, huge changes took place. At the time of his departure, Fripp had talked about the social, economic and ecological changes he believed were about to engulf the world. While his predictions of global catastrophe were wide of the mark, at the micro level Fripp was bang on the button as punk caused convulsions through the body of rock music.

Although, in reality, punk did little to sweep away the musical orthodoxy, it *did* prompt the deflection of the UK rock papers' support away from Pink Floyd, ELP and the like towards a movement that was deemed more authentic and connected to people at an ordinary level. The rough, lo-fi and thus accessible immediacy of punk stood in sharp contrast to the increasingly distended, portentous and remote projects of the big groups. Punk looked cool and subversive and certainly made for better copy. What the music lacked in sophistication, it more than made up for in vigour. Bands such as Camel, Wishbone Ash, Jethro Tull et al. were all marginalised by the three-chord rush and anti-Establishment sneer of The Undertones, Sex Pistols and a host of bands with appropriately brief and meteoric careers to match.

But the tired trope of "Punk Killed Prog" was simply a media invention. Away from the hype, those at the top of the pile continued and simply carried on grazing the savannahs of the stadium circuit in America. Mostly, such groups went on to enjoy even greater commercial success, largely oblivious of, or condescending towards, the new music. The groups who suffered the most were those playing the college and polytechnic circuit. Players like National Health's Dave Stewart recalls that a significant part of any band's income depended on being booked by social secretaries. Lots of bands at that niche level went to the wall.

Although London still regarded itself as the centre of musical cool, New York was brimming with intriguing blends of avant-pop and cross-cultural experimentation among playwrights, composers and conceptual artists. Across town, in venues like Hilly Kristal's CBGB in the Bowery, the spread of the New Wave was unstoppable. The cute reductionism of The Ramones, Television's clipped charm and Talking Heads' quirky art-school angularity produced a thrilling tidal wave which swept across the Atlantic.

Fripp's first tentative steps out of musical retirement were with Peter Gabriel. Like Fripp, the singer had "stepped right out of the machinery" as he put it in his song *Solsbury Hill*, despite being on the verge of enormous commercial success. Fripp played on the demos and recording sessions for Gabriel's first solo album and was persuaded to join the subsequent tour band (which also included Tony Levin), albeit often performing unseen.

During the Gabriel period, Fripp was approached about two other high-profile musical projects. The most intriguing was when EG founder David Enthoven got in touch with a view to putting a band back together. This led the guitarist to contact Bill Bruford and John Wetton and for a while it looked as though the *Red* version of Crimson might return. But Fripp sensed that Wetton's preferred musical direction was not for him and called Enthoven to turn down the offer from his room at the impressive Chateau Frontenac in Quebec City while on tour with Gabriel in 1977. Undeterred, Wetton and Bruford went on to form UK with Eddie Jobson on violin and keyboards and Allan Holdsworth on guitar. The year before, the guitarist turned down an approach from manager Tony Smith to join Genesis.

Fripp, in the meantime, ploughed along on tour with Gabriel performing pseudonymously as Dusty Rhodes and receiving a gentle re-introduction into the music industry. Even before the tour, Fripp had decided to immerse himself completely in the high-speed cultural milieu of America by moving to New York. From his apartment near the East River he was able to take advantage of a more hospitable critical climate. Ironically, since the band and its attendant expenses had stopped, Crimson's albums continued to sell and, for the first time, turned a modest profit.

In the city that never sleeps, a re-emergent and re-energised Fripp was the very personification of the small, independent, mobile and intelligent unit he had talked about back in 1974. In 1977, Fripp moved easily between dates with Blondie, sessions in Berlin for David Bowie's *Heroes*, producing Peter Gabriel and white soul singer Daryl Hall and unveiling Frippertronics to the world. Of his time in New York, Fripp told *New Hi-Fi Sound*'s Mark Prendergast: "In America, there was no star trip. People would come up to you on the street and ask you if you were working and, if not, invite you to play. It was magic. I had a flat on the Bowery; I'd walk out and Richard Lloyd of Television would generally be staggering by whatever time it was. There was this incredible openness. The Johnny Blitz benefit at CBGB's was a wonderful event. Chris Stein, you know – 'We're doing a benefit for Johnny Blitz; got involved in a knife fight; needs some lawyers' fee; do you want to play with us?' It was as easy as that. It was a remarkable flowering." Without doubt, this was an intensely creative and liberating time for the guitarist who was now finding acceptance as a musical wild card guaranteed to bring a burning spray of unpredictability to any album or gig.

In July 1977, Emerson, Lake And Palmer, complete with a full orchestra, pulled into town for three sell-out nights at Madison Square Garden. Although ELP were the complete antithesis, both musically and ideologically, to Fripp's new scene, the guitarist went to see the band and was able to get backstage before the band went on. Lake recalled seeing his former bandmate for the first time since leaving Crimson in 1970 as he made his way to the arena. "And as I'm walking past this barrier I see Robert and I was shocked. So I asked him what he was doing there and said to the roadie, 'Get him out of the crowd and get him back into the dressing room and look after him.' So up we go on the stage and we play the show."

As Lake remembered, after the show the pair agreed to go out to eat. "So we went off in the limo and we're going down the road and I said to him, 'You know, Robert, one day we ought to get our guitars out and play together again. It's been so long since we did that.' And he said, 'I don't think so.' So I said to the driver, 'Just pull over on the left here,' opened the fucking door and told him to leg it. I said 'Out you go' and I dropped him off. I thought why was he like that? It must have been jealousy. There was ELP selling out three nights at Madison Square Garden and you couldn't get arrested in King Crimson at that time."

"Not quite accurate," retorts Fripp. "I went to all three of the MSG shows. I believe I went backstage every evening. After the final show there was a visit to a restaurant for the band and entourage, to which I was invited. Greg was vibrating with various suits and, at the end of the evening, sat me down to talk with him. Greg presented, in strong terms, the idea of a KC69 reformation."

Leaving the restaurant in the limousine with Fripp sitting next to the driver and Lake in the back, the pair journeyed to Fripp's home. Fripp recalls the conversation as the car stopped to let him out. Lake asked Fripp what he thought about the proposal of a KC69 reunion. Fripp avoided a direct answer by asking Lake to give him a call. "So that's it? You want me to call you?" asked Lake. Fripp replied: "You already know my answer." A perplexed Lake asked "You mean no?", to which Fripp replied: "That's right." Lake's limo drove off into the night. It would be several years before the pair met again.

In 1977, Fripp produced Daryl Hall's first solo album, *Sacred Songs*, although staid company executives at RCA feared the combination of Hall's white soul voice and Frippertronics would be disastrous for the singer's career. So the album remained in the vaults, not seeing the light of day for more than two-and-a-half years. By now the former cautious pace was replaced by an almost indecent haste as Fripp was seen in the company of the great, the good and the happening. Ever keen on realising methodologies (and perhaps mythologies), Fripp devised a manifesto of intention which he launched in September 1978.

Entitled *The Drive To 1981*, this detailed schemata was Fripp's means of imposing his will on the chaotic and arbitrary environment in which he operated. For him there seemed to be as much a moral as a practical imperative: "A campaign on three levels; first in the marketplace but not governed by the values of the marketplace; second, as a means of examining and presenting a number of ideas which are close to my heart; third, as a personal discipline."

As part of an increasingly accelerating programme of work, Fripp worked as producer of Peter Gabriel's second album. This was conceived as the second part of an "MOR trilogy" – the first instalment being Hall's album – and was released in June

1978. In the January of that year, Fripp had started work on the third part: his first solo album, *Exposure*. Over the period of a year, the album was constructed with the help of Gabriel, Levin, Eno, Phil Collins and XTC organist Barry Andrews.

The recording of *Exposure* saw Fripp sifting through ideas and through a number of rehearsals with musical colleagues. In December 1977, he reunited with John Wetton, the first time they'd worked together since compiling *USA* in 1975. John was more than happy to receive the call. "It was great to hear from him. We'd never fallen out or anything with Robert so it was really easy to do some sessions with him. I also remember being in New York having a drink with Brian Eno in the bar at The Drake in Midtown Manhattan around that time."

Also at those recordings was Phil Collins. The Genesis drummer, now turned lead vocalist, was also eager to take part. A huge fan of *Larks' Tongues In Aspic*, Collins had impeccable jazz-rock credentials, having recently released albums with Brand X. "Phil Collins was the best drummer I've ever worked with," said Wetton. "He's got everything. He's not trying to prove a point and his sense of time is perfect. You feel good when you play with him. At that time we were still mates. I looked at Genesis when Peter Gabriel left and I thought they'd never get through that one but they didn't drop a stitch, did they?"

Wetton and Collins can be heard in the rehearsal tapes at work on a gnarly riff that had the kind of glowering presence Fripp invoked on *Red* three years earlier. Early run-throughs for *Disengage* differed significantly from the finished version, incorporating elements of *Häaden Two*. Especially interesting are sections that would form part of *Neurotica* by the 1980s version of King Crimson.

The scraps that emerged from the second day included a reflective chord sequence that sounds like something else from the '80s quartet, with Collins' work recalling his contributions to *Energy Fools The Magician* from Eno's *Before And After Science* and a quirky blues-bent-out-of-shape riff, a forerunner of the odd-pop vibe The League Of Gentlemen would be playing a couple of years later. We hear Collins ask for "a bit more guitar!" as he prepares for another take of *Disengage*. The players are still getting to grips with the barbed riff as John Wetton's "I can't remember the beginning" comment indicates. "No worries," says Fripp as he shows his old bandmate the introduction before counting everyone in. Had 1974's incarnation of Crimson continued, this may not have been a million miles away from how they might have sounded.

With four different takes of the piece, we hear the anatomy of *Disengage* as it begins to breathe and stretch. Not all of the music is quite under their fingertips yet.

The two hours or so of the sessions made available as downloads on the DGM website indicate just how compelling and powerful this trio was. It doesn't take much imagination to hear them as one of the great "lost" opportunities of the late '70s. The interplay on the prosaically named *Groove* borders on breathtaking. Speaking to *Prog* magazine's Dave Everley, Collins looked back: "That was an interesting experience. Robert doesn't work like anyone else. He's very professorial and very focused – there's no messing around. That's not to say he's not a warm person, because he is, but he knows what he wants from himself, and from you." Collins included *North Star* on his four-disc retrospective, *Plays Well With Others*, released in 2018. He chose it because: "I think it's one of my favourite pieces of music that I've ever played on."

When Collins moved on, Wetton and Fripp were joined a fortnight later by Michael Walden. Fripp had first met the drummer at the Cape Cod Coliseum when Crimson supported the new line-up of The Mahavishnu Orchestra in 1974. "Michael was a sweetheart," says Wetton. "He had loads of energy. He was a tiny man but he was like a volcano when he played. Lots of fun and very easy to work with." This session shows the players responding and shaping their approaches in mid-flight as well as rocking out together on more than one lengthy improvisation. Taken together they are a tour de force, a riotous journey into turbulent areas that include flat-out rock, explosive jazz and funk-orientated blows, sometimes featuring the high-speed chordal soloing that Fripp first served up on *Sailor's Tale*. There are so many miraculous moments tucked away in these tracks.

Afterwards, Fripp continued to refine material with Tony Levin and drummer Jerry Marotta, familiar from their work with Peter Gabriel. On the sessions made available to download more than 35 years later, there's an easy fluency between the players. Two tracks *Chicagoish I* and *Chicagoish II* – have the novelty of Fripp playing a surprisingly bluesy lick, ultimately abandoned. Also intriguing is the presence of three versions of another softer piece. With the provisional title *Ballad* – if you close your eyes it could be Brondesbury Road in the late '60s or even an outtake from the *Poseidon* album. With only a tiny fraction of these sessions making it to *Exposure*, Fripp could easily have topped and tailed them into a significant release that would have stood on its own merits. Talking to *Zig Zag*'s Kris Needs in 1979, Fripp responded to Needs' point that the album was not "Fripp and Heavy Friends" but rather a natural blending: "I think that the music of the '80s is the music of collaboration. Increasing mobility between musicians is the key to the new music – whatever it is that anyone is trying to grasp in the sense of 'The New Music'. It's inter-reacting with other people to find different chemistries, different whatever, but with this, one can occasionally run into problems with somewhat older-fashioned record companies or management companies or whatever, ones that tend rather to be the old world than the new."

The problems Fripp alluded to included Daryl Hall's contributions to *Exposure* being limited by Hall's management and record company. "It's something like wanting to get married to someone you love and the church won't do it. Having put out a lot of criticism of the different parties that surround Daryl, I think the point has been made, but with a view to contributing positively to the situation, as opposed to continuing to put backs up, I'm simply saying how much I enjoyed working with Daryl, what a successful, personal and professional relationship it was, and hoping that in the future those that own him might release him to do some things other than what they consider appropriate for their particular format thinking."

Fripp's placatory comments also refer to the *Sacred Songs* album he produced and played on. Recorded in 1977, its release was delayed until 1980 with some in Hall's corner fearing that working with Fripp on a more exploratory record would have an adverse effect upon Hall's mainstream success with John Oates.

Talking to Pitchfork in 2007, Hall reflected on his work with Fripp. "I met Robert through a friend in about 1974, and we became friends right away. We have a lot of the same interests, and we just got along. I was first starting to spend a lot of time in England then, so I would stay at his house, and he used to stay at my house, and all that. We were really good friends. And then he went away to Gurdjieff Camp, and I was the only person in the outside world he was communicating with. Yeah, he decided he was going to follow the teachings of Gurdjieff, which is basically like the boot camp of the mind. And so I was sort of his touch with some form of reality. And after he came through that period, he wanted to re-enter the music world, because he had stepped away. And so he and I got together, and we said, let's do some projects … I think we made some really interesting music. I think taking somebody who comes from my background, and taking somebody who comes from his musical background, and putting them together, is a very interesting idea … to try and take two soulful sounds from two different cultures, and put them together, and form a third kind of music. And that was the idea. Simple as that. I mean, there was no – well, I won't say there was no conceptual thought, because there was a lot of conceptual thought. But there was no thought beyond that. We were just going to do what came natural to us. Either I would write the words with Robert or he had his girlfriend at the time who was writing some lyrics, and we would just come up with some lyrics, he would put a track together, and I would just sing. Everything was first takes. Everything was spontaneous. And that's how we dealt with it."

Having been blocked from using Hall as much as he wanted on *Exposure*, Fripp brought in Peter Hammill to sing the songs. The pair knew each other well with Fripp having made telling guest appearances on Van Der Graaf Generator's albums *H To He Who Am The Only One* and *Pawn Hearts* in 1970 and 1971, as well as Hammill's first solo album, *Fool's Mate*, in 1971. "Peter Hammill did very well," said Fripp to Zig Zag. "This thing about collaboration without pre-conceptions: Peter is a remarkable singer, but as in all these situations there's a style of English artist where they're unproducable. They determine their own situation, nothing can change it. Bowie, Eno, Fripp, Gabriel, Ferry, Hammill – these are the names that spring to mind. No-one could normally come along and put Peter Hammill in a context where he would have to work outside his own way of operating, and since from the conceptual point of view my way of operating is not very far removed from his, he could immediately respond to it. He'd come in, well-dressed, take off his nice smart trousers, put on this grubby, smelly, flannel dressing-gown and a hefty brandy which he'd brought in himself, and go in. Here's the microphone, here's the words, go 'n' sing. And he did. All he had were the words."

It wasn't until the 2-CD re-issue of *Exposure* in 2006 that Hall's full contributions were finally heard. Taking Fripp two years from writing to recording, *Exposure* was an intense journey, opening up his psyche for scrutiny. It was as smart as might be expected but there were also moments of vulnerability in the music, and in the lyrics and, briefly, the voice of Fripp's then-girlfriend Joanna Walton, who was killed in the bombing of Pam Am Flight 103 over Lockerbie, Scotland, in 1988.

The record's very power and eclecticism kept it fresh and avoided prog-rock pigeonholing. "I was afraid, in a way, the album would be an irrelevancy, that it would be an anachronism or whatever, but all I could do was simply to make it and try and be sensitive to how the album was shaping itself, almost as an entity on its own. I would interreact with that, try and be sensitive to how it was going. Eventually, this is the album and, although I don't think there's anything new about it, in other words, there's no area of music which is wholly novel, it's nevertheless somehow very modern, do you know what I mean?" Fripp told Kris Needs.

When the album was released in April 1979, Fripp's transformation from prog-rock eccentric to New Wave thinker was confirmed by reviewer Nick Kent, who declared: "Ultimately the album proves that Fripp can effectively straddle the abyss that seems to forever separate the super-musician bluffing out over-agitated fusions and the barely competent dilettante full of ideas that his or her lack of training invariably render futile. An example to us all, in fact, it's the likes of Fripp and Tom Verlaine who are going to make truly new music. Because they've appreciated their art's traditions, but are also capable of perceiving and developing their own visions."

The Wire featured *Exposure* 1998 as one of the 100 Records That Set The World On Fire. "Most of Fripp's recorded output showcases his talent as a guitarist, but only *Exposure* offers any serious insight into the man himself. Returning to music after a four-year break studying with Gurdjieff disciple J.G. Bennett, Fripp's psyche had veered from frustrated hostility to enigmatic good humour, and his first solo album captures every aspect of a many-sided personality. Angelic electric guitar drone in the form of Frippertronics serves to frame a sparse, moving re-working of Peter Gabriel's *Here Comes The Flood*. Tape recordings of Fripp's argumentative New York neighbours jostle for space with cryptic spoken comments from Brian Eno. Terre Roche and Daryl Hall sing gorgeous, gentle ballads over mildly unreliable rhythms, but the highlights of *Exposure* see guest vocalist Peter Hammill chewing glass, barking with grisly charisma over cracking rock riffs. There's no stylistic consistency, and no need. Fripp is resplendent in divergence. It's the *Sergeant Pepper* of avant punk."

II

In 1980, Fripp released a further album, *Under Heavy Manners/God Save The Queen*. One side consisted of two lengthy tracks featuring the dance groove-based funk which Fripp called Discotronics. Along for the ride on it were Talking Heads' David Byrne, ex-Sharks and Heads' sideman Busta Cherry Jones on bass and Paul Duskin on drums. The other side was a partial documentation of his Frippertronics gigs in record stores, restaurants, cafés and other unusual venues, a fuller account of which was found on *Let The Power Fall*, released a year later.

Melody Maker's Allan Jones lauded the Frippertronics pieces but somewhat prophetically concluded: "It's to *Under Heavy Manners* that one eventually looks for a key to Fripp's musical future. He, as much as anyone, needs someone to force an entry into areas he's not fully able to unlock himself. *Under Heavy Manners* suggests he's looking in the right directions."

But EG had something different in mind and, in early 1980, called Fripp in for a meeting at which he was told he should do what he "did best" – that is, play in a band. There was little doubt in Fripp's mind that the band his management had in mind was King Crimson.

The guitarist remained doubtful. "In my own personal process, this was firstly too soon for me to form a band. Secondly, were I to accept their encouragement (which I did) the kind of band I was interested in bore no relationship to anything EG could conceive." Paddy Spinks, employed at the time by EG as a tour manager for various acts, recalls the overly optimistic view which Alder and Fenwick had in respect of the guitarist.

"Ultimately, I think EG were realistic about the kind of thing they wanted Robert to do but there was always the hope that one day Fripp would go 'OK let's do it' and make something that was out-and-out commercial. There was always hope but it was unrealistic hope. The potential was there though to rekindle the Crimson fanbase and to build on it."

Described by Fripp as a "second wave dance band with the emphasis on spirit rather than competence", The League Of Gentlemen formed in March 1980 and for seven months toured the clubs and colleges of Europe and the States. Recognising this as a partial return to his musical roots, Fripp recruited keyboard player Barry Andrews (recently departed from XTC), who had played on *Exposure*, bassist Sarah Lee and drummer Johnny Toobad, both of whom had been playing in a punk group called Baby And The Black Spots.

In the middle of May 1980, this was a typical scenario played out behind stage at The League Of Gentlemen gigs: Robert Fripp, Barry Andrews, Sara Lee and Johnny

Toobad have finished their set. The band were playing small clubs, with even smaller dressing rooms, the tiny confines crowded with well-wishers, people in search of a good time and, with grim inevitability, men cornering Fripp to engage him in a fervent discussion of philosophical issues. Barry Andrews: "Robert's connection with Crimson conjured up a lot of boring fuckers in the dressing room, all very earnest, geeky blokes. It even got to Robert, who was single at the time and up for some action, that, instead of basking in the oestro-waves of well-deserved post-show girly adulation, he was being cornered by yet another sweaty bloke asking for some spiritual or musical guidance. Johnny said that if Fripp wanted to get rid of these Seekers-After-Knowledge he could try pretending to sell them heroin. Gamely, Robert did exactly that. His performance as a drug dealer was less than convincing, 'Would you like to buy some smack? It's really good stuff' – but it certainly did the trick."

When considering the reformation of King Crimson in 1981, the importance of The League is often overlooked. It's not hard to understand why. Their short, four-to-the-floor instrumental tracks, with titles like *Inductive Resonance*, *Cognitive Dissonance*, *Dislocated*, *Thrang Thrang Gozinbulx* and *Ooh! Mr Fripp*, contained skewed and quirky melodies delivered with punkish pace. In their live sets, with about an hour's worth of material, those strange riffs were combined with Fripp's extraordinary guitar work to form a pile-driving avant-pop for those who liked their dance music dissonant. With "an emphasis on spirit rather than competence", as Fripp succinctly put it, The League Of Gentlemen totted up 77 shows. They seemed as far removed from the virtuosic rumination of Crimson as possible. Their sole posthumously released eponymous studio album didn't adequately convey their dance-orientated velocity. Yet The League was the testing ground for much of the musical vocabulary Fripp would refine on 1981's *Discipline*.

Fripp recruited Andrews after seeing him at XTC's first gig in the USA at New York's Beacon Theatre, where they supported Talking Heads. "He came backstage and asked if I'd play on his album, *Exposure*," says Andrews. That said, the organist doesn't recall much about the experience. "I mainly remember Peter Hammill being next to overdub after me, necking a half a bottle of brandy before going in the vocal booth in order to 'silence the conscious/critical part of my mind' or words to that effect. I thought that sounded like a rationale that might be useful to me in the future."

The next the organist heard from Fripp, now living once again in London, was when the guitarist pushed an invitation to form a band under the door of what Andrews describes as a "squalid squat" in King's Cross. "I must say I rather liked the idea of him doing that in his nice suit," he says. Andrews remembers a less-than-promising first rehearsal with Fripp, Lee and Toobad. In the pub afterwards, he recalls Fripp being in sanguine mood. "Robert said that he wanted to revolutionise rock'n'roll with the people around this table. I wasn't too sure if this was going to be possible, given what I'd just heard, but, hey, it meant going to stay in a guesthouse in Dorset and they were about to throw us out of the squat."

With his frenetic keyboard as the amiable glue between the rhythm section and Fripp, Andrews had no real desire to add his own music to the mix: "I had not long left XTC because my writing contribution had been rejected and I had decided that I would not give my creative heart again so easily." Instead, he was content to let the guitarist dictate the direction of the music – although that process was not always easy. "I think the fatal flaw in The League Of Gentlemen was that it was clearly put together around Robert's idea and musical proclivities, and me and The Toobads, as they were known, were cast as though in Robert's movie: 'He was a '70s guitar hero – they were a bunch of North London chancers. Now they have to go on the road …' We were encouraged to pretend it was a real band. I didn't really see the point of that. Robert was the guitar star – we were his backing band. What was the problem?"

If there was a problem, it was that Fripp was actively considering a return to a different level of music. In Fripp's model there were three categories – or "divisions" – of making music. His Frippertronics basked in the third division, representing research and development, he said – "interesting ideas and civilised lifestyle, but you won't earn a living. Second division will earn you a living if you graft and you can get professionally respectable, but you won't change the world."

The League hovered precariously between the two, but several pieces in their repertoire bristled with the sizzling lines of cyclical guitar music Fripp was clearly itching to take further in the first division.

Within the heat of a gig it was common for them to hurtle from dissonant and explosive to simplistic and ethereal in seconds. Though sometimes lacking subtlety, the conversion and exchange of different time signatures, with the melodic heavy lifting alternating between the front and back lines, was crucial to the development of Fripp's next step. It was not uncommon for Andrews's Crumar organ to need a strategically-placed screwdriver sticking in it to keep it operating. Sometimes it would break down entirely, an experience Andrews remembers all too well. "Fuck yeah, horrible business. The thing wasn't really man enough for the job having been 'round the block far too many times with XTC. A note, always a high piercing one, would stick and then the roadies would have to come on and hand me tools while I fixed it. It took ages and was best seen as performance art. To be honest, I quite liked it because it wound Robert up."

Released in 1981, the band's album featured Fripp using the Roland guitar synthesiser for the first time on record, foreshadowing the trumpet-like sound he would explore further with King Crimson. However, despite this additional wider palette, the record failed to capture the group's intensity. Fripp's decision to add "indiscretions" – conversational fragments – like excerpts from J.G. Bennett lectures, the pronouncements of TV pundits and a female orgasm recorded during his time in New York, layered an odd patina on to the tracks. While he had used some similar effects on *Exposure* to great effect, here such additions feel like a deliberate act to distract attention from the music. Another reason why the record didn't quite hit home could be the dissipation of the band's chemistry after Johnny Toobad was sacked towards the end of the group's UK tour in November. Toobad's reliance on heroin got in the way of his performances and he was replaced at incredibly short notice by Kevin Wilkinson. "Kevin was the drummer in my band Restaurant For Dogs, who were also the support band for LOG," says Andrews. "Johnny was having one of his periodic heroin romances and Kev rose heroically to the challenge, learning the whole set in a soundcheck."

There's nothing wrong with Wilkinson's work but the overall performances generally lack the sparkle of the gigs. Listeners would have to wait until 1996 – when Fripp and David Singleton compiled *Thrang Thrang Gozinbulx*, an exciting CD of live performances – to hear what they had missed. Easily transcending its lo-fi origins, it packed the punch its studio counterpart lacked.

On that final string of UK dates, Fripp was contemplating a return to the best musicians, better budgets and a much wider audience. When The League Of Gentlemen played their last show at the London School of Economics on 29 November, Andrews sensed the band had run its course. "I think I was feeling more like part of some kind of a Gurdjieffian social experiment gone wrong than was comfortable. And kinda patronised, if I'm honest. I recall we had got together to try and do some tunes together and bring them back to Robert – in a half-baked attempt to try and be more than lab rats and when I rang Robert to tell him, he said, 'I'm putting the band on hold.' One of his reasons was that he was sick of 'playing with people who are drunk'. That was us told. Fair enough, actually. And a bit of a relief all 'round."

The musical limitations and hapless organisation of The League also played a part in hastening Fripp's decision to return to the first division.

Andrews went on to form Shriekback, while Sara Lee became a hugely respected bassist, appearing notably with the B-52s. Toobad, whose real name was John Elichaoff, made a career as a financial advisor and in band management while Wilkinson worked at an international level with Fish, China Crisis and The Waterboys. In a bizarre coincidence, both men would take their own lives, Wilkinson in 1999 and Elichaoff in 2014.

The first division at its worst, Fripp believed, was about achieving a level of success in mass culture. At its best it allowed access to the best musicians, a nonpareil of ideas and the possibility of scaling the very summit of popular culture. There were, of course, risks. "You're on a tightrope," Fripp outlined in his diary. "Either way you have to jump and if you fall you lose your health, sanity and, occasionally, your soul. But, you just might fly away. So there's your choice."

As the LOG's van trundled its way between Manchester and Liverpool, Fripp decided to risk it. *The Drive To 1981* was now approaching the finishing straight.

III

Having made the choice to put a top-flight band together, Fripp informed EG, who sounded out Bill Bruford's availability. Given the aborted reunion of 1977, Fripp was understandably cautious. But for Bruford the approach was timely.

It was back in early 1977 that Bill Bruford finally made the telephone call to EG Management to set in motion a series of bookings that would get the start of his solo career under way. "I had been a team player all of my career up until that point," says Bruford, reflecting on his first album under his own name. "What persuaded me to take on the whole thing myself? I don't know. Probably sheer bloody arrogance." When he checked his diary and asked his management to book him into a recording studio in August, it wasn't the result of a rush of blood to the head. Rather, it was the culmination of a series of deliberate musical experiences and encounters over the previous three years.

The notion of a solo album had probably been rolling around since King Crimson came to an abrupt end in September 1974. However, the gnawing anxiety that stemmed from being cut loose stylised any immediate progress. Having had a red line scratched through several month's of prospective King Crimson tour dates, Bill Bruford had, overnight, become *very* available for work.

Stints touring with Gong and Roy Harper, as well as responding to invitations to contribute to various records, filled the diary but it wasn't until he met up with keyboard player Dave Stewart and National Health that the decision to go into the market place paid off. Although his association with Gong wasn't the easiest of fits for Bruford, it nevertheless proved fruitful by bringing him into contact with Virgin. Best known at that point for his work in Egg and Hatfield and The North, Stewart recalls Virgin co-founder Simon Draper mentioning to him that Bruford was looking for opportunities to stretch out. Stewart had co-founded National Health with fellow keyboard player Alan Gowen who, in turn, had worked with Jamie Muir a few years previously. The group played closely composed material that combined the complexities of a texturally adventurous chamber ensemble with a rock vocabulary. "We had had a lot of trouble finding people that could play this material. We'd auditioned a number of drummers – maybe as many as eight or nine – and very few of them could get anywhere near coping with the metric changes," says Stewart. When Bruford turned up to play at Gowen's flat in South London, the pair were immediately impressed. "Bill could read and he was very disciplined and he could work his way through a chart and do it without a lot of taking it home and having to think about it. After we'd played through a couple of tunes, he said, 'I think you're really good musicians' and we said, 'Well, we think you're a pretty good drummer,' and it went on from there. We invited Bill to be a member of the group and he rehearsed with us between July and December 1975."

During January and February 1976, Bill toured with National Health alongside bassist Mont Campbell, singer Amanda Parsons and guitarist Phil Miller as well as Gowen and Stewart. Fans of Bruford's earlier work were able to experience a frisson of excitement upon hearing the trashy decay of the crash cymbal rescued from the rubbish bin at Olympic Studios and utilised to great effect on King Crimson's '70s swansong *Red*. "Musically he was a really good fit, very solid, which we liked. He didn't drift off the tempo," recalls Stewart. In an enthusiastic review of the band at the LSE in February, the *NME* perceptively noted: "Modern rock music is progressing and National Health represent the state of the art." Stewart remembers that although everyone was extremely happy working together, it was understood that Bill wanted to do his own thing. "He played us a cassette of this bass player he'd found in New York, Jeff Berlin, who was astonishing."

Though by now fully engaged in writing material that would form part of *Feels Good To Me*, the ever-energetic Bruford had also been spending time playing percussion alongside Genesis drummer Phil Collins in jazz-rock outfit Brand X. Collins, a confirmed fan of Bruford, was delighted to be working with Bill. When Collins expressed his frustration at not being able to find a suitable replacement drummer for Genesis as he took over lead vocals after Peter Gabriel's departure, Bruford put himself forward. Collins enthusiastically agreed. From March to July 1976, Bruford played over 60 gigs with Genesis. Having little empathy with the music, he bristled at the demand that he replicate precisely the rhythmic cues built into the material. "I behaved rather badly," he freely confesses, commenting that his time in Genesis had taught him a valuable lesson "that the musician exists to serve the music rather than the music existing to serve the musician … it took me a while to understand that."

Rejoining National Health for another bout of touring later in the year, Bruford seemed equally comfortable playing to a small crowd in a provincial polytechnic as he was in front of hundreds of thousands of Genesis fans. "Bill was pretty down to earth," observes bassist Neil Murray. "Just the fact that he was happy to work with a band with zero money like National Health shows he was really just doing it for the music. It showed that he wasn't desperate to be in some high-profile, world-touring situation, at least not at that time."

Prior to the National Health tour, however, Bruford took part in September rehearsals with John Wetton and Rick Wakeman. Had the planned group, reportedly to be called Bulldog, got off the starting blocks it would have undoubtedly been a very high-profile group indeed. But the plan was scuppered by Wakeman's record company A&M, who refused to allow their artist to potentially damage his very bankable career. In some circles this configuration is still lamented as one of progressive rock's great "what if" moments. However, had it gone ahead, it's likely it would have delayed Bruford's solo album still further. Instead its cancellation spurred him on.

Formally quitting National Health in December 1976, the New Year began with Bill ensconced in the converted garage of his house that acted as his music room working on a set of lines and melodic ideas that would, over the next few months, come into sharp focus. "I wanted to play the drums in a certain way and if you want to hear them played in a certain way you've got to write the song. You've got to control the audio environment in which your drums are going to be heard and, once you're doing that, by definition, ipso facto, you're into a solo career."

But yet again that solo career would have to wait. No sooner had he recorded *Feels Good To Me* than he was joining forces with Wetton and Eddie Jobson, who were now forming a band called UK with guitarist Allan Holdsworth after Fripp declined the offer to play with them. "For me there are musical problems and they need musical solutions of one sort or another. Sometimes you have more control or less control. In my own band, of course, I have a huge amount of control to affect the audio situation, perhaps with King Crimson or UK a bit less, but it doesn't bother me much. I was on a path to make albums from the drum seat and lead a band," he acknowledges. "However you can't predict everything and UK came along and the size and weight of that pushed me to one side as it were and happily so. I was thrilled to be in UK, especially with Allan. I was in heaven for a while and happy to take a break from my own thing."

Bruford brought in Holdsworth as a means of leavening the rich progressive rock mixture with a flash of jazzy spice. Holdsworth initially viewed UK as promising. But, as he recalled in 1980, from his perspective "the rehearsals had almost nothing to do with what ultimately went on the record". Of the band's signature piece, *In The Dead Of Night*, Bruford notes that Holdsworth's contribution to the piece was the *coup de grâce* – "94 seconds of liquid passion married to a blinding technical facility that was to go down in the annals of rock guitar history. All the hallmarks of his brilliant playing were there in this solo: poise, pace, melody, the Slominsky interval-jumps, the whammy-bar, and all over a killer groove." Holdsworth remembered: "We had to try to reproduce those parts live. And I just don't feel at home doing that. I'd rather play something first, and then record it. Now, I'm not against overdubbing – it's great. It's nice to embellish things, but I think that the important things should go down on the tracks so that when you play the songs onstage, nine times out of ten they'll sound *better.* With UK, particularly, we had millions of overdubs, and then we had to try to decide who could play what parts live because one guy doesn't have four hands, and so on." Holdsworth's reluctance to re-create the same solos on a nightly basis confirmed in the minds of Eddie Jobson and John Wetton that he was not the right fit. With the guitarist sacked at the end of a highly successful American tour in October 1978, and with a more commercial direction in the offing, Bruford opted to leave as well.

Describing his time in UK as a "a short fiery furnace", Bruford said the experience taught him that "some of us had a clearer understanding of who we were and what we wanted … When UK finished in really unhappy circumstances, I think I was thrilled to get back to *One Of A Kind*."

Released in 1979, *One Of A Kind* displayed Bruford's growing confidence as a composer capable of composing pieces that weren't simply complex but also accessible. With Dave Stewart's keyboards, Jeff Berlin's supple bass and, for a short period, the astonishing virtuosity of Allan Holdworth's guitar, the band were popular and well-reviewed, garnering appearances on TV and radio. When Holdsworth quit, his replacement, John Clark, provided a weightier, rockier punch and the band's popularity in the USA's small club circuit was helping build a reputation. The group's reception in America was astonishing, remembers Stewart. "Bill had given us some inkling that they could be very enthusiastic. But when we walked out on stage in Albany in New York State to play, the noise from the audience was absolutely deafening. I couldn't believe how much racket they were making." The release of the live album *The Bruford Tapes*, sourced from an FM radio broadcast of the second night of the tour, confirms just how powerful and tight the group were, with terrifically animated performances from each player. "That record reflected the energy of four young people who really loved to play together," said Berlin. "I sometimes hear it critically from the bass-playing point of view but really by looking at the record as a whole I think it is a successful live, energetic, noisy, quirky album. A fine example of one evening in the life of Bill Bruford's band."

During the tour, the setlist was bolstered with new material such as *Manacles*, as it was later titled when included as a bonus track on the 2005 re-issue of *One Of A Kind*. This track dated from one of the very first lines Bruford showed Stewart in 1977. "I guess we didn't include the piece on *Gradually Going Tornado* because it dated from an earlier era and other material we had at the time was considered stronger," observes Stewart. "However, on reflection, I think it was one of our most interesting tunes, and the 19/16 duet between me and Bill, in which I play electronic percussion synth sounds, or 'typewriter rock', as he amusingly called it, could have pointed the way forward to possible new musical directions. I noted in my diary it was fun to play because it was 'fresh and full of challenges'." The track is also significant because, after the dexterous themes and interplay that makes up the bulk of the tune, the coda with its stop-start pulse and solo drumming counterpoint clearly foreshadows *Indiscipline*.

Dave Stewart offers this perspective of the period from 1977 to 1980: "The great thing about Bill is that he's not just a drummer. Sometimes, as he often said, he doesn't think about what *he's* playing. He's thinking about the whole picture; thinking about soundscapes, and the arrangement and the keyboard sounds and so on. He's got this composer/arranger mentality which was there from the beginning and he evolved through the life of the band. He's a deep-thinking musician and it was great working with him for that very reason."

What ultimately saw the band break up was a hefty bill for £11,000 in tour losses.

For Bill this was evidence enough that, whatever its artistic achievements, the band was financially unsustainable. EG Management's demand that Bill would need to repay these costs came with the suggestion that he might like to be a member of the new outfit that his old sparring partner Robert Fripp was forming. "The worst thing about being a musician is being silenced, not having a platform," says Bruford philosophically. "And if the platform of your own band metamorphoses into a platform that includes Tony Levin, Adrian Belew and Robert, then that's perfectly acceptable to me. You've figured out by now that I'm a romantic but I'm also a pragmatic romantic. I may be an all-right drummer but I'm good at circumnavigating the problems that otherwise can kill you and silence you so that you don't play anymore or that you don't have a record out anymore."

IV

When Fripp and Bruford discussed who might play bass in the new band, the drummer was quick to suggest Jeff Berlin who, in Bruford, had combined "the harmonic knowledge of a jazz player and the sonic wallop of a rock guy". Early jams at Bruford's house were inconclusive, with Fripp feeling that the American bassist's style was a little busy for what he had in mind. Yet it was to America the guitarist and drummer headed to audition bass players.

In scenes that echoed the long search for potential Crims in the basement of the Fulham Palace Road Café, the New York auditions were anything but straightforward. "Auditions are fairly depressing in the traditional manner," says Fripp. "One is tested to see if the capacities and qualifications are acceptable. With these auditions, we rather assumed that the abilities were a given but were checking out compatibility and common aims. In fact, not everyone did have the qualifications."

Fripp found body language and personal deportment as useful an indicator of suitability as musical prowess. "The auditioner can tell at a glance if the auditionee will be right for the band. The first four bars confirms one's instinctive judgement."

Bruford winces at the memory. "We had an hysterical bass auditioning day in New York City. Robert and I set up in a rehearsal room and a line rapidly formed around the block and we auditioned them with *Discipline* on the grounds that if they could play that they'd probably be all right. After about an hour of this, Robert announced he was leaving and so I was left to conduct the rest of the auditions from the drum kit."

On the third day, Tony Levin appeared and the search was over. Fripp had met Levin recording Peter Gabriel's first album in Toronto and, of course, Levin's assured playing had been a defining feature on *Exposure*. Fripp had assumed that the ever-busy Levin would be unavailable but had heard via Polydor that he was mistaken. Fripp: "Because Tony Levin is so busy it never occurred to me that he would be interested in a band, otherwise he would have been my first call."

Given his substantial reputation, why did Levin make the trip across town? "By the 1980s I was, in fact, moving away from being a 'session musician'. I had met Robert on the Peter Gabriel recording in 1976 and had been touring since then with Peter," Levin recalls. "That first recording with Peter was momentous for me in that it introduced me to the talent of both Peter and Robert. When scheduling was possible, I would, without hesitation, have joined any project that involved either. So it was the chance to make music with Robert that got me to the first 'rehearsal' of Crimson, back in 1981. I didn't even know yet of the great talents of Adrian Belew and Bill Bruford – but was soon to learn!"

Levin's first appearance on a record was as a child of seven or eight. Levin and his brother Pete were taken to the WHDH radio station in Boston where their father worked as an engineer. With Levin on piano and Pete on French horn, the pair played a piece by Camille Saint-Saëns, which was then preserved on a 78 rpm record and presented as a present for their mother. Born on 6 June 1946, in Boston, Levin continued with his piano studies until he was ten, when he made the switch to double bass.

Although he was playing primarily classical parts, at the age of 11 Levin was playing with The Cavaliers turning out renditions of *When The Saints Go Marching In*, *Kansas City* and the Latin showstopper *Tequila*. For over a year the band played school dances and even indulged in gigs around the state with the help of an agent sometimes doubling the band's ten-dollar fee.

The Cavaliers went their separate ways when they went off to high school but Levin continued performing with the Greater Boston Youth Symphony Orchestra. In April 1962, the orchestra performed on the south lawn of the White House in the presence of the First Lady, Jackie Kennedy, with President John F. Kennedy putting in a brief appearance to give the assembled players a pep talk about youthful talent and aspiration. As well as his bass playing, Levin supplemented his musical education by tackling the tuba.

In 1968, Levin got a place at the Eastman School at Rochester in New York, where he met drummer Steve Gadd. It was Gadd who introduced Levin to jazz and the pair would work six nights a week from 10.00 pm to 1.00 am in nightclub spots with pianist Gap Mangione. Levin cites Gadd as a major influence. "The club gigs were great for me," recalls Levin. "And I learned more and more of the jazz standards, picking up valuable experience from Gap and having Steve there to lay down his solid beats (and urge me to keep playing up on top of the beat whenever I reverted to the inexorable middle-of-the-beat classical style)."

By the time Levin left Eastman, he knew his heart wasn't in a classical career and being in New York found himself getting on to the session circuit, playing with a variety of jazz names such as Herbie Mann and Buddy Rich. His ability to read and work quickly and efficiently endeared him to many producers and by the mid- to late 1970s he had made appearances on albums by artists as diverse as Paul Simon, Kate and Anna McGarrigle, Ringo Starr, Judy Collins, Lou Reed and Alice Cooper.

It was through Cooper producer Bob Ezrin that he was drafted in for Peter Gabriel's debut album, which also featured Fripp. It was at this recording that Levin unveiled the Chapman Stick, an instrument with which he would become closely associated over the years. The acquisition of a Stick was suggested by friends who noticed Levin's habit of tapping on his fretboard between takes. A ten-string instrument with five strings for bass and five for guitar, it came with a low action which allowed the strings to be tapped rather than plucked.

As both sides of the Stick can be played simultaneously, rather like a piano, the instrument offers an enormous range. Unlike a guitar, the instrument lacks any body and seemingly comprises a single wide fretboard and its appearance provoked raised eyebrows when Levin first tried to use it on the Gabriel recording. "Producer Bob Ezrin took one look and insisted I put it away."

Levin became the bass and Stick player of choice for Gabriel and of course went on to play on Fripp's solo album in 1979. His session work continued apace with Levin's name gracing many an album sleeve, perhaps most notably John Lennon and Yoko Ono's *Double Fantasy* in 1980.

Fripp praised Levin for his intuitive grasp of what the band were trying to achieve. "The afternoon with Tony was one of the best musical experiences of my life. Bill was showing TL a rather difficult 9/8, grouped 5 and 4. Tony had it before Bill completed the sentence … Tony, who had never heard *Larks' Tongues In Aspic, Part II* in his life, played it in spirit perfectly, and certainly the best performance of that in the past three days. For five minutes of the afternoon, the music coming out was as good as any I've ever heard by anyone, anywhere, anytime."

Back in 1971, Crimson co-founder Ian McDonald had said: "If you've got Bob Fripp in a band, you just don't play guitar." Clearly things had now changed. For the first time, Fripp needed another guitarist to play the music envisaged for the new group.

Robert Stephen Belew – he didn't adopt the name Adrian until the 1970s – was born on 23 December 1949, and grew up in the city of Covington, Kentucky. Even as a small child, Belew was something of a performer, singing along to Hank Williams and Elvis Presley records on the jukebox in a small bar across from his parents' house. He joined the local marching band as a drummer and two years later, in 1964, joined his first group, The Denems, on drums and vocals. When he was 16, Belew fell ill with a blood disorder and during a period of convalescence taught himself to play the guitar. Belew got to grips with the basics of the instrument fairly easily but was essentially keeping himself occupied during his illness. However, the arrival of Jimi Hendrix on his musical radar made him take the instrument very seriously and he then began an apprenticeship of playing in small-town groups.

Yet Belew went back to playing drums and really began to pay his dues, touring all over the country playing Holiday Inns and even at one point ending up backing an Elvis wannabe. By 1975, Belew was in Nashville, back on guitar and playing with a covers band called Sweetheart. Two years later, Frank Zappa saw the band play and took a shine to Belew, shaking his hand while the band performed a version of the Rolling Stones' *Gimme Shelter* and inviting him to audition for his band. Belew passed the audition with flying colours. "I liked working with Zappa a lot. It was very educational for one thing, he's got all this folklore to pass on and I learned a lot about putting music together, arrangements and orchestration, that sort of thing. He was very strict but we still had fun."

When Zappa's band rolled into Germany, Brian Eno was impressed with what he saw, calling David Bowie and telling him to come and see the young guitarist. "So David came to Berlin and I remember at one point in the show I looked over and saw David and Iggy Pop standing next to the monitor," Belew told *Melody Maker*'s Ian Pye. During one of Zappa's extended solos, Belew walked over to the side of the stage and struck up a conversation with the strange-eyed boy from Brixton to say how much he liked his music. Belew was astonished by the singer's response. "He said, 'Well howdya like to play in my band!' You know I just couldn't believe it." The deal was sealed over cocktails in a 1920s' transvestite bar and Belew found himself touring the world for a year and a half, playing the searing guitar lines Fripp had only recently laid down for *Heroes.*

Fripp first saw Belew performing at Madison Square Gardens in 1978 as part of Bowie's band, a position which had initially been offered to him. Fripp was impressed and attracted to the energy radiating from his playing and onstage demeanour. They met in person for the first time when Fripp bumped into Bowie and Adrian at New York's Bottom Line Club in 1979 where composer Steve Reich and his ensemble were performing *Music For 18 Musicians*.

Their paths would cross again when Belew's band, Gaga, supported The League Of Gentlemen in America. Belew's ear for detail and his astonishing capacity to create elliptical solos of unorthodox and ingenious ferocity were all factors which convinced Fripp that Adrian was exactly the sort of player he needed and he sounded out the guitarist about the pair of them working together. Ironically, when Talking Heads' Jerry Harrison and David Byrne attended the last night of the LOG's tour in July 1980, they were so impressed by the guitarist in the support band they asked Belew to record with them. The very next day, Belew was bound for the Bahamas to take part in the *Remain In Light* sessions.

While Belew was interested in forming an as-yet-unspecified partnership with Fripp, the offer of a chance to join Talking Heads on tour was too tempting to turn down. Thereafter, the guitarist found himself playing to crowds of well in excess of 70,000 as an expanded Talking Heads toured their world-beating blend of quirky, angst-driven funk.

When Talking Heads came to the UK in December 1980, Fripp seized the opportunity and rang Belew once more to renew his offer. "The Heads had just got to England and we were celebrating being in Europe by going to a Russian restaurant. We drank all these hot vodkas and the next morning I was in pain, you know. Well Robert called me up real early, saying that he knew I wasn't the sort of fellow to go out drinking late so he knew I wouldn't mind being woken up!"

It was now or never for Belew as Fripp needed an answer quickly. Having just secured a solo recording deal with Island Records, he was initially reluctant to join what, on paper, sounded like a session musicians' "supergroup". However, Belew recognised a great opportunity to work with not just one of his musical heroes but also Bill Bruford, whom he cited as his favourite drummer alongside Ringo Starr. Ever the pragmatist, Belew understood that the scope for his own material in Talking Heads was next to zero. So, a compromise was struck. Belew would join the band providing he was able to spend a good portion of the year attending to his own career. For Fripp, that was good enough. Belew was in.

Once Belew served out the rest of his contract with Talking Heads and finished a session for Herbie Hancock's *Magic Windows* album, he flew to the UK to begin work with the newly-christened Discipline. Levin was working in Paris and joined the group a few days later. Both Americans had an attack of last-minute cold feet before finally committing, but the four musicians finally began working together in March 1981 in the incongruous surroundings of a thirteenth-century hunting lodge near Badbury Rings, outside Fripp's home town, Wimborne. "This is perhaps the oldest building in domestic habitation in the UK. The walls are three feet thick. We rehearsed in the lounge, and in the kitchen little or nothing was heard," recalls Fripp. "This venue is significant because it is where *The Sheltering Sky* appeared as an improv, right out of the air."

A few days later, the band moved to the small church hall in Holdenhurst. In a location more used to seeing amateur dramatics, whist drives and children's parties, they worked frantically to keep on top of all the musical ideas piling up. Each day, there would be a new sound or timbre to be experimented with, as they played with different dynamics and trying to settle upon arrangements. From where he sat, Bill Bruford judged the gamelan-style motifs which formed the basis for much of the band's sound to be nothing short of brilliant. Fripp could, he observed later, "safely start clanging at the beginning and finish clanging at the end, with minimal requirement for rhythmic adventure in between. And the drums could do the coming and going. Several of the tracks ... are characterised by his guitar providing an unbroken run of 16th notes from beginning to end. He was happy having assigned unto himself the function of providing the continuum. Like a drummer's right hand on a cymbal, he could get going and forget about it."

By this time the new band was managed by Paddy Spinks, who had been tour manager for the Bruford/Wetton UK venture from mid-1978 until the band broke up. He worked with Bruford's own group and for a spell with Killing Joke but ended up looking after the LOG. "That was the first time I'd met Robert and we got on well," recalls Spinks "I was mindful of the person he was and figured out how to work with him. When he started talking about forming a major band again, it was clear that I could be of use to him. I struck a deal with Sam Alder and Mark Fenwick at EG, with Robert's prodding, and became Crimson's joint manager with EG."

Spinks, though aware of the calibre of the players involved, was unprepared for what he heard when he joined them for rehearsals in Holdenhurst. "It was pretty musical, fairly dense, fairly cerebral. I couldn't be sure how it was going to work on record but I knew it was going to work pretty well live. It just had a magic about it at the time."

The new pieces contained a huge amount of musical information compacted into an average of five minutes or so. Belew had the unenviable task of finding words and vocal melodies to transform five of them into songs – no mean feat considering the spiky textures and unfamiliar patterns of the material.

In less than ten days, they assembled seven pieces in a tightly interlocking style which fused gamelan, rock and Reichian minimalism into a form as exciting as it was innovative.

V

Just under a month after rehearsals began, Discipline played their first gig at Moles, a small basement club in Bath, to an ecstatic reception. The new material was shockingly different from the King Crimson of 1974. And yet the inclusion of *Larks' Tongues In Aspic, Part Two* and the live debut of *Red* made comparisons inevitable. The audience recording of the show reveals a band brimming with confidence and ideas.

Spinks remembers the venue well. "My impression at the time was 'what on earth are these monstrous musicians doing in this tiny room?'. It was a ridiculously small venue for a supergroup. But I understand what Robert's thinking was behind that – it was his way of protecting himself at the beginning. He didn't want his first gig to be in a big hall or something because it would be too intimidating for him and it would've raised the expectations of the audience as well. It was incredibly hot and quite tense."

Levin also recalls the quirky nature of the club. "It's a hole-in-the-wall kind of place. Located at the top of the main street in Bath, it's so hidden you have to comb the two-block-long stone wall to find the steps leading down to the club's entrance. It's a pretty odd place, and in its way, a great gig. I've played there with both Peter Gabriel and Crimson, in each case warming up for a tour. I guess we were sure to have no Press present there – they wouldn't fit. Trouble is, the audience don't fit too well, either – only those in the front row could see the band – and the restrooms are located behind the band, so during the set people would constantly squeeze between me and Bill to get to the loo. But hey, no place is perfect."

At 1.00 am, an excited Fripp noted in his journal: "Well, we did it. This band will be colossal – it's that good … The band enjoyed it. TL doesn't think it's commercial; I said 'It's a top 30 band'. TL isn't convinced but will take the cheque. For me, this is the band I've spent four years getting ready for."

The balance between the business of music and the music itself has always been delicate with one side capable of undermining the other if certain provisions were not in place. Fripp's agenda included trying to restrict the amount of interference from the big record companies he regarded as being terminally inclined to waste and inefficiency.

It was agreed from the outset that all money from royalties would be split equally. The arrival of the American contingent necessitated another amendment to EG's standard operating procedure. King Crimson had always played live in order to promote the album. Any monies paid out to individual musicians therefore came from album sales. EG initially expected the new band to do the same but the notion was laughed off by Belew and Levin, who were incredulous at the suggestion. Discipline ensured that the musicians would be paid wages while touring.

There was also the matter of trying to find the right level for the band to operate. Large venues might make more sense economically but tended to leach away the possible connectivity between the audience and performer, an essential ingredient in the performances. So Discipline preferred venues accommodating 1,000–1,500 people at most. During May, Discipline played a short tour taking in some of the provinces and a brief sortie into Europe. The Press reaction was largely favourable. Audiences were stunned. John Kimber was studying at York but travelled to Manchester when Discipline came to the polytechnic. "I was astonished at the power of the music. It seemed as though they'd gathered all of the strands of Talking Heads, *Exposure*, LOG and King Crimson and made it into something really powerful. It had such an edge to it. The two guitars had an incredible dynamic to it – I don't just mean the interlocking stuff but the sheer energy they generated."

In the elegant surroundings of Her Majesty's Theatre, London, three days later, the band played to a packed house. Crimson fan David Symes was struck by the collective nature of the playing. "I didn't really know what to expect. It was radically different from any Crimson material I'd heard before. There didn't seem to be any members of the band trying to out-perform each other; it was a whole rather than four people. There were certain points where Robert would visibly raise his head and count in the rest of the band through key changes."

At Manchester, Kimber had felt the inclusion of material from the Crimson catalogue seemed natural without being backward-looking in any way. "When they played *Red* I thought 'Wow, this band can go anywhere'." However, *Red*'s inclusion didn't meet with everyone's approval, even if these 1981 shows were its first-ever live performance. Session musician Chris Smith was at Her Majesty's and regarded *Red*'s appearance as a retrograde step. "My own feelings were 'Oh no! He's sold out!'. At the time, however, it seemed like all the bravery of knocking Crimson on the head when Fripp did and the 'no surrender' posture he'd taken afterwards had just gone out the window." Symes recalls: "When they went into *Red*, a whole line of Japanese guys started head-banging in unison. It was an extraordinary moment. One guy behind me shouted out 'Welcome back', which seemed to be quite an appropriate comment."

Belew's onstage presence was a key factor in winning over audiences. Above all, Belew made the soloing and riding through the inherent complexity within the music look easy, his broad smile beaming out to the audience as if to say: "It's OK, folks – just follow me and you'll be all right."

"The reason I'm actually smiling a lot is that it's just natural. I really love playing music and you know, the rest of the day, the other 22 hours might be shit. But when you're on stage suddenly there you are and it's the thing you wanted to be doing the whole day," observes Belew. "I think the hardest thing that I do is all the dance work on the pedals and things. You've got to get that to be so second nature that you don't have to be looking down all the time. By the time I've figured that out and it's started to become what we call in Crimson 'in the body'. What that means is that I can actually be playing in one time signature and my body is feeling that and I don't have to worry about that and I can sing something in a different time signature. It's similar to what a pianist does when they play the bass with the left hand and the melody with the right. I think it's just a natural thing. I'm so attached to guitar and it feels so natural to me. It's my voice. It's like talking; I don't have to think about everything, I just do it."

During rehearsals, Fripp met EG to talk about the name of the group. From the early rehearsals, Fripp was convinced that the music he heard was that of King Crimson, yet changing the name would have all kinds of ramifications, both positive and negative. The name had a certain stature but also had backward-looking associations. He was perhaps mindful of the Press statements in 1974 when he had proclaimed that Crimson had ceased to exist forever. A name change might mean accusations the band was trading on former glories, which would be hard to dodge.

"There was a brand value to an established name that had serious credibility," says Spinks, who admits there was pressure from EG for the band to revert to the old name. "It had a known fanbase and there was the potential to expand that fanbase. I think, however, at the end of the day Mark Fenwick and I knew that Robert was going to make up his mind one way or other and there wasn't much we could do about it. The name King Crimson was a franchise in itself at that point and it was always going to attract more interest. Robert's tactic was that he didn't want it to be Crimson right from the beginning because he wanted to see whether it was Crimson or not. He wanted to take the band out as Discipline to find out if was really worthy of being called King Crimson. And once he'd established that it probably was then it was fine to change the name."

September 1981 would be the seventh anniversary of Crimson ceasing to exist and also marked the end of Fripp's *Drive to 1981*. Fripp and Spinks reasoned that this would make an ideal time to release an album under the Crimson moniker. While that might be true, the name change coincided with the arrangements being made for tours of Japan and America – places where the old name was well-known, even revered. "It was tortuous going out as Discipline because promoters would immediately halve the money because nobody knew the name," recalls Bruford. "Whereas we saw the money double when we went out as King Crimson. I quite liked the name Discipline actually because I'm British and I knew what Robert was getting at with it, but when somebody told me it had changed to Crimson I thought 'good' because at least it removed one obstacle to the band's progress."

Getting the business side of the band organised was vital for Fripp, still striving to find a way of being both a part of, and yet apart from, the music industry. Fripp believed a new Crimson could usher in changes in the way business should be done, seeing the band and its surrounding business structure as a tool to achieve that goal. "If I'm going to uncover my backside it has to be on my terms. But if all this band does is one album, it'll be worth it."

On 18 May 1981, the band entered Island Studios in London's Basing Street, accompanied by Rhett Davies, who has the distinction of being the first producer external to the band to complete a King Crimson album. Spinks suspects that EG wanted a rounder, more commercial sound for the new Crimson. "I think Mark and Sam were particularly anxious not to let Robert produce the record entirely on his own so that it would have a broader appeal. Rhett was a very sensitive producer and really understood that his role in the process was not to remodel the band but to get the thing sounding right as far as he could."

Davies' association with King Crimson went back to 1969, albeit at some remove, when he had crammed a window at Harlequin Records in London with copies of the sleeve of the band's debut album. Davies started his studio career at Island's Basing Street studios in the mid-1970s, working his way up from tape operator to engineer. "Then it was originally Island Studios so you'd have all of the Island artists hanging around, waiting for the sessions to end at midnight or whenever they ended so they could get in there and jam all night long. So, I used to hang around and cut my teeth doing some engineering covering whoever was there wanting to jam that night. It was a really good atmosphere."

Although recording King Crimson presented no technical challenges for Davies, he admits to being initially confused by the sound they made. "When they came into the studio they were very well rehearsed. I remember micing up the band and never having heard a Stick in my life. When they started playing I can remember thinking 'Who the fuck is playing what?' (*laughs*). The noise they made was just incredible. You couldn't work out who was doing what. I had to keep soloing out the instruments: 'OK, *that's* the Stick doing that,' and then, 'Oh, Robert's doing that line' and so on. It was just so … interweaving. It was an eye-opener in terms of the sound and the quality of playing. I was blown away when they first started playing, wondering how I was going to deal with it all. As Paddy Spinks said, my job was really to make it sound as truthful to the sound they were producing."

Davies recalls that, although they were booked in for four weeks, such was the pace and progress that the album was completed in three.

The record was a surprise for any Crimson fans expecting the new album to pick up from where *Red* left off – the musical terrain couldn't have been more different. The move to a 50/50 Anglo-American line-up and Fripp's assimilation of American and world culture were central to the new music. Recalcitrant European fans perhaps wrong-footed by the difference between Crimson 1974 and the 1980s' incarnation weren't the only ones playing catch-up, as Bruford remembers. "Robert had spent the previous seven years, or quite a lot of it, in New York, absorbing a number of influences that I hadn't. There was the whole business about new wave loft music in NY and the beginnings of world music. There was also all these things with David Bowie, Brian Eno and David Byrne and Steve Reich which were floating around in Robert's head more than mine. So perhaps I had further to go in 1981 to catch up with Robert. Indeed I was almost given a reading list as well."

In this context, *Elephant Talk* is a kind of beginners' guide to the new Crimson. On *Under Heavy Manners*, David Byrne declaimed a series of non sequiturs provided by Fripp. A similar list was given to Belew for this song but, uneasy about such a recitation, Belew came up with his own catalogue of words arranged alphabetically.

Indeed, the perceived similarities to Byrne were often the focus of attention in the media. In an interview with Radio One DJ Tommy Vance, Bruford met the criticism head-on and defended Belew. "It sounds to me like Robert playing the guitar beyond all doubt and we have a Talking Head in the group who is singing. It must be inevitable when parts of groups merge together that bits and pieces rub off. I should imagine that it's the narrative vocals but these aren't a new thing and not the province of Talking Heads alone."

As well as being one of the best frontmen a group could have, Belew's instrumental presence enabled Fripp to make his coveted new interlocking parts a reality. Perhaps the most telling example is *Frame By Frame*, whose phase-shifting pointillism draws heavily on Steve Reich's minimalist aesthetic. Paradoxically, although *Frame By Frame* is an adrenaline-driven joyride, it is also a tightly controlled test drive, providing an excellent opportunity to see the two different approaches of the new Crimson front line. Belew acknowledges that the lyrics comment upon the differences in approach between the two halves of the band: "In the 1980s quartet, Robert and Bill, the Englishmen, favoured verbal jousting while the pragmatic Americans, Tony and me, tuned up and waited to play."

More than anything, the album is an exhilarating convergence of imaginative and associative leaps of faith, a strange crossroads at which the likes of gamelan, minimalism, bright dynamic rock, inquisitive, experimental sensibilities, and phenomenal musicianship all meet to form something uniquely Crimson.

Although the framing concept initially came from Fripp, *Discipline* is anything but the work of one person. The title track and its stylistic counterpoint, *Indiscipline*, are both a consolidation and a departure. Constructed from several different and independent lines, each one in itself quite fragile. Yet when all the strands are woven together, the remarkable results are as strong as they are flexible.

Paddy Spinks regards the title track in particular, and the album as a whole, as pivotal. "*Discipline* set the pace for all three of those albums and as a defining piece of music it was very influential in the music community worldwide. It was a seminal album. If you listen to music today you can hear the influences of all three albums but the *Discipline* one in particular. I remember right through the '80s you would hear a new band and you would be able to tell that they'd been listening to King Crimson."

Much like the knot-work relief which graced the spartan cover, *Discipline* is about the interconnectedness of ideas and experience harnessed together. Remove any one element of those threads and the whole thing will unravel. While some of Crimson's contemporaries had been content to either rest on their laurels or make a straightforward dash towards commercialism, every sinew of the *Discipline*-era group and its sound glistened with a dazzling freshness, a supple brilliance that effortlessly surfed the post-punk new wave zeitgeist whilst remaining consistent with its core principles.

VI

The UK music press greeted the release of *Discipline* with measured praise and a grudging respect for the musical skill on offer, along with expressions of bafflement as to the reasoning behind resurrecting the old name. Not that the band waited around to see how things played out with the critics, embarking on a touring schedule that would take in Europe, Canada, the States and Japan. The creative flow which began back in April was continuing with new songs such as *Neil And Jack And Me* already being included in the set, with *Manhattan*, *Sartori In Tangier* and *The Howler* not far behind.

For Fripp, the gigs in America began to tap into the "otherness" he encountered in 1969 and in Central Park in 1974, with the series of gigs at The Savoy in New York in November cited as "out of this world". Fripp later said: "The band as four individuals ceased to exist. Music played the band. When I came offstage I wasn't thinking. I was being."

This was the whole point of being in the group. All the hullabaloo of being a rock band on tour was worth putting up with to get to such an ineffable and mysterious point.

Paddy Spinks agrees that the dates at the Savoy were something out of the ordinary. "The place was crammed every night with people queuing 'round the block and people calling me all hours of the day for tickets because after the first night the word got out that this was something that needed to be seen. On the first tour in the US particularly, when Robert and Adrian were completely in sync with their playing with tracks like *Discipline*, it was extraordinary. You could feel the roof moving."

Yet, by February 1982, the creative heat was already beginning to cool. Bruford recalls that February rehearsals in New York's Garment District were hard work, the band struggling to regain the momentum of the previous year. What had been a new and innovative vocabulary was infiltrated by the musicians' natural instinct to avoid repetition. "We weren't sure how much to continue the heterophonic weaving of the guitars. Adrian was finding this a very difficult style to write a song over. The thing that had started the band had already seemed to become a millstone around its neck and I'm not sure if Adrian knew quite how far to proceed with it."

Given the various extra-curricular activities of the band, the decision to enter the studio so soon after the release of *Discipline* was Fripp's, a bid to maintain momentum. But there was too little time to develop material, leaving Crimson without surplus ideas as they booked into Odyssey Studios. As is so often the case in the Crimson story, people and locations have a habit of interconnecting. Though it played no part in the decision to use Odyssey, the studio was owned by Wayne Bickerton, producer of *The Cheerful Insanity Of Giles, Giles & Fripp*.

Belew recalls he was 19 when he first read the *Beat* writers. "I revisited my interest in their works around the end of the recording of *Discipline*. Robert saw me reading Kerouac and suggested spontaneous prose as the lyrical underpinning of the next record. He prompted me with a note saying 'I'm wheels, I'm moving wheels'."

Perhaps the most obvious homage to Kerouac, Neal Cassady et al. on the album, Belew's autobiographical lyric for *Neal And Jack And Me* perfectly captures the listless, indeterminate state of travelling but never quite arriving. Either side of the two hours on stage, life on the road with a rock band has always been a mixed bag of boredom and homesickness.

Appropriately, there are many musical allusions to Kerouac not least of which from the second verse, a thin chattering ticker-tape of percussion invoking an image of Kerouac's continuous roll of teletype paper on which he wrote *On The Road*.

The band that had once struggled with America now wholly embraced it. Bruford acknowledges that the song is a world away from the more staid, sometimes arcane subject matter of previous Crimsons. "I think it took an American to write it. Adrian knew about that stuff, he understood the size of America. He knew what it was like to see a Studebaker in 1966 or whenever. I thought that was great stuff. I loved it all."

Neurotica blends the qualities of a tone poem and a stream-of-consciousness lyric to perfection. Originally an instrumental titled *Manhattan*, it audaciously constructs a teeming cityscape which hurtles along in a high-speed chase that threatens to become a destruction derby of police sirens, whistle-blowing traffic cops and swarming crowds. The lyric, written during the band's three nights at The Savoy, is a triumph, easily meeting the challenge thrown down by the music. "I thought *Neurotica* was terrific. I just love the idea of it and on the middle section Adrian was just great. One of his perennial gripes was that he's been a bit under-recognised as a songwriter and I think there's a lot of truth in that. I know it took a lot of him to do it all."

By the time the song was recorded, the parts were well-established and fully realised to create a piece pulsating with excitement and electricity, without doubt a landmark track in the band's catalogue.

In sharp contrast, Crimson's penchant for ballads was met by *Heartbeat*. The soft edges of this FM radio-friendly song seems almost startling against the more angular and acerbic material elsewhere. A Belew song through and through, its author has since said that wished he had kept it back for himself. Spinks remembers things differently. "Well that's ironic because he couldn't have pushed it harder at the time, I tell you. He wanted it there on the album."

Rhett Davies laughs when asked about the biggest problem on the album:

"Getting Bill to play a straight 4/4!" Bruford admits he had difficulty in finding the right part or feel. Fripp offers this assessment: "This is a Belewbeloid classic, although the band weren't the best team to deliver this song: the Anglos weren't ideal players for this little sucker. As limp an RF solo as one can find anywhere. Nowadays on a session I have the courage to say: 'There is nothing I can contribute to this.'"

"I disagree with all of them," says Spinks with some passion. "I think the song was an important part of humanising King Crimson, that they were capable of doing something that was, if you like, fairly trite but played in an intensely musical way. When they played it live it was great. It's a classic Crimson track at the end of the day."

But real tensions emerged during *Beat*. Rhett Davies observes that they spent twice as much time on the follow-up as on *Discipline*. "There were no technical problems at the time … but they were at loggerheads creatively, perhaps, and it was tough. I had to spend a lot more time with Adrian on the vocals. He was under a lot of pressure because he had to write all the lyrics and he was really struggling. He needed to get home but he had to finish this record, so toward the end of it, there was a lot of stress."

Davies also recalls the period as one that was relentless in its pace. "From Monday, 22 March, we worked to Friday; and then on the Saturday, Sunday and Monday, I flew to New York for Roxy Music and was back in on the Tuesday, 30 March, with King Crimson. That's what it was like then. And my wife was in hospital as well. It was all go. We were *all* under stress. I remember Robert getting more involved in the mixing. He insisted that there was no reverb on anything. When he came in and heard reverb on anything he made me turn it all off. So I devised a way of putting reverb on without him seeing it on the desk," laughs Davies, "only a *little* bit where I thought it would enhance certain things."

Sartori In Tangier wasn't always intended to be an instrumental but during its writing Belew was uncertain what to contribute. For a while it remained a trio outing. "I never could find anything to sing in the song, and it seemed rather complete as an instrumental," Belew said. "I play mostly in the middle, where it changes into this plush aural carpeting." Holding the slide rather than wearing it, Belew rolls the device along the strings creating a continuous shining note, adding one or two overdubs to create the rich final effect.

Not every track stands up to scrutiny, especially from the band members themselves. Fripp has remarked that, in his opinion, *Two Hands* shouldn't have been on the album and that *The Howler* is less than convincing. "It illustrates the difficulty of writing in the studio, and not having the opportunity of playing material live prior to recording it. There are some good ideas, but they haven't been allowed the time to mature and find their place."

A piece called *Absent Lovers* was aired at some of the play-in gigs prior to the sessions and, although they recorded it, the song resisted Belew's attempts to find a suitable lyric or melody. Deciding that it was unable to stand on its own as an instrumental, the band abandoned it, leaving the album with a very short running time indeed.

Tony Levin recalls: "We had finished all our 'composition ideas' on the album and were short on running time. We decided to do an improv as an experiment to see, if edited, whether it might stand as a piece, and relieve us of composing another."

Indeed, without what would be later titled *Requiem*, the month's studio work would have netted only a scant 29 minutes of music. "I was broadly in favour, not just because there was a shortage of agreed written material, but because I think the aleatoric stuff can have just as much worth or 'meaning' as the carefully prepared material," says Bruford.

Set against the menace of a Frippertronics loop from Fripp's 1979 tour, it contains some of the most free-spirited and engaged performances on *Beat*. Levin's measured descending run reinforces the pensive air, although Bruford's dancing cymbal work pushes the track into a strange hybrid territory which mixes jazz and metal, what Allen Ginsberg might have described as a "bop apocalypse".

"We did it in one, very long, take in the studio," Levin recalls. "All together, listening to each other but with the 'headphone mix' limitations that are always there in the studio and that make real improvisation difficult. So, in my opinion, we were each a bit more musically isolated than is usually the case when we improvise onstage."

The underlying tensions simmering within the group came to a head during the recording of *Requiem* when Belew returned to the studio alone and overdubbed further guitar parts. Fripp followed suit, as the two guitarists seemingly vied for position. With typical diplomacy, Levin observes: "I seem to recall that Adrian was less than thrilled about this." Far away from home and under pressure to come up with lyrics and melodies, Belew pointedly told Fripp to leave the studio. Visibly upset, Fripp left for Wimborne and played no further part in the recording, leaving Davies to mix the rest of the tracks alone. This rift caused consternation at EG and Spinks was worried that it might lead to the premature break-up of the group. "Robert fled the studio and we didn't hear from him for about three days. I remember driving down to Dorset and banging on his door but he wasn't there. Eventually he came back out, we talked by phone and we slowly put it all back together. It was the culmination of a whole bunch of things, Adrian trying to establish himself as a creative force in the group and making sure people understood that he was important in the group."

Though he normally kept his head down in personnel issues, Bruford voiced his distress at the situation, writing Fripp a supportive letter, and Belew apologised. In light of all this, it is perhaps no surprise that the playing on *Requiem* is as fiery and caustic as it is. Indeed one can hear the aggrieved groaning of scraping metal as the two guitars move about the track. Levin rates the track very highly, feeling that it caught a powerful atmosphere. "And perhaps the slight out-of-balance alienation of the end-of-album mood is there if you want to hear it."

Spinks is philosophical about the band's conflicts. "This was not a band that had grown up together as young kids. This was a band of strong people. Adrian was not very strong at the beginning but became very strong because of the success. He could display some immaturity through that process but, then again, so could Robert."

Looking back, Belew is unequivocal: "*Beat* was the most awful record-making experience of my life and one I would never choose to repeat."

For Fripp, Crimson all but died during the recording. "At the time Bill and Adrian thought that *Beat* was better than *Discipline*. For me, this is an indication of how far the band had already drifted from its original vision. The group broke up at the end of *Beat* … I had nothing to do with the mixing of *Beat*, nor did I feel able to promote it. Somehow we absorbed the fact, and then kept going."

VII

Beat was released in June with a press kit including badges of the cover symbol and copies of Kerouac's *On The Road*. In broad terms, the UK Press gave the album a cautious welcome, although some doubted Crimson's ability to invoke the spirit of the Beat Generation via the tight musical structures of the album. *Rolling Stone* accorded *Beat* three-and-a-half stars with reviewer Chip Stern applauding the band for moving into new areas: "Crimson creates a new kind of electronic string music that achieves an orchestral density without resorting to ersatz art-rock bombast."

The band were well received on tour. Although Crimson's *raison d'être* was based upon the relationship and interaction between band and audience, a rather less welcome aspect of this arrangement for Fripp was the degree to which photography and illicit taping had begun to impinge upon his connection to the process. Of course Crimson regularly taped their own performances and Levin had documented the life of the band both on and off stage. In Discipline, Fripp would sometimes remind the audience that Tony Levin was the only authorised photographer for the evening, reasoning that such practices were consensual and thus acceptable.

Taping and photography where the public were clearly asked not to was clearly a violation of the spirit of the performance. Not everyone in the band felt the problem as acutely as Fripp, it has to be said. Levin himself gently lampooned the situation in the comic track *The King Crimson Barbershop*. Bruford preferred not to get involved in the debate. "There were so many themes and sub-plots going on in King Crimson with all the stuff about cameras, and Inclines to 1984 and so on, that the best thing I could do was just keep my head down and practice. I was not in control of any of those things."

What effect did Fripp's increasing aversion to photography have upon the band? Paddy Spinks believed it caused stress. "Robert made no secret of his dislike of the photos when they did happen and it sometimes caused the mood of the show to be dramatically altered. The fans who came to see King Crimson did not understand the reason for it unless they were already a disciple of Robert's thought process and many of them were not. They just wanted to see/hear some great music and were not concerned about their own lack of respect for Robert's wishes."

In fact the majority of audiences observed the "no camera" requests, though the drummer recalls an incident when the policy seemed to get a little out of hand. At a 1981 gig in Germany, the audience was subject to screening by a metal detector or body search on admittance. "By the time the audience got in, the concert was running late and everybody was pissed off as hell by the time we went on stage. We then played not a lot of old King Crimson and a very short set of 55 minutes, being all we had. Then we left the stage to a considerable amount of disapproval from the audience. As we were leaving the stage I heard a thump nearby and a great big piece of raw meat had been thrown onstage!"

The part-time nature of the group was a source of frustration to Spinks. In 1982 Crimson managed less than five months' active service. "Because they all had side projects going on there were a lot of late-night calls trying to figure out when Tony was going to be off with Gabriel, when Adrian was off doing his own thing, what Bill was up to and so on. It was a real headache figuring out when we could get them all in the same place at the same time. It made the job much more difficult than it otherwise would have been.

"Also Tony was making a lot of money from sessions and he was taking a pay cut to come and play for King Crimson. And he knew it. Therefore he could dictate to a certain extent when he was available. If he got a call to do a Gabriel album or a Paul Simon record, well he had to go and do it. So you had four busy schedules, but Tony's part in all that should not be underestimated – it was a pretty critical part of it, quite frankly."

Still, this was better than the following year. In 1983, Crimson disappeared entirely as the members tended to solo interests. Bruford formed a duo with ex-Yes and Moody Blues keyboard player Patrick Moraz, Belew concentrated on his solo career, Levin went to work with Peter Gabriel and Fripp started working with old Bournemouth chum Andy Summers, now guitarist with The Police.

There's little doubt that the turbulence between Fripp and Belew during the making of *Beat* marked a break point in the shared sense of vision and momentum of the group. While a lengthy stint on the road following *Beat*'s release in June may have smoothed away the rougher edges, by the time the band stepped offstage at Munich's Alabamahalle in September 1982, their last live date of the year, as a collective entity King Crimson was now running on empty.

Making an album is never a straightforward affair. Even at the best of times, when a group is riding high and firing on all creative cylinders, the process can still be something of a struggle. So when a band is in a less-than-optimal state, things can be very tough indeed. As Levin notes: "In the studio it's always a battle; wielding guitars like weapons to fight the clock, the headphone mix, budget, record company demands – we struggle to capture some of the magic that happens effortlessly every night in front of an audience."

That magic was conspicuously absent by the time the group reconvened, three months later, for writing sessions at Champaign-Urbana, Illinois, in January 1983. In other circumstances, the 13 days they'd allocated should have been enough. Yet at the end of it nothing substantial had emerged. As Belew returned home to finish work on a second solo album, *Twang Bar King*, and Fripp prepared to embark upon a string of Frippertronic concerts in the US, Bruford and Levin returned to their respective session work.

At the end of May, King Crimson reconvened at Arny's Shack in Parkstone, Dorset, where Fripp had previously recorded with The League Of Gentlemen and with Andy Summers in September 1981 for their *I Advance Masked* album. In a dormitory town tucked away in a corner of the South West of England, Crimson set about constructing formidably strange and angular sounds that would ultimately coalesce into *Industry* and *Dig Me*. Given the oppressive intensity of the pieces, it's no surprise that Levin recalls they would step outside the studio to take frequent tea breaks and read the newspapers, "anything to get out of the studio and clear our heads".

From June, King Crimson transferred to Marcus Studios in London, occupying the downstairs recording room of the building while Yes worked on *90125* upstairs. "Yeah, easy to solo over that," Bill Bruford can be heard saying to his colleagues as they pick over *Dig Me* once again, but there was nothing easy about it. Though never intentionally profligate when it came to utilising valuable studio time, the band still had little to show for their efforts. It wasn't for lack of ideas, though that also seems to have been part of the problem. Without anyone willing to step into the role of advocate or director, a by-product of the simmering resentments steadily corroding the group's infrastructure, the building blocks for material stubbornly refused to meld into place. For a second time, in 1983, the four individuals parted company empty-handed; Levin rejoining Peter Gabriel's live band for three months touring, and Bill Bruford hooking up with Patrick Moraz to tour the US and record *Music For Piano And Drums*.

With Belew's *Twang Bar King* released in August, Fripp arrived at the guitarist's studio in Champaign the following month to write, bringing with him some of the more amorphous ideas thrown up earlier in the year. King Crimson returned to the recording studio, this time at Bearsville, in November – the same month that Yes released *90125*. Finally, things fell into place.

Taken together with *The Champaign-Urbana Sessions* (KCCC 21), the work-in-progress sketches, outtakes, bright ideas, dead-ends and cul-de-sacs gathered on KCCC42's *Rehearsals & Blows* provide a kind of alternative history to King Crimson's catalogue; a shadow album that traces the points where things came together or fell apart. *Steinberger Melody* continues on from the Champaign-Urbana sessions at the start of the year, albeit with a slightly truncated bass groove and the addition of some of the decorative introductory chords from The League Of Gentlemen's *Farewell Johnny Brill*.

The delicately unfurling *Shidare Zakura* flowers briefly but then dies away, though something of it can be discerned in Fripp's solo on David Sylvian's track *Upon This Earth*, released three years later. *Working On Sleepless* showcases the right place/right time principle in full sway. Listeners will readily recognise that the theme abandoned in 1983, itself an orphan from 1974, eventually found its proper home a little over a decade later within *VROOOM VROOOM.*

Speaking after the release of *Three Of A Perfect Pair* in 1984, Bruford commented upon the album that took the group a year not so much to make as it did to find. "It did take quite a while … It's kind of the fourth album with this version of the band. You see, we recorded one LP and more or less dumped it. We couldn't quite see the way it was working out. When we reconvened, the problems we had just evaporated! Sometimes, time is the only thing you need. Just to get away. And then suddenly the project was on its feet again and we knew where it was going and what to do."

For all the difficulties in sifting through material for *Three Of A Perfect Pair*, the album did yield a couple of Crim classics. The title track stems from a Belew riff which the band threw around in concert prior to *Beat.* The resulting tune has such a lightness of touch it's impossible not to be charmed and intrigued. Ostensibly an everyday tale of a dysfunctional couple, it's tempting to apply the "can't live with them and can't live without them" aspect of the lyric to Crimson itself. The recording of the album was hardest in the band's immediate history with each track slowly emerging from hours of determined playing – though there is little evidence of such difficulties in these sparkling guitars and assured vocals. "The title came from nowhere," says Belew. "It popped into my mind and was quickly acknowledged by the boys as an apt title for the '80s trilogy."

Breaking through into the mainstream was something which other groups from a similar vintage to Crimson had managed. Genesis and Yes both entered their most commercially lucrative periods during the early '80s. Yet there was never any serious prospect of Crimson following them. While tracks such as *Matte Kudasai*, *Heartbeat* and *Sleepless* offered something more streamlined and less abrasive, they sat next to material that made few concessions to commerciality.

Crimson's penchant for angular, hard-edged experimentation came to the fore during 1983 partly out of necessity as formal songs remained elusive. *Dig Me* is a bold attempt to fuse the improvised and written halves of the group's collective personality. Rock music's love affair with the internal combustion engine has been well documented from the clean-cut frat-boy cruising of *Little Deuce Coupe* to Springsteen's blue-collar grease monkey. Yet few songs have attempted to delve into the soul of the machine itself. *Dig Me* gives the car's take on being dumped on the scrapheap.

In doing so it bravely questions preconceptions about what a "song" might consist of and it's certainly true that the track fits into the noble Crimson tradition of combining opposite elements. Belew's litany of umbrage emerges from the dark squalls of atonal scraping into a bright, dazzling poppy chorus, suggestive perhaps of happier times on the freeway. Belew recalls that the song's origins lay in the attempts to come up with a different style. "I told the guys I wanted to lay down this very awkward guitar part and then have them play to it, but in a way that would sound like we're really not playing together as often as we are. The song sounds like it's falling apart."

Collective improvisations such as *Industry* and *No Warning* also set the band far apart from any supposed contemporaries.

"It was suggested at one point that we go into the studio and really not pay attention to each other, but still try and go in the same direction, if you know what I mean," Belew explained to *Musician*. "That's how a lot of the industrial-sounding stuff came about, by just going in there and trying to make an 'almighty noise', as Robert calls it."

Taken as a whole, this "industrial approach" is probably more jazz than rock. Fripp recalls: "We played for around 90 minutes. After 30 minutes I stopped, leaving the others going for an hour. (I've done a lot of free-jazz work, although mainly as a producer.) When we were listening back, when the 30 group minutes were up, Bill wanted to keep listening."

Certainly Bruford believed this kind of aleatory playing to be fruitful. Some of the guitar effects used in these industrial areas are not unlike those of Pat Metheny, at the time another Roland guitar synthesiser user, in some of his more interesting tonal explorations like 1982's *Offramp*. Bruford recalls playing Belew a Metheny album around this time only for the guitarist to mistake it for one of Crimson's recent improvisations.

In the press release for *Three Of A Perfect Pair*, Fripp noted: "The album presents two distinct sides of the band's personality, which has caused at least as much confusion for the group as it has the public and the industry. The left side is accessible, the right side excessive."

Why had the album taken so long to make? "There was no-one in charge," is Fripp's quick answer to that particular question, adding that with gradually deteriorating relationships and a division of royalty income that was in theory equitable but failed to encourage those doing most of the compositional work, the process of making an album wasn't likely to get on track.

When the album was released in March 1984, reviewers, even some of the hostile ones, praised the band for avoiding what John Gill in *Time Out* termed the "creative dotage" which seemed to be the fate of Yes and other contemporaries. Reviewing the album for *More Music*, Pete Ravens commented: "You won't be disappointed. Confused, scattered and ultimately disorientated but not disappointed. King Crimson has become a constantly challenging institution. How many other bands can boast this?"

While certain critics may have applauded the band's sense of invention and tenacity, Fripp laments the absence of hazard. "The novel musical approaches of *Discipline*, including the double-guitar interlock, Roland guitar synths, and Chapman

Stick and Simmons' drums without much cymbal and hi-hat, set up a series of challenges; like, it wasn't so easy to fall back on clichés. But, after a year, players who have exerted themselves and worked in unfamiliar ways begin to hanker for their more established modes of expression. So, rather than developing what we had achieved in 1981, we moved back to more conventional forms."

After an absence from the concert stage of over 17 months, the group returned to Japan at the end of April 1984. If some of *Three Of A Perfect Pair* had sounded slightly stilted in the studio, on stage things loosened up. *Industry*, in particular, acquired a much more oppressive feel on stage, its relentless repetition calling to mind *Mars* from an earlier Crimson.

In concert, the band appeared natural and relaxed but what many didn't realise at the time was that they were playing with the aid of a click track programmed by Tony Levin and maintaining an orderly, measured pulse. The need for such a device was not due to any musical deficiencies but because of a disagreement about the assignment of roles within the group.

As Bruford saw things, the role of the drummer had changed. In days gone by and in less creative situations, the drummer had simply laid the part down while others overdubbed the glory parts. In concert, the drummer became little more than a timekeeper. Bruford's rhythmic ambitions and temperament within Crimson had always gone far beyond such a rudimentary approach. He had come to resent the notion of having to merely "keep time". However, in the rehearsals in Champaign, Bruford admitted that his habit of changing his parts on an almost daily basis provoked irritation in his colleagues and ultimately led to the decision to introduce the click. In an interview with *Musician* magazine in 1984, Bruford was bullish: "We have to assume by now that Robert Fripp can keep time. And if he can't, well, that's tough. But timekeeping is also something we need for the audience. The machine can handle it, leaving me free to stand and play a vertical rack set-up of Simmons SDS 7s, embroidering the top."

In the same article, Fripp responded in a similar tone, suggesting that Bruford's approach to playing had become invasive and increasingly presented an obstacle to the performance. "I can understand Bill not wanting to be the timekeeper in a band, because I'm not interested in being a rhythm player … which is an entirely honest, worthwhile, interesting role. But it's not one I go for. Now, my response to Bill's not wanting to keep time is that I don't mind him not keeping time for me, because I can keep my own. What I object to is his *disturbing* my time."

The personal antipathy between Fripp and Bruford reached a new low after the publication of the article. Bruford was angered by the tone of some of Fripp's observations. "We were all denounced, which I took exception to. I didn't know whether to laugh or cry. It was absurd that we should be so continually undermined at the peak of the band's popularity. We were doing really well in business terms. These were definitely the actions of a guy who, if he wasn't actively trying to sabotage the group, was doing very well at it."

With the release of *Three Of A Perfect Pair*, the band's contractual obligations were fulfilled. By the end of the tour in July 1984, with no more immediate plans for live work, the band was free to play together again if it wanted to. However, not everyone was certain that they did. "We just have to sit down and consider that at the end of all this touring," Adrian Belew told journalist Bill Milkowski in 1984. "Personally I'd like to see it take a break for a while, mainly because I feel a real need to fulfil a lot of musical ideas that aren't fitting for King Crimson."

With these kinds of tensions pulling at the personal fabric of the band, it was inevitable that things wouldn't last much longer. The irony is that the band had never sounded better. The material from *Three Of A Perfect Pair* had begun to breathe and knitted well into the set. By the time of the band's final gigs in Montreal, the music was tight, incisive and moving at a stunning pace. In 1998, DGM released *Absent Lovers,* a 2-CD set from the Montreal shows. It showed Crimson on triumphant form. Indeed the performances surpassed many of their original versions – *LTIA2* especially hadn't sounded so animated and full of vim and vigour for quite a while.

On Sunday, 12 July, the morning after the last show at Le Spectrum, the team were having breakfast in their hotel. Bruford recalls Fripp joining them and announcing to his colleagues that the band was no more. Although there were expressions of disappointment, nobody was really surprised.

Fripp offers this perspective: "We compressed the making of three albums into three years, which was probably too short for the music to emerge organically. But, with different career interests and tensions in the band, had we waited longer maybe little more would have developed organically anyway. Regardless of what the albums achieved, *Absent Lovers* validates the group as a live unit, right up to the end. That particular end was a finish, a conclusion and a completion. No discussion followed the end of the tour, to address either working together or not working together."

Crimson's return to the first division was at an end. As Spinks sat in Montreal mulling over his breakfast, there was a despondent air. "I think we all kind of knew that if there wasn't going to be an actual end to the thing at the end of the tour then there was certainly going to be a long pause. And if you think about it, there certainly was a hell of a long pause."

Reflecting on the period in his autobiography, Bruford had this to say. "It is for me an article of faith to expect nothing whatsoever from audience or colleagues in return for any treasures – that way, at least I am unlikely to be disappointed. Some of this may have determined the short life of our collective working relationship, but we did plenty in the time allotted. Ultimately, the magic of the '80s Crim could be spun out for just four years and three albums ..."

In 2011, Adrian Belew floated an idea that the '80s line-up might consider reconvening to celebrate the 30th anniversary of the quartet's formation. What made that Crimson such a special band for Belew? "Oh, I think it was probably the best band in the world at the time! You can't really go back, and I know that, and I know a lot people thought I was crazy for even saying that I wanted to get that line-up back together. And maybe I was, but I guess there was just a moment in time where I realised just how special that band was to me, and I wanted to celebrate it again. It wasn't that I felt like we'd get back together and we'd be the same. Of course not, because it's never the same. But I wanted to celebrate it and show people who didn't get to see it – and there are a lot of them, especially younger people – what a fabulous band really sounds like."

"The Crimson of '81 was just the perfect line-up, perfect combination of things; heavy, light, fun and dark. The sounds were incredible because each of the members had brand new tools that nobody else was utilising; Robert and I with the Roland guitar synths, Tony with the Stick – I'd never seen anyone do that – and Bill with electronic drums. I just think there was something absolutely marvellous about that band. That first record we did is the proof. It's still ground-breaking. It still doesn't sound like anything else you've heard before. A 20-something can put that record on and think that it must have been made yesterday and I still don't understand it! I guess I got nostalgic. I love the guys in the band and love what we did. There's sometimes I look back on that and I wish I knew then what I know now. Because I think I could've enjoyed it more. It was really a difficult thing for me and I was always upset or depressed about something. I wasn't with the spirit of it like I'm supposed to be, like I am now. If I could only go back and relive that, what a different person I would be. But you don't know what you have until it's gone. It's only human nature. I'm sure Robert would look back and say, 'Gee, you know, I wish I'd have done things differently too.' But you know it was a great band and made great music. If I was able to do all that again you'd see the happiest guy in the world!"

VIII

Having completed *The Drive To 1981*, and with *The Incline To 1984* nearing its end, Fripp wanted to take stock of things at a personal and professional level and planned to enrol at the American Society for Continuous Education in Claymont Court in West Virginia. The Crimson-free months ahead enabled him to clear the decks and, as he put it, allow the future to present itself.

Everything Fripp had witnessed in his time in the various incarnations of King Crimson convinced him that there had to be another way of doing things, an alternative means of connecting with music outside the mosh pit of the industry. His personal solution was to devise Guitar Craft – a self-sufficient movable collegiate whose aim would be to create an environment where students would be encouraged to develop a more holistic approach to making music.

In its intensive residential atmosphere, the relationship with oneself was equally important to improving or developing technique. The New Standard Tuning which Fripp had discovered in 1983 was the means by which old preconceptions and habitual approaches to playing were stripped away.

The first Guitar Craft course began on 25 March 1985, and Fripp's personal commitment to it was absolute. The League Of Crafty Guitarists became the performing wing of Guitar Craft with a line-up that initially included Trey Gunn.

Gunn was born on 13 December 1960. His musical education started in San Antonio, Texas, when he began playing piano at the age of seven. His mother, a university professor, taught English while his father's side of the family had been in the car business since 1916. "My great-grandfather became the first Chevrolet dealer west of the Mississippi River," says Gunn. As a piano student, he was weaned on the classics and Gunn particularly remembers having to tackle Bartok's six-part *Mikrokosmos*, which he describes as "a very clever way of getting small children to play some truly whacked-out music".

As he grew up, Gunn listened to The Beatles, Prokofiev, Hank Williams, Charley Pride, Ravel and Dvorak. In 1971, he took up the violin and played it until he was 14. By now his musical taste extended to Blue Oyster Cult, Rush and Alice Cooper. By 16, he was playing guitar.

His musical education continued when he enrolled at the University of Oregon in 1978, obtaining his degree as a Bachelor of Music Composition. He was now a fan of The Mahavishnu Orchestra, Weather Report, Santana and other luminaries of the fusion world. "However I 'balanced' my tenure in the university by playing in punk bands such as Punishment Farm and The Magic If, and working in several different recording studios as an engineer/producer."

By 1985, Gunn was a member of Guitar Craft, enrolling for the course at Charlestown, West Virginia, and beginning an association with Fripp which lasted 18 years. Also on the course was guitarist Tony Geballe. "I remember Trey from my first GC course in May 1985 as 'the guy who moves his head while he plays'. I didn't mark him much more than that at the time. That summer his band, The Magic If, came to Seattle, and shared the bill with some friends of mine, Jeff Greinke and Rob Angus."

Geballe met Gunn again on the GC Level 2 course later that year. Gunn participated in GC craft courses in 1986, including a stint at Red Lion House in Dorset (along with California Guitar Trio members and Diane Aldahl – who would later become the manager for Fripp's independent record company Discipline Global Mobile). Geballe regards Gunn as being an important core member of the GC team, contributing "excellent playing and starting to write pieces in a distinctive and beautiful voice".

Around this time, Gunn began playing Chapman Stick, commenting: "It was like I'd spent my whole career getting ready to play it." In 1987, he appeared on the Robert Fripp/Toyah Willcox album *The Lady Or The Tiger* as a member of the League Of Crafty Guitarists and as part of the Fripp/Willcox touring band Fripp, fripp.

In 1991, Geballe worked with Gunn again on Willcox's album *Ophelia's Shadow*. "I was tremendously impressed with his ability to create wonderful sounds, and his knowledge of studio technique," he recalls. "Trey is very balanced between intuition and intellect in his work and is one of the most serious and conscientious musicians I know, in terms of developing his innate knowledge of music and broadening and deepening his relationship to music. He thinks deeply about all aspects of his music: sound, form, technique, texture, dynamics, etc. But he doesn't lose sight of the essential motive force and meaning of music either."

During 1991, Fripp and Willcox toured under the name of Sunday All Over The World with Gunn on Stick and Arny's Shack session drummer Paul Beavis, releasing an album, *Kneeling At The Shrine*, that year.

As Fripp alternated between Guitar Craft and the band, the affairs of his managers at EG began to encroach upon his professional life in an unwelcome way. After 1977 and the departure of David Enthoven, EG was now run by Mark Fenwick and Sam Alder who, for a while, steered the company into even greater profitability. The pair were also members of a Lloyds insurance syndicate and had diversified into property.

But a combination of huge insurance losses and the collapse of the property market meant that they struggled to keep their various interests afloat. As money moved from one company to another via consultancy fees and loans, EG moved from profit to loss. Suddenly there were difficulties paying artists' recording and publishing royalties. In 1991, Fripp, on tour with the League of Crafty Guitarists, was dependent on these payments to keep the show on the road. When the money failed to materialise on time, he was forced to sell one of his rarest guitars.

Despite promises from EG, payments continued to be late and, in March that year, ex-Crimson drummer, Michael Giles instructed his solicitors to write to the company. From his hotel in Lisle, on tour, Fripp faxed through his resignation to the company, only to be threatened with legal action forcing him to remain as an artist with EG at a meeting a few days later. For Fripp, this event marked the actual termination of his relationship with EG.

At the same time, Alder and Fenwick sold the EG Records catalogue to Virgin and, in July, the publishing side of EG went to BMG in a deal that was estimated to have netted up to £4.5 million. Fripp notes that none of the artists were consulted over these sales nor were any of the proceeds distributed their way, a fact which ultimately led Fripp to serve a High Court writ upon his former managers in March 1992. Thus began a legal battle that would take many years to resolve (characterised by Fripp as a period of "Endless Grief") but which would eventually see him gain control over his own solo material and the King Crimson back catalogue.

Though debilitating and distracting in many ways, the break with EG pushed Fripp into setting up his own label – Discipline Global Mobile – which would enable him to maintain a much closer connection between the music and the business side of his affairs. "Ironically, had Messrs Alder and Fenwick explained to me frankly and fully the reasons for their inability to pay royalties which they had received from Virgin Records and BMG Publishing, the licencees, they would have found me, the most loyal of EG artists, willing to continue supporting them," Fripp explains. "And today I would probably be an EG recording and publishing artist. Sadly, regrettably, and to my present good fortune, after 20 years they didn't know the artist they had managed for so long. Perhaps my loyalty, to me a quality, was for them a weakness."

In the '90s, the founding of DGM was both a philosophical and economic necessity, providing Fripp with an opportunity to not only run a business on ethical lines but also provide a vital conduit for releasing music that otherwise would never see the light of day. Talking to journalist Vic Garbarini in *Guitar World* in 1995, Fripp offered a stark insight into the differing economies of scale between the indie and the major record label. "Terrifying statistic: Robert, an artist, sold 10,000 copies of *Soundscapes: Live In Argentina* in less than three months with no publicity. How many records does Virgin have to sell off the rack for Robert to get exactly the same amount of money? 210,000! Scary, right?"

Importantly, DGM would be able to straddle the major and the indie sectors, the embodiment of the small, mobile unit he talked about in the '70s. "The question behind creating this label was, if the relationship with Virgin fell through, could King Crimson continue? And the answer is yes," Fripp told Garbarini.

IX

Fripp served notice of DGM's intention to do things differently, re-writing the usual small print of the copyright notice to become a manifesto in miniature: "The phonographic copyright in these performances is operated by Discipline Global Mobile on behalf of the artists, with whom it resides, contrary to common practice in the record industry. Discipline accepts no reason for artists to assign the copyright interest in their work to either record company or management by virtue of a 'common practice' which was always questionable, often improper and is now indefensible."

It's no coincidence that the 1990s also saw the emergence of a major re-issue programme that ranged from Fripp's remastering of the back catalogue on CD (as "Definitive Editions"), via an extensive historical perspective with *Frame By Frame: The Essential King Crimson* boxed set and a series of archive releases beginning with another stunning boxed collection, *The Great Deceiver*, and leading, ultimately, to the establishment of the King Crimson Collectors' Club in 1998.

Frame By Frame was Fripp's eye-view of the band's music. "In 1991 there was almost no public interest in King Crimson. In the media the name continued to provoke abuse, often linked to the words 'dinosaur' and 'excess'. *Frame By Frame* was my attempt to develop a dialogue with Virgin, protect the catalogue within the new control structure, and present an overview of the history," recalls Fripp. Setting new standards in design, the lavish package was the work of Bill Smith and went on to win the American NAIRD award (a design subsection of the Grammys) for 1991.

Smith is justifiably proud of his involvement with the project, spending long hours overseeing every aspect of its production. Using the boys (Smith's sons) on the cover suggests the innocence and aspiration of youth, while the individual jewel case sleeves seem to argue that the prime elements are inextricably threaded and bound to the act of making music. Given the synergy that exists between the visual and aural content of the *Frame By Frame* set, it's hardly surprising that out of the numerous Crimson and Fripp-related projects, and indeed the 3,000–4,000 sleeves with which Bill Smith has been involved, *Frame By Frame* is among his favourites.

In compiling the set, Fripp asked Belew and Levin to add new parts for *Cadence And Cascade* and *Bolero* respectively. Talking to journalist Anil Prasad in 1992, Belew explained: "I was going to visit Robert over the summer for a couple of days and he suggested that 'Since you're here, why don't you do something on this new compilation?' So, it was entirely his idea, but I enjoyed singing it. I always liked that track even though I had no involvement in the original version." Though unfamiliar with *Lizard*, Tony Levin overdubbed his part with the minimum of fuss. "I hadn't heard *Bolero – The Peacock's Tale* before and learned it by listening to the track," commented Levin. "Robert was helpful about what he wanted from the bass part, and we did it quite quickly and easily."

Around the time of the set's release, Fripp met criticism that he was tampering with the band's history by arguing that he regarded Crimson's recorded output as malleable and subject to change and review. While this may well be true, Haskell's long-held ire with Fripp, which had been verging on litigious, was also a factor in the decision to air-brush the bassist out of Crim history.

1992's *The Great Deceiver* featured the live work of the '73/'74 incarnation of Crimson. For Fripp, the four-CD set was designed to help "rewrite the knee-jerk school of prog history by presenting primary materials for a new generation to come to its own opinion on Crimson's place in that history".

The albums were once again housed in a package designed by Smith. "We hired a real magician (stage name: The Great Kovari) to do the shoot and I think he was worried that he'd get drummed out of the Magic Circle if the shots revealed his tricks of the trade," laughs Smith. Aside from bearing an unintentional passing resemblance to Jamie Muir, the magician is a representation of The Great Deceiver. "It's like someone behind the stage pulling the strings, which funnily enough is very Robert. I think he is The Great Deceiver. In all of the King Crimsons, Robert is there pulling the strings. Robert's the magician." Smith's designs went on to win a *Music Week* award as well as other industry commendations.

Despite this focus on the past, Fripp felt that King Crimson was beginning to manifest itself once again. "Music bearing an unmistakable Crimson accent had been flying by my ear since 1986/87. I took the personal decision to put King Crimson back into action during the second half of 1990 but without a clear idea of how that might be."

After starting to write the music for a doomed film version of cyberpunk SF author William Gibson's *Neuromancer*, Fripp approached singer David Sylvian in late 1991 to ask him to be part of a new Crimson. Although Fripp had previously appeared on Sylvian's *Alchemy: An Index Of Possibilities* (1985) and *Gone To Earth* (1986), it was a startling suggestion. "Though very flattered, I decided that I didn't feel equipped to take on the whole baggage and history that comes with being a member of King Crimson," Sylvian explained to journalist Paul Tingen in 1998. "So instead we took the offer of the tour as an opportunity to write material for an album."

Trey Gunn toured in the three-piece version of Sylvian and Fripp in early 1992 and was one of the first people to hear some of the music which Fripp thought bore the taste of King Crimson. "I knew he was working on it," recalls Gunn. "There were even inklings of it before Sylvian and Fripp. He'd show me a little figure and we'd experiment with it, and I'd think 'that sounds a little like Crimson to me'."

As the Sylvian–Fripp project started working, the shape of the new King Crimson occurred to Fripp in a typically unconventional manner. "The picture of a Double

Trio formation appeared in a flash while I was driving past our village church towards Salisbury one afternoon in the Autumn of 1992," Fripp noted. "The Double Trio was not what I intended, expected nor wanted, but I trusted this point of seeing sufficiently to act upon it."

Prior to Sylvian's arrival for the recording of *The First Day* in December 1992, Trey Gunn, drummer Jerry Marotta and Fripp found time at Dreamland Studios in upstate New York to work on several pieces, in particular a skeleton of what would become *One Time* and the "Fairy Fingers" section of *VROOOM*. Though these are not on the finished album, parts of *The First Day* – such as the jagged chordal see-sawing on *20th Century Dreaming* – are not unlike the future KC.

Was Gunn surprised at the emergence of a new King Crimson? "I knew that Robert had been thinking about King Crimson since 1987. I knew he was playing around with ideas – you hear them and you know it's Crimson. But I don't think he could bear the concept of putting the band together back then. He didn't really ask and I didn't hustle him or anything. Right place, right time, I guess." Gunn laughs at the daunting prospect of joining the band. "I'm already at a disadvantage being in a band that's 30 years old and has one of the world's best bass players on the planet in it already. It's a no-win situation really."

Following the departure of Marotta, auditions for a drummer for Fripp and Sylvian were held at Peter Gabriel's Real World Studios in Box, near Bath. Local resident Michael Giles was one of those who tried their hand. Another contender was a drummer who had flown all the way from Los Angeles to have a shot at joining the group.

Pat Mastelotto – born in California on 10 September 1955 – began playing drums when he was ten and taught himself by playing along to The Beatles and tunes on the radio. King Crimson was always one of his favourite groups – he recalls hearing *In The Wake Of Poseidon*, in particular *Cat Food*, on headphones at the local library when he was a teenager. Later still, his future wife Connie had a copy of *Islands* on her turntable when they started dating. Mastelotto cites Michael Giles as a tremendous influence on his playing.

After a succession of local bands, Pat moved to Los Angeles and earned a living as a session drummer before finding commercial success in pop group Mr. Mister. The group sold over three million records but broke up after three albums. Mastelotto returned to session work. Among the records on which he made his mark was XTC's album *Oranges And Lemons*, released in 1989. He also played with The Rembrandts, most famous for *I'll Be There For You*, theme from popular US comedy show *Friends*.

It was Crafty Bill Forth who provided Mastelotto with the information that Sylvian and Fripp needed a drummer, putting him in contact with Trey Gunn. Gunn, in turn, passed him on to Richard Chadwick, who was managing Sylvian and Fripp. Chadwick tried to dissuade Mastelotto on the grounds that he did not know any of the material and auditions were due to commence in just two days. But, realising that he was not to be put off, Chadwick pencilled in a slot and the drummer cashed in his Frequent Flyer Miles for the 3,000-mile journey to Britain.

Arriving in the UK, he used his contacts at Virgin to acquire a tape of *The First Day* and then made extensive notes on a drumhead to act as an *aide-mémoire* during the audition. Mastelotto had no real expectation of landing the job but, as a long-time fan of Fripp and Crimson, figured it would be worthwhile for the experience. After only a couple of numbers, Fripp stopped playing. Mastelotto assumed that the guitarist had had enough and had walked out through the door behind the drummer. In fact, Fripp had moved behind Mastelotto to watch him play more closely. At the end of the audition, Fripp gave Mastelotto a note and said: "That's my home number. If you ever need a referral have them call me and I'll give them the highest recommendation."

Somewhat awestruck, Mastelotto produced a snare drum and asked for Fripp's autograph for his then-partner. When Fripp asked if there was anything else he could do, the drummer said: "I'd like to stay around and see if it's possible to meet Michael Giles because I'd heard he was coming." Mastelotto recalls: "I went way off across the field at Real World and coincidently met David Bottrill, who had co-produced *The First Day*, for the first time. I didn't know who he was then but we hung together and he took me on a little tour of the place and that's when I got to realise that he was a friend of Trey, who I really didn't know at that point."

Back home in Austin, Mastelotto was greeted by a message from Richard Chadwick telling him that he had the gig, subject to them working out the details about the money. Mastelotto smiles when he recalls Chadwick's words: "We're not cheap and you're not greedy so this should be easy."

At the end of a successful European tour, the band – Sylvian, Fripp, Gunn, Mastelotto and "infinite guitarist" Michael Brook – broke up and Mastelotto expected that to be the end of it.

But, in January 1994, a provisional King Crimson took its first tentative steps into the world. Tony Levin, Adrian Belew, Trey Gunn, Robert Fripp and Jerry Marotta began work in Applehead Studios, Woodstock. "I'd never met Adrian before other than maybe once backstage at a Sylvian and Fripp gig," says Gunn, who was also meeting Levin for the first time. "I was pretty nervous because he was the guy that was not only the great bass player of all these albums, he was the guy who I knew as *the* Stick player, he was the guy who did *that*," laughs Gunn.

Yet Gunn observed that not everything was going to plan. "I could tell Adrian was going along with Robert's idea but not wholly into it, and that night I think I saw Robert the most distressed I've ever seen him in his life; he was like, 'It's not working.'"

Despite the line-up having played together for only a few hours, Fripp was not convinced and decided to carry on minus Marotta. On 7 January, he made the calls that would bring the Double Trio into being.

X

Gunn recalls being somewhat awestruck at the prospect of working in a line-up that included all four members of the 1980s incarnation of the group. "For me, *Discipline* was *the* record … I liked a lot of other stuff but that was the shit that just kind of landed from Mars for me. I think if I'd just gotten a call from Robert and he said, 'Do you want to join King Crimson?' I probably wouldn't have known how to handle it. But I'd spent so much time with Robert hearing him think about Crimson. So although I wasn't expecting ever to be asked, I wasn't totally surprised when he did. Then it was less about being in the band but more about being with those guys."

Mastelotto was surprised to hear a message on his machine from Fripp, suffering from a heavy cold, with a proposal to join a new Crimson. "He said that things hadn't worked out with Jerry and that he'd had a vision of using two drummers. 'It'd be you and Bill.' And I said: 'What does Bill think about this?' And he said: 'I don't know. I haven't called him yet. I called you first.'"

By March 1992, Bruford had completed several lucrative months on the road with Yes following the release of *Anderson Bruford Wakeman Howe* (1989) and *Union* (1991). It's probably true to say that he could have worked with any group in 1994, though Bruford disputes this. "Really there were very few groups that I'd want to have joined. King Crimson's my spiritual home. Robert's always had a great big pair of open ears for drums and drummers. I think I've always seen King Crimson as one of the very few so-called rock outfits that could begin to accommodate my particular small vision of what it is that drummers can do. Not many other outfits can do that. I mean they have other agendas; they might want songs that are played extremely well or they might be following some other guy's compositional approach or something, but King Crimson is, or was, and may remain, a nominal democracy, which is the way I grew up – where you could bring whatever you had to the table and negotiate with others and see if you could make it work in a group format."

Upon hearing that a new Crimson was in the offing, Bruford lobbied Fripp. "I believe I contacted him by letter and I was very insistent that this next King Crimson of the 1990s would include me, and Robert appears to respond to that."

The creative antipathy between Fripp and Bruford had reached an all-time low at the end of the 1980s. Yet, despite the tensions, Bruford still viewed Crimson as one of the best places for a drummer to be.

In fact, Bruford's "last-minute" addition hinged on the fact that he was still managed by EG until 18 April 1994 – the very date the new line-up of King Crimson formally opened for business. Why did he want to be part of the new formation so badly? "Well, there's a career in place here. In the *THRAK* days, being in the band meant that some

250,000 people could hear your latest rhythmic inventions and that I liked and that I wanted to be part of. Added to which, there are very important peripheral issues – namely Tony Levin is one of my best friends and I love playing with him, Adrian is terrific and so there were lots of reasons to want to join." Bruford states that one aspect to his return was a tacit acknowledgement of Fripp's leadership. He does, however, readily admit that Fripp's stewardship in the past had provided the right guidance and musical direction. "Some great music has been made as a result and better music than I could have done on my own. Had the boot been on the other foot and Robert said to me, one month before *Discipline*, 'All right, Bill, you run the band. What shall we play?' I don't think I would have come up with anything as creative as *Discipline*, *Beat* or *Three Of A Perfect Pair*. So my hat goes off to him. My empathy is with him but he's still a difficult bugger."

In February 1994, with Adrian Belew unable to make it to the UK, Fripp, Levin, Mastelotto and Gunn convened at Bruford's house in Surrey to start tackling some of the new material. Mastelotto was working behind a kit which Bill had borrowed from his neighbour, Kenney Jones of The Who. "There was a huge volume discrepancy; Bill's on his jazz kit and I'm about three feet away from him on a big kit he used when touring with The Who, with a massive 26-inch bass drum and power toms," says Pat who admits to being somewhat awestruck at being in the room with these players. "You can understand that it's such a fantasy of a young Californian kid to get to play music with these kinds of musicians you admire from afar. I went out and bought a musical dictionary because I couldn't understand some of the things that were being talked about. For example, a coda – I didn't know what that was. I'd heard *Hey Jude* a million times but nobody ever told me that that was a coda. I bought a small pocket-sized one which I could keep near me so I could pull it out of my coat pocket during rehearsals!"

Mastelotto readily confesses to being a little starstruck. It was the first time that he'd met Tony Levin and recalled that he had once met Bruford in 1974 when Crimson played the Shrine in Los Angeles. "I've never told him this before but I was standing outside when he walked out with a six-pack of Coors under his arm. I was just a poseur standing by the backstage door watching them get in their limousine." Pat was also a little baffled by Bruford's habitual use of the English phrase "You're a brick". Meaning "You're a good person and someone I can depend on", it was lost on Mastelotto who'd never heard the term before and thought Bruford was saying, "You're a prick." "That kinda threw me!" he laughs.

Bruford smiles when recalling the slightly awkward beginnings of the partnership. "I said hello to Pat and Pat said hello to me and we really started work. I'd never heard of Pat before other than from the theme song of *Friends* and I wouldn't have known that at the time. I didn't really know what to do with him nor him with me. We sat and practised a bit and initially it was fairly fruitless and we couldn't think what to do until the penny dropped: what you do is adopt a character, a musical identity to make this work. Pat was essentially Ringo Starr connecting with the audience and I was essentially Jamie Muir or Elvin Jones upsetting, or terrorising or floating 'round and causing confusion with that connection. Once you'd adopted those kinds of characters and agreed that that was a great way to go, then everything else is easy and after that everything fell into place. In a way it was a reversal of Jamie Muir's playing off of me on *Larks' Tongues In Aspic*; I was the straight good boy and Muir was this creature from hell. I didn't know what to do with him or him with me. My function was to locate a beat and play it. So, something of a reversal and I think it worked really well."

The initial sessions played around with early sketches of *One Time*, *Inner Garden*, a Fripp piece for the two drummers called *Trappist Holiday* and the main themes from what would later be called *Booga Looga. THRAK* also received its first unveiling in a King Crimson rehearsal room. Fripp outlined his plans for the new phase of Crimsonising which detailed the intention to prepare material for a mini-album to be sold to Japanese record label Pony Canyon as a means to finance the next stage: full band rehearsals and recording at Woodstock in April and May; concerts in Buenos Aires during September and October and the recording of a full-scale album in November and December in the UK. It was going to be a busy year.

On 18 April, all six members convened for the first time at Applehead Studios to pull together material through a mixture of blows and formal presentations. Pieces included Belew's *Cage* and *I Remember How To Forget*. On the *VROOOM* sessions, the latter track is entitled *Krim 3*. Unhappy with the result, Belew withdrew it. "I played a demo of that one for the band and we learned it. After hearing the band play it, I preferred the demo version which featured a single trio not a double trio. That's the way I wanted the song produced and, in fact, it's the same demo version which appears on my album *Op Zop Too Wah* (1996). Robert asked jokingly, 'How does it feel to have your child beaten?' I didn't feel the band had beaten my child. I simply wanted a different approach." It was early days for the new group and people were still getting to know each other. The general approach to material presented or improvised in a King Crimson rehearsal room is that people are expected to find their own parts. "Robert's approach is pretty hardline: this is what I'm doing so have at it," observes Gunn. "He really hardly ever told anyone what to play. It was more like *this is what I'm doing and what are you going to do?* So it was up for us to negotiate what we were doing. A good example is Tony's bass in the *VROOOM* fairy fingers section; I was struggling with that for weeks trying to figure out where I could even find a note that fits in that thing. Robert had nothing to offer; he just said 'We'll run it again' (*laughs*). Tony just went off and wrote that entire fretless bass melody to go over the top of the fairy fingers."

Bruford says: "Not being told what to do is a great thing. It requires mature musicians and fairly confident guys, I think. There wasn't much point in me telling Tony Levin what to play or even barely suggesting things. However, within our pairs, that is to say with Pat, I felt perfectly at liberty to say, 'You play this and I'll play that.' He'd say the same thing to me. That worked well with us two. How Tony and Trey got on I don't really know. I also found it took Trey a while to find a particular spot – I think two basses is very tricky."

For a while it looked like the Double Trio might not survive their first week. Three or four days into the rehearsals, Belew called a band meeting in the kitchen and asked to step out of the band. "I was kind of blindsided," says Mastelotto. "I didn't sense or see any of that coming." Belew recalls: "The first few days had not gone well for me personally. My gear had been destroyed by the airlines on the flight to rehearsal so I arrived with literally nothing to play. That certainly hampered my ability to contribute in my usual fashion. Also there were certain pressures inherent in the band which I had struggled with in our first run in 1981 to 1984 and early on I could see they would continue, but such was my excitement to be part of the new King Crimson, I resolved to simply ignore them. The real issue for me was the proposed touring schedule which was posted on the kitchen wall around day three of rehearsals, which if I recall correctly was ten months in the first year. I knew that amount of touring would not allow me to keep all my plates spinning. Since everyone else seemed enthused by the schedule, I felt I might hold them back and that would be unprofessional of me, so we had a meeting." In the spirit of compromise, it was agreed to scale back the touring to around six months, enabling Belew the freedom to pursue his other interests.

In May 1994, the band recorded *VROOOM*. Mixed and co-produced at Real World later that month by David Bottrill, who'd worked alongside Sylvian and Fripp, the guitarist described *VROOOM* as "a calling card rather than a love letter". Opting for the tried and tested KC trick of the calm before the storm, the twilight world of Fripp's opening Soundscapes gives no hint of the truly monstrous and remorseless onslaught of the title track – which isn't so much a calling card as a brick through the window. The hard metal edge and unforgiving density of the sound piles marks it out as one of the most exciting Fripp compositions since *LTIA2*. It was certainly a quantum leap from the 1980s' style. Bruford recalls some discussion about sounds a new Crimson would create. "There was no question of me getting out the log drums and pitched drums playing light fabrics and melodies. That was all gone. This was going to be big, dark brooding stuff like *Red*, only with two drummers."

Cage began life as a Belew composition which he brought to the rehearsals with the instructions to play it "frantic", which the band certainly achieved. Delivered at breakneck speed with alternating time signatures of 7/8 and 4/4, the lyric portrays a dysfunctional present where society is in chaos. Beginning with a sharp intake of breath from Belew, this chunk of urban paranoia, coming in at less than two minutes long, is a frightening display of musical and lyrical dexterity containing two echoes of former Crimson glories – a further refinement of the interlocking guitar style which KC made their own, and a pattern reminiscent of the second guitar section of *LTIA1*. The pained animal-like bellowing throughout the piece comes from a purple-faced Levin playing a spare didgeridoo that had been left in the studio.

Clocking in at a little over 30 minutes, the EP succeeded in not only in whetting the appetite of fans around the world but provided the finance for the next stage – the recording of the first full King Crimson studio album in ten years.

There's no doubting that the Double Trio was an unwieldy beast at times. Belew recalls: "Getting everyone to land on the same downbeat was hard – we used to joke about it, calling it the 'Crimson downbeat'. Instead of BAM! it was more of a BRRUUUMPH! Precision playing was not as easy as with the '80s line-up."

In July, after Fripp had completed mixing *VROOOM* at Real World, he rejoined the band at Applehead to run over the new material and refurbish and retool older repertoire for the band's trip to South America in September. Working out parts for the '80's material brought its own challenges. Trey Gunn recalls: "First of all, what the hell do you do on *Elephant Talk*? It doesn't need anything else. So do you *not* play? Or who do I double? *Frame By Frame* doesn't need it. Also Robert and Adrian have a density to them; there's not really the room to do the subtle little thing that you could perhaps do on the record. They already fill up the space. Adrian's sound is quite small when you listen to him alone but in the band he's got totally the right sound. So, yeah, what do you do? For most of the *Discipline* stuff I didn't feel there was a place for me but Tony found things for us – we eventually started trading off things for *Elephant Talk*. Tony found things like later in *Neurotica* in the second verse he sings harmony with Adrian and he was never able to really play the Stick part and sing the harmony, so I took the second verse as the bass. Once you loosened the mortar on the structure, there was a lot of stuff you could do, and kudos to those guys for trying it. Once you have a piece then it's really about the orchestration of it."

XI

To outsiders, Argentina may have seemed an odd location for the new Crimson's formal live debut. However, Fripp had established links with the country via the Guitar Craft network and, in June 1994, after the recording of *VROOOM*, undertook a Soundscapes tour whose venues included the Prix d'Ami, Buenos Aires, where Crimson would play three months later. Time in Estudio El Pie was spent on the newly developed pieces, refining older repertoire and, when the occasion demanded it, pulling out pre-existing material. After his earlier experience at Applehead with his songs, Belew was initially reluctant to share more, but as the sessions progressed he proffered *People*, a song he'd demoed himself in 1992. "Over time I recognised the songs which were most successful, i.e. the ones that made it to the records and sounded most Crimson-like, were always started with Robert and me writing *together*. To bring a song of mine to the band, less so. It was never my aim to burden Crimson with songs of mine which already had a place to exist on my solo records regardless. I usually offered them when there was a perceived scarcity of material. *People* is a good example. At the time I offered it to the band during writing sessions in Argentina, it seemed more uptempo material was needed to round out the record we hoped to make."

As the six rehearsed, Hernan Nunez, a member of Los Gauchos Alemanes and South American supremo for Possible Productions, took on the task of ensuring that Crimson's return ran as smoothly as possible. In other countries it might have been easy to book a venue and advertise the concerts. Yet, as Nunez explains, in Argentina things are rarely that straightforward.

"This old El Broadway had been closed and was in bad shape, totally abandoned except for Ricardo, a man who acted as 'housekeeper' and lived in the basement, with his cats and dogs. He was known as 'the phantom of the opera'. Possible Productions Argentina took him on to bring up El Broadway to good condition in order to have KC perform there and cut a direct deal with the owners. We had two huge power generator trucks outside by the door because the electricity situation was feeble and couldn't handle more than 3000 watts. Meanwhile, the dressing rooms, backstage and stage were painted and several major repairs began taking place."

Having erected a large marquee outside the theatre to advertise the forthcoming shows, Hernan's people kept a wary eye on ticket touts and other "arrangements" that were common practice. "One afternoon, Ricardo, 'El Fantasma', having been properly 'oiled' (paid) was very co-operative and he called us to tell us that our marquee was being removed and that a box office had been opened in front of ours in the entrance hall for another group."

Racing across town in ten minutes on a fast motorbike, Nunez was surprised to see two people taking down King Crimson's marquee in favour of one advertising forthcoming concerts by Yes, who were then promoting *Talk*. "A team was preparing to sell tickets with a big Yes poster, a few days prior to King Crimson. This was done by a big promoter. We 'oiled' the two guys and they left, after re-fixing the KC marquee. Later that day, the 'Yes in Argentina' story hit the media, using an exact copy of Crimson's press release, even including the phrase 'the return of Yes to active service'."

Nunez recalls that Fripp and other members of the Possible Productions team saw the concerts by Yes, which Nunez reveals helped the Crimson shows. "We got the venue back in better shape than when we first arrived. We had saved lots of money and sold many KC tickets to the Yes audience. The Broadway had been tested by the PA-Stage Monitoring Team (El Toro Martinez) in a full-performance situation, which was very useful to us. We had the lights tested and they just left the PA, power amps, cables in there which meant we were able to use them."

Fripp cites King Crimson's formal return as being on 1 October at the Prix d'Ami Disco. "The dress rehearsal the evening before was a poorly kept secret: I suggested to the promoter that he invite friends to come and listen." Nunez recalls: "At the time, the Prix d'Ami was a hot club-disco and was converted into a live rehearsal-warm up club for KC. The first show was a dress rehearsal, open only to invited guests, particularly the Press, who attended in full formation, including journalists from other South American countries. Then two more performances, also for invited guests – personalities, many rock stars, actors, politicians and, of course, also journalists, but these two performances were also open to the public."

The shows at the Prix d'Ami caused quite a stir, he says. "The tickets were gone in two hours, lots of people outside, police and security team in red alert mode. There are of course many other juicy details to this whole story of King Crimson in Argentina, but this gives you a feel of what was going on and why I began to smoke again after seven years ..."

Looking back on the period prompts good memories for Gunn. "Argentina was awesome," he says. "I'd already been there twice before, and over the decades there are certain periods when you can't go there because it's completely fucked up. Not fucked up like Iraq-fucked-up, but just financially fucked up. Then there's some renaissance and there's money available. Then it goes haywire for another period. I went a few different times in those slots and this was a good one. Buenos Aires is one of my favourite places on the planet. I really can remember almost nothing about the rehearsals. I do remember the shows and that we had to sign 5,000 flats (booklets) for *VROOOM*. So for every day and for every show we had hundreds of them on the table set up like a factory line. We'd end up taking them to our hotel rooms to sign."

Mastelotto has similarly fond memories: "The Prix d'Ami was pretty dingy. It had a pretty high stage, about six feet, and then a dance floor. We couldn't quite all fit on the stage so I went to the extreme at one side in sort of a cage made out of a kind of chain link thing. Maybe it would've been a DJ's booth or something, but essentially it put the band on stage as a five-piece and I was this guy over on the side. That was fine with me; I liked being in the dark and off to the side."

The shows in Argentina allowed the Double Trio to find where each person could begin to build their parts and contribute to the group's sound and overall development. Reflecting on the period, Belew observes that one drawback was that: "It was hard to get someone *not* to play, which is only natural. Soundchecks were a horror show (I can still hear parts of them) but this was all made up for by the intensity of the music; the Double Trio was a thunderous, explosive instrument capable of nearly anything and truly awesome to behold in concert."

Just eight days after their final show at Teatro Broadway, the band reassembled in Real World Studios outside Bath. Opened in the late '80s, Peter Gabriel's studio complex offered a comfortable environment for the group. Yet, despite its state-of-the-art status, the arrival of the Double Trio stretched Real World's facilities from the very beginning of their initial four-week stay. "I always remember technical complexities with the recording. We were largely invisible to each other at Real World. I'm not even sure that Pat and I even had eye contact. Very tricky," recalls Bruford. "We were very dependent on a headphone mix. In those days the idea of six people all playing at once was going out of fashion rapidly and studios were really just elaborate overdub booths with one pair of headphones and one person playing at a time. I think we caused some uproar in trying to be able to listen to each other. It was technically difficult to hear what was going on when we were all playing at once, and of course we had six people saying, 'Can we play it again from C?'"

Mastelotto agrees: "We had six guys who wanted six different headphone mixes. I ended up tracking in the stone room and Bill in the wood room but originally I was in the wood room. For the first day or two I had a decent headphone mix; it was Bill, the last guy furthest away from the control room, who had the worst headphone mix and visual vantage points. So, somewhere around the first or second day, in order to keep Bill on course and having him in a more pleasant environment where he could see and communicate better, I swapped rooms. We agreed my drums in the stone room worked better. Then the headphone mix became my big problem. The further you went down the chain meant that everyone had a problem and by the time it got to me it was the worst. My tracking room was connected more for the other control room which is where the Kronos Quartet, who were there at the same time as us, were mixing an album. As time went on, it became an issue being the loud drummer adjacent to where they were mixing. I forget what arrangement we made but we made it so that they would have some quiet time, so while we did guitar or vocal overdubs they could be fine-tuning one of their mixes without drums pounding in the wall right next to them."

While the set-up was complicated, for producer David Bottrill the aim was simply to capture the music with as much clarity and fidelity as possible. This was not without its challenges. "The first day had really just been setting everything up. So we started up on the second day and the first track they want to run through is *THRAK*. Bear in mind I've not heard a note of what's going on. They play through this song once, and I mean once, and they go 'Yeah, we like that'. But Bill says to me, 'OK, on the end section where it goes into this thing in 5/7, can you drop me in on the third beat, please,' and I'm just staring blankly at the desk. I look up and see Tony and Trey at the back laughing because they know I'm completely lost and I have no idea what's going on. Bill assumes that I've heard it before or had been able to glean it from one listen through this entirely improvisational thing! So, I said: 'Yes, Bill, I can but you'll have to give me a few minutes to do a little education on the tune and start counting.'"

Trey Gunn remembers Bruford being a little wary at first of Bottrill, knowing only of his work on Sylvian and Fripp's *The First Day* album. Any initial doubts were quickly dispelled once Bruford saw Bottrill at work. "I remember Bill saying: 'That guy's got his phase figured out for all the drum mikes. He knows what he's doing.'" Bruford is emphatic about his respect for the producer. "I liked Bottrill a lot. He had the key qualities which were patience and calmness. Five people can turn on you at once; it sounds weedy; it should be louder, or my bass stinks – and everybody says it at once and you do need to be very calm. I thought Bottrill made it sound really good. When it went to tape I thought it was a mess, but the final result has this wonderful quality; very ballsy, very big, very strong rock music but it's also got an airy quality as well. You can see around the instruments. As the sound of a record I love it, it's absolutely great."

Gunn also attests to Bottrill's terrific ear for pitch and tone and the consummate professionalism of his bandmates. "There was one unbelievable overdub for *VROOOM*. Tony's fretless bass melody in the fairy fingers section. Check this out, I bet Tony won't even remember this, or he probably wouldn't be impressed because he's Tony: Bottrill was like, 'Is there something slightly out of tune in this section?' So they listened to the guitar players – Robert doing the fairy fingers and Adrian doing a line. I think what they figured out was that one of the guitars was slightly sharp or flat, I mean *slightly*, and Tony was pitching to the other guy. So he just turned that guy down a little bit and replayed the whole thing. To be honest I couldn't hear any difference, I couldn't hear anything wrong with the first one. I think Tony just did a single pass again and it sounded fucking amazing."

"My philosophy was that if we were going to have two drum kits, one's got to be the engine and one's got to be the colour," explains Bottrill. "For me, Pat was this huge thumping, driving thing so he went into a room that supported his playing, I thought, and Bill was much more precise and needed much more articulation on his sound, so it wasn't as big size-wise but the detail was all there. Other than the odd minor ego thing like that going on, I felt that the rest was really good. I think as Adrian said at the beginning of the project when we started at Real World, 'I've detailed my sounds in my monitors here so that they can fit in and amongst what Robert's doing,' because Robert's sound is enormous. It takes up a lot of space. There was this idea that if we were going to have two guitar players and a Stick and a bass, we were going to have to find sonic positions for everybody to be able to fit and to play. And I think they really did that in the rehearsal rooms. So for the recording process, although it was still a challenge, there were no impossibilities. It all seemed to work out in the process. The mixing process was really interesting actually because we didn't use any automation. Now bear in mind there are two drum kits, two bass players and two guitarists and a vocal from time to time. There's a lot to carve together. Robert would give me two or three hours and say: 'Are you done yet?' And I'd sometimes say, 'No, can you give me another hour?' and he'd be OK and come back 45 minutes later and ask if I was done yet. So I'd say, 'OK, let's try.' So I would ride the volume faders and he would ride the pans, and every time I'd change something on the volume, he'd change something on the pan. His whole thing was the stereo picture; volume for him was as much in the stereo position as it was in actual volume. It was a really fascinating process. I would just try to keep out of the way as much as I could and make sure the band's colours all came through when necessary. When they were more in a support role, they'd still be audible but they wouldn't be as featured, shall we say."

"My main goal really is I feel that if you've written something there should be enough clarity to understand it and for the listener to be able to hear it. What I really attempt to do with most of my projects is to make sure that the compositions that the band is proud of writing are heard. Whether it's a vocal or a guitar part, things that are fundamental to the composition and make-up of the song ought to be audible. That's what I hope I've achieved on those King Crimson recordings – trying to make sure that the two drum kits are featured enough so that it makes sense to have two drum kits. Otherwise, what's the point?"

Bruford reveals another element which came to bear upon the approach to drumming on *THRAK*. "I was highly influenced by the magnificent Gavin Harrison, who I have been proposing as the country's hidden national treasure for several years. Of course, now he's in King Crimson. Gavin at the time was a real specialist in drumming and had released a variety of drum books, manuals and pedagogical stuff that I found to be highly influential, about beat displacement and all sorts of metrical tricks of one sort or another."

The future member of King Crimson sent Bruford a manuscript copy of his book *Rhythmic Illusions* to Real World during the recording. "This became a bit of a bible for me and Pat to work with. I'd play the same thing as Pat but a 16th note late for example, or play a meter within a meter. That kind of approach. Often Gavin's theories depended on one rhythm being played and then another one played against it. So what more fun could you have with two drummers? To me this came to fruition on *Sex Sleep Eat Drink Dream* which has what I'm talking about in bucketloads, especially around the guitar solos where the thing goes completely berserk. It might sound like the drummers are playing anything they want for a minute but this is absolutely not the case. I could notate entirely for you those passages and Gavin probably has recognised them already as being highly informed by his work."

Mastelotto, who would go on to share the stage with Harrison in 2008 and 2014, recalls: "I wasn't aware of Gavin or Gavin's book until a year or so after that. It wasn't really until we were up in Nashville when the band decomposed in 1997. By then I'd worked with Gavin's book for a couple of years. That was the time when Bill and I openly discussed Gavin's stuff. During *THRAK* Bill may have been into it but I wasn't privy to it."

The rhythmic vocabulary of the band is well to the fore on the title track. Trey Gunn laughs: "We joke that the version on the record *THRAK* is the kinder, gentler *THRAK* because it's a little bit sweeter and not very long at all." Mastelotto recalls that the track was a particular favourite of David Bottrill. "We'd just done *THRAK*. As I approached the control room I could see through the glass that Bottrill was jumping and gyrating (*laughs*), like a fish thrown up on to the land, moving in these spasms. I realised he's actually found a rhythm inside of *THRAK* that makes his body twitch. He looked like a puppet, his arms flexing in weird ways – man, it cracked us up."

Dinosaur started life in Woodstock after Fripp presented Belew with a five-chord sequence that consciously re-addressed the cut-and-thrust minor thirds of *Cirkus* from 1970's *Lizard*. Fripp had hoped that a Crimson equivalent of *I Am The Walrus* might be possible. Belew added a few more chords to accommodate the melody he had in mind, but was unsure as to where the song should go next. It wasn't until the team decamped to Argentina that Belew came up with an approach that opened the piece up.

"When I first heard the term 'double trio' I imagined it to mean a sextet which would on occasion operate as two separate trios instead of always performing as a six-piece band. The tenor of the earliest instrumental pieces we were creating like *VROOOM VROOOM* or *THRAK* tended to be 'epic' in nature. I wanted to apply the 'epic' part to an actual song and at the same time break the band into one of the many trios available. So I wrote the middle chamber piece. I envisioned Robert and Tony and me suddenly turning into an 'orchestral trio' in the middle of a (more or less) pop song. Robert approved but declined to play, so the chamber section became me, Trey and Tony. It should be pointed out that *Dinosaur* was already an epic piece. My album *The Guitar As Orchestra* provided me with the necessary guitar synthesiser orchestral sounds I had programmed, but otherwise had no relevance."

Pat Mastelotto still finds the track to be one of the highlights of the Double Trio's brief career. "When that song came together I thought it was fucking brilliant. It had been developed in pieces and when Adrian presented that song, including the whole orchestral bridge, that was Adrian all by himself. The other guys found ways to get into the arrangement. I thought the lyric was just perfect. It clearly defines what the band is, or what we as individuals in the band are! (*laughs*) And it's got a good pop hook on top of that!"

The album is bookended by two of the most powerful pieces in the Crimson repertoire – *VROOOM* and *VROOOM VROOOM*. Fripp had defined the term *VROOOM* as "an inevitable and remorseless forward motion which carries all before it". The first sounds heard on the record emanate from the very same Mellotron used on *In The Court Of The Crimson King* in 1969. Here the sounds coaxed from the venerable keyboard are intentionally awkward, creaking and wheezing – suggesting, perhaps, the old world swept aside by the new. Precisely which old order and its institutions are being rent asunder might be discerned in *Coda: Marine 475*. Alongside the screeching guitars, Fripp and Gunn can be heard intoning the names and designations given to a Lloyd's insurance syndicate which suffered huge financial losses and whose members included Sam Alder and Mark Fenwick from EG.

A startling and uncompromising edifice, *VROOOM* – with its apocalyptic what-goes-around-comes-around coda – defines the Double Trio at its thrilling best. Perhaps with a touch of gallows humour, Fripp describes it as "an example of remorseless and unforgiving inevitability where one is called to honour one's liability without limitation". Belew might well have had *VROOOM* in mind when he made the following comment at the time of the album's release. "To me, this record needed to have its foot in the future and its foot in the past at the same time – to serve as a wake-up call. I think the music is still traditionally King Crimson, and yet it's progressing onward and forward, as King Crimson always does."

While the band recorded at Real World, Bill Smith was commissioned by Virgin to design the album's cover and co-ordinate the packaging for the electronic press kit and general publicity photos. Unusually, Smith had to tout his ideas to all six members of the band for endorsement before he could proceed to a final design and spent some time at Real World absorbing the feel of the music.

"I have to be able to hear the music for an album cover that we're doing. It seemed to me to have a very hard, metally kind of vibe to it and that's what gave me the idea for the cover." The piece of metal he eventually used was a section of a computer security cupboard in Smith's premises which hadn't quite lived up to the manufacturer's guarantee during an office burglary.

Smith also co-ordinated the publicity shoot with photographer Kevin Westenberg. The session at Real World was very difficult as the band were such reluctant subjects. Fripp's well-known aversion to photography resulted in Smith personally having to go and fetch the guitarist and cajole him into taking part. "We had a serious argument about it. He just didn't understand why he needed to be there at that particular time."

"The photo shoot ruined a full day's recording, for which time we paid anyway," argues Fripp. "To prejudice the recording session for photography is unacceptable, in my book. Kevin didn't appear to take this into account at all."

Fripp was by no means the only member less than keen to be there and Westenberg almost walked off the shoot. Smith continues: "They argued about who stood where and about the Polaroids – 'I look all right in this one' or 'I don't look good in that one' and I'm pretty sure we might have put one head off one shot on to another because it wasn't quite right." Smith reveals that this was one of the reasons the *THRAK* tour booklet was overprinted with silver to allow the band and their evident discomfort to be layered into the background.

The logo Smith designed, which acted as a kind of corporate stamp, was nicknamed the electric cockroach by some band members. Smith adds another layer of meaning to the total package by printing the lyrics against a backdrop containing various onomatopoeic words in reverse. Held up in front of a mirror, the single words are revealed but of course in doing so, the lyrics themselves are now rendered unreadable. These words themselves connect to the images printed on the other side of the inlay card. Thus "Vrooom" matches the fast-moving car, "Snap" coincides with the fractured bone and so on.

Not everyone in the band was happy with the results. Belew, for example, didn't like the way the printed lyrics were fully justified across the page width, resulting in some lines ending up with only two or three words and the sense and momentum of the printed words nulled and fragmented. With six people to consult, perhaps it was always going to be an impossible task to please everyone. However, Smith admits to being very satisfied with the total package of CD cover, booklet and metal box, believing that all the design elements worked well together, adding extra layers of visuals to interact with the music. "It was about trying to give another storyline to the existing music."

Work on *THRAK* was completed in December 1994 and the album was finally released in April 1995 to surprisingly receptive reviews. In the UK, *Q* awarded the album four stars and praised Crimson's continuing inventiveness "with jazz-scented rock structures, characterised by Robert Fripp's noisy, angular, exquisite (gizmo-drenched) guitar interplay over an athletic, ever-inventive rhythm section". In the USA, *Rolling Stone* accorded the album three stars, asserting that Crimson's passionate virtuosity was "grayed but not gone", stating "these veterans can keep pace with young noisemakers when it comes to well-wrought sonic violence".

THRAK's appearance represented a dramatic and forceful return for King Crimson as a band and indeed a brand. At any one of King Crimson's concerts around the world you would be able to buy stickers, badges, tour boxes, elaborate programmes, singles, the official live in Argentina bootleg *B'Boom* (1995), the improv suite *THRaKaTTaK* (1996), the *Live In Japan* video – all adorned with the electric cockroach. This was probably the most marketed of any incarnation of the band to this point. Partly this was simply a by-product of the merchandise-savvy times but there was also an economic imperative at work: the beast had to be fed. With six band members and eight road crew, as Belew points out: "It took $40,000 including flights from two continents, hotels, rentals, shipping, etc., just to bring the band together for a rehearsal!"

XII

Several months elapsed between Crimson's last hurrah in Argentina and their European debut on 1 May in Dornbirn, Austria.

Pat Mastelotto remembers it all too well. "It was our first gig after we'd recorded the record. I was surprised how under-excited the audience was, yeah. The place didn't exactly explode, you know? It reminded me of when we started the Sylvan and Fripp tour in Japan where everything is so quiet and sedate. You kind of think, oh well, I guess the material is not that exciting then. It's played well but it's functionary, getting the audience off but not taking them to the next level. At Dornbirn we probably felt like the show was a turd (*laughs*) – we'd be like 'did it work?' but the next night was Milan. That was a whole different story. The Italians are verbal, you know what I'm saying?"

And so it would go on, each gig gathering momentum, energy and pace.

"*VROOOM VROOOM* was always a favourite of mine and I think it was because of the ultimate double trio piece where every player really found their role within the group. I always loved watching the audience rock out to this one," says Paul Richards. Along with colleagues Bert Lams and Hideyo Moriya in the California Guitar Trio, Richards saw and heard the Double Trio incarnation over 130 times when they provided support on KC's first major tour since 1984.

Though Richards had played with Fripp and Gunn in the League Of Crafty Guitarists, supporting the Double Trio was his first experience of Crimson in concert. "I enjoyed watching the band develop and experiment over the course of shows that we did together. The ups and downs, the good shows and bad, I always found something that I enjoyed about this band."

At first, Richards listened to the band as a whole but after 20 or 30 shows he focused on each individual player and their contribution. "It seemed to me that the concept was to have each guitarist, each drummer, and each bassist in a complementary role to his counterpart, which supported the overall sound of the group. My initial impressions were of astonishment, amazement, intensity, joy and ferociousness."

"Robert was continually uncompromising in a supportive role of the music," comments Richards. "Many people see him as being uptight, unfriendly and egocentric, but it is simply that he has his own way of doing things to support the musical event in the best way that he knows how. From my perspective, it seems to me that almost everything Robert does on tour, eats, sleeps, drinks, thinks, is somehow in support of preparing himself to be available for the music."

Paul goes on: "One of King Crimson's specialties has always been improvising.

After seeing the show 40 or 50 times, I became very interested in the improvisation sections of the show. Every night was very different; I always waited with anticipation to see what was going to happen next. There was a show at a theatre in Montreal where the improvising really took off, and I was jumping up and down with excitement. Over the course of the 130 concerts that I saw, the guys were always changing things, trying new things, some ideas worked, and others didn't, but it was a continual process of experimentation and discovery."

"With six monster players on stage, it was a must that each of them find their way of fitting in. I remember several times when Tony Levin was just listening, not playing a single note, waiting, listening for the right time to join in. One of the things that I was most amazed about is how they recovered from mistakes. There were a few trainwrecks, but somehow they always pulled out of it and kept going."

Richards recalls *Indiscipline* at the Wiltern Theatre in Los Angeles on 1 July 1995, the last date of the band's American tour. Featuring a devastatingly controlled revved-up solo from Fripp, it also showcased Bill Bruford's free-ranging inclinations. These apparent contradictions locked into the same piece of music had long provided Crimson with a source of tension.

For Paul, Mastelotto's inclusion defused some of the difficulties that had historically arisen. "There was a show at a theatre in Boston where there was a doorway in the upper level of the backstage that opened to the lighting rigging right over Bill Bruford's drum kit. Bert and I sat and watched the entire show just over Bill's head, listening mainly to Bill and hearing the acoustic sound of his drums. Wow! From this vantage point, I could see clearly how having Pat in the band, freed Bill up in a way. I had the sense that Bill could play anything, no matter how complex, but Pat was there to keep things grounded while Bill went into the outer limits of rhythm."

While some would criticise the Double Trio for its unwieldiness, Richards disagrees. "I personally never felt like it was too many players, as I saw many, many shows that the combination of these six players worked exceedingly well. The main thing I remember about the audience was how glad they were to see King Crimson after a ten-year break. After meeting Crimson fans from all over the world, I'd have to say that they are indeed some of the most avid music enthusiasts that I've ever seen. Of course there were a small group of complainers asking: Why are they doing it this way? Why don't they have Greg Lake or John Wetton? Why is Robert sitting in the dark? Why two drummers? I just always felt like saying, 'Fuck that shit and just listen to the music.'"

As someone who saw the Double Trio probably more than anyone else on the planet, what does he know now that he didn't know then? "That this may have been the only chance we had to see/hear Adrian, Robert, Trey, Tony, Pat and Bill all playing together live. One of the many special moments in King Crimson history."

Fripp believed the 1 July gig at the Wiltern in LA to be a major show and wanted to release it straight away. Belew agreed and a mix was partially completed but the tapes were lost. The planned record was shelved – it only saw the light of day in 2005 as a 2-CD King Crimson Collectors' Club release – superseded by *B'Boom* and the all-improv album *THRaKaTTaK*. In the concerts, with the exception of the duets between Levin and Gunn and the fleeting use of *Soundscapes*, collective improvisation was largely sandwiched between either end of the *THRAK* theme. These sections came as a welcome contrast to the tightly drilled songs, allowing the thunderous clamour of Crimson's suppressed dissonant tendencies to burst forth.

Several improvisations were collected together to form *THRaKaTTaK*. Housed in a witty sleeve designed by Bill Smith Studios, complete with a warning sticker bearing the legend "57 Minutes Of Improvised Music and Poster", the album imagines what a night of Thrakking (as Fripp puts it) might sound like. Packed full of fearsome and fearless playing, *THRaKaTTaK* contains the sound of six psyches sizzling on the hot plate of their own invention.

In *The Wire*, reviewer Chris Blackford hailed the album for capturing the spirit of the band's improvised past and possible future. "The scale and density of this music sometimes borders on the terrifying, as layer upon traumatic layer of noise, distortion and warped tonality build up … Yet this is distinctive Crimson music, so much so that for all its MIDI sophistication, Fripp's 'Soundscaping' system is often used to create the sort of overarching, nightmarish string/choral sounds that emerged from two temperamental Mellotrons in the mid-seventies. As powerful a collision between improv and avant rock as you're likely to hear, *THRaKaTTaK* is King Crimson's finest hour."

It wasn't until May 1996 that the group reconvened for brief rehearsals and further touring with 24 dates throughout Europe before 23 shows in the USA.

On stage, the Double Trio proffered a musical onslaught which led reviewer Tobias Hill in the UK's *Sunday Telegraph* to observe that "Fripp, Belew, Levin and Gunn play like Four Axemen of the Apocalypse". On a raised platform, the backline of Mastelotto, Fripp and Bruford looked down upon Gunn, Belew and Levin. Phil Wiffen's impressive stage design and lighting got 'round Fripp's well-known aversion to the spotlight although, ironically, his impassive silhouette somehow served to draw even more attention to the guitarist.

As the *Live In Mexico City* set (made available as a free download-only album in August 1999) testifies, the band were in fine form although it was interesting to note that there was no new material on offer. On this tour the band revived *21st Century Schizoid Man*, to the evident delight of fans. There could be no doubting the Double Trio's standing as a delivery mechanism for powerful and biting renditions of Crimson's repertoire – but the question as to whether it lived up to its full potential remains open.

The 1972–74 period managed to find an original voice a world away from the original line-up and its predecessor. Similarly, the *Discipline* era fashioned a new vocabulary. Given the versatility of the musicians and the bewildering sweep of digital sounds available to them, it could be argued that the Double Trio had the potential to become a kind of avant-rock-orientated chamber ensemble of vociferous firepower.

The notion of the Double Trio as a chamber orchestra may not be as far-fetched as it seems given the use of orchestral timbres and techniques in *Dinosaur* and the attendant experimentation of Fripp's *Soundscapes* and Belew's *The Guitar As Orchestra* album. Additionally, the deployment of percussion pieces such as *B'Boom*, *Conundrum* and Pierre Favre's *Prism* are more suggestive of a contemporary classical feel. Certainly, the intriguing contrapuntal and polyrhythmic possibilities in material such as *THRAK* and *Sex Sleep Eat Drink Dream* were somehow unfulfilled.

At the close of the tour, the band took a break and Fripp returned to Dorset to oversee the final stages of the *Epitaph* project. This four-CD set was the product of over four months' careful sifting through bootleg, radio and soundboard recordings of the band in 1969. Fripp describes David Singleton's painstaking restoration of the tapes as "rites of necromancy" given the sonically dubious condition of the source material. Most noteworthy was the original Crimson's last performance at the Fillmore West in San Francisco. It was recorded by Richard Vickers, who handed the tapes to Ian McDonald at the end of the show. McDonald recalls: "I had them in my possession for 25 years and no-one had heard it … I played it from time to time and then I transferred it to DAT at one point just in case the tape started to deteriorate."

When the proposal for *Epitaph* came up, McDonald admits to being reluctant to hand back the recording. Rather poignantly, some 25 years after having been given them, McDonald handed them back to Vick who in turn flew them back to the UK. The tapes give some indication of the impact of the original band and their release was marked by a celebratory playback held on 15 March at the Hotel Inter-Continental near Hyde Park, where Crimson's career had originally taken off.

Well over 1,000 fans from all over the world came along to hear the remarkable music and see the original Crimson, their friends, road crew and managers reunited for the first time. Dik Fraser laughs at the memory of it. "It was great seeing everybody again and going up behind Michael Giles and saying 'How you doing?' and him looking at me totally blank. That's not a personal jibe at Mike – it's just we hadn't seen each other since 1969!"

Rumours circulated that the group would actually perform, although this was not to be. "We should have had the band play a song," said Greg Lake. "I think most of the band would have done it. I think they would have played just for the sake of posterity, to do one last show or one last video or something like that."

Away from the crowds, the band members and road crew reflected on the past. For several ex-Crims around the table that day, there was a mixture of emotions. Genuine pleasure at seeing old colleagues mingled in some cases with unresolved resentments. McDonald felt the need to open the band discussion by apologising for having precipitated the split. "I just said I want to apologise to everyone for leaving and something about the effect that it might have had on everyone's lives and Pete immediately said, 'Oh, it's all right, we've not done too badly.' Maybe it made them feel uncomfortable but it was very important to me to say that to everyone."

The event and the release of *Epitaph* at least offered a chance to lay old ghosts and draw a line under some of the band's niggling tensions. The set greatly added to what *Q* reviewer Rob Beattie cited as the "precious few examples of the ferocious musicianship shoehorned into the first Crimson line-up outside of their seminal debut, *In The Court Of The Crimson King*." He awarded it four stars out of five and praised the remarkable breadth of the playing.

A slightly scaled-down version of the reunion event took place in New York a few weeks later, although Peter Sinfield was unable to attend due to illness. But old resentments resurfaced when Fripp did part of the press conference on his own while the rest of the band waited outside.

An indignant Lake bristled with anger at the memory. "We get there and we're standing on the rooftop of this building, record company offices or something, and Robert is inside doing an interview with the journalists. Mike, Ian and I wait outside for one hour and when Robert's finished he leaves the building. Doesn't say a word to any of us and we were ushered in like the backing band. Bearing in mind we'd gone all that way to support his record on his fucking record company. I felt that really that was out of order."

Whatever happened behind closed doors, as far as many fans were concerned such public appearances suggested that a reunion might be in the air. Fripp recalls that such a proposal was made as far back as 1991. "Some/all of the other original members had already been discussing between themselves re-forming and touring, which I was not party to, but which I discussed during 1991 with Peter Sinfield. The plans, as presented to me, were ambitious. They included filming the stages of the reformation process." Fripp expressed willingness to play in principle but was unsure how to put the idea into practice, given that he had already decided to re-incarnate Crimson for the 1990s.

But the initial proposition of a past Crimson stepping into the present prompted the original thinking behind what would come to be called the fractalisation of Crimson. While working on the *Epitaph* and *Night Watch* CDs, Fripp was struck by what he heard. "The power in the music, in the repertoire, and in the players excited me. My criterion for judging critical excitement level is simple: I want to reach for my guitar. This was the response while listening to the stunning, humming little sonic suckers of Crim's living history. So, my suggestion, and proposal was this: A quartet of Ian McDonald, John Wetton, Michael Giles & RF would focus on the 1969-74 repertoire, rehearse together for a week, play-in the group for a week in US clubs, and then visit Japan for a week. All of the performances would be recorded (as per current Crim/RF Standard Operating Procedure). Four good players would get their teeth into whatever (still powerful) repertoire material appealed to them, and rock out. After this first period, the players would then have a sense of whether they wanted to take the quartet further."

Such a line-up would not have been King Crimson in Fripp's eyes and so he argues would not be hampered by the expectations and excessive promotion which often surrounds such reunions. "I was excited," recalls Fripp. "I spoke to Michael and John, who were both very interested. I telephoned Ian (in New York) from Chez Belewbeloible, Mount Juliet, and presented the idea to him. Ian was so locked into the idea of a KC69 reformation that he couldn't hear what I was proposing. His fixity was so strong that it passed down the telephone line, up my arm, into the telephone and locked my neck solid in turn. A headache developed throughout the day into a migraine."

McDonald agrees that at the time, he would have preferred the original line-up to another agglomeration and recalls discussing the idea again when the members were in New York for the *Epitaph* event.

"I was with Mike and we were talking about re-forming the original band and he said: 'I really don't like the idea of re-forming because it would seem like it's for the money and I hate it when you see things like Fleetwood Mac and The Eagles – it smacks of just doing it for the money.' I told him that there's a big difference with us. We broke up before even a lot of the fans had a chance to see us. It wasn't like it had run its course or anything. It would be giving something to those fans, not like re-forming for the million-dollar tour."

Despite a flurry of faxes and phone calls, the deteriorating relationship between Greg Lake and Fripp effectively cancelled out any prospect of such a reunion. In the day and age of heritage acts and corporate sponsorship, reunion tours have always been a tempting prospect for musicians and are reasonably commonplace. From an artistic viewpoint, successful revivals are altogether rarer. At best, one can usually expect serviceable renditions of old favourites. At worst, it's a demeaning spectacle for all concerned. There can be few groups who have come together after an absence of so many years to produce music that comes near to matching or even surpassing the impact of their original output. While Crimson was blessed with some startling talents, the potential for the creative jigsaw to lock together in the same way it had in 1969 was questionable.

XIII

In April 1997, Fripp joined Trey Gunn in Seattle for a recording session with Bill Rieflin. In common with Gunn, the ex-Ministry drummer was a Seattle resident and a member of the extended Guitar Craft community. Rieflin, along with Steve Ball (Crafty guitarist and designer of the DGM "knot logo"), had been in contact with Fripp over a series of prospective Soundscape concerts in the city.

In the course of their discussions, Rieflin mentioned work on his first solo album, *Birth Of A Giant*, and invited Fripp to participate. "A week or two later he called to say when he was coming to town: on which date and for how long and was this a convenient time and that he was coming to play with me," recalls Reiflin. "It wasn't convenient but of course I said, 'Yes.' So, for three days, Robert, Trey and I sat behind or strapped on our instruments, rolled tape and played."

Recorded at The Soundhouse studio in Seattle, the three produced a series of improvised pieces of startling expressiveness. After amassing many hours of material, the editing and mixing was done at Gunn's house. As they worked on what they thought were going to be rough listening mixes, Rieflin was complaining about some of the details in playing. "I was whining about this and that – generally unhappy about little specifics. 'Who cares?' came a quick reply from Trey. 'Listen to these guys. They're really going for it. Who cares about a missed beat here or a dropped note there?' Trey added: 'When I listen to this, what I hear is aspiration.'"

Although not formally part of the ProjeKcts series, the album is a forewarning of where Fripp and Gunn were moving – a looser and structurally more open direction than anything achieved in the Double Trio. "It's such an important album," comments Gunn. "It was the first ProjeKcts album, really, and neither of us had played like that before. And I will say it was recorded on analogue tape. I think it sounds better than any of our records. Not to diss them but I think Robert's guitar sounds better on this than any of our records. It's down and dirty on two-inch tape."

Released in 1999 as *The Repercussions Of Angelic Behaviour*, the free-ranging, joyous intensity of the music makes it an indispensable companion to the ProjeKcts series. Rieflin recalls Fripp and Gunn being excited about their upcoming session with Belew in Nashville. "During the sessions, I remember Trey and Robert being coy about future plans involving Adrian but they weren't saying – just tittering like schoolgirls. Obviously, this became ProjeKct Two."

The musical development of a band is always a delicate matter and the combination of personalities, motivations, costs and competing careers made King Crimson even more fraught. When the Double Trio met again in May 1997, it was to begin the process of threading together various ideas and sketches for new material.

The bulk of the contributions came from Fripp but largely failed to ignite much in the way of passion from the band. As the edited version of the sessions (released as KCCC 13) reveal, much of what would be covered in the ProjeKcts and the *The ConstruKction Of Light* album was already in evidence in crude form.

Despite some intriguing explorations such as the pensive *Sad Woman Jam*, *Tony's Jam* and the ebullient scuffle of *Big Funk*, there was little agreement about what was worth pursuing. "The prime writer presents a piece and has the other guys trash it, without sympathy, respect or consideration, perhaps even play a detailed piece of writing for a week without settling anywhere near a basic part. This is an acute form of suffering for the initiator," Fripp candidly said of the process.

But these sessions – and with them, the Double Trio – came to an abrupt end.

Fripp recalls: "Adrian had invited all of the band to his house, en route to dinner together at nearby Loco Lupe's Mexican restaurant. That is, this was a social event for everyone to see Adrian's new home and studio. We went downstairs into the studio and Adrian played a tape of a Crimson demo: this was an Adrian song that he wanted to use on a solo compilation album."

"Bill became very negative and critical. Even, rather nasty. This surprised Adrian, at least. Bill then went on to criticise, negate and undermine the whole concept that underlay DGM and Crimson's business structure in the post-EG world. Bill completely blasted six years of my work setting up a new structure for Crimson as if it was all a worthless, ill-conceived approach."

"The comments appeared to come from nowhere. I don't know what triggered Bill's outburst, and I doubt that Bill was aware of their effect on me. A leitmotif of Bill's life in Crimson is that he often appeared to be unaware of the effect of his actions."

"We went to the restaurant afterwards although, for me, something had been spoiled. This had been a very different level of critical negativity than might normally arise in band discussions, even band disagreements. Bill had missed the point of the band's business plan and structure, to a destructive degree, and had gone on to undermine the *raison d'être* of the group. Clearly, this view is subjective."

"The next day I woke up and developed a migraine, seeing no way forward. Adrian went into rehearsals without me. Bill called to apologise. What he said to me was: 'You shouldn't take any notice of what someone says after they've had a beer.' What Bill failed to mention was that his destructive comments were made prior to the beer, not during or after."

Characteristically robust, Bruford responds: "Clearly Robert's view is subjective.

The words 'over' and 'reaction' come to mind, but then perhaps he needed a pretext. I was aware of my injudicious comments, but unaware that my fulsome apology the next day had not been accepted in good grace."

"I was also unaware that I had apparently managed to 'undermine the whole concept that underlay DGM and Crimson's business structure in the post-EG world'. This was a surprising achievement, especially in the light of my many public statements of affinity for Robert and his work vis-à-vis DGM's business structure, both before and after this event, and which I take this opportunity to re-state; and my continuing, happy and fruitful use of this structure for my own musical endeavours."

Bruford gives his personal summary of that period. "Exasperation was thick in the air in those Nashville rehearsals, and Robert will understand he was not alone in feeling it. For me, the futile sterility of that period allowed me to sever the lifeline that tethered me to the Good Ship Crimson, and allow the old thing to recede slowly and elegantly into the twentieth-century mist, as I sought more productive pastures for the new millennium."

"It remains my oft-stated case that, despite the odd abrasion, I found my time with the band musically and intellectually stimulating; I remain grateful for its existence, and full of admiration for its leader, as its leader well knows. I, of all the group's members, was not the enemy, but I did have the thickest skin, well used to receiving the sharpest barbs. King Crimson was for 25 years my spiritual home with a bed of nails. Time, now, to move on."

It would appear that for now at least the Fripp and Bruford partnership, which had lasted over 25 years, was effectively over.

They say time is a healer and, in the case of *THRAK*, some of the heated animosity that surfaced in the Double Trio has receded. Speaking to the band, there's a tremendous sense of affection for the period. *THRAK* and *One Time* are personal favourites of Adrian Belew, "because between the two they represent the crucial balance of extremes which is what made King Crimson unique".

Thinking about the pieces that for him represent the Double Trio achieving its potential, he cites *Sex Sleep Eat Drink Dream*. "It is one of the best examples of the definition of our Double Trio, especially in the sections where our drummers are playing in different time signatures together; it sounds like two bands at once. With a killer bassline from Tony and blistering solos from Robert, it's quintessential Crimson. The lyrics are a reflection of the madness of the music."

Mastelotto similarly cites *Sex Sleep Eat Drink Dream* as one of his favourites. "It's the first one that comes to mind. But I loved *Dinosaur* and *Walking On Air*. When I got married to Deborah, we used that as our tune at the wedding. The song makes me cry, man."

In common with many other musicians, Bruford rarely listens to his old recordings. "I found the gestation and generation of this music, of all the records I've been on, particularly with Robert, difficult. But at the end of it, and in retrospect and hindsight, it was probably the only way it could have been done and I'm enormously proud of the result. You don't play this stuff for ten years and then you play it like I did today and you go: 'WOW, this is great!' They don't make pop music like this anymore! Or rock, or jazz or whatever we did is called. I do love the album. It just seems to have so much musical information on it in comparison to a standard rock record that you would think of today. It's oozing hot spices and extra special gravy. A rich meal indeed."

Gunn's memories are also positive. He offers this assessment of the album: "I like making records. For some it's about capturing a performance and I totally get that, but for me it's more about making a sculpture and that's what *THRAK* is." Gunn recalls that in the big room at Real World, David Bottrill had large sheets of paper put up on which details and notes on each of the pieces would be entered and then were put under the band's scrutiny. "At the start it felt fairly fragmented, you go in dealing with it piece by piece. Then at a certain point you start dealing with the *whole* recording, like what's going to work, what's missing. When it was all put together it felt like one complete thing. I haven't heard the record in a long time but I do think it's pretty remarkable that we could pull it off and it not suck, actually. We were really experimenting and you can hear that. I think it came out pretty well."

With Steven Wilson handling the 5.1 surround sound mix for the Crimson catalogue between 1969 and 1984, Robert Fripp asked current King Crimson guitarist and vocalist Jakko Jakszyk to give *THRAK* a different perspective. With years of professional mixing and mastering under his belt, Jakszyk also mixed the surround sound for the King Crimson ProjeKct *A Scarcity Of Miracles* and has subsequently been hired by Anathema, ELP, Jethro Tull and Ian Anderson for mixes. "It was probably 2012 when the tapes arrived. At the start of this project I was working on an older system and computer and I'm pretty sure this was the first thing I did where the files were all 96/24 quality. Back then my computer was struggling to cope with all the information. *THRAK* is 48 tracks and that's a lot of information. There was an ongoing joke between me and Steven Wilson. When Steven was remixing something that came from eight-track reels he'd ask how many I was working with. Thanks, Steven!" laughs Jakszyk. "There's just so much on *THRAK* and you're aware of the intense amount of information that's going on all at once with this six-piece line-up, and if I might paraphrase the great Vic Reeves, it sounded like trying to shove a duvet into a bread bin!

"One of the decisions I made really early on was to have one of the kits at the front and one at the back. I'd never heard an album with two drummers mixed in surround so I didn't know what you were meant to do. With so much going on, it seemed to me to be a logical approach to utilise the fact that we've got this open, 360-degree space and then place instruments within it."

In approaching the new mixes, Jakszyk was keen to preserve what he believed is a key factor in King Crimson's sound: dynamic range. "If you look at a stereo mix of *Dinosaur* as a piece of audio you'll see peaks and troughs, like a little mountain range. If you look at some of the more modern post-mastered mixes, they look like a thick line drawn by a marker pen. I really hate that and I don't think it does the music any service. This is music being played live by musicians and it has a dynamic range. That's particularly prevalent in *Dinosaur*. There's the small chamber piece in the middle section of the song which then falls to complete silence, and then when the band comes steaming in, it's *really* dramatic. That's what I love about King Crimson."

Listeners to the new mixes will hear occasional lines and sequences of notes not previously heard or used on the original recording. "You're trying to traverse the line between being true to the original but also, there isn't an original surround mix so it's a case of finding out what is on the tape. There were things that you didn't hear or were buried in the original mix that suddenly you hear anew. If I hear something I like that perhaps wasn't used on the original CD release, I'll put it up on another track and bring it in. As with all of these things, Robert comes around and then tweaks them. Ultimately, if he doesn't like the things I've done he will ask me to change them. He's the final arbiter."

"When we eventually finished the surround sound, it seemed so successful that the stereo equivalent became a real challenge. Every time we thought we'd mixed it, when Robert came back he'd listen and be disappointed. In the end, in the stereo version we became quite ruthless and it's a bit like mixing a '60s record or a Tamla Motown track. For the vast majority of the stereo version of *THRAK*, the drums are hard left and hard right in mono reverb, so they are really extreme. We took that idea even further in stereo and I'd like to think that the new stereo has the kind of clarity and detail that the surround has."

Jakszyk believes the drummers are chief among the beneficiaries of the revised mix. "Suddenly you're getting a much greater sense of clarity as to who is doing what and how they interact with each other. Also, I think Trey comes out more. I think Trey is very underrated. I think he does some amazing things on this record. When I was mixing it I would get very confused at times as to who was playing what. There'd be moments when I'd think, 'Oh that's Robert' and it was Trey. Other times I'd think well, that's definitely Tony and it wasn't. It was Trey. Then, on another section I'd think, well that's Adrian, and it wasn't. It was Trey. Very underrated. If ever there was an album that benefited from the 5.1 format, this is it."

LEVEL 5: *The jaws of life, they chew you up …*

It's the end of July 2014 and Robert Fripp is in Elstree Studios' Stage Seven, behind his extensive array of effects processors, amplifiers, monitor speakers, pedalboards, laptop and midi-keyboard. As he hones his already manicured nails with an emery board prior to climbing up the steps of the stage, a small invited audience of 20 or so "friends and family" file in, taking refuge from the summer heat in the secluded cool of the huge soundstage.

On the riser next to Fripp's workspace, guitarist and lead vocalist Jakko Jakszyk plugs in, checking levels and the settings of his gear. Tony Levin takes a few snaps of the new arrivals. Surrounded by his array of saxes and flutes, Mel Collins pencils final additions on a piece of manuscript paper. Below them, facing the assembling punters, the three drummers make their final arrangements. Pat Mastelotto adjusts the ornately percussive metallic sculptures surrounding his kit. Bill Rieflin dials up patches on the midi-keyboard nestling within his circle of drums and, just beyond his expansive kit, Gavin Harrison furiously drills upon a tiny practice pad.

Inside, there's a laminated sign detailing some of the movies that have been made here: Kick Ass, Hot Fuzz, Under The Skin, Gravity, Star Wars – A New Hope, *and, appropriately enough as Fripp steps forward to make a short announcement,* The King's Speech. *Impeccably turned out in a three-piece suit and dapper tie, he looks more like a provincial bank manager about to give a short talk on fiscal prudence than one the most innovative and influential rock guitarists of his generation.*

"So welcome to King Crimson. This is our 12th full day rehearsal together and this is an informal rehearsal run-through to our invited guests. If we break down, we reserve the right to begin again, or someone in the band may shout 'Urgh, take it from there!' The first King Crimson principle is, let's enjoy what we're doing. That's a novelty for King Crimson. The second principle is, if you don't want to play a part, fine: give it to another guy. There's enough of them. The sixth principle is, if you don't know what to play get some more gear. The seventh principle is, if you've got some more gear and you still don't know what to play, play nothing. The third King Crimson principle is, all the music is new, whenever it was written."

Returning to the raised stage, Fripp lightly dusts his fingers with talcum powder, plants a glancing kiss upon the body of his guitar as he straps it on and finally takes his seat. There's a pause much like the one before the starting pistol is fired at the start of a race; music muscles flex and stretch, nervous glances flit between players, silent nods of encouragement and support. There's a single note from Fripp, a count-in from Mastelotto and, 45 years after it was formed, King Crimson launch into a two-hour set filled with fiendish complexity, jaw-dropping prowess and hair-raising degrees of intensity. As the numbers fly by, there's an alternating sense of surprise and recognition: The ConstrucKction Of Light, The Letters, Larks' Tongues In Aspic, Part One, Pictures Of A City, Red, Sailor's Tale, Starless. *These were not off-the-shelf accounts of some of the most celebrated tracks from the back catalogue. Instead, they've been remade and remodelled, often benefiting from bold arrangements that sparkle with a contemporary-sounding freshness. As they played, there was a palpable sense that anything was possible, that this was a group that could go in any direction.*

Not everything is nailed down, not everything works as it should. Some pieces work well, others exceptionally well, and others don't quite perform to specifications. Larks' Tongues In Aspic, Part Two *breaks down at the start, requiring Mastelotto to kick-start it again. There's also new material receiving its first outing. In addition to pieces from the 2011 Jakszyk, Fripp and Collins album,* A Scarcity Of Miracles, *there's untitled improv-based pieces as well as three-headed drumming-only intervals which both intercut and connect the set.*

In the testing ground of a rehearsal, things soar and fly, crash and burn, and everything in between. What was consistent in this otherwise provisional landscape was an undeniable sense of fun and discovery, a keenness of considerable intensity, enthusiasm and an undeniable power. At the end there was applause and cheering from the small band of supporters who had gone through the gamut of closed-eye concentration, open-mouth surprise, grins, goosebumps and, above all, engagement. "It's amazing how much of a difference even a small audience makes," says Gavin Harrison afterwards. "We were all fairly nervous!"

A few days later, Fripp offered some reflections on the formation of what he reckons is the eighth line-up of King Crimson. The enthusiasm with which Fripp talks about this incarnation is pretty much off the Richter scale. Given all his well-documented problems with the music industry and the pressure associated with all-things Crimson, is he really sure he wants to do it all again? "I spent this morning at the American embassy sorting out a visa and it's things like that that put me off doing it again," he sighs heavily. "But one of the things I was doing when considering this, was actually listening to the music. The music brings us to life. We've had two batches of rehearsals so far and the tour of America is booked, So yes, I'm pretty sure!" he laughs heartily.

I

With the 1997 sessions at SIR Studios coming to an abrupt and inconclusive ending, something which would have brought earlier Crimsons to a complete standstill, Fripp came up with a novel solution.

By splitting the group into smaller components (or fracKctals), work on current and emerging ideas could continue and, by playing live, the outcomes could be continually shaped and moved forward. "The practical difficulties of King Crimson working together are immense," Fripp wrote at the time. "Our current and alternative approach – for smaller units with the Double Trio to work together privately and publicly rather than for all six of us to clatter and bang away simultaneously, which is often wonderful and frequently invigorating – has already loosened up the band's view of itself and our sense of possible futures."

With hindsight, those "possible futures" appear incredibly brave and largely off the map. While such musical splintering is commonplace within jazz or improvised music, it's hard to think of any other band in a rock context that would dare to adopt this high-risk approach. The genesis of the ProjeKcts can be traced to the April 1997 Seattle sessions which produced Rieflin, Fripp and Gunn's improvised album *The Repercussions Of Angelic Behaviour*.

When Fripp listened to the album in 1998, he offered readers of his online diary this verdict: "More than rehearsals, more than blowing, less than high art and fun: three players playing together for the first time and seeing where they might go. And then going there."

Released in 1999 and bearing an enigmatic, elemental portrait by Rieflin's wife, Francesca Sundsten, whose work would adorn King Crimson releases in the 21st century, the free-ranging, joyous intensity of the music makes it an indispensable companion to the ProjeKcts series.

After those recordings, Fripp and Gunn's next stop was similarly free-wheeling work with Adrian Belew in what became ProjeKct Two.

In 2018 when Trey Gunn thinks back to what he calls the "insane output" generated by the ProjeKcts and King Crimson between 1997 and 2003, he frequently laughs out loud, incredulous at the audacity of taking all-improvisation outfits out on the road. "There was a thread for us but for everyone else, the listening public, there wasn't. The thread moved pretty quickly. We're playing around P2 but I think the original idea was that Adrian was going to be on guitar and it was going to be the three guitars. I don't know what we were thinking but it seems to me like we were saying, 'This is cool! People will like this!' (*laughs*) So there was that."

However, Belew could not have known that his most recent acquisition of a set of Roland V-Drums would suddenly steer the string-driven ProjeKct Two in a radically different direction when the trio assembled at the end of November 1997. The music that unexpectedly emerged was as far away from Belew's original conception of the trio as it was possible to be.

"I thought we might do some Crimson classics with a new twist," says Belew, "using our guitar synths to create a string-trio-with-vocal rendition of *Frame By Frame* ... I was revved up about this new compact V-Drum system I had just seen at the NAMM show and I quickly mentioned the idea of taking along such a small kit so we could on occasion be a power trio of sorts. Then next time Trey, Robert and I met it wasn't to form a trio but to continue working out new Crimson material. We began, the three guitarists, playing a piece called *ConstruKction*. We took a coffee break. Just two days earlier my V-Drums had arrived and were set up in the corner of the studio. When we started again, I asked what we would like to do next. Robert requested a demonstration of the 'wonder drums'. As I started playing, Trey and Robert joined me in an improvised 20-minute piece ... So you see there was no grand plan, I simply became the drummer so we could play together as a band. Within three days, we made a double record and decided to do more live shows as ProjeKct Two. By that time the thought of three guitarists playing Crimson classics no longer seemed exciting."

With other sessions in Belew's studio basement being committed to tape just as rapidly, a tangible spirit of rhapsodic release and good humour pervades the two CDs that comprise *Space Groove*. As Fripp and Gunn rove over Belew's solid drumming, they are clearly having fun. Gunn admits to a fondness for the quirky album. "*Space Groove* is so ... silly and strange. It's really like a *Jetsons* episode or something, y'know? Like the little Martian in the Bugs Bunny cartoon? It wasn't contrived, at least to us, and there was such a freedom for Robert and Adrian to be silly. Coming after *THRAK* it was pretty much about freedom and using it well. It just seemed like the vibe was so strange and seductive enough. It didn't seem heady to me like Crimson can be ... I felt like we could just drop into that vibe and we'd be OK."

Listening back to ProjeKct Two while preparing P2's *Live Groove* album for release in 1998, Fripp pondered the ambiguities that seemed hardwired into the ProjeKct process. "It is impossible for me, listening to the drummer in ProjeKct Two, to know his influence. He's not a jazz drummer, but not quite a rock drummer; and he's also not a jazz-rock player. So, how is the drummer defining/shaping/driving the music? Then, I listen to the other two guys in this trio. The bass player isn't, because he plays the Warr guitar. But sometimes he is. And when he solos, or plays bass, I can't tell his influences either. Then the guitarist – he interests me, too: I have no idea, from listening, what are his influences. A lot of the time he doesn't sound like a guitar. So, is he a synthesiser player, or what? When he doesn't sound like a guitar, the structural elements of his vocabulary are not those of a guitarist ... What are any of those guys thinking? What's going on in ProjeKCt Two?"

Less than a fortnight after the ProjeKct Two album sessions, the action shifted from Nashville to London's Jazz Café and four nights of improvisation with ProjeKct One, consisting of Fripp, Gunn, Levin and Bruford. There had been talk on previous occasions about the possibility of Fripp and Bruford performing as a duo though this had fallen victim to Crimson's scheduling and the widening gulf between the pair since SIR. Yet with the fraKctal process now under way, the opportunity seemed too good to miss. Bruford added Tony Levin's name to the roster and Gunn entered on Fripp's suggestion.

Twenty years later, the concept underpinning the ProjeKcts now seems an obvious solution to King Crimson's problem in developing repertoire. But outside the doors of the Jazz Café in December 1997 for the first of four nights of the line-up, there was a feverish excitement and anticipation in the air, a sense that what was going on with King Crimson was strange, new and revolutionary. The venue was an interesting choice – an intimate supper club that gave those standing in the room the opportunity to be inches away from the players – a stark contrast to the last time these four musicians had shared a stage in London at Shepherd's Bush Empire, 18 months previously, on the last leg of King Crimson's 1996 European tour.

ProjeKct One's sound hovered somewhere between the expansive spirit of Crim improv *circa* 1973/74 and an amorphous area that had yet to be fully defined. Over the course of the four nights, with visitors such as Michael Giles and ex-Led Zeppelin bassist John Paul Jones looking on, at certain points ProjeKct One broke down into four individuals in search of a groove, theme or point of entry. Some of the playing reverted to the safety net of habit. But things turned viscerally exciting when all the elements lined up and suddenly took flight. The audience became a kind of fly-on-the-wall documentary team witnessing musicians going about the sometimes-difficult business of finding the music.

Delving into the unknown wasn't an activity exclusive to the punters at the Jazz Café. When he set out from his home in Woodstock in upstate New York at the end of November, Tony Levin didn't have a lot of information about the exercise. The day allocated to rehearsals at The Premises, an east London facility, was simply an equipment check. "The first gig was a lot of fun for me, not knowing where things would go … Big challenge for the audience – a whole night all improvised – they seemed to like it. At least nobody called out requests," Levin remarked at the time.

There were smiles all 'round as Bruford leaned over his kit to tap his sticks against the strings of Levin's upright bass. As if liberated from shouldering the weight of expectations within King Crimson, Fripp was often in a puckish mood suddenly unleashing the sound of a phat bass guitar sound from his rig and taking everyone, including his bandmates, by surprise. "All of us had new arsenals of sounds and that really was a big thing; let's play with this! Our tools were really a sandbox right after Christmas. We weren't stuck with our old sound anymore and the door kind of opened up with new possibilities," notes Trey Gunn.

Often dense, fiercely energetic and richly atmospheric, the four nights at the Jazz Café frequently evoked something of the rhythmically driven improvisations of the *Larks'* era. But it was also heading somewhere new. Far removed from the tightly scripted lines of the Double Trio, this quartet drilled down deep into the reserves of each musician. However, when it came to sifting through over six hours of material for the *Live At The Jazz Café* release, Bruford – who had been brought in as a consultant – was less than impressed: "I hated it so much … and the little of it that seemed achievable was the bit that I tried to put on the record because the other stuff just seemed so excruciating to my ears."

It's perhaps not surprising that the record failed to convey the range and depth of what had been attempted. The full extent of this would not be apparent until all four gigs were made available as downloads via DGM Live. Regardless of Bruford's misgivings, the residency at the Jazz Café felt fresh and different, yet paradoxically recognisable and familiar, a kind of missing link between 1974 and 1994. Despite a fan blatantly ignoring the "No Photography" signs posted around the venue, and in doing so bringing an abrupt end to Robert's first KC-related stage announcement in over 13 years, nothing could take away from the fact that it had been an amazing week of momentous improvisations with the fourth and final evening particularly strong. After it was all done, with the crew packing up, Bill Bruford chatted to straggling fans, signed a few autographs and eventually picked up his cases, walked out into the night to his car and said goodbye for the final time to his life as an active member of King Crimson.

For many watching in Camden, perhaps the biggest revelation of these shows and the subsequent gigs by ProjeKct Two was seeing Trey Gunn's playing given free rein after the constraints imposed upon him in Crimson. "Before the ProjeKcts I'd never played like that, so to me it was a total blossoming. Actually goes back to the John Paul Jones sessions when he brought me in to solo on his record, *Zooma*, released in 1999, and I found some things that led me to that. But I wasn't doing any of that in *THRAK*. I did a lot of stuff but there wasn't space for that kind of soloing and nor was it appropriate. Robert and Adrian were there so why would I take the solos?" laughs Gunn.

In February 1998, Fripp and Gunn went to Belew's house and studio to rehearse for ProjeKct Two's live debut at The Cannery in Nashville on 20 February. "Wow! What a blast this gig was," commented an excited Gunn on the difference between the studio and the world of live performance. "Unlike our studio CD, *Space Groove*, which had some very silly and mellow-ish moods to it, this performance really kicked out hard. Some of it was downright terrifying! We found that most of the sounds that we had used in the studio were far too subtle to carry through in the live show … and we had to compensate 'on the fly', adjusting as we went. I think we learned a lot about what kind of sounds to approach with in the future."

Taking something of the frantic pace of the drum'n'bass genre, Belew radiated his infectious good humour from behind his pretzel-like array of V-Drums, laying down regular and repetitive beats, sometimes utilising the V-Drums' built-in and programmable bass sequencer. By laying down such a dependable, driving groove, he provided Gunn and Fripp the space to follow their instincts as they worked on many of the themes and ideas which Fripp had presented to Crimson the previous year.

With 35 appearances, ProjeKct Two was the most widely seen and well-travelled of all the KC fraKctals. The *Space Groove* album merely hinted at the energy the trio was capable of summoning onstage. Fripp and Gunn opened up with some untamed, aggressive playing. Sometimes the full-on soloing didn't work, as Gunn noted in his diary after the band's second gig in the Great Western Music Hall in San Francisco. "We probably pushed too hard in the beginning of the first set and couldn't bring the music in. So we countered this with more space in the second set and everything came to life. Improvisation is so delicate."

But the default setting for this group was firmly geared towards rocking out, as Gunn later admits. "We ended the second set in a savage groove that reminded me more of early Clash then anything Crimson."

In April 1998, Bruford Levin Upper Extremities, or BLUE as it quickly became known, joined forces with ProjeKct Two for three concerts in Japan. Though not formally part of KC's fraKctalisation, trumpeter Chris Botti's cool, urbane lines and guitarist David Torn's caustic loops and splintered forays along the fretboard, BLUE illustrated the harmonic and rhythmic areas that had interested the different parts of the Double Trio. In his 2009 autobiography, Bruford describes their first performance. "The offer from the Japanese promoter had at the top of the bill Fripp's ProjeKct 2 … and BLUE opening the show. Coming only months after the stultifying rehearsals in Nashville, the backstage atmosphere at the Alaska Blitz in central Tokyo was bound to be chilly. Our group was little more than an absurdly confident jam band, rough and ready, and I don't remember much that anyone could call a rehearsal. We had never been on stage together before, but the intrepid professional kind of likes that. It means that at the least we are all going to be as interested in the proceedings as the customer. It turned out that, in our embryonic trumpet star, we were fielding a secret weapon of considerable potency. Unfeasibly good-looking, and in possession of a beautiful warm round tone, Chris Botti modelled himself on Chet Baker, the much-photographed cultural icon of the '50s West Coast school of cool jazz. In that school, nothing was done in a hurry, and it was done with a minimum of fuss and the maximum of restraint. This could naturally be very appealing to the ladies and following several years of picking up tips as a sideman with Sting, Chris was to go on to make a substantial international career as a smooth-jazz artist on Columbia Records.

"But tonight he was the lark's tongue in aspic, the delicacy in the aural roughage. Slowly patrolling the front stage area, and bathed in a hazy spotlight, he would equally slowly deliver the fewest, longest, slowest notes he could get away with, the preparation for which was almost as interesting as the notes themselves. Behind him, I watched all this flirting with a great deal of amusement and interest, and resolved to inject a whole lot more control into my own performances. Get them to watch the sticks, not me. The trumpet's bell-like purity of tone cut clean through the clouds of Torn's stereo guitar loops, and with the ex-Crimson rhythm section on fine form smouldering beneath the proceedings we were a tough act to follow. None of us had much idea what Robert's ProjeKct 2 would sound like, and in the event its performance was overlooked in the backstage celebrations."

BLUE's mix of smooth melodic textures and rhythmic finesse contrasted sharply with ProjeKct 2, illustrating the divergent musical concerns which occupied different hemispheres of the Double Trio. While there were certainly crossovers on BLUE's eponymous 1998 studio album and (especially) their posthumous 2000 live album *BLUE Nights*, those records show Bruford's head and heart leaning in quite a different direction to the others in the Crimson fraKctals.

II

Throwing numerical logic aside, it was ProjeKct Four which appeared next, assembling in Nashville for rehearsals and a tour of North West America with a short sortie over the border to Canada in October and November 1998. As Belew went back to his production and writing commitments, the personnel now included Pat Mastelotto on V-Drums and Tony Levin on various basses and Stick. If P2 had merely hinted at a drum'n'bass sensibility, then P4 actively embraced the genre and a whole lot more besides. Admiring the work of artists such as Germany's Alex Empire and the UK's Photek and Talvin Singh, Mastelotto brought their influence into the mix as he cut a dizzying array of beats and grooves of quivering intensity and pace, propelling his colleagues headlong in the club-orientated electronica-based Crim which Fripp had envisaged. The rapidity of the shifting rhythmic base within the group and their respective and collective responses to it was astonishing. For some attending these concerts, it was too much. In Boulder, Colorado, on the tour's opening night, several people left in disgust at the perplexing barrage of hyper-dance grooves. The next night, however, the Fox Theatre was even more crowded as word spread about the hot band. While the new direction alienated a minority of diehard Crimson fans, the ProjeKcts were succeeding in appealing to a much younger audience with more women – an always rare commodity in the demography of KC fandom – attending. With each successive gig, the material was honed and tested in different tonal and timbral combinations. With Levin and Mastelotto's decisive contributions, *Heavy ConstruKction* and *Light ConstruKction*, cautiously worked on in ProjeKct Two, acquired a more fluid and liberated personality. ProjeKct 4 was also the spawning ground for an important development within Crimson's quest for new material.

Sometimes you get lucky. You get to be in the right place at the right time and bear witness to something extraordinary, something that feels like the future arriving. For the members of ProjeKct Four's road crew – Robert Frazza, Ronin Chris Murphy and John Sinks – meetings with remarkable musical events might have begun to seem relatively commonplace on this and the other ProjeKct tours they'd help to make happen.

The improvised nature of much of the music ProjeKct One and Two had performed in Europe, Japan and North America in 1997 and 1998 was a volatile, often incendiary mix that found the players working at the edges of what they knew was possible or could depend on. Essentially this was research and development at its most visceral, all of it in front of a paying audience. Yet as the crew quickly and diligently converted piles of boxes and wires into a coherent working environment in Richard's On Richard, a large club venue in Vancouver, the usual routine soundcheck gave way to something more focused and demonstrative, drawing the sound crew's attention away toward the stage.

Beneath the circular balcony running around the rostrum, as Pat Mastelotto set up his V-Drums, Robert Fripp, Tony Levin and Trey Gunn come to order. "Can we try it, please?" and Fripp counts them off. Within seconds twisting, scattering notes take a hard form, like some vast murmuration where the individuals suddenly swoop together to become as one body. Almost as soon as it starts it falters and falls away. Fripp counts them off again. And again. Gunn is quickly on top of the notes that initially sound like a potpourri of *21st Century Schizoid Man*, a smattering of the opening to *Larks' Tongues In Aspic, Part Three*, and even a sprinkling of Fripp's *NY3*. That Gunn settles in so rapidly is, he later admits, a result of spending a few hours every day running through the sparkling lines. Levin is struggling to land his fingers in the desired places and refers to a scrap of paper retrieved from his pocket in between counts for guidance. The scrabbling begins anew and it suddenly acquires a new momentum, a keener, sleeker shape that suddenly feels dangerously heat-seeking in nature.

The ripples of this ever-tightening theme spread beyond the stage, away from the road team and hit the house crew and staff of Richards. The person ferrying bottles of beer to the bar stops to watch. One of the cleaners leans on his mop and bucket. The battle-hardened, seen-it-all-before employees who assist with the get-in and load-out stop yakking and as their jaws sink to the floor watching Fripp, Levin and Gunn take yet another devastating pass at what would later become *Larks' Tongues In Aspic, Part Four*, one of them is heard to exclaim: "What. The. Actual. Fuck, Dude!" The quartet also unveiled the formidable *Seizure*, an idea brought in by Tony Levin which centred around Levin's pulsing ostinato on the note of C. With Fripp layering in some ominous strings and *THRAK*-like back-and-forth chords from Gunn chopping against Mastelotto's fizzing beats and accents, it all built into a piece of awesome, thrumming energy. Not for nothing would the Double Duo revisit this piece in the improv sections of their 2000 tours.

The final iteration of the ProjeKcts – ProjeKct Three – had, in fact, made a brief debut back in the rehearsals for P4 when Tony Levin and his gear were delayed (Fripp can be heard exclaiming "ProjeKct Three! ProjeKct Three!" at the end of *Masque 6* on the P3 album *Masques*) although their first formal appearance was on 21 March 1998, at the Electric Lounge in Austin, Texas. In the audience was Adrian Belew, making good his promise to go and cheer on the gang when Fripp first outlined his plans for a line-up consisting of Gunn, Mastelotto and himself the previous year. Gunn recalls the moment with some affection. "Right when Pat and I were walking out to go onstage (Robert had begun the show with Soundscapes on his own) there was Adrian laughing at our surprise. He had been very careful not to let any of us know that he was coming. Robert didn't even find out until the middle of the show when he turned to look at the monitor desk and there was Adrian with a big grin on his face."

Gunn had other reasons to regard the gig with some fondness as he explains. "There was an utterly beautiful moment during *The Deception Of The Thrush* when we were playing so quietly with huge amounts of silence around the sound and the audience was sucked right in with us. The music drifted along getting quieter and quieter, and then there was an enormous gap with only this long tail of echo off of T.S. Eliot's voice sailing into the silence. The audience was absolutely still, and I'm sure that my watch stopped running. It is for this, that I am a musician."

While each line-up has its own inherent value, P4 emerged as one of the most musically viable and challenging of all of the ProjeKct groupings to date. Looking back on their work, Gunn singles out ProjeKct Four as his favourite. "Because to me it sounds like super-electric John Coltrane, like heavy intense blowing that's searching and I still don't even know what we were doing! I don't know, it's got a Mahavishnu-vibe as well."

Admittedly not quite King Crimson but with a sustainable potential that went beyond research and development, the combination of P4's players and their respective strengths would have surely supported a searing, cutting-edge instrumental unit. Despite its lack of maturity, by the time P4 broke off in San Francisco it was already a group of considerable force and stature. The full-blooded adoption of *VROOOM* as an encore certainly proved P4's capability at convincingly interpreting Crimson repertoire. The ProjeKcts had served their purpose, providing Crimson with a next step and a clearer picture of how the material might be performed. With Bruford now committed to pursuing Earthworks and Levin signed up for a world tour with the singer Seal, the new King Crimson coalesced around Belew, Fripp, Gunn and Mastelotto. It had taken the best part of three years and over 50 gigs by the ProjeKcts for this particular version to present itself.

III

In August 1999, Fripp joined Belew at his home in Mount Juliet in Tennessee. As the pair listened to the discs from the forthcoming ProjeKcts box set release, Belew raised the possibility of including Tony Levin in the new line-up, particularly in light of the news that the bass player was now available following the unexpected collapse of the Seal tour due to poor ticket sales. Although the inclusion of Levin would have been popular with fans, Fripp was inclined to stick to his original conception. Levin was sanguine about the new line-up in his online diary. "Robert has wisely decided to go ahead anyway, with the invitation to Bill and me that we can come back for the next incarnation. I agree that it's time for a Crimson release and tour – if we wait for everyone to be available, it could take years."

Fripp had devised another three-year plan for the group which would see a huge amount of touring with a strong bias toward the American market, playing smaller club venues. The band would undertake numerous live dates and then move into the studio to put down tracks.

But Fripp and Belew still needed to knuckle down and start carving material out of the raw material of the ProjeKcts. During the week, they worked on ideas which would make up *FraKctured* (at that point referred to as *Larks' Tongues In Aspic, Part Five*) and hit upon an outline of a King Crimson blues. For the first time, Belew elected to play in Fripp's New Standard Tuning, alongside other tunings of his own devising, and the duo began to revisit the interlocking guitar style from the '80's.

Fripp flew back to England to attend to DGM, which was now developing in several directions. This would lead to the establishment of a sub-company (eventually called Bootleg TV) which would record all the Crimson shows, making them available for internet broadcast or CD releases. Although initially the company would be on the road with Crimson, clearly the concept could easily be transferable to other bands. In a short space of time, David Singleton and Steve Ball recruited staff, rented an office suite in Seattle and began to try and enlist other companies and bands.

But Belew wasn't entirely convinced that there was a role for him in the new line-up. Moreover, he was worried about the degree of Crimsonising Fripp envisaged. In September, as Fripp was packing his bags at his house in Dorset, he received a call from Crimson's manager Richard Chadwick. Adrian Belew had quit.

Fripp wryly observed: "Crimson usually breaks up after tours or during rehearsals. The Double Duo is a first in that it has broken up before rehearsing, recording and touring. Even for Crimson, this is an achievement. Two Crimsons have broken up around Christmas time. This year, Christmas has come early."

An hour or so after talking to Chadwick, Fripp called Stan Hertzmann, Belew's manager, for clarification. Belew had proposed that ProjeKct Three and a ProjeKct consisting of Belew, Levin and Bruford record a double album, presenting two different faces of the Double Trio. This didn't interest Fripp. "If Adrian would like to take the initiative with any ProjeKct, it has my support," he replied. "But my own current concern is directed towards King Crimson. Stan emphasised that Adrian had wanted to call me direct, but knew I was in London."

Two hours later, Fripp and Belew talked directly and were able to address their main concerns. Belew was feeling uncertain about his role and position within the new line-up. The pressure of coming up with new songs not only for a new album but also a debut performance in November, as well as the prospective three-year touring regime, caused him to question his commitment. A conciliatory Fripp was keen to accommodate Belew. "I don't have doubts that when the four of us get together in a room, stuff will happen. If the November shows at 12th & Porter overload the recording process, we'll do them later. If more than four months touring in a year is too much, then we'll tour for three months. In other words, when there are legitimate concerns to be addressed and goodwill involved, a personal and direct conversation rarely fails to find solutions."

Looking back on the experience, a phlegmatic Belew remarked: "After Robert left, I began to have doubts about my place in the new band. Perhaps I've read one too many mean ET ramblings. And I worried about the planned three-year touring schedule. But I never actually 'quit' the band. Instead I worked out my concerns and talked to Robert … We revised our touring schedule to a one-year plan. Musically, Robert asked me to trust his vision of the new band. His feeling was that, when the four of us play in the studio together, great things will happen and my place in the scheme of things will naturally occur."

Fripp's judgement was correct. From October to December, the Belew studio was the hub of extraordinary industry. The making of the new album marked a departure from standard Crim operating procedure. With the exception of *Lizard* and one or two isolated tracks like *Red* or *The Howler*, material would usually be honed and sharpened in concert and then recorded.

This time around the process was turned on its head – studio first, then out on the road. Perhaps the defining characteristic of the sessions was the velocity at which the material became available and the immediacy of the writing, playing and recording.

Often as a precursor to formal passes at material, the band would play live in the studio, creating impressive but very different interpretations of ideas. With so much activity in one small location, Crimson seemed unable to contain everything that was being uncovered and thrown up as they experimented and improvised. It became clear that there was a separate enterprise – dubbed ProjeKct X – emerging.

Belew's regular studio engineer Ken Latchney was supplemented by Bill Munyon, who had worked with Mastelotto on the drum'n'bass-orientated Radical Dance and ProjeKct Three sessions. In addition to the complexities of the V-Drums and other devices Mastelotto operated, the pair worked on editing together rough mixes and blows generated when Crimson adopted the PX persona. Working seemingly around the clock, Munyon and Mastelotto (known as BPM+M) would quickly generate scratch mixes and edits for the band to listen to or overdub.

It was clear that PX was a significant musical presence. In effect, two separate albums were slowly being constructed from the ground up, one with its foundations rooted in a smeared-up techno-ambient groove and the other in another variant of intelligent metal.

On several mornings Fripp would emerge from the Belew guest room having finished a bout of writing – "pencil frenzy" as he calls it – which was then immediately road-tested by the band. Belew was working long hours with Ken Latchney, producing demos of his ideas for instrumental pieces which would then be transformed into songs. With so much going on, some found it difficult to keep up. Gunn proposed a new approach. "This new way of working is essentially an old way of working. That is: we made a demo of the material," wrote Gunn in his diary. "We coerced Robert into laying down his whole part to the multi-track. He did this alone to a click track. You can't imagine how hard this is to do. It is as cold and sterile a way of playing music as anything in the world. But he was a trouper and gave us what we needed."

Understanding the material was now made easier with Gunn and Mastelotto providing a route map of how various arrangements and segments hung together. Or not. The ProjeKct Four piece *Seizure* continued to elude them, despite several attempts to capture it.

Gunn also pushed heavily for the title of the album to be *The ConstruKction Of Light.* "I really liked the P.J. Crook stuff but as soon as we settled on that title I knew I wanted it to be different from the other covers. I wanted it black and stark. It seemed so obvious to go with space and darkness." During the sessions, Gunn was busy filming around the studio pointing his camera at anything that caught his fancy, later dumping the footage on to his computer and fooling around with it. The image which would eventually grace the album sleeve is one result of this kind of experimentation. Gunn thinks it's a shot of either his or Mastelotto's equipment: "But I can't be sure, you know. That stuff would get so messed around, I can't remember where it all came from."

Despite the challenge of finishing both writing and recording in an eight-week period, the synergy produced in the low-ceilinged room created some remarkable results, even if Mastelotto was less than happy at having to go with the V-Drums set-up. *ProzaKc Blues*, featured Belew's slowed-down and pitch-shifted vocals, designed to emulate a gravelly-voiced blues singer, wryly addressed the love–hate relationship between fans and musicians. Directly referencing Elephant Talk, an online message board which would regularly contain posts questioning whether Belew was up to the job, it poked a snarky finger in his detractors' direction.

Belew wasn't the only target. After Bruford's departure, some observers doubted that Mastelotto was capable of carrying the band. Fripp had no such reservations. "For anyone who has doubts of Pat's capacity to Crimsonise (and doubters appear to be falling away) the part Pat played on the 'blues' completely threw me. I've no idea where he was, other than he was there. And this from someone who worked with Giles for three years and Billy B for 27 years (so far). As Pat was leaving I asked him: 'What were you playing?' 'Well everyone was centred on the guitar playing, there's no need for me to play it too, is there?'"

Into The Frying Pan, with its doom-laden counterpoint hailing directly from the ProjeKcts, and the juddering 11/8 mayhem of *The World's My Oyster Soup Kitchen Floor Wax Museum*, which came out of a studio jam appropriately entitled *Demolition*, push gleefully into extreme territories. *Frying Pan* adds to the feeling of disorientation with Belew's processed vocals, while on *Oyster Soup* Fripp's guitar solo, at Gunn's urging, is transformed into a frantic, detuned piano. "Oh my lord, this was the perfect thing for this track!" said Gunn regarding the flurry of notes Fripp produces as "Spider Fingers". "It was as if a wild and disturbed ferret had gotten loose inside an old tack piano during a bar-room brawl. Fantastic chaos!"

Upon his return to Crimson in 2008, Tony Levin described the title track's bassline as one of the most difficult he had ever encountered. When the track was revived in 2014 with the new seven-piece incarnation, it remained the piece that caused the seasoned bassist the most problems, requiring him to actively calm himself mentally and physically prior to playing it onstage. Written by Gunn, from the twisting lines entwining themselves around a radiant circulating motif provided by Belew and Fripp's interlocking guitars, Gunn's superbly agile work provides the instrumental section of the track with such forward momentum, it makes this one of the most exciting parts of the album. At around three minutes, the notes from Belew and Fripp spin around like the reflections from a glittering mirror ball, brilliantly dancing over Gunn's lithe ascending bass line. If that wasn't impressive enough, Gunn is also playing the stabbing chords which lightly dance around the beaming centre. These are not overdubbed but played live in the studio using the Warr guitar. Gunn recalls: "I was so up about this track I wanted to do more but I ran out of hands!" Fripp describes Gunn's contributions to this track as both stunning and exceptional.

With *FraKctured*, Fripp revisited some of the ideas thrown up by the *moto perpetuo* of 1973's *Fracture*. With Fripp allowing himself to reference any musical materials which he found convincing and which resonated with what the band was attempting, the track not only echoes the past but points toward a potential future. Similarly, *Larks' Tongues In Aspic, Part Four* also digs into Crimson's past but comes up with a fresh interpretation of the processes that helped initiate a musical journey that began in 1971 with the *Islands*-era band. But the piece which first came to life in that ProjeKct Four soundcheck in Vancouver caused tension. Belew originally envisaged that he would sing a coda outlining a litany of all that he felt to be wrong in the world, with Fripp playing acoustic guitar. Unconvinced, Fripp declined, leaving Belew to record his own acoustic version alongside the full band version that finally appeared on the finished album despite reservations from Virgin and Fripp himself. Originally, *I Have A Dream* would have signalled the end of the album but the inclusion of *Heaven And Earth* from the ProjeKct X sessions took the album's conclusion into a less obvious and more ambiguous mood.

Given the heavy demands of writing and recording a new Crimson album in just eight weeks, it's surprising that anyone found the time to develop ProjeKct X. However, PX proved to be a creative lifeline for Gunn and Mastelotto with both of them less than happy at the way the overall sound of the parent record was going.

With mixing being done in Nashville, Mastelotto would take CDRs of the work as it neared completion and listen to them in his rental car on the way back to his accommodation. "It was still daylight outside and I sat in the car and I was really depressed. This album was almost done and it's almost embarrassing how weak and crappy the drum sound is," sighs the drummer. "I started the car, thinking 'Fuck man, what are we going to do to fix this thing?'" In the end, Mastelotto decided to let go of his frustrations but couldn't help but feel the album didn't live up to his expectations.

"I remember when *THRAK* came out I would put it on and say to visitors and friends, 'Hey check this out.' I don't think I ever did that with *TCOL*. There was never enough time or energy for the ideas that Trey or I might want to introduce," explains Mastelotto.

Turning a seeming disadvantage to an advantage, as the Guitar Craft aphorism goes, Gunn and Mastelotto sought a conduit for their own threads and directions. The outlet became ProjeKct X, co-ordinated by Gunn, Mastelotto and Bill Munyon.

The resulting album, *Heaven And Earth*, was released in May 2000 as a companion to *The ConstruKction Of Light*. Perhaps understandably overshadowed, PX was viewed as an interesting curio. However, the wild collages and collisions of sounds, voices and ideas now seem to be closer in spirit and more of a bolder extrapolation of the whole research and development ethos that had initiated the fraKctalisation process than its parent record. Nearly 18 years after it was made, Bill Munyon offered this overview: "To really appreciate PX's *Heaven And Earth* fully, one must engage it from the beginning and stay to the end. Which I had recently done driving from Austin to Houston. In that listen, I began to think how the flow reminded me of Dante's circles. Each level has its own sound design. Pat did the sequencing, one of his superpowers. Alex R. Mundy and Robert Fripp did an excellent job on the mastering. It was unconventional in the world at that time. It was unconventional for King Crimson, and that says a lot. I believe it is an important part of the King Crimson legacy. I think the world may be readier now to take in this kind of dangerous sonic journey. King Crimson has been ahead of its time and continues to be timeless. I think ProjeKct X's *Heaven And Earth* deserves another listen, still."

IV

The ConstruKction Of Light was released in May 2000. The Press reaction recognised that Crimson were still a potent force despite still being associated with the musical crimes of prog rock. For the *Sunday Times*, Stewart Lee wrote: "Just because King Crimson emerged from the dreaded 'progressive era', don't confuse this vital British group with anything involving Rick Wakeman." Lee goes on to invoke the names of Tool, Tom Waits, Radiohead and the drum'n'bass genre in his praise for the album.

Elsewhere, Stuart Maconie awarded the album three stars, stating: "Sardonic, angular and super-heavy, it takes only a few minutes of *ProzaKc Blues*'s fractured riffing and air of menace to remind the listener that this KC is no sunshine band." Crimson supporter John Bungey, writing for *Mojo*, pointed out: "There's not much here for lovers of pop tunes, and after 30 years of recording it's by no means clear whether Fripp wants to widen his devoted cult following; but there's more going on musically in 12 bars of Crimson than in some entire albums."

In fan circles and on the internet, some commentators noted that *TCOL* failed to deliver on the radical promise of the ProjeKcts. To some degree this is a fair criticism. Certainly, the production of the album is curiously indistinct and staid compared to PX and it certainly stands out as the most self-referential of Crimson albums to date. As he listened to the final version before its release, Fripp had this to say: "My current sense is that the album is flawed but with several gems. In a perfect world, every track works and the album has integrity: a consistent and developed vision. There are few albums (of any artist) where I'm interested in more than two to three tracks. Playing unrecorded music live allows the audience the space to report back on whether an idea is worth pursuing. But very few musicians of my professional acquaintance have been sharp enough to take a hint."

"At this point in Crimson's process I don't believe we would have generated new repertoire unless we had set ourselves the challenge of writing an album. So where there are limitations and weaknesses in the recorded outcome (or report on our process), from my subjective critical perspective, I recognise they are mostly inevitable even where unacceptable. In performance most of the new music will develop and take on a sense of knowing-of-itself."

Gunn offers this view: "*TCOL* isn't the best Crimson record, that's for sure. The best quote I heard about the album is from Bill Rieflin. He said: 'It's the map but not the treasure.' Isn't that good? It's really concise and it's completely true. You get the treasure in the live show."

At the beginning of May, the band began rehearsals in Nashville for their live debut at the small club 12th & Porter. Diana Maio was a resident of Nashville at the time. "I'd hear talk about Adrian Belew every once in a while on Lightning 100 (Nashville's coolest radio station) but had frankly never heard of him. Then the station really started talking the King Crimson concerts up, calling the band 'legendary' and saying the concert was a 'MUST SEE EVENT'. I decided I'd better go too! They were great. I enjoyed the concerts thoroughly and was surprised at the number of fans who came from out of state just to see the band. I had no idea they had such a devoted following."

Kade Graves was one of the out-of-towners, travelling in from Oklahoma. "Since this was a 'warm-up' performance, there were a few kinks in the system to be dealt with. During *FraKctured*, Fripp's space module took a dive before he was to do the 'burning guitar solo' section. The whole group stopped and Fripp excused himself while he rebooted his gear.

"Fans in the audience did take this opportunity to heckle Fripp but in a very non-threatening fun way. When a fan said, 'Start from the beginning!' Fripp returned a 'I challenge that gentleman to come up here and play!' For me, this being my first King Crimson live experience, it was quite awesome and astounding! The synchronicity and the energy between the four players was amazing! The ability to pull off these compositions and do it seemingly effortlessly with a smile is something that I will remember forever."

Also in the audience was ex-Crimson member and Nashville resident Ian Wallace who was cheering loudly, despite reservations about the V-Drums. Notwithstanding sorting out the odd musical trainwreck, Crimson flew to Europe and began the European leg of the tour in Copenhagen. Two months later, the band rolled into London. Among the concertgoers at the Shepherd's Bush Empire were Bill Bruford and Michael Giles.

Reviewing this Crimson's one and only UK appearance in London for the *Guardian* newspaper, Adam Sweeting declared: "Musically, nowhere is off-limits. Pieces might begin with slow, treated percussion and synthesised voice samples, separated by chasms of silence, then kick up a couple of gears into a smooth, flowing motion with Fripp sailing along in pastoral mode. Crimson's version of funk resembles a multiple air crash, shaking the floor with enormous syncopations before uncaging interludes of freeform mayhem."

With *TCOL*'s release, King Crimson was once again touring. Out in the clubs and halls, the new material now began to fully unfurl itself to become road-hardened. Something similar had happened in 1984 when the studio-originated material of *Three Of A Perfect Pair* was performed in concert and so it was with *Oyster Soup*, *Frying Pan* and the album's title track in particular, all of the songs gaining greater definition and potency. The three-disc set, *Heavy ConstruKction*, released in November 2000, documented the degree to which this new generation of repertoire strengthened as it was toured. It also demonstrated the way in which the Double Duo were attempting to augment their regular setlist with improvisations and blows based upon some of the areas mapped out during the ProjeKcts, including ProjeKct Four's *Seizure*. Mastelotto's gradual introduction of real drums into his kit over the coming months also assuaged his and others' dissatisfaction with the V-Drum sound, adding yet more vitality to the pieces.

Containing over 184 minutes of music (with an additional 50 minutes of video footage of the band in concert in Rome), the release was a comprehensive overview of Crimson 2000's repertoire, including *TCOL* in its entirety and an electrifying assemblage of improvisations showing the band's continuing love affair with the unexpected.

What it also revealed was the relative tameness of the studio counterpart and began a train of thought that would take nearly 20 years to come to fruition: to delve back into the master tapes and remix the album. However, at the point at which Crimson reconvened, all such considerations were put to one side. In the 50 years of the band's history there is a clear pattern: the current Crim is ignored during its lifetime but plaudits are heaped upon it with the benefit of hindsight. "Part of the pressure of working with Crim is that it takes so long before what we do is heard and accepted," says Fripp. "So any current Crim works under the weight and burden of what earlier Crims were doing." In waiting for the critical penny to drop, Crimson at this point adopted an active strategy of retiring from the big stages – and the accompanying industry badgering – to a smaller niche market, where the band and its business structure could operate on its own terms. This necessarily painted Crimson primarily as cult operatives – critically influential but occupying the very margins of the first division. Looking back, with the exception of the very first line-up, perhaps it was ever thus.

V

In June 2001, Crimson gathered at Belew's Nashville studio to begin again. Trey Gunn said: "This is kind of a strange time for King Crimson. And it feels slightly odd talking about the band at this very moment. We are at a huge crossroads where the 'past of Crimson' AND the 'past way of doing things KC' are no longer of use to us. We have to find a new way, and not just in the world but between ourselves as musicians. And we haven't found that just yet."

Appearing once again at 12th & Porter, the band integrated new pieces *Dangerous Curves*, *Response To Stimuli* (later known as *Facts Of Life*) and *Krimson Blue* were all integrated into the setlist. There was also the dramatic introduction of *Level Five*, though it had yet to bed down. The piece would become a mainstay of every Crimson tour from this point. Now regarded by Fripp as being *Larks' Tongues In Aspic, Part Five*, even at this point in its development, the piece resonates with a glowering malevolence. Packing in more musical weight and density in several minutes than many groups manage over an entire career, like other entries in the *LTIA* canon it retains a capacity to mix horror and humour for those playing it. During rehearsals for the 2001 tour, Fripp recalled: "At the end of a falling interlocking guitar sequence in 5/8 from *Level Five*, abrasive and acrid enough to shave the fine hairs from an inner ear at a distance of miles, Adrian looked up and said:

AB: I played it right. Beginning on G.

RF: G sharp.

AB & RF: You don't get much closer than that."

The track featured in the set when Crimson supported Tool in August 2001. Gunn remembers that touring with the massively successful alt-metal band had been a long time coming. Tool were huge Crimson fans and the "Nuevo Metal" concept which Fripp had been touting as a route for Crimson found empathetic ears in the Tool camp. "The first show was at Red Rocks in Denver and it was the biggest audience I'd played with Crimson," says Gunn. "We knew it was sold out and we knew no-one was there to see us. And we'd heard all these stories about bands that had opened for Tool – even Primus was pounded with bottle caps and booed off the stage! Fuck! What do we play? We only have 30 minutes. Do we do the mellow songs? Do we play *Deception Of The Thrush*? It was still daytime when we played, so there wasn't a concert vibe but it went over really well. I felt we were the perfect opening act for them because of how we were demanding the audience to listen. It's probably just egotism but it seemed like such a great combination for the audiences."

Mastelotto agrees that the gigs were incredibly important for the band. "They put us in front of a different audience and our music was interpreted differently, the feel was different. Robert wanted the whole Nuevo Metal phase; we could get heavier. Those gigs gave confidence in a way to Adrian and Robert that we could maybe find a younger audience."

Mindful of the differences in opinion regarding *TCOL* when it came to making the band's 13th studio album, Fripp and Belew asked Gunn and Mastelotto to come up with a shortlist of studios. The Tracking Room in Nashville was Gunn and Mastelotto's favourite from the four or five they presented. "We never thought for a second that Robert and Adrian would go for it. It's mondo, dude. That place is where Mutt Lange works. You can put a 90-piece orchestra in there. There is a stone room, a wood room, it's just the most over-the-top place I've ever seen. The budget was maybe $3,000 a day for this place. There's no fucking way they'd ever pick this place," laughs Mastelotto, "but that's what Robert did!"

Just as significant was the decision to ask the rhythm buddies to source a producer. After some sifting and tentative selections, the name they eventually came up with was Gene Freeman, better known as Machine. Having initially met up with Gunn in a New York pizza house to discuss the prospect of working with Crimson, Machine was keen to take the job.

"I was a Crimson fan from college. I would play them on the college radio station where I DJ'd. It was things like *Discipline* and *THRAK*, so I was well up for working. *Matte Kudasai* was such a beautiful song. Then I would smoke weed and listen to the earlier more progressive stuff but that later stuff stuck out for me to play on the station for more regular people," laughs Machine. Music had always been part of Machine's upbringing, although he recalls his father, a clarinetist in the New York Philharmonic, was both baffled and annoyed to see his son max out his student credit card on buying a sampler. "He was outraged. 'What are you doing? This is not how you manage your budget.' And I'm like, 'Dad this is a sampler, a musical instrument. I'm going to make money with this one day. I'm going to be a professional with this one day, you'll see.' He just didn't get it."

Best known for his work in remixing and utilising the vocabulary of hip hop, metal and industrial dance rock, Freeman might not have seemed the obvious choice. Yet the experience with Tool and the growing realisation that the home-grown approach of *TCOL* had stunted their sonic reach, King Crimson embarked on working with an external producer for only the fourth time in their career. "I don't think it was a big deal to them. It's more about an engineer, someone who's really good at capturing a band in a studio, and King Crimson in a way largely produce themselves live," observes Machine. "They have production as a part of what they do. Their guitars have midi pick-ups and are simultaneously feeding synths. Trey's Warr guitar splits to multiple amps, has a bass register and an upper register. The same for Adrian. It was insane and this would all be recorded live. Whereas I'd worked with a lot of younger bands and this stuff is all done in layers in the studio. It's not all performed. Not only is King Crimson's music performed but then there are portions of it which are improvisational and you are recording this massive session." Machine worked with the group in a rehearsal space before the full-on recording. Although Mastelotto originally wanted two weeks of preparation, this was vetoed and the team was given five days before Fripp and Belew came in to begin their work. Machine says the period without the guitarists was crucial to his getting to grips with the material, creating a tempo grid that would act as a map for himself and the band. Originally a drummer, Machine was no stranger to working with grooves and beats but he remembers being amazed at what he calls "this lesson in music theory". "There were times when I'd get stuck with the time signature and I'd have Pat come over and he'd go, 'Oh yeah, well that's an 11/4 bar into a 6/8 which then goes back to 4/4.' And I'm like 'Oh. Right'." He laughs. Machine admits how daunting it was as the sessions got properly under way. "I remember being terrified at the number of inputs. It was like 40 inputs to my digital audio workstation at the time. I mean, that was a lot. When we were recording sometimes there'd be a click track and sometimes there wouldn't be, and we would do these whole takes of 40 inputs at once! And then the drums. Well, there's the real drums and then all the drum machines that Pat is triggering off and everyone's got toys as well as their guitars and it's happening live! Then it's somewhat different from take to take depending on the song. It could be very different. Then it was left to me to put something together. There might be three or five good takes and then Robert would disconnect and I was left to put something together that I liked."

Pat recalls that Machine's way of working sometimes baffled his older band colleagues. "When we finished doing our tracking, they went to Adrian's house to do the guitar solos and the vocals. They were done in a few days and I would call up there to ask how it was going. Adrian says, 'I don't know what Machine's doing. He comes into the studio every day looking at that screen typing all day.' I said, 'Dude, he's going through everything bar by bar, beat by beat, you know the way we make modern records,'" laughs Mastelotto. Machine has nothing but respect for Belew. "The way Adrian does his solos is just insane. It's amazing. When Adrian was doing his solos he would say, 'Give me a pass' and he would rip out an incredible solo. Then he'd say, 'Give me another pass,' and he'd rip out another one that had nothing to do with the first one. Then he'd do a third one that had nothing to do with the other two. He'd do about five of these and he'd go, 'Make something out of it, Machine.' And he'd walk away and I would take these pieces, these insane, wild, crazy-sounding pieces and construct something and show it back to him. And then he would listen to it and go, 'OK, well that's cool. Punch me in right there so I can seam that together a little better,' and he would then replay that whole thing! I mean it was effortless for him!"

Released in 2003, *The Power To Believe* seemed to prove the long-established convention that Crimson albums benefit from having material that's been played-in live prior to the studio. After the deceptively gentle a cappella opening of *The Power To Believe I*, the brutal power of *Level Five*, with the band's patented bulldozer riffing, re-establishes another Crimson tradition: beginning an album with a sucker punch, a quiet feint followed by a rapidly-moving metal-edged thump hitting the listener hard. And that's not the only callback. In the same way that Fripp's *Peace* theme balanced 1970's *In The Wake Of Poseidon*, the repeated use of *The Power To Believe*'s melody – adapted from *All Her Love Is Mine* from Belew's 1996 solo album *Op Zop Too Wah* – gives the album an architectural coherence and a sense of epic proportion made possible by instrumental tour de forces such as *Level Five*, *EleKtriK* and *Dangerous Curves.*

Belew's wry sense of humour dominates *Happy With What You Have To Be Happy With*. Gently poking fun at the often difficult business of coming up with words for music that often doesn't make many concessions, they also satirise the content of many a metal band's songs. Belew's more introspective side flourished on *Eyes Wide Open*, a beautiful ballad providing a thoughtful contrast to the extraordinary bursts of fretboard mayhem and percussive fury served up in *Facts Of Life*, a prime example of the metallic crunch and crush of King Crimson's heaviest-sounding work since *Red*.

Machine is intensely proud of the album. "Nuevo Metal was Robert's description. What he meant by that was a new sound for metal because there was a term Nu Metal for music like Korn, Incubus, and those bands were all part of that. There are so many metal bands that are influenced by King Crimson. For Robert it meant something different. It was about the sound. The fact that I've worked with King Crimson comes up often when people meet me, especially among these really educated metal bands. They're very proficient on their instruments like Crimson is and, for them, KC is a very big deal, like we all know Tool is very vocal about the King Crimson influence over the years. For me, it's pretty awesome that I got to be part of that in a small way for a small amount of time."

A significant element which informed both the ProjeKcts and Crimson's subsequent sound was Mastelotto's inspired use of electronica – not only his ability to dial up samples of Jamie Muir's aerophones, Wimborne Minster's bells or Adrian's voice sampled on the fly and played back in concert, but also the heavy glitch-edited sounds more normally associated with acts such as Boom Boom Satellites, Squarepusher, Photek and others. To refine that for *The Power To Believe*, Mastelotto teamed up with Machine at Pat's garage.

"We were there for five days. The one he really helped me with was *The Power To Believe II*, which used to be called *Virtuous Circle*. I'd done two drum takes, one in the bigger room with the snares on and one in the stone room with the snares off. We started to cut the phrases. It's what I played but it's not where I played it," laughs Pat. "We really tightened up the drum and percussion sounds to the bassline. You think you know where you are but you don't realise how complicated it is until you play along with it. It's not repetitive. So he helped me a lot with that. Then I asked Adrian and

Robert before we go to mix, can we have a pre-mix. Same kind of thing as with the pre-production – can we get in a room and listen to things so that when we go in the expensive mix room we already know what we want: the slap on the vocal or the reverb on one section, that kind of thing. We're not guys that hang out together so it's like a really good way to get down what we want but they didn't want to do it. I think *Level Five* was the last thing we mixed. The first time 'dddddrrrrrr' went by on the drums, Robert was like, 'What?' And I'm like, 'Oh shit. He fucking hates it.' He was really disturbed by it. We turned around and thought Robert was getting coffee but he'd left."

Back in the UK following some additional Crimsonising of the album by Fripp and David Singleton, Mastelotto was relieved to receive a call from the guitarist. "He told me that he and David had saved the record and that he was very happy with it. I was delighted. Anybody that I played the mixes that I took home were going 'fucking hell – this is a great record'. Robert had started to believe in the album. To me, it doesn't sound different with all the fairy-dusting they did on it from the original. The individual things sound largely like what they were is what I'm saying. The sequence and flow of the final record is something they decided. The idea of putting in the inserts and haikus that was all done over there in the UK and that certainly made the whole record hang together. My impression when I first heard it was that this was a record to be proud of."

The beginning of the ProjeKcts had seen Bill Bruford depart the ranks. Now, at the culmination of the entire cycle some six years later, it was Trey Gunn's time to leave. Unhappiness at an attempt to redistribute the way in which the band's money was apportioned, with a bigger cut going to Belew ahead of the tour following the release of *TCOL* album, had soured his relationship with the band. However much it was publicly stated that Crimson was a democratic institution in which all four members were equal, it didn't always feel like that on the inside. It wasn't just the money issue that unsettled Gunn. The difficulties which he and Mastelotto experienced in getting the guitarists to alter their approach or go with some of their musical directions and ideas had also been a factor in reinforcing the sense that as relative newcomers they were very much regarded as junior partners. Though each man dealt with this in different ways, that difference permeated the fabric in which Crimson operated.

Now in 2003, there was talk of Tony Levin being brought back into the band. While Gunn bore Levin no ill will whatsoever, when the decision was finally made that the fifth man, as Fripp had dubbed the bassist, would return in October, Gunn handed in his resignation after the end of the European tour. It might have all gone smoothly – except for the fact that nobody had ascertained if Levin was actually free. As it turned out, he wasn't and, with only weeks to go and faced with the possibility of extremely expensive cancellations, Crimson's management asked Gunn to return.

His initial impulse was to say no but, after some determined financial negotiations, he signed up for the American tour on wages as a sideman. The tour was arguably one of the most powerful of the period, with several gigs reaching outstanding levels of energy and Gunn's contributions as savage and as incisive as they ever were, earning every cent he'd negotiated and more. After the band's run of rapturously received gigs in Mexico City which marked the end of the year's commitments, Gunn publicly announced his departure.

For fans who'd started out wondering what Gunn did in the Double Trio and then been ever more impressed by his distinctive contributions to the ProjeKcts and the latest Crimson, his decision to leave came as a complete shock. "Earlier this year, at the inevitability of the closing of this phase of my musical life, I spent some time looking back. I thought back to the original aims I had as a young musician. And much to my surprise, I discovered that I have realised them. They were simply and elegantly stated to myself at the time: I want to play with the best musicians on the planet and make the most powerful and unusual music possible. I have done that. And done it with this band: King Crimson. And I don't need to just keep on doing it over and over again."

VI

In the aftermath of Gunn's departure, Tony Levin joined the remaining Crims at Belew's studio in September 2004 and, while work there produced some interesting moments, it failed to truly gel and, for Mastelotto, there was once again the frustration of recording in Adrian's studio. "Any time I hit a snare drum it was too loud. We were using quilts and all sorts to make a canopy for the kit. It made it very hard to do a rock record. We could do ballads and we did some trippy things but soon you're listening to the playback and it's a bunch of slow, ambient 'something'. We had this thing in five called *Buzzsaw* which was uptempo. Those just squirted out but we never went back to work on them."

In 2006, Belew and Fripp worked live as ProjeKct Six. With Belew back behind the V-Drums and Fripp extending his Soundscapes into a rockier context, the pair found their feet at a variety of gigs in America supporting Steven Wilson's outfit, Porcupine Tree. DGM released a compilation of the duo's shows in the support slot in October 2006. It offered a snapshot of the duo grappling with the task of combining the harmonic ambiguity of Soundscapes with some straight-ahead rock grooves. With so much of Fripp's public work that year being taken up with Soundscapes, it was almost a novelty to hear him rocking it up as he does on *Time Groove* from Boston and *Queer Jazz*.

Despite all the technology involved, this was a pared-back sound compared to previous ProjeKcts and there's a tentative, exploratory quality to much of the music – two players in search of that often elusive moment, an intriguing aspect which provides much of the tension and appeal. As well as the big set pieces, there are some little jewels to be found in small places – the Frippertronics-like ending of *Berklee Strut* and the beginning of *End Time*. Of one gig, the *Boston Herald* reviewer commented: "With Belew pounding on an electronic drum kit, Fripp tore into a set of improvised sound sketches, mixing in hints of electronic programming under his searing guitar explorations."

All of the gigs were later made available as downloads. The pick of the bunch, though, comes from the Keswick gigs which push some of the ideas and themes a little further. As ever Fripp's own commentary is more circumspect: "An enjoyable performance. Probably, we played well, but I have no idea."

Elements of ProjeKct Six's rapturous soloing against regular rock-orientated beats had echoes of Fripp's Discotronics as heard on 1980's *God Save The Queen/Under Heavy Manners*. The ProjeKcts were always a means of developing new material but in this instance, despite some fiery and inventive moments, the ideas stayed somewhat half-formed. Nevertheless, Fripp remained keen, but a planned P6 tour of Japan with Porcupine Tree later in the year was hastily rearranged as a series of solo Fripp gigs after Belew abruptly bailed.

Fripp spent much of 2006 operating as a solo artist, taking his Soundscapes to dozens of venues in the US and supporting Porcupine Tree, where he admired the playing of drummer Gavin Harrison. There was a short run of dates on the West Coast of the States with so-called ambient supergroup Slow Music, convened by his long-time friend Bill Rieflin. Additionally, performances with the League Of Crafty Guitarists and his ongoing commitment to Guitar Craft continued to be an important focus.

In 2003, Fripp had written: "Crimson is presently in the completion stage of a small cycle; the next step is a completion of a large cycle. A completion is a new beginning – something becomes available to the future. But this is not a mechanical action and there is nothing inevitable in continuation. What is available may be actualised, or may remain in potential. The next step in the world of Crimson is to conceive and present a view of Crimson as Small Mobile Intelligent Unit to the members and see whether it appeals to them. In the life of DGM, mobility is now mostly achieved. Crimson, however, has become locked into the functional restrictions of a professional touring and recording band. This is probably inevitable and has happened before, on a regular basis. Unfixing is the strategy that has conventionally followed fixing."

The prospect of a return for King Crimson seemed remote given the failure of the post-Gunn line-up to come up with anything substantial. While seasoned Crim-watchers know never to say never, the announcement that Gavin Harrison would be joining Levin, Mastelotto, Fripp and Belew for a series of gigs in 2008 nevertheless came as a welcome surprise. Harrison knew little of Crimson's material – which, in other circumstances, might have been a problem. In this instance it was an advantage. What Fripp was looking for was a fresh approach and in Harrison, already regarded as one of the key technicians and conceptualists of the drumming world, that's precisely what he got.

When the new quintet convened at SIR in Nashville in 2008, there was a spirit of optimism compared to the previous occasion when the Double Trio's run in the rehearsal complex ended in acrimony and disarray. There were early suggestions from Fripp that new material could be tested and explored but Belew's commitments to other work effectively limited his time with the band to an afternoon-only basis. This meant focusing on the familiar and the repertoire for the tour was mainly drawn from the 1980s with a smattering of *THRAK*-era pieces and only one song each from *The ConstruKction Of Light* and *The Power To Believe*. The mornings were spent with Harrison and Mastelotto running through their arrangements and swapping ideas to be honed, refined or rejected before the rest of the band arrived. Although Harrison was Crimson's newest recruit, his work had informed the Mastelotto/Bruford partnership of the Double Duo through Gavin's 1996 book, *Rhythmic Illusions*. Mastelotto relished the opportunity to be working with Harrison. Their opening duet, featuring guitar and voice samples triggered by Pat, posits early ideas for multi-part drumming which would be further developed by Harrison for the 2014 incarnation of the band. Putting

Top: The original lineup of King Crimson at Heathrow Airport, 27th October 1969. Their first tour of America would also be their last. **Bottom left:** Pete Sinfield the man who wrote the words and came up with the name of the band. Photo: Willie Christie. **Right:** Playback at Wessex Studios during the recording of *In The Wake Of Poseidon*.

Top: Peter Sinfield & Robert Fripp keeping the name of King Crimson alive following the original band's breakup in 1969. **Bottom:** Hyde Park, 4th September 1971: just one of several gigs performed around the recording sessions for *Islands*.

Top left: Boz Burrell and Ian Wallace recording backing vocals on *Ladies of the Road* during the *Islands* sessions 1971. **Right:** Percussive alchemist & avant-garde catalyst Jamie Muir in concert with King Crimson, 1972. **Bottom:** A Crimson quintet with magical abilities recording 1973's *Larks' Tongues In Aspic* at Command Studios. Photo: Willie Christie.

Top: Discipline in the act of reincarnating King Crimson. Photo: Tony Levin. **Bottom:** 1980s KC: A period of stability. Photo: Tony Levin.

Top: The Double Trio recording *THRAK* at Real World 1994. Photo: Tony Levin. **Bottom left:** A Crimson fraKctal: Project 4 in 1998. Photo: John Sinks. **Right:** In the forecourt of the Crimson King: L-R Robert Fripp, Sid Smith, Ronan Chris Murphy, Trey Gunn. On the road with P4 somewhere between Vancouver and Seattle, 1998. Photo: Tony Levin.

Top: The Double Duo - a new Crimson for the new millennium touring *The ConstruKction of Light*. Photo: Bill Munyon. **Bottom left:** On stage in Barcelona in 2003. It would be another 15 years before a very different King Crimson would return to Europe. Photo: Bill Munyon. **Right:** Another Crimson quintet - Gavin Harrison adds his percussive firepower to a short-lived lineup. Photo: Sid Smith.

Top: 40th Anniversary series launch event 6 October, 2009 Air Studios. L-R Michael Giles, Peter Sinfield, Bill Bruford, David Cross, Robert Fripp, John Wetton, Mel Collins. Photo: Hugh O'Donnell. **Bottom left:** A quiet moment with cake at Air Studios 6 October, 2009. John Wetton, Robert Fripp, Jakko Jakszyk. Photo: Sid Smith. **Right:** The last time the *Starless & Bible Black* team would be reunited. 6 October, 2009 Air Studios. Photo: Sid Smith.

Top: After an absence of six years King Crimson, boasting a three-drummer frontline, returns to the stage in America. Photo: Tony Levin. **Bottom:** The Crims in Japan, December 2018. Photo: David Singleton.

in long days paid off for the two drummers and the results were patently obvious throughout a tour for which their playing was flawless throughout. While Fripp, Belew and Levin undoubtedly worked on their respective parts away from SIR, the cohesion of the unit took longer. At a friends and family show on the eve of the short run of dates, there was almost a party atmosphere in the large room. While there were plenty of rough edges, they were largely confined to the frontline. The general consensus was that the wrinkles would be ironed out as the band got into its stride.

All afternoon a line of expectant fans snaked around the block from the Belcourt Theatre under the punishing Nashville sun on Saturday, 2 August. When they entered the small foyer, the evening excitement was palpable. Many of those present were local but some had come from as far away as Europe, Asia and Japan. Although it wasn't captured on the board recordings of the tour, the audience gave the players an ecstatic welcome in a venue that felt more akin to a small club date. As the new quintet unveiled itself, there was a surprising degree of nervous tension among the players – perhaps only to be expected given the last time Belew, Fripp and Mastelotto had gone out on stage together was in 2003. For Tony Levin, 12 years had elapsed since he'd performed with Crimson. Normally this would not have been a problem to a seasoned gigster like Levin whose duties with Peter Gabriel had taken him around the stadiums of the world. However, it was quickly obvious as he manfully struggled with the complexities of Trey Gunn's parts for *The ConstruKction Of Light* that he wasn't as up to speed as he would have liked. Nor was he the only one tripping over the material as the chiming guitars in the piece occasionally moved from interlocking to unlocked and hanging wide open. In a somewhat reserved and tentative performance, it was interesting to note that sometimes the pieces that caused the greatest difficulties were those that had been around the longest. *Red* saw more than one Crim mixing up fingers, chords and cues, not to mention various pedals failing to deliver as intended on setlist stalwarts like *Elephant Talk* and *Thela Hun Ginjeet*. The set culminated in a calamitous *VROOOM* – it was all very well to approach the music as if for the first time but it was better if the players were all on the same page. None of this mattered to the cheering crowd. In a pattern that would be repeated as the band moved on to Chicago and Philadelphia, had you been in the room on any given night it simply seemed enough to have Crimson back after five years. The second and the third night at Chicago's Park West, one of King Crimson and Fripp's favourite venues, found the group on a wild high. Large portions of these shows possessed a carefree quality that prompted a sense that it could all fall apart at any minute, with the band teetering toward the end of the show in a giddy, exhilarated rush. That kind of energy and drive carried forth into the combined velocity of *The Talking Drum* and *Larks' Tongues In Aspic, Part Two*, on which the band really gelled for the first time on the last night in Chicago. *Frame By Frame*, which sounded precarious at the start of the tour, was now bedded down while *Level Five*, with percussive cymbal chokes newly added, continued to provide a full-frontal assault despite some unsteady moments.

What audiences were getting was raw and unvarnished. Whatever it lacked in the way of KC's customary precision was to some degree compensated for by its spirit and verve. On the second night at Philadelphia's Keswick Theatre, the focus seemed to slip away entirely. When the band launched into *Red*, large swathes of the audience usually, to use the colloquial Philadelphia phrase, "lose their shit" and the second night at the Keswick was no exception. At this point there were some members of the band who had been playing this piece for well over a decade. However, there were still razor-sharp man traps waiting to snap at any unwary Crim whose fingers go astray. As with all Crim clams, it was really about the recovery and so as they rumbled along it was possible to witness many moments of heroic resurrection and redemption on material that shouldn't have had the capacity to unseat them at this stage in their careers. Fripp turned in a concise and powerful solo on *Dinosaur* and an energetically-paced *The Talking Drum* and *Larks' Tongues In Aspic, Part Two*, once again built into something special. Overall, however, despite the considerable efforts of the drummers, while there were some fiery individual moments, as a whole the collective spirit was weak. This was not Crimson's finest hour.

It was possible that the frequent flash photography sapped something. A restless audience, including significant numbers getting up to go to the bar, exacerbated a feeling that whatever magic Crimson might have conjured was dissipated by the time the sound hit the back rows.

There's a Guitar Craft aphorism that goes: "Begin with the possible and move gradually towards the impossible." However, every night of the tour King Crimson disregarded this advice by placing *The ConstruKction Of Light* at the head of the set. Like a mountain demanding to be climbed, it loomed ominously before everything else on the setlist. The complexities of the piece and the demands it placed upon those called to perform it were considerable and, on the tour, so far it had exerted an exacting price on anyone whose concentration or fingers experienced even a momentary lapse. So far, on a nightly basis, the band tackled the seemingly impossible and came off slightly worse for wear but just about surviving the experience.

However, tensions offstage were also exerting their pull. Belew was increasingly feeling resentful about the way in which he was overlooked by critics, some punters and online commentators. Fripp's phobia of flash photography had been a huge issue in 2003. While they were supportive to a point, there was a sense that Fripp's unhappiness leached into the psyche of the group. It seemed an insoluble problem and, although touring should be an enjoyable experience, Fripp's method of dealing with it, by playing unlit and half-hidden behind his rig, created a physical and psychological barrier between the guitarist and others in the band. At the end of a performance, Fripp would stay briefly by his rig as the crowds applauded with him, in turn, applauding the three players taking a collective bow at the centre of the stage.

It was the same in 2008. When, at the end of one show, Mastelotto gestured and shouted to a reluctant Fripp to join them, it earned the drummer a stinging rebuke afterward. Mastelotto never issued such an invitation again. Fripp was by now not only unlit but completely hidden from two-thirds of the audience. Depending on the seat they were in, only a fraction of punters would be able to see the guitarist and even then in profile only. Some felt disgruntled and expressed their unhappiness at the box office demanding that confused staff give them their money back.

From Belew's perspective, it didn't matter how well he played or sang on an individual level, or however hard he worked at presenting a smiling, animated point of contact to an otherwise static stage presentation – all the attention, all the credit and all the glory was directed at Fripp. The issue that had irritated him in 2003 was now writ large, leaving him wondering if it was worth all the effort. No matter what he did, Fripp got the critical acclaim. The "no photography" edict was, for him, hypocritically undermined by DGM's last-minute decision to have the tour documented by members of the road crew taking photos in soundchecks and from the wings during performances. These, along with short video sketches from each venue, were uploaded on to the DGM website on a daily basis to give fans unable to attend a small taste of the Crims' return. But nobody had informed Belew and the process of documentation got under his skin so much that by the time the band arrived in New York, a note from his manager and wife Martha requested that no photo or video of Belew be made public without prior permission.

Whether this helped or not, in New York Crimson began to sound like they were finally getting in the groove, discernibly sharper than before. An incredibly powerful *Larks' Tongues In Aspic, Part Two* offered proof. From the extended screech through to furious double drumming and superb percussive embellishments from an energised Mastelotto, it felt and sounded like King Crimson 2008 really began at this point. Over the run of four shows, the band began to come together. In the afternoon soundcheck on the second day in New York after the others had finished, Fripp began a Soundscape. This wasn't unusual – it was the guitarist's practice to create an atmospheric sequence to play as the audience arrived. It was his way of "tuning the air", as he put it. As staff and crew prepared the stage and seating prior to opening to the public, Fripp began to solo over the top of the drifting string chords. Long surging notes flowed out across the PA and one by one people stopped and stood or sat utterly spellbound. The playing was so poignant and yearning that more than one member of the Crimson road crew was moved to the point of tears. Throughout the piece, as it built in layers and waves of impassioned playing, Fripp's face was impassive as he channeled some of his most heartfelt, inspired, playing of the tour. After 10 or 15 minutes, it subsided and silence crept into the room, broken by scattered applause from entranced cleaning staff. "I hope that was recorded," said one of crew looking expectantly at the sound engineer. After a long pause, Fripp keyed in the more usual ambiguous bell 'scape that would greet the audience and left the stage to eat and undertake his own preparations for the show. The sense that something special had been inadvertently witnessed by the handful in that room was tangible.

Despite a rough and uneven start with a setlist that was relatively unadventurous, by the last night in New York the quintet were ready to think about the future. Afterwards, in the dressing room as a bottle of champagne was uncorked, Fripp asked if everybody was on board for another round of Crimsonising? In typically unconventional fashion and appealing to Fripp's dry sense of humour, King Crimson's 40th-anniversary tour took place in its 39th year. Now with that portentous anniversary in a sense neutralised, the band's 40th year would see them stepping forward, perhaps with new material. With everyone signing up to another round of touring in 2009, glasses were raised, toasts were made and Crimson's return seemed assured.

A few weeks later, however, things became less certain. After Fripp had circulated a suggested block of tour dates for April and May 2009, Belew's management came back to say Adrian was unavailable due to a planned solo tour. It wasn't the first time Belew had initially committed to a series of dates only to get cold feet at a later stage. It had happened at the very start of the *Discipline* era when he joined Talking Heads' expanded line-up and later, in 1982 and 1984, Crimson's live activity had been organised to accommodate Belew's solo career. The early days of the Double Trio were thrown into doubt when Belew initially thought the new line-up was not for him. More recently, ahead of ProjeKct Six's Japanese dates with Porcupine Tree in November 2006, Belew's pursuit of a greater fee and for all visa work to be handled by someone other than his own management had resulted in Robert undertaking the gigs in Japan on his own.

Now with Belew apparently unavailable and Fripp perhaps sensing that things would only get more complicated, the Crimson convenor cancelled the dates. Within a few days, Belew's team advised him that the solo dates were now scrubbed and he would be available for Crimson in April and May 2009 after all. For Fripp, however, the moment had passed. Any plans King Crimson had for live work during its 40th anniversary were now permanently shelved. And with them, as it would turn out, Belew's position as a member of King Crimson.

VII

It's late in the afternoon of Tuesday, 6 October 2009, and the tiny café next to the spacious hall No. 1 in London's AIR Studios is filling up with excited people. There's lots of smiles and grins as the accents bouncing off the high walls reveal this to be a cosmopolitan crowd. America, Japan, New Zealand, Poland, France and places closer to home are all represented in varying degrees of loudness and animation.

What's brought these various writers and broadcasters together is the unveiling of the new surround-sound remixes of King Crimson's back catalogue by Steven Wilson. Every few minutes, one of the assembling crowd buttonholes a harassed-looking organiser enquiring politely but firmly when they'll be able to enter the main hall. "It won't be long now," he says before dashing off to welcome a new arrival and usher them into the now less-than-commodious café.

When the doors are finally opened, the journos quickly take their places on the thirty or so chairs set squarely inside a sonic perimeter of high-quality speakers. It's like a game of pass-the-parcel but in reverse – you only get to set down when the music starts. Given that the impressive building was once a church, it seems bizarrely appropriate that when he walks to the front of the small crowd, Fripp bears more than a passing resemblance to a Church of England minister about to address his flock. When he starts you half expect him to begin "Dearly beloved, we are gathered here today …".

Instead, he notes wryly in his opening remarks that King Crimson's relationship with the media, particularly the British music press, hasn't always been so cordial.

Next up is Steven Wilson. He's talking about the process he went through in remixing the music. Beforehand he looked slightly nervous. That may seem odd considering that the guitarist is regularly playing to huge crowds. This audience, however, contains some of the musicians whose work helped to shape his own musical path. At heart, Wilson is still very much a fan. This was music that he grew up with and which inspired him. Such was his ardour for Crimson, he had no hesitation in putting himself forward for the remixing job: "I suppose that's because this music has been part of my DNA. I instinctively knew how they should be approached."

Sometimes musicians are fixed in their attitudes towards a given album because of what occurred during the recording sessions. Wilson knew that with an album like *Lizard* he would have to break through the barrier which Fripp had erected around its making since 1970. "I can see why so many players don't want to revisit their past. It's not just the music but the politics and the problems of the time that they can hear. Talking with Robert during the whole remixing process has been interesting. Every record that Crimson ever did was a battle of one kind or another, either between the players or the record company or a hostile or disinterested press, especially in the UK.

There were so many factors stacked up against these albums, and sometimes it's like they are on the verge of falling apart, that it's a wonder they ever got made. But in a way that's what makes them so extraordinary."

Wilson would work largely on his own and then invite Fripp to listen to the results. Often Fripp would suggest deletions or significant alterations which Wilson would then have to resist, in a sense defending the original instrumental decisions. "I'd say: 'No, you can't do that, Robert,' which is odd really I suppose but he would nearly always defer, saying that he trusted my judgement as a fan who would know what other fans would want."

So enamoured was Fripp of Wilson's efforts that, in the case of *Lizard*, he was able to hear the music – rather than re-enacting the disputes of the time – for the first time. Wilson's remixing certainly paved the way to rehabilitating *Lizard* to the extent that nearly two-thirds of its material, unloved for so long by the guitarist, now sits on the KC setlist. The remixes and Wilson's work opened up the door to the idea that a live incarnation of King Crimson could revisit and re-imagine material that had otherwise lain dormant for 40-plus years.

As the music gets under way, a small group of men in their late '50s and early '60s sit, as though in some large-scale public seance, listening to the ghosts of their youth creating sparks burning just as brightly as it did when they first laid down the tracks. During the playback of *Larks' Tongues In Aspic, Part One*, Bill Bruford can't contain his enthusiasm, annotating various points in the track with whoops of excitement or surprised chuckles. He draws bemused looks from some of the people around him, as though they've ended sitting next to the nutter on the bus. Not that he cares. Bill is enjoying himself immensely, just as he always did when he was in the thick of Crimson's music. Take a listen to the many live recordings from his time with the band and you'll find them peppered with similar shouts of encouragement from the drum stool.

After *21st Century Schizoid Man*, *In The Court Of The Crimson King*, *Larks' Tongues In Aspic, Part One*, *Red* and *Starless* have rattled both the windows of the building and the recesses of individual memories, Michael Giles, Peter Sinfield, Mel Collins, David Cross, John Wetton, Bill Bruford and Robert Fripp line up to have their collective photograph taken. The body language is good, the atmosphere between warm and inviting, with lots of laughter. Whatever enmity may have existed, it's been forgiven and forgotten about. While the photographers snap away, this utterly unique gathering of musicians look surprised and thrilled to be there. At the end of it all, one awe-struck punter correctly concludes that this was a remarkable reunion of men who made remarkable music.

As various interviews are conducted between the two scheduled playbacks, the one musician they'd all like to talk to stays silent. Much to the frustration of many an editor, Fripp refuses now to include interviews in his job description, declining all offers to talk about his work. What has been very much part of his brief, however, has been the careful curating of King Crimson's audio legacy. Some bands have little or no say over what gets re-issued or licensed. For many, the royalties they receive are unlikely to keep their budgerigar in seed for six months.

Had Fripp not gone through the period of six years or more of what he called "Endless Grief" and won back control of the Crimson catalogue, it might have been the same for him and it's a safe bet that this audience and countless others out in the real world wouldn't be enjoying the 40th Anniversary editions. In addition to Steven Wilson's revelatory renditions in 5.1 and the refreshing new stereo mixes undertaken with Fripp, the original albums have been accompanied by all manner of extras. Prior to these re-issues, whenever Fripp has been asked about the existence of alternative versions of tracks or outtakes, he'd always maintained that since Crimson's time in the studio was so short, they didn't really have the luxury of a real budget to run up multiple takes. The Crimson ethos was always "get in and get out as quick as possible". However, Wilson's delving into the vaults uncovered a treasure trove of material which, when pulled together with the original albums, documents the Crimson process in hitherto unimagined detail.

While Fripp is clearly pleased with the results, how do other Crims regard the prospect of their work being remodelled for surround sound? John Wetton was unequivocal in his support. "You wouldn't like some music executive type coming in and remixing it. That wouldn't do at all. But Steven's got the ears. He knows the music, understands it, and knows what's going on, so it's great!"

Yet, as Declan Colgan of Panegryic, the company responsible for co-ordinating and releasing these editions reveals, the appearance of the 40th Anniversary series was by no means guaranteed. Not everyone was convinced that the expense of digitising the original multi-tracks, and then the amount of time and effort spent restoring the music, made any kind of sense. "There were a number of people saying to us when we were starting this process that there was no point because there wasn't an audience or market for it. But Steven Wilson was very persuasive with Robert in wanting to get it done, saying there was a valid musical reason for doing it first, and that there would probably be an audience for it if it was done. We started out quite tentatively last year, thinking we'd have one ready (*Court*) but, when *Lizard* and *Red* became available to us, we decided to put them out as well and got a tremendous reaction!"

These releases essentially created a bespoke market which labels large and small across the industry would soon emulate. That King Crimson is taking the time and trouble with this ongoing set of re-issues to create new benchmarks and standards in terms of looking after and presenting its archive to the public seems entirely consistent with its reputation for going against the prevailing flow and shaking up expectations.

Colgan finds it reassuring that Crimson should be doing so at precisely the point in time when the media and the industry tells us that people prefer convenience over quality. "It's very refreshing to know that there's not just an audience, but a decent-sized audience, that's willing to support an initiative that actually goes in the opposite direction and says, 'We're going to make the music sound the best it can be and not the weakest that the consumer will put up with.' It's about respect for the music and respect for the audience – which is what Crimson has always been about."

Wilson, who would soon see his own career move into a bigger league, quickly became the remixer of choice for re-issue campaigns that would include classic albums by Yes, ELP, Jethro Tull, Hawkwind, Caravan, Roxy Music, Gentle Giant, XTC, Tears For Fears, Tangerine Dream et al. However, that night at AIR, all of that lay in the future. At the end of the evening, members of Crimson past and present lined up to have their photos taken by the journalists and photographers. It was impossible not to feel a moment of history being made as Giles, Sinfield and Fripp stood together. Similarly, seeing the *Larks'* quartet smiling and laughing. There was a poignancy seeing Mel Collins and Fripp together, the last surviving players in the *Islands* line-up reunited once again.

But the event wasn't just about the past and the present. What nobody beyond a very small number of those in the room could have known was that when Mel, Robert and Jakko Jakszyk stood to have their pictures taken, the lenses were capturing the future of King Crimson.

VIII

In January 2010, Jakko Jakszyk (pronounced Jack-Chick) found himself sitting opposite the guitarist who had inspired him so much back in 1971 at Watford Town Hall. That 13-year old boy would never have believed anyone who told him that 39 years later he'd be improvising in a studio with Robert Fripp. The pair spent a day at DGM's sound studio trading ideas. Jakszyk confesses he felt a degree of trepidation at Fripp's invitation. "When I drove down to Broad Chalke that afternoon I had no idea what Robert had in mind, I had no idea what he was going to play or what he'd want me to play, but we sat there, hit record and we improvised. At the end of our day together, we'd improvised four or five pieces and Robert suggested I take the hard drive away and do something with them, though he didn't tell me what to do."

When Jakszyk was growing up in Croxley Green, near Rickmansworth, he could have had no inkling that stumbling upon his first King Crimson album, *In The Wake Of Poseidon*, in 1970 would change his life. Hearing it immediately made him want to pick up and play the guitar, something he did professionally upon leaving school. "When I first heard Crimson I didn't have many reference points, but even at that age I could tell it was coming at things from a completely different point of view. It wasn't coming at it from the same place as everyone else, you know, the blues and pentatonic scales. It was coming from a whole other place."

In an incredibly varied career – which includes a period in the late '70s signed as a solo artist to Jake Riviera's Stiff label and to Chiswick Records – Jakszyk has collaborated with a diverse array of artists including Mick Karn, Richard Barbieri, Tom Robinson and Slapp Happy's Peter Blegvad, as well stints in bands such as Rapid Eye Movement (along with ex-Hatfield stalwarts Dave Stewart and Pip Pyle), The Lodge with ex-Henry Cow bassist John Greaves and Golden Palominos' Anton Fier and, in the '90s, Level 42, where he replaced Allan Holdsworth.

Jakko's presence at Broad Chalke hadn't come out of the blue. Fripp made contact when the guitarist and singer was fronting the 21st Century Schizoid Band, which featured Ian McDonald, Peter Giles, Mel Collins and Jakszyk's father-in-law Michael Giles. Fripp recognised that handling such a diverse group of players, not to mention taking a tour on the road – all tasks which had fallen to Jakszyk – was no easy feat. Nor had the fact that Jakszyk was playing fiendishly complex guitar parts *and* singing, often at the same time, gone unnoticed by Fripp. He'd occasionally ring Jakszyk to find out how things were going. "Now someone else understands what I went through in Crimson," Fripp would laugh upon hearing about some of the tensions that had surfaced in the Schizoid Band.

In 2002, in a bizarre case of history repeating itself, Michael Giles unexpectedly quit after the band's final performance on a Japanese tour. But this time Ian McDonald was in no hurry to join him. Instead Ian Wallace joined the group and in some ways the band was better for it. "It meant people could stop treading on eggshells," says Jakszyk.

Away from the band, in 2005 Jakszyk invited Fripp to guest on his fourth solo album, *The Bruised Romantic Glee Club* (2006). Back with the Schizoid Band, the addition of Wallace gave the band a greater fluency and the drummer's unalloyed enthusiasm at being reunited with the music was palpable. Released in 2006, *Pictures Of A City – Live In New York* is the definitive account of the group's ability to carry the tunes with an astonishing authority. *Record Collector* was just one of a number of publications to be surprised and delighted.

"This album's title track is often dismissed as a poor man's *Schizoid Man* ... by the same token, it's probably legitimate to enquire whether 21CSB can ever amount to anything more than a glorified King Crimson tribute. Happily, they're very much more than that. Robert Fripp's recent incarnations of KC left this repertoire behind, but there are still plenty of us who appreciate hearing it ... drummer Ian Wallace, bassist Peter Giles, horns and keys men Ian McDonald and Mel Collins, are all evidently qualified to play it, and frontman Jakko Jakszyk makes light work of filling in simultaneously for Fripp on guitar and Lake (or Wetton) on vocals. Nor is this the KC legacy set in aspic featuring as it does one new composition (*Catleys Ashes*) and an item from McDonald's solo career (*Let There Be Light*), plus re-workings of the classics. *Epitaph* sounds more pertinent than ever as a piece of social commentary, though on this form, it's way too early to be writing one for 21CSB."

Mel Collins was especially satisfied with the results. "I think with this live album we got somewhere close to playing with the same amount of passion and ability that I was hoping for when we put the band together in 2002."

Whatever the differences or circumstances that had led each member of the group to leave King Crimson, by playing parts that in some cases they hadn't touched in over 30 years they were at least reconciled with the music. The acrimony of the split with Fripp meant that for many years Collins, for example, turned his back on his time with Crimson. Back in August 2002, Mel was at home in Germany transcribing music for 21CSB when, in a moment of extraordinary synchronicity, his telephone rang. It was Robert Fripp calling from Nashville where he was in the middle of preparing material for *The Power To Believe*.

"We were offering each other congratulations on the various things we'd done since playing together," says Mel. "I told him how good I thought what we were doing back then was, and in the course of this he apologised for the hurtful things he'd said to me 30 years ago. He felt he could have put it all in a different way and that he wished he had. I'm glad we made our peace."

At the time, Fripp mentioned to Collins that they would perhaps work together in the future but the saxophonist hadn't truly expected it to happen. However, the call did come, albeit several years later when Jakszyk was working on the improvisations he and Fripp had produced in January 2010.

Sifting through several hours of material was a daunting but exciting task for Jakko. "I approached it like a sculptor, really. The obvious thing to do would have been to have gone through it and found sections that had a cohesiveness and then chop them up and create compositions in a cut-and-paste fashion. I decided against that and to follow the improvisations we'd done wherever they went. I divided them into sections and worked on them bit by bit creating a kind of musical Consequences. After spending a week working on each little section, it was only when I played it all back that it revealed itself. I wasn't using it as source material to chop up into an arrangement. I decided that what was already there was the arrangement and I'd follow where it goes."

As each piece came into clearer focus, Jakszyk then improvised vocal melodies, scat-singing words and phrases in free association then listening back and surprising himself by the unexpected themes that emerged from his subconscious. Some titles came from those vocal improvisations and others were supplied after the fact by Fripp.

Mel Collins, playing with Fripp for the first time since 1974's *Red*, delivered a series of takes of breathtaking lyricism, delving deep into the scales within the chords to tease out new melodies. While the young Collins had channelled John Coltrane's spiritual howl in his early '70s work in Crimson, several decades later he sought his way to the heart of the music, focusing on concise but telling commentaries rather than obvious soloing. Playing back the tracks, Jakszyk's ears picked up on a descending line Collins improvised on *The Price We Pay*. Struck by the way it inadvertently provided a new transitional bridge, he doubled the melody on guitar and had Collins return to play what was now a fixed part adding alto harmonies to the original soprano. The use of the soprano sax was largely determined not by Collins or Jakszyk but Fripp, who was especially keen on the sonic space and frequencies the instrument occupied in relation to the Soundscaping, echoing his approach when working with Theo Travis.

Across the rumbling grooves of *Secrets*, Collins turns in mocking soliloquies and some spectacular soaring choruses. The sombre mood of the album is matched by a restraint which only breaks cover for the explosive paranoia of *The Other Man* and the discursive atonalities of *The Light Of Day*, on which an especially bleak Fripp/Jakszyk improvisation is adorned by multi-tracked voices and gouging scrawls of acidic sax. It's dark and powerful stuff.

The addition of Tony Levin, who flew his parts in via the internet, and Gavin Harrison, working on the pieces in his own studio on a vintage jazz kit, gave the tracks a substance and presence that hadn't been planned or anticipated. A precedent might be found in the song *Forgiving* from *Bruised Romantic Glee Club* which features Fripp and Harrison and, in some respects, foreshadows the brooding quality of this album – which was eventually credited to Jakszyk, Fripp and Collins with Levin and Harrison and dubbed "A King Crimson ProjeKct".

In December 2010, Fripp mastered the finished album with Simon Heyworth with whom he had worked on all of the King Crimson remixes. "JFC is a superb album. I have not heard stereo quite like this since the early 1970s, and much of that was not of this quality," enthused Fripp in his online diary. "Our stereo-positioning & balancing is exquisite. If the sonic & musical pattern/picture is not rightly placed and positioned, it hurts, I twitch, I cannot settle. Dealing with this, I impose on the patience of others – recently Jakko, Steven Wilson and Simon Heyworth ... JFC is one of my favouritest albums, of those where I am a determining element. It has the Crimson gene, but is not quite KC. It is a Crimson ProjeKct, although this was not the intention. Given the gene pool, I suppose this counts as evolution. If JFC were named as a ProjeKct, which would be legitimate IMO, then all manner of expectations, categorisations, limitations and dopey commentaries would be launched to deter the ears of innocent audients."

At other points in Fripp's career, Frippertronics and its digital successor Soundscapes had been used within the context of a song. The emotional rawness of the stripped-back version of Peter Gabriel's *Here Comes The Flood* from *Exposure* is subtly complemented by the *Water Music* prelude and Fripp's delicate shadings within the verse and chorus. Daryl Hall's *Babs And Babs* from *Sacred Songs* has a more dramatic use of Fripp's loops as the vocal track drops away leaving the drums and bass adrift in washes of notes. In later years, Fripp would often respond to a request to collaborate or appear on an album by gifting bespoke or pre-exisiting Soundscapes. Future Sounds Of London, FWWD, The Beloved, Robert Miles, John Wetton, Porcupine Tree, Ten Seconds, Iona and Cheikha Rimitti and many others had benefited from this approach. *The Wine Of Silence*, released in 2012, took the orchestral personalities of Fripp's evolving approach to Soundscapes to their logical conclusion. In the summer of 2000, California Guitar Trio and one-time League Of Crafty Guitarists member, Bert Lams, handed over his painstaking transcriptions of Fripp's soundscapes to composer Andrew Keeling who then worked up fully orchestrated renditions with Keeling's own compositional extrapolations of the source material.

After they were performed by the Metropole Orchestra in Amsterdam in 2003, a further eight years passed before the pieces were deemed ready. Just as Keeling himself used the original soundscapes as a starting point for further melodic and harmonic exploration, Crimson manager and producer David Singleton took the Metropole concert recording and generated multiple layers of the orchestra in much the same way as Fripp might manipulate his guitar during a Soundscapes concert.

The results were immensely powerful. While Keeling's sensitive orchestrations emphasise the contemplative reverie of *Pie Jesu* and the elegiac *Midnight Blue*, it's the middle of the album where he vividly and persuasively articulates the more challenging elements contained within the soundscapes equation. The pensive atmospheres of *Black Light, Miserere Mei* and *Requiescat* coalesce into what is in effect a 34-minute suite of impassioned ferocity. Their shimmering tonality encompasses luminous passages of gorgeously transcendent melody, turbulent percussive rumblings, glowering, sepulchral brass undertows and achingly beautiful strings. Perhaps the most impressive passages come from the startling choral sequences, which in part take their text from the Anglican burial service, and provide some truly arresting and awe-inspiring moments found on the album. Occasionally evoking the works of Pärt, Górecki, Tavener and others of the "holy minimalist" school of composition, *The Wine Of Silence* burns brightly with Fripp's intense musicality even though he does not appear on the recording.

With King Crimson on hold since their short-lived return in 2008, the release of JFC's *A Scarcity Of Miracles* in 2011 provided a surprise instalment of the ProjeKct series. An album of finely crafted, mid-paced songs rather than the fast-moving, genre-blurring instrumentals that characterised previous ProjeKcts, the collaboration wrong-footed many listeners. But the ProjeKct experiments were never about a given style but about evolving beyond a creative impasse. While Fripp's playing was rightly lauded for its "wild card" properties and the quirky angularity of his soloing, there was always a deeply emotional quality to his work that found its most haunting expression in Soundscaping. Jakszyk's work in extrapolating the material from their initial improvisations was something special indeed. The aching melancholia within the Soundscapes was homed in on by Jakszyk as a springboard for his writing. *A Scarcity Of Miracles* is an important release, representing the most fully-integrated use of Fripp's Soundscapes in a rock-orientated context. Here, far from an adjunct or mere decoration, they were absolutely central to the finished sound – a tightly woven tapestry of memorable melody and often heartbreaking atmospheres. For some listeners, however, the restraint was a turn-off and it was not uncommon on forums and social media to see the responsibility for what was regarded as an unwelcome blandness laid at Jakszyk's feet.

Ironically, the relative lack of sharp dynamics was something Jakszyk had raised in production meetings with Fripp as a potential concern. For example, *The Light Of Day*'s original bass and drums were removed at Fripp's direction. Ultimately, the responsibility for the downtempo mood and direction belonged to Fripp. Jakszyk, trusting his senior colleague's judgement, happily acquiesced. Fripp later declared the completed album to be "a stunning sonic tapestry, carefully woven and satisfying to the ear".

The album picked up a brace of positive reviews. All About Jazz's John Kelman stated: "*A Scarcity Of Miracles* returns Fripp to a nearly all-English line-up for the first time since the '70s, and while impossible to define *why*, possesses the most decidedly

British feel of any group project in which Fripp has participated since his 1990s work with David Sylvian. It may lack the sharp corners, jagged edges and harder surfaces of latter-day Crimson, and there's none of the overt symphonic prog of early Crim, but Jakszyk's refined vocals, soft-spoken playing and haunting songwriting, Fripp's searing lines and orchestral Soundscaping, and Collins' soaring melodies make for the best group record – Crimson or no – to come from the Fripp camp in nearly 30 years."

The Sea Of Tranquility website wrote: "*A Scarcity Of Miracles* is easily the most different release ever put out under a King Crimson-related banner, and also the most intriguing. Who knows whether this line-up will produce anything after this, but let's hope so. I'm sure most folks never thought that Robert Fripp would take KC down into pop and jazz waters, but that's kind of what you get here, and it's quite refreshing. Don't expect this CD to jump out at you on first listen, but give it a few tries and all the rewards will surely reveal themselves to you. Beautiful stuff."

The Prog Rock Music Talk website offered this perspective: "Don't expect speedy payoffs with this album … I immediately liked it better the second time around, and the pleasure increased with each subsequent spin. I believe this will be the case for most listeners, each time revealing subtle nuances previously missed. Albums like this rarely reach the point of diminishing returns. Though not technically complex or cluttered, there is a lot to take in on these six tracks. More than most should expect to pick up on in one go-round. Be patient – both with this album and with yourself – and the rewards will be comparable to the time you put in."

IX

If *A Scarcity Of Miracles* represented a comprehensive and successful assimilation of song and Soundscape, it also held another significance: heralding a future incarnation of King Crimson. Just as in the late '90s when the ProjeKcts cycle of R&D had moved ideas and material towards the next stage in Crimson's evolution, there were plans for the *Scarcity* line-up plus Pat Mastelotto to work live as ProjeKct Seven during 2010 with potential dates in Spain and the UK. A combination of Fripp's personal and business priorities saw the moment pass for ProjeKct Seven with Fripp using the time to renew the partnership with Theo Travis which had begun in 2007 with their debut album, *Thread*, released in 2008.

Travis was a long-term admirer of Fripp and Crimson's work. The cover to his debut solo album, *2am*, released in 1993, had a knowing wink to *Red* on its sleeve with Travis's portrait half in shadow with the colour scheme of the lettering on the cover echoing that of Crimson's '70s swansong album. 2004's *Earth To Ether* included a mid-paced swing at the fast-running lines in a lively cover of *21st Century Schizoid Man* with a striking bop-edged solo from Travis. Travis almost encountered Fripp during the making of *Snow Borne Sorrow* by Nine Horses, a collaborative project between David Sylvian, Burnt Friedman and Steve Jansen, released in 2005. "I was invited down to play and I heard that Robert Fripp had been in on the same day earlier in the morning playing on some of the same tracks that I had played on," recalls Travis. "I hadn't met Robert at the time and I was excited at the prospect of maybe meeting him but it never happened. Anyway, I did the session which went pretty well and they used a lot of my stuff. Subsequently, I heard they'd not used Robert's material. A couple of years later, I got in touch with Robert to suggest a collaboration and he wrote back, 'Ah yes, you played on David Sylvian's album on the same tracks that I did but they used your solos instead of mine.' Of course, I thought that things had gotten off to a terrible start and I wrote back somewhat apologetically, but he wrote back saying the decision to use my solos was 'quite right. They were much better'."

Fripp was keen to see Travis in concert and in 2006 arrived at the Pizza Express in Dean Street, London, to see Travis with Soft Machine Legacy. Following the death of Elton Dean in February that year, Travis joined the group on a permanent basis, going on to become one of the band's principal writers as it dropped the Legacy part of its name to revert to Soft Machine.

"The night Robert came down to see us play, Soft Machine founder Mike Ratledge had also come along for a drink." For any progressive rock/jazz fan the image of Fripp and the reclusive Mike Ratledge, who retired from live work and public view in 1976, sharing a drink and a chat is enough to cause palpitations. Travis laughs and quickly adds: "They weren't in the building at the same time. I think there would have been a rip in the space–time continuum or something if they had been. Robert and I had a chat and a pizza and he offered to contribute some soundscapes to my album *Double Talk*, which came out in 2008. When we did the session in the studio at Broad Chalke, we got enough improvisations down for us to make the first Travis and Fripp album, *Thread*. It was the very first time we'd ever played together."

When the duo appeared together as part of Coventry's 2009 Jazz Festival, the passion, eloquence, lyricism and sense of grandeur in the vast sacred space of Coventry Cathedral was so strong, it was astonishing to think that this gig was only the duo's fourth time playing in public, and only the sixth time they had played together in total.

Around 300 or so people gathered in the impressive location where Tangerine Dream made a memorable appearance in the '70s to witness something magical as Travis's looped flutes and icy-edged soprano sax met Fripp's midi-generated orchestral washes in mid-stream.

Travis and Fripp emphatically created far-reaching music that transcended the sum of its parts. A mixture of entirely improvised musings and visits to previously agreed themes, including a then ultra-rare meditation on King Crimson's *Moonchild*, resonated with a haunting presence.

Lamentation, the last piece of the tour and the longest in the Coventry concert, grew from shrill, single notes into an enormous, complex cloud of shifting density and mood. Travis's use of a delay system he calls Ambitronics, in a nod of deference to Frippertronics, slowly swirled in dark layers while his soprano added piercing shafts of light. Filling the cathedral to the roof and beyond, Travis and Fripp's music was both profound and moving. Released on CD in 2010, *Live At Coventry Cathedral* documents a special experience for Travis: "To this day that was one of the most amazing concerts I've ever been involved in in my life. It was astonishing."

When it came to doing another album, Travis was keen to push the duo's work into a slightly different direction. "Pretty much everything we've done has been performed and created in real-time together. But with 2012's *Follow* I wanted to go panoramic and widescreen. I thought it'd be quite interesting if I had a flute choir with bass flutes and concert flutes, and a clarinet choir. This wasn't done so much using live looping but using structured pre-recorded parts. I thought it would be interesting to explore some more muscular areas which we had been doing live in any case. And the other aspect of this I wanted was to do the whole thing in surround sound with Steven Wilson mixing it. He was totally up for doing it. It certainly takes the Travis and Fripp project a step forward."

Reflecting on his work with Fripp over the years, Travis says: "I love Travis and Fripp. It's an unusual music because it's improvising and it's pretty dark in places but to be able to play that music and play somewhere like Coventry Cathedral or in Madrid to play in the same venue to roughly the same sized audience that Pat Metheny had had recently … The thought that we could do our strange and dark improvising to the same-sized crowd that Pat Metheny gets is astonishing to me. I know Robert has a public reputation of being quite austere but my experience with Robert in the studio, live, on the road, in the van and in restaurants, has been fantastic. He's great fun to be on tour with. He needs a lot of personal space, as do I, but he's a complete pleasure to be with."

In the aftermath of the cancellation of 2009's proposed Crimsonising, ProjeKct 7 signified a radical shift in Fripp's thinking as to where things might be heading. However, in 2011, any kind of King Crimson activity seemed a remote possibility. Not for the first time in his professional career, the outright deceit of the music industry diverted Fripp's attention from making music.

Having gone through the Endless Grief period in which his dispute with ex-managers Sam Alder and Mark Fenwick had stalled his ability to make music in the early 1990s, in 2003 Fripp's unwillingness to let UMG get away with flagrant abuses affecting his copyrights meant taking on the corporate lawyers. It's common practice that large corporations will sink anyone opposing their interests or practices by piling on lawyers and deliberately move things at a glacial pace – causing complainants to run out of patience, money or both, and then give up. A constant refrain from musicians of a certain age is that although they knew they were being ripped off they simply didn't have pockets deep enough to fight back. It was factored into record company thinking that the musician would eventually just sigh in resignation, shrug their shoulders and give in.

If UMG thought this strategy would work in this instance, they had severely underestimated Fripp's resolve, his keen eye for detail and a forensic ability to cut through legal verbiage and disassembling. As Fripp would later note in his diary: "Most working players of my acquaintance accept it is not possible for them to change the nature of how the industry works, the cynicism and carelessness, the restraints of money, the nature of the working life, its grinding remorselessness. But we may choose to act otherwise. King Crimson does act otherwise. King Crimson has a great reputation. Fripp has a terrible reputation. That's a good combination."

Nevertheless, the ongoing negativity again exerted a distorting effect upon his ability to play and perform. In 2005, in an interview with the *Daily Telegraph*, he quickly disabused anyone who still held any romantic notions that being a musician for a living involved simply picking up an instrument. "Being a professional musician doesn't mean you spend 12 hours a day playing music. It means you spend up to 12 hours a day taking care of business, dealing with litigation, with the various characters who've stolen your interests, or fending off hostile lawsuits from former members of the band … I recommend my students not to be professional unless they really have to be. I tell them, 'If you love music, sell Hoovers or be a plumber. Do something useful with your life.'"

Things hadn't especially improved by 2012 when he declared to the *Financial Times*: "My life as a professional musician is a joyless exercise in futility."

With ProjeKct Seven merely a footnote on Fripp's online diary, the closest anyone would get to see anything remotely resembling King Crimson in this period was either Stick Men, a trio founded by Tony Levin and Pat Mastelotto, joined by ex-Guitar Craft alumnus Markus Reuter on touch guitar, or the Adrian Belew Power Trio featuring bassist Julie Slick and drummer Tobias Ralph. Each band featured King Crimson material in their respective repertoires. In 2011, the two camps went on the road together under the Two Of A Perfect Trio Tour banner, playing over 30 dates in the USA and Canada.

When the opportunity arose for the two bands to join forces again after being offered a slot supporting prog-metal outfit Dream Theater in 2012, Belew and company jumped at the chance. "It started three years ago, on the 30th anniversary of my and Tony Levin's joining King Crimson," Belew told Basil Francis on the eve of a 2014 tour. "We thought, 'Wouldn't it be nice to celebrate this music?' So we spoke to Robert, and he joked, 'I'm all for it, as long as I don't have to do it.' So it had his support ..."

The name of the new venture happened to have been coined by Fripp, as with The 21st Century Schizoid Band. "Tony and myself discussed the not-easily-doable name of The Stickmen and The Adrian Belew Power Trio That Do A Set Of King Crimson Music. Tony's suggestion was ProjeKct Krimson. Mine was The Crimson ProjeKct," Fripp noted in his diary.

"The idea was to put it all together as one big show; you have the Stick Men come and play for 45 minutes, then you have the Power Trio for 45 minutes. After that, you have yet another trio, which is Pat and Tony and I – something that has never happened before – we play a couple of Crimson songs together," enthused Belew. "Then, all of a sudden, we turn into a gigantic six-piece band with two bassists, two drummers and we play more than an hour's worth of full-on King Crimson material. It's quite a night! When we first started it, I really thought we'd just do it once for the US audience but it's now become something that people are asking for all around the world."

Given that there was no question of any ex- or current members going out as King Crimson without Fripp's presence or blessing, Belew saw the Crimson ProjeKct principally as a way of keeping the music alive. Fripp had rejected Belew's earlier suggestion of the two of them going on tour with Julie and Eric Slick on bass and drums. It might have been Fripp and Belew with the Slick Kids but it wouldn't have been King Crimson. When it came to Crimson ProjeKct, Belew was at great pains to say this sextet wasn't setting itself up to be a "new" version of King Crimson. "There's nothing new being written, or trying to be offered up except the intensity and intent of our performances. What The Crimson ProjeKct is, is a celebration of the music that Tony and Pat and I were a part of and King Crimson music in general. We feel like we're the right people to go out and keep this music alive. I suppose that makes it differ a lot from being an actual King Crimson. Robert's role in the band in The Crimson ProjeKct is very well covered by Markus Reuter; he's a student of Robert's. He plays all of Robert's parts expertly, even the Soundscapes and all the different sounds. You don't really miss the sound, but let's face it we can't legitimately call it King Crimson. In my mind, King Crimson is always about moving forward and making new music and trying to re-invent the musical wheel. Crimson ProjeKct is really a band that's simply celebrating that music already and we're not trying to re-invent it. But our shows are dynamic, they're very impressive and strong, you won't hear this music in an authentic way like this anywhere else in the world. It has its own attributes that I really enjoy. Personally, having been so involved in this music for half of my life, it's really a pleasure to get up and play it again. I feel so excited about it and yet so comfortable with it."

On 16 July 2013, another group of musicians gathered to discuss the prospect of playing King Crimson's music. DGM's David Singleton had returned from a business trip in Japan where he'd seen Steve Hackett's band playing the music of Genesis. Impressed by the power and authenticity of the performance, his enthusiasm for such a project with a Crimson hue caught Fripp's interest. At his invitation Jakko Jakszyk, Gavin Harrison, Mel Collins and John Wetton met at DGM HQ at Broad Chalke to discuss the practicalities of working together.

Christened Crimson DNA, it wouldn't have involved Fripp joining them onstage but it would have his enthusiastic endorsement and practical support. Jakszyk and Harrison got as far as working up demo tracks and the four of them met up at Harrison's studio to play together. Having been initially happy to be simply the catalyst for Crimson DNA, Fripp found himself unexpectedly attracted to the possibilities of becoming involved in actually playing the music. For the briefest of moments, the potential formation that would have matched the eras of *Islands* and *Red* with a new generation of younger players hung tantalising in the air.

However, when John Wetton's management intervened, arguing that the new group should go out under the banner of John Wetton's King Crimson, Fripp quickly pulled the plug.

However, the idea of bringing King Crimson's music back to a live audience had clearly piqued his interest. Less than a week later, Fripp attended a social event with his wife and friends in London. In his online diary for 22 July, he recorded, albeit in cryptic and coded terms, a vision as to how a new King Crimson might unfold.

"While the rich conversation and comments continued around me, I looked at a situation-of-interest and how it might be approached: it spoke back, directly. Earlier in my life, an experience like this would have set the next period in motion. Presently, choices generate rich repercussions and are to be nicely considered. But, good to know that creative insight remains available to enquiry."

At key points in Crimson history Fripp has experienced what he refers to as a point of seeing – a moment of profound insight in which he claims to explicitly and directly experience how a new band will look or sound. It happened in 1981 as he was driving to meet Bill Bruford, and again in 1994 when the concept of the Double Trio presented itself to him. Now, in July 2013, the answer to the question "If King Crimson were playing tomorrow what form would it take?" presented itself in clear and unambiguous terms.

Just six days after the meeting of Crimson DNA in Broad Chalke, and on the same date that the birth of Prince George, third in line to the British crown was announced, the heir to an entirely different throne had been conceived.

History doesn't always record the small occurrences or the daily milieu that in some obscure way connect to a significant moment or event. On the day that would herald the beginnings of the next phase of King Crimson, Fripp could be found standing on a stage in a field with a microphone in hand addressing the public. For a man who'd spent several years playing just beyond the reach of the spotlight and out of the sightlines of punters, he was relaxed and in great spirits. On Saturday, 7 September, in the company of his wife Toyah Willcox and Bill Rieflin, who were working together on their Humans music project, Fripp was guest of honour at the Wick village fête and, in that capacity, declared the event – featuring a working steam engine, a magician, a dog show, photography competition, craft display, children's games, skittles, coconut shy and wet sponge throwing – well and truly open. After a day spent enjoying the fête, Fripp returned home and sent off an e-mail to Rieflin, Jakko Jakszyk, Mel Collins, Pat Mastelotto, Tony Levin and Gavin Harrison, all members of what would now become the eighth official incarnation of King Crimson.

> *dear brother crims,*
> *we have one year to prepare for action of the savage variety, and be in Go! mode for september 2014 … but essentially, King Crimson is in motion.*

X

The new line-up – and, more specifically, the positioning of the players – was a radical departure even for Crimson. Having three drummers at the front of stage altered the assumptions most people make about what constituted front and back lines in rock music. When Fripp talked about "seeing" the formation did he mean this literally, a vision in which he could see and hear precisely who the players were?

"Oh yes. I could see every one of them," Fripp says enthusiastically. "The first point of seeing was: there's the three drummers at the front and here's Mel, Jakko in the middle and Robert in the backline with Tony Levin somewhere in the front line with the drummers-ish but not quite. Point of seeing version 1.2 when Tony, rather than hovering somewhere between Bill and Pat, so obviously had to be in the backline. Yes, all the people were there. This shouldn't be surprising, I mean what is creative thinking? You look at something and the answer appears in front of you. It's not a rational process. A creative insight is instantaneous. You hold all the factors together and if there's enough necessity then something speaks back to you. When we arrived at Elstree's Stage Seven and I turned up on the first day, there it was actually set up: the point of seeing I'd had and there it was set up before me. To actually see it – the three drummers in the front line, the four characters in the backline, I knew immediately. This is serious stuff, I mean, I'm already convinced and there's nobody even behind their instrument!"

Beginning in February, and operating in small units, the band began the process of getting to grips with a setlist determined by Fripp. The three drummers worked together on parts which were developed and written by Harrison. Fripp and Jakszyk worked initially on their own at Jakko's studio and then were joined by Mel Collins and Tony Levin. It wasn't until June 2014 that the full band assembled for the first time at Elstree Studios. Over the years, King Crimson rehearsals had frequently been tense affairs. But as the week got under way, all seven players were laughing, joking and generally having a good time. The novelty of hearing all those separate elements come together in such a powerful way was like putting a jigsaw together and only when the parts were all in place finally getting to see what the bigger picture looked like.

When that small invited audience assembled to look at Collins, Levin, Jakszyk and Fripp at the back of the stage and Mastelotto, Rieflin and Harrison at the front, it looked and, more importantly, sounded different to any previous King Crimson despite the fact that it was re-imagining material that in some cases had not been heard live in 40 years or more. With the tour dubbed The Elements Of King Crimson, the personnel Fripp had chosen meant different strands of the band's history were represented in person – Collins fronting *Poseidon*, *Lizard* and *Islands*; Levin, with his yellow Music Man bass and Stick, personified the *Discipline* era and the Double Trio, alongside Mastelotto whose array of electronics and sampling brought alive the Double Duo. Meanwhile, Harrison's tenure in the short-lived 2008 configuration,

Jakko Jakszyk and Bill Rieflin represented a new and previously unseen potential in the court of King Crimson.

Rieflin had been with Fripp the day the e-mail went out to the others. "I knew that he'd been considering new Crimson possibilities, but if I ever did entertain the notion of playing in the band it was only as a passing entertainment. When Robert asked me to do this, by my reckoning I spent about half an hour, if not longer, attempting to talk him out of it; basically me just me just saying 'Are you sure?', 'Do you know what I do?', 'Is this really what you want?'. And then it came to be at the end of the conversation that I was the right guy for the right job and at that point you can't say no. If I'm the right guy for the right job then you have to say yes."

Rieflin had a lot of history with Crimson. "The first time I saw them was at Seattle's Shoebox Theatre, 30 November 1981. One of the guitarists referred to a particularly disruptive audience as 'a wart on the ivory skin of innocence'. These facts are easy to tell. More difficult to describe is the significance of the music's impact on my life. I remember wishing it was louder. I could sit and tell you stories about every record I heard and where I was and what it was like, and all the shows but if I can distill it in any way, I would say that to me the records had life. There was a life in those records as well as intensity. Those two qualities go hand-in-hand. Maybe the intensity was simply a characteristic of the life I was hearing within the music. So within the music I heard life and a quality of that life was intensity. That's a fucking quote for you!" he guffaws.

"The first time I knowingly heard King Crimson's music was in Seattle, in Dan Rabinowitz's bedroom. It was *21st Century Schizoid Man*. I was 15 or 16. Interestingly, it was familiar to me, although I couldn't say where I'd heard it before. I assumed it was the radio. Another possibility is that I'd actually never heard it before but yet it was still familiar. This is what listening to The Beatles was like as a young boy. I knew I'd never heard it before and yet it was familiar. I remember thinking this at five or six years old. My second King Crimson encounter was *Red* in San Francisco at 16 or 17 years old. Rich Werner played it for me. Erich and I were in a band together when we were teenagers, called The Telepaths. We played *Schizoid Man* occasionally but only after Mike Davidson joined. He was the only guy in town we knew who could play it. I have a cassette of a radio performance somewhere. Funnily, I was the one who sorted out the fast guitar run section and had to teach it to the guitarist. It never quite got there."

From bands on the local rock scene, Rieflin found himself playing in the "industrial" scene with Ministry and KMFDM in the '90s and from 2003 worked with REM. He had already worked with Fripp in Guitar Craft and in rock settings including *Ten Seconds* in 1996, 1999's *The Repercussions Of Angelic Behaviour* and Bill's solo album *Birth Of A Giant*. However, the lack of opportunities to explore an entirely improvised vocabulary led him to convene a group of diverse players under the banner of Slow Music. On their live debut at Seattle's Crocodile Club in 2005, Rieflin, on keyboards and acting as ensemble director, was joined by REM's Peter Buck – Rieflin was REM's drummer from 2003 – on guitar, bassist Fred Chalenor, Hector Zazou on keyboards, ex-Bowie drummer Matt Chamberlain and Fripp.

In a culture where doing your "own thing" and doing it as loudly and conspicuously as possible is often the norm, there's something almost quaint about music as unselfish and as egoless as that created by this sextet. Given the firepower of its line-up, it could have been marketed as an ambient "supergroup" but it was really just a bunch of guys who wanted to play and see what happened.

2006's *Live At The Croc* was an exotic collection of tiny knots of whoops, whirs and sizzle sounding like they belonged to a humid cyber rainforest. An exploratory first stab in which *not* making a sound held as much kudos as doing so, there was a distinctly European sensibility to the group, evoking the quiet but austere minimalism on David Toop and Max Eastley's sparse 1975 work *The Divination Of The Bowhead Whale* or the artful composite structures of David Sylvian's *Steel Cathedrals*. In May that year, the sextet undertook a series of gigs in California and Oregon, all of which were later made available as downloads on DGMLive.

Such was the organic, interlocking nature of their improvisation it was often difficult to tell who was doing what. The notion of playing only what felt right rather than what was expected added a rigour that kept the six concerts highly focused, avoiding the usual lapses into habitual tics and comfort zones. Slow, of course, doesn't always mean sedate and there were many points when the transient mesh of tones and textures built to surprisingly intense levels with dynamics including Buck's exemplary butter knife-induced glissando guitar.

Rieflin's work in Slow Music might be said to foreshadow the fairy-dusting role he would later come to occupy within King Crimson. "In Slow Music I am nominally the director. I play keyboards and noises and electronic percussiony things. I set a parameter and create the world in which something can exist. I steer it in a way. However, in performance all bets are off; in performance everyone has the reins because it's improvised."

Fripp's placing of Rieflin at stage centre was no accident. "My role in Crimson is that I'm the man in the middle at the front and I'm also the middle point of the big triangle behind me. The role or the job of any musician in or out of Crimson is to be present to the performance, to the experience. I'm in a position physically where I can take in the big picture in a way. As I understood, I came to see that as my role as a drummer in many rock bands. Behind everything I can see out and really keep the overview, keeping my attention wide open for as long and as of as great an intensity as possible. I think one of the primary currencies of King Crimson is intensity in my view. Intensity can manifest in a variety of different ways. It doesn't have to be loud. It doesn't have to be abrasive. It can be quiet and very quiet and still gripping."

Viewed from the audience's perspective, Rielfin's physical position was a fulcrum, a balancing point between the two great forces at either side. Applying the techniques of focusing attention on a given performance honed through his Guitar Craft practice, that location gave him a particular vantage point. In rehearsals in 2014, he was often heard making suggestions to other members. Never one slow to come forward and express a view, Rieflin's abrupt, direct manner rubbed some of his English colleagues up the wrong way. Was that something he was aware of? "You mean being an arrogant cunt in a band of seven people?" He laughs.

While Fripp may have had a professional and personal connection with each one of the new line-up, and an overview as to how they might interact, for the players the rehearsals were as much to do with learning how to navigate each other's foibles, habits and idiosyncrasies as with getting to grips with the notes.

"Crimson is a living, vibrating organism – it's like all of the points on a circle; each one has equal value but essentially it's an organism working to find its way," says Rieflin. "Each step of the process has its own rules and aims. The aims of rehearsals are going to be different of performance, for instance. Even in rehearsals there are different stages. The early stages are familiarity with the material, familiarity with the parts, just physically learning to do it, keeping the pattern alive in your mind as your body gets to know the stuff. What was surprising for me would be something personal which is that I felt at home. I felt accepted in the group. That's what surprised me. It has nothing to do with the others, nothing at all to do with them. I felt part of the team. I'm the new kid on the block and arguably I'm a less skilled player than the others so I had concerns about that but I felt very welcome and in feeling welcomed it made it easier for me to do what I need to do for the explorations to find my place. That's an ongoing process. It was like 'Oh this is fun, I'm enjoying this'. Maybe that's an easier way to put it. What surprised me was how much fun it was and how much I enjoyed it as well as feeling a part of the team. Maybe that's the best way to put it without getting into heavy psychological inferences."

Psychology played another part in the new King Crimson. Fripp's long-documented aversion to non-consensual flash photography had been a significant impediment not only for him but also for his colleagues since the '80s. In the Double Duo and in 2008 his way of dealing with it was to become increasingly obscured and resolutely unlit. But, in 2014, he was in plain view on a riser. That shift was something to do with the band moving from a prohibition to an invitation. The "no photographs please" policy was replaced by a request for everyone to take as many photographs as they liked with the proviso that it was at the end of the gig; when Tony Levin picked up his camera, the audience was encouraged to snap away to their hearts' content. This shift was thought to have been brought about in part at least by Fripp receiving coaching sessions with a sports psychologist. The efficacy of the course was plain to see at the end of every concert from 2014 on. In a remarkable break with what had sadly become a tradition in which the guitarist was the first person off the stage, now he was very often the last member of the group on the rostrum, looking out and taking photos of the crowd and their appreciative applause. In the general scheme of things, this might be thought a small thing but it represented the first of two significant changes in the way band and audience interacted. The second qualitative difference was the way in which this incarnation dispensed with the need for a front man. There was no-one making announcements, nobody in the spotlight, no star. In much the same way as a classical chamber orchestra might be presented, the visual focus rested solely upon the ensemble.

This neatly avoided any understandable comparisons between Jakszyk and Adrian Belew. With Jakko standing on the backline next to Fripp, his playing and singing was simply another section of the septet.

Fripp understood that some would find it difficult to envisage a Crimson without the second guitarist who had been such a significant presence since 1981. Yet he was utterly unshakeable about the necessity of "unfixing" the old way of doing things, tacitly acknowledging that the old way had been problematic.

"There's always been a tension between Adrian's solo career and his life in Crimson, which we've always sought to accommodate – although it hasn't always been easy, and sometimes it's simply hasn't worked. From my point of view, in terms of seeing what is necessary for this Crimson, this was not a Crimson which I could invite Adrian to join because it's not Adrian's material. He's out playing with Crimson ProjeKct so he's fine. But this isn't a Crimson for Adrian."

In March 2014, Fripp attended Crimson ProjeKct's London show at a largely deserted Shepherd's Bush Empire, one of 24 dates around Europe. That tour, along with a short run of gigs in Australia and New Zealand in June, and another leg back in Europe during July, had been planned prior to the announcement that King Crimson would be returning. For as long as the real thing wasn't around, gigs by Crimson ProjeKct gave fans a value-for-money show that largely drew upon Crimson's 2008 setlist. On the evidence of their sole official live CD, despite occasional sparks – such as an incendiary *Industry* – there was a cursory aspect to performances of road-wearied material. Lacking focus, despite the energetic efforts of some of the younger players, the album was adequate rather than inspired.

With his energetic, and animatedly affable persona and guitar-is-the-star soloing well to the fore, the largest percentage of the band's earnings went to Belew, an arrangement which Levin and Mastelotto thought fair as they regarded Belew as the band's main draw. While King Crimson was moribund, Crimson ProjeKct was able to step up into larger venues than they could in their respective trios. However, any chance of Crimson ProjeKct being able to coexist with a renewed King Crimson was questionable. Given the choice, fans would understandably and inevitably opt to see the genuine article rather than a cheery facsimile.

Though he didn't say anything in public at the time after leaving the Crimson ProjeKct show in London, Fripp was appalled by what he saw and heard. Speaking at a press conference in April 2019, the guitarist gritted his teeth in anger at the memory of the gig. "I went to see the Crimson ProjeKct, very excited may I say, prepared to jump up and down and shout out loudly, demanding *Schizoid Man*. And what I saw with the excellent Stick Men, the excellent Adrian Belew Power Trio, and of all the King Crimson music they played, they had the notes and none of the music. In other words, King Crimson had not *left* the building; King Crimson had not even *entered* the building. And I was *angry*."

At this point, Fripp closed his eyes, gritted his teeth and, lowering his voice, repeated: "I was *angry* and I walked out! I walked out of the Shepherd's Bush Empire wishing never ever again to play a note of King Crimson. Awful. Two great trios and nothing to do with King Crimson."

To see players he respected dispatch the repertoire they had all shared in developing in such a casually "professional" manner shook his confidence in going forward with the new lineup.

"The next day I had to make the choice of whether the seven-headed beast of Crim, the 2014 incarnation of Crimson, would go ahead or not and it was a hard choice because I was *really* fucked off," Fripp admitted.

Crimson manager David Singleton's persuasive argument was that for Crimson to not go ahead would be the real tragedy and, after reflecting on the matter, Fripp decided to continue with plans for Crimsonising in 2014: "I had to accept that, for King Crimson to be King Crimson, Robert has to be there."

Although nothing was said, nor any ultimatum issued, given the gravitational pull of the parent band and the likely demands it would make on their time, Levin and Mastelotto were never likely to carry on with Crimson ProjeKct once their touring commitments had been fulfilled. In any event, the future of Crimson ProjeKct would have been severely restricted, if not entirely curtailed, by Belew's decision to join Trent Reznor's Nine Inch Nails, announced in February 2013.

Belew's association with Reznor began when he guested on NIN's 1994 platinum-selling album *The Downward Spiral*. From there he became a regular contributor to subsequent releases by the industrial metal outfit. This time he was coming on board as a full member with 15 months of touring ahead of him in support of forthcoming NIN release *Hesitation Marks*. The night before the news went public, Belew rang Fripp to tell him, quipping that if Fripp had any plans to re-form Crimson without him then now would be a good time.

In a case of being careful what you wish for, Fripp took him at his word and just a few months later did exactly that. Had the stint with NIN worked out, it's likely that Belew wouldn't have worried too greatly about not being included in Crimson. However, with just seven weeks to go before the start of NIN's tour in June, Belew announced on his Facebook page that he was out. "Hey folks … I greatly respect Trent and the music he makes. No-one is at fault. We both agreed it just was not working … NIN will do an amazing show and I am back where I belong: creating Flux."

This message, however, was later deleted and replaced with a somewhat starker valediction: "Concerning me being part of the 2013 Nine Inch Nails band, it didn't work."

Whatever went wrong created a significant gap in Belew's schedule. Although Crimson ProjeKct's 2014 dates were still on the diary, he retrenched to his power trio and continued to work on the development of a music app called Flux which promised to blend Belew's music and art into an interactive experience which guaranteed never to play the same thing twice.

The loss of Adrian Belew was taken hard by many Crimson fans who'd grown up with the band since the '80s. Adrian's assured, winning stage presence, songwriting and prowess at pushing the guitar into all manner of contentious spaces had been a crucial part of Crimson's modus operandi for over 30 years. Responding to the now-public news that he'd been excluded from the new Crimson, whatever ire he may or may not have felt was kept to himself as he adopted a sanguine tone in a Q&A-style statement about the matter on his Facebook page.

Q: are you in the new King Crimson planned for next September 2014?
A: no. after 32 years I am no longer in King Crimson.
Q: were you asked to be in the new King Crimson?
A: No, I was not. Robert informed me in an e-mail that he was starting a 7-piece version of the band. He said I would not be right for what the band is doing.
Q: So, how do you feel?
A: Happy with what I have to be happy with … which is quite a lot

Belew ended his post by positing this final question.

Q: What would you like to say to crimson fans about the new King Crimson?
A: "My advice is to check it out and if you like it, support it."

The post sparked hundreds of messages of support, ranging from sympathy and commiserations to something akin to condolences along with a few posters outraged that Adrian should be cast aside so casually after years of loyal service. While Belew put on a brave face, a measure of just how difficult things were for him was found in his Facebook post at the end of the year.

> *Goodbye 2013!*
>
> *I have to say, I'm happy to see you go. back in January you held such promise; a big name world tour and the security of big name world tour money and exposure.*
>
> *instead you became the year I lost my position in not one, but two major rock bands.*
>
> *the year in which I learned firsthand that "life is not a beach. life is a mountain".*
>
> *still there were high points and things to be thankful for.*
>
> *the health of family and friends, awards and honors, and the appreciation of wonderful fans.*
>
> *FLUX in particular helped me through the dark times. without creativity I am nothing.*
>
> *so I am eager for a new year.*
>
> *bring it on 2014!*

XI

They didn't know it at the time but when the new King Crimson gathered in Elstree Studios for their final rehearsal day on 29 July 2014, it was exactly 45 years to the day since the first incarnation of the band were ensconced in Wessex Studios working on *In The Court Of The Crimson King*. The seven players were there to watch a videotape of the previous day's public rehearsal. "The first thing I saw what is necessary is that we play the music, and if all we do is play the music, that's 85% of it," said Fripp of the video. "Well, that should be it, shouldn't it? I mean what you have to do is play the music – that's 85% of it." Honing in on his own performance, the guitarist remarked: "What I saw is that I do very little. I'm actually playing very little but I do nothing very well," he laughs. "I think Bill Rieflin's example of that is the trombonist in the Berlioz Symphonie Fantastique, who does nothing for about 54 minutes, then picks up his trombone does a quick blast and that's it. If that's entirely acceptable for a symphony orchestra why should it really be any different for anyone else? If there is no reason for you to play, better to play nothing. A lot of players on stage feel they have to do a lot. Well actually, you only have to do what is necessary and sometimes what is necessary is that you do nothing."

Offstage, however, doing nothing wasn't an option for Fripp who involved himself in the minutiae of touring plans and preparations with American manager Andy Leff. Yet, even here, Fripp's demeanour was positively sunny. Contrary to his austere and stony-faced public persona, or his obvious unhappiness on tour at varying points of 2003 and parts of 2008, Fripp was more often than not seen in the company of the other Crims smiling and laughing. If it looked like he was having the time of his life, that's because he was.

"Well, it's the first Crimson I've been in where there isn't at least one person in the band who actively resents me. I'm not used to that," he explained. "Everyone in the band is one seventh member of the band. It's a group. Now conventionally the singer steps forward and is the focal point of the attention. Well, with Jakko, although singing, when he sings he's still one seventh of the band. When he's playing the guitar he's one seventh of the band. The role of singer is not as front man. This is a band of seven equal members; there's no foregrounder exactly. Clearly within that, the drummers are the stars of the show. How do you know a group is a group? They share the money. So when everyone said yes, they were up for this Crimson, the e-mail went out; the business terms are it's a 1/7th equal split all around the band."

Prior to leaving Britain for America, with all the excitement that had been generated for a tour largely sold out, there was a lot of speculation and anticipation about what King Crimson would be playing. There was also something incredibly satisfying about the symmetry that brought the different strands of Crimson together. By the time they hit the concert halls in the States, it had been 42 years since Fripp had shared a stage with Mel Collins. Did that have a special resonance for him?

"Yes but it's not about nostalgia. He's a wonderful player. Having had the point of seeing, I called up all the characters or e-mailed them, and I said to Mel, if any of them had said no, if you, Mel had said no, then that would have been the end of it. I suppose I could have called another sax player. I could have called Theo Travis. But the right man was Mel."

Uniting elements of the band's past, and with new repertoire beginning to percolate, there was a lot to take in with this radical re-invention of the Crimson wheel. What, Fripp was asked at Elstree, was the one thing people should know about this incarnation? Pausing for a moment, guitar in hand, he hurriedly, and even a little excitedly said: "I think they should know the first King Crimson principle which is 'let us enjoy our playing'. That is, let us be joyful." He leans forward, smiling: "Hopefully for the audience too."

It was immediately obvious when King Crimson stepped out on to the stage of The Egg in Albany that the band had been utterly revitalised and rebuilt from top to bottom. Finely tuned and firing on all cylinders, there was a pin-sharp accuracy in the standard of playing of the backline which had been only fleetingly present six years previously. The rehearsal period alone for this seven-headed Crimson had been longer than the entire lifespan of 2008's iteration. The differences between that Crimson and the present configuration, were, as Tony Levin points out, substantial.

"Of course it's different personnel but more than that the underlying ethic of us getting back together has been completely different. Before, I think we got together, rehearsed older material and played it the way we had played it before but with two drummers. But even that we had done before in the old Double Trio. There were no new elements and there wasn't much rehearsal time, and there really wasn't the desire to head off in a new direction. This time it's been completely different. New and different members and the gigantic challenge of three drummers and also the usual King Crimson challenge of let's not do it the easy way or the way we did it before; let's attack it as new territory and as Robert has famously said, it's all new material even if it happens to have been written in a previous time. So it's really different."

"What's in common or similar is that King Crimson is always the most challenging musical situation for me because it's the band that challenges itself musically, and it's the band in which I'm most expected to challenge myself in what I play on my instrument. I like to do that anyway, but King Crimson is to me the context where that's most appropriate so I bear down the hardest on myself. I say, 'I did that way before and that was nice but what's the way I'm going to do it this time.'"

Levin admits to being surprised at getting the news that Robert was putting Crimson back together. "2013 had been a very busy 12 months for me and I'd not been at home hankering for more music to play and wishing I could get called for something. So it came at a time I was fairly busy and it completely changed my future the way the call from Robert always does."

"I was thrilled. I had mixed feelings about the line-up. I was glad to see the new guys but sorry to see Adrian not there. I have great admiration for him and he's a good friend. But that's the way with Crimson – it's always surprises and new line-ups."

Levin admits that when he was allocated the "fifth man" status – technically a member of the band but in spirit only – with the formation of the Double Duo, he'd have preferred to have been in the group.

"I was somewhat honoured to be called 'the fifth man' but, of course, I would rather have been doing it. Now, with a historical look at these parts, the more I play them I feel like I'm really glad I wasn't there, because Trey got to fully be the bass player in King Crimson which he could never completely do with the two of us doing the bass parts, and what he came up with is something that would never have happened in the way it did if I had been there. The more I play them, the more I feel that that was the best bass music that's been written for touch guitar."

"That means two things. First, I'm really glad that I get to learn them and play them, and second, in the end in the big picture I'm actually glad that I wasn't in that band. History can be funny in that way. In the same way, this incarnation of Crimson will do things that wouldn't have been the same had Adrian been here. I'm so old and so experienced that I look at myself in a historical context of my career but I'm mightily thrilled to be back in King Crimson. I've done some of my best musical work in the band and I hope there's more for me in the future."

One person in the new line-up without any baggage regarding Crimson, at least until 2008, was Gavin Harrison. "I didn't grow up as a teenager hearing these songs in the way that say Jakko or Bill or Pat did. I only ever had one KC record and that was *Discipline* on vinyl. I grew up in a different musical dimension. I wasn't listening to rock or what is now termed progressive. I was aware of bands like Pink Floyd, Genesis and Yes, but I wasn't listening to them. I didn't have any of their records. A lot of my friends that I was hanging out with around that time weren't listening to any of those kinds of groups. When I first got together with the band in 2008, Robert came to my house and gave me a list of the songs he wanted me to learn. I said, 'Robert, I've got to hold my hand up here and say I don't know these and I haven't got them.' He said: 'Great. I see that as an advantage. I want you to come at the songs like they are brand new.' So maybe it was a good thing."

Gavin had the distinction of being the very first person Fripp called in 2013 when putting together the septet. Though he didn't know it at the time, had Harrison declined, Fripp would not have continued with the idea.

"I could have saved Robert a lot of calls had I said no," Gavin laughs, going on to say that the call came as a complete surprise. "As far as I knew, he'd retired from live performance. So I was completely shocked when he called up out of the blue and said, 'I've got an idea. Let me run this past you.' I really liked the idea. Afterwards he said 'Great, I'm going to call the rest of the guys' and I think by the end of that evening he had spoken to all the guys in this current band."

Harrison was more than pleased to be working with Fripp again. Although to some ex-members Fripp's methodology was problematic, the drummer argues that it was precisely this aspect of the guitarist's outlook that made Crimson an attractive proposition. "I like the way he thinks. The things he says sometimes, and in 2008 he said things to me which didn't immediately make sense to me. But as I've thought about them over the following hours, days, weeks, months, they started to make more and more sense. I think as I've got older and my playing has progressed more and more, you do start to think in more abstract ways. You don't need to think about the way you're holding the stick or what drum or cymbal you're hitting next. You're miles beyond that. It's more interesting when you think in abstract ways because it'll make you play differently."

"I think Robert's obviously got a skill at making suggestions to players to make them play in ways that perhaps they'd not previously considered. I think that's probably true of all the people who've gone through King Crimson; they probably played in a way in King Crimson that they never played like before or since. In 2008 I asked him what I should play in a particular song and he said, 'Play what you've always wanted to play in a rock band but were never allowed.' I thought well, that's completely useless. I was hoping for something specific to do with this particular song like play the hi-hat and bass drum. But in saying that he was essentially saying, 'There are no rules; do whatever you want.' I remember one night in New York on the 2008 tour in my little drum solo during *Indiscipline*, partly as a joke, I decided to do my impersonation of the drumming in a band called The Shaggs. I looked at Robert and he was laughing his head off, and at the end of the night he came over and said, 'Yes, that's exactly what I mean. You can play anything, it's just how far you're willing to open up your mind and go there.' Conditioning from doing lots of other gigs, once you've played about four or five fills, people are going to start saying you're over-playing if you're playing a pop gig or something. But Robert's attitude and thought processes lead the players in a way that you can be creative and do whatever you want."

With his role as an acclaimed teacher and innovator in the world of drumming, it was natural that Harrison takes on writing and arranging parts for the three drummers. "There's a lot of challenges because not only are you thinking about what you've got to play but you've also got to consider what the other two guys are playing from their point of view of playing the parts, and also thinking from a perspective of frequencies so that it's not too muddy in the low end, so that we're not playing bass drums and floor toms. A lot of the challenge is staying out of each other's way and finding frequencies and rhythms that are going to fit together. We don't necessarily have to play what was on the original record for example, and in fact it quite often works better when we don't.

"I've come up with some small amounts of arranging and tried to think of it as one drummer with six legs and six arms. So you think someone should be playing hi-hat in this part; who's got the right sound in the hi-hat for this part. What kind of sounds have Bill and Pat got available to them that I could utilise if I was arranging a song like *Level Five*, for instance. We're not playing the way the original record was played, where Pat played drums with a lot of electronics – we're coming at it from a completely new angle and it's an interesting challenge really to think about what three drummers could really play. We've almost never played the unison thing where we all play exactly the same part, although that can be an interesting effect in itself but it's a sound that's been done to death. It's more interesting having all those other sounds available to you. Not only have I got the sounds on my drum kit and the things I can do, but I can see and hear what Pat and Bill could also come up with from their collection of sounds, be it electronics, different-sounding drums or even the different styles that they play in."

The positioning of the drummers at the front, though generally novel, was something Harrison had experienced once before. "When I was playing in the singer Paul Young's band, I was playing a very small kit, part-percussion and I was right down the front of the stage which I'd never done in my life. All I could hear were these women talking to each other (*laughs*) and in those days they were smoking so you were getting a right face full of smoke as well. It was a bit alarming to be so up close."

"When I was playing with Iggy Pop, the guys at the front would get spat at and things would get thrown at them – a glass of beer in the face was all part of the punk madness. I got hit on the head with a wig and a bible one night. Someone threw a metal ashtray which hit me on the arm. Usually when you're on drums you're at the back and there's a detachment sometimes from the audience, which I generally don't like. In this set-up with Crimson, it's the most engaging experience of being at the front of the stage. It's almost unheard of to have drums at the front. It's a great idea."

The necessarily tighter arrangements resulting from three drummers playing articulated parts that circulated notes and beats in much the same way in which themes and chords circled between players in the Guitar Craft tradition came with a price tag. The capacity for any open-ended improvisation of the kind practised by the *Larks'*-era band or even the Thrakking of the Double Trio was never going to be possible for this group. While arguably technically the most gifted of all Crimsons, when it came to extemporisation this aspect was going to be limited to small variations within a predetermined structure.

Because of the use of a click-track, something which the '80s Crimson introduced towards the end of its life, it didn't matter how fired-up Fripp might have been in the storming solo section for *Larks' Tongues In Aspic, Part One* or carried aloft on the raging waves of *Sailor's Tale*, irrespective of wherever the urgings of the muse pointed, whatever he was playing would be brought to an end because of the primacy of the arrangement's fixed bar length.

Over time, *Easy Money* grew into a looser arrangement and the instrumental section of *The Letters* became elasticated, often led by Mel Collins' interrogations of the baritone with others following his lead. The introduction of stand-alone cadenza sections in the later years of the new Crimson provided a sense of improvisational space.

The use of in-ear monitoring effected a subtler change in the interaction of the musicians. The ability to mix in or out those you shared a stage with created a unique bespoke aural picture which might, for example, exclude the vocal, or the bass, or another instrument, because it distracted attention from a crucial point in the song. The reverse was also true, of course. Tony Levin always mixed Mel Collins' sax up in his monitor mix because he enjoyed listening to Mel's playing whether it provided cues or not. It was, in theory, possible for any one of the players to leave the stage at the end of a gig having heard only a fraction of what the audience encountered. That envelopment in an individual's sound world extended to the audience itself with any reactions or cheers rendered inaudible. Indeed, the combination of in-ear isolation and stage light shining into players' eyes was for some disconcerting, and for later tours the crew half-lit a portion of the hall in order to combat the sensory isolation.

The confidence and momentum gathered by the band during 2014's concerts was remarkable. Often the gasps from the audience at the sound of *Larks' Tongues In Aspic, Part One*, which opened most of the shows, were so loud that some observers in the crew thought it was a previously unannounced and unrehearsed sound coming off the stage. Dressed in sombre, formal suits the band looked as though they might be on-stage to sell home insurance. Yet the music they unleashed on a nightly basis frequently blew out the doors. When it came to the three drummers, Mastelotto represented the emotive and emotional heart of the band, Rieflin a more playful capricious spirit and Harrison personified both the piercing intellect and surgical precision. While there had been many sceptical voices about the wisdom of having three drummers on stage, as the news spread about the impact King Crimson were having across the 19 official dates, Fripp's vision was utterly vindicated.

At Seattle's Moore Theatre there was a palpable sense of celebration, not only among the ecstatic capacity crowd but also clearly visible on the faces of each member of the band. Evidence of their enthusiasm was peppered throughout the set: wry smiles between Fripp and Jakszyk during *The ConstruKction Of Light*, now adorned with an alto sax solo which sounded as though it had always belonged to the song ... Levin throwing his head back and laughing out loud in response to Mel's solos … indulgent grins from the entire group as they watched Harrison's virtuoso drum break during a blistering performance of *21st Century Schizoid Man* …

King Crimson had authoritatively and definitively blown the cobwebs off a repertoire that had been ignored for far too long. Pieces such as *One More Red Nightmare* had never been performed live before. Some criticised the setlist as being too backward-looking, but conveniently overlooked the fact there were several tunes being played live for the first time in well over four decades. As corny and clichéd as it sounds, it was common to see people in floods of tears at the thundering climax of *Starless*. Unheard in concert for exactly 40 years, its return, in such a triumphantly regal manner, was a powerful, cathartic moment. Progressing from the yearning ballad into the ominous bassline, the evening's only light change took place, slowly almost stealthily, as the intensity built, eventually bathing the stage in a glowering, infernal red light.

Along the road from Albany to Seattle nobody knew for sure if this was a one-off event or an ongoing concern with a future. They hoped, they suspected – but nobody knew for definite. There was so much vitality and energy within the music and the connection between the players was so strong it seemed inconceivable that it would not continue. There was a mixture of relief and overspilling elation when they gathered in the cramped dressing room at the Moore Theatre after the show.

With a glass of champagne provided personally by Fripp, they raised their glasses and toasted the future. When he asked them if they were all up for another year of Crimsonising in 2015 a collective hurrah went up. Whatever plans and commitments people might have had, they would be put to one side in order to make space for the return of the King. Unlike 2008, nobody in that room that night would be changing their mind.

XII

The King Crimson rehearsal room has always been a crucible into which ideas are poured and tested. Greg Lake recalled how sessions in their 1969 basement headquarters on the Fulham Palace Road could be intimidating. John Wetton always liked to tell the tale of how he presented the demo of the ballad section of *Starless* to a total lack of response. More often than not, soundcheck was the place for throwing ideas around. Parts of *Red* had been tried out on the road in 1974 and Vancouver played host to a remarkable pre-gig unveiling of what would ultimately become *Larks' Tongues In Aspic, Part Four*.

As the 2014 tour progressed, small snatches of new material appeared during soundchecks. As the various Crims arrived and took up their positions, Robert leaned towards Jakko's workspace, saying "Try this one" and playing a small repeating pattern. Jakszyk recognised the motif from a writing session before the start of the tour. The pair swapped notes. Meanwhile, the others went about their business, making sure everything was to hand. One by one, though, they picked up the lines. Levin was the first to join in the cycle, in an almost absent-minded way as he found his volume levels and adjusted his in-ear monitoring. Suddenly he began adding chordal jabs and undulating bass notes from the Stick.

Mastelotto, Rieflin and Harrison, previously engaged in the seemingly never-ending task of tiny adjustments and fine-tuning of their kits, one by one began to add their take on the sequence of notes, testing out patterns, laying down tentative, exploratory but uncommitted grooves. Having finished working on his sheaf of repertoire notations, Collins reached down and took his soprano sax from its stand to add and subtract flourishes and vamps. Fripp, on the riser behind Harrison's kit, leaned forward and spoke to the drummer. Within seconds, following that small suggestion, what had been provisional and somewhat inchoate achieved definition and clarity of purpose as Harrison put in a foundation upon which everyone was able to find their place. A wholly new King Crimson piece, later titled by Fripp *Radical Action (To Unseat The Hold Of Monkey Mind)*, had come into being for the first time.

"I knew from the first day that we started rehearsals in 2014 that it was going to work," says Mel Collins, whose return to the line-up delighted fans and band members alike. Tony Levin remarked that one of his greatest kicks is listening to Mel's solos in the set, never knowing quite what he's going to get. "I can't play the same thing each time. It's not in my make-up," Collins admits. "It changes every time as I interact with what the others are doing. And, of course, my playing goes up a notch working with players such as these where the standard of the musicianship is so high. I feel I have to raise my game. There's no slacking. It lifts me up when I'm in Crimson. There's so much depth in the playing. It's actually given me a kick up the backside, to be honest."

"As with any band, the more you play the better you get; the better the communication and the mix of the chemistry and the personalities becomes better," offers Gavin Harrison. "Everyone's at different levels of how comfortable they are – some of us have got charts on the floor and are still reading but that's the whole point of rehearsals, trying to get it into the system and get it into your blood. There are bits where something goes wrong and we look at each other and start laughing, and there's Robert, doubled up with tears of laughter rolling down his face. We do have a good laugh."

Levin regards the hours spent in rehearsal – and this line-up has been in more rehearsals than most other incarnations of the group – as leading to one outcome. "I've been doing it about as long as you can be doing it, to realise that it's all about the music; that two hours on stage and the interaction with the fans; the sharing of something very special musically with people that makes it worth it and gets you through the other 22 hours of the day. I have always approached it with the same sense that I'll throw myself into what there is and what we have booked and I'll thoroughly enjoy doing that, and whatever the future brings I'll be glad of it. I hope there's more. What's consistent in all the King Crimson incarnations that I've been involved in is that, of course, I want to do more. I'm one of those guys who loves touring and recording and I love doing old and new music."

If the appearance of so much vintage repertoire is a surprise to thousands of people who filed into the halls in America in 2014, it was a surprise shared by members of the band. "I wouldn't have expected a lot of those songs to be on the songlist, not because I don't like them but because I didn't expect that Robert would want to do them," says Pat Mastelotto. "Look, just talking about this stuff I'm goosebumpy, do you see it? I'm not faking it, dude. Every time you hear the chords from *Starless* start I know the chills that *I* get, so I know it's going to be a very heavy experience for a lot of people. I said when we were going down the stairs at the last rehearsal, 'Robert you're going to make a lot of people *really* happy.'"

2015 saw a lot of people in the UK and Europe made very happy indeed with the return of the band to locations and venues it had not performed at in decades. Because so much of the older material from the '70s had not been aired for so long, and the way in which it was so convincingly delivered, it felt brand new. Reviews from fans were rarely less than enthusiastic and frequently bordered on the ecstatic. When the band performed at the Brighton Dome in September, John Wetton and his wife Lisa attended the gig. Both were impressed by what they saw and heard. Lisa recalls that John would glance over to her with a smile, as they watched Jakko perform the songs he regarded as his, such as *Easy Money* and *Starless*. Jaksyzk had an affinity with the material from the '70s. It was in his DNA and that level of connection came through loud and clear. His vocal performances of *The Letters* guided Crimson from violence to silence with a degree of vulnerability that perfectly captured the state of mind of the song's distraught and resigned narrator. His vocal extemporisation during an increasingly spacious middle section of *Easy Money* offered up a kind of cleansing purgative quality, letting go of the structure around him and entering into the moment, fully committed without regard or worry as to whether he'd get to the other side. Wetton was impressed. "He said he was confident that 'the Great Crim had found just the right singer'," Lisa recalled.

When it came to the British Press, however, the disdain always reserved for that generation of musically progressive groups who'd emerged in the '60s and '70s couldn't help but surface once again. The *Guardian*'s review by Ian Gittins of the band's London show exemplified much of this attitude in a grudging, somewhat sneery fashion. "This return of quintessential '70s progressive rockers King Crimson marks a major volte-face by the group's founder, Robert Fripp. Having announced his retirement from music in 2012, he has since not only re-formed the band but also overseen the writing of their first new material in 12 years."

"It's major news for the venerable group's baby-boomer fans, who are excited still further when they learn that the band are playing classic tracks that have not been heard live for over 40 years. They're doing so with a highly unorthodox set-up: Fripp, saxophonist Mel Collins, bassist Tony Levin and singer/guitarist Jakko Jakszyk line up across the back wall behind no fewer than three drummers."

"Fripp always envisaged Crimson melding rock and classical tropes, with their music a cluttered fusion of psychedelia, free jazz and acrobatic electronica. These elements are all firmly in place in tonight's opener, *Larks' Tongues In Aspic, Part I*, a dense 1973 album title track and faux-freewheeling symphony in which instruments actually dovetail with forensic precision."

"Really, it's a curious evening. With Fripp a simultaneously avuncular and aloof presence at the rear of the stage, the seven players never say a word all night. Instead, they focus meticulously on offerings such as 1971's *The Letters* and *The Sailor's Tale*, whose guitar spasms, sax squalls, seismic percussion and dramatic crescendos could have inspired Spinal Tap's *Jazz Odyssey*."

"Porcupine Tree drummer Gavin Harrison produces a prodigious solo on *21st Century Schizoid Man*, famously sampled by Kanye West on *Power*, before the evening closes with a prog-rock sacred text, the vermilion gash of sheer cosmic hogwash that is 1969's *In The Court Of The Crimson King*. King Crimson may be an immersive experience, but sometimes you don't half wish that you were stoned."

Although older material featured prominently in the setlist, it had the virtue of being relatively unfamiliar, certainly in a live context, and the degree to which it had been redrawn lent it a freshness that worked in its favour. Newer songs such as the quirky *Suitable Grounds For The Blues* found Crimson in that playful yet provocative state of mind, with a wryly skewed take on a popular form bent awkwardly out of shape. Perhaps most bafflingly, however, material such as *A Scarcity Of Miracles* and *The Light Of Day* appeared increasingly rarely despite the fact that the former had the magical quality that imbued earlier Crimson ballads and afforded Fripp an opportunity to play some of his most romantic and plaintive soloing, and the latter took the entire band into a freer, less regimented, space.

One song that inexplicably didn't make it on to the setlist at all in 2014 or 2015 was *Separation*. Written by Jakszyk, it had been demoed up as far back as 2010 when the *Scarcity* ProjeKct was active. A small extract appeared on the band's 2014 Tourbox but the full track remains unreleased and unheard. It's a pity because the force and power it conjured fully anticipated the sound of the new King Crimson a good four years before the seven-piece line-up was conceived.

The steady release of archival boxed sets chronicling Crimson's past raised the bar in terms of packaging and quality. When it came to documenting the new era of Crimson, there was a sense of taking time to get things right. The release of *Live At The Orpheum* in 2015 offered a snapshot of the septet but didn't quite convey the impact of the band in concert. Partly this was down to fastidious fixing and mixing by Jakszyk and Harrison whose instincts were honed in the studios of the '80s and erred toward a cleaner sense of perspective. It wasn't until the release of 2016's *Live In Toronto* double album that something approaching the full effect of the band in 2015 was available to those who hadn't seen a gig. It pinned back listeners' ears with *Pictures Of A City*, sounding more potent and assertive with every date, and a bulldozing encounter with *Level Five*, which found its true home with this incarnation. John Kelman's perceptive review said: "With the triple drum set arrangements, twin guitars, reeds and woodwinds, and bass and stick, all played by top-drawer musicians capable of respecting every song's formal construction while, at the same time, introducing interpretive variations and impressive solos, this is no tribute band; this is a Crimson … bringing the music firmly into the 21st century." *Prog* magazine also recognised the special qualities of the release and Crimson's 21st-century *raison d'être*: "Part wholesale re-invention, part meticulous refinement, the … new material crackles and pops with exuberance and the infectious thump of hearts buoyed by fresh adrenaline."

Classic Rock thought that this Crimson, perhaps more than any other in recent years, was far more friendly to the wider rock punter beyond Crimson's niche audience. "As someone almost said, you don't have to be a Crimson fan to buy this, but it helps. But if you are new to KC and pick this up, you might be pleasantly surprised. The prickly, jazz-rock beast of old isn't exactly tamed, but the modern septet are at their most accessible and dynamic – minimally free-form, no extended jams – on this official bootleg from one particularly high-quality night on the band's 2015 Canadian tour."

In a sense the release acted as a placeholder for the six-disc CD/DVD/Blu-ray boxed set *Radical Action (To Unseat The Hold Of Monkey Mind)*. The cover art bore the enigmatic and, for some, unsettling countenance of a Cyclops – Cy as he was known affectionately in the band. This was the work of Francesca Sundsten, also the wife of Bill Rieflin. Fripp, Gunn and Rieflin's 1999 pre-ProjeKct release *The Repercussions Of Angelic Behaviour* had featured her work and Fripp was an enthusiast of the archetypal style she favoured, buying the Cyclops, painted in 2008, from her collection when visiting Seattle in 2013.

Recorded on the Japanese tour of 2015, the video in the box gave a full performance, while the three CDs offered the fullest account of the band's set so far, zoning the songs into Mainly Metal (disc one), Easy Money Shots (disc two) and Crimson Classics (disc three). *All Music Guide* noted the strength and impact of Crimson's performances. "This band is a juggernaut and hearing them tackle not just the '70s repertoire they hadn't performed in decades, but some '90s tracks as well, is something fans could not have dreamed of at the turn of the century. Rarely has a band that's been around for 45-plus years sounded so vital. This is essential for fans."

XIII

Three years after the line-up was announced, 2016 saw the first change after Bill Rieflin requested a sabbatical from the band. With Fripp's full support, Rieflin left on a temporary basis, leaving a significant gap. There weren't too many drummers who played keyboards but Jakszyk and Harrison knew Jeremy Stacey. Running his name past Fripp first, Harrison got in touch with Stacey in January that year.

"After getting that call from Gavin, we got together in April because he'd written a lot of the parts for the three drummers so I had time to listen to stuff and I got sent songs. In April and May, we got together for three sessions of three days each. That was just drums at that point but there were keyboards to learn."

Like Harrison, Stacey wasn't particularly knowledgeable about Crimson. "I remember hearing *Frame By Frame* in the '80s and really liking it. I'd heard some of *Red* and *Larks' Tongues* and, of course, *In The Court Of The Crimson King*. So I only knew bits and pieces really, so I had to start from scratch."

Stacey's background in jazz and rock is long and deep. He has played with artists as diverse as Noel Gallagher, Chris Squire, Mark Wingfield, The Waterboys, Ryan Adams and Steve Hackett. The newest member of the group, at 55 Stacey was also the youngest. He regards himself as very fortunate to have had such a varied career and a level of work which demands he keeps kits ready for use on both sides of the Atlantic. However, he admits that King Crimson is at another level.

"It's the most different thing I've done. Well, it's kind of obvious when you consider there are three drummers but it's the fact that I play keyboards which I hadn't done for a while. I'd played on records but I hadn't played them live in a band since the early '90s and I hadn't practised or played much piano during that period because I was mainly drumming. I had a long jazz background and the thing about jazz is that while you're improvising over a form – that's like 16 bars followed by another 16 to an eight bar section in the middle followed by 16 bars which we call an A-A-D-A form – you learn those sorts of things in jazz which pop musicians probably don't do as much. That's fine. With jazz there's a deeper understanding of form and how to play over it which kind of prepares you for Crimson, although with Crimson it's more rehearsed and less improvised than a jazz situation. All that stuff I learnt from doing straight rock gigs and jazz has helped. I do think that Crimson isn't a gig that just anyone can do unless you have some background or understanding of the intellectual side of music for it to be possible. Pat Mastelotto is incredible because he doesn't read music, but he makes his own notation in his own language which I've never seen before, the way he writes stuff, but it totally works for him. So it shows that if you've got the mind to understand it then, whether you've got a formal trained background or not, you'll find a way to do it."

With Stacey filling the gap centre stage, the band went back out on the road. Their appearance at Aylesbury's Waterside Theatre, on 3 September 2016, marked not only the first and only date in the UK that year ahead of an extensive European trek, but an obvious uptick in the band's energy, with Stacey's presence being an obviously significant factor.

"The first gig I was learning what it was like to play a whole show and try not to mess up," he recalls. The underlaying swing and playfulness which Rieflin had brought to the mix was there, but so too was a greater firepower which made the drumming exchanges take on a ferocity that took many observers by surprise. With a set that now boasted material from *Lizard* including *Cirkus*, last played live in 1972, and *The Battle Of Glass Tears*, receiving its live premiere, the music acquired an increased savagery especially in the latter piece with Stacey's piano excursions comfortably echoing Keith Tippett's frenetic extemporisation. What was especially interesting about the selection from *Lizard* was the way in which the music dating back to 1970 sounded as though it had always been waiting for this particular incarnation to bring it to life."

That sense of music from whatever period converging with the present-day lineup applied on future tours to *Suitable Grounds For The Blues*. The song found Stacey pitching atonal runs and scattering spiky notes into the air in a manner that unconsciously evoked Keith Tippett's work on *In The Wake Of Poseidon* and *Lizard*. As the uneven metre of Crimson's mangled take on the blues unrolls, Stacey maintains the barrage. Adding a dissonant freshness, its spontaneity lights a spark to one of the band's newer pieces. "I don't practise anything beforehand. I close my eyes and start and see what happens. I feel that's an element of what Crimson is about. I could obviously do something more harmonic and prearranged but when it comes to those cadenza moments, I'm improvising every night. It's sort of terrifying but also lots of fun. That's if it works which it sometimes doesn't. But that's the whole point. If you improvise it's not necessarily supposed to work. You're taking a risk to put yourself out there and seeing if something magical can happen."

Stacey assumed he would be covering one tour as a sideman but such was his evident value that Fripp offered him a permanent post.

The seven-piece version with Stacey was documented on *Live In Vienna*, recorded toward the end of the tour. The triple album received a limited release in Japan in 2017 and had been intended for the European and American territories. However, while worthy enough, the octet's gig at Chicago on 28 June, with Bill Rieflin back in the lineup but now on keyboards, rendered it utterly redundant and it would not be out in most of the world until 2018. Fripp commented: "If we are looking for a KC live show; Chicago was exceptional," a view endorsed by Levin who regarded it as one of their best.

They were right. *Live In Chicago* was rushed into release less than four months after the last cheers had faded at the Chicago Theatre and it captured something special. Now with two keyboard players and Fripp's occasional Mellotron embellishments, the band's sound became much deeper, bringing out details in the older material that had never been available before. Stacey welcomed Rieflin's return. "It's fantastic because a lot of the keyboard parts that were on the record are now being played fully. One keyboard player couldn't pull off all the parts live without cheating and Crimson isn't the kind of band that cheats."

In his notes to *Live In Chicago*, Fripp wrote: "Overall, my sense of KC 1999–2003, and 2007–2008, was of dis-satisfaction. Something was not quite realised. This was not how I wished to let go of Crimson. So, in 2013, in a flash before my mind's eye, a picture of the Seven Headed Beast and its onstage configuration presented itself (22 July 2013). The Seven Headed Beast (2014) may be considered KC formation 8.1; Jeremy replacing Bill (2016) as Formation 8.2; Bill returning (2017) as Formation 8.3. But please read on …

"My two prime aims in the re-formation of KC in 2013 were Redemption and Completion. Acts of Redemption took place during 2014, 2015, and 2016; at which point completion was realised. A completion is a new beginning, and the eight-piece KC of 2017 constitutes a new beginning in the process of King Crimson."

The band's appearances over five nights at Mexico City, presented on 2018's 3-CD/1 Blu-ray set *Meltdown*, ushered in what he now counted as King Crimson Formation Nine, which Fripp said was the Fourth Definitive Formation of King Crimson since 1969, the others being the 1969, 1974 and 1981 bands. He concluded by asking a question, and helpfully providing the answer.

Q: What is a Definitive Formation?

A: Nothing is quite the same afterwards.

XIV

In the wake of his tumultuous 2013, Adrian Belew directed his energies into work on his Flux app and gigging with his Power Trio. Whatever frustrations he may have had appeared to have been resolved. In 2014, he was asked to provide a score for an animated short film and in 2017 Pixar's *Piper*, about a sandpiper bird overcoming its fear of water, was nominated for an Oscar. With the gala Oscar night coinciding with the eve of an extensive American tour, the trio were finalising their preparations. Bassist Julie Slick beautifully captured the air of anticipation and nerves at Belew's house that night. Via Facebook she wrote: "So we ate dinner at the Mexican restaurant again tonight … Adrian was much too anxious to watch the Oscars. We even stayed late, had another round … when we got back to Casa Belew I looked online to see if they'd declared a winner."

> "'Adrian, you should probably turn on the TV … I think they are about to announce it …'
>
> "Oh gosh Julie, I'm way too nervous … I just don't know …' He held out a shaking hand.
>
> (*3 minutes pass*)
>
> (*the TV clicks on*)
>
> 'And the Oscar for best animated short goes to …'
>
> 'What a surreal moment.'"

Later on, Belew, with considerable and understandable pride, would say: "Scoring this Oscar-winning film has been one of the greatest honours of my life."

With that kind of fillip adding to his creative capital, later in the year Belew's membership of The Police's Stewart Copeland's new group, Gizmodrome, was announced. Belew had originally gone to Italy to add his distinctive soloing to what he thought would be a few songs, but it turned into something much more extensive. Along with Level 42 bassist Mark King, who coincidently used to be Jakko Jakszyk's employer and ex-PFM keyboardist Vittorio Cosma, the band's self-titled debut album of quirky but nondescript pop-rock tunes was released in September. During August, Copeland and Belew did the press rounds. Appearing on the Jim and Sam radio show, uploaded on to YouTube, in a wide-ranging interview Copeland was answering a question about dealing with the ego of frontmen – specifically, in this instance, Sting. As Copeland defended the singer's decision to walk away from The Police and pursue an at-times unorthodox solo career, he ended by saying that Sting was "a loyal guy".

On the video Belew's previously relaxed demeanour visibly changed. Now looking vexed, Belew interrupted: "You see this is how I know I've lived my entire life in an alternate universe because I was in a band for 33 years and I was the frontman and the other guy was the guy who had all the big issues." The hosts, who clearly knew nothing about Belew's tenure in Crimson queried who that person was. "He played guitar and Mellotron," Belew said.

Fripp's name was not mentioned but Belew went on to cite some of his grievances. "He *was* the band in his mind … how I dealt with it? Well I dealt with it for 33 years, first of all by having a great relationship with the person and loving him, and then I get an e-mail one day saying 'You're not in the band'."

Amid the shocked reaction, somebody mentioned being thrown under the bus. Belew replied that he had just been thrown from the bus and that the couch from the bus had been thrown on top of him. When asked what reason had been given for his dismissal, he replied in measured tones with his eyes fixed on the console in front of him: "I have yet to ascertain that but I think it was probably a mistake on his part."

Copeland, possibly attempting to defuse the situation with a light-hearted remark, said: "It was to make room on the stage for four drummers." Stoney-faced, Belew replied: "That's it … that was done over e-mail … it was a terse and laconic e-mail."

One of the show's hosts asked: "Did you regret putting up with his nonsense for 33 years? Like, 'If this is how it's gonna end, I would have told him he was an asshole from the beginning!" At this point, Belew attempted to cool down the increasingly excited comments. "Now, come on, I do love this person," he said. Had they talked to each since, the host asks? "No. I'm writing postcards. I just don't send them," laughs Belew. "It's OK, I went off and won an Oscar and toured the world a bunch of times and joined a supergroup. I'm doing OK."

The conversation moved on but the damage was done. Despite the passage of time, it was obvious from Belew's unprompted comments that his departure from King Crimson still rankled. Within hours the falling out between Fripp and Belew was once again circulating around social media, generating lots of heat but not much light.

Belew's unhappiness at a new development in King Crimson had been simmering away since June. The addition to the setlist of a version of *Indiscipline* in which Jakszyk set Belew's spoken words to a new melody had been at Fripp's urging. Some fans initially took against the new arrangement but for others it worked surprisingly well, gaining many converts.

When Belew learned of this via his Facebook page, he commented: "We had an agreement they would not perform anything I wrote. Hmmm."

Despite maintaining in public, and on the radio show, that he had no contact with Fripp other than the "terse" e-mail, the pair had, in fact, talked on the phone on 9 September 2013, and it was this call which Belew regarded as the origin of his agreement. Unusually coded in his online diary, on 22 August 2017 Fripp disclosed that the telephone conversation was "more monologue than dialogue: dudgeon was high, grapes were sour. Adrian made an opening statement, followed by three demands, and a final declaration (that Adrian was not prepared to be The Eighth Man, and was quitting the band)."

In the most revealing public insight into the workings of the relationship between the pair, Fripp went on to note: "Adrian's concern prompted a telephone conversation between Adrian, Martha Belew, Adrian's *de facto* manager, in Mount Juliet and David Singleton, King Crimson manager/minister, in KC's Denver Hotel-Quite-Acceptable on June 23rd, 2017 (nominally a day off). Several matters were discussed, including Adrian's understanding of the 'agreement' between Adrian and myself by telephone (September 9th, 2013). I did not know, until the 'phone conversation with David, that Adrian viewed the 'agreement' as conditions upon which he was prepared to *walk away from the band without a fuss.*

"Another point raised by Martha: ... *if Adrian was in this band, we'd want the others paid as sidemen*; this preceded by the comment that she thought it may be why Adrian wasn't asked to join the current line-up."

"The basis on which Martha and Adrian considered Tony, Jakko, Bill, Mel, Pat, Jeremy and Gavin available and willing to be hired as sidemen to Adrian, and why they might wish to, was not mentioned. But Martha's assumption is correct: this is one of four primary reasons why the current KC is not for Adrian, and reason sufficient on its own to preclude membership of King Crimson's equal-sharing group endeavour."

"Martha's comment evidences an attitude developing in Chateau Belewbeloid through the Noughties which, despite much good musical and personal history, I felt myself increasingly unable to engage. Today, it strikes me as an attitude out-of-touch, a misjudgement of Adrian's station. Views of the Crimson Universe from Planet Belew appear to be remorsely pre-Copernican. As might have been said in the Dorset of my youth: *Our Ade's gettin' a bit above himself.*"

"Adrian's expressed concerns regarding the repertoire: he has learned that KC sings his lyrics and melody in *Neurotica*. Adrian does not consider this a 're-imagining' but an actual performance of Adrian's words and melodies without his permission. Regardless of the extent of Adrian-associated songs included in current KC repertoire, he does not want this. Adrian's concern goes beyond 1980s material: he does not want another singer to sing or perform any of his songs from Adrian's entire tenure as lyricist, singer, songwriter. For Adrian, the lyrics and the melodies belong to him, although it is fine with him if the songs are performed as instrumentals. Adrian worked for a large portion of his life on those melodies, lyrics; recording and touring the world to establish them, make them memorable and beloved. It is not OK with Adrian to have Jakko singing, even changing his work, in an embarrassing way. Should DGM release any live KC recordings of material Adrian considers as belonging to him, without his permission, this is another issue as well."

Following the phone call to Belew, David Singleton at his diplomatic best sent the following e-mail.

"I am happy to do anything I can to resolve this. It is tragic that two people who worked together for so many years to create so much wonderful music should be in such violent disagreement."

"I know you are very unhappy. Equally Robert pulled me aside yesterday morning, quoting your recent Facebook post, and suggesting that he therefore maybe needed to respond with a public statement explaining the current and historic situation between you as he sees it. This seems a recipe for despair."

"Robert also sent me a recent setlist from your Power Trio, pointing out that it included nine King Crimson songs, many of which, in his words, were highly collaborative or written on templates which he created. He made no explanation, but I assume his point was that he sees these as being as much his songs or King Crimson's songs as your songs, and that if it is fine for you to play them, why should it not equally be fine for him to play them?"

"In that sense, it comes back to where I started, which is that the two of you have a shared musical legacy. As the singer and lyricist, I can, of course, understand why you feel that 'the lyrics and the melodies belong to me', and marvel at the time you spent making them memorable and beloved. Equally, I am sure that Robert would feel that the originating guitar lines are just as key to many songs, and that he has devoted just as much energy and time taking these songs into the world. Tony Levin and Bill Bruford doubtless feel the same. In that sense, both legally and morally, the songs in their entirety belong to all of you. And, of course, the right to perform or record them belongs to the whole world. You are upset that King Crimson are playing them 'without my permission, but no-one needs permission from anyone to play or record any of the King Crimson catalogue."

"It occurs to me that King Crimson, like many bands, has often played historic material with changed line-ups. There were many examples in the 1970s, but even after 1981, you played *Red* and *Larks' Tongues* from the Wetton/Cross era, the six-piece added *Talking Drum* and *21st Century Schizoid Man* from 1969, and the double duo in 2000 continued to play songs co-written by Tony Levin and Bill Bruford after they had left the band. From an external perspective, this seemed entirely normal and natural. No-one sought or needed any permission from earlier members ..."

"While I am very happy to do all I can to resolve this, I struggle to see how to square the circle. Martha is right that your belief that the other members of the band should be paid as side-men would have made it difficult for you to be a part of the current incarnation, which has eight equal members, but even so, I know the circumstances of you leaving the band were strained. As such, I suspect that this is a situation that dates back to unresolved issues at the time. I have already spoken to Robert about the points you raised in your phone-call (as in my reply), and I will also copy this e-mail to him. I fear that your Facebook post may already have set this on a more public path, but it would seem best for everyone if possible to avoid a public spat, which seems a waste of both of your creative energies when everything in both worlds seems to be going so very well."

The exchange on Belew's views on sidemen as one of the main reasons why this Crimson wasn't for him highlighted a previous theme that had circulated between Fripp and Belew. Belew's initial suggestion when the Double Trio had first been posited was that he and Robert essentially take King Crimson as a studio project supported by a range of guest players. A different variation came when he suggested that the pair of them go out live as King Crimson with Julie and Eric Slick on bass and drums. Whether true or not, there had been a feeling from some that, during the Double Duo, Belew had never fully accepted that Gunn and Mastelotto were equal partners from an artistic standpoint, a view which seemed vindicated by the singer and guitarist's request around the time of *The ConstruKction Of Light* that he receive a greater share of the tour receipts.

Having opened a particularly unpleasant can of worms and with a clearly annoyed Fripp publishing more detail than they would have wished for, the Belews sought an amicable resolution. A few days later, Fripp's diary for 3 September reported that peace had broken out. "My own with-benefit-of-hindsight: after sending Ade the e-mail in 2013, to have called afterwards rather than wait for Ade to get in touch. That is, to take the initiative, as with this telephone call. (*There is no mistake, save one: the failure to learn from a mistake.*)"

"Adrian presented his own views, and I asked Adrian if he were prepared to be KC's Ninth Man. Happily, Ade agreed (which makes David Singleton Tenth Man). The status of Full Band + 1 role is, continuing on in the Crimson family while not on active service. T Lev held the Fifth Man status between 1999 and 2003. Hooray!" On Facebook he added, "There are no current plans for Adrian to come out with the current formation; but in Crimson's strange history there is a tendency for things to come around. So, Adrian has rejoined the larger family – hooray! – and doors to the future are open. So, no plans, but who knows what the future holds?"

XV

The future for King Crimson took another unexpected turn in October 2017 when Bill Rieflin required a further sabbatical whose immediate consequence meant finding someone to fill his spot on keyboards. An obvious solution would have been for Stacey, already handling some of the more virtuosic flourishes, to add the textural work to his duties. This wasn't discussed, however, as Rieflin, having an idea as to what to do, went with his own instinct and got in touch with Chris Gibson.

Gibson cites King Crimson's 1969 debut as where he began his journey into the band's music. But, like many, Gibson didn't listen to the records in chronological sequence and his next port of call was *Discipline*. "I was really into the Adrian Belew era. *THRAK* was timed just right for me as I was a 22-year-old aspiring musician at the time," he says.

Originally hailing from Utah, Gibson was well known as part of the Seattle music scene and as a member of the Guitar Craft fraternity. Although Gibson knew Rieflin well, he had no inkling when he received a call from Bill on Friday, 22 September 2017, that just under four weeks later he would be on stage with King Crimson.

"The phone call with Bill went something like this. 'Hi Chris, how are things … how's your piano playing these days?' At that point I knew what he was going to ask and my breath was taken away and my heart sank. Next question was 'Are you available to sub for me with King Crimson in the upcoming Fall 2017 US tour?' I said let me talk it over with my wife and less than 60 seconds later I called back and gave him an emphatic 'Yes!'"

Rieflin said he would check with Fripp. Later that day, Gibson arrived at Rieflin's house to discuss what was required. "As you can expect I was quite excited. I met with Bill that day to go over the list of over 30 pieces that I would need to learn in the next two weeks. Leaving Bill's home that night, I had a folder full of charts and a plan to meet at my studio ASAP."

By Sunday, Fripp had agreed Rieflin's plan with an instruction that Chris would need to get himself a suit. Over the next two weeks, the pair worked together intensively, and after a couple of sessions they moved Rieflin's stage gear into Gibson's studio.

"After the first week I came to the conclusion that I would need to ramp up my focus and I began working 12-plus hours a day. Tai chi breaks throughout the session helped to keep my learning process moving. During the middle of the process I had the inevitable fear and doubt creep in. Bill and I would speak about this process as making the impossible possible. Our shared background in Guitar Craft gave us a language and ways of working together that did indeed make it possible."

On 11 October, Gibson and Rieflin flew to Texas and began rehearsals for the first performance set for six days later. At breakfast in the hotel, Gibson became aware of someone approaching his table. "I looked up and it was Robert; a handshake, a smile and 'Welcome to the team' was all that was said."

Being the only person ever to deputise for a serving member of the band meant Gibson occupied a unique position in King Crimson's 50-year history, but the weight of that expectation was nothing to the challenge of assimilating the material. Working late into the night and drilling deep into the music, by his own admission he pushed himself way beyond tiredness. "It's sometimes a good way for me to let things soak in because I'm out of the way a little more. And I *know* I'm tired but I just keep going anyway, not expecting anything. And then the next morning things are a bit more solid."

As the band waited in the wings of Austin's Bass Concert Hall they gathered together. Led by Fripp, they joined in a tight circle, lowered their clenched fists to the centre and then, raising their voices from a low murmur to a loud roar, slowly raised their arms high in the air and at the crescendo flung open their hands, releasing their collective energy into the air. The pre-gig ritual, performed since the '90s and done before and after every gig, acts as a kind of invocation, a summoning and a physical expression of intent and joint endeavour. With that done, the band walked out to huge applause. Getting his charts in order on top of Rieflin's keyboard rig, Chris Gibson dived deep into the baptismal fire. "This was my first professional gig on the keyboards. There's been a huge burst of confidence in seeing that I *can* do this, but it's been very hard."

Over the course of the next few weeks, Gibson played 23 shows. The sheer amount of technical and musical heavy lifting he had to do was daunting. Rieflin, who returned to King Crimson in 2018, had nothing but admiration for Gibson's tenacity. Gibson highlighted some of his favourite moments onstage in his brief period as a member of the band: "*Epitaph* for the sheer magnitude and depth of the lyrics and songwriting, and *Neurotica* is also a fun and exciting piece to play, especially as the opener – it really sets the stage for the audience and gets the excitement buzzing. Same for *Larks' I* and *II*. *In The Court Of The Crimson King* was a particular highlight. I felt a very strong connection with the audience every time we would play this piece. Hearing the crowd sing along to every note was transformative and very special."

All of us, to a greater or lesser degree, have moments when we think to ourselves, if only briefly: "How the fuck did I get here?" Jakko Jakszyk has had more than a few in his time.

In the late 1980s, he was living in Los Angeles, an Englishman abroad at the behest of the publishing company who had signed him up as a songwriter. A call came in from Gavin Harrison asking if Jakszyk wanted to join a backing group for Italian singer Alice on a tour of her native country in 1989.

"Gav said I should bring my driving licence because we were travelling separately to the Italian members of the group. He also mentioned we were all going to share the driving. So when I got to Italy I had my driving licence and, from what I remember, no other fucker had brought theirs," he laughs.

Ending up doing all the driving and being the last band member into the hotel as he parked up, he recalls that the further south the tour went the more disdain drivers had for anything resembling the Highway Code.

"I remember saying to the tour manager, 'Fucking hell, man, what is going on?' It didn't matter what colour the lights were, people just ignored them and did what the fuck they wanted.' And he said: 'The trouble with you English is you treat the traffic lights like they are the law.' I said: 'They are the fucking law!' He said: 'No – not in Italy. They are merely a piece of friendly advice.'"

In 2018, Jakszyk and Harrison found themselves in Italy once again. This time around, Jakko didn't have to worry about the driving. He had other things on his mind as the band prepared to go onstage in Pompeii. It's not only ancient history which resonates there. For a music fan of a certain generation, it's impossible not to associate the location with Pink Floyd's celebrated (and filmed) 1971 appearance. "Having walked down the stone tunnel, the 2,000-year-old stone tunnel where presumably, if you'll excuse the melodrama of the allusion, gladiators would have walked before us, the hairs on my arm were on end," says Jakko with a note of incredulity. "Walking down there bathed in this weird blue light and from there out into the open air with a full arena and then standing under a clear, moonlit sky on stage as a member of King Crimson with Vesuvius behind me; if that doesn't count as a 'how the fuck did I get here?' moment, then I don't know what does."

If Jakko had to pinch himself, he wasn't the only one. Crimson fans had been doing exactly that since Robert Fripp's re-imagining of the group brought the radically different three-drummer configuration to life in 2014. Yet if the history of King Crimson has taught us anything, it is that you underestimate Fripp's tenacity at your peril. For a while it looked as though King Crimson's legacy would be left to reside in the setlists of Stick Men or Adrian Belew's Power Trio. Had Fripp not returned to the frontline then the only way to hear a very partial account of the repertoire would have been the Crimson ProjeKct. By returning with a lineup able to connect with all aspects of Crimson's past, Fripp preserved the band's integrity and legacy by rescuing it from scratchy approximations and good-time cover bands.

Moving on without Belew, a significant presence in the life of the band, caused tribal divisions and left many fans disgruntled that their favourite band had the temerity to move on without asking their permission. In the pre-internet age when a group opted for a shift in direction or personnel, unhappy followers had the option of moaning about it to their mates or, if they were really, really peeved, possibly writing a letter to *Melody Maker* or *New Musical Express*. Nowadays the digital democracy enables fans to broadcast their praise and grievances through the blunderbuss of the world wide web. In his days in the group, Adrian Belew was regularly on the receiving end of abuse that questioned his abilities or even his right to be on the stage with Crimson, something he playfully immortalised on *ProzaKc Blues*. These days, it's Jakszyk who comes in for a knocking. "Yes, there's a handful of the militant wing of the Adrian Belew Fan Club who have got it in for me regardless of who I may, or may not, be. I regularly see myself referred to by some of them as the worst singer King Crimson has ever had. I understand that music is subjective and you may not like tone or phrasing, but when somebody writes something that's so preposterous it's difficult to be offended by it," Jakszyk says.

One criticism that does rankle, however, is the accusation that this version of Crimson is backward-looking and less experimental than its predecessors. People with long memories will note that when Crimson returned to live work in 2008, despite the presence of new recruit Gavin Harrison, no new material was forthcoming as the band opted instead for a celebratory, nostalgic setlist of well-worn items by the latter-day bands. However, the three-drummer-fronted ensemble not only has its own freshly composed songs but its gigs have also resounded with material previously unplayed for over 40 years. The inclusion of items from every single Crimson album bar one, with material spanning the years 1969 to the present day, confirms that this band offers the most extensive presentation of all the elements of Crimson to date.

"In general terms, this is a very popular version of the group playing to bigger crowds and larger venues than before, and I guess that's because we're encompassing the whole repertoire. We don't neglect any era and the fact that we can do and it all sounds incredibly different and yet somehow there's a genuine glue and thread that connects it all together." Ticket receipts and a string of sell-out shows would seem to bear out Jakszyk's argument; this line-up is attracting greater numbers than ever before.

In the Double Duo's time, the band were playing smaller venues with smaller audiences. As the 2008 and 2014 lineups found out, after time away from the spotlight there was always an uptick in interest. However, along with the expected older fans, younger people are increasingly prevalent and, whisper it softly, larger numbers of women – traditionally a demographic in short supply when the group comes to town – are showing up.

Jakszyk: "I was in the car with my son last week and he said his two most favourite bands ever are Everything Everything and The Beatles. That's quite a spread and what I take from that is that in more general terms there seems to be a lack of tribalism among young people today. You've got these young fans who are getting Crimson on some level regardless of whether we're cool or not, and they're going to the gigs. I look down from the stage and I see these young women singing along and they know the words better than I do! It feels like a weird regeneration thing which is partly to do with the nature of this version of the band."

Jeremy Stacey agrees that there's something in the fabric of this configuration that makes Crimson a must-have ticket. "I think it's so fantastic for the audience that suddenly after all these years they are able to go and hear material that's not been played live before. It's not the same as it was because there's three drummers and new arrangements but there's enough of the original stuff suggested for people who want to hear an element of the record but it's moved forward, as music should."

When in Rome there was talk in the band that things had somehow moved into a different gear. Jakko says he had a sense of it, as did their agent, that Crimson might be achieving a potential that had hitherto eluded it. "Robert said to me one night that he felt a change in the band," says Gavin Harrison. "I didn't perceive it myself, but Robert has a good overview and masterplan when it comes to looking at the band."

With over three-and-a-half hours of new and re-imagined pieces at the band's disposal, Harrison is pleased with its evolution though he admits to the occasional disappointment that in the course of a performance the octet will only scratch the surface of their repertoire.

"It can be frustrating but I know Robert spends a lot of time planning each setlist. We could do two entire evening performances of completely different material but that wouldn't necessarily make either night a great night if you only came to one of them. That would only work if you bought tickets for both shows of course. Frank Zappa used to do virtually a different show every night. He had so much material that he could do that. I saw him twice at Wembley and I think there was only one song the same on both nights. You should always play the set that you feel flows the best and that's what Robert does. He can see and perceive things that on the surface others might not realise. He senses these shifts that others might not. In my eyes, it's his band. He's steering the ship and he decides when we're going to work and where we're going to work."

XVI

In 2019, the band's touring will take them into some decidedly non-Crimson terrain such as the Doctor Music Festivals in the Pyrenees – where they'll be sharing a stage with pop-rock, progressive rock, electronic, metal, hardcore, World Music and R&B acts – and, perhaps even more unlikely, the multi-stage Rock In Rio festival, said to be one of the biggest music festivals on the planet. Crimson are seeking to move beyond their usual base because Fripp clearly believes that this band is one for a wider audience, one including younger people and others outside stereotypical older rock fans or prog rock devotees.

The 50th anniversary will also see the release of *Cosmic FuKc: Prog-Rock Pond Scum Set To Bum You Out*, the first documentary on the band, directed by filmmaker Toby Amies. Amies has spent time talking to as many Crims past and present as he could. Crucially, his approach is not as a fan but as someone tracking down witnesses to a phenomenon and having them relate their direct experience. *Heaven And Earth*, another in the band's series of multi-disc boxed sets, this time detailing the ProjeKcts and King Crimson from 1997 to 2008, will complete a sequence that has made Crimson one of the most scrupulously documented groups this side of The Grateful Dead.

One thing that won't be appearing in 2019 is a new studio album. Fripp has long maintained that, while a studio album was a love letter, Crimson in concert was a hot date. With six releases already showcasing the present era's stage abilities, Crimson has been positively promiscuous when it comes to putting out live albums. Yet a recurring question is: "When will they make a studio album of new material?" The answer would appear to be: not anytime soon.

"There are several things about this. One, the modus operandi has changed completely," says Jakszyk. "Historically, touring was a device to promote an album that you'd released. That world no longer exists. It's gone. I've also thought that the irony of any education is that it prepares you for a world that won't exist by the time you get there. That seems truer than ever because it seems to be moving quicker than ever. Those transitions seem to be quicker with every step. So what's the imperative of recording a new album?

"I tell you what people don't seem to see, or are blinded by, is this; if we went on stage and played for an hour and a quarter and played all the new music we've come up with since we began back in 2014, then over half the set would be brand new music. And would people think 'that's what we want'? Well, you know what? We did do that except that we're on stage for three hours. So the 50 minutes of new music is engulfed in the midst of a three-hour sandwich. So I quite often think 'What the fuck are these people talking about?' When we were kids an album lasted 40 minutes. Was there a time in King Crimson's career where they went on stage and played the whole of one album? I don't think so. From what I can see, the previous version of King Crimson that was together and did a short tour in 2008 didn't play any new music at all.

"All the people whingeing about the new music in light of the fact that there is new music within the set, I really would be intrigued to know how many of the people that regularly complain in forums and on social media have actually been to any of the gigs and how many they've actually been to. Because sometimes I get the impression that they are so appalled and outraged that they don't go to see us. So it's all based on what?"

The prospect of getting all the band into a studio to make a record as they did for the previous KC album, 2003's *The Power To Believe*, is not one that finds any resonance with the present Crimson. "I don't think any of us want to do that," continues Jakszyk. "I think there's a way of recording a new album but that's not it. It would be difficult and costly to record this band in a traditional manner. I think there's a way of doing it where you utilise some of the live stuff as a basic backing track and then work on overdubs. But is it cost effective? Why would we do it?"

The writing of new material in any incarnation of King Crimson has never been easy or straightforward. As the principal co-writer of songs, Jakszyk thinks it's impossible to second-guess how Fripp will react to new compositions. "I don't know what he's hearing and not hearing. Sometimes I'll do something and I'll think he might not like that – and he'll really like it. And sometimes the opposite. Frequently Robert will say when I present him with a finished piece, 'I think it's marvellous. What a fantastic song. What a great new song for your next solo album!' So as a result, I now have quite a lot of material for my next solo album!

"I think you have to just do what you do and play it. I think if you start to take it personally it would be distressing and upsetting. There's no point in trying to second-guess him because then you'd be writing stuff for the wrong reasons. I think if I'm moved to write something then I get on and write it, and if Robert likes it then it becomes one of a pile of things that we at some point hopefully add to the set or at least explore in rehearsals."

"At the beginning of every year Robert will suggest some tunes from the repertoire that we might add to the set. What normally happens is that Gavin and I will produce a demo of that King Crimson song. I'll learn all the parts and record them and Gavin will come up with a new drum arrangement. What that enables us to do is have accessible to the rest of the group members a virtual band with which to rehearse on an individual basis prior to when we all get together."

"That's particularly relevant to the drummers of course, because when they get into the rehearsal room it's handy to have a demo with all of the bass and guitar but none of the drums. But when they're on their own they can add one of the drums or two of the drums. Putting all that together can be time-consuming because some of the music is quite elaborate and you're recording them from scratch. Sometimes Robert and myself will get together and we'll assess parts and sometimes re-voice them. Last year we got together with Bill and Jeremy as keyboard players and worked with them. At another time, Gavin, Pat and Jeremy will work separately and we do all that before we get together and rehearse collectively."

"By the time we come to do gig number one of the tour, we've done an awful lot of work. There's been all the preamble – the recording of demos, people woodshedding at home, then rehearsal in small ensembles and then rehearsing collectively as a band for two or more weeks. It's a lot of work before we hit the stage for the first time."

The band is conspicuously happy and not for nothing is Fripp, once notorious for lurking in the shadows, playing boldly in the light these days, standing alongside his colleagues at the end of the set to take the applause. How long King Crimson will continue, given the ages of Collins, Levin and Fripp, is hard to determine. Harrison suggests that people should give up speculating on what may or may not happen and concentrate instead on being in the here and now. "This band is unfolding right before you in real time. I can't say where we'll be in six months or what we'll be doing. I really don't know. Robert's plans tend to be more the type of audience he thinks we should be reaching and the areas we should play more than 'I think we should play the songs like this'. That is left to the individual to play the way you think is correct for the song at that time. The band's sound is the sum of all the personalities and the chemistry. For better or worse. If you change one member the band will sound different. The way the personalities click together, or not in some cases, is the sound of the band. Some bands have lots of bad vibes and arguments and animosity and that will produce a certain type of sound or songwriting or album. Surviving each other is usually the hardest part of any band. King Crimson is not a rock and roll band where we get drunk and start punching each other. Yet."

As King Crimson moves into its 50th year, it appears radically different to the quintet that embarked on its journey back in 1969. In the intervening years much has undoubtedly changed. Yet within the turbulence, transience and triumphs documented in these pages, it's possible to see recurring patterns and motifs that transcend the people and places which gave rise to it all.

Regardless of the disagreements or perhaps even the accord that have been part of the story, there's a prevailing continuity or integrity present with all of the varying forms and directions which King Crimson has taken and, in some cases, not taken over these five decades. Speaking with members of King Crimson over the years, it's clear they have experienced first-hand the good and bad that comes from spending time in the group. For many of them it's been perplexing, frustrating and infuriating.

As these pages have shown, the court of King Crimson can be a deeply unsettling and upsetting place to be. Nor was being a member ever a good way to make money. The only album that had any kind of significant commercial viability was their 1969 debut. Paraphrasing Orson Welles talking about *Citizen Kane*, they started at the top and worked their way down, at least when it came to sales.

Greg Lake, Ian McDonald, Peter Sinfield, Boz, Mel Collins, Ian Wallace and John Wetton all went on to enjoy much higher-profile and more lucrative careers after King Crimson. Yet a majority of members, even some of those whose time was marred by rancour or adversity, will tell you that being in King Crimson led them to some of the most satisfying musical moments of their entire career.

Perhaps, the success of King Crimson isn't to be measured in box office receipts but in the long-term legacy and impact upon those it has touched. Over time, in a quiet way with barely any coverage in the mainstream media, Crimson's stock has incrementally risen.

On the admittedly non-scientific evidence of my Google alerts alone, hardly a day goes by without Crimson being namechecked either as an influence upon a band or a go-to comparison when assessing the quality of a new artist. The effect and impact Crimson had upon musicians coming up in the '60s and '70s, and later generations of aspiring players, was considerable. Players as diverse as Nick Cave, David Bowie, Craig Armstrong, Mark Hollis, Steve Vai, Tool's Maynard James Keenan, The Unthanks, Björk, Phil Collins, the hotly tipped Weyes Blood and many more have all pricked up their ears and taken notice of Crimson's output. Kanye West's sampling of *21st Century Schizoid Man*'s chorus on 2010's *My Beautiful Dark Twisted Fantasy*, an album with recorded sales in excess of 1,300,000, took King Crimson, albeit obliquely, out towards new and possibly receptive ears.

While they remain a relatively niche underground act, the music of King Crimson has begun seeping out into popular consciousness through the occasional movie soundtrack. A video of a performance of *Starless* from a Japanese tour in 2015 is, at the time of writing, well on the way to notching up seven million views on YouTube.

Half a century on from the formation of King Crimson, the world is a profoundly different place. In 1969 it looked and felt as though music could, and might, change the world. Whether explicitly or implicitly, it suggested a Technicolor alternative to the post-war monochrome. It wasn't just about escapism. Wrapped in the rhythms and chords were questions about what kind of world might be possible. Optimism, hope, freedom, change, innocence, experience and truth was what the music of that generation was about. Today the role and purpose, importance and centrality of music within culture and commerce is radically and irrevocably altered. Where it once was the only game in town it has now become incidental music on a game – or a muted soundtrack to a much bigger game. Atomised, accessorised, it is but a small detail in a bigger, distracting and distorting, picture. Where once it *was* the mood, now it is simply mood music, an aural air freshener drawn from a pot pourri of playlists. Where once it defined the zeitgeist, it has been largely exorcised from the body electric.

Music has joined wisdom in William Blake's "desolate market where none come to buy". Here in the 21st century, the civics and polity, rationality and order that framed our world are convulsed and fevered by a viral madness coursing deep through the veins, self-administered through the daily poison of social media and demagoguery disguised as discourse. In a world bent out of shape by greed, cynicism and paranoia, it turns out that nothing we've got, we really need.

This is an understandable conclusion to come to, given today's diet of despair, doom and catastrophe. But while music's pan-cultural importance has diminished, the intensity of feeling, albeit to a smaller portion of the populace, has deepened.

For many of us, music is one of the ways to make sense of the chaos, a still point for reflection, an act of both communion and community; a rallying point at which disparate ideas, emotions and connections come together at a speed and depth that mere language can't compete with.

When asked to describe King Crimson in just one word, a couple of hundred fans on social media responded in rapid succession. This small sample is pretty indicative of the general gist: *intense; inspiring; unmistakable; true; eternal; sharp; challenging; groundbreaking; bountiful; cathartic; visceral; uncompromising; transcendent; original; dense; complex; vital; unique; indomitable; fearless; magical; angular; dangerous; unexpected; sensational; brutal; complex; astonishing; deep; visionary; unexpected; diverse; powerful; inventive; compelling; innovative; different; powerful; restless; precise; reckless …*

And so on.

Listening to music wakes us up both superficially and profoundly. It makes us feel fiercely alive, or as though we are discovering some arcane, secret knowledge. It can make us experience a clarity of thought that borders on the mystic. That it can do all of this, and so much more, speaks to the remarkable, transformative power it carries.

Fifty years on, King Crimson, even with all its inherent dilemmas, quarrels and complications, still carries with it that power – the power to move us, the power to annoy us, the power to exasperate us, the power to exhilarate us, but perhaps most importantly, the power to change us. That power to change is something it has continually exerted upon the one member to have been constant throughout Crimson's five decades.

At a press conference held in Bloomsbury's October Gallery in April 2019, Fripp talked for more than four hours to journalists who had flown in from all over Europe and the United States. Elegant and dapper in a smart blue suit, the guitarist held forth on topics covering all points in King Crimson's history and taking the opportunity to announce that saxophonist Theo Travis would be joining King Crimson as "the ninth man" for all of King Crimson's live performances in 2019.

This being Crimson, of course, nothing was as it might first appear. With Bill Rieflin taking time away from performance to attend to family matters, Travis would not be playing sax but instead taking up Rieflin's role on keyboards, Mellotron and fairy dusting. Even as Fripp made the announcement, Travis had already put in rehearsal time the previous month with Jakko Jakszyk. Though Fripp didn't go into the details at the press conference, he had lined up Travis as early as the previous year to join Crimson depending on Rieflin's commitments. "I regard Theo as a member of the Crimson family," he told fellow Crims at a rehearsal that year.

The current King Crimson was the first in the band's history that had the capacity to be able to embrace the full extent of the 50-year repertoire, Fripp said. Speaking of the players he was proud to be on stage with, he commented: "Their breadth of musicality and experience is utterly astonishing to me."

Reminding the audience of Jamie Muir's remonstration to Bill Bruford in 1972 that they were there "to serve the music", he went on to observe: "Well, that's a very lofty aim but this is the first band where that's actually fully happened. No-one has an agenda. Alternatively expressed, there are no prima donnas in this band."

While the conference was formal and structured, there was a relaxed, almost intimate, atmosphere. Standing on a small dais with a laptop containing his notes nearby, Fripp spoke freely, one topic associatively leading to another. He was overcome with emotion more than once talking about meeting Hendrix and the experience of coming into direct contact with what he called the "inexpressible benevolence of music" or, with tears streaming down his face, reflecting on his friendship with John Wetton in the latter years of the bassist's life.

Of what the future might hold, Fripp relayed the story that he'd only just received an e-mail from Mel Collins on that very subject. A journalist in Chile, where Collins was on tour with Dire Straits Legacy, had asked the sax player if he could confirm the rumour that, when Crimson appeared in Chile in October 2019, it would be the band's very last gig ever. Collins was, Fripp said, understandably concerned.

Fripp laughed. "Well, it's news to me unless David Singleton hasn't told me something," he smiled, going on to confirm that as far as he was concerned King Crimson would be continuing. By playing larger venues such as Chile's 12,000-capacity Movistar Arena in Santiago, as well as large-scale festivals such as Rock In Rio, Fripp stated his intention was to take King Crimson to "innocent ears" in its anniversary year. The fact that the first of two dates in Chile sold out within an hour of the tickets going on sale suggested a significant appetite for Crimson's music.

When asked by *Record Collector*'s Andy Rawll whether King Crimson could exist without Robert Fripp, the guitarist replied: "No." "So," continued Rawll, "does that mean when you stop performing that is the end of King Crimson?" "Yes," came Fripp's instant reply.

This was, as many seasoned Fripp-watchers in the room confirmed, the first time that Robert had been so unequivocal about the matter in public. He'd been trying to give the band away to someone else for at least 45 years, he said, noting that in 1974 he suggested Ian McDonald rejoin Bruford and Wetton after the recording of *Red*. Then there had been the groups playing King Crimson material such as 21st Century Schizoid Band and, more recently, Crimson DNA and Crimson ProjeKct. While some of these had been initiated by others, they had sought and received Fripp's blessing and support. However, after seeing the Crimson ProjeKct performance in London, Fripp said: "I have accepted that for King Crimson to be King Crimson, Robert has to be there."

As 'convenor' of the group, Fripp's habit of bringing things to an end when success – and the attendant distortion of the band's ideals and goals – beckoned has had the effect of preserving Crimson's integrity. Given the obstacles facing a large-ensemble rock band operating in economic and politically uncertain times, the fact that King Crimson continues to exist, with plans to carry on working beyond 2019, is nothing short of a miracle. And we know how scarce they can be.

May 2019: King Crimson is hard at work in a large rehearsal facility near Bedford. The rehearsals are efficient and business-like. Each player in the eight-strong team makes adjustments to settings and sounds on their various instruments. The newest recruit, saxophonist Theo Travis, located behind a keyboard rig sits in for regular Mellotronist and sonic fairy-duster, Bill Reiflin. The ensemble rumble through some new additions to the concert repertoire which already clocks in at over three hours of available music that has to be ready to go in case Fripp decides to include it on the setlist. After just three days, with his customary directness, Fripp moved to tell his friend Travis that his time in Crimson was over. Writing in his diary, Robert said: "Theo was first choice as Bill Rieflin's dep for 2019 touring. But not every idea works out, even good ideas among excellent musicians – no blame! – and should in no way be considered any form of failure on Theo's part," explained Fripp. "Theo's response was with the decency, straightforwardness, and graciousness that I know in him. I also mentioned to Theo that I do not see this as the end of our professional work together, merely this particular aspect of it. At 13.02 King Crimson decided, in Bill Rieflin's absence, to proceed as a Seven-Headed Beast. The decision was taken unanimously by all Crims. Tacitly, we accepted: regardless of the quality of player depping for Bill, simply, Bill is irreplaceable. It's not the notes that are played, it's the Billness of Bill that Master Rieflin brings to the group."

For his part, though obviously disappointed, Travis accepted the decision with equanimity, noting that "Robert and Bill are very close both musically and personally and I understand and respect this decision. The rehearsals I attended were very enjoyable and the band sounds great. I particularly enjoyed getting to know Mel Collins a bit better and hearing his wonderful stories and fabulous sax and flute playing." As Fripp notes: "So, a surprise for all of us. But – hey! – this is King Crimson. The good news: Theo is out and stomping with Soft Machine; and King Crimson is beginning again, again."

Beginning again is something King Crimson has been doing on a regular basis since their dramatic arrival on the music scene in 1969.

Writing in March 1999, Fripp's perspective on the Crimson story was this: "The band would be better named 'King Crimsoning'. Crimson was always in process, and continues in process. The next Crimson (group and album) will be greeted by disappointment, approval and disappointment. After 10 or 15 years, the next step will be seen in the perspective of what went before and what follows afterwards. Enthusiasts will continue to have their favourite periods, players and repertoire. In time, all this will make more sense then than it does now, even Crimson's history (to anyone who cares) isn't available to easy generalisation or simplistic assessment.

"The key is this: be there when it flies. Look at the flying, not the flight plan (although there will be framed flight plans hanging from the bedroom walls). And the standard advice, to those generous enough to take interest: when Crimson comes to your town, see it now rather than wait until next year."

"Always the same, always different, always the same, always …"

After Crimson

ADRIAN BELEW (born 23 December 1949)

After King Crimson's 2008 tour, Belew released *e* (2009), featuring his then-regular power trio band Julie and Eric Slick on bass and drums, and in 2011 he was invited to work in Amsterdam with the Metropole Orchestra on an orchestral version of *e* performed at the Paradiso venue. Speaking about the experience to Nick DeRiso, he recalled: "I think *'e' for orchestra* came out every bit as good as I hoped it would, and in some ways better. Even though I had, in my mind, imagined as best I could do what I thought it would sound like, and what I thought it would be like, and what I imagined the experience itself would be, of course none of those things turned out exactly as you predict them. But in this case, happily, they turned out even better. I had a sound in mind that I thought *e* would end up being. But it turned out more powerfully than I thought. Somehow, once it was arranged and scored by myself and Tom Trapp, and put into the hands of such a great orchestra as the Metropole, it just turned out more powerful – and a bit more unusual than even I thought. I couldn't exactly say that the orchestra was going to be what it turned into, such a powerful and modern version of orchestral music. A lot of people have said this to me – and I take it as a compliment – it's got a lot of Zappa and King Crimson attributes to it, orchestrally speaking. Still, there's not much to refer to in that area. There aren't many pieces of music like this yet that have come from that fraternity of music – the Zappa/Crimson fraternity.

"As I got to know the orchestra members, and the different factions of the orchestra, I began to realise that many of them did have an appreciation of my music already – both Adrian Belew and King Crimson."

"But it's a different fellowship, what goes on with orchestra players, who are used to getting sheet music with dots on it as opposed to the rock world that I've lived in all my life. They are separate worlds, though they do have an appreciation for each other. It was scary as hell for me because, even though I am the composer of the music, not being a traditional composer in that I don't sit down and write it on paper like someone would usually do, there was a little worry on my part: How would I interface with these people? This is all they know how to do, and it's exactly what I don't do. It turned out in the end though – it fascinated them just as much as it fascinated me. For them, they're thinking: 'How is this guy playing this 43-minute piece of intricate music with no sheets of paper?' They were just as intrigued by my way of doing it, as I was with theirs."

Following his departure from King Crimson, in addition to scoring the Oscar-winning *Piper* in 2017 he launched his FLUX app. The developers describe FLUX thus: "Belew imagined, created and recorded several hundred different effects, tracks and sonic clips … at its core FLUX is an engine. It links hundreds of musical tracks, audio snippets and art into a visual language that conveys Adrian Belew, his ideas and his avant-garde style into an intriguing app. Through a roulette of digital algorithms, FLUX by Belew offers an infinite number of musical combinations to discover. An enthusiastic bench review of the app by *Sound On Sound* magazine concluded: "The manual states that more effects are in development, but there aren't any gaping holes at present. This is a professional-feeling, imaginative effects processor with an interface as slick as they come. For me it's the one by which others will now be judged."

Belew was also part of the Celebrating David Bowie tour featuring ex-Bowie alumni and special guests. The tour played the USA, UK, Australia, Japan, Mexico and South America in 2016, 2017 and 2018. More dates are planned. He continues to tour with long-term bassist Julie Slick and drummer Tobias Ralph, and in 2019 announced that guitarist and keyboard player Saul Zonana would also be joining the band touring to support his new album *Pop Sided*. Adrian described the tour as "a more complete picture of most things I've done. More songs, new songs from the award-winning FLUX app, King Crimson material I haven't played for years, and a dose of classic Power Trio. It's my intention to make this the best Adrian Belew show ever!"

BILL BRUFORD (17 May 1949)

Bill's departure from King Crimson after the rehearsals in Nashville and ProjeKct One's four-night residency at Camden's Jazz Café in 1997 provided a stepping stone into the next phase of his career as a bandleader. *If Summer Had Its Ghosts* (1997) was a collaboration with guitarist Ralph Towner and bassist Eddie Gomez. Bruford said he was aiming for something "more poetic – softer, hazy autumnal". Recorded over four days, the album achieved his goal with elegant, often beautiful, music that sold well.

The second incarnation of his Earthworks group picked up to some extent where the mid-'80s left off with Bruford extending his compositional abilities. 1999's *A Part, And Yet Apart* drew praise in *Jazz Times*: "The tremendous quartet of drummer Bruford, saxophonist Patrick Clahar, pianist Steve Hamilton and bassist Mark Hodgson deliver endlessly intriguing compositions, featuring reoccurring riffs to hang a hat on, but riffing into unexpected, yet satisfying directions." The album also marked the end of his association with the DGM label, and in 2001 he launched his own Summerfold label, providing a home for his acoustic work, while sister label Winterfold was earmarked for archive electric/rock-orientated outings. In 2004, he embarked on a partnership with Dutch keyboard Michiel Borstlap releasing the album *Every Step A Dance, Every*

Word A Song. Surpassing anything he had recorded in the '80s with Patrick Moraz, the combination of Bruford's quicksilver responses and Borstlap's lyrical invention made for a truly remarkable and highly creative partnership that yielded two albums and a live DVD.

A highly popular lecturer on the drum clinic circuit in Europe, America and elsewhere, in 2008 Bruford completed work on his biography and took the decision to retire from live work. He wrote that all the hassle and anxiety and worry about not being at the top of his game could be stopped if "I could just mouth six little words: 'I no longer perform in public.'"

Published in 2009, his biography was well received. The *Guardian*'s judgement was that "Bruford's autobiography not only provides a humorous insight into the daily detail of a successful musician's life but also grapples with the big existential issues of what it takes to be an artist of any sort in the modern world. The account is loosely organised around a string of questions that Bruford has found himself parrying for most of his life: Why did you leave Yes? Is it difficult, with a family? Do you like doing interviews? (The latter receives a resounding "No!" conveyed in one of the most entertaining passages in the book.) But the perennial question that irks him most is: Yes, but what do you really do? Now we know."

Away from public performance, Bruford continued to produce a series of releases via his labels and fully embraced the opportunity to lecture in universities about the role of the creative artist in the commercial world, a subject close to his heart. In 2011, while continuing with public lectures, Bruford enrolled as a postgraduate student at doctoral level in the Faculty of Arts and Human Sciences at Surrey University and in 2017 gained his doctorate.

Bill was briefly reunited with his old bandmates in Yes when he was inducted into the Rock and Roll Hall of Fame. 2017 saw the release of a Bruford band archive set, *Seems Like A Lifetime Ago*, which included new stereo and surround sound mixes for *Feels Good To Me* and *One Of A Kind* by Jakko Jakszyk. The boxed set immediately sold out and a second edition was made available later that year.

In 2018, the University of Michigan Press published, *Uncharted: Creativity And The Expert Drummer*, a more accessible account of the research undertaken for his PhD.

In 2019, Bill is overseeing production of another multi-disc boxed set that will cover his period with Earthworks.

BOZ BURRELL (1 August 1946–21 September 2006)

After King Crimson broke up at the end of the *Earthbound* gigs in April 1972, Mel, Ian and Boz continued to tour with Alexis Korner who had been working on the same tour. That year, under the name of Alexis Korner and Snape they recorded and released *The Accidental Band*, and in 1973 followed it with a live album. Later that year, Burrell successfully auditioned for Bad Company featuring Free's singer and drummer Paul Rodgers and Simon Kirke and ex-Mott The Hoople guitarist Mick Ralphs. Their self-titled debut went to No. 3 and No. 1 of the UK and US album charts in 1974. Burrell went on to record a further five albums with the band until it went into hiatus after the release of *Rough Diamonds* in 1982.

When I was writing the first edition of my KC biography in 1999, I was pleasantly surprised how many ex-members were keen to talk about their time with the band. Even the couple who were at first reluctant eventually agreed to talk. The one person who declined was Boz Burrell. He had only recently quit a re-formed Bad Company with whom he had spent the previous year. He was always polite when I rang him at his home. Sometimes his wife, Kath, would answer and she'd say "Oh hang on, he's just out playing some golf. I'll just go and get him." I think I spoke to him three times in total. On each occasion he'd politely enquire how the book was progressing. Sometimes I'd tell a little of what someone had said, hoping it would spur him into a response, but Boz was too seasoned a pro to be caught like that. Instead he would offer neutral comments. "Well it might have been like that but, you know, I can't really remember" was about as far as he would be drawn.

Boz spent time working with ex-Family vocalist Roger Chapman and was in Alvin Lee's touring band in the '90s. In the '00s, he was a member of Tam White's Celtic Groove Connection. White was with Burrell at his home in Puerto Banús in Marbella when he died. Groove Connection guitarist Neil Warden remembers: "Tam was there along with his friend Billy. They were ready for going out to a small party and play a few tunes with some friends. Tam was sitting in Boz's apartment singing, Boz picked up a guitar and sat back in his seat and slumped over and passed away. Efforts were made to revive him before the emergency services arrived but no luck." Boz was 60 years old.

Keyboard player Tim Hinkley, who guested on the Snape album, recalls that Boz was from Saracen's Head in Lincolnshire and sheds light on the origins of Boz's chosen name. "Back in the day, we all rode our bicycles to school. Raymond Burrell was collecting his bike from the local bicycle repair man who for some unknown reason had put the name of 'Boz' on the repair ticket. The nickname stuck with him for the rest of his life.

"I spent a lot of my life growing up with Boz from the heady days of the 1960s when he was absolutely blowing everyone away with his jazz singing to the great stomping bass lines he played after taking up bass (by the way, I don't think Fripp taught Boz anything about playing bass, or for that matter music, that he didn't already know) in the 1970s. Check out his great vocal rendition of *Part Time Love* on the Steve York *Cameo Paradis – Manor Live* album. Boz and I also recorded together at Rudy Van Gelder's studio in New York for producer Creed Taylor along with drummer Ian Wallace that was released as the Esther Phillips album *Black Eyed Blues*. Boz was very demanding of himself and was rarely satisfied with any of his musical performances especially the most commercially successful ones, i.e. the King Crimson and Bad Company bands. Boz lived life to the full and was determined to go out with a song on his lips and an axe in his hands … this he most certainly achieved. As Boz would say 'Later, Man!'"

After Burrell's passing, Peter Sinfield said: "Ah dear Boz … he owns too much of my heart, not to say my liver, to ever be really gone."

Bandmate Ian Wallace offered this poignant remembrance: "Bozzle did a remarkable thing when he joined King Crimson. He started to play the bass. Of course the story is well known amongst Crimson fans; after auditioning several hundred bass players he picked up a bass someone had left and started noodling on it and one thing led to another with him becoming the new King Crimson bassist. He probably saved the band. We'd exhausted all the possibilities of getting a bass player and Robert would probably have called it quits. But for that moment there would have been no *Islands* band, no *Larks' Tongues*, no *Elephant Talk*, no more King Crimson. So to my mind, I owe him a debt that can never bc repaid.

"Boz became my rock. Mel and I talked about this during a Schizoid Band tour. As the *Islands* band progressed, and particularly after we'd broken up and the restraints were lifted whilst we continued to fulfill our contractual obligations, Mel and I and Robert too, were able to fly off in all kinds of weird and wonderful directions knowing that Boz wouldn't move, anchoring our base, allowing us to always be able to return to the one. That is an essential part of improvisation, and Boz was as good as they get at this. A rare talent indeed. That was why Mel and I loved playing with him so much. I wish there were more like him."

"What saddens me is that I don't think he ever knew just how good he was in King Crimson. And why should he? Just about everything that has been written about him on the various sites has been about how awful he was, not just as a bassist, but as a singer too. To my mind he had a beautiful voice; pitch perfect, with a fine jazz sensibility to it. If he'd wanted to, he could have held his own with most of the great jazz vocalists. But he chose a different path; he fell in love with the bass guitar and became a great player. Boz, wherever you are I hope you don't rest in peace. I hope you're playing your balls off somewhere with people you love, to appreciative audiences."

"Save a place for me, my brother."

DAVID CROSS (23 April 1949)
Perhaps more than any ex-Crim, David Cross has actively embraced his Crimson heritage and has been enjoying a late-in-life renaissance as a live performer and recording artist. Having gained an MA in the performing arts at Middlesex University in 1993, he went on to teach at London Metropolitan University.

With a series of early albums in the '80s and '90s, his reputation as a solo artist gained momentum following the release of *Closer Than Skin* (2005), including contributions from Richard Palmer-James, and of which Robert Fripp said: "It continues a line of the work we did together in 1973 that no-one else has quite followed."

In 2006, he released *Unbounded*, an impressive album of contemporary classical-sounding improvisations with pianist Naomi Maki, and, in 2009, *English Sun*, a more pastoral, gentle semi-improvised set with composer Andrew Keeling.

In 2015, he released *Starless Starlight*. Co-credited to Cross and Fripp, it featured Cross' variations on the *Starless* theme and his improvisations against soundscapes provided by Robert Fripp. *Classic Rock* magazine said: "The way in which Cross's violin excursions take Fripp's original thoughts and turn them into a regime of emotions is not only an exercise in virtuoso excellence, but also spirited. Cross has the knack of never allowing technique to overshadow his compassionate desire to keep everything warm and inviting. It also serves as a template for what could be live variations. Truly progressive."

In 2015, Cross guested with Stick Men – Pat Mastelotto, Tony Levin and Markus Reuter – for a series of concerts in Japan subsequently released as *Midori* by Moonjune Records in 2016.

Also in 2016, the David Cross Band released *Sign Of The Crow*, again with lyrics by Richard Palmer-James. *Prog* magazine described Cross's soloing as "so flamboyant and intense, one can imagine him sprouting horns".

Uniting two separate eras of the Crimson continuum, Cross continues to tour and record with Stick Men. Other notable releases include *Another Day* (2018) with ex-VdGG sax player David Jackson, who now also plays with Cross's band.

JUDY DYBLE (13 February 1949)
After her stint with Giles, Giles & Fripp in the cramped confines of Brondesbury Road in 1968, Judy went on to join forces with ex-Van Morrison associate and singer Jackie McCauley to form Trader Horne. They recorded just one album, *Morning Way* (1970), now revered as a "lost" psych-folk classic. When the record received its 45th anniversary reissue, *Record Collector* said: "Dyble has been one of the most underrated British singers of the '60s since debuting with the first Fairport Convention line-up in 1967. Here her voice gambols and intertwines around McCauley's huskier tones against the lustrous guitar-autoharp tapestries of tracks such as *Growing Man* and *The Mutant*, particularly shining when traversing the spectral luminescence of *Velvet To Atone* and *In My Loneliness*."

In 1971, Dyble married DJ and music journalist Simon Stable and during this time worked in reception at Command Studios. The couple also took in lodgers, including Ian Wallace and, around the recording of *Islands*, Robert Fripp. "He moved into our flat, filled up the fridge with melons and told us off for using coloured toilet paper," she laughs. Judy also reveals that Fripp would occasionally join them in a card game called Spite and Malice. "It's a bit like double-handed Patience. You can really throw your opposition by fouling their next move and Robert was really very good at it. He was vicious and would really knock you off the board. He was very private but his eyes would light up when you'd say 'Spite and Malice?'."

She co-founded a tape duplicating firm, Somewhere Else, with Stable which they ran until Stable's death in 1994. "He always liked to go around saying he was the man from Somewhere Else," laughs Dyble. In March 1997, she attended the *Epitaph* playback celebrating the original KC line-up and was reunited with Ian McDonald and others from the period. She mentioned to McDonald that she had received an offer to play with Fairport Convention at their Cropredy Festival in August for the first time since she'd parted company with the band nearly 30 years previously. "I was unsure about doing it after so long but Ian said to me 'You've got to do it!' And he even rang me from New York afterwards to tell me to do it. But if I hadn't have gone to that playback and talked to the people there I'm not sure I would have done the Fairport thing again."

Her appearance with Fairport marked the beginning of a return to music for Dyble and in the '00s she began an interesting journey that took her through electronica, folk and prog-tinged arrangements to which her cut-glass diction and fragile vocal added beauty and purity. *Talking With Strangers* (2009) looked back on Dyble's life and times with the 19-minute *Harpsong* becoming something of an epic sentimental journey, and featuring guest spots from some of those who were there with Dyble back in the '60s. Thus, Ian McDonald and Robert Fripp, Celia Humphris from Trees, Pentangle's Jacqui McShee and Fairport Convention's Simon Nicol become part of a swirling chorus, echoing reminders of meetings in what were undoubtedly remarkable times on a track which also includes Pat Mastelotto on drums and percussion. What could have been an ill-advised stylistic disaster is instead a surprisingly sophisticated triumph. The triple album *Gathering The Threads* (2015) offered a comprehensive through-view of her career. In 2016, she published her autobiography, *An Accidental Musician*, and she continues to play live.

MICHAEL GILES (1 March 1942)

In the aftermath of McDonald And Giles, Michael Giles threw himself into studio work as a hired hand. "Throughout the 1970s I was so busy with session work, revving 'round London with drums packed in the back of a wide-wheeled yellow Morris Minor, playing in most of the major and minor studios. The phone was always ringing with calls from session fixers, producers and musicians," remembers Giles. In the space of a couple of years, Giles' drumming ended up on numerous recordings including library music albums, singer-songwriter Kenny Young, Duffy Power, BJ Cole, Hunter Muskett,

Luther Grosvenor, Leo Sayer, Kevin Ayers, Anthony Phillips and Jackson Heights, to name but a few. Giles recalls that the sessions for Jackson Heights' *The Fifth Avenue Bus* and *Ragamuffins Fool*, both 1972, were unusual. "Throughout recording history, at least since the advent of multi-track machines, it was and still is common practice to record a good drum track before carrying out overdubs. After that, all other instruments and performances can, if necessary, be re-recorded, replaced, repaired, enhanced, edited and improved by overdubbing on top of the drum tracks. This means that the drummer's responsibility is to give his best performance in one take, even though the other musicians may only be giving 'guide' performances, with the luxury of recording their final best takes later via overdubs. With most or maybe all the Jackson Heights tracks I worked on, this regular process was completely reversed – namely, I was invited to overdub full drum kit on the tracks the band had finished recording. So I was alone in the studio with drums and loud headphones listening hard to every change, shift and development in their music in order to make my contribution sound as if we'd all recorded it together as a four-piece band. This involved making written and mental notes so that I could anticipate and lead into different sections while going for my best performance. I think there are one or two tracks on either or both albums where it was not possible to do a complete take from start to finish. The drums were then dropped in maybe halfway through, and edited to make a complete drum track in sync with the other instruments. I enjoyed the very rare challenge of working this way which required intense concentration."

Michael wasn't just confined to the recording studio. In the mid-'70s he toured with Neil Sedaka in a band that included Matching Mole's Dave MacRae and future Police guitarist Andy Summers. The resulting album, *Live At The Royal Festival Hall*, was produced by Wayne Bickerton who had produced *The Cheerful Insanity Of Giles, Giles & Fripp*. In another example of cosmic Crim coincidence, Michael also played on 1974's *Streetwalkers* by ex-Family outfit Chapman-Whitney alongside Mel Collins, Ian Wallace and John Wetton. In the 1980s, Michael's appearances became increasingly eclectic, working with Simon Jeffes' Penguin Café Orchestra and a collaboration in 1983 with ex-Crim Jamie Muir (who had recently returned from his sojourn in a Tibetan monastery in Scotland) and Flying Lizards supremo David Cunningham, who recalls: "We decided to do something but we didn't know where to start. We couldn't play live. Jamie didn't want to cart all his gear around; Michael, sensibly enough, wanted to get paid properly, and I was a liability who couldn't play the same thing twice unless it was a tape loop. The three of us met and talked about the world and played some things to each other."

"I was very impressed to meet Michael who, from my 28-year-old perspective, didn't think or behave like other 42-year-olds. Instead he was wise, optimistic, constructive and adventurous."

The trio ended up providing the soundtrack to Ken McMullen's film *Ghost Dance*.

"Michael took the structuring of the film score very seriously, making notes and plotting and planning all sorts of specific sections and scenes. Jamie and I thought we'd just make it all up on the spot and use it as an excuse for improvising." The extended soundtrack was released on Cunningham's Piano label in 1995. Giles has fond memories of the sessions. "Jamie and I did stuff in my studio in Dorset in the '80s which I've still got on tape and which hasn't been released – very much in experimental mode."

Around the same time, Giles worked on a series of songs with guests including Peter Giles, Dave MacRae, Caravan's Geoffrey Richardson, John Perry and several horn players, including old Trendsetters colleague Michael Blakesley, who also guested on *McDonald And Giles*. The tapes lay unreleased until 2002. Giles described the record – entitled *Progress* – as an "impression of a railway journey in summer, departing from the city at dawn on a bright sunny morning and travelling through the English countryside with a variety of experiences, to arrive at dusk in Cornwall".

In 1994, Giles auditioned at Real World studios for the Sylvian Fripp band. Pat Mastelotto also auditioned that day and after his audition was over he recalls specifically asking if he could wait around in order to meet Michael Giles. "I wandered the grounds at Real World to get far away as another drummer arrived to audition, met Richard Chadwick, future road manager Tim Hook (he was being interviewed for SF tour) and producer David Bottrill. David gave me a private tour of facilities, even Peter Gabriel's room upstairs. Then in the distance I could see a Land Rover coming over the hill and in the back seat was a silhouette of a drum kit; toms still mounted on kick drum, cymbals still on stands, etc. It was Michael Giles. So I met Mike and helped him unload, told him his drumming changed my life and that I hoped he'd get the gig so I could actually see him play."

The release of Giles' *Progress* album in 2002 coincided with the formation of the 21st Century Schizoid Band that included Giles' brother Peter and son-in-law Jakko Jakszyk. The band performed the title track from *Progress* in its live shows. When Giles unexpectedly quit after a successful tour of Japan in 2002, there was talk of Giles working on another solo album. In 2009, he released *The Adventures Of The Michael Giles MAD Band* by a collaborative experimental outfit with Adrian Chivers on found sounds/horn and guitarist Daniel Pennie. The album contained a manifesto of sorts: "MAD Band music is made in the moment without composition, arrangements, rehearsal or great expectations. The only idea is to have no ideas and be completely spontaneous. In a spirit of freedom, the MAD Band explores the universe of sound, silence, space and time." In 2011, another MAD Band album, *In The Moment*, featuring guest player Keith Tippett, was released. Tippett displays his customary command and focus, mixing quixotic splashes of notes or brewing ominous bass-heavy patterns brimming with thunderous intent. Giles confines much of his contribution to that of colourist rather than timekeeper, accenting the luminous electronica and magical allsorts emanating from Chilvers and Pennie. A crucial feature is the speed at which they pull off heart-stopping mood swings. Passages of industrial clattering, pastoral airs, eerie abstraction and avant-rock are vigorously pursued. Such leaps into the dark are exhilarating and entertaining. During the last quarter of the album, what had been riotous knockabout unexpectedly topples into an exquisite ballad which in turn shimmers towards a haunting guitar/piano coda.

For several years, Giles has been working on a book which he says "takes a full-frontal philosophical bash at the incongruous rhythms of the human condition in the 21st century. The book explores the causes of socially sanitised insanity with anger and humour, and rudely exposes those who desperately depend on their fellow humans' deluded collusion. Schizophrenia is not just the hush-hush hideaway of a few disturbed intelligent people. Politicians, corporate men, warmongers and religious leaders are but a few examples of the schizoid personality operating in public. The book will be published when it's ready."

PETER GILES (17 June 1944)
After GG&F and his appearance on *McDonald And Giles*, Peter left the music industry and spent many years as a solicitor's clerk taking statements and assessing cases. His eye for detail found him spending time working on behalf of the Performing Rights Society, tracking down the unpaid royalties of its members. In 2001, he oversaw the release of demo tapes he had originally recorded in Bournemouth and in the flat at Brondesbury Road with GG&F, Ian McDonald and Judy Dyble. Featuring several interesting pointers towards King Crimson – compositions such as *Peace* make early appearances in nascent form – it provided a more rounded view as to what GG&F were aiming at rather than their idiosyncratic Deram album. Released as *Metaphormosis* on Tenth Planet Records in 2001, a CD edition entitled *The Brondesbury Tapes* also saw the light of day that year. Giles picked up his Fender Jazz bass once again to record and tour with the 21st Century Schizoid Band. In 2009, he appeared on *The Giles Brothers*, a compilation that gathered together early demos and recordings of Peter and Michael's pre-GG&F outfits such as The Dowland Brothers and Trendsetters.

Always a keen athlete, Giles proudly noted that in 2015, at the age of 71 no less, "I came 2nd in the 1500 m, and third in the half marathon, at the World Masters' Track and Field Championships in Lyon, France. I also won team gold in the half marathon to complete my set of medals. Additionally, I won my age group running for England in the British & Irish Masters Cross Country (in Ireland) for the first time in November that year."

In 2001, Peter was playing gigs with his wife Yasmin as Aluna. Making occasional live appearances in the London area, Peter talked about an album the pair were recording. "It's the culmination of everything I've done so far. If somebody asked how long it has taken to do the album I'd say 'my life so far'." And so it proves to be. In 2018, on an online bassist forum, Peter wrote: "My wife, Yasmine (who is a keyboardist/

vocalist), and I are currently producing our first album of original songs. This will be finished some time this year. We have an analogue studio at home with two Tascam MSR24S tape machines and a synchroniser! Now that's what I call Sex-on-Reels!"

TREY GUNN (13 December1960)

With a string of exceptionally creative albums released under his own name and as The Trey Gunn Band, Gunn formed the multi-media project Quodia with Joe Mendelson, and in 2007, they released *The Arrow: A Story In Seven Parts* (CD/DVD). "It was a multi-media performing project with storytelling, film and integrated live music," Gunn told *Ultimate Guitar* in 2016. "It didn't quite take off. It was very powerful but we were a little early on the curve. I was a little impinged by my Crimson history because we would show up to do gigs and people really wanted to see me wheedle wheedle on the guitar. Also the venues weren't really set up to bring in multi-media at the time and that project kind of fell apart."

Along with Pat Mastelotto, Gunn formed KTU with Finnish accordion legend Kimmo Pohjonen. Their live work and their 2009 album *Quiver* gained widespread praise with the *Guardian* saying, "tracks such as *Nano* question the conventions of guitar rock with the irony and skill we expect from King Crimson alumni Gunn and Mastelotto. But it's the tracks *Womb* and *Purga* that make best use of Pohjonen's artistry."

Back in 2007, Gunn joined forces with Eddie Jobson's project UKZ, formed in the wake of a faltering UK reunion with John Wetton. The quintet, featuring drummer Marco Minnemann and guitarist Alex Machecek, released an EP, *Radiation*, recorded entirely by file-sharing without any of the musicians meeting. Gunn remembers getting a call from Jobson at the start of the UKZ project. "I was kind of surprised because I felt like I've met almost all of those guys from the '70s prog world. I mean there are some I haven't met but Eddie's so off my radar I was like 'Oh yeah, I've seen you play', which is kind of a rare thing because most of these guys I haven't seen play. But I saw UK (Terry Bozzio, John Wetton and Eddie) on their last tour opening for Jethro Tull in 1979 at the Municipal Auditorium at San Antonio, Texas. When he called me I was in New Mexico and driving down to the airport in Albuquerque and we talked for two hours straight! I knew he was up to something because I don't get calls from people like Eddie unless they're up to something. Basically, we were just talking about likes and dislikes, and we were very much in synch with a lot of our opinions. Eddie told me he was starting this project and asked me if I was interested. After being in King Crimson for ten years, the last thing I wanted to do was be in a band so, bearing that in mind, I said I would be. It sounded interesting and he presented it as very low-level going out into the world, recording just five tracks and do one show. That was all he wanted to do and I was fine with that. The funny thing for me was that a lot of time people talk and nothing happens for whatever reason because other things come up or you can't get the puzzle to fit, because it's like a giant jigsaw puzzle to make something even simple happen. That's why most of the bands I play in are two guys or three!"

UKZ made their live debut at New York City's Town Hall in January 2009 to coincide with the release of *Radiation*. Gunn recalls, "When we realised we weren't going to have enough new things to put on a whole show we had to do some old material. We ended up doing more older material than I thought we would and so Marco and I learned a couple of UK tracks. Man, they're fricken hard! They're harder than some of the Crimson material for me because they're so quirky. It's maybe like it's more going from the jazz world into the rock world whereas with Crimson it's more of the rock world going into the avant-garde classical world. It's just a little bit outside my vocabulary – rhythmically and harmonically. The UK stuff was definitely more harmonically sophisticated than some of the Crimson material. It was pretty hard and hearing some of the keyboard parts I thought ,'Man, can that guy still play this stuff?' It was rocking. There's some stuff where John and Terry are wailing on the original and Eddie's all over it but we worked it out and Eddie was just great. I guess the short story was we were as nervous but it went off pretty well.

"Of course you learn so much from a first show. Eddie rebuilt his rig after that before we went to Japan to make it simpler. Being able to access all these sounds for him is really complicated. For him and some of the fans of UK, the original sounds are critical on tracks such as *Alaska* or *In The Dead of Night* ... some of the sounds themselves are the essence of the track so he needed to get those sounds and it's complicated to pull all that off. The UK stuff did work and *In The Dead Of Night* worked fantastically. It was a really exciting piece of music to play. *The Only Thing She Needs* – fucking hard, man. There's some really tricky shit in there. Eddie really had to pull out the chops! There wasn't any rest for him. He was always going from one thing to the next."

From exploring some more traditional progressive rock areas with Eddie Jobson, Gunn went on to join The Security Project in 2012. Formed by Jerry Marotta, with whom Gunn had worked with on the Sylvian Fripp album *The First Day*, the band tours and celebrates the music of Peter Gabriel's first four albums. To date they have notched up four official releases. Gunn is also a member of the Deep Energy Orchestra whose album *Playing With Fire* was released in 2018. An eight-piece band that includes string players, tabla, electric violin, electric bass and percussion, the band combines traditional Indian music, jazz, classical and progressive rock. In 2019, the band collaborated with the Seattle Metropolitan Chamber Orchestra. Maintaining his 7d record label, Gunn offers musical and performance coaching and has run many touch guitar workshops.

GORDON HASKELL (27 April 1946)

After quitting King Crimson in acrimonious circumstances, Haskell continued his career as a solo artist. *It Is And It Isn't* (1971) featured John Wetton and contained a song called *Worms* which would be later covered by Stackridge on their 1975 album *Extravaganza*, under the title *No One's More Important Than The Earthworm*. Though he continued to record sporadically, Haskell experienced times of great deprivation, including time spent as an entertainer on cruises, "playing to people too pissed to care". Occasionally his King Crimson past would come back to haunt him with requests at solo shows to sing *Cadence And Cascade*, a song he grew to detest. Haskell was invited to attend the annual reunion of his old '60s group, The League Of Gentlemen. "I turned down the first one where they drank to my health like I's sick or something but the second time I thought, well I'm really going to enjoy this with the old boys. Then Fripp comes waltzing down the passage shouting 'Respect! Respect! *Butterfly In China* (Haskell's 1996 album)' like a lunatic. We hug each other and I say to him, 'It's just like the old days when we were kids,' and he says, "Did you ever grow up?""

When playing dates in the USA, Haskell found himself in Nashville and got in touch with Adrian Belew who had replaced Haskell's vocal on *Cadence And Cascade* on the *Frame By Frame* boxed set. "We had a lovely chat. He told me he couldn't do *Cadence And Cascade* as well as I did and I said that anybody could have done it better than me."

Haskell hit something of a purple patch late in his career with *Harry's Bar*. Released in 2002, it contained the song *How Wonderful You Are* which had been released the previous year and was narrowly denied the coveted Christmas Number One slot by Nicole Kidman and Robbie Williams, managed at the time by ex-King Crimson manager, David Enthoven. Despite receiving a reputed £2.8 million advance from Warner Brothers, Haskell ended up in debt to the record and management companies after his follow-up album *Shadows On The Wall* (2002) failed to reach the top 30 in the UK. After being dropped by the company in 2006, Haskell published his autobiography *The Road To Harry's Bar – Forty Years On The Potholed Path To Stardom*, which details his life and treatment in the industry. After spending several years living on the Greek island of Skopelos, he returned to the UK and in 2019 is releasing a new album, *It's Me And You And Them And Us*, and planning a UK tour. Ahead of the release of the album, Gordon writes: "I want the tides to turn. I will not pretend that everything is OK in the world just to be in 'show business'. But I do still want to lift people's spirits if I can. I believe that is part of my job. I don't really want to repeat which bands I have played in for the millionth time in talk shows. It's today that matters to me. People have always loved me for my honesty. I don't do baloney. It is an impossibility for me. My new record makes me feel good and smile. I hope it does the same for all of you, children and adults of the world."

GREG LAKE (10 November1947–7 December 2016)

Keith Emerson wasn't so struck with King Crimson when they supported The Nice in the UK and America in 1969. He was, however, extremely impressed with Greg Lake's abilities. Having made his final vocal contributions to King Crimson's *In The Wake Of Poseidon*, Lake joined forces with Emerson and Carl Palmer to form ELP. Given Emerson's status as a senior figure on the rock circuit of the day, it might be assumed that Lake came on board as the junior partner. If that was the case, nobody told Greg. While accepting Keith's pre-eminence as composer, Lake saw the producer's chair was empty and immediately filled it. While that could have been viewed as arrogance, it was, as Lake recalled, a matter of expedience. "I was the only person who really knew anything about recording. So, it fell to me to do it. Also, Keith was very keen on playing and then leaving (*laughs*); he wanted to get it done and go, you know? He didn't want the tedious technical stuff, sitting there for hours, getting a mix right. He wasn't into that aspect of the band at all. So it came down to me."

When 1973's *Brain Salad Surgery* was sitting high in the charts in just about every country on the planet that sold records, ELP weren't just a rock band. They were an imperial force with a fleet of liveried trucks, bound for venues with audiences bigger than some of the towns they swept past.

When he wasn't on the road, Lake could be found holding court in his London townhouse enjoying the spoils of his success. Smoking Sullivan Powell Turkish cigarettes, he would sometimes refer to the music his band played as "art". For sniffy critics, such ostentation was proof of his soulless vulgarity. For Lake, who'd come from the humble background of an asbestos-lined post-war prefab in Poole, there was nothing pretentious about it. Unlike some rock stars from middle- or upper-class backgrounds feeling awkward about their station in life, Lake, having had no money in the past, had no such inhibitions when it came to grabbing his stash with both hands. As Greg saw it, things were simple: he'd earned it through bloody hard work. If you didn't like it, well, too bad. In 1975, he released *I Believe In Father Christmas*, co-written with Peter Sinfield, which became one of the best-selling Christmas songs of all time.

In the '80s he released solo albums with players such as Gary Moore and Cozy Powell and briefly joined Asia in a strange cosmic crossover that saw him replacing John Wetton. 2001 found Lake touring as part of Ringo Starr's All-Star Band and guesting with The Who, playing on their track *Real Good Looking Boy*. In 2010, Lake and Emerson reunited, performing a series of stripped-back acoustic-style gigs, and Lake developed his Songs Of A Lifetime tour which involved a mixture of songs and anecdotes about his career. ELP managed to reunite for one final show at the High Voltage festival in London's Victoria Park and, although Lake was keen for the band to continue, Carl Palmer felt the group was technically not up to the standard the music demanded.

The last time I talked to Greg Lake was in March 2016 after the shock announcement of Keith Emerson's suicide. He talked frankly about his old bandmate and their often difficult relationship. "One of the things I think Keith got to resent about me was that I would tell him if I thought something he'd written was not very good … It's not an easy thing to tell someone that … if we argued about music it's because we were both passionate … That's when people clash but that's where you'll find great music."

He told me that he also took pleasure in revisiting the music he made in his heyday. For him nothing beat the thrill of hearing some of the early ELP records on vinyl again. Things have a habit of going in and out of fashion, he observed. "You know what? There's a metaphor in there somewhere," laughing with gusto.

What I didn't know as he talked to me to provide a quote about the death of an old bandmate was that he was facing death himself. Although Greg's cancer had been diagnosed for some time, there had never been any announcement about him having the illness. So, when the announcement of his death was made by his long-term friend and manager Stewart Young via Lake's website on 8 December 2016, it came as a bolt out of the blue. While some cancer sufferers have found it therapeutic and even comforting to share their struggle in public, that approach wasn't one that interested Lake. For a man who'd spent the bulk of his entire adult life in the glare of publicity, when it came to his personal life, and that of his family, he was intensely private. While understanding the professional applications of social media, Lake was bemused at the modern-day obsession with selfies, pet portraits and political rants. As one close friend observed, he couldn't see the point of letting fans know what he was having for breakfast or what television show he was watching. Speaking to Martin Townsend of the *Daily Express* in an interview given in 2015 but only published after his death, Lake explained: "If I announce that I'm ill it'll be all over the internet but, I know it sounds awful, I don't want all the sympathy that will bring. I don't want to have a Facebook death."

Understandably daunted by his diagnosis, he faced the illness without fuss or drama, enduring rounds of nausea-inducing chemotherapy with stoicism. After years of fighting cancer left him unable to play the guitar, he told Townsend he decided to abandon treatment. "I'm not frightened of dying but I don't like the idea of leaving so many people that I love behind, and I want to enjoy this time with them. I don't want to be feeling sick and tired from the drugs."

Lake's posthumous autobiography *Lucky Man* was published in 2017.

Tied in with his lack of enthusiasm for social media, Lake subscribed to the now old-fashioned view that a bit of mystery about the life of an artist was a good thing. I made the point to him that fans often have a very deep sense of personal connection to a player through the music. He agreed.

"In the sense that there's no veil over the music. You play it from the heart, or you should do, and there should be a direct passage into your soul. People sometimes like to give off an image of themselves which is not necessarily who they are. So maybe you could tell more about a person I think from the music than you can from the Press or things you might read, or even what the person themselves might say."

What Greg Lake was saying was that if you want to know who the person truly is you're probably best to look for them in the music they made.

IAN McDONALD (25 June 1946)
Following the release of *McDonald And Giles*, the pair went their separate ways. After appearances on records as diverse as T.Rex's *Electric Warrior*, including the hit single *Get It On*, and, at the other end of the commercial spectrum, *Septober Energy* by Keith Tippett's Centipede, McDonald went into production work including *Canis Lupus* by Darryl Way's Wolf (1973). After McDonald's guest spot on King Crimson's *Red*, he went on to produce Fruup's *Modern Masquerades* (1975) and American act Fireballet's *Night On Bald Mountain* (1975). Leaving the UK for the USA, McDonald settled in New York, teaming up with ex-Spooky Tooth guitarist Mick Jones and Ian Hunter associate drummer Dennis Elliot to help form Foreigner. Their 1977 self-titled debut was largely ignored in a punk-fevered UK, with *Sounds* offering a derisory 1½ stars in a review that seemed be more about the writer's unresolved hatred of King Crimson than the album in question. "REMEMBER IAN McDonald? That's right, the geezer who used to mess around something chronic on keyboards for King Crimson back in the early days when they were just as awful as they were later, only we were all too stoned to realise it. Words of portent, florid images and magic music, right? Tawdry, shallow fustian more like it. Now McDonald's back with, get ready for it, more of the same. He's only one of six in Foreigner but, although judging by the credits Mick Jones (no, another one) is the technical leader, this album has ''69 in the park' stomped all over it. The days when even bad acid was good, 'cos it's like a karmic yin and yang balancing act, ain't it man. Not that the words or the music come to that are McDonald's but they're still wedged tight in the same cosmic illusion that Crimson used to peddle. And it still sounds like a musical accompaniment to some kind of destruction avenue sci-fi imagination psychedelic Operation Barbarossa. Forget this being the Blank Generation. Foreigner have so little musical or literary grey matter that it's almost embarrassing."

It's unlikely this review would have bothered anyone in the band, however, least of all McDonald. The album went platinum in the US and Canada and a string of hit singles assured their success on the radio. McDonald was a member until he was ousted in 1981, a victim of the band's internecine politics. After taking part in the *Epitaph* playbacks in London and New York in 1997, he teamed up with Steve Hackett in 1999 alongside John Wetton to play a series of gigs in Japan with a line-up that also included drummer Chester Thompson. The resulting album, *The Tokyo Tapes*, had McDonald revisiting *The Court Of The Crimson King* and *I Talk To The Wind* as well as material from Genesis and Asia and the solo album catalogues of Wetton and Hackett. Through his association with Hackett, McDonald released his first solo album, *Drivers Eyes*. With a broad range of styles that reflected McDonald's wider musical interests, the album briefly reunited McDonald and Giles on *Demimonde*. Further ties to his past were found on *Let There Be Light*, which echoed early Crimson's stately grandeur with lyrics by Peter Sinfield. McDonald wanted Greg Lake to sing but when Lake was unavailable the song was performed by Procul Harum's Gary Brooker. All Music Guide gave the record a four-star rating, saying: "*Drivers Eyes* is a surprisingly complex album, and one that might have charted 25 years ago, when it seemed as though a small but aggressive part of the public was clamouring for any Crimson-related releases. It's still well worth hearing."

In 2002, McDonald joined Peter and Michael Giles, Mel Collins and Jakko Jakszyk in the 21st Century Schizoid Band. Performing King Crimson's music from *In The Court Of The Crimson King* to *Red*, the band also played *Let There Be Light* and part of the *Birdman Suite* from *McDonald And Giles.* In the notes for the double album *Pictures Of A City – Live In New York* (2006), after Ian Wallace replaced Michael Giles in early 2003, McDonald wrote: "It's been great to be reunited with Peter for the first time since recording *McDonald And Giles* in 1970, and at last I have enjoyed the opportunity of working with Ian again, having spent about six weeks on the road with him in Foreigner in the '70s." After expressing his admiration and thanks to the others in the group, he goes on to highlight what makes the experience of playing live with them so special. "One of the most enjoyable aspects of doing these shows is meeting audience members after the gig, to sign autographs, and shake hands, etc. It's really good to hear their comments and stories. It's very gratifying to hear such things as 'I've been waiting 30 years to hear these songs!' In some cases, so have I."

In 2011, McDonald began an association with actor and singer Ted Zurkowski, scoring music for Zurkowski's productions of Shakespeare's plays – which led to McDonald joining Zurkowski's group Honey West. Speaking to the Improper Music website, McDonald outlined his involvement: "I didn't really want to form another band initially. After being excused from Foreigner, I went through a period of readjusting, and I did do various other things. Flashing forward a number of years, I felt that I still wanted to get involved in something that I could really dig into, and that's when I met Ted Zurkowski. That opportunity arose after I heard his original version of the Honey West band. I felt I could help in some way and that they could also help me get back into something major. I saw this mutually beneficial opportunity to create an album and to enhance the band, which I feel we've done, and I'm very proud of it."

The band's 2017 debut *Bad Old World* was warmly received on websites such as Sea Of Tranquility: "If you've heard *Drivers Eyes* then what you'll find on the Honey West debut, *Bad Old World*, won't come as too much of a shock, a mix of AOR and gentle prog riding a strong rock'n'roll heart and Zurkowski's wry overview of everyday life. Self-deprecating, yet never flippant, it's clear to see why McDonald was so taken by the musings of his writing partner, the sideways glances the likes of *Dementia* and the title track provide, sharp enough to make you smile and shake your head simultaneously."

ANDY McCULLOCH (19 November 1945)
After McCulloch's first post-Crimson band, Fields, folded he became a founder member of Greenslade. "We played together in Stanmore, where Dave Greenslade lived, in the village hall there. It was really good. That was really nice because the band was from scratch. It wasn't like the Crimson thing where you're moving into someone else's seat and carrying on. I learnt a hell of a lot in Crimson and I don't

want to knock it but later on, in Greenslade, you were allowed to develop your style in the way that you wanted to do. You were a part of the band and you were expected to fix your part – this is the song, let's arrange it, develop and then the whole band would play it. I was able to do a fair bit of what I liked to do." The band made their live debut at Frankfurt's Zoom Club in November 1972 less than a month after the *Larks'*-era Crimson had unveiled their new line-up. Later that month, Greenslade recorded their self-titled debut record, released by Warner Brothers the following year, the first of four albums for the label until their demise in 1976.

"Unless you're a composer, drummers don't make a lot of money," says McCulloch. "Jon Hiseman, for example, made his money writing the lyrics. It's quite sad in a way and as we had a bit of time free between albums and touring I wanted to make some new flight cases for my drums. They came out pretty well, so somebody asked if I could make some for them and from there it took off really and I formed a company called Bulldog Cases and did that for a few years."

McCulloch also worked with Peter Gabriel. "I liked his work enormously. We did a try-out session where we played some tracks and things, and knocked around some ideas. He was playing with lots of people and trying to make up his mind how he was going to do it and who he was going to play with. He ended up doing a lot more with American musicians but I really enjoyed playing with him."

McCulloch eventually retired from music in order to build a successful career as a yacht master running his own commercial boat hire around the Mediterranean. He says that sailing and travel was always in the family's blood going back generations. "My father was in marine engineering and I've always been fascinated with boats but it took me until about age of 30 to step on a sailing boat and say 'this is what I want'. I took it up quite seriously and became an instructor and examiner and I've done races across to America and things like that. After you get six years of bashing around in the heavy seas 'round the UK then you want to do the Mediterranean (*laughs*). I spend most of my season out there. I love the life and I love the sea."

RICHARD PALMER-JAMES (11 June 1947)
Looking back on his time growing up in Bournemouth, Richard Palmer-James remembers experiencing an epiphany with John Wetton at Lagland Street Boys' Club. "It was a cellar in a church-run youth club and it had a heavy R'n'B scene. In 1964, we saw a band called The Classics playing Chuck Berry stuff. It was a very important night for John and I and we were introduced to the fact that rock'n'roll was more than just Cliff and The Shadows. They had everything going for them; they smoked on stage and their clothes looked like they'd been wearing them for the last two weeks."

Palmer-James recalls that Wetton became friends with Fripp, who already had a reputation as a guitarist to watch. "In Bournemouth, Fripp was already a legend because of the stuff he'd been doing and because of his dexterity. He was a legendary guitarist because he didn't play like anyone else and his playing isn't blues based. Right from the very beginning, he was very skilful at surrounding himself with an aura of question marks. The things he did with The League Of Gentlemen in Bournemouth was quite adult, tricky stuff. His name was mentioned in awe. He was renowned as an exceptional instrumentalist. I didn't know him personally but I'd seen him play in the mid-'60s in places like the Bure Club which was just outside Christchurch on the eastern side of Bournemouth."

Palmer-James formed The Corvettes, going on to work with The Palmer-James Group and in 1968 forming Tetrad. "We tried Tetrad a year. We managed to pay off some of the debt to my parents which had been pending for some time for a Vox AC30 and various bits of equipment although we'd built our own PA system which was pretty adventurous. Then we decided the name Tetrad was too obscure and sounded too academic, so we called the group Ginger Man after JP Donleavy's novel which was very in at the time because it was a bit risqué, generally about drunkenness and debauchery not realising, of course, that it's Cockney rhyming slang: Ginger Man > Ginger Beer = queer. We didn't twig that at all which shows how naïve we were. It didn't help.

"We were kiboshed anyway. We weren't earning any money and we were realising that playing covers wasn't the way to go and so we amicably decided to call it a day. We had a great final gig in a girls' school in Salisbury or somewhere which was absolutely wonderful and that was it."

Parting company with Wetton, Palmer-James co-founded Supertramp in the summer of 1969. "It was a beautiful late summer, September going into October, and we started putting songs together for the first Supertramp album. Then we were in Germany for six weeks at the PN Club which was a baptism of fire. It was really professional stuff. We weren't playing about anymore. I was the lyricist because nobody else wanted to write the words and that's what started me off. I wasn't too comfortable with that at first. Considering that I've more or less lived from writing lyrics since then, if you ever aspire to be a rock'n'roll star then it's a pretty boring part of the job writing the goddam lyrics. But on the other hand, of course, as I didn't know at that time but discovered later, you could hit the jackpot through some freak of chance and be part of a song that then went on to be very successful. The reason I was happy about joining Supertramp in the first place was there was a retainer. In 1969, when we were living out in the country we only got £6 a week. Even that seemed like El Dorado in the rock and roll scene at the time, getting regular money. It's the kind of thing you can do when you're 21 or 23. It was incredibly idealistic in some ways."

After Supertramp's debut album, Palmer-James left the band. "We were very disparate characters involved. We weren't really made for one another, and I was aware that I was rocking the boat. I hate to admit this but I really thought I knew a lot more at the time than I did. In fact I knew practically nothing at all. I was a complete greenhorn but I had this arrogance I carried with me of having been to college. It makes me cringe to think about it. It was basically my fault. I was superior and pompous and I must have been absolutely unbearable and not easy to get along with."

After a spell back home in Bournemouth, Palmer-James returned to Germany and established himself in Munich in 1971. After working once again with John Wetton on lyrics for *Larks' Tongues In Aspic* in 1972, he joined a band called Emergency. "They were doing a kind of jazz-rock, strenuous and very nervy. The year after in '73, we did lots of stuff. Lots of touring, lots of gigs. We made a record and I was working on music for a TV series."

After his work with King Crimson, Palmer-James continued to work on the Munich scene and at one point was an active producer in German disco. After years in the industry, continuing to supply lyrics for Wetton's solo career and also for David Cross's band, in 2017 he released his first solo album, *Takeaway*. "Having spent the last few decades writing words for other people to sing, and thus being obliged to comply with the ambitions and sensibilities of others, I wanted to present a collection of songs that are uncompromisingly my own. I've been trying them out in club and pub appearances as a singer-songwriter, and they seem to work, but I'm very curious to see what sort of reaction this album production, which was realised with the indispensable help of a few talented colleagues from the Munich music scene, might elicit. The recordings differ stylistically from most of the stuff I worked on as a hired hand – probably because I enjoy playing acoustic instruments and writing pieces which involve storytelling."

PETER SINFIELD (27 December 1943)

In the aftermath of King Crimson, EG Management nudged Sinfield into production work and, in the summer of 1972, he helped guide Roxy Music's debut album to fruition. He provided lyrics and production for *Photos Of Ghosts* (1973) and *The World Became The World* (1974) for Italian group PFM, who were signed to ELP's Manticore label. After Manticore released his post-Crimson solo album *Still* (1973), in 1974 he published a slim collection of poetry and lyrics, *Under The Sky*, which has since become a highly sought-after collectors' item. Sinfield's association with Greg Lake continued in ELP, with Sinfield providing lyrics for *Brain Salad Surgery* (1973), *Works, Volumes I & II* (1977) and *Love Beach* (1978). During the '80s and the '90s, he was responsible for co-writing highly successful hit singles for artists such as Cher, Bucks Fizz, Five Star, Cliff Richard, Celine Dion and others.

Sinfield has contributed lyrics to solo projects by David Cross, John Wetton and, perhaps most notably, Ian McDonald's debut solo album *Drivers Eyes* (1999). He also provided revised lyrics for Jakko Jaszyk's rearranged cover of King Crimson's *Pictures Of A City* on Jakszyk's solo album *The Bruised Romantic Glee Club* (2007). Recast with sitar-like guitars, tabla and vocals from Pandit Dinesh, it was retitled *Pictures Of An Indian City*.

In 2014, Fripp invited Sinfield to provide an updated take on the lyrics of *21st Century Schizoid Man*, renewing their partnership, albeit briefly and at a distance, in line with Fripp's mission to have the music, and in this instance, the lyrics reimagined for the new Crimson. He wrote:

Cat's foot, iron claw
Sykes, Picot and the fat cigar
Knuckles dragging in the desert sand
Twenty First Century Schizoid Man
Blood rack, dark wire
Politician's funeral pyre
Cursed and poisoned
Bless his heart
Twenty First Century Schizoid Man
Death seed, Blind men's greed
Poet's starving children bleed
Nothing he's got he really needs
Twenty First Century Schizoid Man

Highlighting the shift of American foreign policy from Asia in the original lyric to later Middle East adventures, it was sung for the new Crimson's first tour in 2014 before the band reverted to the original lyric. Sinfield took part in 1997's *Epitaph* playback and the Steven Wilson/King Crimson playback at AIR Studios in 2009.

A keen cook and gardener, living on the Suffolk coast in the town of Aldeburgh, famed for its international music festival, Sinfield has now largely retired.

KEITH TIPPETT (25 August 1947)

Although best-known in rock circles for his work with King Crimson, Keith Tippett is surely one of the most important composers and players to have emerged from the UK in the 1960s jazz scene. "David Bowie told Robin Lumley, who told me, that in America I'm known as an avant-garde rock piano player. And if people are moved by my work with King Crimson then I wish they'd go and hunt out my own stuff. If they liked my piano playing on *Islands* then they'd surely love my piano playing on my solo work."

Over the years Tippett released many acclaimed albums, including 1978's large-scale work on the double album *Frames (Music For An Imaginary Film)*, and in 2011 guested on the Michael Giles' MAD Band album *In The Moment*. 2015 saw the release of the stunning *Live In Piacenza*, a 50-minute continuous performance encompassing touching lyricism, tottering playfulness and ground-shaking thunder chords, digging rich emotional seams and personal resonance.

In 2016, he released *The Nine Dances Of Patrick O'Gonogon*, a score for his octet.

Intense and bracing, with plenty of wild, horn-dominated punches tempered by thoughtful use of tender melody, it is music of depth and beauty, an absorbing work by one of the greatest players of his generation. In 2018, ill-health forced him to take time out from playing live though it is hoped he will return to the stage in 2019.

IAN WALLACE (**29 September 1946–22 February 2007**)
It's almost easier to write a list of the people Ian Wallace *didn't* play with after his time in King Crimson such was his ubiquity on the live circuit and recording studios in his adoptive United States. Among his colleagues were Peter Frampton, Jackson Browne, The Travelling Wilburys, Alvin Lee, two separate stints with Bob Dylan in the '70s and '90s, Warren Zevon, Crosby, Stills and Nash, Jon Anderson, Eric Clapton, Steve Marriot, Joe Walsh, Don Henley, Bonnie Rait and many, many more. His rapprochement with Robert Fripp came when the guitarist was in dispute with EG Management attempting to wrest control of the KC catalogue and gain unpaid royalties.

Moving to Nashville in the late '90s, Wallace later became friends with Adrian Belew, occasionally meeting up with Robert Fripp on his visits to Belew's house and studio complex. In early 2003, Wallace recalls he was on the road and "depressed in a van somewhere in Colorado when Mel rang me on my phone and asked me if I wanted to join the band". Replacing Michael Giles, he played Russia, Italy, Greece, Holland, Belgium, France, Spain, Japan, Mexico and the West and East coasts of the USA with the 21st Century Schizoid Band. With no label or finance behind the group, playing in the band was a labour of love, Wallace said, going on to forcefully point out: "Without Jakko pulling everything together, we wouldn't have been able to play a single solitary note."

Writing in the liner notes to *Pictures Of A City – Live In New York*, Wallace recalled the shows at BB King's as being particularly good. "As a rule I enjoy playing two shows in one night. The first show gets you used to the sounds on the stage and loosens you up for the second show where you can forget about the technicalities, enabling you to relax and just blow. And we did just that. Playing this music again after 30 years was just so much fun. It made me feel like I was 25 again. Especially doing it with my old mate Mel, who hasn't lost a step. I hadn't played with Peter (Giles) previously, though I had played with Ian (McDonald), albeit briefly in the late '70s, though I'd got to know him and he's a good friend, but Jakko? Now there's a revelation. Do you know how difficult it is to sing so superbly and play those extremely difficult Fripp licks at the same time?"

Wallace's love of jazz had previously been expressed on an album with pianist Brian Trainor. Working under the name of the Wallace Trainor Conspiracy, the partnership's 1997's *Take A Train* contained an idiosyncratic merging of Thelonious Monk's *Evidence* and Crimson's *21st Century Schizoid Man.* Dubbed *Evdoid Suite*, it also contained a guest appearance from Ian McDonald.

Wallace's desire to blend KC with jazz was consolidated with the formation of the Crimson Jazz Trio. Their first album, *King Crimson Songbook, Volume One*, was released in 2005, featuring pianist Jody Nardone and bassist Tim Landers. The CJ3 reworked KC tunes including *Three Of A Perfect Pair*, *Ladies Of The Road*, *Red* and *Cat Food*. Reviewing the album, All About Jazz's John Kelman noted that the music was "not only surprisingly faithful to the essence of the eight songs it covers, but the general arrangements as well, while shifting them firmly into the jazz mainstream", going on to note: "The title track from *Red* – a hugely influential song to progressive metal groups like Tool – works best. It clearly references the elements that define the original, but it's more liberally worked over, with a funky rethinking of the orchestral middle section featuring a powerful drum solo from Wallace. *King Crimson Songbook, Volume One* is an intriguing reshaping of material from a band that has always had a tenuous relationship with the jazz aesthetic. If there's a *Volume Two*, perhaps more time together will find CJ3 taking more risks with the material, a move more in keeping with the ongoing Crimson spirit of Robert Fripp."

Wallace maintained an online diary on the DGM website and after Robert Fripp's own journal it was the most arrived-at destination on the site. Wallace regaled readers of his life with his wife Margie, their dog Hagi and his often-hilarious take on the events going on in the world around him. Always happy to engage with fans, Wallace announced in 2006 that he was suffering from oesophageal cancer. In a response both baffling and upsetting, the owner of a Crimson fan website used his platform to belittle Wallace and make fun of the diagnosis with a series of offensive remarks. Even after Wallace's passing the abuse continued, though now directed at Margie.

At Ian's memorial service on 22 March 2007, at the Amadeus Centre in London's Little Venice, Jakko and Mel performed *Islands* and Robert Fripp gave the eulogy. "Ian Wallace was a man of faith: he believed that the power of music could give life value. Few professional players retain, through a long career, their passion for music. The finest tribute I can pay to Ian, the musician, is to acknowledge that, after 40 years of professional life, his passion continued undiminished, Ian's musicianship a reflection of his humanity.

"In Ian's playing, both as a young man and an older man, I never saw him, I never heard him, going through the motions. And, Ian's playing was getting better."

"A tribute to Ian, the human being, is the observation that over the period of 35 years in which I knew him, I saw no malice."

"There is no loss in a life well lived, and to its fullest extent. Perhaps, Ian's life was not lived to the extent that was available. But what do we know, standing where we are? Shortly before Pal Wallace flew away, Ian told Margie that he felt he was needed elsewhere. And I'm inclined to the view that Ian knew what he was doing, better than any of us; and I trust Ian's sense of timing."

The Crimson Jazz Trio's *King Crimson Songbook, Volume Two* was released posthumously in 2009 and the appearance of Mel Collins on soprano and tenor saxes widened the scope of the trio on the *Islands* material in a setting that invoked John Coltrane's *A Love Supreme*. Introduced by a meditative drum solo, and some McCoy Tyner-like scene setting, rather than a straightforward cover, the *Islands* suite was a more abstract reading with familiar themes recast into darting motifs, scurrying runs and deft games of hide-and-seek phrasing. At the end, Landers' intimate acoustic bass solo almost steals the show. Like the very best of jazz drummers, Ian Wallace's final recording has him constantly adding subtle shades via nimble cymbal work, ensuring either melodic or rhythmic emphasis are achieved with precision and an irrepressible *joie de vivre.* In this life you never know what you'll be remembered for but there's a good chance Ian would've been happy with that.

JOHN WETTON (12 June 1949–31 January 2017)

In the aftermath of King Crimson's implosion in 1974, John Wetton admitted that he didn't quite know what to do with himself. "I had to completely change tack. I just thought I'd tread water for a couple of years. I think Bill did exactly the same thing. He went to Genesis and I went to Roxy Music … it had thrown my plan into disarray."

In 1978, he co-founded UK with Bill Bruford, Eddie Jobson and Allan Holdsworth, their eponymous debut album selling 250,000 copies. After Bruford and Holdsworth were ousted, UK recruited former Frank Zappa drummer Terry Bozzio and released *Danger Money* and live album *Night After Night* in 1979 but the band dissolved.

"The right thing to do for me in 1974 would've been to move to America," Wetton told me as he looked back on his career. "That's exactly what I should have done. I should never have done that fiddling around that I did from 1974 and 1980. The difference in living in America is you walk into someone's office and it's a 'yes' before it's a 'no'. In the UK, it's a 'no' before it's a 'yes' unfortunately."

America gave John and specifically, his next band, Asia, an emphatic "yes", providing him with the large-scale canvas he'd yearned for.

"I think in the early days I was very much a bass player who sang and by the time we get to Asia around 1981 I'm a singer who plays bass. In fact it happened about two years before Asia with a solo album called *Caught In The Crossfire*. By that time I was feeling that the bass wasn't going to carry me through this career. In order to express myself I was going to have to put the emphasis on the singing. If you look at *Caught In The Crossfire*, Asia was almost an extension of that album. That's where I laid out my stall, and now I need to get some guys to play that kind of thing and we can launch it on the public."

The global success of Asia took everyone by surprise. Wetton recalls that executives at Geffen Records were decidedly underwhelmed. "I was in Los Angeles and they were looking at the record. They didn't like the cover, hated the logo and said they couldn't hear anything commercial on the thing. Of course it took off and sold somewhere in the nine million ballpark. I remember *Heat Of The Moment* was on a compilation album which sold four million in Germany alone!"

The success came with a price tag, though, and Wetton's drinking soon got the better of him. In 1983, after the release of their second album *Alpha* (1983), Wetton was forced out of the band. Speaking to *Classic Rock Revisited* in 2012, Wetton talked about his battle with alcoholism and how it had marred his career and his time with Asia. "I'm a dyed-in-the-wool alcoholic, but I don't drink these days. All I can tell you is that people would say 'Oh it was the pressure', but no it wasn't, it was just the course of that particular illness. It gets worse no matter what happens. If it's a lovely day, it gets worse; if it's a bad day, it gets worse. Yes, I was in a shocking state. I'd like to say that I wasn't the only one, but the responsibility ultimately lay with me so I have to take that responsibility. If I had been the rest of the band I'd have gotten rid of me too."

The root of John's unhappiness may never be known but his long slide into alcoholism dragged him into the depths. I witnessed John in the grip of the illness in 2000 after being invited to Bournemouth to scour his personal archive for King Crimson-related material. Though we'd often spoken at length on the telephone when it was obvious that John was drinking, I had no idea how ill he was. I arrived a little after 10.00 am and John offered me a can of lager, already a few tins ahead of me.

The months and years ahead were very difficult times for John who went on to experience a variety of personal and professional setbacks. This is not to be sensationalist but to convey the extent of John's spirit and determination after he was able to achieve sobriety and come back from the brink. His recovery from alcoholism was aided by the urge to go back to doing what he used to do so well. The love and support of a good woman, his soulmate and now widow, American musician Lisa Nojaim, meant his later years were productive and filled with a giddy happiness, despite the fact he needed emergency heart surgery in 2007 – about which he wrote *An Extraordinary Life* from Asia's aptly named *Phoenix*, released in 2008.

In 2014, Wetton was diagnosed with cancer and, after a period that included contracting sepsis, he died on 31 January 2017, just a few days after marrying Lisa.

Lyricist Richard Palmer-James had a special appreciation for John's ability to bring out the best in songs. "In John's whole body of work there are a few moments that implicitly open the floodgates and you hear very deep, emotional things coming through. He doesn't sing it emotionally but somehow in the background, if you want to hear it, then he's talking directly to you about his own disappointment or pain or whatever. I'm thinking specifically of *Who Will Light A Candle?* from 2003's *Rock Of*

Faith album. There's an emotional outpouring that I didn't intend in the lyric but he grabbed it and took it far beyond anything I would have dared to. There's a little bit of that in King Crimson's *Starless* and I think that's part of the impact of the track."

In a touching tribute to his old Asia bandmate, Carl Palmer wrote: "John was a gentle person who created some of the most lasting melodies and lyrics in modern popular music. As a musician, he was both brave and innovative, with a voice that took the music of Asia to the top of the charts around the world. His ability to triumph over alcohol abuse made him an inspiration to many who have also fought that battle. For those of us who knew him and worked with him, his valiant struggle against cancer was a further inspiration. I will miss his talent, his sense of humour and his infectious smile."

On the news of John's passing, Robert Fripp said: "During the past decade, JW became a hero of mine, courageous and exemplary in dealing and speaking frankly of his alcoholism. Visiting John during not-so-good times, and then good times, we became closer than in the three previous decades; John's conversation was wonderfully clear, honest, positive, encouraging. And then Lisa. Hooray! to whom thank you for making my friend a happy man."

John left behind a solo career that saw over 20 albums released under his name and numerous collaborations that included stints with Phil Manzanera, Steve Hackett, Wishbone Ash and Icon, his project with Geoff Downes.

Track by Track

GILES, GILES & FRIPP

THE CHEERFUL INSANITY OF GILES, GILES & FRIPP

North Meadow
(P. Giles)
Peter cites the land surrounding Bournemouth as the inspiration for this bucolic reverie. "I've always loved the country and it was just an imaginary thing about a rural setting. When I was in the school holidays in Bournemouth I just used to bugger off for the whole day going bird nesting and chasing squirrels and getting up to all sorts of mischief. I love the trees and the wildlife. It's not based on anything, it's just purely imaginary." With its bright clarion introduction and rich harmonies lovingly varnished in reverb, the track is as quintessential a piece of 1960s sunshine as you're likely to hear.

The Saga Of Rodney Toady, Parts 1–5
(Fripp)
This unkind script is played for laughs as Fripp affects to stutter out the tale of a young misfit and his parents. Its inclusion fatally wounds the album, despite being an indicator as to what made the boys laugh during the long winter evenings in Brondesbury Road. "I believe Peter Sinfield thought it was autobiographical!" says Fripp. "The story was longer than appeared on the record and featured a tale I had learnt from a college chum in Bournemouth, whose mother worked at Boscombe Hospital. Apparently a man came into outpatients with a vacuum cleaner attachment stuck on his pecker!"

Newly-Weds
(P. Giles)
With a lilting introduction reminiscent of Pink Floyd's psychedelic whimsy, this cautionary tale about the dubious merits of early marriage counts as one Michael Giles' favourite examples of his brother's writing. "*Newly-Weds* was all about young people getting together: 'Don't they know it's their lives that they're gambling?' I mean, where does he get that from? He had no experience of marriage or relationships!" In

fact, it was Michael himself who had married in his teens, having two children with his first wife. "Maybe he was looking at me? I don't know – I'll have to ask him!" His younger brother only recalls the song was simply based on observation and an engaged imagination.

One In A Million
(M. Giles)
Michael had in mind the kind of territory which Ray Davies made his own, as he chronicles the foibles of the bourgeoisie at home and play in this short song with a jaunty, comedic presentation. In this humble, unassuming setting, the Mellotron makes its debut appearance on the album, the beginning of its long association with Fripp.

Call Tomorrow
(P. Giles)
Peter Giles recounts this lachrymose tale of unrequited love and unwanted pregnancy, largely unaccompanied over a suitably mournful Hammond organ. The descending chords of the chorus beautifully capture bitter rejection and loneliness, as the narrator forlornly trudges away to lick his wounds.

Digging My Lawn
(P. Giles)
Small but perfectly formed, the track remains one of Michael Giles' favourites. "One of the titles of Robert's songs was *Erudite Eyes* but it's Peter who had the erudite eyes in terms of the words. I don't know where it comes from but I'm just glad it was there. 'There was a man that I didn't know digging my lawn.' I mean, what the fuck's that about?" Played to perfection with a knowing poise, the humour is perfectly balanced by the pastiche cocktail lounge jazz setting. Light, witty and easily the best of its kind on the entire album.

Little Children
(Fripp)
Though not without a certain charm, *Little Children* is not to be confused with the tale of thwarted lust which Billy J. Kramer and The Dakotas took into the charts in 1964. Michael Giles' vocal has an agreeable warmth but the genteel arrangement and pace merely highlight the fact that there is little of substance in this piece composed by Fripp at the Majestic Hotel in Bournemouth. Fripp agrees, describing the track as "utter crap", and adding: "It should have been rejected."

The Crukster
(M. Giles, Fripp)
Peter Giles remembers that *The Crukster* began life as a piece of poetry his brother had written two years earlier. "We tried that at home and it was an idea by my brother which was like a spoken thing which Fripp accompanied, very free-form-ish. I used the

tape delay echo to make it explode at the end. I was just practising my recording while the other two just did what they wanted."

The guitar parts reveal the fast cross-picking style which Fripp had developed in Bournemouth under the tutelage of Don Strike, and in places one can detect a glimmer of the kind of playing he would deliver in the fast section of *21st Century Schizoid Man*. Michael Giles explains the origins of the word Crukster. "Well Crux sounds a bit like the crux or the cross or the crutch. It's all in that area. 'The Crukster', I suppose, is someone who is having difficulty with the crux of the matter."

Thursday Morning
(M. Giles)
Michael Giles demonstrates that it wasn't just his brother who was inspired by the beauty of nature in his native county. "It's meant to be a slice of English pastoral. It's meant to be a celebration of the summer, no problem with the world; you can just be, you can just float."

How Do They Know
(M. Giles)
With a punchy opening, this rousing number sees Michael Giles asking questions about popular demagogues and manipulation in modern life. It's the closest the band gets to rocking out. Despite its brevity, the track demonstrates what an effective and inventive drummer Giles is. Built upon three rhythmic motifs, it is probably the best mix of relaxed walking jazz and potentially powerful pop on the album. It is also one of the few tracks where the trio play without embellishment or the accompaniment of Decca's in-house arranger Ivor Raymonde – and sounds all the better for it.

Just George, Parts 1–4
(M. Giles)
The sentence "I know a man and his name is George" probably speaks volumes about the tedium of life on the road and the humour needed as a coping mechanism. On the other hand, it might well be the kind of thing which relieves the boredom of a slow afternoon, looking through the classifieds for dance band gigs. "Where did that come from? Why did I write 16 lines all based on one – turning it all 'round?" asks a bemused Michael Giles.

Peter recalls the piece enabled the pair to go through their repertoire of daft voices recalling the time spent with Trendsetters.

Elephant Song
(M. Giles)
Written quickly in the summer of 1967. Underneath the comic upper-class twit accent lurks someone who feels like an animal in a zoo, poked and prodded and open to

ridicule or indifference. By Michael's own admission, this is pretty surreal. "What I love about writing words and music is when it comes quickly and freely and then of course it's a question of organising it. It wasn't any struggle to write it. It just came and it's about the absurd performer/audience situation one finds oneself in."

The Sun Is Shining
(M. Giles)
Ivor Raymonde pulled out all the stops and provided the song not just with top-notch backing vocalists but two trombones, two violas, two celli and six violins! It's likely that this track alone will have accounted for most of the album budget. Peter Giles recalls it as "a complete piss-take on heavy ballads. We had The Breakaways on backing vocals, who really hammed it up beautifully without overdoing it." They sail fairly close to the wind, though – and, even if the band knew it was played for laughs, did the listener? Once again, in slightly improbable circumstances, Michael Giles provides a solid vocal.

Suite No. 1
(Fripp)
Sounding like Jacques Loussier on speed, Fripp whips along at a rate of knots in this awkward agglomeration of sketches and scraps. Not so much a fully fledged composition as an exercise, it nevertheless is clear evidence of just how handy Fripp could be with a plectrum. Fripp later recycled the calm reflective section hummed by the Giles brothers and called it *Prelude: Song Of The Gulls*. Slightly expanded, it was arranged for a small chamber orchestra and can be heard on the Crimson album *Islands*, released three years later.

Erudite Eyes
(Fripp)
The success of King Crimson meant that the GG&F album was later eagerly sought out and examined by enthusiasts far more closely than during the time of its initial release. For the most part, fans seeking clues to where Crimson came from were baffled by the overall lightness of the album. Perhaps only this and the preceding track offer any hint of what lay ahead. The modal nature of *Erudite Eyes*, with its free-form section, offered new possibilities which excited all three players. Michael: "We'd found an area of freedom where you weren't a jazzer or a rocker, you just got into this other zone. It's an exciting place to be. There are some fabulous moments where you've got an instrument in front of you and you've got the ability to manipulate this set of tools, this instrument. You get to a higher level and something else is playing you, something else is telling you what to do."

Peter Giles confirms the springboard nature of the track. "This wasn't me playing, it was another part of me playing and I was just the agent for that. So make yourself into a channel for that kind of music and that was brilliant … part of the spirit was about being able to disregard all the rules in music, because you've followed them so carefully for so long, you're then in a position to break them."

Of these last two tracks, the guitarist adds: "These two pieces are my distinctive contribution to the album. It highlights the growing conceptual distance between Peter and myself, as the young man from Dorset begins to find his feet and his own approach."

IN THE COURT OF THE CRIMSON KING
21st Century Schizoid Man
including **Mirrors**
(Fripp, McDonald, Lake, Giles, Sinfield)

This track deservedly became one of the most celebrated Crimson pieces. Its origins lay in disparate pieces like a jigsaw, only coming together when the wider picture was fully available. Fripp came up with the precocious fast middle section during 1968 and Greg Lake recalls a sense of mounting frustration as they tried vainly to make it work.

Fripp remembers: "Greg's idea was the first part of the opening heavy riff, telling me to play a C minor block chord while he sang over it. Ian suggested the F, F#, G addition to the riff. I donated the fast running lines. Michael suggested the band phrase the stop section together. A group effort."

Although opening the album, it was the last to be recorded, completed in one barnstorming take in the early hours of Friday, 1 August. Any self-congratulation was strictly curtailed, as McDonald explains: "Well, we're a funny sort of band because we didn't remark on that sort of thing. We didn't pat each other on the back and say, 'Hey great, we did it in one.' We just said, 'OK, that's it.' We were just too busy getting the album made to even relish too many moments like that, apart from later on when things were taking shape and we were coming to the end of the album, then we could start to see what we were making."

Opening with the sound of air blowing through the reed organ, the song quickly moves into one of the most definitive and recognisable chord sequences in rock music. Brought into the band by Greg Lake, the weighty brutality of the opening riff is suggestive of George Orwell's visualisation of a totalitarian future in the novel *1984*: "A boot stamping on a human face – forever."

Summoning an anti-capitalist/war message with startling lucidity and force, the lyric avoids evoking a specific time or place. It is this very ambiguity which has lent the song a universality making it applicable to Kosovo or Syria as it does to Vietnam and Cold War hawks policing the policy of Mutually Assured Destruction.

Lake's overdriven and filtered vocals lend a rasping dehumanised aspect over the stabbing guitar, itself subjected to a slightly altering filter with each stroke in the verses. The snarling menace of the first section and the verses is in fact executed without any of the leaden or ponderous thumping which bedevilled many a future prog and HM copyist, where "heavy" often meant loud or blundering. Crimson's refusal to opt for lumpen riffing is perhaps the distinctive feature of this album.

After Lake's opening gambit coupled with McDonald's ascending chromatic wind-up, the track accelerates into a bebop-like phrase dating from Ian McDonald's Army days. The tune was originally part of a big band composition of his called *Three Score And Four* which stayed with him, finally finding its true home during the rehearsals in January 1969. As Lake's unfaltering bass deftly locks together with Giles' crisp snare, the band captures some of the adrenaline drive and fervour which made them so vibrant in concert.

Recorded three days after the backing track on the evening of 4 August, the guitar solo lasts a little over a minute but is brimming with tension and urgency. Like the rest of the band, Fripp had been in attendance as McDonald worked on the elements of his solo and only when that was finished several hours later did he lay down his own contribution. Perhaps it was this which gives his solo its sense of pace. Although the solo was laid down in around 30 minutes, it had taken him 12 years of practising and preparation to be ready for this moment. Fripp himself regards the solo as "worthwhile in context but as a solo not exceptional".

The remainder of the instrumental section is occupied by McDonald's malefic solo and here he decides not to extemporise on the principal themes and phrases established so far, instead ploughing across the driving 12/8 pulse, suggesting an affinity with the New York experimentalism of Ornette Coleman.

The brash sneer of the double-tracked solo belies the painstaking method of its construction, as he explains: "I do remember I was having trouble with that solo, getting it angst-ridden enough. It was coming out too nice and so I remember putting myself into uncomfortable positions, sort of like kneeling on a hard floor and making myself uncomfortable because it wasn't coming out angry enough. So what you hear, I'm probably contorted. The end of that solo's funny too. We were only on eight tracks and it ends very abruptly because we had to punch into that track to record something else." The end result of those hours was to produce a writhing knot, seething with paranoia, stridently post-Parker and utterly caustic.

After momentarily re-establishing the *Three Score And Four* theme, the track unexpectedly veers off into an ascending flurry of notes before coming to a breakneck halt. This device – along with the 6/8 + 3/4 figure – was Fripp's compositional contribution, though it was Michael Giles' suggestion to play it in unison. In this audacious moment of dynamic unity, one can hear the hours of endless rehearsing which made this section so razor-edged.

The effect stunned the audiences. Even when Crimson resurrected the piece with the Double Trio on tour in 1996, the twisting spiral of notes and the punch of silence at the end of each section remained immensely powerful.

As a whole, the piece also avoids the lengthy bombast which blights much of the progressive oeuvre in which Crimson is often placed and for which the track became something of a template. But, though many would try, very few would get anywhere near the economy and flair of Crimson's original.

As the track finally burns into the chaos that has been threatening to engulf it since its beginning, one has the sense of a world spinning madly out of control. What lends *21st Century Schizoid Man* its continued potency is the certainty of the performances and their astonishing delivery.

I Talk To The Wind
(McDonald, Sinfield)
This pastoral respite briefly illustrates the folk-tinged side of Crimson. Recorded on Tuesday, 29 July, the day after a well-received gig at Friars in Aylesbury, it was the second track tackled at Wessex. Opening with a charming flourish on double-tracked flutes, Lake's honeyed voice is augmented by an ephemeral harmony provided live by McDonald at the same time. Though the timid nature of his vocal contribution still causes him regret, it's his strength as an arranger and soloist which capture the attention. The ruminative introspection of the clarinet adds a dark veneer to the bright air of naïveté.

In concert the song was taken at a much livelier pace and, of course, originally began with McDonald playing acoustic guitar at Brondesbury Road. "There's been a quote that's been floating around for years that 'When you've got Robert Fripp in the band you just don't play guitar'. In fact, I should have played guitar on the album version in my opinion but it was out of the question because I was doing all the woodwind and keyboard stuff and all the rest of it. At that point it was performed in A, but this was changed over to E once it became part of the Crimson repertoire in order to accommodate the flute solo."

The track as a whole is cosseted in a halo of smudgy reverb, which helps trace the passage of McDonald's graceful flute solo and does much to create the piece's laid-back complexion. By comparison, Fripp's spartan passage is hazy and somewhat cloying. Dancing interplay between the flute and drums finishes the track. However, on this occasion the perfect solo eluded McDonald and so two separate takes were combined. The edit point can be heard at 5:23, as McDonald explains: "The drop-in on the coda is quite noticeable because the stereo panning is different. I did two solos on different tracks and what that is punching out of one solo and going into another one and the flute drops down an octave. The beginning of one was good and the end of the other was good."

Epitaph
including **March For No Reason** and **Tomorrow And Tomorrow**
(Fripp, McDonald, Lake, Giles, Sinfield)
Unlike *Schizoid Man*, whose constituent parts are more easily assigned, there are

competing claims as to who wrote what parts of this classic tune. Lake is certain that he contributed the main melody while McDonald resolutely holds that the melody and main chords are his. Fripp simply says: "This piece was collaborative. Period."

The track was a while in the making and the "Tomorrow I'll be crying" section only emerged at the band's rehearsal on Tuesday, 27 May. On Friday, 6 June, McDonald wrote out the lead sheets for *Epitaph* as well as *Cadence And Cascade*, so it seems fair to assume the piece was only finally completed by this date.

Recorded on Wednesday, 30 July, the song took a marathon ten hours to complete. When the session started a little after 11.30 am McDonald had been out the previous night and had had little sleep. If the backing track proved difficult to capture then tiredness may therefore have been a factor.

The song is a sombre consideration of the precarious Cold War situation toward which the planet appeared to be slouching. Yet, despite the piece's doom-laden nature, it has a disquieting and awesome beauty and sounds as fresh as the day it was recorded. Lake was born to sing these words and his phrasing and delivery are faultless. His task is helped by a quality production hardly to have been expected from a relatively inexperienced group whose average age then was around 23.

The maturity of *Epitaph* and its realisation is arguably the album's crowning achievement, littered as it is with numerous subtleties, the Mellotron's Arctic bite and Michael Giles' bracing signature drum sound. Not that Giles would agree with this assessment. "I hope the signature is in the playing, not the sound. It's not the sound I asked for. It was something which throughout the short span of King Crimson that I was continually frustrated with. Outside of those couple of sessions at Morgan, everything we did at Wessex or Tony Clarke was just compressed and fucked about with. There was not a lot of reality about the drum-kit from my point of view."

The timpani at opening and closing appear almost by accident, having been left over from another session. Their inclusion does much to give the track its sense of stature and scale as, of course, does the Mellotron which receives its first dramatic outing here. One of the great spine-tingling moments occurs in the opening moments of the first verse as Lake sings "Upon the instruments of death/the sunlight brightly gleams." It's at this point the Mellotron frostily spreads underneath the vocals, the eerie strings underlining the sense of dread and pessimism.

If Giles has reservations about the drum sound, McDonald has none. "I think it's my favourite track on the album. It's just a beautifully structured song and a perfect vehicle for Greg. In my opinion, it's Greg's best vocal performance – anywhere. I think the song is perfectly suited to him and he sings it brilliantly. I think it's very atmospheric – it has this doom-laden thing about it but I think it's beautiful in its own way."

Lake cites the track as his favourite. "I think it is a poignant song. There's a finality to it and in a way it encapsulates a lot of the feelings that there were about the cracks in society. There was this idealistic view of love and flower power and so on but there were cracks and that song somehow typifies that period in time with all its naïveté. As to how well it was sung – well, it was a job. When I listen back to my vocals from that time they sound to me very naïve – all the singing techniques that I didn't find out about until later aren't there and I wince a lot and think, 'Oh fuck you could've done that a lot better.'"

The *March For No Reason* section (beginning at 4:15) contains a sulphurous woodwind arrangement positively simmering with looming peril. The tension is maintained by alternating strokes from the drums and slashing acoustic guitar, wreathed in echo and moving in the stereo mix.

This point in the song is reminiscent of the Moody Blues' 1967 epic *Nights In White Satin* and its middle eight containing Ray Thomas' flute solo, although any suggestion of direct influence is firmly rejected by Crimson's members.

Up until this point, *Epitaph* has been tightly controlled but, once Lake completes his plaintive retelling of the first verse, the playing opens up. At the beginning of the *Tomorrow And Tomorrow* section (6:56), McDonald introduces a searing mixed line on the Mellotron and Giles provides a rallying drum. The Mellotron is particular effective here, shimmering with a glacial beauty.

During the mixing of *Epitaph* and the title track, McDonald developed a technique designed to add a little life to the Mellotron, which could sound rather static in the mix. "I would keep the faders moving continually between the two channels, undulating against each other like waves in order to give some sense of movement and dynamic to the thing, so it's not just sitting there leaden. If you listen carefully the strings have a very slight motion to them."

Moonchild
including **The Dream** and **The Illusion**
(Fripp, McDonald, Lake, Giles, Sinfield)

The backing track to *Moonchild* was recorded on Thursday, 31 August, and is the most fragile piece on the album. Because of this, the track is often overlooked and, indeed, the improvised section was excised completely by Fripp for the 1991 *Frame By Frame* boxed set. Yet the inclusion of *The Dream* and *The Illusion* (or "the free thing", as the band knew it at the time) captures a different side to Crimson, one just as vital to an understanding of the group's psyche as the breakneck *Schizoid Man* or the Gothic title track.

The ballad section was first rehearsed in the café basement in February – Fripp: "The melody was mainly written by RF and Ian fine-tuned its details. The middle section is all RF, I believe. The guitar line and solo was a guide track, which was kept. The available time was perhaps also a factor here" – but the decision to include an improvised sequence was as pragmatic as it was artistic, given the band's shortage of material.

From their live set they had available *Get Thy Bearings* (a tune by Donovan from his 1968 album *Hurdy Gurdy Man*), *Travel Weary Capricorn*, *Drop In* and *Mars* but none were deemed suitable, even during the Tony Clarke sessions.

A willingness to explore areas of musical abstraction had long been a characteristic of the group. "We gained increasing confidence in free sections and played without a 'safety net' sometimes resulting in some cliff-hanging moments – very exciting for us and the audience," explains Michael Giles.

The drummer was a frequent visitor to The Old Place in Gerrard Street and the Little Theatre in St Martin-in-the-Fields, behind Trafalgar Square. One of the groups which particularly impressed him was the Spontaneous Music Ensemble, an influential outfit led by drummer John Stevens and featuring some of the leading exponents of the UK free jazz scene, including guitarist Derek Bailey and young percussionist Jamie Muir. Short dissonant strands, a random, atonal scattering of notes and silence performing as much of a role as the playing itself – all were features which applied just as much to anything the SME were doing at the time as they would to the improvised section of *Moonchild*.

The song section opens with Fripp's guitar, taut with sustain in a production enveloped in a wraithlike sound. With its dampened percussion the song has something of a stately pace to it, not unlike a slow, medieval pavane. The courtly dance aspect of the piece obviously appealed to film actor and director Vincent Gallo in his 1998 cult movie *Buffalo 66* in which the track is used in an off-kilter tap dance sequence!

The luminous presence of the vibraphone, an instrument left over from a previous session and played here by McDonald, was very much a last-minute decision. Yet again chance provided a defining sound, setting the tone and feel for the entire piece.

Lake and Sinfield sat in the control room as the others improvised. "We'd just recorded *Moonchild* and Mike's drums were set-up with the muted sound to them. He had towels and things all over them," recalls Ian McDonald. "What's strange about that is that I had the vibes set up in a vocal booth and I had no sightline between me and the other players. I think Fripp and Michael could see each other but I couldn't see them and so all that stuff I'm doing on vibes, I'm just doing totally on headphones. So, there are no visual cues or anything like that. Which might account for part of the sound of the thing."

As the song section finishes, a hazy cloud of vibraphone languidly stretches out, setting up the improvisation between McDonald, Giles and Fripp, in what must be the very first King Crimson fractal. It's well over a minute before Giles joins in with the lightest dot of cymbal, a testament to his desire to listen rather than fall foul of habitual playing.

A few moments later, Fripp turns on the treble pick-up on and the piece takes on a spikier, fragmentary feel with clipped accelerations and slivers of melody abruptly curtailed. It's a kind of musical blind man's buff where the players are trying to guess the identity of what the other is playing. (At 9:50 pm, Fripp plays a snippet of the *Oklahoma!* tune *The Surrey With The Fringe On Top*!)

For Giles, the track continues to provide an example of moving into an area of playing where the musician becomes the vessel. "I do remember on those sessions, that thing about being directed by the great mistress of music in the sky, not being totally in control. And then going back into the control room and playing it back and thinking 'Did I play that? Where did that come from?' There was a moment where Ian is playing the vibes and he does a fast flurry and I do exactly the same on the cymbal. Now where did that come from? How did that happen? There were only the three of us playing. He was at the other end of the studio and there was nothing pre-arranged and yet at the same time we both do a trill. You couldn't have designed it. You couldn't have thought it out."

The Court Of The Crimson King
including **The Return Of The Fire Witch** and **The Dance Of The Puppets (McDonald, Sinfield)**

Sinfield started putting together these words – then set to a Dylan-esque/sub-Donovan tune of his own devising – in 1968. He happily admits that, were it not for Ian McDonald auditioning for his band Infinity, the song as we know it would never have happened. It was McDonald who took *Court* and fashioned it into something spectacularly different. Listening to the stirring sweeping chorus of massed voices and Mellotron on the album, it's hard to imagine such an imposing piece of music being written entirely on a humble acoustic guitar. Most definitely a case of "from little acorns do great oaks grow".

The long gestation of the song is charted in McDonald's diary. His entry for Tuesday, 4 February 1969, (typical of most) records: "Up at 4 pm. To rehearsal at 6 pm. Went to Standard Restaurant for meal with Pete. Went over to Andy's (DJ Andy Dunkley) at 12. Listened to records until 1.30 am then went to Pete's to write. Had some success with *Court of the Crimson King*. Home at 7 am Bed 7.15."

This is the first mention of the song in the diary, suggesting it was still some way from completion. A week later, after rehearsals and McDonald and Sinfield's work on the stage lights which Sinfield had been constructing, the pair went back to Sinfield's flat and "made another attempt writing *Court of the Crimson King*. Home at 2.15. Sounds. Bed 4.15."

By Tuesday, 11 March, the full band were rehearsing the track and Sinfield recalls: "I was entranced, as the saying goes. I truly thought I'd died and gone to heaven." On Friday that week, the rehearsal was again taken up with the song. As the band prepared for their first gig, the basement room in the Fulham Palace Road attracted a regular crowd of admirers and music industry apparatchiks and word was spreading about the band's power and intensity.

McDonald notes that a rehearsal on Thursday, 3 April, was especially overwhelming: "Played some numbers, best solos ever. Cried during *Court of the Crimson King*."

Less than a week later, Crimson took to the stage for the first time at The Speakeasy and the buzz really began to mushroom. Inside a month, the band were booked to record a session for John Peel's BBC show *Top Gear* and, on the afternoon of Tuesday, 6 May, along with *Schizoid Man* and *I Talk To The Wind*, the song received its first official recording. The tracks were broadcast a few days later – on Sunday, 11 May – although McDonald had to ask his father to record the programme as Crimson were playing at The Country Club in Haverstock Hill with The Pretty Things.

Notwithstanding some last-minute additions and revisions during the recording, the song's anthemic theme was going down well with audiences. However, playing the track live was not without its problems and, because of the Mellotron's sometimes wayward tuning, its use in the chorus could often undermine the harmonies sung by McDonald, Giles and Lake. In the studio there were no such problems and, on Monday, 21 July, the band began laying down what many still regard as its definitive track.

Tuesday was spent adding and tightening the song further with Mellotron and vocals finally added the following day. The opening sweep on the Mellotron was a fanfare fit for a king, as McDonald explains: "What I like about it is the sweetest note – the F sharp, a major third in the first chord, and by continuing it to the next chord, it becomes the sourest note (a flattened fifth). So it goes from a sweet note to a sour note without actually changing, which actually is reflected in the lyrics. And then the run-up that follows is actually a rip-off of James Brown if you can believe that! There's an undercurrent of all kinds of influences that actually goes into Crimson music."

There are only two (restrained) solos, both by McDonald. Firstly the stirring Mellotron strings theme at 2:21, carried aloft by Giles' breezy cymbal work, and the gentler pastoral of the flute solo after the third verse. McDonald worked hard to get his flute to sound as effortless and as distinguished as this. Indeed, McDonald reveals that the closing phrases of the solo (5:11) borrow from Rimsky-Korsakov's

Scheherazade, in particular the twisting clarinet theme in the opening passages of the second movement.

Though several members of the group were unhappy with Wessex as a studio, it did supply the album with some important instruments. Their chance inclusion provides several signatures sounds, without which the album would be unthinkable. The timpani and reed organ both added to the sonic palette but it was the discovery of an old Baldwin rock harpsichord, neglected and unused for several years, which really fired up the band's imagination.

Once the machine was connected up to an amplifier they discovered it was horrendously out of tune but still fell in love with its enigmatic sound. It fell to McDonald to dust the innards and get the thing tuned up and its sparkling presence is found all over the record.

These instruments were subjected to rigorous inspection and testing to see how they might be used. For example, the sound of the air being blown through the reeds of the pipe organ found their way into the introduction of *Schizoid Man*. McDonald and Giles were just doodling around on the keyboard when they created the section known as *The Dance Of The Puppets* at the end of the title track. McDonald: "It's up in E played by me and Mike. I'm doing the top part of that and Mike is sitting next to me playing the bass end – totally improvised. We just sat down together and goofed on that. It wasn't written but is just another example of collective improvisation."

After the funfair sounds of the pipe organ, a newly recorded end section slams back in, driven by Giles' tumultuous drums and the stabbing of the Mellotron on the unlikely accordion setting. As all manner of fills and licks are thrown up, the music sways in an alarming, bilious manner before finally swirling to an abrupt, heart-stopping conclusion.

IN THE WAKE OF POSEIDON

Peace – A Beginning

(Fripp, Sinfield)

A recurring theme throughout Crimson's career has been the bringing together of opposing forces and concepts. The tension within Crimson's music is often created when those opposites collide and crash.

Sometimes this is achieved in very subtle ways, such as on the *Peace* themes which open and close this album. In just under two minutes, using nothing more than Greg Lake's plaintive voice, the distance between the artificial and the natural is discretely measured out and connected as his vocal makes its transition from a bed of numinous echo to the Spartan surroundings of a converted chapel in West London.

The lyric may contain the vast imaginings of a world and the colossal forces moving above and below, but it is presented in a reductive, minimalist package – there's nothing as simple or as sophisticated as the human voice.

Pictures Of A City
including **42nd At Treadmill**
(Fripp, Sinfield)
Not for the last time in Crimso's career, the peace is shattered by a mischievous thump as the album gets under way with a riotous, cartwheeling fanfare. Brimming with testosterone, this track is arguably one of the most overtly macho pieces in the KC songbook. Burgeoning with cavalcades of guitar overdubs, it swaggers with ebullient virtuosity.

As in *Schizoid Man*, Sinfield maps out a nightmarish, dystopian vision of the modern city, riven with chaos, inevitably running down into ruin and loss. "This was influenced by when we first arrived in New York … you know the drive from Kennedy Airport," Sinfield told *NME*'s Nick Logan. "We were horrified. The song is about the nastiness of New York … a place with cold hands and a warm heart where it's difficult to reach the heart." As Lake spits out the words, blistering distorted fuzz guitar blows through the snarling cityscape like a vengeful wind.

What follows next is a white-knuckle ride as Fripp takes us on a whirlwind tour of a series of frighteningly fast lines. At times, the daredevil bravado almost sounds too clever for its own good but there's no denying its licence to thrill. Throughout this spectacular section, Fripp supplies a horn-like arrangement which punctuates the section as though the guitarist Fripp were a member of a mutant hybrid metal be-bop band.

A truly awesome experience? Well it would have been, but for the fact that *Schizoid Man* had charted much of this territory before. Indeed, the piece is now dismissed by Sinfield as consisting of an inferior *Schizoid Man* arrangement and cheap words.

The piece was untangled from a composition called *Trees*, played live in 1969. At that time it featured an introduction of haunting beauty written by McDonald and performed in three-part harmony by Giles, McDonald and Lake. It seems likely that the placing of *Peace – A Beginning* before *Pictures Of A City* was designed to re-create that pastoral contrast.

Cadence And Cascade
(Fripp, Sinfield)
A calmer mood is introduced as the door slams shut on the howling chaos of *Pictures Of A City*, which has its origins in a tune written by Ian McDonald in the spring of 1969, subsequently amended by Fripp with new words by Sinfield.

Cadence And Cascade is the story of two groupies and their ministrations to the young men of the road. The delicate nature of the song belies the carnal subject matter and features some appropriately ravishing flute from Mel Collins. "I just remember it as being very relaxed at Wessex and the sort of situation in which I would normally have been very nervous," recalls Collins. "I didn't work off charts and it was just listening to it and going for it. I would have had a few stabs at it for sure but it was very quick."

With celeste overdubbed by Fripp for extra decorative sparkle, Haskell's fragile vocal is delivered in little more than a tremulous whisper. His vocals were recorded a semi-tone lower and then sped up to the required pitch.

Haskell admits being baffled by the lyrical content and frankly underwhelmed by the song. For him the genteel ballad was a few thousand miles short of his beloved American influences and heroes. "I didn't know what the song was on about. To me it was at the other end of things from Otis Redding. I couldn't imagine Otis singing *Cadence And Cascade*, so I didn't know how to sing it either. I was directed like an actor and that wasn't where I was coming from either. So I acted the song. I didn't know what *Cadence And Cascade* meant. I didn't know anybody called Cadence and Cascade! I was really a fish out of water."

It was a point of view with which Fripp had some sympathy. He says: "An increasing difficulty for myself, as well, was Peter's proprietorial attitude towards the recording of his words." But then the guitarist adds: "Actually, I love the words to *Cadence And Cascade*."

Though he wasn't impressed with the song at the time, it has nevertheless remained closely associated with Haskell's subsequent solo career, as he recalled in 2000. "I did an American tour a couple of years ago and all these Crimson fans come out of the woodwork and insisted that I sang it and it was the first time I'd sung it for 30 years. So I sang it like I sing now – I put it down into a better key and I sang it with as much soul as I could muster and pretended that it was a Tony Joe White song. They loved it. It got the biggest cheer of the night!"

In The Wake Of Poseidon
including **Libra's Theme**
(Fripp, Sinfield)

There's no denying that the luxuriantly soaring theme instantly kindles memories of *Epitaph* and – toward the end – the title track of the first album. Yet, despite this handicap, these lofty chords have a resplendent grandiosity all of their own. It's the kind of anthemic song for which Lake's voice was made and it's hard to imagine any other singer who could bring it off with such impact and conviction.

Speaking to the *NME*'s Nick Logan following the release of *Poseidon*, Sinfield confirmed the marriage between the lyrics and De Jongh's imagery on the cover was not something that came easily or quickly, revealing that he "re-wrote the words to this 25 times. The faces on the cover are mentioned in the song, a character every two lines. The idea, according to the artist who did the cover, is that out of combinations of the four elements – earth, air, fire, water – come 12 archetypes ... the faces on the cover."

The inclusion of Libra in the title stresses the concern for equilibrium but this is not just a lyrical allusion. The contrast between the chill, austere perfection of the Mellotron and the ruminative, intuitive interventions from the acoustic guitar and drums seems to provide another metaphor, describing the need for balance and justice in matters of both the temporal and spiritual, the mechanical and human, the compassionate and the greedy.

For all the impressive scale, there are some fine points of detail, including the dignified shimmer of piano (provided by Fripp) during *Libra's Theme,* the two strikes of finger-cymbals during the last verse and Lake's valedictory choir wheeling high above the drama below in hymnal splendour.

Peace – A Theme
(Fripp)
Fripp wrote this piece in 1967/68 at Brondesbury Road. He explains: "The original draft notes were written on score without guitar, with a string quartet in mind. The middle section drew influence from a Carcassi étude."

A midway point between past and future, a natural place to take stock. This warm pentatonic melody offers a folk-tinged take on the *Peace* motif. Bright and warm, it wouldn't have sounded out of place in London venues such as Les Cousins.

Cat Food
(Fripp, Sinfield, McDonald)
Recording and releasing *Cat Food* was not without controversy, not least because of a dispute over who wrote which part of the song. McDonald recalls being outraged upon hearing that the track was initially credited to Fripp and Sinfield alone. He contacted David Enthoven and a meeting was arranged in the manager's mews house in central London to hammer out the question of attribution.

McDonald had worked with Sinfield on *Cat Food* over two days in Detroit the previous November. Though unfinished, it was played to the group. After McDonald and Giles' departure, Fripp returned to what he regarded was a brilliant lyric and he and Sinfield now set about finalising the tune.

Fripp says: "I remember hearing Ian's demo once, I believe in the US, and acknowledge the importance of Ian's 6/8 turnaround, and that both versions are rock songs. But Ian's original demo is very different to the 'rewritten' *Cat Food*. I asked Peter Sinfield for his opinion. Peter's view, expressed to me, was that, given a writer writing to the words, the writer would have to write a 6/8 turnaround. (Actually, I don't agree with this.) I believe the key bass riff is also mine, and the shouted melody (on a minor third) is a standard rock 'melody'."

"They weren't going to credit me at all," recalls an indignant McDonald. "Fripp claimed to have written the whole thing and I called a meeting with the management and I said, 'Look, I wrote this song' and it was finally agreed that I did. I wrote the riff and the verses, including the 6/8 riff. Fripp just wrote the little bridge part – 'no use to complain', etc. And that's all."

Lake's yelp of laughter – "At the critical juncture I dropped my pants in the control room and mooned Greg through the window to the vocal booth," recalls Fripp – gives some evidence of the relaxed atmosphere in the studio. It certainly adds to the sense of uninhibited exuberance evinced by Keith Tippett's flaying of the piano in a dazzlingly anarchic fashion. Regarded by Sinfield as the best song on the album, this scathingly satirical lyric on the fast-food culture and rampant commercialism is given a boisterous and effective reading by Lake.

The line in the song about poisoned Hurri Curri may well have stemmed from observing Fripp's eating habits at the time. "I recall in the studio that he ordered beef curry (before becoming a veggie) 13 nights in a row," remembers Sinfield. "That night I persuaded him to order a variation. He did and 15 minutes after eating said variation, having carefully laid aside his guitar – he threw up."

Fripp recalls the sense of revulsion the song provoked in an old school chum, Barry Amor, who accosted him one evening at the Exeter Hotel in Bournemouth not long after its release. "His argument was along the lines of, well, the music was upsetting/disturbing/different; and somehow he was implying that this wasn't right to present to an audience." Fripp still regards this track and *Groon* as the two forward-looking pieces to emerge from the *Poseidon* sessions.

Remarkably, the song was covered by jazz singer Annie Ross and her version was included on her long-deleted 1971 album *You And Me Baby: An Evening With Annie Ross*. The band, featuring the talents of Rick Laird (about-to-be Mahavishnu Orchestra member) on bass and Dave MacRea (Nucleus/Matching Mole) on keyboards, take the tune at a fair pace, as Annie extemporises a few meows in between the verses.

The Devil's Triangle
(Fripp)
Merday Morn
(Fripp, McDonald)

The Devil's Triangle is a patch of ocean just off the coast of Bermuda in which numerous unexplained disappearances are alleged to have occurred. The only thing to disappear here was the original name of the piece, *Mars*, thanks to the problems with the Holst estate.

As well as alluding to the tritone (the dominant musical force within the piece), the title tied in with the release of a documentary made by Richard Werner. Werner had seen Crimson at the Palm Beach Festival and approached them with a view to using the darkly atmospheric *Mars*. The resulting low-budget movie utilised excerpts of the track accompanied by a lugubrious voice-over from horror veteran Vincent Price.

After nearly four minutes of sinister building, one of the most hair-raisingly infernal sounds ever produced from the Mellotron heralds the approach of extreme 'tron madness with Keith Tippett in tow. The Mellotron never sounded as dark and as savage as it does on this frenzied concoction. Perhaps it's just ignoring the maker's recommendations about what should and shouldn't be twiddled, poked and prodded. Perhaps it's another example of balancing out the opposites contained on the album – the dissonance of *The Devil's Triangle* against the harmony of the title track?

The Hand Of Sceiron
(Fripp)
In Greek mythology, Sceiron was a character slain by Theseus, whose name was then given to a biting wind which any argonaut would know as "the hand of Sceiron". At around the seven-minute mark, the furore is blown away by a howling wind. The ambiguous clicking of a metronome perhaps symbolises the passage of time, but in any event, offers a momentary though welcome cessation of the aural hostilities.

Garden Of Worm
(Fripp)
Amid the pyroclastic splintering of guitar and piano innards, dense layers of sound are folded one on another in the anarchic melée. When describing the recording process to Nick Logan at the time of the release, Fripp wearily noted: "This one took a long time to record. You have three basic things go on. The basic rhythms of guitar and drums. On top of that you have piano and drums fighting, and above that there are various pieces making a commentary on what's going on underneath. Keith is playing bits of nursery rhymes on harpsichord and there are snatches of reggae and *In The Court Of The Crimson King* in there as well."

Occupying more than 11 minutes and the lion's share of the second side, *The Devil's Triangle* is a courageous attempt to take a stage favourite and shift it into new territories of sonic trepidation. It harnesses atonal experimentalism, chance procedures and bold, self-referential expression. While such unorthodox exploration was entirely consistent with Crimson's reputation and interests, it is more than likely that its appearance on *Poseidon* has as much to do with a shortage of formally written material as a desire to nail their collective colours to the avant-garde mast.

Peace – An End
(Fripp, Sinfield)
Naked and vulnerable, Lake's voice brings the album to a close and all the vocal and instrumental aspects of the *Peace* theme are finally brought together in perfect balance and harmony.

McDONALD AND GILES
Suite In C (including **Turnham Green, Here I Am** and others)
(McDonald)
Though he will admit to the odd cringe here and there, Ian McDonald's lyric faithfully documents a fairytale romance to warm the hearts of even the most cynical listener. On Sunday, 22 June 1969, McDonald was travelling on the London Underground's District Line to meet David Enthoven. He noticed a beautiful girl and her friend. The girl had a cat sitting on her lap.

Spellbound, McDonald watched the pair until they alighted at Turnham Green. McDonald met up with the others and went on to the Marquee to see The Strawbs. After socialising with Dik and others, he played guitar before eventually going to bed sometime after 4.00 am. However, the image of the girl continued to haunt him and he knew he had to see her again. A few days went by and he placed an advert in *International Times* asking the girl to contact him, though he hardly dared to hope for a response.

The girl in question was Charlotte Bates and she recalls that Kay, her friend from the train, told her about the advert in *International Times*. It was Monday, 7 July, 25 days after McDonald saw Bates on the train. "I knew straight away it was him (McDonald) who'd put the ad in the paper. I had a boyfriend at the time but I thought I'd phone him once – that was the thing to myself. Anyway, I did phone him once and it just so happened that he was there and he'd just got in from the studio because he'd been recording all night."

Arrangements were made to meet on Sunday at 2.00 pm at the Albert Memorial and the couple spent the afternoon walking and talking in Hyde Park. Within a few weeks, the pair started living together, sharing a flat with Peter Sinfield and Stephanie Ruben. "I think I was only 17 or 18, so I was quite young," Bates recalls. "My parents weren't over the moon about it but they quite liked Ian despite the fact that he was some kind of disreputable rock musician. Up until then I was into people like Mick Jagger so they thought that Ian was a vast improvement."

Unsurprisingly, the music is joyous, effervescent and brimming with good humour. Delightfully loping guitar, sweeping strings, jaunty whistling, rising heartfelt harmonies, freewheeling flute, riotous shouting and jokey doo-wop, not to mention a parade of pushy, virile horns all evoke the feeling of a young man falling in love for the first time.

As he sings the line "soft pussy on her knee", the other side of McDonald's unalloyed adoration is represented by the sound of Giles rubbing his hands together, as if in knowing expectation. Lasting from 36 seconds until 1:03, such a witty and idiosyncratic form of rhythm pre-empts Jamie Muir's forays into similar territory by a couple of years.

Giles' playing throughout is wonderfully light and crisp, without ever being showy, and his mastery of moving the beat around with the snare makes even the most conventional of time signatures a source of enjoyment and delight. Though Giles will probably always be remembered for his work in Crimson, his contribution to *Suite In C*, and across the album as a whole, continues to attract admirers and devotees.

Giles recalls being in the bar of the Horton Inn, Dorset, one day in May 1981, when a fan came up and made himself known to the drummer. Surprised that he'd been recognised, Giles discovered that this particular enthusiast was enamoured with the funky bass drum and snare punch at 8:20 into *Suite In C*, which also happens to be a personal favourite of Giles himself.

In the course of their conversation, Giles discovered that this discerning listener was none other than drummer-turned-guitarist Adrian Belew, then rehearsing in the nearby Holdenhurst Church Hall with the new line-up of King Crimson.

Flight Of The Ibis
(Fallon, McDonald)
In May 1969, Crimson were rehearsing a new McDonald and Sinfield composition called *Cadence And Cascade*. However, the split destroyed any opportunity to hear the song in its original state as Sinfield took the lyric and McDonald kept the tune.

McDonald and Giles' new words were supplied by Island PR supremo and Crimson confidante BP Fallon. In a charming song which features an agreeably mellow vocal harmony arrangement, the highlight is the gossamer-like, glittering solo by McDonald on the zither, which glides skywards with masterly ease, expressing both contentment and aspiration.

Looking back, however, he regrets the splitting of the original *Cadence And Cascade*, and regards the results on both this album and *Poseidon* as being one strong piece made into two lesser songs.

Is She Waiting?
(McDonald)
A gentle but perhaps overly winsome ballad describing life on the road when your love is left at home. The subject of the song, Charlotte Bates, recalls: "I did go to some of the gigs but there was a policy from the managers that girlfriends didn't traipse around with them a lot."

The lyrics paint an idealised portrait of the domestic life of the patiently waiting woman. Stephanie Ruben remembers that when McDonald and Sinfield shared a flat together, the women weren't the only thing waiting for the returning men. "We were living at Wevern Mansions and we had a long corridor. When Ian and Pete came home from gigs, their lovely place was just peppered with cat trays, cat food and cat smellies – it was just a mess!"

For McDonald, the track is flawed by a lack of energy in the performance and some rogue feedback between the first and second verses provides some evidence that the clock (and the finances) were against the duo.

Tomorrow's People – The Children Of Today
(Giles)
Giles had written elements of this song back in 1967 though it was strangely overlooked by GG&F. It was the played by Crimson in rehearsals during the early part of 1969 but never performed live. Giles was never a prolific writer and *Tomorrow's People* is his only composition on the album. Although he and McDonald worked very closely on the content, arrangements and the supervision of the album as a whole, they never collaborated directly as writers.

When writing the parts, Giles hit upon the idea of renewing his acquaintance with trombonist Michael Blakesley, whom he hadn't seen since their days together in Trendsetters Ltd. "Although he wasn't a name session player, it's better working with people you know because you haven't got a lot of explanation to do and you can get on with the job," recalls the commonsensical Giles.

Instrumentally, the main action lies in an irresistible and irrepressible extended percussion work-out following the third verse (1:45 into the track). With every bar packed with kit drums, shakers, milk bottles, nutboxes, and timbales, it's a wonder in the age of plunderphonics that the section hasn't been spirited away to re-appear on a chart-topping confection.

Clearly, they had a ball recording it as Giles and company can clearly be heard yelling and shouting just before the hustling drum roll, which ushers in McDonald's sprightly flute solo. In Crimson, Giles had increasingly taken a back seat in respect of his voice, letting the euphonious tones of Greg Lake take the limelight. Yet *Tomorrow's People* demonstrates that he was more than equipped to step into the limelight as a singer.

Birdman
involving **The Inventor's Dream (O.U.A.T), The Workshop, Wishbone Ascension, Bird Man Flies!, Wings In The Sunset, Birdman – The Reflection (Sinfield, McDonald)**
Lyrically, *Birdman* dates back to early 1968 when Peter Sinfield and future EG factotum

Dik Fraser used to make, paint and sell kites to passing tourists in London's Hyde Park as a way of keeping body and soul together. Happily, Sinfield's fascination with aeronautical matters had lyrical as well as practical applications, when he started sketching out the bones of what would become this suite.

The cathartic changes and shifts in McDonald's personal life found their way to the surface of his music and there's a lightness of touch here more life-affirming and considerably warmer than anything Crimson had produced. While most of the songs on the previous side are self-explanatory, McDonald views the more abstract *Birdman* as about seeing the world with open eyes. At a little over 20 minutes, the track was not only the longest but the costliest track to record, using a real string section as opposed to the trademark Mellotron. Despite the expense, McDonald could no longer bring himself to use the wretchedly unreliable instrument.

The Inventor's Dream (O.U.A.T.)

The various sections of *Birdman* are brimming with tiny touches and nuances evidencing the time and care which went into its construction. As with the hero of the story, attention to detail is what makes the piece triumphantly fly and it shows how extremely diverse musical influences were brought into play by McDonald. The vocals heralding the opening show something of his talents as an arranger and his unerring ear for gorgeous harmonies, setting up the startling take-off sequence achieved by manipulating the sound of the studio's resident Hammond organ.

The jocular nature of *The Inventor's Dream* is emphasised by a tune inspired by the theme tune to an old TV sitcom that McDonald saw during the 1960s. Called *My Three Sons* and starring film comedian Fred MacMurray, the series had signature music composed by Frank De Vol featuring a series of dashing triplets, here re-invented by McDonald, who plays the stabbing phrase on the organ.

The Workshop

After the vocals, a biting sax solo energetically weaves over fusillades of handclaps and the fussy clutter of Giles' snare and hi-hat. Indeed as the hectic pace picks up, such is the drummer's dedication to re-creating the sounds of a workshop in use that one can just make out the rasping of a handsaw as it moved through a block of wood. As the tape rolled, the sawdust gathered on the floor, causing studio engineers to fear for the safety of Island Studios' fixtures and fittings had the track required any further takes.

Wishbone Ascension

After the soaring Hammond theme, the piece goes into the "Slowly up and slowly down" section which had previously seen the light of day as part of the Crimson piece *Trees*.

Birdman Flies!

From a tentative shimmer of cymbals, there emerges a delicate theme on the flute, inexorably building to a grandiose climax. The ever-inventive Giles adds sundry percussive effects to each successive statement of the main theme, which is in turn incrementally layered with guitar, electric piano, flute, strings and horns.

Once again, there is the suggestion of another musical influence when, at 12:39, McDonald's guitar – processed through the organ's Leslie cabinet – seemingly re-creates Eric Clapton's famous guitar bridge section from *Badge*.

Wings In The Sunset

Bringing together the varying themes that had been carefully suggested and placed throughout the piece, *Birdman*'s flight is over. For Sinfield the realisation of the track was something of a personal anti-climax when he visited the duo in the studio during its recording. "I had always envisioned *Birdman* as a much longer, light operatic thing – to include his travels. However, on *McD&G*, he goes up and he comes down. Ah well … one day?"

Birdman – The Reflection

Another rich theme is given a gradual send-off complete with huge sweeping strings and horns, flurries of Giles' patent tom-toms culminating in a massive crescendo which takes the breath away. Prior to the ill-fated American trip, McDonald and Sinfield had been working on the *Birdman Suite*, which Fripp described in an interview with *Rolling Stone*'s Mark Williams in 1969 as having "a catchier chorus than *Crimson King*. It's pretty long and shows the direction that King Crimson is going in." Speaking of the track in 2001, Fripp still regards the piece as a stunning piece of writing. "I had hoped that this would be the centrepiece of the second Crimson album," he said. "But Ian, whatever his other concerns, didn't like my feel as a guitarist on his music."

LIZARD
Cirkus
including **Entry Of the Chameleons**
(Fripp, Sinfield)

Like the lion at the top of an MGM motion picture, the snarling growl of mixed-brass Mellotron gets the third King Crimson album well and truly under way, documenting weird scenes inside the big top. *Cirkus* bears all the hallmarks of a classic Crimson tune; a delicate introduction leading to the massive punch of the chorus. Collins is particularly graceful as he surfs over waves of the Mellotron in what Fripp calls the Mantovani section, though it's unlikely that the English light entertainment conductor, famous for his singing strings, ever had to cope with anything as unruly as this.

The lyric, which rails against the hedonistic vagaries of the rock lifestyle, had its origins in Sinfield's upbringing. As a child, Sinfield was exposed to the excitement of the circus when his mother's German housekeeper, Maria Wallenda, took him to a visiting Bertram Mills show. The housekeeper herself had been a member of the Famous Flying Wallendas high-wire act.

Talking to composer Andrew Keeling, Sinfield remembered: "I was introduced to various animal trainers, acrobats, the stern, red-coated, black-top-hatted ringmaster and in particular I remember it well, her gentle, just an old friend, Coco The Clown. He glowed! I became by affection/infection honorary circus folk at a very imperishable age. Add that to my later fascination with funfairs. The envy/admiration for the 'wild' greasy haired, black leather jacketed , 'allo darlin' guys who ran the bumper cars as Buddy Holly belted out *Rave On*. Throw in *Those Who Are About To Die Salute You*; a couple of tomes by Robert Graves plus Vance Packard's timely revelations in his book *The Hidden Persuaders* ... and you will get a 'Megaphonium Fanfare'!"

The barely contained chaos of the track is interspersed by some truly startling acoustic guitar by Fripp, adding razor-edged footnotes to each line. The guitar in question was a Martin which Fripp recalls was eventually bought by none other than the legendary UK guitarist and fellow spectacle wearer Hank Marvin.

Indoor Games
(Fripp, Sinfield)
With the backing sounding like an off-kilter hotel dance band, Collins' fruity baritone ushers in this curiously crooked take on domestic ennui, dilettantes and vacuous chancers, all engaged in a round robin of self-important delusion. Writing in his diary of 1969, Ian McDonald noted that on 10 May there was a party at Sinfield's house in Kensington Hall Gardens where indoor fireworks amused the revellers. McDonald goes on to note that he didn't get home to bed until 5.45 am, so a good time appears to have been had by all.

The Hammond organ-induced middle-eight is suggestive of monkeys and organ grinders while the next couplet perhaps evokes some ex-Harrovian bikers known to the lyricist – a joust at the expense of the band's management. It's interesting to hear the use of the VCS3 to simulate the revving of a motorbike engine, a trick that Sinfield would re-create with Roxy Music two years later when he produced the classic single *Virginia Plain* – though on that occasion the budget stretched to a real motorbike.

Here the VCS3 – nicknamed Vick at the time – is utilised largely for its comedic tone and errant beeps until the bridge into the third and final verse where it resembles a fairground calliope, reinforcing the circus motif, which occurs at various intervals across the album.

In terms of performance, *Indoor Games* veers somewhat uncomfortably between hesitation and commitment, pulling its punches and lacking in tang or zest. Fripp's spirited comping on guitar reveals his undoubted prowess while stylistically alluding to his days in the Majestic Hotel house band. But however deft the chord work may be, there is less to this lacklustre track than meets the ear. In the end, only Collins' sax solo partially saves the day.

Perhaps the most striking moment on *Indoor Games* is the maniacal peal of laughter at the end. Sinfield recalls making the singer laugh as a means of trying to relax him, although this is hotly denied by Haskell himself. "I was in a booth on my own with the lyric sheet in front of me and the lyric ended with 'Hey Ho'. When I saw the line come up I thought, 'I don't know how to sing this.' I thought this was fucking insane so I just went 'Hey Ho'! Who says 'Hey Ho'? And I just burst out laughing. The Flowerpot Men and me used to use a lot of silly voices and my 'Hey Ho' came from that. I couldn't believe they were taking it all so seriously. It was just a joke. It was the worst thing I'd ever heard up to that point and there I was actually doing it."

Whatever the cause of Haskell's guffaw, Fripp and Sinfield responded to the surreal qualities of the moment and there his laughter hovers, disembodied and disturbed – eerily echoing, consigned to haunt the album, and Haskell himself, from that day on.

Happy Family
(Fripp, Sinfield)
The break-up of The Beatles is documented in some of Sinfield's driest and well-observed lines on the entire album. Sinfield recalls that the decision to process the words through the VCS3 was as much to do with reservations about the quality of the tentative vocal performance as any sonic experimentation. Adding another layer of obfuscation to the legendary tale of the Fab Four, Haskell's voice is sent through ring modulation, square waves and saw tooth filters. The ominous descending fanfare opening the track was also produced by using the monophonic keyboard that came with the primitive synth. On this occasion, Fripp played it, but Sinfield controlled the effects for the vocal processing.

Sinfield recalls how he came to be beguiled by the VCS3. "Before my career in music, I worked on early mainframe computers as an operator and programmer in the early '60s when they had 64 bits of storage, paper tape and punched cards and it was a revelation when we got it to play 'Daisy, Daisy'. I met the guys that made the VCS3 at their workshop in Putney in 1969 where they had very early experiments in pitch to voltage, etc. I must have bought either the first or second VCS3 and it really was simple for me to understand its basics and its limitations as I, er, pushed its envelopes. I loved it!"

Through the convoluted swirl of the instrumental section, Fripp and Keith Tippett provide a splintery bedrock of dense staccato as Collins and Nick Evans swoop and bellow respectively. Yet apart from the odd moment, there is little more on offer than bluster and ballyhoo. Suffering from a case of Micawber's syndrome (i.e. all the players sound like they are waiting for something to turn up), *Happy Family* is a brave experiment that doesn't quite catch. The jazzy sensibility that pervades the piece is saddled with a distinctly un-Crimson lack of rhythmic ambition. No matter how good the words are, the music just doesn't quite lift off, ending – much like The Beatles – not with a bang but with a whimper.

Lady Of The Dancing Water
(Fripp, Sinfield)
A plaintive ballad of lost love and times past. The sparse instrumentation highlights Haskell's delicate, gentle vocal with Collins' exquisite flute hovering like the memory of a butterfly on a long-lost summer afternoon. The whole song is given added piquancy by Nick Evans' mournful trombone, which manages to keep the track from becoming overly sentimental.

In fact, Evans regards the track as a favourite. "As far as my memory goes, I think there was a vocal track on *Dancing Water* but it may have been a guide vocal and not the one that actually appears on the record. I also have a memory that my part for *Dancing Water* was scored, although there was room for 'artistic interpretation' as long as it was in keeping with the track's character. It's one of my personal favourites, although with an album like *Lizard* it is not easy to dismantle the overall record into individual tracks – it is one piece in its own right."

The track also holds special memories for UK composer Andrew Keeling, who was then 15 and had in fact written to Fripp asking to join King Crimson. He was surprised to receive a reply from the guitarist and an offer to write an arrangement of *Lady Of The Dancing Water*. "Robert had quickly written it in pencil (the melody line plus chords) and invited me to do an arrangement of it. I did so and sent it to him. When *Lizard* came out and I heard what Robert had done with Peter Sinfield's words I learnt a great deal about not what to do with an arrangement: Robert's original was a wonderful indication of control and simplicity done so as to heighten words. Mine was an overblown monster of a thing! I think Robert set my future in motion by inviting me to arrange something."

Lizard
Prince Rupert Awakes
(Fripp, Sinfield)
Crimson's association with Yes was further strengthened by the guest appearance of Jon Anderson on vocals. Invited in by Fripp and Sinfield, the singer worked quickly, overdubbing his parts near the end of the sessions. It was always known by the duo that Haskell would not be have the right voice for this track, which kicks off the lengthy title suite, and the singer himself recalls no attempts at a recording.

The second chorus marks the first appearance of a backwards guitar part –

achieved by working out the desired notes and then turning the tape around – influenced by The Beatles' deployment of such intriguing studio tactics. A few moments later the same technique is applied to Anderson's wordless chorale as it swarms back and forth over limp handclaps.

Despite its grandiosity, the track is not without its moments of levity, as Fripp told Richard Williams in *Melody Maker*. "Gordon said to me the other day that he was worried we – and me especially – were too serious about the musical side of things, and that's true to a degree. I believe very much in what we're doing, I have tremendous faith in all the men involved, but at the same time we always manage to mock ourselves a little, just to show that we're aware of when it gets a bit heavy."

"For example, there's a section on the new album, one of the parts of *Lizard*, where there's massed Hollywood strings complete with timpani rolls, cymbal clashes, grand piano … so we stuck a second grand piano on and really overdid it. But I hope nicely so – I can still enjoy it very much … perhaps that's a comment on my poor taste, but it's very moving and hilarious at the same time."

In the years since its recording, the humour has palled somewhat. While remastering the album in 1999, Fripp caustically remarked of *Prince Rupert Awakes* – "Rupert would have done better to stay in bed that day."

Bolero – The Peacock's Tale
(Fripp)

The incorporation of classical instruments into jazz and rock isn't particularly new. Sax player Yusef Lateef brought the oboe into his playing to startling effect back in the late '50s. Close to home, Karl Jenkins (later to find international success as the classical crossover Adiemus) was playing oboe first with jazz leader Graham Collier and Ian Carr's Nucleus in the late '60s.

Here the oboe is beautifully played by Robin Miller – at the time co-principal oboist with the BBC Symphony Orchestra under conductor Pierre Boulez. Miller's involvement hinged around the fact that he was married to Stephanie Ruben's sister.

Miller recalls that the parts for *The Peacock's Tale* were all written out for him by Fripp and that the pair talked at some length about what was needed, with Fripp being particularly keen on Miller's ability to produce notes of extraordinary length and purity. Here Fripp is cast in the role of conductor or musical director, content to contribute the tender, autumnal Mellotron underpinning the yearning beauty of the main theme.

However, this track also suffers from the slightly inhibited playing of the featured soloists (excepting Miller). This cannot really be blamed on their capabilities but rather on the way Fripp and Sinfield would record them.

Nick Evans: "The improvising passages were done a 'section' at a time, although after each section the recording was checked to ensure the style of my improvisation suited the record's overall structure/feel." Despite this, there are points where the track momentarily catches fire as Charig's fiery blasts mesh with bandmates Tippett and Evans (7:50 onwards). Yet as the piano seems about to spiral out of control, the fireworks are cut short by a brutal edit (8:44) and a new theme is set up by Evans and Collins.

The Battle Of Glass Tears
Dawn Song
(Fripp, Sinfield)
Miller plays the eerie opening on the cor anglais (an alto oboe). The moment seems supremely cinematic, a musical jump-cut from the warmth of *The Peacock's Tale* to the chilly battlefield. Fearfulness and foreboding are perfectly conveyed by the stark electric piano, cymbal and rolling timpani, as the cor anglais disconsolately threads between Haskell's delivery of the lyric. Perhaps here more than anywhere else on the album, Haskell's apprehensive low-pitched vocal seems perfectly at ease with Sinfield's brilliant evocation of a medieval battle scene.

Last Skirmish
(Fripp)
Amidst the turmoil and furore of the battle, a conflict of a different kind was taking place in Wessex. Gordon Haskell admits to totally losing his way during the recording. "I get to the end and they say 'That's great!' and I think 'Well that's probably as good as your drum sound. You don't have a clue what you're doing. Thank Christ that's over!' Eight minutes of a bloke wandering around up his arse. Great. That's art."

Fripp's main role in the *Lizard* suite had been to add the texture and propel the principal themes via the Mellotron. Indeed, Fripp as guitarist has been entirely absent for more than 12 minutes but the vexed yowl of its return (at 15:37) shows that he has lost none of his acidulous edge.

As the chaotic melee proceeds, the instruments seems to jostle for position as they simulate the disarray and flight of the battlefield and, once again, it's the Mellotron which sets the pace making frenzied wails like some deranged company of buglers. The first let-up comes at 17:49 where the bass and guitar occupy a similar position to the quiet section in *Pictures Of A City*, only augmented by the needle-like shards of Tippett's piano echoing in the distance – alluding to the glass tears of the title. The pace becomes altogether more incensed and seething than anything yet heard, ferried along by the roll of McCulloch's angry snare, hurtling abruptly into silence.

Prince Rupert's Lament
(Fripp)
The sombre ostinato provided by the bass and drum overwhelmingly creates the

impression of a weary funereal procession making its lonely way through the remnants of a shattered army. Having spent the best part of the album shielded behind the dense armoury of the guest players, Fripp breaks out from behind the ranks to produce an intensely emotive performance brimming with intensity and tragedy. A mournful pibroch, wreathed in echo, the notes drift across the stereo picture, each one seemingly wrenched from the very soul of the guitar. A landmark moment in King Crimson and a triumphant conclusion to a brave, but uneven, album.

Big Top
(Fripp)
After the solemnity of the lament, the album's postscript is a humorous fade out on an ascending melody line, slowly speeding up and shooting off into space. Clockwork drums, fairground sounds, all the fun of the circus and Robin Miller having a lot of fun improvising a few twists and turns of his own.

ISLANDS
Formentera Lady
(Fripp, Sinfield)
Uncharacteristically, this Crimson album begins with a languid ten-minute stretch as Burrell delivers the tale of Sinfield's tour of the sun-drenched Balearic Islands. Veteran jazz pianist Jules Ruben (later to become Peter Sinfield's father-in-law) was invited to play piano for this track and for *Islands* itself. Despite several attempts the music somehow didn't click and his contributions went unused.

The pianist who replaced Ruben was, of course, Keith Tippett. In his own music, Tippett had now travelled far away from the big band whirl of Centipede into the more intimate world of small group improvisation. The opening minutes of *Formentera Lady* would not sound out of place on either of the Fripp-produced *Blueprint* or *Ovary Lodge*. If the track owes something to Tippett then perhaps, with its use of ostinato and building textures, there's also a nod towards the modal explorations of Miles Davis' *Shhh/Peaceful.*

Over an unobtrusive and slightly leaden backing, Paulina Lucas, a soprano from the Sadlers Wells Opera, sonorously wafts over the proceedings but in truth finds little with which to engage. For, as pleasant as the piece undoubtedly is, it takes a long time to say very little. Only when the string section and brass usher in the darker theme from *Sailor's Tale* (at 8:41) is any real tension injected into the piece and by then it's almost too late. Not even the prodding of the wonderful (and woefully under-used) Harry Miller on string bass can shake the track from its torpor.

"It sucks," says Fripp.

Sailor's Tale
(Fripp)
Although the backing track for *Sailor's Tale* was completed earlier in the month, the guitar solo which is the highlight of the entire album was recorded against the clock right at the end of the sessions.

A little after 2.00 am on the morning of Friday, 8 October, as Sinfield and engineer Andy Hendrickson looked on, Fripp made two passes at a truly astonishing solo. Broiled in a lacquer of short delay, VCS3 sweep, spring reverb and chopped repeat of Sinfield and Hendrickson's devising, the guitar sounded like a steroid-enhanced banjo and utterly unlike anything else which Fripp had done before in Crimson. It's the sound of the rock guitar solo rulebook being ripped, shredded and thrown aloft like confetti.

Small incremental adjustments build the sense of occasion as the track unfolds – the ghostly materialisation of Mellotron strings just after three minutes, Wallace moving from rimshot to open snare at 3:37, dissonant Mellotron flutes clamouring in the background at 4:11 – all dramatically underpin this passage.

Over the years, the Mellotron has enjoyed a reputation for being unreliable and unwieldy and, deserved as this might be, it was also capable of providing some of the most spine-tingling moments in rock music. This, the Mellotron rushing and weaving between the tremulous thickets of Wallace's drumming, is one of them.

On the fade-out, the ominous purr of the mixed-brass drone rises and falls like a slumbering beast. Fripp recalls: "The Mellotron tapes didn't go that low. We recorded with the tape running faster, then returned it to its normal speed."

Ultimately the guitar solo and its clattering coda is the leap from the symphonic and jazz styling of the earlier albums into a spikier, more metallic world waiting to be fully realised. Somewhere in that fractious skewering of notes and chords, Fripp was fashioning a new idea of where he wanted to be.

Fripp explains: "It is difficult to convey the level of exhaustion during this last week. My landlords were then Simon Stable and his wife Judy, née Dyble, just off Ladbroke Grove. I'd get home about 3–4 in the morning from the studio, pull out a pencil and write orchestral parts for *Song Of The Gulls*, before getting to bed anywhere between six and eight. Up around ten to leave for the studio for noon. The final night began around 18:00 and never ended for me – Peter bailed in the early hours and I carried on. Richard Williams came in to listen to the playback/run-through the following late morning, then the van arrived after lunch. I got in, fell asleep, we drove to the first show of the tour, and I woke up shortly before we arrived."

"The solo was, and is, from some other world. Technically, the right hand could only have been developed by someone familiar with the banjo. My connection to this was through Don Strike. Other references would include Sonny Sharrock (notably with Herbie Mann) and the *idea* of Peter Townshend's flailing. And maybe a subversion/perversion of early Scotty Moore, with echo delay, at the Sun sessions. But none of this seems relevant somehow. Late at night, faced with a solo to be played, for which there was no solo available, something happened: a young guitar player was confronted by necessity. And then something remarkable happened ..."

The Letters
(Fripp, Sinfield)
In this tale of deception, betrayal and tragedy, the mood is full of foreboding and given a stark, suitably washed-out production. Crude shock dynamics are deployed after two quiet verses followed, almost inevitably, by a blunt and thumping sax-led chorus. The sustained shriek of horror deployed by Fripp's guitar echoes the Grand Guignol of Sinfield's tragic tale, the anguished howl abruptly cauterised into silence, amplifying the pain and loss.

The Letters had its origins in Fripp's *Drop In*, played by the original 1969 line-up (two takes are captured on the *Epitaph* boxed set). Then it was a fairly trite exhortation to the hippie community to actively engage with their circumstances rather than simply drop out. Here, with new Sinfield words, it is transformed into something altogether darker. Perhaps a touch too melodramatic and literal for today's tastes but gripping stuff nevertheless, with a riveting performance from Collins. In the improvised middle section, his intimate baritone sax solo dredges up a mixture of emotions with an economy and focus which marks him out as one of the best players of his generation.

Ladies Of The Road
(Fripp, Sinfield)
When remastering the album for its 2000 re-release Fripp made the following observations about this song: "Bozzell the Vox is singing into his BBC brass wastepaper bucket. He is not dealing with the unfortunate after-effects of late-night partying (although the night before was a late-night party) but to create a halo around the voice. *Ladies* is the defining song of this particular Crimson. The lyrics are stunning: witty and drawn from observing the rich tapestry of life available to a young person on the road when rock still had a measure of innocence. A measure of a kind of innocence!"

Looking back on that kind of innocence, Ian Wallace recalls: "There were a lot of girls at that particular time, both in the UK and USA, and we had our moments. On the last tour in Grand Rapids, Michigan, we played a non-denominational church and there was a fluctuation with the power which meant we couldn't use the Mellotrons. After the show, the pastor of the church invited us all to his house for a bite to eat and a little party. So we went back and there were a lot of people there and all these girls.

"Mel used to do this thing where he would disappear to the bathroom and come back with his hair braided with toilet paper, his trouser legs rolled up and shaving cream all over or whatever and so he did that at this party. A couple of us paired up with some girls and we started necking with them and whatever and, before you know it, the pastor's got his Polaroid out and he's taking pictures. Anyway, when the party finished, we all paired up and went back to the hotel and carried on in our own rooms."

Fripp adds: "The pastor's wife used to give out condoms, she told me. She was what might be called 'a liberal thinker'."

A master of understatement, Wallace concludes: "It was a very wild night."

The track is perhaps the best example of the four principal performers seeming perfectly in balance. Fripp's lopsided subversion of clichéd blues licks, Collins' shrill blasting, Burrell's uninhibited and earthy vocal and Wallace's sure-handed but riotous grasp on rock, lock together in a way hardly matched anywhere else on the album.

Prelude: Song Of The Gulls
(Fripp)

This charmingly simple melody provides a lilting diversion between *Ladies Of The Road* and the more meditative *Islands*. The tune dates back to the slow section of *Suite No. 1* from *The Cheerful Insanity of Giles, Giles & Fripp* album in 1968.

Clearly, Fripp thought highly enough of it to go to the trouble to arrange it, with modifications, for a small string orchestra and the plaintive oboe of Robin Miller. Fripp recalled: "I conducted the string ensemble, of hardened London session players, with a pencil. They had the professional courtesy to ignore all my directions. I've never known which one of them was discreetly giving the cues."

Islands
(Fripp, Sinfield)

In 1642, it was John Donne's belief that "No man is an island, entire of itself; every man is a piece of the continent, a part of the main", and here Sinfield fleshes out this concept with the haiku-like beauty of the chorus. Though we may be drifting towards isolation there is underneath it all a common humanity binding us all together if we could but see it.

"Heaven's sea" was also given a graphic depiction on the album sleeve. Having previously involved another artist in the commissioning of album covers, Sinfield now became the sole executor of that task. In the UK, the album was presented in an unmarked single sleeve with a photograph of the Trifid Nebula in the constellation of Sagittarius. The inner sleeve was a fragile cream-coloured gatefold with delicate islands created by Sinfield's patented method of food dye on blotting paper on the outside, and a collage of five individual portraits and three group shots of the band in concert. This was the first time the faces of the band had ever appeared on an album sleeve.

On its release in the USA, the inner gatefold was used as the outer cover. In the fractious history of King Crimson, there is still some ill-feeling over this. Fripp: "The change of cover for the US was because the UK cover was considered so feeble. The cover artist for the UK cover was Peter. Peter's 'move onstage' through use of the VCS3 now expanded to include designing the cover as well. If this works, fine. But Peter's cover wasn't striking, and wasn't in the same league as the other Crimson covers. The Nebula really wasn't much of a cover either, because it hadn't been chosen as a cover."

Burrell's vocals are sparingly augmented by the delicate chiaroscuro of Collins' bass flute and the translucent chords and passing notes of honorary Crim Keith Tippett. The pianist, well known for his adventurous and dynamic scrambles around the keyboard, here demonstrates an almost glacial poise and control. The minuscule duet between Tippett and Fripp, setting up the introduction of the keening oboe, is a point of marvellous internal reflection on the lyric.

Here the musical relationships are direct and presented without artifice. Wallace's percussion is kept to a stoic brushed hi-hat and bass drum pulse and the guitar provides only fleeting tonal colour. It's left largely to the churchy burr of the harmonium with its rustic dignity to carry the melody. Only the introduction of a paper-dry tracery of Mellotron hints at former glories.

Mark Charig provides a rousing wake-up call with his robust and playful cornet solo, an antidote to any potential mawkishness hovering over the track. Charig's bleating phrases dance over the understated rhythm, accumulating tension and generating expectancy in a rush of smears and flurries.

The naturalness of the performances, including a fluffed chord change by the harmonium at 6:13, and the sparse production give the track, in Fripp's words, "a strange charm: the openness and vulnerability of the players and parts".

Tucked away right at the very end is a few moments of Fripp and the ensemble about to perform *Prelude: Song Of The Gulls*. A tiny documentary fragment, it acts both as a humorous sign-off and also reveals the mundane aspects of life in the recording studio. This is not a place of glamour but of seasoned professionals, chatting to each other as they prepare to go to work.

LARKS' TONGUES IN ASPIC

Larks' Tongues In Aspic, Part One

(Cross, Fripp, Wetton, Bruford, Muir)

This glorious patchwork of contrasting dynamics begins unassumingly with a bright dialogue between thumb piano and glockenspiel almost reminiscent of Steve Reich's epic *Drumming*. However there's an edgy, haunted feel underlined by David Cross's terse, hovering motif until, after almost three minutes, the track explodes with a raucous, grinding piece of ensemble playing.

One of Fripp's most intricate and fiendishly complex guitar lines so far weaves around Bruford and Wetton's fearsome brand of steroid funk. The sheer brute force of this section makes it a fearsome overture – Bruford regards it as one of the best things from this period.

In respite, Cross then offers a beautiful solo which has drawn comparisons with Ralph Vaughn Williams' *The Lark Ascending*. Cross claims that at the time of the recording he was unfamiliar with the Vaughan Williams piece but that his intention was to create some light and space in the proceedings: "Years later, when I played *The Lark Ascending* I, too, was struck by the similarity with that *Larks' Tongues* intermezzo passage. It is a very well-known piece of music, so it seems likely that I must have heard it before that date but I wasn't consciously referring to it at the time. I think the biggest coincidence is the name."

Richard Palmer-James recalls visiting the studio and saw Fripp working repeatedly on the dextrous cross-picking figure on *Larks' Part One,* trying cleaner, jazzier tones before alighting on the final version. Palmer-James remembers Fripp and engineer Nick Ryan attempting to record the guitar unamplified as at the beginning of the piece's coda.

From there, ghostly voices percolate through a clipped staccato guitar part slowly climbing from silence towards a remorseless climax. It was Muir's idea to use voices in this way and Bruford recorded them directly off his radio at home. The play he recorded – *Gallowglass* by John and Willy Maley – was chosen totally at random. Making the word "dead" coincide with the dramatic G major chord of the coda was time-consuming and required several attempts, yet the results are more than worth the effort, providing a chilling end to one of Crimson's memorable pieces. As the track winds down with a fleeting glockenspiel theme, more voices are heard in a frenzied but subdued babble. Again, it was Muir's idea. Along with Bruford and Cross, he read out words and phrases from anything to hand in the studio, such as tape boxes and newspapers.

Book Of Saturday
(Fripp, Wetton, Palmer-James)
Lyricist Richard Palmer-James remembers writing the words. "Over the years I had forgotten about the amount of work I devoted to this lyric: it seems to be just another stream-of-consciousness job of the type that was popular at the time such as *The Windmills Of Your Mind*, *A Whiter Shade Of Pale*, *MacArthur Park* – though I think all of these are better lyrics than *Book Of Saturday*. But a while ago I dug out the manuscript and was surprised to discover all the corrections and variations – five foolscap sheets,

in fact. I think what I was trying to do was to create a sort of collage or scrapbook, containing simultaneous images of a love affair before, during, and after; a sort of Cubist approach, if you like; combining different viewpoints in space and time in the hope of getting nearer to the story in its entirety."

When Palmer-James visited Command during the recording, he recalls speaking to Fripp. "Robert and I exchanged some polite remarks; I don't think we had ever spoken before. As a gambit, I mentioned that I thought my couplet 'As the cavalry of despair/Takes a stand in the lady's hair' was perhaps a bit over the top (a new expression back then). He said that was one of his favourite bits. Could I be right in saying that this is his sole known commentary on the 1972–74 lyrics?"

For Wetton there was also the burden of laying down vocals, knowing that any of his previously recorded performances to date had never reached as wide an audience. Though a bassist of immense capability, he was then less sure of his capacities as a vocalist. But he threw himself into the job and came out with a more than credible performance in a relatively short number of takes.

In lesser hands, the yearning melancholia of the piece might become mere cloying sentimentality. Happily, Wetton's emotive, smoky vocals are beautifully delivered. Instrumentally, the piece contains many sublime moments, despite its brevity. Recalling the song with obvious affection, Fripp observes: "*Book Of Saturday* continues to exert its magic upon me even today. It somehow manages to hold a place outside the flow of time and seems to be young men expressing the thoughts of old men."

"The action begins with voice and bass close to centre positions, and guitar accompaniment on the right. The left speaker is empty long enough for an audient to wonder if the mixer fell asleep on the pan knobs. Then, the backwards guitar comes in: it's another Crimson set up! The left speaker was left empty long enough for us to sense emptiness, a space opened and held open; then our patience is rewarded and in comes the backwards guitar moving against time."

A basic demo version recorded at Bruford's house in 1972 appears on a scrapbook CD called *Monkey Business 1972–1997* by Wetton and Palmer-James (Voiceprint). Also included on this CD is a taped conversation between Fripp and Wetton, where Fripp comments: "Epic ballads are at a premium nowadays. It's very easy to get the hard playing thing together – it's comparatively straightforward. But good songs, good tunes … I don't think you can ever have too many of them."

Exiles
(Cross, Fripp, Palmer-James)
On the Bremen Beat Club version of the song, Muir can be heard adding some circumspect phrases on trombone – quickly curtailed following a withering glance

from a certain colleague. Needless to say, there was no possibility of the trombone making a re-appearance in the studio.

From a slow fade in, far-off indistinct sounds slouch their way to the foreground. Muir rubbed glass rods and manipulated the sound on tape, providing a hazy mirage out of which Fripp's recycled *Mantra* theme gloomily emerges, framed by Mellotron on a dark cello setting, making this perhaps the most cinematic of all the tracks.

Wetton's yearning vocals are closely miked though at times a touch strained. However, they deliver Palmer-James' exquisite tale of remembrance, loss and hope with a convincing passion.

Palmer-James: "When I wrote it I was just beginning to realise – after about 18 months of self-imposed exile in Europe – that my umbilical cord to our native island was about to sever, and that I probably wouldn't be wanting to live there again. This thought was both exciting and mournful. The atmosphere of the piece is influenced by the last couple of paragraphs of Joyce's *A Portrait Of The Artist As A Young Man* ('Away! Away!'). And it's a glorious melody, the kind of thing that gets a lyricist's pencil sharpened. I soon discovered, incidentally, that facing the call of fame and making a drunkard's name for oneself are not mutually exclusive."

The middle-eight features uncredited compositional contributions from Wetton and his similarly uncredited piano accompaniment. Cross plays flute, also anonymously. But it is his violin playing which makes the track so warm, propelling the poignant swooning backing vocals to greater heights.

Fripp adds lustre with a radiant sustained-effect solo. But the real star is his acoustic playing, weaving with graceful precision around the main melody.

Easy Money
(Fripp, Wetton, Palmer-James)

Certainly, Bruford and Wetton were less than inspired by the choice of studio and their opinion was not altered when engineer Nick Ryan botched the editing of *Easy Money*. Fripp: "What happened was that Bill's drum part was recorded over on a verse section. Astonishingly stupid error. Bill went back out and played drums almost blind to the track, which dropped him on to the blank space: it was an impressive piece of playing."

Needless to say, it would be the last time Crimson would record at Command.

But the real problem with this version of *Easy Money* is that the song fails to ignite in the way it did live. The guitar solo fails to build into anything other than meagre prickliness, until it sparks to life in the last verse when Cross produces some compact doubling with the coy funk of Wetton's (again uncredited) electric piano. *Easy Money* sounds like punches were pulled during its recording. It's the most unbalanced, and perhaps weakest, track on the album.

Muir's inventive flair is always present, whether he's hissing gently into a nearby mic or crumpling a piece of paper. This kind of ironic, self-deprecating air was largely unheard on previous Crimson albums. The most obvious examples are the sloshing mud in the introduction and a joke-shop laughing bag at the end. Surprisingly, the device was not part of Muir's bag of tricks but was introduced by Fripp, who loved it.

Many of the sounds suggested and produced by Jamie Muir required close and careful miking. Regarding himself and his methods as intuitive and "messy", Muir felt that Fripp in the studio had a propensity to be more "clean and tidy", resulting in tension and a feeling that Muir had to fight to have many of his ideas and suggestions included at all.

As the hours ticked away, Muir came under pressure to turn his intentions into reality, a position exacerbated by the unpredictable nature of the instruments he was working with. "With all these found instruments, they've got a mind of their own and you don't quite know if they're going to do what you want them to or not." Assuming they worked, there was a substantial degree of experimentation to get the desired sound and appropriate level in the microphone placement and mix.

The track was always popular live – and, with its abrasive opening riff, it's easy to hear why. Palmer-James wholly approved of the comedic mien of the piece, claiming the lyrics were written by way of a joke aimed at people guided by the lowest motives. This might go some way to explain the infamous alternative verse used in concert and its reference to sex with a minor. Often assumed to have been a politically incorrect vamp by Wetton, it was, in fact, written by Palmer-James.

The Talking Drum
(Cross, Fripp, Wetton, Bruford, Muir)
The strange trumpet-like noises – like drunken bees – at the beginning and end are produced by one of Muir's hybrid arsenal: a brass mouthpiece attached to a length of tubing blown and whirled around his head to achieve a shifting Doppler-effect. This is made all the more effective by placing it in the desolate wind sound of Fripp's fuzz-driven wah-wah pedal.

Muir recalls playing the agitated hand-held drum solo too fast and having to slow down when Wetton came in with the simple but insistent bass figure upon which the track is built. The guitarist's judgement is less than effusive: "*The Talking Drum* is really a weedy sounding track to ears which accompanied it around the world live over a period of 24 years. But John Wetton's crunchy bass sound makes up for some of it."

The band had several passes before plumping for the final version. Muir recalls David Cross being anxious about his solo. "He was much more reticent than he had any cause to be. He was a much better player than he thought he was. He was a bit nervous about the solo, but as we got into it he had no need to be." Bill Bruford is less than impressed with the finished version: "It's a tempo and a dynamic which is meant to get from very quiet to very loud – that's the only instruction in the music and all you've got to do is get from A to B and on the record it doesn't get very loud. It's feeble and singularly failed to build momentum."

The track erupts into an ear-splitting finale of Jamie Muir's devising, as he explains: "The screeching at the end was produced by bicycle horns – the ones with the black plastic bulb on the end – and if you take that off, they've got a little reed and if you bend the reed and blow it with your mouth you can change the sound. I did it and I think Bill might have done some as well just so we didn't use up too many tracks."

While there's no denying that the track lacks the driving energy the band generated in concert, it still manages to produce a spine-tingling anticipation. The climactic screech sounds like it could have erupted from the terrified mouth of the face on the cover of the first King Crimson album.

Larks' Tongues In Aspic, Part Two
(Fripp)
As grating guitar breaks through the banshee howls, so begins one of the classic Crimson pieces, containing a clear homage to Stravinsky's *The Rite Of Spring*. With dissonant bells and chimes, the exhilarating piece alternates between a 4/4 and 5/4 pattern with Muir and Bruford re-creating their double drum kit trick, furious drum rolls mixed with cruelly dented baking trays and other household objects. Over all this domestic mayhem, Cross's solo is majestic and maniacal. Fripp forgoes any grandstanding and concentrates on powering the piece along with his raucous guitar, culminating in a marvellous crescendo reminiscent of the coda from *Sailor's Tale*.

Talking to *NME*'s Ian MacDonald in a very tongue-in-cheek interview five months after its release, Fripp claimed the enormous bump and grind of the track might have as much to do with sexual as with musical technique. When digitally re-mastering the album in July 2000, he remarked: "*Larks' Two*, as a piece of writing, addresses the paradox of being simultaneously within the conditioned and unconditioned worlds. This partly explains the depictions of contradiction, forms of resolution, longing, loss, anger and despair, evolution, arrival and respite. The (musical) metaphor of physical union is particularly obvious (surely?) during the ascending sections (10/8 with an opening bar of 11/8 to throw the beat off and introduce a dual downbeat). *The Nascent Soul's Journey Into Light* might be a more literally descriptive title but I wouldn't have had the courage to use that in 1972; and probably not today either."

STARLESS AND BIBLE BLACK

The Great Deceiver
(Wetton, Fripp, Palmer-James)

The album's opening track kicks off all guns blazing with Fripp and Cross shooting off a fiery unison line which wouldn't sound out of place in The Mahavishnu Orchestra. Despite clocking in at only a little over four minutes, *The Great Deceiver* packs a terrific punch and contains an almost absurdly confident vocal from Wetton. This is not to say that he got it right in one go. At 1:52 he is heard to yell "You don't!" – a phrase coined by Mark Fenwick and in common use around the EG office to convey disapproval or disappointment. Wetton had just fluffed a take but the exclamation worked well and was left in.

The track initially sprang from a Wetton bass riff combined with an altogether different piece from Fripp. Wetton recalls the song originally had a much funkier feel to it with the bass playing all the rhythmic emphases, later appropriated by Bruford. This left Wetton the job of anchoring the track with a quirky stop-start line.

Wetton wanted Fripp to double the bass line on the lower octave of the guitar but the guitarist was unconvinced. One evening after the others had gone home, Chkiantz set the tapes rolling and Wetton doubled the basslines on his black Stratocaster. The following day the results were played back to the band, gained Fripp's approval and remained, oddly uncredited.

Fripp makes a rare lyrical contribution with his caustic observation of a commercialised Vatican in the chorus "Cigarettes, ice cream, figurines of the Virgin Mary". The line originated in Crimson's visit to Rome the previous November and was, as Wetton recalls, later enthusiastically and volubly recited by band members in the manner of Monty Python's "Albatross" sketch.

Many years later, Fripp saw the Palmer-James lyric "Health food faggot" mentioned in a book on gay references in rock music and in 1997 took the opportunity to question the lyricist about the line. "Richard had no gay reference in mind: his notion of 'faggot' was the health food version of a meatball. The insulting gay connotation only occurred to him later."

The track was released on a single ahead of the album as the B-side of *The Night Watch*.

Lament
(Fripp, Wetton, Palmer-James)

Palmer-James' story of life in a rock'n'roll band perfectly evokes an industry, as someone once said, oiled by deceit, riven with theft and fuelled by greed. Sadly the music fails to live up to it. Essentially bolted together from different fragments dating back to 1971 and the *Larks' Tongues* sessions, it fails to gel. Wetton: "It should have been cataclysmic but fizzles out." Bruford agrees and admits its inclusion on the album was down to the shortage of composed material available at the time.

There are some interesting percussive flourishes and many individual moments of interest but overall the track fails to add up to a convincing piece of writing.

We'll Let You Know
(Cross, Fripp, Wetton, Bruford)
Recorded live at the legendary Apollo Theatre in Glasgow on 23 October 1973, this dense improvisation begins cautiously, Wetton clearly seeking to drive the pace with a brutish funk motif. Bruford resists the temptation to fall into line, prolonging the sense of flippant anticipation as he whoops and clatters around his battery of metallics.

As Cross makes fragmentary stabs on the electric piano, Fripp and Wetton set off bursts of jarring squeals and petulant slapped notes but still Bruford resists the pulsing, building rhythm. The strange brew continues for almost three minutes and when Bruford finally obliges with a killer bee funk work-out the sense of elation is palpable. Listening back to it, Wetton observed: "I realise that Bill and I weren't completely in sync and that we were hearing beat one in different places but it works. It sounds more complex than it actually is. Bill played against what I was playing and I think that's what gives it that kind of unusual tension."

The sparks really begin to fly with Fripp's guitar careering and spiralling like a Catherine wheel. Sadly, David Cross's electric piano seems severely under-mixed but the careful listener can hear him ducking and diving between the fireworks. The full improv can be heard on disc two of 1992's *The Great Deceiver* boxed set and discs 1 (CD) and 23 (Blu-ray) from 2014's *Starless* box.

The Night Watch
(Fripp, Wetton, Palmer-James)
The first two minutes of this beautiful ballad are taken from the 23 November show at Amsterdam's Concertgebouw. The location couldn't be more apt, given that the subject is a painting by Rembrandt. Palmer-James is particularly fond of the song. "I always found that the subtle change in atmosphere caused by the edit pricks up the listener's ears, and adds to the effect of the following – 'recital' seems to be just the right word for it. The piece has a timeless, chamber-music feel; it's difficult to categorise. That's what I like."

"Unfortunately, this may have served to make the lyrics much more mysterious than they were meant to be. In the '70s, nobody seemed to have the foggiest idea what I was on about. More recently, however, I get the impression that people recognise the song for what it is – a thumbnail sketch of Rembrandt's situation as an artist in

17th-century Holland. Practically lifted from sixth-form art history notes. There's nothing obscure about it at all."

Wetton had his work cut out delivering a lot of words in a short time and, in a live setting, the song often sounded rushed and jumbled. Here, however, it's a perfectly balanced performance. Not for the first time, Wetton adds value to the piece by double-tracking his voice and processing it through a Leslie cabinet. These vocal washes are immensely effective, adding an extra patina to the overall sound.

There are perhaps allusions to bygone eras other than that of Rembrandt's age in the song. Fripp's use of harmonium is suggestive of the bucolic reverie of *Islands*. The guitar solo, completed in one take, certainly counts as a personal best for the 27-year-old guitarist. The timeless grace and ardour which seems to flow through every note is only matched by the lyrical, ascending bassline which underpins it. Fripp recalls that Wetton wasn't initially convinced by the solo but was eventually persuaded of its charms – "I persuaded John to listen to it twice," he says. The compactness of the production and its arrangement, with its unerring eye for detail, makes the painterly comparisons unavoidable and entirely fitting.

Trio
(Cross, Fripp, Wetton, Bruford)
The gentle incline of Wetton's bassline, played above the 12th fret, which grounds this piece had, in fact, been presented to the band on previous occasions and sometimes featured in soundchecks and rehearsals. But the piece that emerged that night at the Concertgebouw was totally improvised.

The band was, as David Cross puts it, "long-term and deep down tired" and these few moments provided Crimson with a brief hiatus from the energy-sapping thunder of that night's set. Little wonder that Bruford opted to sit out the number with his sticks symbolically folded across his chest. This not only had the benefit of enabling him to pace himself for the rest of the show, but the absence of any percussive intervention perversely made a telling and decisive contribution to the dynamics of the performance as a whole – hence his writing credit. Wetton had nothing but admiration for Bruford's ear. "Most drummers would have played something on the brushes but he didn't do anything at all. He was just saying 'I think you guys can handle this one' but it wouldn't have happened with anyone else."

As Fripp takes to the Mellotron on flute setting, Cross swoops and soars over the crowd, providing a little over five minutes of delicate beauty. For Wetton, the interplay between Cross and Fripp was astonishing. "When you hit that level of confidence, things start happening and that track makes you start to wonder about telepathy and so on – it's definitely *X Files* stuff on that track. I can't think of anything else that we did that was that sensitive."

The Mincer
(Cross, Fripp, Wetton, Bruford, Palmer-James)
This small excerpt from the band's performance in Zurich on 15 November 1973 is snipped from an improvisation that lasted over 13 minutes. The brief section omits the six-and-a-half minutes of thrashing, atonal funk that preceded it in concert. The pensive mood is enhanced by vocals overdubbed in the studio. Wetton recalls the words were inspired by a well-coiffured character in close proximity when Crimson played *Midnight Special* in Los Angeles on the singer's birthday on 12 June 1973.

After the vocals, the track appears to be building up but dribbles to an end as the tape runs out. Wetton recalls that the track was an experiment in trying to find new methods of composition, using improvisation as a foundation on which to graft melody and lyrics.

The abrupt ending caused controversy with Bruford and Wetton wanting the piece to stop properly. However Cross and Fripp preferred the ragged tailing-off and their view prevailed. Listening back, Bruford, Wetton and Palmer-James still regarded the track as filler material.

Those wondering what happened next had to wait 18 years for the release of *The Great Deceiver* boxed set to find out. The track *The Law Of Maximum Distress, Part One* cuts out just before *The Mincer* section is about to start, though it should be noted that this itself is incomplete. *The Law Of Maximum Distress, Part Two* takes up the story a minute or two later from where *The Mincer* petered out. The full sequence is re-created on the *Starless* boxed set, where it can be heard on discs 1 (CD), 21 (DVD-A) and 23 (Blu-ray).

Starless And Bible Black
(Cross, Fripp, Wetton, Bruford)
Recorded at the Concertgebouw, where it was the first improvisation of the set, that might explain the slightly cautious, edgy beginning. Wetton breaks open the piece, establishing a thumping pulse on the bass as Bruford emerges from the glockenspiel to snake around the beat with sundry implements. The front line slowly inches forward, gathering up a tightly woven theme to produce the molten core of what Wetton regards as one of their finest improvisations.

The track highlights Cross's role as texturalist as he skilfully utilises the Mellotron and piano to offer a palette of rich tones, generating a swirling mist through which Fripp shines. Indeed, in the early part of the piece, Cross makes inventive use of the electric piano's volume pedal, letting dark blotches of timbre bleed up underneath the guitar lines.

After nearly four and a half minutes, the band fuses together over a characteristically off-kilter 4/4, crackling with a bristling energy and interplay that corkscrews off into the Amsterdam night. Cross's ethereal shifting Mellotron raises the piece above the rhythm section's determinedly rockist groove and propels Fripp's scorching guitar to rare heights. Because of this cohesion, many listeners believed that the piece was composed rather than improvised.

Sensationally, after eight minutes, the entire band bites down on a strident, descending flourish from Cross – now on violin – punctuated by Bruford and Wetton with customary exactitude. The fact that the group was capable of producing a piece of such focus and clarity while so tired is a testament to their prowess and talent. Anyone in any doubt about what Cross could do should start here.

Fracture
(Fripp)
The album closes with yet another Concertgebouw track that defies expectations. Just when you think it can't get any more complex – it does. Just when you think the main theme can't get any higher and faster – it does. Just when you think you can't possibly dance the Watusi to it – you can! Talking to *Circus-Raves* in 1974, Cross recalls Fripp's unassuming introduction of the piece at the writing rehearsals in Kingston. "He said 'I have this idea …' and proceeded to play this incredible, complicated guitar solo. The rest of us sort of stopped and clapped, 'Oh very good!'"

When asked which Crimson piece was the most difficult to play, Wetton offered *Fracture* without any hesitation. The bassist would often feel sorry watching Fripp trapped inside this cage of his own making – but not as sorry as he felt for himself as he grappled with the intricacies of its elaborate, obsessive timings and interlocking sections.

Fripp has often been described as the musical glue holding Crimson together and nowhere is this more evident than on *Fracture*. Fripp confirms that the piece remains one of the hardest pieces he's ever played in public. "During the moto perpetuo, in the middle of the piece, if the group's time drifts then the guitarist is hung out to dry. Often, the time drifted in the group. The guitarist is stuck with and endless (it feels) series of equal semi-quavers at 124–136 bpm with cross-picking over two and three strings."

Also in perpetual motion is the rhythm section, which roves under and over the main themes carried by Cross and Fripp. And who else but Bruford would have had the idea to restate the theme on glockenspiel and xylophone? The effect is to introduce a brief comedic respite while emphasising the stridently manic nature of the main theme, before the track drives on, shifting gears and throttling up. The power of this piece is extraordinary even by Crimson standards and, on this recording, Bruford can be heard excitedly signalling his evident enjoyment.

In 1974, Cross recalled: "When I went on stage the first time we played *Fracture*, I still had no idea what I was going to play. I had five alternatives for each section. It took me a month of playing every night, of walking on stage and not knowing what the hell I was going to play, and just going from there." If *Larks' Tongues In Aspic, Part Two* (and the cross-picking themes of *Part One*) are Fripp trying to find his voice as a composer, then *Fracture* heralds that voice's dramatic arrival in full.

From the early cross-picking of *Suite No. 1*, his fierce riff for *21st Century Schizoid Man* and then into the principal themes and dynamics of *Larks' Tongues In Aspic*, Fripp had been moving inexorably towards *Fracture*, both logical extension and quantum leap forward. But its significance as a composition lies not so much in its origins as in its implications. *Fracture* is a pivotal moment in Fripp's emergence as a composer. The moto perpetuo middle section lays the seed for the pointillistic style of The League Of Gentlemen – and *that* defined the next further step of the interlocking, rock gamelan, at the point when Fripp's concerns shifted decisively away from classical European tradition towards new and world music.

In this version of *Fracture*, one or two overdubs were felt necessary. To compare the original recording without them, listen to the version on 1997's *The Night Watch*. Fripp recalls: "I double-tracked the lead line on the return in the moto perpetuo. George Chkiantz was impressed: double-tracking that sucker from a live recording wasn't easy."

RED
Red
(Fripp)

The first piece the band tackled at Olympic was the monstrously heavy *Red*, the main riff of which was first tried out in a soundcheck in Salt Lake City's Terrace Ballroom. Aspects of the tune had also been thrown around in some of the last tour's improvisations, but it wasn't until Olympic that the piece was finally constructed. Immediately impressed with its power, Wetton remembered a contrasting piece called *Blue* being discussed, but coming to nothing. (Fripp: "I still have the manuscript notes for the theme of *Blue*, which I had presented in an earlier rehearsal and had been tossed around without quite arriving anywhere. It has never re-appeared.")

The piece oozes the controlled potency and simple economy now a signature of Fripp's compositional style. Redolent with expectancy, the power in *Red* lies in the sheer weight of Wetton's fuzz bass, a smoking core to the music. When this murky undertow is set against the caustic, jarring chords of Fripp's guitar and the volatile hail of Bruford's meticulous cymbal work, the combination is devastating.

But when the piece was presented to the band there was some discussion about its merit, as Fripp recalls. "Bill didn't 'get' *Red*. He didn't have a feel for it. I said fine, we don't have to use it. John urged for its inclusion. Bill said something along the lines of, 'I don't get it, but if you both say it's good I believe you.'" Looking back, Bruford isn't sure if he did or didn't originally "get" *Red*. He does recall, however, that his initial impression of the composition was that it reminded him of *Tea For Two*.

In the light of this, Fripp presented a case for the royalties for the track to be solely assigned to him – a change from the band's usual practice of dividing songwriting royalties equally, regardless of the composer(s). "I said that if we were going to use *Red*, I wanted all the royalties, because I wrote it. My reasoning was this: if one of the members is getting as much as the writer for the piece, and can't tell whether the piece was any good or not, I think it's better that the writer keep the writing royalties! I discovered about two years ago that EG misfiled: royalties have been divided three ways since the beginning."

The piece's cello section originally contained another portion, excised at the time by Fripp. It would resurface 21 years later in *VROOOM VROOOM*!

Fallen Angel
(Fripp, Wetton, Palmer-James)
In this lachrymose combination of Elvis Presley's *In The Ghetto* and *West Side Story*, Crimson are helped out here by Robin Miller (oboe) and Mark Charig (cornet), both of whom last appeared on 1971's *Islands*.

Miller recalls Fripp being almost apologetic about the tune. "He said something about it not being as good as some of the other pieces he'd given me to play. I thought it was delightful." Miller's delicate oboe adds a distinguished, courtly feel summoning up memories of the older Crimson amid the more metallic elements.

The song is bolted together from two separate elements. The principal arpeggiated chord sequence is faintly reminiscent of the lick which opens *Ladies Of The Road*, and more particularly of the bridge following Fripp's guitar solo on that track (at 4:11). Of course, it had been road-tested as far back as The Zoom Club in October 1972, where it was incorporated into an early reading of *Easy Money*.

It's amalgamated here with a plaintive middle-eight section of a Wetton ballad called *Woman*, delivered via a fanfare of multi-tracked basses which sing the lead melody on this section (a demo version of *Woman* can be heard on the Wetton/Palmer-James CD *Monkey Business*).

It's interesting to hear how Fripp's raking staccato figures accompany Marc Charig's beefy cornet, perhaps providing a further insight as to how Crimson's sound might have developed had gone on to consolidate the experiment with the re-introduction of Ian McDonald.

The twinkling harmonics of Fripp's acoustic guitar overdubs, which shower the first two verses like falling snowflakes, mark the last time Fripp would play an acoustic guitar on a King Crimson album.

One More Red Nightmare
(Fripp, Wetton)
The thunderous opening riff was thrown around by Fripp in concerts such as at Toronto's Massey Hall (see *The Golden Walnut* from Disc 4 of *The Great Deceiver* or Disc 11 of the later boxed set *The Road To Red*). In that context, it is tentatively dabbled with, making fleeting appearances in the full flight of improvisation. One month later in the studio, it becomes a weighty piece of brazen power-play.

A relentlessly ebullient Bruford steals the show as he rattles and clatters his way around the kit and adjoining metals. Bruford had found a discarded cymbal dumped in the rubbish bin by the previous users. A 20-inch Zilket, upturned at one side like an Australian bush-hat, it awakened some of his fascination with found objects from the Jamie Muir period. "I fished it out of the rubbish bin and discovered it had this fantastic short trashy sound which was really great. To this day, there's never been a cymbal to sound as good as that and everybody wants one. Nobody's been able to make one. It lasted for the album and a few months afterwards and died. Nobody ever had a cymbal like it before or since."

Engineer Chkiantz noted a significant expansion in Wetton's vocal abilities. At Olympic, dummy microphones were no longer required to boost the singer's self-esteem. "I just used a very natural set-up but that was because John had been doing vocals a lot longer. He had more confidence and his voice had developed, and it was therefore projecting much better which made it easier to handle." Wetton agreed that this was one of his best vocal performances in a studio but was less than convinced by his own lyric, dismissing it as half-formed.

What set the heart beating, however, for most Crimson enthusiasts was the re-appearance of Ian McDonald. The importance of McDonald in the birth of KC cannot be overstated and, were it not for Fripp's determination to keep things going, McDonald's departure in 1969 might have delivered a fatal blow to the band. His re-appearance on a KC record has a mighty resonance. While Fripp concentrates on building and developing the texture in the background, McDonald whips up a storm with a garrulous alto sax.

McDonald weaves between the tightly regulated knots of Bruford's cymbal work, creating some of the track's most memorable peaks. If Bruford and Wetton were looking for an instrument that could compete with them, then they had found it in McDonald's electronically viscid sax.

Although the tape ran out during the recording of the solo, the band were so impressed with McDonald's playing that they wanted to keep it. It was Chkiantz who came up with the solution, as Wetton recalls: "George turned the tape upside down and recorded a very long fuzz bass note and turned the tape the right way 'round. Of course, what you then get is a bass note that comes out of nowhere, building up until the tape runs out."

Providence
(Cross, Fripp, Wetton, Bruford)
The second improvisation from Crimson's show at the Palace Theatre in Providence, Rhode Island, on 30 June 1974. Cautiously emerging from Bartokian gloom, *Providence* positively glowers with menace and foreboding as Cross's violin nervously haunts the outer edges of a frail, skeletal melody.

For more than four minutes the ensemble rides a series of dramatic swells over which Cross and Fripp (at this point still on Mellotron flutes) distribute dissonant, sclerotic exchanges from either side of the mix. Listening to this, it's possible to imagine the personal cost every mile had exacted from the players on their way from the beatific *Trio* to this exhausted point.

After almost five minutes of precarious atmospherics, Bruford introduces one of his patented rim shot and bass drum parts. A scurrying Cross hurriedly reprises the skittering motif as the band reach critical mass and all hell breaks loose with Fripp letting out a shrill, caustic bellow of sustained notes heralding one of his most perilous and coruscating solos.

Bruford opens up the throttle and Fripp and Wetton vie for position over an embarrassment of riches – there's so much for the listener to choose from. As the pair lock horns, they resemble a pair of irritable heavyweight prize fighters driven by adrenaline, instinct and a desire to get to the other side intact. Simply put, there are few improvisations before or since which have the clarity and authority of *Providence*.

The complete version of the improv appeared on *The Great Deceiver* and *The Road To Red* boxed sets complete with Cross's full contribution and a somewhat ragged ending.

Starless
(Cross, Fripp, Wetton, Bruford, Palmer-James)
Starless was one of the first tracks recorded for *Red* but Wetton asserted that it was always set to provide the album with one of the most thrilling and emotional conclusions of any Crimson recording. "We always knew that *Red* should start it and *Starless* should finish it. All we had to worry about was the middle. It makes the album sequence like a live show."

The yearning ballad section had originally been presented to the band – but rejected – the previous January. As ever with Crimson, the scarcity of written material forced them to re-examine what was lurking in their collective back pocket and out came *Starless And Bible Black*. Having already used the title in March, the band shortened it to avoid confusion. Despite this, Fripp often called the tune by its original name in his stage announcements.

The lyric went through several revisions and, despite four attempts, Richard Palmer-James still expresses some reservations about the final version. The bleak abyss of personal loss was never more chillingly represented than in these lines and Fripp observed that Wetton, in delivering them, made the transition from merely singing to becoming a singer. Documenting the dissolution of a long-standing friendship, Wetton's vocals wearily carry the unfolding burden to the heart.

Fripp suggests the song also marks the passing of another epoch. "The song part of *Starless* is Crimson's swansong for the 1970s. This is the death of a certain kind of innocence which continued the optimism of the 1960s, the acknowledgement of this loss, and Crimson's final statement on it. The instruments state their varying positions on what this means to the individuals represented by them."

Wetton's song benefited from the addition of introductory chords provided by Fripp, a lilting reflective melody from Cross (with a finishing touch from Fripp) and quite possibly the band's most monstrously ominous bass riff, courtesy of Bill Bruford. Of this, Bruford nonchalantly remarks: "I was beginning to find my compositional legs and it wasn't something I really thought about. I just knocked it off on the piano at home and thought it might work well." Fripp proves the dictum that less really is more by offering one of his most minimal guitar solos to date. With just two repeating notes, it looms over the 13/8 section as Bruford overdubs a playful levity via his arsenal of percussion, showing just how much he had assimilated from Jamie Muir.

Fripp admits that this deceptively simple tension and release section of *Starless* was a trial for him in concert, claiming: "Bill's time on this section was appalling. At Central Park it was a nightmare playing over him."

Over a thumping figure, Collins bursts in with a furious sweep of notes weaving between Fripp's slashing power chords, making for some of the most agile and acute playing on any Crimson album. As Fripp once said: "The playing from 1973/74 is definitely and comfortably rock, but rocking rock. Never a fusion band, we fizzed and fused." Nowhere is this better demonstrated than on *Starless*.

Ten minutes in, over the deliriously insistent whisper of Bruford's hi-hat, the opalescent gleam of Mel Collins' soprano and Robin Miller's oboe briefly entwine around the main theme.

As the track hurtles toward the final theme, it's easy to miss the brace of furious chords underpinning the corrosive screech of the lead guitar. As the main theme returns, guitar and sax are majestically carried aloft in a triumphant and dramatic fusion of spine-tingling proportions, reinforced by haunting Mellotron and a quartet of overdubbed double basses adding to the gravitas of the piece.

Fripp offers this telling assessment of *Red*'s overall achievement. "If *Starless* represents the end of one theme, *Red* is the beginning of another. Although Crim heavy metal began with *Schizoid* and continued on through *Larks'*, this piece marks a qualitative shift in the function of Crim metal, the implication of which continues to resonate in Crim even today."

DISCIPLINE

(Music: **King Crimson;** Words: **Adrian Belew**)

Elephant Talk

Any fan expecting Crimson 1981 to start where *Red* left off was in for a shock – the musical terrain couldn't be more different. Of course, those who had followed Fripp's progress since his return to music in 1977 would have seen the tone of this new Crimson carefully laid out in the preceding solo releases. *Under Heavy Manners* clearly shows where Fripp's thinking was headed. Similarly, the new wave weaving of the LOG demonstrated the desire to see succinct and self-contained material.

The move to a 50/50 Anglo-American line-up and Fripp's assimilation of certain strands of American and world culture were central to the new music. Recalcitrant European fans weren't the only ones having to play catch-up, as Bruford remembers. "Robert had spent the previous seven years, or quite a lot of it, in New York, absorbing a number of influences that I hadn't. There was the whole business about new wave loft music in NY and the beginnings of world music."

"There was also all these things with David Bowie, Brian Eno and David Byrne and Steve Reich that were floating around in Robert's head more than mine. So perhaps I had further to go in 1981 to catch up with Robert. Indeed, I was almost given a reading list as well. Welcome to the band – here's the reading list!"

In this context, *Elephant Talk* is a beginners' guide to the new Crimson, a dramatic in-your-face assessment of where things now stood. As with *Under Heavy Manners*, Fripp had prepared a list of words to sing but Belew was uneasy about such a recitation. In the end, he came up with his own words, delivered in a joyous declamation.

Originating from an undulating riff on the Stick, the track was one of the quickest to come together in the *Discipline* rehearsals. There's a rippling urgency threading its way throughout the piece and the disorientating clamour is heightened by the stirring arrival of Belew's effect-laden pyrotechnics. Spurning convenient pre-set sounds, the exotic arsenal of sounds at Belew's disposal was a result of rigorous experimentation with all the various elements of his equipment, all carefully documented in a little notebook.

The trumpeting elephant effect was realised by a combination of a Big Muff effect pedal and a flanger set to move the pitch up and down. With Belew manually sliding the note up on the fretboard, the resulting collision of sound and effect sounds remarkably like a highly agitated elephant moving toward the listener.

Rather than competing with Belew's boisterous roar, Fripp offers up a squeaking mouse of a solo. In doing so, he not only provides a lightly comic foil but clearly announces that the two-guitar Crimson will not be a place of trilling histrionics or lengthy solo excursions.

Frame By Frame

The centrepiece of the track is undoubtedly the Steve Reich-like phasing which provides such a turbo-charged opening. A firm favourite with fans, *Frame By Frame* offered spectators a vicarious thrill as the twin-guitar Crimson came into its own. Belew maintains the repetitive figure; Fripp relocates the accent in a different place with each cycle, creating a tension that slowly stretches the piece apart. Sure enough, the guitar lines slowly unravel, spiralling around each other in a decaying orbit, eventually consumed by the fiery burst of Fripp's absurdly fast double-time picking.

Performing such a piece is not without its dangers. A finger in the wrong place could fatally puncture the delicate metrical network. An example of how shaky things could become may be heard on the *Live At Moles* KCCC release.

Over the years, Fripp has gained something of a monastic reputation, foregoing the usual pleasures of life on the road in favour of long hours spent battling the metronome in hotel rooms or backstage areas. While this approach may have unsettled some observers and colleagues, for Fripp it was vital to be able to meet the demands of the music. More than that, practice as part of a personal discipline was a means of staying sane inside the asylum.

Belew, by contrast, had a more *laissez-faire* approach. Although he would devote huge amounts of time exploring the sonic possibilities of a slew of effects pedals, he did not go in for the long sessions of callisthenics preferred by Fripp. Nevertheless, he was endowed with a prodigious technique enabling him to assimilate a range of styles. Interestingly, when he first began to work with David Bowie, he quickly learned solos which had been artificially manipulated and highly edited in the studio. Not knowing he wasn't meant to be able to learn the material, Belew sat down and did just that – a fact which speaks volumes about his tenacity and talent.

The combination of the methodical and intuitive approaches in the new Crimson was the band's secret weapon, producing the sparks to transform a tapestry of eclectic ideas into a compelling blend.

Speaking in 1982 to Ian Stewart, Belew offered his own perspective: "I think there's a kind of common ground we meet on. It has to do with some of the sounds and approaches we use. Robert is fairly inflexible as a guitarist; he doesn't adhere to my style at all. I have had to adhere to his. This is fine with me, because it's a learning process. Therefore, I think we can cross over in certain areas; there is a kind of middle ground that we have. And then each of us has our extremes that the other person doesn't do – Robert can't make his guitar sound like a rhino and I can't play the fast end line at the end of *Frame By Frame*."

The track is a whirlwind *tour de force* around the hairpin bends of the new Crimson music, making for one of the most exciting pieces produced during this era.

Matte Kudasai

The Crimson ballad had been a long and honourable tradition and on this occasion was achieved in the exquisite form of *Matte Kudasai*. With a title purloined by Belew from a Japanese phrasebook – it means "please wait for me" – the track has an incongruous country and western lilt. Belew explains how it came together: "Robert and I sat quietly unplugged working through the verses chords – written by Fripp – which were left with me to expound upon, adding changes to support the melody I had in mind. The lyric was written in the lonely bowels of the Horton Inn and was as painful to write as usual."

The relaxing air that permeates the song is strongly reminiscent of *Julie With* … from Brian Eno's 1977 album *Before And After Science*. Perhaps most notably, the golden shimmering guitar arpeggio which underscores the chorus ("She waits in the air") appears to echo a strikingly similar device at 2:37 in the Eno track. Whether deliberate homage or unconscious lift – Fripp claims to be unfamiliar with *Julie With* … – the effect is to give *Matte Kudesai* a delicious buoyancy, perfectly capturing the motion of the mournful seagulls circling throughout the song.

When the album was originally released, the track contained a purring solo from Fripp. "In Island Studios, recording and mixing of the album completed, Adrian and I agreed that something more was needed for *Matte*. He left it to me to come up with something, flew home, but when he heard my contribution wasn't convinced."

The solo, opening with a reference to the *Peace* theme from *In The Wake Of Posiedon*, was subsequently removed when the album was released on CD. The original version is included as a bonus track on remastered albums from 2001 onwards.

Matte Kudasai was released as a single in 1981 and received a reasonable amount of airplay in the UK. In 1995, as he sat in a restaurant in Canterbury waiting for his wife to join him for brunch, Fripp noted: "To my surprise *Matte Kudasai* slides on to the house muzak system. Does this mean crossover and break-out? Should I be grateful that the unwitting and innocent crepe and cappuccino consumers of Canterbury have their unsuspecting ears accosted by Ade's superlative slide playing?"

Indiscipline

Fripp well understood Bruford's love of pushing the beat around a piece, providing percussive thrills and spills. This aspect of Bruford's musical personality was, in Fripp's eyes, both an asset and a difficulty, given the complex phasing of the two guitars. Levin's inclusion was intended in part to counter-balance Bruford's style and provide a reliable point of reference amid the shifting meters.

Two days into rehearsals, Fripp and Bruford had their first falling out. The cause was the distance between what the guitarist envisaged the drums to be doing and what the drummer thought would work with the material.

Paddy Spinks recalls that Fripp would talk to him about his frustrations. "I came to learn that sometimes the creative process involves friction and sometimes that creates magic. That's what happened with that band sometimes. There were certain situations where it came together in such a way that it was just astoundingly good. Robert knew he needed Bill but hated the fact that he needed Bill. It provided him with a certain creativity which he himself couldn't provide and King Crimson's always been a greater sum of the four parts. Robert would get anxious about Bill's alleged overplaying and I would basically try to just let Robert look at it in a larger context."

Fripp's solution was to present Bruford and the rest of the band with ground rules. Residing within the 15 instructions were such helpful hints such as: "If you have an idea, don't play it," and "If there is space for a fill which is demanded by the music, don't play it: there are three other people who would like to use the opportunity."

How did Bruford feel about Fripp's proscriptions? "He was right much of the time. I have a very thick skin and I'm not in the slightest bit delicate, and if I think somebody is saying something that I think I can take on board them I'll certainly use it. I think I'm the only person who would have put up with this. I think most drummers would have smashed him on the nose. It's only that I sensed that most of what he said was, if not right in inverted commas, was at least intriguing and probably useful to my work that I stayed and rolled with the punches."

Indiscipline is the antidote to Fripp's aphorisms and directions, giving Bruford an opportunity to cut loose.

Levin grounds the tempo on the Stick, unwavering as the drummer pushes the rhythm up, under and over the bar – often all at the same time. "Well, it's not unknown in jazz for the bass player to hold a rhythm while the drummer moves about," explains Bruford. The drummer pitches up a bombardment of percussion to showcase the agility and wit of his playing.

But it wasn't just Bruford having the fun. Belew's ambiguous spoken tale was based on lines taken from a letter from his wife Margaret, describing her responses to a sculpture she had recently finished. The close miking on Belew's oblique monologue draws the listener close, literally and metaphorically.

When the band slams in between the spoken passages, aural flak flies in all directions. Fripp's guitar work seems on the point of critical mass in its ferocity and density. A pity then that it is mixed so far behind the drums and Belew's vibrant playing. With echoes of *Sailor's Tale* and the climactic solo on *Disengage* from Fripp's *Exposure*, the blistering runs are nothing short of extraordinary, the guitarist relishing his freedom as much as the drummer.

"I once asked Adrian Belew how he knew where to start the verse after Fripp's solos," recalls Tony Levin. "He said, 'I look at Robert and when he grimaces in a certain way – and his hands are at the top of the neck and there's no place else to go – then I know.'"

Thela Hun Ginjeet

As the band prepared to unveil their new material at Moles Club in Bath, the lyrical ideas for this track existed only in outline. They knew it was going to be about life in the street, crime and the pressure of life in the urban jungle. Fripp explained to Belew how he had illicitly taped the sound of his New York neighbours arguing in the apartment next door (heard on *NY3* from *Exposure*) and Belew duly incorporated the "Your house/My house" exchange into the song's debut performance.

Already destined to be a barnstorming classic, the track gained a very real edge when the band moved to Island Studios in London's Basing Street. During a break in the recording, Levin went off to look for carrot cake (a big favourite with Crimson members) and Belew was encouraged to do a little fieldwork in the streets of Notting Hill Gate. While Levin tucked into a moist slice of his favourite confectionery, Belew – tape recorder in hand, saying "This is a dangerous place" – walked straight into a street gang who wanted to know what the hell he was doing.

An anxious Belew hurriedly showed them his Talking Heads T-shirt, explaining that he was a musician making a record. The group finally accepted Belew's explanation and let him go on. Then, as he turned a corner, he was immediately stopped by the police. Belew escaped unhurt but in a sweat, the heat of the urban jungle getting a little too close for comfort on this occasion.

Talking to Tommy Vance, Bruford laughed: "He came back to the studio shaking like a leaf and started to recount all of this and he didn't know it was being recorded and I think we have some *cinema verité*. I think we have a slice of a genuinely upset and fairly shaken young American tourist in the streets of Notting Hill Gate and he definitely got some heat in the jungle on the tape."

The Sheltering Sky

Bruford opens the piece using an African slit drum – a hard wood box with tongues carved in the top, each one tuned to a different note. In concert, Bruford would often be seen wandering around the stage, tapping out the melody with a beater. These rich, dancing tones are complemented by the deep seam of Levin's Stick, threading darkly underneath the lilting palm-tree sway of Belew's rhythm guitar.

The haunting melody (which owes some of its lineage to the rhapsodic flurries at the very end of *Trap* by the LOG at around 4:32) and the solo from Fripp are the focal points, although there are many intriguing points of detail which combine to make the piece one of this Crimson's most enigmatic and beguiling tracks.

The middle section slips into a sultry reverie and away from the arid swirl of Belew's gathering dust clouds.

Both seductive and inscrutable, the gradual unfolding music came about during one of the group's earliest rehearsals. This was wholly improvised, largely in the form in which it appears on album. Thanks to a policy of taping their sessions, the band were able to go back and relearn what had magically appeared.

Talking to journalist Mark Derry in 1984, Fripp said: "Most people assume that a musician creates music, but I don't look at it that way at all – I'd say music creates the musician. In time, one develops a relationship with the music where it's not what one requires of the music but what the music requires of the musician. And it's only at that point that anything worthwhile happens – where you recognise that music not only has a life of its own but that the life the music has is more real than life itself."

The title comes from the novel by American writer Paul Bowles. Published in 1949, the book is set in the desert surrounding Tangier, on the coast of North Africa but also documents the desert of the interior of its two characters, Port and Kit. Bowles was also an associate of many writers of the Beat generation including William Burroughs (who was directly inspired to move to Tangiers by Bowles' novel) and Jack Kerouac. Something of a polymath, Bowles was also a composer, studying most notably with Aaron Copland. In the same interview with Fripp, Derry revealed that Bowles had heard Crimson's track and that "he considered it an interesting musical rephrasing of his novel".

Discipline

This piece was the very first musical point of contact between Bruford and Fripp for the new band. The guitarist called over to Bruford's house in Surrey and ended up playing along with the drummer and bassist Jeff Berlin from Bruford's group. "Jeff and I had written this lovely ostinato in 17/16 which became the basis for *Discipline* and Robert was sitting on the sofa and said, 'I've got something that could go with that,' and so we ended up, the three of us playing an early version of what would become *Discipline*."

To the casual listener there may not be an awful lot going within the piece. Yet closer inspection reveals a constantly shifting fabric of layers, runs and riffs which open and close over each other.

There are clear allusions to the New York minimalism of Reich and Glass but also the Gamelan orchestras of Java and Indonesia. An endless tumbling piece, its startling counterpoint has the capacity to appeal to the brain while its mesmerising groove takes care of the body.

BEAT
(Music: **King Crimson;** Words: **Adrian Belew,** except **Two Hands:** words by **Margaret Belew**)
Neal And Jack And Me
The opening interlocking theme dates from the *Discipline* sessions though it was not sufficiently developed at that point. Belew was 19 when he first read the Beat writers and began to re-read them in 1981.

When the song moves into the final section after an angst-ridden collision of Beat allusions and memories of homesickness on the road, the closing section showcases Levin's yawning notes introducing a marvellous resolution underneath the rolling spirals of interlocking notes, restlessly ticking over like cogs in a turning wheel.

"At the ending of it I'm playing a line in 21, which changes every time to a different manner of playing it, and I'm singing against that, and at the same time my singing is really going with Tony's bassline. So I'm dividing my attention three ways – my singing voice is listening to the bassline, my hands are playing this pretty crazy line, and I'm singing at the same time," Belew told *Guitar* magazine's Ian Stewart in 1982.

With considerable modesty, Belew underplays these as simply part of the inventory of techniques required of a professional musician. "I think it's just a matter of being able to divide your attention correctly – focus the right things at the right time."

Heartbeat
Of course, there had been songs dealing with love from Crimson in the past – *Book Of Saturday* being one of the most evocative – but none had dealt with the subject in such a direct manner.

Bright and appealing with its straight time and catchy chorus, the song does, however, seem out of character. Below himself wishes he'd kept it back from the band.

Recognising the commercial potential of the song, a single was released although its coupling with an excerpt of the hardcore squalling of *Requiem* made for a very schizophrenic item indeed. In keeping with the Beat connection, *Heart Beat* was also the title of Carolyn Cassady's memoir of her time with Jack Kerouac and Neal Cassady, published in 1976.

Satori In Tangier

Levin's opening notes had been around for a while and were finally picked up as the band rehearsed back in September 1981. The early versions of the song benefited from an extended introduction, with Fripp using the Roland keyboard as a scintillating backdrop from which the tripping figures would emerge.

When remastering the album in 2001, Fripp made the following observations about the prowess of the bass and Stick player. "What becomes more and more obvious is the sheer quality of T. Baldy Levin. We usually attribute to outstanding musicians a 'world' too high. For example, a very good pro will often be described as a 'master' and an outstanding master is frequently called a 'genius'. We know almost nothing of what genius might be. There are not many players that I acknowledge as master musicians. Very rare for an established studio player, T. Lev is a master. Now returning, after some years, to the Beastly Levintine delivering the goods on track after track is a joy. 'Where did that come from?' I ask myself. 'From music,' comes the reply, straight back. Tony has an access and connection to music which I do not, and which is mysterious."

Bruford endorses Fripp's view, adding: "Tony Levin has taught me volumes about music although I can't ever remember exchanging a full sentence on the subject with him."

Levin's theme provides an effective launch pad for Fripp who uses a setting which Belew refers to as "Robert's Turkish trumpet". The delight here is in a near-rapturous solo which scatters glimmering jewels of burning notes in all directions.

As fiery as this version may be, the rendition featured on the later *Absent Lovers* live double set surpasses it. In Montreal, the incendiary potential of this tune is finally unleashed.

The title comes from a blending of several literary sources. *Satori In Paris*, published in 1966, was Kerouac's account of his search into his own heritage – Satori being a Zen phrase meaning enlightenment. Tangier was also the setting of many a pilgrimage from various Beat luminaries, most notably William Burroughs and was the setting of Paul Bowles' novel *The Sheltering Sky*.

Waiting Man

The bubbling lines of percussion and guitar which open the song suggest the speeding miles while Belew's smoky, wafting vocal again contains the plaintive heartache of travel.

"What happened was that whole tune came about because I had the Simmons drums set up in the studio at a certain wood sounding pitch like log drums or deep marimba, and I just started playing this pattern on them," Bruford told *Creem* magazine in 1984. "Then our bassist Tony Levin came in and picked up on it and played a pattern on his Chapman Stick that related harmonically to what I was doing. Then the rest of the band came in and played in harmony with us. That's something I'm very proud of. And, except for the very last section of that song, there's no conventional kit drumming at all."

If *Neal And Jack And Me* described the progress of the lonely traveller adrift in distant hotel rooms, *Waiting Man* represents the impatience of wanting to be free of all the waiting around of soundchecks, hotel lobbies and airport lounges. This is the travelling player desperate to be back among friends, family and familiar surroundings caused by the increasing difficulties Belew was experiencing in working on the album. Sounding like the roar of a plane taking off or the squealing of breaks on tarmac, Belew's guitar solo is fuelled by an urgency which borders on delirium, insistently pushing the song ever onwards to its final destination. By the last verse, the words have acquired the clipped economy of a hastily sent telegram.

This stunning piece is genuine proof of Belew's talents as a gifted player, vocalist and lyricist.

In concert, the opening section became a popular part of the Crimson set as Belew joined Bruford for an extended work-out at the Simmonds kit. However, it's the studio version which provides the detailed intricacies and nuances. Belew's contribution transforms an interesting and spirited rhythmic exercise into a fully-fledged song of the heart without recourse to louche sentimentality.

Neurotica

Originally trading under the title of *Manhattan*, this was a compelling and convincing recreation of the urban jungle with the guitar synthesisers coming into their own as they emulated the snarling howl of blaring cars and the general chaos of the city that never sleeps.

Fripp has commented that life moved three times faster when he moved up from Wimborne to London. Then, in 1977, he moved from London to New York and this in turn moved three times faster than London! Capturing something of that velocity, this is a wild and disorientating landscape, mixing as it does the sizzling heatwaves of the opening Frippertronics and the creeping paranoia that thrashes about just below the surface. New York was, of course, the epicentre of much Beat Generation activity and the title of the song, suggested by Fripp, is taken from the 1950s' literary magazine of the same name, which published many Beat luminaries.

Without doubt, *Neurotica* is a landmark track for King Crimson, convincingly fusing music and lyrics in a furious display of prowess and judgement. Little wonder that it would also be stunningly covered by Crimson in its Double Trio formation 14 years later and again by the seven and eight-piece incarnations operating today.

Two Hands

With words by Belew's then-wife Margaret, this song is so decorative it seems churlish to be anything other than complimentary. However, it suffers from being a kind of re-run of *The Sheltering Sky*, using almost identical instrumental voices.

Belew himself acknowledges that the song doesn't sit well within Crimson. "As I have said, there are musical boundaries but that's what makes King Crimson unique. There are times I have wandered outside those fences, usually with mixed results. *Two Hands* is a song I wish I hadn't brought to the band."

Even a spirited solo by Fripp fails to move it from being the weakest track on the album. In 2001, in a remark which sheds some light on the fractious atmosphere surrounding the making of *Beat*, Fripp was dismissive, commenting: "This shouldn't have been on the album. To have said that at the time would probably have ended the group."

The Howler

This song was premiered in concerts in the US and UK during February and March 1982, sporting a brooding introduction played on the Roland organ by Fripp, out of which the final gnarled, swirling opening gradually emerged. The original piece was much heavier in character and lacked any vocals.

In concert, the piece appeared as another example of the close interlocking style, operating largely as a framework for some extended soloing. Once inside the studio, however, such displays were shunned and it fell to Belew to search deep into the music to divine scintillae of singable melodies.

Belew's method of not finalising lyrics and vocal melodies until the last minute would often mean that the structure would be slightly altered, causing his colleagues to re-think their parts. Just as *Neurotica* held a spotlight on the bustling public spaces of New York, Belew's lyric here casts a baleful glare on the dark suspicious passages and back streets, filled with looming paranoia and insidious disorder.

Bruford recalls being impressed by the track, believing the insidious grating sounds in the track to be "a very Crimson kind of thing, the general neurosis of the band – I thought it was a very good fit". In between the drilled tightness of the verses, the undertow of Levin's bass falls starkly across the writhing knot of dissonant notes, vast and shadowy, adding to the aura of menace of foreboding.

But Fripp notes: "This didn't convince me at the time, and doesn't now."

In contrast to the regimented structure, Belew's striking solo is the centrepiece of *The Howler*. "I don't play a note in the solo, not a single note, it's just a horrid machine-like, rats scratching their claws on a chalk board, sound," he told *Guitar*. "There is so much of a noise element in it, also because I have a harmoniser tuned a half-step down, and I'm beating on the guitar with a metallic slide."

Requiem

Moving away from the tight structures of the rest of the album, *Requiem* – a superb improvisation – makes a glancing contact with the ghost of Crimsons past.

This move may have been borne out of necessity, as Tony Levin recalls: "We had finished all our 'composition ideas' on the album and were short on running time."

THREE OF A PERFECT PAIR

(Music: **King Crimson;** Words: **Adrian Belew**)

Three Of A Perfect Pair

Surely the most integrated piece within the three albums produced during the '80s, *Three Of A Perfect Pair* unites the pointillist house style and Belew's pop sensibilities in a near-effortless combination.

Over a loping patchwork of cross-rhythms, Belew performs a laconic solo which stands as a testimony not only to his hands but some fancy footwork as he cuts from one effect to another, dicing and splicing the notes in a manner reminiscent of his work on *Born Under Punches* by Talking Heads. It's a joyful noise which belies the tensions in the studio during the difficult making of this album.

Always a popular number with the core Crimson fanbase in concert at the time, the song was resurrected as a Belew solo spot on the ConstruKction Of Light tour in 2000. It's surely one of the most unlikeliest of singalongs, with the vocals and guitar appearing to move independently. Belew's talent was – as always – to make it look effortless.

Model Man

It was in the unlikely confines of Apple Health Spa's sauna on Bleeker & Thompson, in New York in September 1983, that Fripp's alternative to standard guitar tuning first appeared. The CGDAEG configuration appeared, as Fripp has described it, to simply "fly by", in something akin to a vision. New Standard Tuning, as he impishly called it, would come to have profound repercussions on a personal and professional level, although at the time its application and true significance was not fully appreciated by the 36-year-old man from Dorset.

After this revelatory moment, Fripp left New York to join Belew in Champaign to continue the writing process. Starting work on *Model Man*, Fripp was uncertain how to implement the new tuning and the pair continued to develop the song conventionally – although Belew later recorded it using the decidedly unconventional fretless guitar.

The result was an FM-friendly song opening with an agreeable canter and an upbeat bouncy bassline. Despite this outwardly congenial setting, Belew presents an interior monologue cautiously interpreting the actions of those around him – hardly the usual territory of the pop stompalong. It's possible to read many things into lyrics like these, but given that they were written in Bearsville right at the end of the session, it's not beyond the realms of possibility that they refer to the inner workings of a rock band struggling to produce an album.

A pleasant if somewhat lightweight song, it does, however, boast an impressively opulent chorus in which Belew delivers an impassioned, swooning vocal with authenticity and maturity. Without Belew's almost beatific voice to make sense of everything, there would be little distinctive or distinguished about the piece and certainly not much that would mark it out as being convincingly Crimsonesque in hue or character.

Sleepless

In the Crimson rehearsal and writing process, ideas are offered up to see if there are any takers. Sometimes this is in the time-honoured, "Hey fellas, I've got this great idea and it goes like this!" tradition. More often than not, however, it's left to an individual to play a phrase and hope that someone picks up on it.

As the band were searching for ideas in June at Tony Arnold's studio in Dorset, Levin offered up a driving pulse, doubled up in a tight sheath of echo. Simple and stark, it pushed the process forward and the band turned the riff around and around as Fripp and Belew tried out different shadings, accents and effects. It sounded ominous and was clearly going to be important. During a lull in the proceedings, an excited Bruford leaned over and asked Levin "Do you know what it is you're doing?", anxious that such a great groove was not lost.

Yet despite such a good start, the song was left unfinished as the band parted company to go on to other commitments. "When we reconvened in Woodstock, in December, I was in a different mood with my playing, and I did the opening as a slapping part instead of using a pick, as well as playing it much faster," Levin told *Musician* magazine in 1984. "It just took off to a different place then, for no reason; it was just very much in the air."

With Levin having advanced the process a second time, the piece quickly fell into place and became one of the most powerful and brooding songs of this Crimson era. At Bearsville, Bruford and Belew were sharing accommodation and the drummer recalls that Belew would have a lot of trouble getting to sleep. "He maintained that the house was haunted and that he was having some very strange dreams but you do when you're up against a deadline and you've got lyrics to write. Adrian earned every penny for those words."

Appropriately, there is a brooding, oppressive presence throughout, suggested in no small part by Belew's warily breathless vocals and the density of the production. For the most part there are very few alternative studio versions of Crimson tracks. *Sleepless*, however, generated several different edits and mixes. For the most part, this was due to differing perspectives as to the kind of percussive spine required.

In its original format, Bruford had opted to provide a dancing series of rolls on the timbales, avoiding the straight snare laying down the four. For Levin, the originator of the piece, the track lacked what he thought was the required amount of bite and so he prepared an alternative mix. For this he took a sample of Bruford's snare and edited in a stomping backbeat. Sonic trouble-shooter and respected producer Bob Clearmountain adopted a similar approach when he was drafted in. No stranger to having his drum parts manipulated in the studio, Bruford was philosophical about such changes. In the end, however, it was the original mix which appeared on the final album.

All of this attention on one track was sanctioned because of the belief that *Sleepless* had the potential to deliver the band to a much wider audience. This hunch was confirmed when the track was given to 30-year-old DJ Francois Kervorkian. When not pumping out dance music in the clubs, Kevorkian liked to listen to the likes of The Mahavishnu Orchestra, Yes and King Crimson and had been DJing on the New York club scene since 1976.

His mix attracted some good critical reviews when it was released as a single. *Music Week*'s reviewer appealed to listeners to open their mind and bodies to the song. "Forget the group-name background, this is a classy contemporary dance track that has general pop appeal. Could be a Top 40 disc provided people get past the group name and associations and review and play it." Indeed, for a while the song was briefly a hit in London clubs.

The 2001 remaster and subsequent editions of the album gathered together all the principal mixes. On or off the dance floor and whichever mix you chose, *Sleepless* is one of the most powerful tracks this band recorded and is certainly the outstanding cut of this album.

Man With An Open Heart

In April 1984, Crimson started to prepare for their forthcoming tour of Japan in Champaign, rehearsing in the back room of a music store. Several times a day, Tony Levin would lead the troops over the road to a shop which sold carrot cake. Word got out about Crimson rehearsing and soon the music store was filled with fans spending an entire day pretending to shop whilst furtively listening to the sound of Crimson's set list bleeding through the wall.

One of the songs they would have heard being worked on was *21st Century*

Schizoid Man. However, Fripp wasn't happy with the way the song was being played and it was dropped. One of the other less familiar songs they would have also heard was *Man With An Open Heart*. Live, the song was slightly remodelled with a more strident, crowd-friendly feel, lending it a more confident aspect than its studio counterpart.

A jaunty tune, shaped and guided by the smeary lines of Belew's fretless guitar, its inclusion provides further evidence of Belew's keen ear for a classy pop song. However, it remains by far and away the lightest track on the album and its meditation on jealousy comes over as innocuous rather than compelling with little of instrumental interest beyond the slurring guitar motif.

There's an old saying in pop music that if you can't say it in three minutes then it isn't worth saying. Here, Crimson keep to those timeless guidelines, straying over the optimum by a mere five seconds.

Nuages (That Which Passes, Passes Like Clouds)

Opening clouds of Roland-enhanced guitar drift and frostily gather, producing an eerily languorous backdrop which at times barely hovers in tune. This precarious setting provides for the album's one and only appearance of the classic sustained tone with which Fripp was most identified with in the '70s. The curving melody snakes its way across a percolating bedrock of tabla-style percussion triggered on this occasion not by Bruford but Belew, utilising a patch he had devised on his set-up of pedals and effects rack.

At the core of the melody is an aching loneliness, the product of a man who had taken a shot at being in the first division but had still found it wanting. From the initial excitement of putting the band together and the heady ecstasy of those New York shows in 1981, the creative flow had all but dried to a trickle. Whereas *Discipline* had been an album that was "waiting to be made", *Beat* and *Three Of A Perfect Pair* had struggled to be made at all.

Industry

From the dry and "natural" sound of *Discipline*, Crimson had gone on to amass a formidable arsenal of effects, processors and devices. All of the band spent huge amounts of time trying to push and develop sounds well beyond the factory setting and, in some cases, against the express wishes and recommendations of the manufacturer. Levin reckoned by the time of the recording of this particular album there were around 84 effects of one sort or another at the disposal of the group.

Whereas most of the effects and devices are usually to be found embedded within the fabric of Crimson's material, here the technology is placed centre stage and it's a bit like getting a behind-the-scenes glimpse into the band's special effects workshop. For over seven minutes the band thrash, splurge, thrum and thunder away on the numerous knobs and buttons at their collective disposal.

Belew has said that the intention was to go into the studio and make a virtue of not listening to each other. So that's largely what happens and the problem here is that there's relatively little substance behind the literal and somewhat lumpen portrayal of heavy machinery at work.

It's interesting to compare this version with the one which appears on the live album *Absent Lovers*. There, the track has a better balance between the spiky punctuation of the bass keyboard and drum figure, Belew's winding solo and Fripp's orchestral-like backdrop. The theme is fleshed out with an additional top line which etches an altogether more eerie aspect to the piece and Belew's harmonic histrionics have an impact which seems entirely missing from the studio counterpart.

Dig Me

Rock music's love affair with the internal combustion engine has been well documented from the clean-cut frat-boy cruising of *Little Deuce Coupe* to Springsteen's blue-collar blues. Yet few songs have attempted to delve into the soul of the machine itself. *Dig Me* gives the car's take on being dumped on the scrapheap.

In some disreputable used-car sales rooms, there are some models whose chassis are actually that of two separate vehicles joined together. Fitting, then, that this song (originally entitled *Dig Me Don't Bury Me*) is essentially just that.

Dig Me bravely questions preconceptions about what a "song" might consist of and it's certainly true that the track fits into the noble Crimson tradition of combining opposite elements. Belew's litany of umbrage emerges from the dark spluttering squalls of atonal scraping into a bright, dazzling poppy chorus, suggestive of happier times on the freeway.

Belew recalls that the song's origins lay in the attempts to come up with a different style. "I told the guys I wanted to lay down this very awkward guitar part and then have them play to it, but in a way that would sound like we're really not playing together as often as we are. The song sounds like it's falling apart."

No Warning

For the bulk of its brief career in the '80s, Crimson had pursued a succinct, self-contained musical language. Although some tracks – notably *The Sheltering Sky* and *Requiem* – had their origins in group improvisation, most were composed by a process of accretion and considered layering. *Requiem* came into being because of a shortage of material. So when it came to the next record and the lack of consensus within the group, it was agreed to try a series of improvisations.

Like the old animal impressionists on the variety stage who would invite their audiences to join them for a stroll in the countryside or the farmyard, Crimson take the listener for a walk through the hard-hat area of the Industrial Zone. *Industry*, *No Warning* and two more examples included on the 2001 remaster all came from this process.

In these abrasive tone poems, it's interesting to hear how many of the sounds and motifs jostle for a place in the final version. In rock terms, at least such musings may sound radical although most are well-rehearsed "licks", albeit fairly stark and experimental. While the structure is fairly open-ended, the path between the various sound events is, it must be said, fairly well trodden.

No Warning is a painting in sound. While containing some impressive points of detail, the overall picture delivers little convincing or viable. Compared to other practitioners in the free improvisation sphere, this is pretty plain fare.

Larks' Tongues In Aspic, Part Three

The familiál resemblance in this latest instalment of the *Larks' Tongues* saga can be clearly seen when stood next to the introductory section of *I May Not Have Had Enough Of Me But I've Had Enough Of You* from *Exposure*. If not an actual brother, then *LTIA3* is a very close cousin indeed.

The unmistakable double helix that threads through the compositional body of Robert Fripp is well to the fore in the opening flurry of blistering notes, and the driving theme pushed along by writhing guitars is among the best of such devices used in Crimson. Although Bruford confesses he wasn't overly keen on the track as a piece of writing and arrangement, he can be clearly heard in the studio enthusiastically shouting from the behind the kit (2:21).

Indeed a defining characteristic of this body of compositions has been the degree to which carefully layered themes and motifs build into a satisfying system of ascension and climax – although the climb may be hard, the view at the top was nearly always worth the effort.

After a storming beginning, the track levels out to a plateau on which Fripp unleashes a squalling storm of notes that fly and flay with remarkable ferocity, adding to the mounting sense of expectation. All of which makes the decision to fade the track out all the more puzzling, fatally undermining any sense of resolution or completion which might otherwise have been achieved.

Earlier attempts to arrive at a workable piece in the studio included a different structure. Fripp recalls an early Bruford idea of Fripp and the drummer playing the opening guitar solo section as a duet, but says: "We tried this, and I abandoned the piece as not working."

Another attempt opened with the mighty flighty picking, it then veered off into a menacing chopping ostinato complete with brooding shadings not dissimilar to the middle section of *Red* or *VROOOM VROOOM*. After several repetitions, the driving unison guitar theme was introduced and after the familiar stop/start slash and burn motifs, the interlocking guitar parts were punctuated by a series of ascending bridges, like a series of steps up to a stomping solo section. This section was taken at quite a canter when compared to the final version on the album and the expected resolution was delivered via the *Red*-like ostinato before the whole thing came to a dead stop. This was, of course, a provisional reading and, in fact, the final version benefits from fewer frills and garnish. In concert, the lack of a suitable ending was solved by segueing into *Thela Hun Ginjeet* as per its appearance on *Absent Lovers*, where the track really comes into a sharper focus.

THRAK
(Music: **King Crimson;** Words: **Adrian Belew**)
VROOOM/Coda: Marine 475

Following a short string fill from the accompaniment and effects side of the same Mellotron which appeared on *ITCOTCK*, *VROOOM* begins the first full album by the Double Trio incarnation of King Crimson. Whereas the version on the previous mini-album to which it gave its name was taken at an almost magisterial pace, this reading fairly clips along. Of this change, Mastelotto commented that the band had stopped "feeling" the track at the original tempo and were itching to get it going.

Another more significant variation, however, was Fripp's decision to opt for a mix which saw the two trios contained within the group, separated out into the right and left channels of the stereo image. Although the track lacks something of the impact of its American-recorded counterpart, the extreme separation is almost like opening a pocket watch and being able to see the various interactions of the internal mechanism as they tick time off and spin away.

While Bruford, Gunn and Fripp operate out of the left side, laying down the foundations of the track, Belew, Levin and Mastelotto explode from the right moving rapaciously over the track in a less-disciplined manner. In fact, it's Mastelotto who occupies the role of percussive terrorist, filling the bars with a stream of subversive volleys which crash away at the underside of the piece.

Fripp defined *VROOOM* as "an inevitable and remorseless forward motion which carries all before it" and so it does. As the coda winds inexorably downwards, the climax is every bit as mordant and astringent as the opening section with Belew and Fripp's guitars exchanging shrill howls of pain. The voices of Fripp and Gunn intone the names and designations given to a Lloyd's insurance syndicate which suffered huge financial losses and whose members included Alder and Fenwick from EG. With characteristic humour, Fripp calls the track "an example of remorseless and unforgiving inevitability where one is called to honour one's liability without limitation".

Dinosaur

Up there with any of the classic Crimson repertoire you might care to mention, the achievement of *Dinosaur* is to combine a killer riff, a knowing wink to Crimhistory, a punchy, richly ironic chorus and a Robert Fripp solo with a sting in its tail.

Answering fans' questions via *Elephant Talk* in 1997, Belew offered this insight into the processes which led to the realisation of the track. "I have noticed the songs which seem to work best are the ones which at least start with Robert and me writing together. I would say '*Dinosaur*' is a successful Krimson song. It began with Robert showing me a sequence of five chords he had written. I added more and more changes to accommodate the melody I was writing and ended up with an epic! The point being it had started with Robert and therefore sounded more Krimson-esque than, say *People*, which I had written alone."

It was also Belew, using the Roland GR-1 guitar synthesiser, who devised the opening sound which emulates the timbre of the Mellotron, lending the track an orchestral quality. "There are times when I'm able to cross over into 'composing', an area usually reserved for Robert," says Belew. "The middle instrumental section of *Dinosaur* is a good example. It was a separate piece I had intended for a solo record but, when I wrote it into the middle of *Dinosaur*, it fit."

Walking On Air

Belew's vocal performance is strongly suggestive of John Lennon, one of his musical heroes. Indeed, one of the first times Mastelotto met the guitarist – at a post-gig party on the Fripp and Sylvian tour – Belew and his wife were dressed as John and Yoko. Emerging from one of Levin's lyrical basslines, the charming song from Belew is as gentle and refreshing as a light breeze – making it something of a rarity on this album.

Though at times it borders on being a little too sweet, it nevertheless contains a middle section in which tiny ripples of notes are scoured and shaved from the fretboards of Gunn, Fripp and Belew. These small but intense clusters illuminate the languid, seductive air pervading this tune.

B'Boom

Of the new double drum set-up, Belew revealed: "There was a running joke in the band: 'How do we have two drummers and not sound like the Allman Brothers?' Pat and Bill worked very hard on orchestrating all sorts of different possibilities."

Indeed they did. There can be few drum solos in rock music which translate well to the studio and usually their appearance is either an opportunity to go and make a cup of tea or press the skip button.

Bruford looks back on the piece with some fondness. "The technical interest in the drums for me was fantastic and great fun and, right there, there was enough of a reason to join King Crimson. Because Pat would be the very solid time keeper, the link between the band and tempo, which would enable me to be the terrorist which was great. So I could play the fancy shit and he'd play the bit that connected the fancy shit to the listener. A lovely scenario and a very clear and simple understanding of what the two drummers would be doing and I could work well with that."

The title is Bruford's pastiche on Max Roache's multi-percussion group M'Boom. "I thought King Crimson should have its own little percussion group on that track – Bill Boom as opposed to Max Boom," remarks a proud Bruford.

THRAK

When the band (minus Belew) convened for the first time at Bruford's house, Mastelotto recalls Fripp explaining what he was after from the two drummers. "He asked me to play the five and Bill the seven and only to play the stressed notes of the meter." As the guitarist went through the idea, a quizzical look came over Bruford's face. The memory of it still makes Mastelotto laugh out loud. "When Robert suggested this, Bill said, 'But Robert, I can play both parts!' And there I was wondering about just playing my part!"

In fact, the piece had been crashing around in Fripp's head for quite some time. Tobin Buttram, a member of the League Of Crafty Guitarists, recalls that a piece bearing all the hallmarks of *THRAK* appeared around 1986 at Red Lion House in Dorset and forming part of the group's 1991 repertoire. (*Larks' Thrak* from the LOCG's *Intergalactic Boogie Express* released on DGM in 1995.)

In terms which might well apply to Guitar Craft, Fripp offers the following definition as to the meaning of *THRAK*: "A sudden and precise impact moving from intention, direction and commitment, in the service of an aim." Alternatively, he suggests it could be "the sound of 117 guitars almost striking the same chord simultaneously".

Severe and inhospitable, this is a vision of Hell or at least a sonic snapshot of Hell's house band. But this outing (and its counterpart on *VROOOM*) sounds tentative and cautious compared to the freewheeling opportunities that would appear in later months on the road.

Inner Garden I/Inner Garden II

Essentially a Fripp composition with embellishments by Gunn and Levin, the song originally had drums when it was first aired during the *VROOOM* sessions. Stripped down to a tolling guitar arpeggio, this reflective interlude contains a particularly evocative lyric.

People

Replete with short, dazzling runs from Fripp, this tune by Belew bursts into life with a skewed rhythm that would defy an octopus with a penchant for adventurous tap-dancing.

Brimming with fun, this is Crimson's own take on super-charged funk. The piece settles down into an impressively driven stomp complete with exhilarating reversed guitar lines, manipulated in real time by Belew courtesy of his effects rack.

Complete with a catchy chorus, a promo single of the song was issued in 1995, although Belew regrets bringing the song to the band, wishing he'd kept it for himself. He laid down a demo version of the song back in September 1992 (which can be heard on his 1999 collection *Coming Attractions*).

Radio I/Radio II

After an absence of 11 years, Fripp returned to the stage as a solo performer in June 1994 in Argentina, a month after the *VROOOM* sessions in upstate New York. Now the analogue looping of Frippertronics had been replaced in a digital upgrade to become Soundscapes. With some relish, Fripp asserted that the new system was "the best way I know of making a lot of noise with one guitar". Somewhat darker in character than the older system, Soundscaping was to provide Fripp with an ongoing means of connecting with the process of making music at an extremely intimate level.

The release of *1999* (an aural souvenir of those first performances in Argentina) was the first of six such albums, culled from numerous performances undertaken usually prior to or immediately after tours by King Crimson. The inclusion of *Radio I* and *Radio II* seems to act as a cleansing of the musical palette, establishing a calmness and slowing down the pace of the album.

One Time

The task of writing lyrics was always something of a lonely job within King Crimson and, during the *VROOOM* sessions, once the rest of the band had retired for margaritas and dinner in a nearby restaurant, Belew would start work alone on the words and vocal melodies.

In order to keep the creative juices flowing, various members of the band took to smuggling refreshments out of the restaurant and up to Belew. Sadly, on one such mercy run, Mastelotto was busted by the door staff and for a while the lyrical progress seemed threatened. "Once we explained who the drink was for, the bar made the arrangements to have the drinks sent up themselves!" laughs the drummer.

The track had originally emerged from the rehearsals at Applehead with Gunn, Marotta and Fripp. Here, *One Time* is an essay in understatement in which all six players adopt simple, delineated parts which combine to produce a delicate web of balance and harmony.

In a song which manages to be both sultry and haunting at the same time, Belew's plaintive lyrics describe the pernicious whispers of internal doubt which undermine and censor our everyday lives. Such themes find form in the middle section where Gunn's gorgeously sparse solo peerlessly shimmers in the heat-haze of the pedalled guitar lines. Thankfully, this early rendition lacks the woebegone choirs which would sometime tip the song into maudlin theatricality when played in concert.

Sex Sleep Eat Drink Dream

Described by Belew as "an occurrence" rather than a pre-planned idea, the song came together at Woodstock. A typical part of Crimson's *modus operandi* has been the skilful accretion of opposing factors or parts. Here, Bruford and Mastelotto's rhythmic duelling splits the song into two different tempi at the same time, causing a gnawing undertow of tension as the song thrashes about itself.

A different kind of collision can be found in Belew's lyrics and their tumbling associative interplay. Their surreal qualities find an echo in Bill Smith's stunning design for the inlay cover. In some cases, the words are typographically cast adrift, strangely distanced from their original meaning and relationship, while bringing to mind the works of US poets such as e. e. cummings and William Carlos Williams.

VROOOM VROOOM/VROOOM VROOOM: Coda

If *VROOOM* was "an inevitable and remorseless forward motion which carries all before it" then *VROOOM VROOOM* as defined by Fripp was "the same but here it comes again". Fripp also notes that the track contains a middle section originally written for *Red* but left unused. This barnstorming white-knuckle ride through the scales – with its opening retrograde inversion of the opening theme of *VROOOM* – benefits from a jarring, dissonant undercoat of some truly malevolent Soundscapes presaging some moments from Fripp's 1997 epic *Gates Of Paradise*. In amongst the entropic freefall, a Mellotron can be heard gamely straining through the morass of howling guitars almost harking back to the celebratory chaos of *The Devil's Triangle* from *In The Wake Of Poseidon*.

Fripp had two Mellotron 400s shipped to Real World for the recording of *THRAK*. These, however, saw little in the way of action – except from Mastelotto and Levin, who rested their laptops on them. Eventually, the two machines were shipped back and the original Mellotron from *ITCOTCK* arrived in their place – along with a request from Fripp for it not to be used as a workstation.

Appropriately enough, the last track of the album was recorded right at the end of the sessions, as drummer Pat Mastelotto recalls: "Around the last day, Robert suggested a musical blindfold test, he gathered us around and laid out a plan – 'four beats of this chord, seven beats of the next, etc, etc,' as we all scribbled notes. Then we went out to play. We did one take with some of the team falling out on the way. When we finished, we said let's go again, but I asked to lay out, as I thought I had stayed true to form.

"Bill questioned me, saying I had made mistakes and I should replay but I suggested that they all go again and then I would fix the time to them. Well, that's the last track on the *THRAK* record and I did not go back to punch in anything."

After the last note fades out, there's a burst of cocktail lounge music from the Mellotron. Mastelotto recalls the moment. "My big surprise on hearing the CD was my voice at the end going 'Yeah!' I had said that as I got up to leave my kit, long after the track had died out, but after additional overdubs it appeared right at the end of the Mellotron decay."

THE CONSTRUkCTION OF LIGHT
(Music: **King Crimson;** Words: **Adrian Belew**)
ProzaKc Blues

In 1991, long-standing Crimson fan Toby Howard established an online message board for Crimson fans called Discipline. In 1994, at Fripp's suggestion it changed its name to Elephant Talk and became a focal point for online debate and discussion between Crimson fans around the world.

Fripp and other members of the band contributed posts to the forum, in some cases responding to suggestions made on the newsletter, including the release of *THRaKaTTaK* after many posts suggesting an album comprised of Crimson's then-current improvisations.

Given the long history of the band, it is natural that there exists a wide diversity of views about the merits of one era over another. A particularly strong and recurring thread in fan discussion of this period was whether Adrian Belew should be in Crimson at all (ironically, nowadays the complaints are usually about Crimson carrying on without him). Posters would often lament the fact that Belew's penchant for pop was diluting the instrumental integrity of the Crimson body. Several implied that Belew was simply not up to the job.

An occasional reader of ET, Belew was particularly offended by the tone of several posts and in December 1996 was moved to fire off a Kipling-esque stream of consciousness admonishment to his detractors.

He wrote: "Regarding the ongoing debate 'Is Adrian Belew any good for Crimson or what?': If you can write songs which are good enough for the approval of King Crimson; songs like *Elephant Talk* or *Matte Kudesai*, *Neurotica* or *Heartbeat*, *Thela Hun Ginjeet* or *Three Of A Perfect Pair*, *One Time*, or *Dinosaur*, and when I say write I don't just mean write some chord changes, but ALL the melodies and ALL the words, words which include even the title of this digest, and if you can then perform those songs consistently and fluidly at the front of the band well-lit and in full view of audiences from all over the world who are willing to pay to see you, keeping in mind that often times the guitar parts are in a different time signature from the singing and the singing is often in a difficult range and if at the very same time you can provide a plethora of guitar styles and sounds from animals and pianos to oboe and E-bow, not merely the required shrieking spooge solos but the interlocking precision-picked parts as well and tap your foot and make it all look easy, night after night and if you can withstand the pressure, the criticism, the comparisons, the indifference, and unkind remarks you'll receive knowing that in the end you may never see credit for your work and the huge investment it will take from you … If you can do all this as well or better than I do, please, by all means, step up on the stage. I'll offer you my place in KING CRIMSON. I'd be quite happy to sit at the back and just play guitar with my pal Robert. It's so easy to criticise. But as the saying goes PUT UP or SHUT UP."

Of course, such a heartfelt outpouring did little to convince or silence the critics but it did show the extent to which unthinking commentary from fans can impact upon the psyche of the artist concerned. The danger of wanting to know what the fans think is that you just might find out.

When asked why he read the online Crimson newsletter Elephant Talk, Fripp replied: "Humiliation."

Three years later, in October 1999, as the band worked on ideas for their new album, they hit upon a strangely twisted take on the blues starting out from a Belew riff. This being Crimson, however, there was no straightforward reading of one of the most enduring and quintessentially American musical forms.

"The Crimson blues has been unsettling Trey and myself," Fripp opined in his diary. "We feel it as a four, while Ade has it as a 12/8 shuffle as does Pat, except Ade and Pat have different downbeats within the same 12/8. The Crimson solution: Trey and Robert play a bar of 7/8 + a bar of 5/8 which neatly matches the 12/8. Then T and R reverse their 7+5 to offset each other (and go into a 12/8 for the subdominant). If this sounds arithmetical, don't worry: it rocks."

In early December, just over a month after first running the idea through, the track was nearing completion. Perhaps against his better judgement, Belew went online and took a peek at Elephant Talk. As Fripp recounts, sometime later, an exasperated Belew called in to the studio.

"AB: I've been reading the latest Elephant Talk. What a turd that is! What a turd! Those people are really mad.
RF: May I quote you on that?
AB: What a turd!
RF: You know you shouldn't read that.
AB: I haven't read it for weeks."

Instead of sending off an indignant post, Belew began further work on the track which by now was called *ProzaKc Blues*. Wittily satirising the world of artistic vanity, writer's block and poking fun at sections of Crimson's audience, Belew recorded the vocals in the digitally enhanced persona of Hooter J. Johnson. Belew also provides a thrilling performance on guitar which glides and surfs over the seismic shifts in tempo caused by his bandmates.

Fripp related a point which referenced another ongoing debate on the cyber-pages of Elephant Talk – whether or not Mastelotto was good enough to be in Crimson. "For anyone who has doubts of Pat's capacity to Crimsonise (and doubters appear to be falling away) the part Pat played on the 'blues' completely threw me. I've no idea where he was, other than he was there. And this from someone who worked with Giles for three years and Billy B for 27 years (so far). As Pat was leaving I asked him: 'What were you playing?' 'Well everyone was centred on the guitar playing there's no need for me to play it too, is there?'"

The ConstruKction Of Light

Gunn joined his colleagues in Nashville straight from having finished the mastering of his fourth solo album *The Joy Of Molybdenum*. Now, from being a band leader, he was having to make a mental re-alignment in order to apply himself to the task in hand. And not for the first time. Having spent much of his musical career playing bass, in Crimson he had slowly carved a new niche for himself. Figuring that in the Double Trio there didn't seem a lot of point in competing for the low end of things with Tony Levin, Gunn had gone on to find his own voice as a versatile soloist, particularly in the more liberated climes of the ProjeKcts.

But with Levin out of the line-up, Gunn was now back to supplying the bass (courtesy of the Warr guitar, a Stick-like touch guitar) and, early in rehearsals at Belew's studio, reflected on this change in direction. Clearly uncomfortable in the early stages of recording the new album, he wrote: "What I think a lot of people don't realise is that 'playing a bass part' takes an entirely different kind of thinking, as compared to 'playing a lead part'. It is not simply a matter of being supportive as opposed to being directive. It has something more to do with being foundational." In adopting the role of what he called a "monster low-ender", Gunn had to dig deep within his own reserves and experience.

On the title track, it's evident that he managed to make the change with considerable success. Seasoned Crim-watchers might understandably want to focus on the re-appearance of the interlocking guitar style from the '80s. However, from the very outset, Gunn's supple playing is every bit as worthy of consideration as the glistering work of Belew and Fripp.

From the twisting lines entwining themselves around the radiant circulating motif, through to climbing, inquisitive patterns, Gunn's work provides the instrumental section of the track with the forward momentum required to make this one of the most exciting parts of the album.

At around three minutes, the notes from Belew and Fripp spin around like the reflections from a glittering mirror ball, brilliantly dancing over Gunn's ascending bassline. As if that wasn't impressive enough, Gunn is also playing the stabbing chords which lightly dance around the beaming centre. These are not overdubbed but played live in the studio using the Warr guitar. Gunn recalls: "I was so up about this track, I wanted to do more but I ran out of hands!" Fripp describes Gunn's contributions to this track as both stunning and exceptional.

The title has a provocative ambiguity about it. Fripp, who coined the phrase, reveals its origins. "I visited a Church of England clergyman in 1975, a rare one; one who knew J.G. Bennett and visited Sherborne. He gave me some very practical and profound advice: 'There is a law: light drives out the dark. Do not concern yourself with driving out the dark: concern yourself with bringing in the light.'" Fripp adds: "It is not possible to construct light."

The use of astronomical imagery in the cover may offer further clues or red herrings. Then there's the search for personal enlightenment. The quest for something that is at once so nebulous but so vitally intimate finds a novel expression in Belew's striking imagery, invoking pop-art iconography and alien genitalia along the way to make his point. Did the phrase have any associations for Belew? "None whatsoever, which is why I used it as a high diving board into a pool of absurdity."

It's difficult to overstate the importance of Belew's contributions to the development and final shape of Crimson's music. Fripp is full of praise for his colleague's skills in dealing with the metrical complexities of the guitar and vocal lines. "My brain is not able to handle the cerebration needed to hold one line, then split it into two lines of alternating notes, and play each in turn as independent creatures. Once the individual parts are in the body this is not difficult. But while the brain and the body believe the two lines are one – pain, suffering, misery, death, terror and bad notes."

Fripp had been carrying the shimmering leitmotif (another Crimson pun) around since at least the time of the Double Trio rehearsals in May 1997, where an early run-through of it can be heard on the track *Circulation* from KCCC13. Of course, elements of it formed the basis of several themes in the ProjeKcts where it moved around in a somewhat itinerant manner, a theme in search of a home. It found a permanent one here.

Into The Frying Pan

Sounding like a beatbox running low on battery power, the lurching slug of Mastelotto's pounding rhythm locates the track in a powerful rock tradition in a manner which is highly reminiscent of *Intruder* from Peter Gabriel's seminal third album. Yet things are not that straightforward, as Fripp observed during its recording. "Pat has become as archetypical a Crimson drummer as any, while being very much his own person. His part on *Frying Pan* is a good example of the Crimson Drummer Virus in effect: choogling along in a heavy pudding at 98 bpm with the singer singing, suddenly the drums shift to the offbeat. Why? It's the Crimson Drummer Virus at work! If everyone else is on the beat, why should the drummer be? Good question. The answer is in the drums."

Another point of subtlety is the dissonant shimmer on Belew's voice, mirroring the divergent harmonies of the main theme. Talking to writer Jeff Perlah of Guitar. Com in 2001, Belew revealed an interest in presenting the vocals in a microtonal, Eastern approach where the scale is cleaved apart. "Instead of it being just 12 notes, it's split up into 32 notes (in the vocals). So you have all these little notes that are in between the normal notes."

The doomy counterpoint which opens the track had been a recurring motif throughout the entire gestation of the ProjeKcts period, where it was perhaps most obviously realised in P2's *Contrary ConstruKction* from the *Live Groove* album and *ProjeKction* from P4's *West Coast Live*.

However, the theme has its origins in the composition *Symbiotic* from Trey Gunn's second solo album *The Third Star*, released in 1996 – well ahead of any fraKctalising. "Are you suggesting that a mere bass player has influenced the work of real guitar gods?" laughs Gunn.

Acknowledging that with *The Third Star* he was beginning to find his real voice as a bassist and soloist, he underplays the extent to which he imported any particular theme into the band. Gunn offered this explanation of the musical relationship with Fripp.

"What Robert does is he goes out in the field and gathers up some apples. I take Robert's apples and make a pie with them. That's kind of what I do really. He brings the apples to the table and I help him make a pie. In respect of the track *Symbiotic*, I bet Robert couldn't even tell you whose apple that was. I don't even know, I mean, it all gets kind of mixed up."

Whilst accepting that *Frying Pan* and other Crimson material is an accretion of several ideas and contributors, Gunn does not hesitate in pinpointing Fripp's crucial role in guiding the entire process. "King Crimson is Robert's vision. Period. We all contribute but we can only contribute with how it lines up to Robert's vision. Now, his vision is pretty wide and it leaves a lot of room but it's his vision. Robert's real happy to share the limelight and the money and all those other things that compensate everybody – hopefully enough to keep the band together."

Frying Pan is a thrilling culmination of numerous musical fragments artfully threaded together and delivered with a devastating panache, making it a high point of the album as a whole.

FraKctured

The appropriately reflective phrase which delicately opens this piece is suggestive of a clock ticking. Only here time is moving backwards, a point underlined by Belew's backward moving guitar at 1:52. This, of course, isn't the only reference to times past, as the ghost of *Fracture*'s *moto perpetuo* is summoned. "This is terrifying stuff for me, right on the edge of what is possible," observes Fripp. "Semi-quavers at 138 bpm, all picked, mostly continuous, written and delineated, awkward time signature, with a rhythm section hurtling along with a linked but separate agenda."

In December, at the very end of the first phase of the recording, the band (minus Gunn) stood in front of the studio white board, considering track titles. Mastelotto was unsure about applying the title *Larks' Tongues In Aspic, Part Five* to the piece and asked Fripp how attached he was to it. When Fripp explained the linkage with *Fracture*, Mastelotto agreed, pointing out that Ken Latchney thought Fripp had, in fact, been playing the piece when Fripp practised it. So the piece became *FraKctured*.

Revisiting one's past can always be a tricky affair and Fripp admits to having some initial reservations about moving on with this fearsome piece consisting of whole tones and fast continuous single-note lines, which he first outlined when he was working at Belew's house in February 1997.

Its inclusion came about when Fripp allowed himself to reference any musical materials he found convincing and which resonated with what the band were attempting.

Whereas Fripp has often censored some of his favoured compositional devices and vocabulary (i.e. the '70s style of playing during the construction of *Discipline* and the interlocking guitars during the Double Trio), and normally rejects any suggestion of trading on former glories, here he positively revelled in this act of historical plunder.

"I'm not sure that I have to rationalise this, and certainly not justify it. But if I were to present a basement answer to the question: 'Why *FraKctured*?', it might be this: I'd like to play *Fracture* again, but it's not a piece for this Crimson," says Fripp. "It's Crimson historical repertoire, and good repertoire, but it's part of the lives of other people, in another country and another period."

"I read enthusiast feedback on how much enthusiasts would like to hear *Fracture* live. If Crimson did play it again, Pat, Trey and Adrian would have to learn the parts of Bill, John and David. That wouldn't work, for several reasons. Like, they were not involved in the process of that music coming into the world. We have an entirely different relationship with a piece if we were a 'parent' to it. And *Fracture* requires more than purely professional skills to make it live. I have some reservations with the piece. If I were going to rewrite or rearrange it, I'd probably begin again. If I did begin again, what would it sound like?"

Fripp argues that this kind of reinterpretation of previous themes is part of a wider strategy which addresses renewal and maintaining a momentum. "The musical identity, 'tradition' or 'way of doing things' is given – King Crimson! – and this is one way, within that tradition, of keeping the creative process moving. The externals may sometimes seem familiar, recognisable, and even appear to be the same, but the inside is fresh."

Fracture itself, meanwhile, would return to the band's repertoire, but not until 2016.

The World's My Oyster Soup Kitchen Floor Wax Museum

A monstrous tune which began life as a blow called *Demolition* by Crimson in their ProjeKct X guise consisting of what Gunn describes as "controlled mayhem and madness".

He attempts to explain how the track operates. "Adrian and Robert are playing together in a certain time signature (I think 4/4, but I'm not entirely sure) and Pat and I are in a totally different universe. OK, not totally different, but we are doing our best to tear everything apart. We are playing in 11/8, with myself on pumping bass and chord stabs, and Pat on crashing smashing drum bits. Plus, I am generally disregarding Adrian's chord changes."

This in part accounts for the feeling of disorientation the listener might experience. As notes are unceremoniously jostled and thrown about, the piece dangerously judders along like some vast machine being tested to destruction.

Matters are complicated further by the appearance of Belew's vocals which take on the leery Sprechgesang of a bilious holiday tour guide as the bus lurches precariously back and forth out over the edge of the precipice. Retaining the original guide vocals, complete with cues and throat clearings gives the track a documentary feel – a mood further enhanced when he namechecks titles from Crimson history along the way. Indeed, Fripp's cameo appearance on guitar-triggered piano (a sound used at Gunn's urging) conjures what a metal-clad Crim might sound like with old associate Keith Tippett in tow. Of the solo, Gunn comments: "Oh my lord, this was the perfect thing for this track! It was as if a wild and disturbed ferret had gotten loose inside an old tack piano during a bar-room brawl. Fantastic chaos! Spidey delivers."

Whereas, normally, Belew might be expected to use a huge array of effects, on the sessions for *TCOL* he stripped everything back to only a few guitar sounds. This doesn't stop him from continuing to experiment with pushing the sounds out as far as they go. On *Oyster Soup* he unleashes the Pixolater – an effect of his own devising which takes the note he's playing and morphs it into another with typically unpredictable results. Gunn admits to being awed by Belew's work at times like this. "I haven't the faintest idea how Adrian was getting these sounds out of his guitar. He calls it his pixelated sound, but I just call it plain hot!"

Larks' Tongues In Aspic, Part Four

Elements of this piece had been around for quite some time. Back in 1997, Fripp ran through the complex driving riff during the sound check of a ProjeKct Four gig in Vancouver. As the road crew of R. Chris Murphy, Robert Frazza and John Sinks went about the business of tweaking the house PA, Fripp took the rest of the band through an intensely ferocious sequence.

Two years later in Nashville, the embryonic piece was gradually reaching a kind of critical mass, being shaped in the studio with pieces added on a daily basis. Eventually the band threaded all the pieces together to form an astonishingly high-octane performance of Herculean proportions.

While some fans have observed that Fripp's ongoing reprise of the *Larks' Tongues* title is a retrograde step, it's difficult to know what else this particular piece of music could be called. If it looks like a Larks' Tongue, smells like a Larks' Tongue and sounds like a Larks' Tongue, then best bow to the inevitable.

From the opening theme, the track pushes along shoving and shouldering its way along like a bulldozer gone amok. The guitars shudder like stuttering buzz saws, slicing jagged cross cuts into the thundering backing.

As the individual chords are batted back and forth between Fripp and Belew, they form a fractious whole, barely contained by the volatile punctuation from the back line. Paradoxically, it sounds chaotic but is finely controlled with an exacting precision which characterises the *Larks' Tongues*' canon.

At nearly three-and-a-half minutes, the whole piece moves up a gear with the arrival of a devastating running line from Fripp. As the racing guitar lines duck and weave between increasingly choleric detonations, Gunn, Mastelotto and Belew convert the studio into a dangerous rhythmic minefield and, in doing so, provide a landmark moment in Crimson history.

It's impossible to hear this section without wondering just what goes on in Fripp's mind as he navigates his way through these blistering clusters. "There are moments when, as if in surprise, I look out at my fingers, trained over many years, almost independent, dancing effortlessly across the strings," observes Fripp. "On the inside of the hands is vitality, lightness. On the outside, only the slightest glancing contact with the strings. This is calisthenic: where physical motion and beauty coincide, dancing in joy."

Gunn characterises Fripp's part as being one of the most difficult he's ever come across. "I mean, you can't feel sorry for the guy because he wrote these parts. Plus, he's been practising for this style of playing for nearly as long as I have known him. But still, this is the most difficult articulation on a guitar that is in any repertoire, period. Of course, it won't come off like that because of all the chaos that Pat and I are laying alongside of it. But, trust me, it is. And, I should know."

In all, Fripp performed four takes with the third being judged the best by the team. The section which follows is a remarkable antithesis. Pausing for dramatic effect, Belew lets the note swirl in the air before bringing it down hard, causing the dust to rise and the sparks to fly. Here the notes are whisked, drizzled, dabbed and spattered with the fevered, sizzling animation of an abstract expressionist painter. Belew acknowledges the painterly connection. "Painters in general influence the romantic notion of the manner, lifestyle and intent of the way I work. The greatest compliment ever given me was from Robert pointing to a print of Picasso's *Three Musicians* which hung in my studio and saying, 'That's what your guitar playing sounds like.'"

There is a vivid crispness to Belew's playing here, which is taut and well considered. Possibly his best solo within Crimson, it's delivered on a high tide of emotive potency and irresistible force.

At this point, the track takes an unexpected twist with the introduction of the Belew-written coda. The remorseless, descending chords are given no quarter by Mastelotto who produces an incessant storm of turbulent eruptions and rolls on the V-Drums, echoing the litany of tragedy, conflict and human failure detailed in Belew's lyric. This highly personalised, broad-brush account of the history of the 20th century is compressed into a little over three minutes and provides a sombre ending to the album proper.

The origin of this part of the track was not without incident and was the subject of rumour, argument and counter-claim between fans and band members prior to the release of the finished album in May 2000.

As Belew sat upstairs in his house, he could hear the band thrumming through the chords of *LTIA4* below, then picked up his guitar and began to play. "I started writing a string of chord changes to their pulse. They were interesting changes," recalls Belew. "Eight chord shapes moving downward chromatically which after 24 bars end up back where they began. The chord voicings were unique due to a new tuning I used throughout the record. The melody I had in mind was sad and mournful but emotionally highly-charged."

Having worked on the chords for several hours, Belew presented the section to the band, describing it as being akin to a power ballad. Belew admits to being slightly surprised when the rest of the band endorsed his suggestion that it provided a coda.

"This was an exciting new area to me because it meant for the first time a Crimson instrumental piece would turn into a song."

As the last days and weeks of the 20th century moved by, Belew wanted to write something which invoked the spirit of the age, the landmark events which had entered the collective consciousness. With a passionate interest in modern history, Belew took to drawing up lists of the major happenings of the century, taping the plethora of TV programmes which on the historic transition from one age to another was marked. "Looking back at the last half of the 20th century, what stands out most, unfortunately, are the bad things. Wars, deaths, crimes, etc.," recounts the guitarist. "Of course, many great and wonderful things happened or were discovered but are not as readily recalled. Why? Because the bad things are 'events' while the good things are mostly 'non-events'."

Belew was bothered by the one-sided nature of the list and talked it over with Fripp, who suggested another verse of good things which would balance the piece out. His suggestion for a title was *In My Lifetime*. Although he tried, Belew says the "emotional sadness" of the chords and melody prevented him from making much in the way of progress. "Eventually I accepted it was a song which could not have a happy ending," asserts Belew. At the tail-end of the sessions in December, the band had listened to the album and all agreed that the atmosphere was far too dense. What was needed was some breathing space.

Belew's suggestion was to record the coda as an acoustic track appearing at the front of the track. Belew believed that this would provide the necessary contrast which was also rooted in an approach adopted in Crimson albums in the '70s – notably *Peace – A Theme* from *Poseidon*. Belew suggested that Fripp play the acoustic guitar while he sang. Fripp declined, however, and, after the other members left for the Christmas holidays, Belew set about finalising and recording his own rendition.

By now the piece was entitled *I Have A Dream* – taken from Martin Luther King's speech at a civil rights march in Washington on 28 August, 1963 – and Belew recorded it on New Year's Eve, with engineer Ken Latchney and friends in attendance.

Belew recalls the awkward moment in January when the group first listened to his work. "For Pat, Trey, and Robert I can appreciate how awful it can be when you've heard a track without vocals for so long and suddenly the lyricist/singer has imposed meaning and melody. Everyone seemed a mixture of unsettled and happily surprised. At the end of *Larks'* Pat expressed concern about the single verse being repeated (which it was at the time) and we quickly agreed it should happen only once at the very end. We now had two versions of *I Have A Dream*: the acoustic guitar/vocal intro to *Larks'*, and the full band/vocal version at the end of *Larks'*."

However, the album was far from finished. In February, Belew received a message from Fripp via manager Stan Hertzmann that Virgin was unhappy with the song's inclusion on the grounds that it was too "controversial". As Belew points out, in the days of death metal and rap, an overview of significant events was an unlikely source of controversy. Unconvinced by this intervention – the first in Crimson's dealings with Virgin – Belew called Fripp. I asked a very direct question: 'Do you want the song on the record, yes or no?' When Robert did not answer 'yes' I should have known the answer was some shade of 'no'. Robert said, 'It's your call, Ade' to which I replied, 'Then I would like the song to stay as it is on the record'."

Yet the discussion between Virgin's Declan Colgan and Belew continued. Eventually, Belew was beginning to feel ill and lose sleep over the issue and on 16 February he rang Fripp. "Simply put, Robert did not want it on the record so it is not on the record. Or to look at it a different way, if Robert had wanted it on the record it would be on the record, regardless of what Virgin might say. So it wasn't 'my call' … and he agreed it was true. I then recommended he 'make the call', knowing he would take it off the record."

The acoustic version was removed, although Belew would later make it available as a free download via his website.

The episode says much about the dynamics within King Crimson, revealing the strength and depth of relationships between the individuals.

Belew points out that, although there is always a degree of cut and thrust about what material should and shouldn't go forward on record, somebody ultimately has to make the final decision. "It works best in King Crimson if someone has the last word in situations such as this and Robert is the right person for the job. He may not always be correct in his judgements (I'm certain I would be worse) but I respect his vision for King Crimson and the dedication he brings to it, even when his thoughts negate my own. And I've learned what it takes to make Robert a 'happy boy'. I accept Robert's need to have things his way. That's not a criticism. There's nothing wrong with it. In fact, I can be the same way. To me the true gift of friendship is acceptance. I only wish Robert had come to me directly and said, 'Hey Buddy, your song gives me the creeps' and we could have arm-wrestled for it."

Heaven And Earth

The challenge for Crimson had been to write and record an album's-worth of new material in just eight weeks. Understandably, the bulk of that time was spent working through the formal compositions. Given the heavy demands placed upon players to achieve the target, it's surprising they found the time to develop ProjeKct X.

Viewed another way, the making of the album could have been made more difficult had PX not emerged as a conduit for the different directions and threads which some members of the band wanted to explore. "There was never enough time or energy for the ideas that Trey or I might introduce," explains Mastelotto. Gunn emphatically agrees: "Pat and I had to beg the other guitarists to play on it. We said 'you guys have all this repertoire so just go in there and play'."

Bill Munyon was crucial to the development of the beat and glitch-orientated electronica that had gradually begun to seep into the group's sound after Munyon worked on ProjeKct Three's *Masque*. "Pat moved from LA area to Austin in the early '90s and needed some help sorting out studio gear and setting up a recording space in his garage. Our relationship gradually built from there," says Munyon who refers to the method of working the pair developed as "guerrilla audio". "That's what I call it when your studio is not a studio but some audio gear and a location like a car garage, an apartment, a tour bus. Project X came about because Pat and I had been developing a project constructed out of King Crimson archives, rehearsals, random samples from interviews and so forth, folding in Pat's mad drumming and beat programming chops in addition to my computer editing and sound design skills."

Mastelotto, Gunn and Munyon shared an apartment during the recording period. On the drive to Belew's house each day, the three talked about the different doors which the PX approach was opening for them. "Pat and Trey were itching, and so was I, to go some places that Robert and Adrian as writers weren't going," recalls Munyon. They began by sorting various phrases and grooves into different sections which could then be recorded in the various moments of downtime on what were supposed to be days off. These, in turn, were downloaded on to Munyon's computer, enabling the rhythm section to continue working on them when they returned to the apartment. Gunn and Mastelotto laid down a track with a dark, surging groove as its centre, which at this time was called *Spy Kritters* but, as Munyon testifies, though they may have been rhythm buddies, as Fripp dubbed them, there wasn't always a consensus as to where the beat might be when it came to the placement and editing of the principal rolling riff. "There was this disagreement that occurred between Pat and Trey that was fun to listen in on. It was truly 'Math Rock'. Pat was tapping on his chest and counting and Trey was tapping his foot and they could not agree on an edit point because they were counting the track so differently."

As work on *Spy Kritters* progressed, Belew and Fripp were invited to contribute solos. Both were initially reluctant but were eventually won over. "Adrian played one quick pass and split. So we took the two bars we liked and looped and arranged it and kept his two great soloing moments just where he played them," remembers Mastelotto. Fripp joined them and offered to play over their work-in-progress without even hearing it. "Trey, Pat and I are huddled around the console and Robert is really into his Soundscape," recalls Munyon. "Some of the notes are rather sour and we are wondering if we should abort and start over with a slightly modified direction." Turning to Mastelotto, Munyon asked whether they should stop but the drummer smiled broadly saying, "I'm not gonna stop him." Munyon and Mastelotto then turned to Gunn. "Knowing that if Pat isn't willing to stop Fripp," says Munyon, "then for me to do so would be overstepping the mark. So, Trey, with authority, says 'Stop it!'"

Munyon recalls the comic embarrassment in the control room as Fripp's sound dribbled to a premature halt. "Robert then shouts out 'WHO TOLD YOU TO STOP?' Pat and I are both pointing at Trey. Trey backpedals. We can tell that Robert is feeling a bit antsy and might not stay long enough to get a take at all but Trey recovers nicely and so does Robert." Fripp did indeed recover to produce a stirringly molten solo.

Between the apartment and Belew's garage, *Spy Kritters* slowly took shape as Munyon sculpted the solos to meld with the main theme. This had its problems, admits Bill. "The rock/funk section went right past me. I never found anything to latch on to and I had to tell them that. So, rather than letting the continuous pointing at the monitor and trying 'move this over there' experiments, I bowed out and let Pat at the driver's seat. I know he was burning with the knowledge of how this track should work. He seemed to have the plan. Later that week, Pat and I were in the garage tweaking and trying things that would make the track better, getting ready to show it to Robert and Adrian."

When Fripp first heard it, he was impressed but unhappy with the coda although in the cut-out-and-keep climate of the time nothing was wasted and the rejected sequence was subsequently recycled to become *The Business Of Pleasure*, the opening track on the PX album.

On 12 December 1999, they got straight down to recording some more ideas with Mastelotto filling the garage with his Taos drums and even trying out the sonic possibilities of the garage door! Working quickly, Mastelotto fashioned a lilting 9/8 groove. Once this was combined with the cavernous swell of Gunn's bass notes and the tender orchestral folds of soundscapes, Gunn, Mastelotto and Munyon had produced a classic blissed-out piece that merged fusion, electronica and rock in one triumphant suite. Belew and Fripp gave *Spy Kritters* a nod of approval. "Robert provided the title, *Heaven And Earth*, almost the first moment he heard it. Later I learned that it was also the title of a TV show in the UK that Toyah helped to present," says the drummer.

THE POWER TO BELIEVE
(Words: **Adrian Belew;** Music: **King Crimson**)
The Power To Believe I
There's a hymn-like quality to the opening of *The Power To Believe*. Belew's voice, through its gauze of electronic processing, has a plaintive vulnerability. The tone and sentiment is about giving thanks, a devotional paean that acknowledges there's a powerful external force capable of exerting redemptive life-changing effects upon the everyday.

A series of experiments were carried out at writing sessions in Belew's studio in 2002. Fripp sent his voice through the processor and the results were eventually dubbed on to the title track of his album *Love Cannot Bear*, released in 2005. With his voice sounding somewhat awkward and moving against the flow of the slow-moving soundscape, part of what he was intoning certainly resonated with the theme that would eventually emerge throughout *The Power To Believe*: "Can it be true that music might redeem our fallen world? Can it be true that music can heal our world?"

Belew's experiments with the process were more successful. His short lines, enveloped in a subtle digital halo, seem to embody something fragile and human wreathed within technology – the ghost in the machine. Some of these experiments appeared on 2002's *Happy With What You Have To Be Happy With* EP. *Bude* has the artist framing the view of an ocean in one small window pane encapsulating the micro and the macro, while *She Shivers* stresses the cause and effect of human contact. *I Ran* describes a bleaker place: "I ran into a man with whom I had nothing in common. I ran into a man with whom I had no conversation."

With a melody originally alluded to on the soundscape track from the *Happy With* … EP, *Mie Gakure*, which (very roughly) translated from the Japanese means appearing and disappearing, Belew adapted the lyric of *All Her Love Is Mine* from his 1996 album *Op Zop Too Wah* and recast the words into this shimmering opening.

Be it the simple act of falling in love or something far deeper and more ineffable about the nature of music's transformative qualities, the "haiku", as these sections were referred to in the early stages of the recording, is a beautiful set-up for the album. The thematic concept is reminiscent of the sentiments of *Peace*, which opened *In The Wake Of Poseidon*. Just like the earlier track, this is a quiet prelude to a visceral assault.

Level Five

In 2018, *Level Five* was officially rechristened *Larks' Tongues In Aspic, Part Five*, a reversion to its original working title when the Crims met up at Belew's home studio in March 2001.

From its opening descending theme, which sounds like it's being detonated as much as played, the subsequent jagged see-sawing riff went deep into the formation of the *Larks' Tongues* band in 1972. The *LTIA* form had nagged away at Fripp's fretboard for several decades. Whatever it was called in 2001 or here in 2003, this latest studio variation on a recurring motif possesses a fresh, bracing power that's utterly convincing. Little wonder it formed the flagship number of what Fripp liked to call Nuevo Metal.

With more than a suggestion of the *Heavy ConstruKction* theme outlined back in the ProjeKcts, *Level Five* was first road tested at the band's run of four gigs in the sweaty confines of Nashville's 12th and Porter in June 2001. At that point, the rigidity of the principal theme was tempered by a nervy fluidity in the arrangement and in Mastelotto's driving cymbal work.

Hot-wired with percussive jump-start whizzing and thrumming under the surface, chest-hitting sub-frequencies ratchet up the drama. All of the glitch-editing was done over a period of five days with producer Machine and Pat working at Mastelotto's studio in Texas after the main recording sessions. "I might play dat-a-dat-a but I want to hear it going 'Vrrrrring-Vrrring' It takes time to do that kind of thing. You have to listen, figure it's not right and do it again. You can easily decide it's shit and throw it away but no, take an hour and work on it and you'll get it. It's a process," he says.

The thrakking guitars and rippling unison notes from Gunn and Fripp reprise the spirit of their corkscrewing twists from *Larks' Tongues In Aspic, Part Four*. Just after the four-minute mark, Fripp's lead theme, referred to in the band as "the *Star Trek* section", soars and dips above the gnashing blocks laid down by Gunn's snarling baritone guitar, leading into Belew's typically liquid soloing. Whatever sonic deficiencies plagued *The ConstruKction Of Light* are utterly swept away by this piece which positively screams "Crimson is back". The plunge into the final section, with its seething electronica, churning cymbal work and, in the dying seconds, the cheering crowd drawn from Paul de Villiers-mixed live version from 2001's *Level Five* EP, stands as a widescreen highpoint in King Crimson history.

Eyes Wide Open

After eschewing the Crimson ballad on *The ConstruKction Of Light* the band bring a familiar sense of balance back with *Eyes Wide Open*. Belew's well-observed lyric about being aware of events seems especially apposite when it comes to this deceptively simple piece. The undulating guitars mark a return to the way in which Fripp and Belew worked at the formation of *Discipline* in 1981. The middle section with Belew's lead guitar articulating the principal melody is artfully framed by Fripp's wafting strings and Gunn's purring bass sweeping between the gentle tug of Mastelotto's graceful percussion. Gunn's solo is understated but provides a brief burst of light. A different mix of the song with alternative percussion and layering on the vocals, alongside Belew playing acoustic guitar, appeared on the *Happy With ...* EP. The track is a particular favourite of Machine's. "I'm a big sap for vocals and I loved *Eyes Wide Open* which was a sober, melodic, beautiful track. Recording vocals with that was pretty serene, doing it one on one with Adrian."

EleKtriK

Opening with quasi-woodwind voices that sound like they could have been part of the chorus from Belew's underrated and largely overlooked 1995 album, *The Guitar As Orchestra*, a series of mirrored dovetailing sections intercut and loop back upon each other in a manner which, if translated into a drawing, would surely give M.C. Escher a run for his money. This Fripp-composed piece dates back to 2000/2001 and showcases the way in which an initial idea becomes exposed to the influence and ideas of the rest of the band. Describing his process, Fripp noted in his diary: "The bulk of this work is mechanical: writing out ideas by hand which, of themselves, move by very quickly.

Then, breaking down how the parts are allocated. Then, learning my part. So, an original idea might take a minute to grab as it flies, an hour to write down, and a week to develop before it's available to be presented to the Team. Until I have developed a relationship with the idea, I'm not able to pass it on – it's only notes, not music. When I have a relationship, I can pass on the music."

The piece circulates between all four players, demonstrating their skill at being able to collectively marshal and control a sense of escalating urgency peppered with expectant pauses in the flow with Gunn's savagely ragged bass offering an extreme contrast to otherwise precision-tailored instrumentation around it.

As the band grappled with the piece in March 2001, Fripp wrote that the track combined whole-tone and symmetrical elements. "In response to the helpful list of modes which might be used in Crim writing, posted on the Guestbook by a helpful poster: if the question is 'why not use these modes of which I have helpfully provided a list?', the answer is simple: they lack necessity. Crim writing is not arbitrary; it is not an exercise for me. I write in a vocabulary which speaks to me, which has a resonance. If my suggestions resonate with the Team, we move forward with everyone contributing."

"In terms of a list of scales, the selection provided were not what I would call overly exotic. As exercise, in the past I have considered many different modes. To adopt a scale, or meter, simply because it is different, has a value: it interrupts mechanical thinking. This can be useful, and lead into novel areas. An example: the mode which gave rise to *Matte Kudasai.*"

"But the value is limited in writing-writing. I don't present my exercises to the band. If the poster is suggesting that my compositional skills are limited, I agree. Fortunately, my suggestions are only part of the musical materials used by the band and (this is almost like boasting now) I'm actually making suggestions which are not only outside the two modes mentioned above, but also in 12/8! Hold me back."

"My approach to choosing a mode is not usually to consult a scale encyclopaedia or lexicon, but to assemble the notes which speak to me. Then, to discover what mode this might be so that my brain can then get engaged. *EleKtriK* wasn't meant to be a combination of the whole-tone and symmetrical scales: that's what it is."

It's a quirky piece that flirts with busied, almost cautious, figures which then opens out into something altogether more assertive and at times grandiose. Teasing out such tensions is a well-known Crimson device and while it undoubtedly provides a challenge to even the most well-drilled of players in the group it doesn't always take off entirely successfully. A curious interlude within the context of the album overall.

Facts Of Life Intro/Facts Of Life

Heralded by Fripp's sepulchral atmospherics, yet another Fripp-initiated motif is brought convincingly into being with a textbook example of how to pack a lot of punch into a small amount of clock-time. In just a little over five minutes, the band well and truly stomp across the rockiest terrain found on the record.

When the band unveiled the piece at their residency at 12th & Porter, it was called *Response To Stimuli*, a title conjured on the fly in the room by Adrian when he bellowed the words out across the shifting meters of the music. If the audience were surprised then they were in good company – none of the band had any idea that he was going to make a vocal addition to the piece.

After a series of increasingly tightly contracted sequences, the band back up like a bull pawing at the ground about to charge. The piece then hurtles headlong into a raging, chordal guitar solo that is classic Fripp. By the time you catch your breath, Belew has dispatched his thoughts on the merits or otherwise of the prospect of an afterlife and it comes to a pounding resolution. This couldn't be anybody else but King Crimson.

The Power To Believe II

Previously known as *Virtuous Circle*, with several variations on spelling and capitalisation along the way, the piece dates back to the writing and rehearsal sessions at Belew's studio in March 2001 where it had developed into free-standing life from an early version of *EleKtriK*. At the time, Fripp noted in his diary: "Trey has been urging this one forwards, and we are urging forwards, with a click track at 160. Not quite music without Pat (who had briefly returned to Texas on family business during the rehearsals) but the openness and clarity give us room to examine the musical mechanics. No room for concealment provides an opportunity seized by all to slither off notes, slither on notes, miss the beginning of sections, and calumnies worse than this; all of which is noted mostly with good humour, if not outright laughter, by your Rhythm Buddies."

The piece was first heard live in 2001 at the Nashville warm-up gigs in June and presented on the *Level Five* EP that year. But it wasn't until the appearance of Belew's haiku that it assumed its final, most satisfying form. From Fripp's diaphanous vectoring, Belew's sarangi-style processed guitar slowly emerges to perform a courtly dance. When Gunn enters here it is on his tiny Ashbory Rubber Bass, an instrument first used in the ProjeKcts. Listening back to his performance 17 years after he laid down the track, he notes: "But, damn, if I am not playing in tune decently enough on this track. Which is really hard to do. In fact, it is so hard to do that I am surprised I pulled it off so well here." Gunn also recalls using his Warr fretless bass. "In the middle of this track around 4:30 and again at 6:30, when the bass comes back in, this is definitely the Warr fretless. You can really hear the difference between the two."

The track then passes into a beguiling, hypnotic reverie provided by the glittering interplay of various Roland Handsonic devices. These translucent bell-tones add to the ringing sonorous quality of the preceding guitar solo and presages the one that follows. The reprise of Belew's vocal is cosseted in dreamy clouds of strings and Mastelotto's shifting rimshots and gentle cymbals. Fripp's surging solo holds a favourite melody of his that he'd been using live for several years and which he'd previously partly featured, albeit in an entirely different setting and tempo, on *Bringing Down The Light* from Sylvian and Fripp's *The First Day*. Mastelotto has nothing but praise for Machine's work on the track. "I'd done two drum takes; one in the bigger room with the snares on and one in the stone room with the snares off. We started to cut the phrases. It's what I played but it's not where I played it (*laughs*). We really tightened up the drum and percussion sounds to the bassline. You think you know where you are but you don't realise how complicated it is until you play along with it. It's not repetitive. So he helped me a lot with that."

Dangerous Curves

Not for the first time, the album echoes *In The Wake Of Poseidon*, specifically *Merday Morn* from *The Devil's Triangle* in the orchestral-style strings gradually unfurling against Belew's insistent bolero-like guitar figure.

Trey Gunn recalls Machine's presence was crucial in shaping the sound design within individual pieces. "I'm playing my fretless Warr Guitar on *Dangerous Curves* with a pick run through an amp and with some direct distortion. The strings on this guitar are actually nylon strings, so, just like super fat classical guitar strings. Because there is no metal in the strings, a standard magnetic guitar/bass pickup won't work with it. So, it has only a piezo pickup like an acoustic guitar. That gives it, naturally, a kind of rough upright sound. Then during mixing, Machine added some kind of envelope filter on the sound so it kind of opens up like a weird wah-wah sound."

From its appearance in the live set in June 2001, the track quickly became a highpoint and stayed with the band until with the end of the Double Duo's final gig in Mexico in November 1973. The insistent heartbeat of Mastelotto's pulsing bass drum gave a physical presence to the band's forward momentum. Often left open-ended in performance, here in the studio it ends with the chord of doom, a dissonant sign-off which Mastelotto sampled and would use as part of the introductory drum duets with Gavin Harrison in 2008's run of gigs.

Not for nothing did Fripp note in May 2001: "The Demon Beast Mastelotto is a Crimson Propulsion Unit. This is part of Pat's function in this band: he propels us along. This differs from Bill, who (for much of the time) used the group as a background to foreground commentary from the drums. Pat learnt a lot from Bill. I'm not sure how much Bill learnt from Pat. Anyone who might see Pat's role in Crimson as 'the timekeeper' misses most of what is going on, although Pat is better able to keep time than any of us. More impressive, he is able to follow the group as they speed up, and without making it obvious. Pat has a quality I respect: he continues to learn, facilitated by his deep modesty."

Happy With What You Have To Be Happy With

Belew's brilliant deconstruction of the writing process is surely one of his most inspired contributions to late-era Crimson. Not only does it address the process facing every writer but it affectionately lampoons a direction of travel in metal music which Crimson had partly helped kick off, going all the way back to *Red*.

That these witty and incisive lyrics were only meant as placeholders until something better came along makes their presence all the more remarkable. "We had this thing we were doing musically, where the band is playing in distant time signatures based around 11. I thought this is going to end up on the cutting floor, unless I can formulate something to sing over it. Once I find something to sing over it, it legitimises the idea somehow," Belew told *Vintage Rock*'s Shawn Perry. "So I worked for three or four days trying to come up with exactly the right phrase to sing against it. It ended up in a phrase 11 syllables long: happy with what you have to be happy with. Once I played that for the guys, it became a song. Suddenly, we're strapping to see what ideas would go with it. We put together a lot of different arrangements and finally came up with one that everyone agreed on. Then they asked, 'Now, what would you sing over this?' And I said, 'I haven't had time to write the lyrics, but I know what I would do melodically.' And they said, 'Well, why don't you send us a tape of what you think the melody would be, because we're not sure of what to play until you develop the melody.' So they went away and I quickly wrote down this sort of funny thing (*sings*). 'Well, if I had some words, I'd sing them here and I'd sing them like this and this would probably be the chorus.' I did it in a joking manner for them to learn the melody. And everybody liked it so much that we kept it that way."

An edited version appeared in 2002 on the *Happy With What You Have To Be Happy With* EP. The cover, chosen by Fripp, is a P.J. Crook painting of a family eagerly clutching their lottery tickets and awaiting the results.

The Power To Believe III/The Power To Believe IV: Coda

Commenting on the progress of writing for the new album in April 2001, Fripp offered this perspective: "There is a raft of interlocking and related ideas which currently fall under three titles: *Larks' Tongues In Aspic, Part Five*, *eleKctriKc* and *A Virtuous Circle*. I'm not sure where they are leading me although, knowing that they are leading me, I trust my feet (and hands, and ear, and sense of smell) to follow. At the end of this particular process I shall stand back and look, and listen, and see and hear what has been revealed: a wheel (or two, or three). This is the Crimson process of re-inventing the wheel, once again. If Crimson were a blues band we'd have a conventional template, or series of customary templates, to begin. Crimson does have its own templates, and vocabulary, but somehow they are not so obviously available. The discovery and re-discovery of them is somehow necessary for the music to come into the world. And sometimes, without any effort whatsoever, new Crimson music appears as if of its own volition, without discussion within the band. Two examples: *Deception Of The Thrush* and *The Sheltering Sky*."

The Deception of The Thrush had appeared in ProjeKct Two's early outings and quickly established itself as something of a classic in concert across the other ProjeKcts in which it was co-opted and, later, when King Crimson returned in 2000.

In concert, and here on record, the piece took time to build a slow, smouldering journey in which Fripp would summon forth multilayered harmonies that were simultaneously bitter and sweet, slowly lifting itself upward before dramatically falling back to silence. The piece gained its full stature with a set of string chords from Fripp (in their way, every bit as heart-rending as *Starless*) acting as a backdrop to Gunn's frequently astonishing closing solo. For many who saw and heard it performed live, it felt like the clocks stopped to make way for something otherworldly. If ever there was a piece of music that played the musicians, this was it.

So when it came producing a definitive recording the stakes were high. The band recorded a couple of versions of the piece which went well but, when clearances to use the voice of T.S. Eliot (originally triggered by Gunn's rig) couldn't be obtained, a different approach was required. Fripp's vocoder processed voice was used and Gunn himself attempted to read some poetry. "I tried and tried and it felt so lame to me, for so many reasons, that I said I can't make this work," sighs Gunn. Eventually, Fripp and David Singleton determined that the album should come to an end with another reprise of Belew's *The Power To Believe* haiku combined with an extract from a Fripp Soundscape. The becalmed tones were recorded at St Peter's Church, Newlyn, in December 1997 just two days after ProjeKct One's gigs in London, bringing together, albeit obliquely, two separate timelines involving the fraKctalistion of the group and the formal Crimsonising of 2002 that would ultimately end the following year.

Some would argue that the sense of resolution that comes from *Thrush* would have made a more satisfying ending to the album. Trey Gunn isn't one of them. "I kind of feel like it was a very auspicious thing that *Thrush* is *not* on that record, that there isn't a definitive studio version of that. It was kind of a weird thing to pin down a studio version of something that is so free and really has much more to do with the audience and the performance on the night more than any other piece that we did, really. The pauses were so determined by the audience in that piece, like if they could listen with us as the sound would decay away into nothing, we could only hold it as long as they could listen. As soon as they stopped listening we had to jump in. I can remember in Montreal they just sat there with us for the longest time. How can you do that in the studio? You can only contrive it. It's music, but it's not that. So we probably auspiciously slipped through that. It would suck if there weren't any recorded versions of *Thrush* but there's plenty."

Released in March 2003, *The Power To Believe* has the honour of being the last studio album to date and the last studio outing to feature the talents of Adrian Belew and Trey Gunn. As final statements go it is powerful, wiping out the deficit resulting from *The ConstruKction Of Light*'s material being untested on the road and further hampered by a weak production. If the last instalment of the old-world approach of the tour–album–tour treadmill is *The Power To Believe* then it's a not a bad way to say farewell to that part of the band's story.

Annotated Gigography 1969–2003

Over the years since the publication of the original book, I've had numerous people suggesting that my show notes for downloads on the DGM website be gathered into one handy place. "But it's all on the internet," I would say. "Well, yes but as we've already said: we'd like it in one handy place while we're listening to a given show," I'd be told. So, here it is.

Please also take into account that this annotated gigography was written over a period of nearly twenty years. As shows would be readied for download by DGM's Alex "Stormy" Mundy, I would be asked to come up with some words primarily intended as a guide as to whether said show was a 'good' gig or not.

Although presented here in chronological order they were written very much out of sequence, appearing when required for download; several years might separate my comments on two consecutive nights.

Along the way, therefore, there will be occasional repetitions of phrases where I get excited or the overly-frequent use of adjectives where my vocabulary has flagged. I would ask the reader to be forgiving of these instances where they encounter them.

1969

FRIPP McDONALD GILES LAKE SINFIELD
5 JULY 1969 – HYDE PARK, LONDON

A gig that is not only an iconic moment of the sixties but one that announced Crimson's presence on the international stage. If you think about the rest of the music on the bill at Hyde Park that day, you get a sense why tracks like *21st Century Schizoid Man* and the solos on *Get Thy Bearings* were so powerful and utterly shocking. This is a band playing far beyond their years; nothing and nobody else sounded like it. Faced with a daring display of vibrant styles and influences compacted into a hurtling musical express, the assembled hippies had to make a choice and make it quick; get on board or get out of the way. If the boys sound a little hurried in places or the vocals a touch brittle at times, who can blame them? Gigs don't get much bigger than this one. In his diary, RF wrote: "Mammoth success, of importance which will take time to appreciate. We'll look back to see this day in years to come and fully realise its significance." He was right on the button.

6 JULY 1969 – MARQUEE, LONDON

Clearly it wasn't just their musical reputations that had been enhanced by appearing at Hyde Park the previous day. In his diary, Ian McDonald noted: "Up p.m. Dik and Vic came over … Mike (Giles) picked me up and went to Marquee. Did gig. Came back to flat with 9 chicks(!)" During this gig, they zipped through rock, pop, folk, jazz and classical – sometimes all in one song. It's little wonder that they had a spring in their step. After all it's not often you play to most of hippiedom one day, return to your word-of-mouth supporter (499, to be exact) the next and then roll into Wessex Studios the day after to record *Epitaph* with Moody Blues producer Tony Clarke.

9 AUGUST 1969 – PLUMPTON RACECOURSE

For King Crimson's appearance at the 9th National Jazz, Pop, Ballads & Blues Festival, the band were low down on the bill with Idle Race, Dry Ice and Groundhogs, and situated in a tent well away from the main stage. "Can I tell why we played there?" Fripp explained to Vic Garbarini in 1981. "The agency that booked it hadn't been completely straight with us, so we said, you're no longer our agents. So instead of putting us on front stage – where we'd wipe out anything they had – they stuck us in the tent, so we wouldn't touch anyone. It was a deliberate agency move to fuck up our careers."

On an audience recording, an incendiary rendition of *21st Century Schizoid Man* opening the show suggests that Fripp's assertion that Crimso would wipe out anyone else is pretty much on the mark. Aside from the shock and awe of the bone-crunching opening, the fiery details were really unlike any other of the rock acts appearing that day. The telepathic qualities between Giles and Lake are quite extraordinary. Check out the audacious slow-down in tempo under Fripp's solo. Just as it seems they're about to grind to a halt, the pair take off again, adding to the drama underneath Fripp's angular workout, ahead of the transition to Ian McDonald's frenzied burst. An incendiary sequence of improvisations within Donovan's *Get Thy Bearings*, *Mantra* and *Travel Weary Capricorn* showcased a determination to break away from the verse-chorus-extended solo, the accepted norm of the day, and adopt a collective approach that was open-ended and, above all, open-minded. And if all this sounds rather serious and sombre, there were plenty of examples within these fascinating pieces where the band was clearly smiling and having a lot of fun.

6 SEPTEMBER 1969 – CHESTERFIELD JAZZ CLUB

When King Crimson appeared in Chesterfield, the recording of their album had been completed though some post-production work was still being undertaken. But the record was still a month away from being released. So outside of a couple of appearances on BBC Radio 1 and word of mouth, the audience would have had little idea of what to expect. Given the weight of history that presses down upon KC's debut album, it's often something of a surprise to discover that gigs such as this (their 47th) have an almost carefree sense of abandon. The improvisations were clearly amorphous zones where ideas were thrown up in the air to see where they might land. Sometimes the intention was playful and obviously designed to entertain both crowd and band members alike. On other occasions the music was deadly serious with a sense of steely purpose to the proceedings.

21 NOVEMBER 1969 – FILLMORE EAST, NEW YORK

A tired Ian McDonald records in his 1969 diary that the band had spent the previous day rehearsing *Pictures Of A City* and ran through it on the afternoon of the 21st just to nail down the arrangement. The lyric was still being written, differing slightly from the album version which would be recorded the following month by the remnants of the group. Of the gig itself, McDonald notes that they "Played really well, went down OK." A classic slice of Crimhistory and as David Singleton says "that rare treasure – a virtually complete and audible show from 1969". The band played a shortened set list as they were part of a large bill, headlined by Joe Cocker – with two shows a night. Years later, by seamlessly joining an audience recording of *In The Court* to Michael Giles' own cassette of the gig at the first night of the Fillmore East (which was missing the bulk of the song), DGM re-created a small slice of KC history – although the majority of this show will be familiar to anyone who has KCCC25.

1971

FRIPP COLLINS WALLACE BURRELL SINFIELD

12 APRIL 1971 – ZOOM CLUB, FRANKFURT

The debut show for Mel, Boz, RF and Ian and what a fantastic atmosphere! The band are incredibly animated, clearly delighted to be away from their basement rehearsal room and obviously enjoying being onstage. The shouts of encouragement and approval being exchanged – often in mid-song – give this recording an astonishing intimacy. Highlights included Fripp's razor-sharp lines in the chorus section of *Cirkus*, an enchanting version of *Lady Of The Dancing Water* with winsome backing vocals from Ian, trimmed with some rich baritone sax, and the running lines and slashing chords from *LTIA1* making their debut during a radically different and experimental *Sailor's Tale*.

13 APRIL 1971 – ZOOM CLUB, FRANKFURT

Cirkus moves at a fair rate here. Played at this kind of speed, with the stabbing massed brass Mellotron lines provided by Mel, it sounds close – very close – to *Dinosaur*. Also noteworthy because it must be one of the few times that RF slipped in those *Lizard*-quick guitar lines during the chorus. Two versions of *Get Thy Bearings* were a platform for brave and fierce free-form exploration veering excitedly between chaos and control; Collins and Wallace tore the place apart in the first set while fans of *Lizard* thrilled to Fripp's allusions to *Prince Rupert's Lament* in the second *Bearings*.

14/15 APRIL – ZOOM CLUB, FRANKFURT

Only the second set from the last night at the Zoom remains in the DGM archive with an abruptly truncated intro to *Pictures*. *Sailor's Tale* – a track so new that Boz couldn't even recall its title – was the star of the show. A week after the residency, long-standing supporter Richard Williams heard the tapes and observed in *Melody Maker* that "the recordings show that the band has grown together in a remarkably short time, and is already developing its own personality" and that "it's a very strong blowing band with particular emphasis on Collins's extraordinarily confident alto and tenor". Elsewhere in his preview he notes: "Bob Fripp was almost bubbling over with joy, after having confessed to extreme nervousness after such a long time away from audiences." Five months later the band were recording *Islands*.

11 MAY 1971 – GUILDHALL, PLYMOUTH

Seventeen months after KC last played the UK, Boz, Mel, Ian and Robert made an out-of-town debut showing the band overcoming initial nerves and sounding far more confident during the *Islands* material. Even so, these versions were still brand new and the paint barely dry on them as a somewhat sticky version of *Ladies Of The Road* demonstrates. Fripp sounds curiously subdued throughout while the undoubted man of the match was Mel Collins. When Fripp described Mel's talents as "beyond belief" it was no idle flattery; the ground Collins covered during this gig was astonishing, especially his blazing solos during *Bearings* and *Schizoid* and the sheer stamina on display during the nascent *Sailor's Tale*.

28 MAY 1971 – GREEN'S PLAYHOUSE, GLASGOW

For an opening number, *Pictures Of A City* is performed in a remarkably relaxed fashion. Indeed there are moments where the band deconstruct the piece almost to the point of collapse. It's a fine line between chaos and brilliance but, rather than easing themselves into the set, Crimso opted to walk that particular highwire straight away. A jazzy guitar interlude on *Sailor's Tale* appears as it did in Plymouth only tonight it's completely unaccompanied. Aside from a couple of atonal swipes it's a remarkable opportunity to hear Fripp play in a traditional style he would only very rarely revisit after this tour. Ian Wallace is on great form throughout and clearly enjoys his solo spot during *Get Thy Bearings*. Fripp also provides a hair-raising sustained guitar solo including a liberal quote or two from *Prince Rupert's Lament*.

29 MAY 1971 – CITY HALL, SHEFFIELD

Mel Collins' sax work on *Pictures* and *Sailor's Tale* continue to amaze. His flute solo towards the end of *Tale*, as Fripp plays the "Mantovani" licks on the Mellotron, is a non-stop flurry of invention. After the serious subject matter of *The Letters* (a pretty good rendition with a smouldering middle section), Fripp sweetens the pill with a sugary coda ending on a jokey flourish. It sounds odd now but it was for a while his standard operating procedure when they played the piece. Collins once again steals the show on *Get Thy Bearings*, delivering a torrent of twisting choruses that touch on Charles Mingus and a bit of rock'n'roll. After a rather perfunctory *Ladies Of The Road*, and a bit of bicker/banter with the punters, an impatient crowd get an angry-sounding *Schizoid Man*.

9 AUGUST 1971 – MARQUEE, LONDON

A very relaxed-sounding King Crimson returned to the legendary London venue that they first played in 1969. Fripp recounts talking to ex-John Mayall and Fleetwood Mac guitarist Peter Green in the bar at the Marquee. "It's good to see you making a comeback," said Green. "I've never been away," Fripp replied.

"That's what I like to hear!" The *Islands* material had by now been shaped by touring during May and sessions in Command Studios with *Ladies* and *The Letters* largely finalised and *Formentera Lady* making what might be its live debut.

The improv section contained early sketches for parts of *LTIA1* and *Lament*. While some of this had been worked out in their rehearsal space on the Fulham Palace Road, there was very much a sense that the paint was still wet. After a couple of run-throughs in which Boz virtually dropped out entirely and Wallace sounded as though he was struggling, the piece broke down into a bravura solo for Mel Collins in which he wittily quoted from Sonny Rollins' *Tenor Madness* and Victor Sylvester's tea dance classic *You're Dancing On My Heart*.

10 AUGUST 1971 – MARQUEE, LONDON

One of the greatest finds in Mister Stormy's trawl through DGM's archives was a previously unheard set from the second night of the band's stint at The Marquee. Having only had the fairly grim-sounding bootleg to go on, it was wonderful to hear the band in pristine sound. Fascinating also to at last be able hear some of the vocal harmony ideas that they had in mind for *Formentera Lady*.

After a thumpingly good *Cirkus* (with crystal-clear Mellotron duet and Ian Wallace's double bass-drum thundering in the coda) Boz introduced "yet another newie" in the shape of *The Letters* featuring an exceptionally good free section, followed by arguably the very best *Cadence And Cascade* played by this line-up. It's interesting to note that at this stage the as-yet-untitled amalgam of *LTIA1* and *Lament* was clearly under active consideration for inclusion on *Islands*, according to Fripp's stage announcement. Although the band did record a studio version (available on the 40th anniversary edition of *Islands*) it clearly wasn't thought to be ready enough to make it to the final running order. It's interesting how similar in feel this version is to parts of *Emergency!* by Tony Williams' Lifetime.

11 AUGUST 1971 – MARQUEE, LONDON

The improv (elements of *LTIA1* and *Lament*) feels more flowing and there's a terrific Mel Collins solo after the main section. Once Mel goes unaccompanied the band veers into good-humoured duck calls, in-jokes and larking about. Wallace nevertheless whips up a storming solo. After an impromptu break, the VCS3-treated drum solo ushers in a wall of screeching sax and another stunning sustained guitar solo. Fripp sounds more comfortable here than on the previous evening. As it ends, a cash register rings and the band slips seamlessly back into the *LTIA* running lines: cue HUGE audience response. An energetic *Schizoid Man* contains a scorching guitar solo followed by Collins on devastating form, pushing and driving the piece along with inventive ferocity.

28 AUGUST 1971 – WEELEY FESTIVAL, CLACTON

Although scheduled to appear on Friday, 27 August, at around 9.00 pm, it wasn't until midnight that the band took the stage. Although only three numbers survive on bootleg, we know they were contracted for an hour and eyewitness accounts suggest that the set included *Formentera Lady*, *Ladies Of The Road*, *Cirkus*, *Sailor's Tale*, *Court*, *Cadence And Cascade* and *Schizoid Man*. At the end of *Pictures* you can hear the crowd shouting "Doctor". Mike Ferguson, who was in the crowd, shared his memory of the event with the BBC. "King Crimson playing *Cirkus*, a rousing rendition, but someone was ill in the crowd and people were calling out for help, and it was all sounding quite desperate – all of this building to a crescendo as the music itself built to a climax. Eventually, someone shone the tower lights in the direction of the shouting just as the music reached a peak."

Claire Whitaker was also at the festival and remembers: "My lasting memory is trying to sleep under the stars in the main arena and listening to King Crimson playing *The Devil's Triangle* in the middle of the night!" Judging from the mayhem of the version captured for posterity, Claire wouldn't have been the only one whose sleep was interrupted that night.

19 SEPTEMBER 1971 – GREYHOUND, CROYDON

"Totally amazing band," says a happy punter at the end of this audience recording. Although not pristine quality, the DGM Archive's recording captures the full Crimson set. The band are on strikingly good form with Fripp's solo on the opening sections of *Sailor's Tale* especially adventurous. There's a wonderful reading of *The Letters* with a splenetic improv featuring furious guitar bursts and grumbling baritone sax. Collins is on searing form as *Groon* builds up nice and slow, barking and roaring one minute and turning out sweetly flowing melodic lines the next. Ian Wallace's drum solo is beautifully constructed, again building nicely into the VCS3-processed section, though Fripp's unaccompanied coda struggles to find any real substance, eventually breaking down into humorous interplay. A fierce reading of *Schizoid Man* ups the ante with a fluidly twisting guitar solo. Good fun ahead of *The Devil's Triangle* with Fripp quoting *Sleepy Lagoon* (signature tune to the BBC's long-running radio series *Desert Island Discs*), hence Fripp's quip: "It's really great to be on your show, Roy" referencing its host and creator, Roy Plomley.

9 OCTOBER 1971 – PUBLIC HALL, PRESTON

The second night of Crimso's autumn tour gets under way with *Pictures* and *Cirkus* as knock-out punches. As *Formentera* gives way to *Sailor's Tale*, Fripp unleashes a scalding solo, after which Collins' flute solo isn't quite able to maintain the momentum. *The Letters* gets a huge reception after Boz's unaccompanied vocal on the end verse after a rather dramatic moment of silence, and "O'Rafferty's Pig" (as Ian Wallace jokily retitles *Cadence*) also gets a large round of applause. There's also a barnstorming *Ladies Of The Road* which Fripp introduces, as was his long-standing habit, as being about "rude ladies". *Groon* has an almost introspective quality after the main theme and first sax solo blow themselves out. The squalling blow towards the end swirls like a gathering tornado as Wallace whips up a white noise roar on his cymbals and Collins shrieks dementedly. Fripp's sustained solo carries over some of the mayhem before fading out and reintroducing the main theme. An enthusiastic crowd even briefly joins in with *The Devil's Triangle* – surely the most inappropriate clap-along song ever!

15 OCTOBER 1971 – WINTER GARDENS, BOURNEMOUTH

The quality of DGM's archive bootleg makes your ears squint. Interestingly the concert contains side one of *Islands* played in album running order. Here, for the first time in the archive, we hear Fripp's revved-up chordal solo as it was played on the studio version of *Sailor's Tale*. It's just a pity that a lot of the detail is sadly subsumed. Also of note is *Islands* itself. From what we know of this band's setlists, this song wasn't played too often. Here recast as something of a Mellotron power ballad (in lieu of Mark Charig's playful cornet solo), it's just about possible to make out how lovely it was in concert, although the coda seems slightly fluffed just a second or two before the tape cuts out.

16 OCTOBER 1971 – DOME, BRIGHTON

This concert was originally issued as KCCC 30 in 2004. In his liner notes Ian Wallace, responding to criticism of Boz's contributions, wrote: "This is obviously a band at its peak, enjoying one another's playing and it shows. Mel, Robert, Ian are stretching out whilst Boz is anchoring the whole thing, steady and ultimately reliable, enabling the others to take it out as far as Pluto and back without ever getting lost. A musical lighthouse if you will saving the others from an impending train wreck … That was the thing about Boz that so many people didn't get. Apart from being lyrical, his playing was solid and reliable. Something that is so necessary in playing this kind of music where anything can happen at any given time. I guess many of the listeners didn't get that. But the players sure did."

You can hear Boz stretching out during the improv section of *The Letters*, as well as a rare Mellotronic interjection from Fripp in the climactic moments. Also of note is *Islands*. The sound quality of this bootleg is notably better than the boot from the previous evening which means we get a clearer ear-view of Fripp's picking and embellishments on the track. Despite the lo-fi provenance this is a thing of joy.

18 OCTOBER 1971 – DE MONTFORT HALL, LEICESTER

While the sonic quality of the covert cassette recording masks the fine detail, in the broad strokes it provides an audio snapshot of a band very much enjoying itself as the humorous asides coming from the drum and guitar stools demonstrate.

The audience would have been familiar with the tunes from *Poseidon* and *Lizard* and, of course, a blistering *Schizoid Man*, featuring intense, white-hot soloing from from Fripp and Collins. While "heavy", as the heads used to say, it also stretches the fabric of rock to its very limits, pulling both band and punters into a turbulent free-jazz vortex. It's not until the piece hooks back into the spiky unison lines that you realise how far out into uncharted waters this Crimson sometimes travelled.

A slightly different feeling of discovery is present earlier in the show when, after a particularly caustic *Pictures Of A City*, Boz announces "a song now which we've just finished recording". *Formentera Lady* heralds 30 minutes featuring five of the six tracks from *Islands*, nearly two months before its December release date. Fripp adds some licks that wouldn't be out of place in a West Coast jam band, as Boz provides a serene, blissed out croon.

Although *Sailor's Tale* had been in the band's repertoire since March/April, it's now properly codified and delivers a substantial punch. By contrast, *The Letters*' quieter moments keep the crowd as rapt as the blow-out chorus and middle section. *Islands* is a thing of beauty. It was soon dropped from the setlist but this outing is simply exquisite. Yes, the sound is lo-fi but the clarity of the tune and the luscious playing comes across loud and clear.

The ending of *Ladies Of The Road* demonstrates that not everything was nailed down and the early section after the head in *Groon* sounds like a work-in-progress melody being tossed around. The sustain-laden *Peace – A Theme*, with stylistic echoes of *Prince Rupert's Lament*, is a fascinating moment of Fripp in truly rhapsodic form. All told, this is one of the best, most complete accounts of the KC setlist from this period.

19 OCTOBER 1971 – CITY HALL, SHEFFIELD

The archive's very clear and extremely listenable audience recording has the band in fine form. *Cirkus* has a somewhat eerie beginning with Wallace hissing out the title over Sinfield's VCS3-generated waves. After an equally authoritative *Pictures*, Wallace once again delivers his Monty Python-inspired *My Hobby* (heard more clearly perhaps on the Denver Summit recording KCCC 35). From the ridiculous to the sublime with a lovely reading of *Formentera* and into a scorching *Sailor's Tale*. As Collins supplies a spectral Mellotron this builds into one of the best versions of the piece. As ever, there's lots of fun to be had during *Groon*, and listen out for Fripp's unaccompanied solo at the end which seems to be flirting with the *Peace* theme from *Poseidon*. An exceptionally powerful gig.

11 NOVEMBER 1971 – MASSEY HALL, TORONTO

The archive's often fuzzy and at times indistinct audience recording captures Crimson on the second date of its North American campaign, Peter Sinfield's final tour with the band. The double-whammy of *Cirkus* and an extremely aggressive *Pictures* lets the punters in Toronto know the band mean business. The huge rise and fall in dynamics of these tracks is nicely contrasted by a gentle *Formentera Lady*, embellished by Mel Collins' lightly skipping flute. The volatile and explosive sax on *Sailor's Tale* might make you think that you're hearing two entirely different musicians. Fripp's revved-up solo provides a hair-raising and dramatic interlude and, although slightly scrambled by the audio quality, the duelling Mellotrons on the outro sound bizarre and other-worldly. Wallace's solo erupts out of *Tale* and the whole piece concludes with a controlled sustain fade-out. A strong *Schizoid Man* sounds jazzier than usual in the winding instrumental break with Collins on devastating form.

13 NOVEMBER 1971 – EASTOWN THEATRE, DETROIT

The second of two performances in Detroit on this Crimson's first foray into the USA. In his 2001 liner notes for KCCC 18, Ian Wallace wrote: "Of all the live concerts of this band that I've heard so far, I think this has by far the best sound. Also it's a sonic representation of the band at the peak of its powers, before the rot set in and the music changed."

David Singleton notes: "The audience link after *Pictures* has been repaired. A few obvious faults remain. The introduction to *Ladies Of The Road* is missing, and there is a break in the middle of *Groon*, where the original tapes were changed. *Lady Of The Dancing Water* remains an incomplete fragment."

Wallace explains the origins of the bluesy rendition of *The Court Of The Crimson King*: "Backstage during the applause for an encore we plotted. Sick of having to listen to people shout out *Epitaph* and *In The Court* we retaliated. 'So you want *In The Court Of The Crimson King*, do you? Well take this, you bastards!' What you hear next is a hilarious and unique version of a familiar song that could be titled *In The Court Of The BB King*. Did they get it? I doubt it. My reference [on the tape] to being an All American Boy was no doubt some sarcastic allusion but I can't remember what it was now. Still we had fun."

Closer inspection reveals an unfocused quality to the gig, though this might be down to the crowd as much as the band. "If you're clapping, clap in time – don't muck us about," Boz tells the audience as he mangles the first verse of *Ladies*. Even the normally stellar Collins sounds crestfallen here. Though reviving after Fripp's comedy intro to *Groon*, he neglects to offer a solo on a truncated *Schizoid Man*. The band's frustration at remaining in the shadow of '69 is evident during Fripp's initially diplomatic attempt at crowd control. Boz on the other hand just tells those baying for Court and Epitaph to "shut up for fuck's sake". If ever there was a case of band versus audience then this is it. You decide who won.

24 NOVEMBER 1971 – ACADEMY OF MUSIC, NEW YORK

"Ladies and gentlemen, you see before you a phenomenon which is interesting if not rare; it's a Mellotron which has just broken down." Eight gigs into the North American tour and Fripp's Mellotron has given up the ghost, forcing him to valiantly comp for all he's worth during an otherwise storming reading of *Cirkus*. Thanks to on-stage support from the crew, normal service is soon restored. The DGM archive's bright and often hissy audience recording clears up nicely for *Formentera Lady*, containing some choppy picking from Fripp as though he's slightly impatient and wanting to get on to the next piece. The outro is momentarily chaotic with Collins' brass setting Mellotron somewhat swamped by Fripp's scorching tone. A superb *Schizoid Man* gives the punters in New York the kind of clout they were cruising for all along.

1972 (February)

FRIPP COLLINS WALLACE BURRELL

11 FEBRUARY 1972 – ARMOURY, WILMINGTON

Since Crimso last played the States they'd not only parted company with Peter Sinfield but had managed to break up during their first writing/rehearsal session in January. Despite this setback, the band fulfilled what it believed to be its contractual obligations. There were two performances at the Armoury, the second set providing material – including the celebrated version of *Schizoid Man* and the storming *Groon* – released on *Earthbound*. In the first set, Mel Collins is as raucous as ever on *Pictures Of A City* with sophisticated moving of the rhythm by Ian Wallace during the improvised section. Overall, Fripp seems subdued, particularly on *Groon* where he fails to pick up the gauntlet thrown down by Collins' bruising solo. Consequently there's a degree of drift, rectified by an energetic *Schizoid Man* for which the crowd were especially appreciative.

17 FEBRUARY 1972 – GRANDE BALLROOM, DETROIT

On the archive recording drawn from the same clutch of cassettes that gave you *Earthbound*, this gig can be summed up in two words: Mel Collins. From the monstrously belligerent *Pictures Of A City* to the frenetic scrambling of *21st Century Schizoid* Man, Collins dominates the solo spots and everything in between! Collins is constantly adding lines between the parts as though he can barely contain himself. Even on a relatively sedate *Formentera Lady*, his spirited and energised flute work spins and glides. Once Collins switches to sax, Ian Wallace moves the piece into an extended percussive shuffle with Mel hollering like there's no tomorrow. There's a wonderful bit of freeform rough and tumble as they work on the transition to *Sailor's Tale.* Fripp appears unsettled during his solo, adopting a more acerbic chord-thrash midway. Fripp gets an electric shock from the microphone while making his customary announcement. A rueful Burrell can be heard complaining that he's had to put up with that all night. There's a more reflective than usual start to *Groon*, perhaps reflecting the tiredness of the band. While Fripp comps from the sidelines, Collins, Burrell and Wallace absolutely stomp this particular sucker flat, then set about building from scratch up to a blistering, frenetic hybrid. Unfairly maligned and dismissed for many years, this KC line-up - Collins especially – rips down the barriers between jazz and rock.

19 FEBRUARY 1972 – ARIE CROWN THEATER, CHICAGO

A couple of intriguing mysteries. First, where exactly did this gig take place? The DGM Archive has it happening at the Arie Crown Theater. Yet the same date is listed in the *Frame By Frame* and *21st Century Guide To King Crimson* scrapbooks as the Grande Ballroom, Chicago. Just to make matters even more confusing, bootleg listings have the band playing at the Grande Ballroom in Detroit, on 19 February! Another mystery is why this set is so short. *Cirkus* wasn't usually next to Groon in the running order yet, with no apparent cut in the tape, here they are side by side. Although the recording quality is ace, this is in truth a subdued outing. *Cirkus* never quite lifts off, even though Wallace's deftly shifting kit work beneath Mel's solo is an eloquent testimony to his skill and subtlety. Just before the outro there's some marvellous honking between the Mellotrons – something fans of this mighty beast always look forward to. *Groon* begins well with some spirited blowing from Collins but the attention is grabbed by Fripp's series of nimble pointillist runover some rock-solid, if unadventurous, time-keeping. Ian's drum solo lacks the frenetic energies of other occasions and the coda also fails to ignite in the usual manner. Nevertheless, this is still an intriguing fragment.

25 FEBRUARY 1972 – AUDITORIUM, MIAMI BEACH

The talkative punters in the vicinity of the partially concealed microphone on the archive's audience recording were indeed highly appreciative of a band on cooking form. A sprightly *Pictures* has Mel Collins scaling a steep incline of vertiginous notes. After the languid song section of *Formentera Lady*, the team are quick off the mark in the blowing section, with Mel quickly swapping from flute to alto. The folks in Miami certainly voiced their approval of Mel's solo as Fripp takes over for *Sailor's Tale*, sounding like molten silver seeping across the ruminative backing. Fripp's request for a moment of indulgence as he checks his tuning prior to a slow-bumping *Ladies* also draws applause. Witty asides from the guitar between the lyrics and a sneaky flirt with *Day Tripper* make this is a fascinating insight into how the band had fun playing the same material night after night. The grainy audio renders the sax solo and cymbal work on Groon into a strange white noise haunted by ghostly echoes of Albert Ayler and John Coltrane. Fripp's solo is another slow-burning and achingly lyrical intervention, erupting into Wallace's splenetic drum spot. *Schizoid Man* bubbles with malevolent energy and although the edge is blunted by the audio quality there's nevertheless plenty of excitement being generated. At its explosive conclusion the crowd rightly go ape!

"'Scuse us as we make it up as we go along," says Boz as the team embark on an improvised encore, which sees Boz gamely scat as Fripp tiptoes on the wah-wah. After the storm comes the gentle rain of *Cadence And Cascade* (warmly applauded) to calm things down. It's a lovely, light as air, and a perfect way for the team to say goodnight.

26 FEBRUARY 1972 – BASEBALL PARK, JACKSONVILLE

Pictures is taken at a medium pace and, after an uneven beginning, an assertive solo from Mel Collins makes the punters sit up and take notice. Certainly a belligerent *Ladies* pins back their ears as well. The same can be said for a tumbling and extended improvisation between *Formentera Lady* and *Sailor's Tale*. Up until then, the concert had been dominated by Collins. Now it's the guitarist's turn to drop jaws. The solo maps out a different space from anything preceding it – a deeply emotional outpouring that sounds as though the notes are being squeezed from as deep within the psyche as the fretboard. It's one of Fripp's best moments, and the end theme where Fripp's weaving tone is chased by the Mellotron brass is utterly thrilling as the band hurtles over the edge and disappears into Wallace's exuberant drum solo. However it's *Schizoid Man* that steals the show. The way in which the seemingly anarchic titanic forces unleashed by Fripp and Collins are suddenly marshalled into precision-guided weapons of shock and awe is what gives Crimso such an edge.

An edited version of *Sailor's Tale* from this concert appeared on *Earthbound*, released in 1972. This gig was chosen for the second disc in the King Crimson Collectors Club series, released in 1998.

27 FEBRUARY 1972 – KEMP'S COLISEUM, ORLANDO

Confidence or bravado? Whatever it is, you know Boz really means it when he scats "my kind of boogie" during encore improv *Earthbound*. The contemplative guitar solo that follows suggests Robert prefers a different kind of bag altogether. Of the singer and novice bassist, Mel Collins wrote: "Boz, thrown in at the deep end and much maligned over the years, swings like mad on *Schizoid Man* … I can't think of many musicians who could get that together in so short a space of time." Given that the lively crowd responded so well to the one-chord workout, ending this gig with a ballad like *Cadence* might appear a risky choice but it's a sublime conclusion to a solid gig having regained some of the energy that eluded them in Jacksonville.

This concert is also available as a two-disc set, originally released in 2003 as King Crimson Collectors Club 23. *Earthbound* first appeared on the 1972 album of the same name.

6 MARCH 1972 – WARNER THEATRE, PITTSBURGH

"This next song is aptly titled *Cirkus*," says Boz with a slight edge. Here's the band at the halfway point of what they know is their last tour together. Certainly there's a lot of clowning around masking some of their unresolved tensions and resentments.

"I feel lost, I feel out of control, I feel I'm going MAD!" declaims Fripp as he fails to quell a call to party from the rest of the troops on stage. A case of many a truth said in jest, perhaps? Alongside such psychodrama there's some good music; *Formentera Lady* is a rootsy, gutsy affair, with Boz's crooning especially good over Mel's thorny soloing. For fans of the vintage sustained tone that Fripp made all his own, *Sailor's Tale* will not disappoint. *Ladies Of The Road* features some laugh-out-loud banter and Fripp's blues guitar pastiche. Perhaps because of all the fun and games, *Groon* lacks bite and, while *Schizoid Man* rescues things with a revved-up guitar solo, the encore improv is probably Fripp's most uncommitted performance of the era. *Cadence And Cascade* is robbed of a proper conclusion when the tape runs out. It could almost be a metaphor.

8 MARCH 1972 – RIVERSIDE THEATER, MILWAUKEE

What a difference a day makes. After their uneven performance in Pittsburgh, Boz and the boys spent a day travelling to the Riverside Theater. Twenty-four hours away from the stage has made them hungry again. Arguably the best live *Formentera Lady is* found here; Fripp's chords and timing are tight and consequently Boz's vocals are focused and sharp. Collins moves from supportive flute to bracing salvos of alto sax fired over the rhythm section's inquisitive wanderings which range from sparse funk to R&B shuffle and Elvin Jones workout. As the piece becomes *Sailor's Tale*, Collins' frenetic soloing is jazz rock but not as we know it, Jim.

Groon is cut into two sections in the archive, thanks to the tape running out and being reinserted into the cassette machine. While some of the internal tensions are referenced by Boz and Ian (particularly when a member of the crowd yells for *Schizoid Man*), it's relatively minor stuff compared to the previous gig. Not even Robert's guitar breaking down at the start of *Schizoid Man* dents the confident air. Ever wanted to hear what Crimson without Fripp would sound like? Well, here's your chance. When they start up again with Fripp in tow they deliver a version which comes pretty damn close to the jaw-dropping rendition of *21CSM* at Wilmington the previous month.

10 MARCH 1972 – THE BARN, PEORIA

Although this recording begins with a sadly incomplete *Cirkus*, at least we do get to hear a full and unexpurgated chorus of *The Happy Wanderer* performed (played might be too much of a stretch) on what Fripp describes in his announcement, as "a bird warbler", courtesy of the Bozzel. Clearly the boys are enjoying themselves as Fripp's one-step-at-a-time solo builds up the tension. Partly obscured by Boz and Ian's vocals on the chorus, and Mel's sax, Fripp goes Vesuvial a la the studio version of *Sailor's Tale.* His parting-shot sneaky Beatles quote tonight is *Lucy In The Sky With Diamonds.* The good people of Peoria were immortalised following the release of *Earthbound* in the summer of 1972. What we didn't know back then was that the track cunningly entitled *Peoria* was edited from *Groon*. It's a joy to hear Mel's fruity baritone solo gouging and harrowing the groove in this way – and, if the shouts of encouragement from Boz and Ian are any indication to go by, the band thought so too. On *Earthbound* the track faded out during Fripp's comping but in the full version we get to hear Fripp's nippy, darting runs for the first time, and a menacing syncopated set-up for Ian's drum solo. A riotous *Silent Night* concludes a delightfully skewed *Groon*. *Schizoid Man*, including a fiery guitar solo, fades out just as Boz gets into the final verse. The improv encore is interesting with Fripp laying down one of those wonderfully fluid, molten solos at the very start before giving way to Boz's scatting and Collins' sax. The polar opposite contrast between this and the following *Cadence And Cascade* is astonishing.

11 MARCH 1972 – FAIRGROUND COLISEUM, INDIANAPOLIS

Missing its claw-hammer intro, a slow-burning *Pictures* allows Fripp to run at the fast-moving guitar sections like a greyhound out of a trap. Mel's sax over the slow middle section swings precariously between funky jabs and a roiling free-jazz alchemy. "A song from *Lizard*. This is *Cirkus*," announces Boz. Alas we don't get to hear it in this shortened set and leap straight to Boz announcing the next number. Fripp is clearly having some trouble with his custom-built pedal-board and we hear Boz suggesting the band start up with Robert joining in once his equipment problems are fixed. So the band (initially minus RF) start a tentative groove. Collins, of course, just blows the roof off as the band maintain a holding pattern (via the swooning croon usually heard on *Formentera Lady*) until the shift into the *Sailor's Tale* theme more than five minutes later. Fripp's sustain pedal clearly isn't fixed and so Collins carries the main theme with Fripp's natural-sounding Les Paul adding what it can. The drama is resolved when Fripp's pedal sparks into life, and we get a gorgeously plaintive outpouring that wouldn't have sounded out of place in *The Night Watch!* Ian's solo spot, which runs directly from *Sailor's Tale*, is rather compact and the haste with which they go into *Schizoid Man* suggests the band are up against the clock. At the end it becomes apparent that the band have had their set cut short not because of any equipment problems but because of local regulations concerning the use of the hall.

12 MARCH 1972 – SUMMIT STUDIOS, DENVER

Surely a contender for the strangest gig in the archive? It's hard to imagine a KC concert as odd as this: excerpts from *Symphony Sid*, *Flight Of The Bumble Bee*, snatches of *LTIA1*, Fripp doing the blues, a tribute to Monty Python, a splash of Pharaoh Sanders and what might have happened had James Brown's band backed John Coltrane at his most exploratory. Not weird enough? As this was originally a radio broadcast, throw in some product placement, the intriguing absence of Mellotron and a radio announcer who sounds as lively as Rip Van Winkle on Mogadon and you have the bizarre glory that is the Summit Studio session – all committed to pristine-sounding eight-channel multitrack. This is a quirky snapshot of a band with only 12 gigs left.

This concert was first released in 2000 as King Crimson Collectors Club 9. A new stereo mix and a quadrophonic version were released as part of the boxed set *Sailors' Tales* in 2017.

13 MARCH 1972 – SOUND TRACK, DENVER

The first of two nights at Denver's Sound Track begins with a delightful *Formentera Lady* with Boz giving a lovely reading of a lyric he wasn't always comfortable singing. Collins' flute work, weaving between the words, is always good to hear but tonight he's on fine lyrical form – a vein he continues in as he switches to sax after the main song. It's a faster version than usual, with Wallace adding sizzling cymbal work. Halfway through raucous sax and the crooning arc of Boz's vocals and glancing bass take this into more extreme territory. Though he's sadly under-mixed, Fripp's solo in *Sailor's Tale* nevertheless offers a contemplative alternative. Happily the sound problems are resolved by the coda and Fripp's laser-sharp tone rises through the Mellotron brass like a malevolent beast. An honourable and slightly distracted *Ladies* finds Boz momentarily amused by Ian's backing vocal, while the blowing section of *The Letters* enables the band to scratch and growl with an added chugging rhythmic work-out more usually associated with their encore improvs. With a first-class vocal from Boz, this may well be the best live version of this song.

Schizoid Man once again proves a dependable vehicle from which to take off and head for the stratosphere. Wallace is constantly inventive and supports Fripp's convoluted fretboard gymnastics with unerring precision. Another gig where an introspective interlude takes the piece into an interesting place before revving back up to fire on all cylinders. Agile bass work from Boz also makes this a cracking version. You'll wonder how they did it.

14 MARCH 1972 – SOUND TRACK, DENVER

There's quite a bit of levity in the air here. It all starts off fairly seriously as the pastoral charms of *Formentera* give way to the fearsome sax sorties of *Sailor's Tale*, with an especially gorgeous, slithering solo from Fripp, and *Cirkus* (which Fripp refers to as being a "goodie from the *Lizard* album that didn't work") has a ragged grandeur. However, it's impossible to listen to *Ladies Of The Road* without a smile. From the banter at the top (with Boz's comment about being "past it") to Ian Wallace completely breaking up with laughter as he's about to do his backing vocal in the chorus and Fripp's comedic runs and interjections on the guitar, this is a FUN take on the song.

The Letters is another highlight. In a feisty, combative *Schizoid Man*, the dynamic changes at around four minutes, when the charging pace is dropped and Fripp's solo moves into the newly created space. When the band kicks back in, the vagaries of the soundboard rob us of some of the guitar's volume. Nevertheless we can still hear Fripp really going for it. That it teeters at the end and threatens to fall apart simply adds to the high-octane excitement.

This show was originally released in 2007 as KCCC 35 where it was incorrectly dated as having taken place on 13 March.

21 MARCH 1972 – WINTERLAND BALLROOM, SAN FRANCISCO

The last time King Crimson had been in San Francisco was in 1969 while in the process of splitting up. Now, here were King Crimson in the Golden Gate City, once again in the process of falling apart. That said, the set here has real spirit and many inspired moments. *Pictures Of A City* commands attention and Mel Collins is at his grittiest and most angular grappling with the irregular terrain of the middle section. *Ladies Of The Road* gets a brutal workout from Collins and a lovely stepping stone solo from Fripp which evokes both Crims past and (then) present.

Groon morphs from its jazzy head and its one-chord boogie work into something quite diaphanous as a prelude to the drum solo, showing once again that this Crim can't be dismissed as a mere jam band. This is the sound of King Crimson stretching the boundaries of what being a "rock" band meant. *21st Century Schizoid Man* had also done its fair share of boundary-blurring, although in this instance the only thing that's blurred is the sound; Fripp's wonderfully luminous solo just manages to shine through the murk on what would otherwise have been a wonderful rendition – notwithstanding Boz's far-out ring-modulated vocals on the last verse.

Though the archive's bootleg recording is far from pristine, it's certainly listenable with the boomy acoustics of the hall favouring Mel Collins when it comes to instrumental clarity.

27 MARCH 1972 – ORPHEUM, BOSTON

A truce of sorts had developed between Fripp and the rest of the band as they criss-crossed America. That said, the differences were evident when speaking to Boston-based music writer JP Donlon. "There are two schools of thought," mused Ian Wallace. "One is committed to technique, discipline and virtuosity for its own sake. The other believes that the feeling of a piece, the feeling we give it, is more important. Basically the difference is between Fripp and the rest of us."

The gulf between the two camps was not one which could be repaired at this stage. Speaking to Donlon, Fripp acknowledged that the band was effectively finished, which meant he "would have to start all over" in figuring out how to proceed further.

We can hear a fleeting glimpse of the kind of start-over Fripp was contemplating during the bluesy raunch of *Formentera Lady's* instrumental section. As Mel Collins' sax barrage subsides, Fripp throws out the fast angular lines he would later refine in *Larks' Tongues In Aspic, Part One.*

Despite the personal differences, there are plenty of musical fireworks which the Boston audience are quick to reward with spontaneous applause during *Pictures Of A City*, an exceptionally blistering rendition of *Sailor's Tale*, and a frankly astonishing version of *Schizoid Man*. Whilst Fripp's fluid solo here is enough to make jaws drop on its own, Burrell and Wallace produce some off-the-cuff unison work while the guitarist is in full flight, brilliantly upping the excitement. Not surprisingly, after the funky blues-scat of the improvised encore and the comedown of *Cadence And Cadence*, the band sound all blown out.

This concert was first released in 2009 as King Crimson Collectors Club 40.

31 MARCH 1972 – MUNICIPAL AUDITORIUM, NEW ORLEANS

The penultimate gig from the Boz-era Crim is represented by a grim-sounding bootleg that has resisted the very best necromantic rites available to DGMLive and makes *Earthbound* sound like the sweetest-sounding record you ever heard. The distortion on *Schizoid Man* creates the impression the band are playing in the middle of an astonishing whirlwind. If we could but hear it properly, Fripp's solo goes from laser precision to nuclear wipe-out. Understandably the crowd go crazy at the end. A good audience, nevertheless, and generous with their praise – especially when it comes to Mel's flute on *Cadence*, which, despite the less than optimal conditions, gracefully takes flight.

1972 (October)

FRIPP WETTON BRUFORD CROSS MUIR

13 OCTOBER 1972 – ZOOM CLUB, FRANKFURT

In the excitement before this incarnation of Crimson's debut performance, one of the newly-formed five-piece anxiously enquired: "What are we going to play?" Jamie Muir chipped in: "Oh, let's improvise." And they did. Quite a few in the audience that night would have been at the same club 18 months earlier to see the debut of the *Islands*-era Crim. And it's a fair bet that many were hoping to hear their old favourites. But what they got was something entirely different. What the archive recording of this show lacks in audio fidelity, it more than makes up for in unique musical content: long improvisations and early transitional arrangements of better-known pieces.

This restored bootleg was first released on CD as KCCC20 in 2002.

17 OCTOBER 1972 – BEAT CLUB TV, BREMEN

An old trombone, tuned bleach bottles and a sack of leaves – not the band's backstage rider but all part of the rich tapestry of Jamie Muir's tenure in Crimso. The lengthy improv that makes up the bulk of this session shows the band wasn't to everyone's liking. Of their first formal performance, John Wetton recalled: "We were under-rehearsed, no confidence, we didn't know each other." Yet once the musical introductions are made this TV appearance is brave and action-packed stuff. The picky Crimhead will notice that the coda to *LTIA1* has yet to be written, let alone added, while *Exiles* appears to be coming together rather nicely, thank you very much. Short and sweet, this is a must-have for Muir completists!

10 NOVEMBER 1972 – TECHNICAL COLLEGE, HULL

Following the warm-up shows in Germany and a one-off date in Redcar in October, the new line-up took to the stage to unleash a ferocious sound. The abrasive mixture of freshly composed material and excursions into improvised territory was a dynamic and often challenging combination. Things are clearly still in development. *LTIA1* (still minus its coda) has a rockier feel. The big improvised set-pieces shed light on the protracted nature of KC's compositional techniques as licks from *Fallen Angel* and *Doctor Diamond* are thrown and tossed about long before they were ever distilled into songs. Even the tuning problems which plague *Exiles* fail to dent the excitement of what one reviewer described as "a riveting performance".

13 NOVEMBER 1972 – CIVIC HALL, GUILDFORD

Soundboard-quality recordings of this line-up are few and far between but this one is an especially powerful show heard on the third night of the band's marathon UK tour during November and December 1972. Looking back on his time with Crimson, Jamie Muir felt that one of his personal highlights of the tour was being able to hear Fripp break free of his self-imposed reins and play what the percussionist refers to as "extraordinary guitar". There's plenty of that during the 25-minute improvisation in which Fripp in particular plays like a man possessed. Leaving aside the frustration that the tape runs out, leaving us with only a tantalising snippet of *Exiles* and another improvisation, Guildford is certainly a special occasion.

This concert was first released on CD in 2003 as KCCC24 and as part of the 15-disc LTIA Complete Recordings box set in 2012.

14 NOVEMBER 1972 – TOWN HALL, WATFORD

Five gigs into their inaugural tour and Crimso are on fine form on the archive's decent-quality audience recording. *LTIA1* shows off extraordinary interplay between Fripp and Wetton just before the whole band comes back in for the main theme and the wind-down into the violin and dulcimer duet between David Cross and Jamie Muir. With the coda still unwritten, David Cross's beautiful solo gracefully gives way to *Daily Games*, as *Book Of Saturday* was still known. The extended improvisation begins with the ascending theme that will be familiar to listeners of the Bremen recording, splurging out into a funk-spattered workout whose violent stop-start build-up is given greater urgency by one of Bruford's trademark shuffles. The second, sadly truncated, major improv of the night opens with the arpeggio that would be recycled into *Fallen Angel*. The assertive soloing from Cross against the motif wouldn't sound out of place on an early Mahavishnu Orchestra album. Though Muir's visual theatrics are obviously absent here, his thrashing with chains comes over loud and clear in a superb *LTIA2*. Ian Wildman, who was at the gig and indeed responsible for ensuring the recording found its way into the archive, says: "One thing I remember about the concert is the power of the band and how the audience reacted at the end – totally won over! I also recall Jamie taking most of the stage with his kit, thrashing his metal plates during *Larks 2*. I also seem to remember he did most of the drumming during *Schizoid*. Bill seemed to take a back seat."

25 NOVEMBER 1972 – NEW THEATRE, OXFORD

Oxford's dreaming spires were surely rattled by this performance.

The version of *LTIA1* is about as close as you can get to the album version recorded two months later. The main item of interest however is the lengthy improvisation. Coming out of *Daily Games*, it begins delicately with Fripp pursuing a classical motif with counterpoints from Cross and Wetton. From there it moves up a notch as the rhythm section, primarily Bruford at first, engages. As Wetton maintains the centre of gravity, Cross can be heard mapping out some violin lines later to be revisited in more detail on *Doctor Diamond*. Later as Cross, now on keyboards, lays down Mellotron flute, Fripp really opens up with those sustained lines. Elsewhere his soloing evokes the steroid-enhanced banjo chords of the studio version of *Sailor's Tale.* The music sounds so organised, concise, arranged (and, for long sections, highly melodic) that it's little wonder so many audiences thought they were hearing traditionally composed pieces. While the sonic provenance of the recording fails to do justice to the subtleties of Jamie Muir's more abstract contributions, when Bruford and Muir lock horns behind the kit drums, their awesome barrage ratchets up the intensity factor almost to the point of destruction.

Although only the first section of the concert was caught on bootleg cassette this recording is nevertheless stone-cold, drop-dead classic Crim of the highest calibre. Arguably one of the best performances by the *Larks' Tongues* quintet.

1 DECEMBER 1972 – GREEN'S PLAYHOUSE, GLASGOW

Starting with a truly storming *LTIA1*, Robert seemingly loses focus during *Book Of Saturday*. Whether this was due to a technical issue or some extraneous occurrence of the Green's kind is unknown. Quickly recuperating, the song proceeds towards an orderly conclusion and dives off into an improvisation. Careful listeners will note that not one but two violins rise up from these pastoral beginnings with John Wetton literally playing second fiddle to Cross. John took up the violin when he joined Family in June 1971 to duplicate the parts played by departing bassist/violinist John Weider. Sadly it was the criticism of this Crimson duet spot from members of his former band that led John to put his violin back in its case for good.

The improv soon develops into more aggressive territories with Bruford and Muir building up a volley of percussion over which Fripp's guitar strafes and dives. The white-hot intensity is marred by the distorted audio but, once your ears get used to it, it's all rather exhilarating. As things subside we hear growling Mellotron as Muir's percussion and all sorts are deployed, followed by the emergence of a Mellotron-led theme that sounds like it's been cut from the same cloth as *Sailor's Tale*. Coming out of *Easy Money*, the surviving portion of the second improv contains shimmering guitar elements that Fripp would later revisit for *The Night Watch*. It's interesting and not a little intriguing to hear Muir's solo spot featuring his madcap humour going down so well with the equally boisterous Glasgow crowd. Sadly the incomplete source tape cuts out just as Bruford enters the fray.

8 DECEMBER 1972 – ODEON, NEWCASTLE

"My, my what a nice crowd of people they have in Newcastle. To the gentleman who so kindly passed those killingly funny remarks at the beginning may I say thank you, sir. You're really a scream. The piece was entitled *Larks' Tongues In Aspic, Part 1*. *Larks' Tongues In Aspic, Part 2* finishes the evening's music. But now, we shall proceed to attack culture yet again with a song entitled *Daily Games* and this in turn is preceded by a small demonstration of Mellotron tuning. The gentleman with the loud voice, your indulgence, sir," says the guitarist. The antics of the Geordie loudmouth in question are not preserved for posterity but happily the music, or at least part of it, is.

This previously unknown soundboard tape ended up in the archive after being discovered by ex-KC crew member Chris Kettle and passed on to DGM in 2017. The mad, savage beauty and heroic sense of adventure that made this period so magical is caught on the fly in wonderful up-close and pristine detail. The improv following *Daily Games* moves into what could pass for a West Coast-like "peaceful vibe" with a laid-back groove from Bruford, burbling percussion from Muir, a meandering, almost mellow, solo by Fripp and yearning annotation from Cross on violin. When Fripp's sustain hits up the pace, Bruford can be heard yelling his approval. As the velocity increases there's a line from Fripp that could easily be mistaken for the opening of *Fracture.* Perhaps more than in any other recovered archive recording of this band we get close-up to the empathetic way this team worked. The blow before a beautiful *Exiles* is brimming with invention and a level of collective attention that is especially impressive. *Easy Money* gives way to an amorphous improvisation that centres on a lot of percussion and allsorts with some Fripp-powered Mellotronic surges and swoops which ultimately herald the way out of the nightmare-frightmare zone and out towards *The Talking Drum* and, the climax of the main set, *LTIA2.* Jamie Muir's presence as a kind of agent provocateur comes over loud and clear. Tragically, as Muir flails chains on his sheet metal toward the end of *LTIA2*, the tape runs out.

13 DECEMBER 1972 – RAINBOW, LONDON

You'll need nerves of steel to make it through this audience recording of the penultimate gig of this incarnation's one and only tour of the UK. Chris Charlesworth's *Melody Maker* review reveals that Robert Fripp remonstrated with the audience following *LTIA1*: "If you're not prepared to listen to the dynamics of the music then you'd be better off in the bar." Williams goes on to note: "The latest Crimson is the most bizarre of all. It relies very heavily on improvisation and the visual antics of second drummer Jamie Muir who crawls obscenely around the stage, assaulting a battery of gongs and chimes in random fashion … each piece merges with the next and vocals play a small part in the overall sound. It's a cacophony of sound that hits the mind from the word go and doesn't let up for the whole performance."

No amount of sonic necromancy by Alex Mundy or David Singleton could find the spark of life in a fairly execrable audience recording, though there are some hardy souls who say it's not all that bad. They're wrong. Listen to it at your peril.

15 DECEMBER 1972 – GUILDHALL, PORTSMOUTH

The final night of the *Larks' Tongues* quintet's first and last tour of the UK. It had been quite a journey. Coming out of *Book Of Saturday*, the improvisation quickly goes from amorphous to direct with David Cross's violin making strident headway across solid funk-orientated grooves from Bruford and Wetton. Cross admits to being the most inexperienced member of the group but you wouldn't know that from his work here. As he slides and glides melodies that intertwine with Fripp's soloing, the musical ground becomes incredibly turbulent thanks to the Herculean efforts of the rhythm section.

A beautiful *Exiles* is the perfect palate cleanser after the rich improv but there's little rest for the audience who, *Schizoid Man* aside, was hearing an entire concert of completely unfamiliar music. As the band leaves a particularly rowdy *Easy Money* the transition into the improv is marked by Cross's violent slashing harmonies on the violin. At this distance, given the fuzzy nature of the archive's audience recording, it's not easy to discern precisely what everybody is contributing early on although it's possible that some of the high-frequency tones are emanated from Muir rubbing glass rods close to the microphone. Amid the rocking out it's possible to make out a Wetton-led charge into a motif that would be repurposed for *Doctor Diamond*. Later on, Fripp's riotous solo manifests as a ghostly oscillation between the percussive salvos and Wetton's daunting bass. The gap between the improv and *The Talking Drum* is priceless, filled with Jamie Muir's call and response, a useful example of some of the onstage behaviour that startled audience and band colleagues alike.

1973

FRIPP WETTON BRUFORD CROSS
18 MARCH 1973 – RAINBOW, LONDON

It takes several minutes before ears adjust to the murk of this audience recording even after Alex "Stormy" Mundy has worked his sonic magic. "I have managed to make it ten times more listenable! You should hear the cassette!" says DGM's in-house hero. Regardless of the shortcomings, it's possible to discern the Crims were on fiery form just three days into their UK tour in the week of the release of *Larks' Tongues In Aspic*. The speed with which they tackle *LTIA1* in this period is always a cause for wonder. The swells of the climactic build in *Easy Money*, even though partially diminished beneath the distortion, remains impressive. The real surprise, however, is the segue into the riff that would later form the central instrumental section of *Fallen Angel*. David Cross uses it as a platform for some very effective soloing, gliding over the see-sawing groove before the piece slowly dissolves towards *Exiles*. The ensemble comes out of *Book Of Saturday* with an improv that begins on a slow march that eventually becomes wreathed in swaying lines from Cross and Fripp as Wetton and Bruford stoke up the intensity. The recording may be flawed but the gig is fantastic!

1 APRIL 1973 – RHEINHALLE, DUSSELDORF

If the intention behind *LTIA1* was to demonstrate the full extent of what this incarnation of King Crimson was capable, it more than succeeds. While present-day ears are largely acclimatised to the *Larks*'-era Crimson, the range of colour, tone, and dynamics covered during the piece instilled a kind of stunned awe in audiences back in the day. The quality of this recording of the third date on 1973's European jaunt is somewhat boomy but it nevertheless conveys the startling freshness KC represented at that time. You can tell the crowd is well up for it as they try clapping along to a bass solo that comes out of *Easy Money* and leads into an absolutely epic improvisation that makes the scale of *LTIA1* positively myopic! As the audience's clapping falters, the Crims flirt with something more angular for a moment or two but Bruford's gorgeous *In A*

Silent Way-style shuffle provides stability for Wetton's percussive snaps and a languidly beautiful violin passage before eventually moving into straighter rock territory. Fripp's darting notes at around seven minutes provide a dazzling herald for the next excursion into the components of what would become *Guts On My Side*. Graceful, delicate versions of *Exiles* and *Book Of Saturday* sound all the more remarkable in proximity to the band's often caustic improvisations. The second example of this aspect of their collective personality in the set moves from pastoral themes into a solo rummaging on snare and kit from Bruford. He's out there on his own for a while before a comping Fripp rides in and the intensity builds. When Wetton comes in it's like a bomb being detonated. Perhaps more than anything this concert showcases an energised band taking flight.

5 APRIL 1973 – PALAZZO DELLO SPORT, REGGIO EMILIA

Crimson are hitting their stride but on this murky audience recording John Wetton's sore throat is having an impact – you can hear him straining on *Easy Money* in particular. He manages to rest it up in the following improvisation, turning in some of his trademark monster bass work. The improv that comes out of a delightful *Book Of Saturday*, still being played with accompanying tambourine, continues the reflective mood with some charming interplay between bass and guitar setting up a gorgeous violin solo from Cross. Whether or not Bruford is exercising "admirable restraint" or is simply inaudible is hard to say. However, when he does enter, with crashing cymbals in tandem with Wetton's growling bass, they take the piece in mighty and majestic direction. The rhapsodic overture comes to a slow end and is abruptly replaced by some stop-start funk that drives into the riffs and shapes that would eventually form *Guts On My Side*, with gothic Mellotron slices through the mayhem and horror movie soundtracking that slides into *The Talking Drum*.

Although Alex Mundy has done his best to clean this one up, the level of distortion is significant. That said, hardcore Crimheads will be able to discern what is, without doubt, a substantial performance.

6 APRIL 1973 – PALAZZO DELLO SPORT, ROME

The second night of King Crimson's first visit to Italy is an astonishingly powerful gig. If you ever doubted how formidable John Wetton was as a bassist, you need only listen to this frenetic rendition of *LTIA1*. After the cross-picking section there comes a storming blowing section in which he holds forth between slashing chords from the guitarist, the pair passing the baton as the piece rages toward the violin solo.

It's Wetton once again who takes the lead in the improv emerging from *Easy Money*. Although Bruford's embellishments are somewhat lost to the boomy acoustics of the venue, Wetton's string-popping outing is intensely rhythmic, providing a focal point for the audience. As the funk-flavoured blasts bed down with a Bruford groove, we can hear Fripp introducing the opening section of a motif that would eventually become *Fracture*. As it curls around the drums and bass, it feels like a case of the future reaching back into the present to pull the musicians forward. Fripp brings in another section of *Fracture* to this superb mix of pure improv and speculative sketches knitted together in real time. If that isn't enough to keep you on the edge of your seat then the improv that comes out of *Book Of Saturday* features Cross and Wetton in a stately, elegiac mood that brings to mind the opening section of *Starless*. Things rapidly escalate into a surging riptide of chordal soloing from Fripp and combative, driving playing from Bruford and Wetton. This is one of the best improvs by this quartet on a tour that produced so many breathtaking forays.

9 APRIL 1973 – L'OLYMPIA, PARIS

An astonishing show, opening with *Doctor Diamond* and the assault continuing with a fearsome *LTIA1*. However if that doesn't convince you then in addition to the album songs themselves, there's over half an hour of full-blooded improvisation. The first is based around the themes and motifs that would later be clarified (although ultimately abandoned) in *Guts On My Side*. The whole band storms through the show although special mention should be made of the guitarist who frequently exceeds all expectations.

24 APRIL 1973 – STATE FAIRGROUND, OKLAHOMA

A very powerful, albeit incomplete, *Doctor Diamond* opens this show. Seven dates into King Crimson's first American tour since the end of the *Islands* band, the energy being generated at the State Fairground is enough to power an entire field of Ferris wheels. Although the audience recording is murky, the bulldozing force of *LTIA1* is enhanced by the overloaded recording. You get the idea that this is pretty much how it would have felt to the punters on the night. During *Easy Money*, Wetton's bass carpet-bombs the instrumental section as it builds towards the climb-out and last verse.

The first of two improvisations begins with Wetton's funky chops providing a bedrock against which the other Crims explore. Cross is on fine form, initially adding chunky wah-wahed notes and then threading a soaring melody between the jagged stop-start strafing. Once the piece beds down into a mid-tempo groove, Cross and Fripp trade luminous, rhapsodic lines as Wetton underpins them with a descending bass figure. The bulk of the 11-minute work-out sounds almost too organised to be so entirely improvised. That said, the end section features a theme built a spiky Wetton motif with which the band would tinker for the next year.

After an exquisite *Exiles* and a *Book Of Saturday* sadly minus its introduction, a punter can be heard shouting for *Epitaph*. Instead Crimson set off into uncharted regions once again with a dark and brooding improv. Cross ratchets up a tense, nightmarish atmosphere which becomes a daring duel with Wetton's jabbing bass. As Bruford rocks out, the piece borders on the frantic. Cross's frenzied bow work, normally obscured in such circumstances, is preserved here. In yet another example of just how fearless this group was, halfway through everything drops back to a low rumble and the start of the journey toward *The Talking Drum* and a furious *LTIA2*, concluding with an incomplete *Schizoid Man*.

6 MAY 1973 – PALACE THEATRE, WATERBURY

With *Larks' Tongues In Aspic* having only just been released in the States, Crimson were hitting their stride. Opening with a strident and magnificently confident *Doctor Diamond* they move on to a *LTIA1* that's allowed to go gloriously off-piste. The boom of Wetton's monstrous fuzz-wah bass provides carpet bombing while Cross' violin solo offers serene safe harbour before the final rush into the coda. In his customary têtê à têtê with the audience, Fripp announces: "And now in an attempt to push culture a little further, to ascend to a new height of creative inspiration we're going to surge forth with a burst of enthusiasm and vigour into a song called *Easy Money* …" Tongue in cheek of course but he's not wrong in his description of what's transpired in what is only the first 20 minutes of the show. As your ears become acclimatised to this somewhat grainy audience recording, there are many stand-out moments – not least of which is the *Trio*-like improv, populated with yearning lyricism and expressive space. After a truncated *Book Of Saturday*, we drop into an improv that has David Cross rhapsodising as the band build up the heat around him. It's intense stuff, with Fripp adding layers of Mellotron while Wetton vamps it up and Bruford gets a rolling boil on the go. Brimming with energy and with a devastating conclusion, every reason you love this era of Crimson can be found in this one superb 15-minute improvisation.

8 MAY 1973 – MASONIC TEMPLE, DETROIT

"Hang about," says Robert to a boisterous and lively crowd who insist on shouting out requests during his announcement on this decent-sounding audience recording. "These kind suggestions are very well received but it's rude for me to talk over you. So perhaps you should be quiet?" The improv initially revolves around a searching solo from Robert. As the pace picks up, Wetton adds a descending run which, several months later, will form the spine of *Trio*. Here, however, it's the foundation for some mid-tempo rocking out upon which the band pours various rhapsodic runs. Then that rarest thing: a Bill Bruford drum solo. Though brief, it's a stand-out moment as he breaks into a super-fast shuffle and the band rejoin and blast into the still-as-yet-unnamed *Guts On My Side* riff. This is turbo-charged Crim at its best. The short improv that emerges from *Book Of Saturday* features a gorgeously melancholic solo from David Cross. A moment of true beauty it's in some ways the hidden gem of this performance. Then we are pitched into the set-up for the simmering menace of *The Talking Drum* and a truly scorching *LTIA2*. How do they top that? Well, that would be *Schizoid Man*'s job, of course.

16 JUNE 1973 – COMMUNITY THEATER, BERKELEY

At this fiery gig, where they opened for The Eagles, *Doctor Diamond* and a frankly astonishing *LTIA1* suggest that, in a parallel universe, Crimso could have been a top-notch jazz-rock outfit giving the Mahavishnu Orchestra a run for their money. The section where Wetton solos is made all the more dramatic by dark rumbling lines from Fripp that initially evoke the horror-tinged menace of *Mars* before transforming into a mutant brand of whacked-out rock. Bruford is on terrific form. His abstract ruminations in the set-up to *The Talking Drum* demonstrates just how much he had absorbed from Jamie Muir's short time in the band. The sheer drive and pace never lets up for an instant.

23 JUNE 1973 – RICHARDS CLUB, ATLANTA

The DGM HQ team got very excited when they heard this version of *LTIA1*, with certain voices going so far as to suggest it to be the "best ever" rendition. They have a point. As those spiky guitar arpeggios begin, the rhythm section sprints off ahead, leaving Fripp fighting to stay on the back of the tiger on a turbo-charged gallop. As Wetton turns in an astonishing bass solo, Fripp heralds his guitar break with a pre-echo of *Industry*'s doom and gloom theme. No, really!

Doctor Diamond would go through further stages of refinement on the road but with Wetton having to cram a frantic torrent of words into the verses, it's perhaps no surprise that the song (whose principal riffs had been around since the earliest times of the *Larks*' quintet line-up) never made it on to an official studio or live release at the time. The Spanish modes contained within the first improv make for exotic listening and the second improv – a gloriously spooky Mellotron fest – would have made a great horror movie soundtrack.

20 SEPTEMBER 1973 – CAPITOL THEATRE, MONTREAL

This second date of the band's last American tour of 1973 finds the quartet taking the material written during their August rehearsals for a spin. As Robert makes clear in one of his on-stage announcements, this concert is only the second time that *Fracture*, *The Night Watch* and *Lament* have been heard in public. David Cross's playing is very fluid in *Fracture*, which has an extra expansive blowing section prior to the jagged chords that herald the end section. *The Night Watch* is also of interest, because of the ending – a two-mellotron reprise of the intro theme combined with a gentle backbeat gradually slowing to a halt after a few bars. The band revised this into the standard coda soon after this gig. *Lament* is given a forceful reading but the final verse is delivered over the descending/ascending patterns heard in the instrumental breakdown.

Also interesting is the improvisation. Underpinned by a *Tight Scrummy*-style rhythm box, albeit at a much slower tempo, there's a degree of hesitancy in the embellishments from Wetton and Bruford. Fripp and Cross, however, dive in. The snaking, sinuous guitar has the same howling quality with which modern-day listeners will be familiar from *Asbury Park*, while Cross turns in some gothic Mellotron that adds grandeur and depth. When everything slows down and spaces open up, Fripp ushers in the introduction to *LTIA2*, the band dispensing entirely with *The Talking Drum* lead-in. A boomy but eminently listenable audience recording, along with a couple of laugh-out-loud moments courtesy of Robert's announcements and dynamic, persuasive versions of the *LTIA* material.

23 SEPTEMBER 1973 – ORPHEUM, BOSTON

The opening improvisation has a stirring intensity that eventually takes us to the strident violin introduction of *LTIA1,* delivered with a devastating attack. "Good evening, ladies and gentlemen, how exciting it is to be in Boston once again," says Fripp in the aftermath, going on to remind the punters of King Crimson's long association with the city going back to their appearance at the Boston Tea Party venue in 1969. It's interesting to hear Crimson working through their new material. Fripp's solo in *The Night Watch* is beautifully eloquent and Bruford's light cymbal work and rim shots add a special sparkle in the final verse. *Fracture* is given an especially good reading. The piece is not yet entirely fixed into its final iteration and has a spacious blowing section, of which Fripp takes full advantage, before the biting chords kick in. The end section with the furious distortion between electric piano and the guitar with Wetton's descending bass is hair-raising. If that wasn't enough, after the punchy bombast of *Lament*, yet another track that would have been unfamiliar to the audience that night, Fripp then announces: "We are about to venture into uncharted territories." And off they go into another improvisation. Against the backdrop of the rhythm box various members of the quartet dart and dive across the beats. David Cross turns in an especially robust violin solo between Fripp's spiky jabs and Wetton's funk-driven rumbling broadsides. When Bruford kicks in with a righteous backbeat after some eight minutes, the effect is not unlike the ecstatic release of the title track of Miles Davis' *In A Silent Way*. A stunning moment.

6 OCTOBER 1973 – UNIVERSITY OF TEXAS, ARLINGTON

Crimson play a high-energy show, highlighting their new material. In *Fracture*'s case, there are still a couple of sticky moments evident around the intro. However, the real surprise comes around the 6.30 mark in *Fracture* – with a later-discarded section propelled by a mighty Wetton bassline that reappears on *Red*'s *Starless*. An improvised section prior to those familiar rasping chords adds a pinch of wonder to this tale of the unexpected. A vintage improv, driven by Bill's rhythm box, features great thunking chunks of bass, laser-beam guitar, screeching violin lines, swathes of Mellotron and some ebullient Bruford mayhem. An *Asbury Park*-style must-have. The final 20 minutes are astonishingly good with one of the best versions of *The Talking Drum*. And if you think you've heard all the *Schizoid Man* you're likely to need, then think again.

23 OCTOBER 1973 – APOLLO, GLASGOW

What a dynamite gig this is – full of twists and surprises. There are times when both band and audience combine to make something special that goes beyond the night merely being a "good show". This is one such occasion and thankfully for us recording engineer George Chkiantz was on hand with the mobile studio to capture it all. While hindsight has made us familiar with the setlist, try putting yourself in the shoes of the folks at the Apollo that night. Large sections of the evening were devoted to completely new music that the punters would've been hearing for the first time. Perhaps it's this which makes the atmosphere so electric. Portions previously appeared on *Starless And Bible Black* and disc two of *The Great Deceiver* set; the whole thing is available on the

Starless boxed set and from DGMLive.

When *The Night Watch* appeared on *The Great Deceiver* the original guitar solo was replaced by one from Zurich. But the track sounds just fine without edits – clearly John Wetton thought so as he can be heard enjoying Fripp's playing. We can now also enjoy a superb *Fracture,* again with its jazz-rock middle section (later reused in *Starless*), and a forceful *Lament.* A thrilling gig – just listen to the demands for more at the end of the formal set. As they wait for *Schizoid Man* you can almost hear the astonishment when the crowd realise they're about to hear *Cat Food.* Wonderful from start to finish.

26 OCTOBER 1973 – RAINBOW, LONDON

Although their UK autumn tour consisted of just six dates King Crimson were on stunning form, as this great-sounding audience recording demonstrates. Alongside the warmly-received *Larks' Tongues In Aspic* material, including a truly blistering *LTIAI*, this concert also highlights tracks which would appear on their next release in 1974. It's interesting how well bedded-in *The Night Watch*, *Lament* and *Fracture* (on which you'll hear Bruford exclaim at almost precisely the same point he would 18 gigs later at Amsterdam's Concertgebouw) are. And it's evident just from Fripp's two classic announcements just how the band is enjoying themselves as the guitarist drolly lampoons recent live reviews in one, and threatens to demonstrate the band's new dance move that goes by the name of *The Mince* in the other. The improvisations return to some of the motifs of *We'll Let You Know* from Glasgow just three nights previously and there's a relatively rare outing for Bill Bruford's drum machine, which supplies the groove to a very satisfying quartet rock-out. Contemporary reaction suggests that the band were let down by muddy acoustics but this particular taper struck lucky, capturing an especially powerful performance.

2 NOVEMBER 1973 – AUDIMAX, HAMBURG

"When I was a very young man at school in England I studied German. I gained 4% in my school examination and abandoned the subject," says Fripp as he stands on stage in Hamburg for the first time in his professional career. After a powerful opening with *LTIA1*, which leaves the audience momentarily reduced to silence, the band dive into a blast of *Easy Money*, containing a furious guitar solo. He may have failed his German exam at school but this musical one at the Audiomax is passed with flying colours. In the audience was Reinhard Karasek, who had previously seen King Crimson in 1969 at Hyde Park and the Marquee. "In 1973 we could feel the energy and dynamic in this band and I think the concert was a better experience for me than in '69," he recalls.

On the archive's somewhat grainy but eminently listenable audience recording, there's a lovely rendition of *The Night Watch*, a sadly truncated *Fracture* and a particularly forceful *Lament.* The improv features Bruford's rhythm box providing an insistent click track of sorts. Wetton is quick to jump in and, despite the less than optimal recording, you can easily hear John's muscular yet lyrical counterpoint. A surging, high-octane improv finally gives way to *Exiles*, which sits, somewhat unusually, adjacent to *LTIA2*, which closes the gig from a cold start.

3 NOVEMBER 1973 – JAHRHUNDERTHALLE, FRANKFURT

"It's very exciting to be in Frankfurt yet again. In days of old it was in fact the Zoom Club," says Fripp. "The first simpering whimper of enthusiasm tonight from the band was in fact the legendary *LTIA, Pt 1*." Despite that slightly disparaging reference to the opening number, the cross-picking section is taken at a fearsome pace. After *The Night Watch*, in which Wetton seems to jump into the ascending bass part and thus curtails Fripp's solo just as it was getting going, the band enter the *Fracture* zone. A somewhat down-tempo version makes it more of a bulldozer as they go into the grinding finale. It's nonetheless a real blast by the coda, though not without some tuning issues. The improvisation begins with a cautious, impressionistic sequence making atmospheric use of the volume pedals. As Bruford drops twinkling glockenspiel into the mix, the mood becomes starker and more angular as Wetton makes his presence felt. As the group break into a strange, lurching march, there's a sense of uncertainty. Fripp introduces a plucked chordal solo normally deployed in *Easy Money* and for a while it sounds like a reprise of that number until they make their way into Exiles. A night of varying levels of energy and excitement is captured on this good-quality audience recording, concluding with a tragically truncated *LTIA2*.

12 NOVEMBER 1973 – PALAZZO DELLO SPORT, TURIN

"Good evening, ladies and gentlemen, from King Crimson," says Robert Fripp on a very good quality DGM Archive audience recording that finds the band at the peak of their powers. "It's very exciting once again for us to be in Italy … I would like to request, a considerable number of the audience please, for a little silence. Yup?" With hindsight today's eager ears will recognise many of the initial elements of the improvisation that comes out of this rendition of *Easy Money* – those which appear in *We'll Let You Know*. There's also the bonus of hearing the "jazz-rock" riff that would later be used in *Starless* and, if that weren't enough, stay tuned for Fripp's quotes of the rising theme of *Sailor's Tale* as he solos. The group are still eight gigs away from *Fracture*'s definitive reading in Amsterdam but all the components are in place. The version of *The Talking Drum* that emerges from the final improv is superb, with David Cross's violin soloing a particular high point. And listen out for the breathtaking control of dynamics in *Schizoid Man*.

13 NOVEMBER 1973 – PALAZZO DELLO SPORT, ROME

A boomy but very listenable audience recording, complete with a little coating of fairy dusting from Mister Stormy, provides a pretty comprehensive account of the Crims in Rome. With every piece from the recently released *Larks' Tongues In Aspic* album being performed, the real surprises come from the inclusion of *Peace* and *Cat Food*. The latter was a particular favourite of John Wetton, the prime advocate of resurrecting the 1970 track. There can't have been many people expecting to hear it on this tour. As if that wasn't enough, the set also finds the Crims road-testing *The Night Watch*, *Lament* and

Fracture, the latter particularly well-received. The first improv occupies a sonic space cut from cloth similar to *We'll Let You Know* performed 13 days earlier in Glasgow while the second, preceding *The Talking Drum*, amasses scary strings and blunt trauma from bass and percussion. A powerful gig ending with a high-octane performance of *21st Century Schizoid Man*. Containing some hair-raising soloing from Fripp, there's a chordal duet with Wetton prior to the final verse in which he gives the guitarist a run for his money.

15 NOVEMBER 1973 – VOLKSHAUS, ZURICH

For the 1972-1974 version of King Crimson, developing and writing new material was, as Bill Bruford memorably noted in his autobiography, "excruciating, teeth-pullingly difficult music-making". When *The Mincer* appeared on *Starless And Bible Black* it represented a new way of approaching the process for Crimson; taking live improvisations and then editing and over-dubbing new parts to create an interesting hybrid. Although parts of this show were previously released on *The Great Deceiver* box set, the entire performance has since seen the light of day at DGMLive and on 2014's extensive *Starless* boxed set. Using bootleg sources to restore the section originally excised to create *The Mincer*, David Singleton and Alex Mundy have re-created an evening of music which underscores Crimson's reputation as one of the classic must-see live acts of the 70s.

27 NOVEMBER 1973 – PALAU D'ESPORTS, GRANOLLERS

There's only so many ministrations Mister Stormy can apply to the source material. As the man himself explains: "This was a request from the forum. It's a bit woolly, but once one adjusts it's listenable. I sometimes wonder, after chasing hiss and trying to find the music, if I've improved them or not. Well, it may not sound like it to you, but this is tons better. The first half of the cassette needed retuning, quite a lot of these cassettes do, as the batteries on the machines are sometimes running flat, so the tape slows down. Sometimes they are too fast/high pitched as well but that's the joy of the job!"

Despite the less-than-optimal sonics, it's obvious the Crims are having a good show. When the band goes into the heavy slashing riff in the second part of *Fracture* the crowd bursts into applause. Given that they would be hearing this track for the first time did they think it was *LTIA2*? Well, no, as it happens. The audience frequently shows their appreciation at what's going on, suggesting they are well tuned into the gig. A graceful version of *The Night Watch* and a robust *Lament* are joined by a lovely *Exiles*. The quiet introduction suffers somewhat because of the overall murkiness of the tape but, after some gentle chording, Wetton breaks out his thunderous snap-bass and the team enter a stop-start interlude. Cross can be heard on electric piano with Fripp providing some Mellotron voicing. Despite the audio shortcomings, this is an intriguing excursion for the Crims.

1974

19 MARCH 1974 – PALAZZO DELLO SPORT, UDINE

This ranks with 1972's Summit Studios recording as a contender for the oddest download ever released by DGMLive. Between December 1973 and March 1974, during the writing sessions from which *Starless* emerged, King Crimson came up with a number called *Guts On My Side*. *Guts* and *Starless* were premiered here but whereas *Starless* went on to become an integral centrepiece of the KC canon, *Guts* was only ever played once in concert – as far as we can tell – and totally forgotten until January 2006. The last three tracks of this show existed for years on quarter-inch reels, but the first reel, which would've contained the rest of the show, was missing from the archive. Later in 2006 and in early 2007, better quality boots were sent to DGM HQ and Alex and David worked on restoring it. Sadly, the SADIE equipment died under their very fingertips and the work was lost. The curse of *Guts* had struck! Undeterred, Alex worked on the show when time permitted and eventually completed the work. The bootleg sources only went up to *Fracture* but Mister Stormy appended the remaining soundboard versions of *Exiles*, *Fracture* and *LTIA2* as a bonus. Aside from some first night nerves, this is not only a cracking performance but, in light of the rarity of *Guts*, also a significant one. Alessandro Pizzin and also Mauro and Renzo in Uppotipo were thanked by DGMLive for their help in rescuing this important show.

20 MARCH 1974 – PALAZZO DELLO SPORT, BRESCIA

They don't come much more frenetic or savage than this – a riotous *LTIAI* emerging from a down'n'dirty intro/improv, pausing only to catch breath in David's solo (here with additional guitar shadings) before taking off again. "That was a good ending," says an approving Bill Bruford before they duck and dive their way through an especially crunchy *Doctor Diamond*. The fun continues during *Easy Money* with ornery and cussed clusters taking flight from the fretboard like a bunch of punch-drunk wasps. Listen out for Bruford audibly swooning during a particularly beautiful guitar solo on *The Night Watch*. Of particular note is a storming improv which combines the eerie *Providence* sonics with a blast of *Journey To The Centre Of The Cosmos*. Mind you, the moment when the band set up a seamless transition into *Starless* is nothing short of beautiful. A sadly incomplete version of *Exiles* completes this belter of a gig.

24 MARCH 1974 – PALAIS PAUL VIDEL, AVIGNON

Sounding somewhat tired compared to the Brescia gig, the band have a little trouble finding their focus. Even the powerful *Fracture* teeters alarmingly at times. Yet even when Crimson isn't firing on all cylinders, they still manage to rattle the windows a little as a growling rendition of *The Great Deceiver* demonstrates. Slowly but surely the band pull themselves together and, by the time they reach the screaming guitar section of *Starless*, things are locking together. The end solo on *Exiles*, though brief, is filled with that bittersweet ache that makes this song so attractive. The weaving solo that David Cross dishes up on *The Talking Drum* radiates above the hurtling melee scuffling below. Be warned though, the hoped-for resolution of *LTIA2* is chronically curtailed by a bad case of Tapeus Interuptus – the unkindest Crim cut of all!

25 MARCH 1974 – PALAIS DES SPORTS, BESANCON

Bearing in mind that *Starless And Bible Black* had only just been released, the audience in Besancon would have only been familiar with just one of the nine tracks captured on this soundboard tape. That's quite a journey. On *The Great Deceiver* be sure to listen out for Bruford flying by the seat of his pants with those rolling toms skipping off Fripp and Wetton between the first and second verses and then into some bucking-bronco turbulence during the third verse. It's hairy stuff and they almost don't make it but it's precisely that sense of risk that makes this band so interesting and exciting. There's a storming *Fracture* that never lets up. Even the slightly wayward tuning on the final theme can't derail the crackling energies that this band conjures out of the air. The first improv hovers between bellicose astringency and detached experimentation before coming to focus in on a riff that would eventually become refined into the opening of *One More Red Nightmare*, and then taking flight. That it slides seamlessly into *Starless*, and a gloriously flawless rendition that makes this concert a simply astonishing must-have.

27 MARCH 1974 – AUGSBURG, STADTTHEATER

This gig appears to be a testimony to the recuperative powers of John Wetton. Having been out partying with David Enthoven and Richard Palmer-James in Munich the night before, he still manages an impressive performance on *Doctor Diamond* and indeed throughout the rest of the gig. Though the good *Doctor* would forever elude them in the studio it seems that the band were really beginning to find the soul of this song in concert. *Fracture* has a risky quality; Bruford is in an adventurous mood while David's Mellotron is a touch out of tune. However he wreaks havoc on the Hohner by way of compensation as Fripp and co rock out. Short but terribly sweet, one can't help but wonder where the improv with its gorgeous violin outing might have ended up had it not been prematurely guided into the direction of *Exiles*. While the improv Augsburg appeared on the *21st Century Guide To King Crimson*, the whole concert has been made available online and in the *Starless* boxed set.

28 MARCH 1974 – HALLE DER FACHHOCHSCHULE DIEBURG

"This is the exciting part of the evening where my scintillating personality draws you into the band's close personal magnetism, and I can only do this by announcing the pieces we have just played ..." A tittering Robert Fripp then proceeds to offer up two titles in a deeply impenetrable Dorset accent that produces guffaws from the band behind and utter bafflement for anyone trying to transcribe his announcement. A wonderful reading of *The Night Watch* is no laughing matter, however. In the raised adrenaline levels that come from switching from one high-octane track like *Lament*, a song as delicate as this could easily be over-played and brutalised. Yet the band manage to pull off something powerful without recourse to bludgeoning the audience. Shards of scattering xylophone, simmering bass, squalling electric piano and terse guitar form the bulk of the improv that goes into some hard-edged areas before Bruford kicks the thing off into a groove at around six minutes. The build-up and pay-off are worthwhile, spawning an *Asbury Park*-style solo from Fripp. When Cross cuts in with a rising Mellotron theme, it's a truly magical moment.

29 MARCH 1974 – KONZERTHAUS ELZERHOF, HEIDELBERG

First released on CD as KCCC 29, the opening improv is akin to a gathering storm that suddenly finds its focus in *Doctor Diamond*. Almost overwhelmed in the beginning by Bill's use of the gong, it quickly powers up into a great opening number. Prior to a gorgeous *Exiles*, Fripp deploys his classic stage announcement borrowed from Elmer Gantry: "Right, hands up those who like it those who don't fuck off my eyes feel like pissholes in the snow this is the last one for the evening seeds of space fly by my face." The second improv begins with an agile, funky groove with explosively percussive outbursts from Fripp's guitar and harmonic lines from Cross. Thereafter, Fripp offers up another flowing and often frenetic solo as the band lock down in the manner of the improv they would perform a few months later at Asbury Park. After the storm comes the calm: the Mellotron flutes and sustained guitar lines at the end of the piece offer a wonderful haven for reflection.

It's interesting to note that Fripp then starts playing the intro to *The Night Watch* which is then quickly abandoned for *Starless*. Had Fripp misread the setlist or was this the mood changing mid-stream and the band responding to it? During the especially strong *Starless*, Bruford and Wetton are on devastating form. Dense, acerbic, stirring and moving.

30 MARCH 1974 – ELZER HOF, MAINZ

Want to hear the best rendition of *Doctor Diamond*? This is it. Elsewhere, *Lament* comes close to being the monster Wetton always wanted it to be, while *Easy Money* addicts will need to add this one to their collection – it's among the best "hard" versions, pummelling doubters and flattening opposition. There's a pensive element to the improvisations that pepper this incomplete show, seasoning the standard Crim repertoire with a tinge of exotic mystery. Best of these is the sultry Spanish-style phrasing of *Atria*. Here, David Cross provides great atmosphere and depth alongside Robert's scorching notes. The mighty rhythm section slip the leash, running with a choppy, explosive groove that could well be the signature sound of this line-up.

31 MARCH 1974 – JAHNHALLE, PFORZHEIM

From cautious beginnings, *Improv II* quickly expands into lolloping beast of a track providing what is arguably the best set-up to *Exiles* to date. As Cross and Wetton hurl fuzzed lines across the stage over one of Bruford's slow-burning jazz vamps, Fripp introduces one sustained note that lasts somewhere in the region of 37 seconds. An object lesson in making a little go a long way. Looking back on this little hummer of a gig, lyricist Richard Palmer-James says: "What had seemed robust in the music the night before (at Mainz) now became threatening … the unsettling power of the performance comes through. In the dressing room afterwards, John sprawled naked on a bench, looking like he'd been shipwrecked; he didn't really recover before he went to bed. Even Robert had a few beers later in the pub. There was a quiet euphoria in the air, as if they'd survived a potentially lethal accident."

1 APRIL 1974 – STADTHALLE, KASSEL

This concert was originally released on CD as KCCC 36 and it's another high-energy performance by the band. *The Great Deceiver* is almost brutal as it ploughs open the evening. Wetton's bass really is more akin to a baritone lead guitar in his hands particularly in the first improv, a prelude to a riotous *Doctor Diamond*. The second improv is a superb example of the backline leading from the front; ever eager to get off the starting blocks, Bruford kicks off a fusillade of percussive battering with everyone else caught in the tailwind. Though under-mixed here, Cross's violin is wonderfully effective adding a light and dextrous melodic content to the bluster and braggadocio.

You can hear Wetton's appreciative groans between the second and third verses of a majestic *Starless*. When they go into the ominous bass section, Bruford similarly enjoys himself, detonating all kinds of rhythmic bombs about the place prior to the jazz-rock work out wherein Cross's solo whips up a microstorm all of its own. The third improv is a lovely pastoral interlude with Fripp's introspective chords and Cross's elegiac melody – short but quietly stunning in its own way. *Easy Money* begins in the usual way but the funk-driven shuffle with Fripp's chordal picking in the instrumental section is remarkably effective, punctuated as it is with Wetton's jabs and Bruford's tireless hi-hat.

2 APRIL 1974 – STADTHALLE, GOTTINGEN

"Yeaaah!" yells Bill Bruford as the band tear into *The Great Deceiver*, filling the cavernous-sounding venue with all of their considerable might and firepower. He yells some more as they bulldoze their way from that track into a devastatingly heavy *Doctor Diamond*. During *Lament*, Bruford ploughs into the climb-out section after the second verse instead of joining the others into the staccato unison parts. The band being road-hardened veterans, nobody is fazed and in fact it adds an unexpected and rather welcome swing. There's also an added sense of resolution when all the players lock down into the correct groove and power on.

This and other minor fumbles elsewhere in the set suggest the Crims are feeling a little tired as the finishing line of last show of the tour is within sight. Yet you'd be hard pressed to discern any flagging energy during *Fracture*, *Starless* or the improv preceding *The Night Watch*. Nine days after this concert the band stepped out on stage in America and embarked on the final leg of their road to *Red*. It would be another seven years before King Crimson played in Europe again.

28 APRIL 1974 – VETERANS MEMORIAL COLISEUM, COLUMBUS

We know from the full sets that have survived from this period how hot the band was at this time. *Fracture* is especially good, with a thundering performance from Mr B, while *Easy Money* has a piquant rip with a sting in the tail from the guitarist. The channels on the soundboard have John's vocals a touch higher than he might like and so there's a tendency for his voice to drown out his colleagues. David Cross plays a blinder in the improv that follows *Easy Money* but then experiences equipment trouble in the next number. What follows is a great example of a band thinking on its feet. When David's violin mic fails at the end of *The Night Watch*, Fripp keeps the Mellotron part going and John steps in to play Cross's part on the bass. Better yet, Robert buys the frantically busy road crew a few more precious minutes of repair time when he announces that the band are conducting a survey to see how popular they are: Cue the audience to go bonkers for a much-needed minute. Fripp (who clearly has missed his vocation as a stand-up comedian) then goes on to set up one of his best on-stage jokes yet.

While the good folks of Columbus may well have been treated to yet more chuckles or indeed barnstorming versions of *Starless* and *Schizoid*, these are not heard by audiences 33 years later as the tape ran out. Nevertheless, a great show.

29 APRIL 1974 – STANLEY THEATRE, PITTSBURGH

A cracking, take-no-prisoners version of *The Great Deceiver* opens this defining, much-bootlegged performance from 1974. For those who prefer a pastoral Crim, look no further than the sublime improv *Daniel Dust* that quells a boisterous crowd (including yelled requests for *Ladies Of The Road*) and elegantly sets up a reflective version of *The Night Watch*. This is desert island stuff indeed.

1 MAY 1974 – FELT FORUM, NEW YORK

"Welcome to an evening of karmic retribution with King Crimson," says Robert Fripp after a rousing *Fracture*. He then embarks upon what must be regarded as one of his classic mid-set stage announcements involving the offer to have his penis plaster-casted in Akron the day before and the appearance of Fripp favourite alter-ego Legs Quigley. As we know, life on the road was taking its toll on Fripp at the time. However, he has this boisterous New York crowd rolling in the aisles. Nearing the end of their run of gigs in the USA, the band take interesting liberties with the guitar solo in *Easy Money* which becomes a cooking pot into which all kinds of musical ingredients and ideas are thrown in before it comes to a boil. After a bulldozing *Starless*, Bruford hits the ground not so much running as sprinting with a 100mph rendition of *The Talking Drum*. As good as the music might be, the excitement comes also from seeing if they can maintain the breakneck momentum. Arguably the fastest version of this song anywhere. Needless to say, the punters go apeshit when *LTIA2* delivers its double-punch to the collective kidneys! All this and a great *Schizoid Man* make this a scorcher.

4 MAY 1974 – McMASTER UNIVERSITY, HAMILTON

It had been a bit of a day for the Crims, who travelled from Montreal – where they'd performed the day before – to Hamilton, Ontario. With a couple of the band nearly missing the flight and their luggage delayed, as Robert tried to buy some yogurt he was asked for autographs but records in his journal at the time that he was "not in the mood". The concert itself – in a gymnasium on the university campus – was remembered by a then-18-year-old punter John Harris as an impressive show: "The most memorable moment for me was during *Fracture*. Fripp was mostly in darkness and was wearing black but at the 7.40 mark when the guitar kicks in, a moving light showed Fripp's face with a big grin."

Fracture is indeed memorable but the archive version is a pretty grim-sounding audience recording with enthusiastic conversations intruding into the quieter moments. However, as the sound settles down and ears acclimatise, there's a lot to enjoy, including the improvisation that follows. In terms of the rhythmic part of the improv and the soloing over Bruford's fusillade, this one occupies a territory similar to *Providence*. The Mellotron flute interlude moves into a very different area, including a chord sequence sounding very like a song idea being tossed around. After the show, Fripp noted in his journal: "Thoroughly enjoyable. Interesting and different blow – very twitchy but exciting. Well received."

6 JUNE 1974 – TARRANT COUNTY CONVENTION CENTER, FORT WORTH

Alex "Stormy" Mundy has skilfully reconstructed the third date in on the last tour for this incarnation of King Crimson from a well-known bootleg source and a soundboard cassette. It finds the band on slightly unsteady form in places during the early stages as David Cross's out-of-tune Mellotron threatens to derail *Easy Money*, itself an unusual choice for the opening number. Fripp's solo begins with a *The Zero Of The Signified*-type running-lines pattern, sounding at times as though he's trying to straddle the abyss-like differential between the tuning of the rest of the band and the wayward Mellotron. After a perfunctory *Lament* and a much-needed spot of tuning-up, *Fracture* is where the band begins to gel with Bruford excelling with some precocious percussion, and Cross turning in a wonderfully atonal vamp. The improvisation flirts with the opening lines of *Exiles* but oozes into a groove not unlike the stately ascending middle section of *Sailor's Tale*. There's a brief respite from all the busy density via what amounts to an exceedingly rare – albeit brief – drum solo as we transition into what is arguably the most intense version of *The Talking Drum* the band ever performed. To describe this version as frenzied doesn't get close: *LTIA2* is almost an anti-climax here compared to the ferocity unleashed – Cross and Fripp's interweaving lines are simply magnificent.

Connoisseurs of Clams Crimsonesque will appreciate John Wetton's contribution around the two-and-a-half-minute mark in an otherwise triumphant *LTIA2*. Not to be outdone by his bandmate, David Cross momentarily forgets to engage the distortion pedal on a relatively rare keyboard solo in the climactic section. Such minor errors cannot, however, detract a fantastic performance.

7 JUNE 1974 – FAIRGROUNDS ARENA, OKLAHOMA CITY

An interesting gig, this is Crimson slogging it out rather than letting it flow. Not that this is a bad performance – far from it. However, they've been on the road for almost three months solid and it's beginning to show. You can almost feel the tiredness taking the edge off things; irritable-sounding musical exchanges, missed cues, proffered suggestions being ignored, etc. There's very much a sense that they've got their heads down and are just trying to get to the end of the gig in one piece.

Not that the good folks in Oklahoma are too worried, by the sound of it. Were you lucky enough to have been in the crowd that night then it's very likely you'd have been pleased as punch to have been beaten into the ground like a tent-peg by the massive, monstrous roar of Wetton's bass. John is very much up in the mix. While this might be fine for aficionados of the demon fuzz, his vocals occasionally come across like an overloaded sand-blaster approaching the limits the manufacturer's operating instructions.

There are plenty of superb moments here, though. David Cross's overdriven keyboard vamping on *Starless*, Fripp's solo shriek on *The Talking Drum*, the rhapsodic Mellotron flutes in the second improv. Oh, and a pretty devastating *Fracture*.

There were a few problems restoring this gig for the DGM Archive. *The Great Deceiver* is slightly truncated. Elsewhere bits of the soundboard recording were missing but the ever-resourceful Mister Stormy cunningly stitched in sections from a bootleg of another show. "The end of *The Talking Drum* and the beginning of *Larks II* was missing, but for continuity purposes I took the missing section from their show at Fort Worth from the day before. Basically this amounts to about 32 seconds for *TD* and 1.46 for *Larks'*."

8 JUNE 1974 – CIVIC AUDITORIUM, EL PASO

"May I on behalf of the band initiate a campaign which I'm sure will capture the hearts of millions. Ladies and gentlemen, make King Crimson a top ten band," says Fripp to the crowd in a jokey announcement which only seconds before, had seen him perform what was known in the trade as a "big willie". No, me neither. But what isn't in doubt is the ferocity of the opening number in which David Cross, sometimes lost in the mix on other dates on this tour, comes over loud, clear and incendiary. There's also an astonishing improv in *Easy Money* in which the band sound like they are brawling with each other in the final moments of the climb-out. That pace doesn't slacken as the team slam straight into *Fracture* with Cross's over-driven pianet adding to the sense of the whole thing about to go up in flames. *Starless* sees the band misstep with a fluffed intro and some shaky transitions in the early stages of the instrumental section. Just as they find their feet, tragically an incomplete tape means the action jumps to a madcap pianet solo with the band in full flight, en route to the track's thundering conclusion.

M. Deutrom, who was in the crowd, recalled: "Their sound was almost painfully loud and suffered from a combination of excruciating treble frequencies, and a multi-purpose venue that was more suited for car shows and wrestling. I do remember KC being excellent despite the sound and my unfamiliarity with most of their set. The show was much discussed, with the general consensus being that Robin Trower was someone to watch, and King Crimson was really weird, but cool."

16 JUNE 1974 – COLISEUM, DENVER

With ZZ Top opening and Golden Earring headlining, King Crimson's rocker-on-steroids *The Great Deceiver* quickly establishes that this isn't quite your regular rock'n'roll. The abrupt switch to *Lament*'s more genteel introduction must have turned more than a few heads. Fripp notes in his diary that the band received a polite reception but, if you listen to the cheers and applause after a very strong *Exiles*, the punters seemed to have come around to the Crim way of doing things. *Easy Money* continues the high-energy approach, the intro to the guitar solo being extremely powerful with Fripp's lacerating solo scratching deep into the fretboard. The pace drops but only momentarily as Cross's Mellotron flows and Fripp's guitar goes from the reflective arpeggios of the album version to a screaming howl. Definitely one of the hardest-edged versions. Speaking of hard edges, check out the instrumental section of *Starless* as Bruford takes the ball and runs with it. There's a moment where he goes into an extended snare roll that leaves Fripp hitting that single note like he's driving a piton into the side of a particularly precipitous cliff face. This is another remarkable rendition with the band bringing every last scrap of its considerable firepower to bear on an especially thrilling climax.

Upsettingly, just as a truly savage take on *The Talking Drum* is whipping up a frenzy and is just within a few beats away from the jump into *LTIA2*, the audio goes dead. Has the tape run out? No. The venue is hit by a power cut. The cause? Maurice Cloud, who was at the show, reveals all: "Two give-or-take weeks later I learned from the owner of Independent Records that the cause of Crimson's abbreviated appearance was a ZZ Top roadie pulling the plug on them."

22 JUNE 1974 – PERFORMING ARTS CENTER, MILWAUKEE

The band sound tired and irritable on the 12th date of their last tour together. An incomplete *LTIA2* is marred by the band not being able to hear each other properly, with different players being left on the wrong side of the beat and the violin irksomely flat. *Lament* doesn't fare much better with Cross's Mellotron out of tune and other missed cues abounding in a somewhat dashed-off *Exiles*. Although improvisations are normally a speciality of this incarnation, the one between *Exiles* and *The Night Watch* somehow never quite catches fire. It's driven by a restless Bruford trying out a series of speculative beats, as though taking the temperature of the band. With Cross developing abstract clouds on the electric piano and Fripp sounding strident notes, it's not until around three minutes in that they settle on a fast-moving direction. Yet even then there's a degree of diffidence and none of the flying sparks more usually associated with this band. Wetton's vocals on *Starless* come at a point when the words had yet to be pinned down and so he's heard to be what amounts scatting his way through the verses. Fripp and the bass/electric piano sections struggle to stay on target during Bruford's percussive excursions. The conclusion sounds like more of a stumble than a dramatic resolution. This soundboard tape is missing the set-finishing *Schizoid Man* but, given the rest of the below-par performance, perhaps that's a good thing.

23 JUNE 1974 – AQUINAS COLLEGE, GRAND RAPIDS

It's fascinating how a band simply gets on with the business of playing regardless of their internal politics. A little after 7.00 pm Fripp informed Wetton and Bruford that he wanted to knock the band on the head. As might be imagined, this was unsettling though not exactly unexpected as Fripp had previously expressed his disenchantment on other occasions earlier in the tour. A lively three-way discussion took place about the pros and cons of keeping the band going to give them a chance to become successful, later joined by David Cross. With nothing resolved, the band then went on to the venue, a college gymnasium. In his diary Fripp describes the band mood as "v. heavy from BB".

Can any of this internal turmoil be felt within the music? As tempting as it may be to try and ascribe the ways in which the musicians approach their instrument this night, the truth is the group are professionals who deliver a very good gig. After a blasting *LTIA2* and *Lament*, an improv that begins with a bassline that could almost be *One More Red Nightmare* leads into a terse soundscape that is quickly abandoned and subsumed into the opening strains of *Exile.* A truncated *Easy Money* is compensated for by the band going straight into an improvisation led by Fripp's arcing feedback, which then cools down into something of a soothing mood. Cross's violin steps forward with Wetton maintaining the momentum as Bruford bides his time and exercises his well-known admirable restraint. There's a point during *Fracture* when the guitar drops out of the *moto perpetuo* section as the band races through the piece but the ending has no such missteps with the Mellotron providing an extra chill. It's strong stuff.

24 JUNE 1974 – MASSEY HALL, TORONTO

If you listen carefully to the first improv, *The Golden Walnut*, you'll hear guitar lines that would later form the basis of *One More Red Nightmare* making a tentative, fast-moving appearance. After the gig, opinion in the group was divided – both Wetton and Cross having experiencing difficulties (Cross hadn't been able to hear what was going on in places). All agreed the audience hadn't been the easiest to win over. Fripp's diary entry concludes: "General verdict: hard work, not the kind of gig one would want every day of the week, but a success."

25 JUNE 1974 – CONVENTION CENTRE, QUEBEC CITY

Even though it's an incomplete concert, Crimson certainly hit the ground running. Opening the show with *Schizoid Man* is certainly a way of grabbing the audience's attention. Fripp is on form and David Cross's violin solo adds a fiery piquancy. Even John Wetton gets to take a short, rumbling breakout solo in the handover.

Lament benefits from an amped-up Fripp solo in which he employs the devastating *Sailor's Tale*-style chordal attack. The improv preceding *Exiles* sounds rather non-committal and half-hearted. *Exiles* itself wobbles slightly after the first verse but also contains some good violin commentary from Cross. Swinging out of *Easy Money* on a searingly brutal sustained note, Cross takes the band into a confident but reflective mood at the start of the second improvisation. For the first minute or so Wetton and Cross drift in a lilting duet with Bruford confining himself initially to small points of percussion before opening out on dramatic washes of gong after three minutes. Holding his own against Fripp's twisting tones, Cross emerges as the moving force of this particular episode.

The gig's excellent sound quality is marred only by the incomplete versions of *Schizoid Man*, which opens on "Cat's Foot, Iron Claw", and *Starless* and cuts out during Fripp's final solo.

27 JUNE 1974 – KENNEDY CENTER, WASHINGTON DC

The forgotten show. The performances before and after were recorded on multitrack, while all that remains of this gig is a cassette of the front-of-house mix – presumably the tape that RF refers to in his diary: "Shout at PW after gig for coming in with the tape …" The tape (thank you, Peter Walmsley) is an incomplete fragment of seven tracks – justified by *Easy Money* ("fuzz solo v. effective" – RF's diary). Hearing this, a different diarist 30 years later observes "fuzz solo v. Satisfying". Just when you think it's all over there's a delightful improv featuring David Cross. For a few moments they create from thin air a beautiful tender ballad with a touch of *Trio*. As with many board recordings, the mix can be interesting. The end of *Fracture* almost becomes a bass and bass drum solo – interesting for students of John Wetton's playing.

28 JUNE 1974 – CASINO, ASBURY PARK

Ever wanted to know what happens after the edit on the storming *Asbury Park* or the fade out on that contemplative solo on *Easy Money*? Well now you can find out! The power of this gig is tangible. Despite their internal politics and tensions, the band taps into a ferocious energy that never stops burning. Wetton is especially inventive, infusing the material with a brutal force. At the other end of the sonic spectrum, Fripp's sparkling clarity produces a consistently powerful performance that must rank among his very best. From the grumbling rasp of *LTIA2* through to the ecstatic demands for an encore, this is a classic Crimson show in every respect. Indispensable.

29 JUNE 1974 – PENN STATE UNIVERSITY, UNIVERSITY PARK

Though this particular line-up were edging closer to oblivion, 30 years after the event the energy levels of this show are astounding. In his journal, RF described the show as "Tired. Lifeless. Lacklustre". Maybe Fripp's estimation was informed by his recovering from mild food poisoning, the cumulative effect of prunes and a boil in his ear! Sound engineer George Chkiantz had trouble with the sound in the recording truck, roadie Tex was frightened to turn down Wetton's amp despite the discreet urgings of other members of the band and crew, Fripp was giving tour manager Dik Fraser grief and the promoter wasn't best pleased because the band didn't do an encore!

Despite all of this, the concert isn't anywhere near as bad as Fripp and others judged it at the time. *LTIA2* rips and roars like an angry beast, and the exquisite lead lines during *Exiles* compensate for the liberties taken with the timing. *Fracture* is a major event with Wetton and Bruford seemingly in a race to see who can reach the end first. Thankfully Fripp and Cross manage to keep up with them! The improvs are robust and prove that even with all of the problems and politics, Crimso hit escape velocity: the second improv in particular gives a gently inclined Cross a chance to move out from under the overbearing rhythm section. Oh, and did I mention that *Starless* is a must-have belter?

30 JUNE 1974 – PALACE THEATER, PROVIDENCE

"We weren't aware this was to be a final statement and when we were, we were wrong there too. But we did know we were knackered," wrote RF about the last theatre performance for this incarnation of KC. Despite the band being somewhat road-weary, this is nevertheless a durable set showing a band playing near the top of its game. High points include the two improvisations which RF noted in his diary as being "more spacey than before". While *A Voyage To The Centre Of The Cosmos* structurally echoes *Asbury Park*, the second improv, *Providence*, comes from another place altogether, somewhere well off the musical map. An assertive and highly recommended gig.

1 JULY 1974 – CENTRAL PARK, NEW YORK

Of this momentous concert, John Wetton commented: "If I shuffle off this mortal coil tomorrow that gig would be the one for me. That was the one … it was almost tearful, it was so emotional." Memorable not only for being the last date with David Cross but also for Fripp the first gig "since the 1969 Crimson where the bottom of my spine registered 'out of this world' to the same degree". Of the improv, *Cerberus*, John recalled: "It's very together. It's almost telepathic the stuff Bill and I are doing … the energy level is terrifying." And so it is. An unbelievably poignant gig marking the end of an era but the beginning of something else. Just a week later, without David Cross, they entered the studio to start recording *Red* and, just two months after that, King Crimson would "cease to exist".

1981 (April)

DISCIPLINE
FRIPP BELEW BRUFORD LEVIN
30 APRIL 1981 – MOLES, BATH

The smoky, sweaty atmosphere of the tiny club is tangible; this is the place where *Red* makes its live debut – seven years after it was recorded. The ambition of what's being attempted, let alone achieved, makes for extraordinary listening. This is fast-moving and furious – even the somewhat raggy sound can't disguise the fact that this is astonishing stuff. No wonder that, after the gig, an excited RF wrote in his diary: "This band will be colossal – it's that good. For me, this is the band I've spent four years getting ready for." Material that would form a staple part of King Crimson repertoire for the next 20-odd years is lifted sizzling hot and startlingly new from the creative forge that was Moles. Mind those flying sparks! First released in 2000 as KCCC11.

7 MAY 1981 – POLYTECHNIC, MANCHESTER

Although they only had five gigs under their belt, Discipline entered Manchester sounding confident and ready to take on all-comers. You can almost hear the brashness in this line-up as they launch into a set comprising music that did not exist just four weeks earlier. There's a palpable joy in the bouncy rendition of *Elephant Talk* (reprised also as an encore) and *Frame By Frame*'s incorporation of Steve Reich's phasing patterns sounds as hair-raising now as it must have done at the time.

Red, being played in public for only the sixth time, receives a rapturous welcome. In the post-punk era during which this concert took place, it's interesting to note that a call for *21st Century Schizoid Man* from a member of the audience is met with significantly less enthusiasm. That said, the reception given to *LTIA2* borders on the ecstatic. To some extent the material fashioned during the previous month's *Discipline* rehearsals is still fluid. *The Sheltering Sky*, originally born from an improvisation, is being moulded and shaped onstage at Manchester. Fripp's solo towards the end dramatically incorporates the introductory ascending lines from *Red*.

The archive recording is restored from a bootleg source by Alex "Stormy" Mundy.

1981 (October)

KING CRIMSON
FRIPP BELEW BRUFORD LEVIN
9 OCTOBER 1981 – THE VENUE, LONDON

"Hello, hello and hello very much," says an out-of-breath Belew after a cantering *Discipline* and a decidedly frantic *Thela Hun Ginjeet*. When a punter yells out something about his shirt Adrian responds: "I have no Hawaiian shirt tonight." This off-the-cuff, seemingly trivial, remark is important as it helps date this audience recording to the second gig of a two-night run in London.

By all accounts, ex-Crims Peter Sinfield and Boz Burrell had been in the night before. While posterity does not record their response, this gig is a turbo-charged performance with a dazzling "shock of the new" sheen. The bristling energy percolating through *Frame By Frame* is potently underlined by Levin and Bruford's nimble accents, constantly pushing the piece forwards. So far, so new. But listen to that roar from an ecstatic crowd when they go into *Red*. Back then, hearing this then-seven-year-old piece being played in public was a gobsmacking novelty. The version here, despite some classic clams at the bass end, is devastating.

At this point, Fripp was using a Roland keyboard and its thin reedy tone can be heard on the introductory bars of *The Sheltering Sky* before the trumpet-like tones of the Roland guitar synth take over. The inclusion of *Neal And Jack And Me* provides an early glimpse of the song as a work in progress, some four months before its recording. The cyclical figures spiralling outwards during the coda, later dropped, heighten the tension. After a barnstorming *Elephant Talk*, a Frippertronics loop can be heard above the rapturous applause. A four-minute ovation is rewarded with a savage *LTIA2* and, again, it doesn't require too much imagination to realise how strange and exciting it must have been to hear this piece in 1981. Even more surprising is how well it fits this incarnation.

14 OCTOBER 1981 – STADTHALLE, COLOGNE

It's a newly rechristened King Crimson just eight gigs into their European tour with a brand new album under its belt that is ushered onstage to a fanfare of Frippertronics. With the album, *Discipline*, released the previous month, the archive audience recording shows the band greeted rapturously. *Frame By Frame* is especially ferocious, and devotees of *The Sheltering Sky* will be pleased that not only is Fripp most definitely "on", he also adds a spooky line or two on the Roland keyboard. Also of interest is an early arrangement of *Neil And Jack And Me*, still in a state of flux and nearly being, ahem, fluxed up entirely in places. Having emerged from the first writing sessions in April, it still has a way to go. Briefly unleashed from the structured material, Bruford lets rip on an improvised intro to the encore, *Thela Hun Ginjeet*. When Fripp joins in, it sounds like a precursor to *Requiem* – a small but dazzling vignette of astonishing power. Though marred in places by some tuning problems, this shows just how formidable KC '81 really was.

22 OCTOBER 1981 – EL MOCAMBO, TORONTO

"Sorry, we like to play in tune," says Belew after a barnstorming *Discipline* and *Thela Hun Ginjeet*. "This is our first night in the great North West. How are we doing so far?" Pretty good, going by the reaction. It's the first night of the tour that would deliver a radically retooled KC around 29 cities in Canada and America. *Easy Money*, *Peoria*, *Asbury Park* and *Sailor's Tale* are just some of the numbers which the eager crowd shout out for in the archive's lively, eminently listenable audience recording. They don't get any of them, of course, but they do get rip-roaring music from the newly released *Discipline* album and a foretaste of the future with work-in-progress versions of *Sartori In Tangier* and *Neal And Jack And Me*, the latter featuring some end vamps from Fripp that come as close to blues as this band gets. Crimson feel and sound like they're in command here and clearly eager to get going, with Levin especially on fine form. *Frame By Frame* scorches, *The Sheltering Sky* opens up the roof on the place and *LTIA2* blows the doors out. El Mocambo didn't really stand a chance!

23 OCTOBER 1981 – CONCERT HALL, TORONTO: FIRST HOUSE

The archive audience recording is a little muddy in places but is eminently listenable. The Canadian crowd are on top form – very boisterous but clearly supportive. *Satori In Tangier* opens up a tentative space where notes cautiously emerge and test the air. There's a speculative quality to Levin's Stick work here and the fading-in pulses echoing from Belew's guitar. Fripp introduces thin rays of light via his Roland keyboard and for a short while all three players gracefully orbit around each other waiting for Bruford to launch them off on the main part of the journey. The open aspect of the tune's structure at this point is emphasised by Bruford's stop-start punctuation toward the end. It's a fascinating point of collective improvising within a reasonably defined space that's not unlike some of the grooves which the earlier King Crimson used to excel at.

The run from this through an excellent *Elephant Talk* and the tour de force *Indiscipline* is first-class Crim in action. On the latter, Belew's interactions with the crowd are especially entertaining.

23 OCTOBER 1981 – CONCERT HALL, TORONTO: SECOND HOUSE

"There's supposedly a considerable mystique about being a member of a rock band. In a sense the idea of being on the road in the 1980s is very similar in essence to being on the road in the 1950s … the whole beat mythology of Jack Kerouac, Neal Cassady and so on. This is …" At which point a heckler repeatedly interrupts Fripp's attempt to introduce *Neal And Jack And Me*.

After a couple of pauses to perhaps let things settle down, Fripp addresses the character directly: "Listen up, you're a rude fucking twerp – pipe down!" After a roar of approval from the crowd, he finishes the introduction and the band get under way with the as-yet-unrecorded track. The extended coda, a feature of this run of gigs, is a thing of joy. It's a pity that this part of the song didn't make it to the final studio cut.

The ending of *Sartori In Tangier* wanders out there into atonal psych sounds, eventually neatly resolving into *Elephant Talk*. Belew adds a manic drama to his spoken words during *Indiscipline*, a quality later mirrored in the blistering twin-guitar maelstrom in the final portion of the piece. It's pretty intense! This isn't a bad audience recording – if a little muddy in places.

29 OCTOBER 1981 – THE METRO, BOSTON

King Crimson are on devastating form. For all the general muddiness of the archive's restored audience recording, their musicality burns bright. The occasion is auspicious enough to bring Robert Fripp up from his stool to address a highly boisterous and enthusiastic crowd. "First it begins King Crimson's return to active service in the United States … in the venue King Crimson first worked in America in October 1969. It was also the same hotel in which Bill Bruford last stayed with Yes before joining King Crimson …" Before this, Fripp had played the solo of his life on *The Sheltering Sky*. The material that would make up much of *Beat* the following year pulsates with life. *Sartori In Tangier* is blessed with a spectral introduction featuring some soaring guitar from Ade against the dark undertow of Levin's rumbling Stick work and radiant constellations of notes radiating from the Roland keyboard. It's stunning stuff.

30 OCTOBER 1981 – TOWER THEATER, PHILADELPHIA

There are times when the sonic quality of this audience recording resembles a series of speeding cars suddenly braking and then thudding into each other. Of course, once your ears finally begin to adapt to the shifting murk it's possible to make out a pretty good show. And speaking of crashing cars, *Manhattan/Neurotica* is taken at a markedly different tempo. The piece was still in its early stages of development, coming in as a straightforward 4/4 footstomper rather than the whirlwind overview of the Big Apple it would later become. There's a certain fluidity in the middle section as they work on the business of finding parts for a piece that only made its live debut the previous evening. Elsewhere, following a lugubrious but rapturously received *Red*, a stately *Matte Kudasai* and a gently undulating version of *The Sheltering Sky*, there's a particularly lucid reading of *Neal And Jack And Me*. Whatever concerns there are about the somewhat muddy qualities of the source tape, *Sartori* and a blistering but tragically incomplete *LTIA2* ramp up the excitement regardless.

31 OCTOBER 1981 – CARNEGIE MELLON UNIVERSITY, PITTSBURGH

Some Roland keyboard-generated Frippertronics provide a delicate web of walk-on music before the slow intro to *Discipline*. Once your ears settle into the ambience of the archive's somewhat muddy audience tape, it's possible to hear the crowd enthusiastically clapping along to the early part of this signature piece as the complex lines echo around the rafters. "Happy Hallowe'en," says Belew. "King Crimson right now has two American boys, Tony and myself, and two English boys, Robert and Bill … let's show them a real American Hallowe'en cheer …" or words to that effect before the band launches into a barnstorming *Red*.

Matte Kudasai sends out the sunlight before things get darker and more pensive with *The Sheltering Sky*. A real highlight of this pretty strong setlist, it highlights the more free-ranging aspects of Robert's soloing while giving Ade a fine platform to showcase his skills as a texturalist. Tonight's version isn't quite as out there as on previous evenings but not for nothing does the solo at the end draw appreciative applause from the punters in Pittsburgh.

Especially interesting tonight are the middle section of *Manhattan*, which goes off on an extended wander around some pretty remote back alleys, a decidedly jazzy opening section of *Elephant Talk* from Tony Levin.

3 NOVEMBER 1981 – WARNER THEATRE, WASHINGTON DC

Near the start of this in-pocket audience recording we can hear punters wondering where Fripp might be located on the stage and regaling those arriving late. Needless to say such clueless behaviour means they are missing out on an astonishingly powerful *Discipline* as they do so. Something of that power finally gets through and we settle down to a great show. The sound quality is less than optimal but the band are really on form. "My favourite word of the night is 'if' as it has a lot of potential. It's easy to say and only has two letters. I know some bigger words but if's pretty good as a starter," says Adrian two numbers into the set. "So let's play if tonight. If you remember the album previous to the present King Crimson album, which is *Discipline*, this album is the same colour as my suit." And off they launch into a swaggering *Red*. If you want a clue as to why this line-up caused such a stir when they toured the USA you need only listen to *Frame By Frame*. Taken at a pace that you think they can't possibly maintain, its dazzling guitars spin like fiery Catherine wheels. It's a bravura display of ideas, technical skill, confidence and intention.

4 NOVEMBER 1981 – PAINTERS MILL MUSIC THEATER, OWINGS MILLS

"Hello! Still there?" asks a breathless Adrian Belew after a stomping *Red*. He needn't have worried – the punters are hanging on King Crimson's every note. *Discipline*, *Thela Hun Ginjeet* and the aforementioned piece are all pretty amped up, designed to drive through whatever atmosphere had been building up beforehand and drag it off in a new direction. While that's all part of the dynamics of a rock show it's also not sustainable for an entire concert. That's where *Matte Kudasai* comes in, taking things down a notch, providing a breather and refreshing the palate. The version here is especially good, an oasis of calm. A pity then that a latecomer wondering where his seat might be breaks the reverie which even this audience recording manages to hint at. We hope the wandering audient managed to park his butt by the time the band started a slow-burning performance of *The Sheltering Sky.* Keep an ear open for a rather savage *Neil And Jack And Me*; either by accident or design, there's quite a few liberties being taken with the structure by a roving Bruford, and the extended coda is a wonderful example of band having to think on its feet.

5 NOVEMBER 1981 – THE SAVOY, NEW YORK: FIRST HOUSE

What an amazing noise the crowd make as King Crimson take to the stage. No wonder the band's spines were tingling. This was the start of a three-night stint that passed into KC mythology as containing some of the best moments of the '81-era Crimson.

As with most things, you probably had to be there to fully appreciate it. For those in attendance, both artist and punter, the occasion is etched into the memory with indelible detail. For the rest of us, these audience recordings at least provide a thumbnail sketch. With a set consisting primarily of numbers from *Discipline*, the inclusion of new material in varying stages of progress make this a fascinating way of charting the making of *Beat*. *Neil And Jack And Me* is a beautiful lattice-work of ideas, muscular in places yet remarkably fragile in others. Interesting also to hear *Manhattan* (later to become *Neurotica*) taken at such a slow tempo.

Writing on the KC newsgroup Elephant Talk in 1997, Steven Sullivan noted: "Those concerts were outstanding even by Crimson standards. *The Sheltering Sky* and *Manhattan* were literally hair-raising. And Fripp-raising: the guitar 'conversation' in *The Sheltering Sky* at one of the Savoy shows was the only time I've ever seen Fripp rise off his playing stool in musical transport."

6 NOVEMBER 1981 – THE SAVOY, NEW YORK: FIRST HOUSE

The first of two shows on the second night of King Crimson's run at The Savoy. Want to hear a smoking *Discipline*? Check this one out. Whereas the previous evening's audience recording of the track was incomplete, there's no such problem here. Astonishingly confident, buoyed no doubt by the reaction from a tremendously supportive crowd, it also swings like the clappers. "The King Crimson album previous to one you might find in your record store contained this little song called *Red*," says Belew. No sooner have the words left his lips than the place erupts into a frenzy. Elsewhere, Belew is clearly having a hell of time. His exuberant interventions on *Frame By Frame* act as an accelerant to an already volatile version, and you can picture his beaming smile as he wrangles all those hoots and hollers during *Elephant Talk*. An otherwise intact and devastatingly good *Neil And Jack And Me*, with a variant interlocking section, is robbed of its very ending as the tape cuts short.

6 NOVEMBER 1981 – THE SAVOY, NEW YORK: SECOND HOUSE

"Hello again, New York City," says Belew at the end of a barnstorming *Thela Hun Ginjeet*. "I gotta tell you for a skinny boy from Illinois, this is quite a thrill." Writing on ET some years after the event Charles Jowett recalled: "I saw the second performance on a Saturday night … It was the first time I had ever seen Mr Fripp, or King Crimson, in concert. At the time I didn't even own any KC records, although I did have a copy of *Exposure*. I was completely blown away by the concert. I still consider it to be the most amazing concert that I have seen. Partly because I knew absolutely none of the material, and yet was totally overpowered by it. Adrian Belew was a maniac, bending the neck of his finger-painted Stratocaster and blasting out those wild whammy-bar riffs that he favoured in the early '80s … And Fripp was equally impressive, writhing around on his stool and even standing once or twice? His solos were especially amazing during *The Sheltering Sky*."

7 NOVEMBER 1981 – THE SAVOY, NEW YORK: FIRST HOUSE

On the third night at the Savoy, KC open with a rock-steady *Discipline* that emanates such power that, even from this distance, you can't help but get into the groove. If the previous evening's second house had signs of the team wilting slightly, they sound as though they are back with a vengeance here. An astonishing *Neil And Jack And Me* is so savage that at times it feels as though it's going to blow apart. The solo at the end combines Fripp's love of a yearning melody with out-of-this-world clinches. The cruel, but often accurate, concert-going consensus is that when the drummer strikes up a solo spot, it's time to go the bar. That's not a mistake any self-respecting Crimhead would make and Bruford is in playful form. *Indiscipline* takes things up a notch, as the team revels in being let off the leash. Riotous fun ensues on each of those break-out sections. Listen out also for another tumultuous *Sartori*. Talk about raising the roof!

7 NOVEMBER 1981 – THE SAVOY, NEW YORK: SECOND HOUSE

There's so much to enjoy on this second concert of the evening. Somehow, the energy is even higher than the first set. *The Sheltering Sky* in particular seems like one long masterclass in rapture; notes piling upon notes to create something shimmering and transcendent. Mind you, there's clearly a spot of collateral damage on Ade's voice as his normally elegant vocal is closer to a belligerent roar during *Neal And Jack And Me*. The tempo on *Manhattan* seems like it's itching to speed up to the pace it would later acquire. Listen out also for that bittersweet melody Fripp slips in on the play-out.

Writing in Trouser Press, David Fricke observed the fans packed into the Savoy and noted that they all "... share the conviction that that this is no idle cash-in reunion. These paying customers always admired King Crimson not only for what it played but what it stood for. Thus guitarist Adrian Belew (whose credentials with Frank Zappa, David Bowie and the expanded Talking Heads probably don't carry much weight with this crowd) gets the same enthusiastic reception for a string-bending wipeout as Fripp does for a stirring psycho-solo. The audience hears the same commitment in material from the recent *Discipline* album and new, as-yet un-recorded pieces that they recognise in live reprises of *Red* and *Larks' Tongues Aspic, Part Two*."

9 NOVEMBER 1981 – THE NITRO, DETROIT

Given that the name of the venue is The Nitro you'd hope that the performance captured on this not too shabby audience recording would be, well, explosive. Thankfully, it is and if you wanted a hint as to how volatile a show it is then check out *Sartori In Tangier*. Also worth checking out is the sadly incomplete *LTIA2* which King Crimson had last played in Detroit back in 1974. This time 'round it's Belew who shreds the lead lines like there's no tomorrow. The murky but listenable quality of the archive's audience recording hides much of Bruford's cymbal work though happily he comes through loud and clear on an especially rowdy *Indiscipline*. As you'd expect, Belew's recitation has the punters hanging on his every word. Mind, audience recordings do throw up some truly bizarre moments that border on surreal. Just after Adrian says, "I carried it around with me for days and days," one of the punters suddenly yells, "Where's Allan Holdsworth?" You do sometimes have to wonder what goes through people's heads.

10 NOVEMBER 1981 – PARK WEST, CHICAGO

As the tape loop plays out over the PA at the start, we hear one of the punters ask another: "Which one's Fripp?" Hopefully as the show progressed the answer to that particular question became apparent. Though a bit gravelly and initially somewhat boomy, the audio quality of this audience recording is pretty good!

As a result we can hear a thumpingly good *Discipline* and a *Thela Hun Ginjeet* which oddly enough benefits from the halo of distortion, imbuing Belew's stunning solo with even more urban angst than usual. "So, one night, little Adrian Belew from Illinois ..." he says as he begins his monologue about dangerous places in London and goes on to unleash yet more sonic mayhem. An impressive performance from the guitarist and the band seem lifted up by it.

There's a real sense of depth and space in *The Sheltering Sky*; after Robert's solo and before Belew goes into cloud mode, the guitars hang in the air drifting above the insect buzz of crowd noise. That air of stillness in what was quite a boisterous crowd is something to be savoured, a taste of something altogether rather special. There's a point where Fripp and Belew are taking their respective guitar synths to amazing places before the restatement of the end theme, which again seems to be occurring in a different space and time to the rest of the gig. Extraordinary stuff.

11 NOVEMBER 1981 – SOUTHERN ILLINOIS UNIVERSITY, CARBONDALE

"There are two points I'd like to make ...," says Fripp after explaining how he rarely comes to the microphone, preferring to sit at the side of the stage and keep his mouth shut. "I saw the piece in the university newspaper and it had a piece on King Crimson. It's very rarely that I get angry ... I found that piece most offensive and if the lady who wrote it is here may warts encrust your ..." and at this point the roar of the crowd obscures the body part in question.

"Secondly has to do with the way audience and performer get together with this process of making music. We have the most absurd notion of our performers – in some way they are elevated creatures and we externalise this notion and build stages; we put pits with water and piranha ... so that if you did want to connect with the performer you'd be eaten in three seconds flat. The Shakespearean theatre was constructed in the round so that it was entirely impossible for the event to take off unless the audience got stuck in. You can play rock'n'roll clubs and they're sweaty and uncomfortable and you can play theatres like this and they're, like, cold and uncomfortable ... I'm saying we all have to make a little more effort to bridge this gap."

Writing in his diary on 11 November, 2004, Fripp noted: "A late lunch with Steve Ball, who lived two blocks from the hotel until recently. Steve reminded me that today is our 23rd anniversary of meeting on The Drive To Carbondale. The anniversary links two parts of my history: King Crimson and Guitar Craft. On one GC course, I asked Steve: what brought you into Guitar Craft? Steve replied: seeing King Crimson at Carbondale in 1981."

"The Drive To Carbondale refers to a KC performance at Carbondale University in Southern Illinois on 11 November 1981. It was so named because the date fell in the middle of a three-month tour through the US and on to Japan. The band knew extended touring fucked me over, that the middle was a low-point of energy and enthusiasm, therefore that at Carbondale the English guitarist would be in very bad shape. To acknowledge his easily-anticipated condition of feebleness and despair, they named the tour for the middle-of-the-middle and The Drive To 1981 – The Drive To Carbondale."

"It is interesting and instructive to learn, even well after the event, of repercussions that result from our actions."

13 NOVEMBER 1981 – AGORA, ATLANTA

A fairly muffled audience recording gradually opens out into a brighter sound as *Discipline* threads its way around the venue. As the gig goes on the sound world improves quite dramatically thanks to the heroic work of Mr Stormy. Bruford is clearly having a ball as can be heard in his thoroughgoing exploration of the kit during *Indiscipline*. Mixing straight beats with tumbling rolls and arhythmic assaults, this section is so musical it's perfectly possible to forget that, whatever else it may be, this is a phenomenal drum solo. There's a really dramatic moment in the midst of Belew's monologue when Fripp suddenly unleashes a note-hammer of the kind that augers *Breathless* from *Exposure*. Full of menace, it suddenly alters the tone of the piece. It's gripping stuff. A bulldozing *Sartori In Tangier* takes us inevitably to a stonking version of *LTIA2* – a candidate for one of the best of the tour. Hurtling along at a frenetic pace, the vagaries of the audience recording pick out Levin's stabbing bass in the early parts of the piece and the solo fuzz punctuation in the breaks erupts loud and clear. He's especially lyrical in the first two runs around the principal theme. Clearly Bill Bruford is not the only one having fun. A great gig!

15 NOVEMBER 1981 – CULLEN AUDITORIUM, HOUSTON

"Hello, Houston!" bellows Belew before the final chorus of a rousing *Thela Hun Ginjeet*. The crowd go wild and Belew continues: "I think we're safe in here … unless you have a tape recorder …" Well, of course they did, thus preserving the event for posterity. A slightly boomy audience recording captures a Crimson that takes a little while to get into its stride.

That happens in the middle of *Red*; you can almost smell the fire and brimstone from this infernal lumbering beast, followed by what might be termed the beauty as *Matte Kudasai* makes for an interesting contrast. Belew's vocal is perfectly delivered as is the song itself. As Bruford wanders around the stage tapping the slit drum that begins *The Sheltering Sky*, sections of the audience clap along. It's probably the single most inappropriate clap-along song on the planet; thankfully they soon desist and allow the magic to unfurl. The version here is slightly restrained but there's still a tangible thrill as those clusters of notes from Fripp swirl about the place. *Frame By Frame* is stunning; after the first time around, the two guitarists depart from the usual script and channel the intro of *Neil And Jack And Me* – or at least a close cousin of those guys!

17 NOVEMBER 1981 – OPRY HOUSE, AUSTIN

This is King Crimson up close and personal. You can almost smell the sweat of the crowd on the archive audience recording. Not for the first time we hear the question "Which one's Fripp?" – surely an indicator of how many new fans were being drawn in by this band. A scorching *LTIA2* has an already enthused crowd go off at the deep end as Belew holds a single note and Fripp detunes the low notes to create a dive-bombing effect. "MORE MUSIC!" yells someone and that's exactly what they get with *Sartori In Tangier* as the encore. There's lots of space in the intro which only gradually begins to tighten. It quickly shapes up to be one of the most interesting renditions of the track, cut short when the tape runs out. Oh well.

23 NOVEMBER 1981 – THE ROXY, LOS ANGELES

"*Moonchild*!" somebody shouts. Of course, he hasn't a hope in hell. For his trouble he gets a mesmerising, almost meditative, *Frame By Frame*. With the *Discipline* album still only a couple of months old, this performance has a remarkable authority, catching Crimson on a classic night in which they swing and rock with equal abandon. Despite our hindsight and familiarity with the set there's lots here to surprise and delight. If *The Sheltering Sky* was meant to start with the trumpet theme nobody has told Fripp, who just starts letting rip like he can't wait to get going. Bruford's percussive intro to *Indiscipline* doesn't sound a million miles removed from the electronica textures of ProjeKct 4, no less!

The new material positively smokes; a still wordless *Neurotica* burns between blistering mutant metal jazz and ruminative math rock. The cascading lines of *Neil And Jack And Me* are still shiny new with a rockier-than-usual arrangement. And how about that Fripp solo at the end? *Sartori In Tangier* has Fripp on his trusty Roland keyboard and Belew making monster noises along the stage.

25 NOVEMBER 1981 – PERKINS PALACE, PASADENA

Even after the very best efforts of Mister Stormy, such is the sonic degradation of this audience recording that the instrumental middle section of *Thela Hun Ginjeet* is transmogrified into something resembling an outtake from Lou Reed's *Metal Machine Music. Red* similarly mutates into something not so much heavy as molten. *The Sheltering Sky* suffers when the excitement of the crowd effectively layers out sections of Fripp's opening solo, and a lone handclapper, prior to Belew's cloud sequence, is following a beat entirely of his own devising. Brown moments bedevil *Neal And Jack And Me* although the end of the formal verse, with Belew holding the vocal note and Fripp's emerging solo, has an endearing albeit savage beauty.

There are moments of clarity on *Matte Kudasai* and sections of *Frame By Frame* and, although this is generally a lively and direct performance, it that comes through a prism of distortion which lends it a diffuse punkish ambience that will likely appeal to only the most ardent of completists.

27 NOVEMBER 1981 – OLD WALDORF, SAN FRANCISCO

"It's a very rare occurrence that I come centre-stage to use this microphone," says Robert Fripp midway through the gig. "I normally sit over on the side. I'm a shy kinda guy. Every now and then there are important events which call me to the front and the rest of the guys in the outfit tend to give me a moment or two. World events such as the assassination of all world leaders over afternoon tea – this is the kind of situation that would draw me to the microphone. Today, or rather this evening, we have an event of similar magnitude: my sister is here!" Cue wild cheers and, quite possibly, relieved applause.

Despite being a somewhat murky audience recording in places there's an interesting variation in Fripp's picking between verses on *Neil And Jack And Me* that didn't make it to the finished studio version, and *Manhattan* is especially busy and bustling. Perhaps the most turbocharged piece is *Indiscipline*, with Belew working the crowd to perfection.

28 NOVEMBER 1981 – OLD WALDORF, SAN FRANCISCO

Not for nothing did the SF Chronicle cite these shows as a highlight of the venue's existence when it closed down in 1983. Crimhead Phil Toudic has cause to remember the Old Waldorf well. "It was a 300- or 400-seat club in an office complex in the fringes of the financial district. The band, billed as King Crimson Discipline, played four sets on Thursday and Friday of the Thanksgiving holiday. I had tickets to all four.

"The level of anticipation in the audience was off the charts – and was rewarded with a series of scorching, blistering performances for the ages. *Indiscipline* and *Thela* were so powerful they threatened to upend the tables and chairs. When the band launched into *Red*, though, the place came apart. We didn't know in advance if they would play older material, and to hear *Red* performed live for the first time caused near-delirium. The band's intensity had more than hinted at the presence of the Beast Crim, but *Red* confirmed it.

"Other highlights were the new pieces, a fully-realised *Neal And Jack And Me*, *Manhattan* and *Sartori In Tangier*. During the last piece, which I recall they only played at the end of the late sets, Mr Fripp kindly sprayed the hall with gouts of burning guitar. It was a fitting end to a fiery residency.

"I left out the story of nearly running headlong into Robert on my way to the men's room. He seemed slightly alarmed …"

Phil's assessment is bang on the money. The archive's punchy, in-yer-face audience recording is, to these ears, of a slightly better quality than the previous evening.

1 DECEMBER 1981 – COMMODORE BALLROOM, VANCOUVER

This rather murky audience recording captures Crimson on the last night of their North American tour. Thanks to Mister Stormy's ministrations a picture of a highly charged band emerges. There's an interesting *Thela Hun Ginjeet* with a slightly extended bridge and some intriguing harmonic variations on the bass end during Belew's frankly stunning solo section. After a thunderous *Red*, glacially slow and bearing all the hallmarks of an unstoppable juggernaut, we are treated to a truly transcendent *The Sheltering Sky*. Fripp's scorching solo work rightly raises applause. This astonishing piece frequently seems to be a portal through which something remarkable enters the world. Leaving aside the cruel irony of audience members loudly discussing the control of the guitarists precisely as Fripp does his double-time crosspicking, the punters are volubly excited as Belew tries and fails to introduce what was then a previously unheard song, *Neil And Jack And Me*. Sadly the song is incomplete but we do get to hear the gorgeously reflective play-out from the Dorset contingent of the band. *Manhattan/Neurotica* pummels the place to the ground. *LTIA2* is a flailing monster and the tension is heightened when Robert's rig breaks down, leaving Ade and the rest of the team to do all the heavy lifting. They heroically carry it off. When RF joins back in on the break, it's like a million-dollar firework show going off all at once. Impressive stuff and the crowd go bonkers! As an aside, after *Elephant Talk* a woman is heard to say: "I'm impressed. It's quite good, actually." Welcome to the dark side, sister!

4 DECEMBER 1981 – FRIDAYS, ABC TV, LOS ANGELES

After the final night of the tour in Vancouver, the Crimson crew headed to the studios of ABC for their spot on the network's flagship comedy vehicle. Touted as a rival to *Saturday Night Live*, ABC's *Fridays* enjoyed a run of three years. Crimson played *Elephant Talk* and *Thela Hun Ginjeet* and were sandwiched between show regular comedian Rich Hall and *Easy Rider* star Peter Fonda. The two numbers make for a pretty interesting, not to say edgy, contribution to a show whose musical guests were generally a tad more conventional. Just five days later, the band started a run of shows in Japan to end their momentous year.

1982

10 MARCH 1982 – OXFORD POLYTECHNIC, DORA COHEN HALL, OXFORD

The band had been on a short tour that began in February in the States, and then took them into the UK for this gig – the first of five in old Blighty in March – prior to the *Beat* sessions. Provided you can forgive the less-than-optional sonics from the DGM Archive's bootleg-sourced tape, it's abundantly clear that the group are relishing every minute. On *Discipline* they seem especially reluctant to arrive at the last note and *The Sheltering Sky* takes on truly epic proportions.

This being part of the *Beat* play-ins there are a couple of outings of new material – new to the Oxford audience at least. *Neurotica* is triple turbocharged. *Neil And Jack And Me* stretches time and shifts inside its skin while there's a tiny, almost pastoral, interlude before the band plough into *The Howler*. Buyer beware however – the source tape fades out before the track finishes. Still, Adrian's solo will give your goosebumps goosebumps.

Perhaps of greatest interest to long-term fans will be the untitled track near the end of the show. During the recording of *Beat*, the group laid down the backing track for this tune which was christened *Absent Lovers* but never made the final cut.

30 JULY 1982 – MANN MUSIC CENTER, PHILADELPHIA

With a team-band like Crimson it might seem unfair to single out individuals but in this performance (captured for posterity on KCCC26), Adrian Belew is a dazzling, fiery presence. The material he did so much to shape is presented here as a euphoric concoction that isn't born from rock or pop but is a kind of rocket fuel distilled from ambition, geography and experience. *Thela Hun Ginjeet* packs a devastating punch; a knockout collision between on-the-fly improvisation and canny judgement of what makes a good story great. While Belew cuts the narrative some slack, this song is as sharp as an arrowhead and fired off with a dead-eye precision that brings Crimheads out in a cold sweat.

31 JULY 1982 – CONVENTION HALL, ASBURY PARK

An awful lot about Crimson had changed since Fripp and Bruford were last in the neighbourhood back in 1974: songs about the Beat generation, electronic percussion, twin-guitar synth-noise terror, the whole rock-gamelan groove thang and a dazzling New Wave chutzpah that confounded some critics and old-school fans alike. This is a confident band retaining its reputation for experimentation by pushing the song format to the limit with fiery versions of *Indiscipline* and *Neurotica*. For all its interlocking angularity, *Neal And Jack And Me* is played to perfection, knocking several spots off the version only recently released on *Beat*. *Sartori In Tangier* has Fripp coming in low and lean but quickly running out of fretboard as the Turkish trumpet dervish gets a-twirling. Despite the newness of the sounds, *LTIA2* sounds very much at home. The only note of caution is that what sounds like a world-class rendition of *Frame By Frame* was cruelly cut short when the eight-track conked out.

Nevertheless this is a vital reinterpretation of what a rock group could achieve. Nobody sounded like this band at the time.

1 AUGUST 1982 – PIER 84, NEW YORK

A run of classic shows from the group continues. The power of the group is impeccable even if the sonics from this open-air audience recording leave something to be desired. NYC was treated to two nights of truly fiery performances where the group let go of any inhibitions.

Indiscipline captures this perfectly: Bruford swings a wrecking-ball of a solo, almost dislodging the pulse of the intro, while Fripp takes furious swipes that would knock a heavyweight sideways. While their enthusiasm occasionally gets in the way, it's hard not to smile as the audience join in with Ade's monologue. *Discipline* messes with the space/time continuum, while *Neil And Jack And Me* showcases the animation and effusiveness for which Belew is rightly praised – his work throughout this gig is astonishing stuff. Sadly, an otherwise superb version of *The Sheltering Sky* cuts out at about 8:50, foreshortening the dazzling climax. However, the presence and passion of the group redeem and transcend the bootleg-sourced recording.

2 AUGUST 1982 – PIER 84, NEW YORK

It's clear from the soundboard tape that the band are having a great time – the always ebullient Belew even croons a couple of lines from *New York, New York* during a riotous *Indiscipline*.

Reviewer for The Record, Mark Mehler, noted: "Over the course of a two-hour show that was heavily weighted with material from the band's last two LPs, King Crimson hung firmly to the cutting edge of contemporary music. Theirs was a bold, ballsy, alternately minimal and grandiose, but always intriguing set that never stopped challenging its audience."

5 AUGUST 1982 – PLACE DE NATIONS, MONTREAL

Highlights from this incomplete set include *Neurotica*, which must have ploughed the punters into the back of their seats. *The Howler* is a feral beast and *Indiscipline* bristles with a shocking energy that will surprise even the most jaded veteran of this well-worn wig-out extravaganza. Mention must also be made of a very impressive *Sartori In Tangier*.

Despite heroic audio restoration work, one or two bits are forever lost – *Frame By Frame* cuts out dead and *Matte Kudasai* exists only in the memories of those lucky enough to have been there.

13 AUGUST 1982 – THE GREEK THEATER, BERKELEY

A sprightly performance from all parties. As usual, Belew makes it sound all too easy while the Levin bass demon doesn't so much play the material as possess it. Here the *Beat*-era stuff sounds noticeably buoyant and a touch more exuberant than the studio versions. Certainly *Neil And Jack And Me* and a demented *Neurotica* consume energy like there's no tomorrow. It's one thing to be able to make a big noise and play fast. It's another thing entirely to be able to consistently perform such demanding numbers with this kind of pinpoint accuracy. Exemplary.

23 AUGUST 1982 – MOSCARDO, MADRID

On the second date of a series of gigs in Europe, King Crimson provides a stark contrast to the smoother tones of headline act Roxy Music. Given that Bryan Ferry and colleagues were touring their bestselling album *Avalon*, you'd expect the majority of the crowd would be barely tolerant of the support act. However, in the archive's restored, if slightly toppy, audience recording, there's clearly an enthusiastic enclave cheering on our heroes and, in the case of the opening bars of *The Sheltering Sky*, attempting a clap-along! This piece always manages to provide a shift in dynamics, conjuring a kind of still-space. That they are able to achieve this in the face of a punter determined to whistle louder than the band borders on the remarkable.

Despite the Crims sounding a little distracted, with the opening portion of *Red* turning a shade brown, powerful renditions of *Indiscipline* and the thundering set-closer *LTIA2* are especially effective. Little wonder that in his interview with the popular Spanish newspaper, *El Pais*, published the day after this gig, Roxy Music singer Bryan Ferry declared: "King Crimson … is very good live, fantastic."

26 AUGUST 1982 – ARENA, CAP D'AGDE

This is Crimson wowing the crowds primarily there to see headlining stablemates Roxy Music. And a heroic job they make of it. As Bill goes walkabout on a mesmerising rendition of *The Sheltering Sky*, the sultry Mediterranean weather has to cope with Bobby and Belew raising the temperature with their own brand of sweat-inducing storm-clouds of sonic shock and awe. Robert describes this show as "very good", a classic bit of Dorset understatement. This being Crim, we celebrate heroic brown moments too. During a crackling version of *Neil And Jack And Me*, the heat-seeking fingers of everyone's favourite Stick player momentarily veer off the highway of a song that doesn't ever want to hang about. Clams Crimsonique with that Riviera touch, anyone?

27 AUGUST 1982 – ARENA, FREJUS

The crowd at this show sound very keen indeed, considering that not all of them would have been there to see Crimso. Mind you, situated somewhere between the rich playground of St Tropez and the movie-star haunt of Cannes, this was a perfect opportunity to soak up the band beneath the Gallic sun. Let's be honest: if the rolling intro to *Waiting Man* doesn't put a smile on your face and set your toe a-tapping, then there's something seriously wrong with you. Belew the consummate showman gets Crimson's Roxy Music support slot off to a great start. A glossy *Red* shows Levin to be on devastating form and his nimble work on *Matte* is a perfect reminder as to why this player is held in such high esteem. Despite the sunny weather, *The Sheltering Sky* sends shivers down the spine, with Belew coaxing some of his patented weird-wired sploog from the wood. *Neil And Jack And Me* sounds sharper than its outing the day before at Cap d'Agde.

29 AUGUST 1982 – ARENA, REGGIO EMILIA

What kind of band is it that offers a heartwarming song one minute only to follow it with a heart-stopping sonic monster hell-bent on stomping you into the ground? Dear reader, the name of the band is King Crimson. Their setlist has always been a celebration of contrasts. For example, with hindsight the encore of *Heartbeat* and *LTIA2* looks either incredibly brave or bloody-minded. Or possibly both. *Indiscipline* sounds particularly dangerous while *The Sheltering Sky* gives an impressively strong account of itself with some outstanding work from Adrian. There's a real vivacity on display, despite sound quality which never scrambles above the level of the historic Moles release.

10 SEPTEMBER 1982 – WILHELM KOCH STADIUM, HAMBURG

Somewhere from the murk of this audience recording King Crimson emerge full of vim and vigour. Opener *Waiting Man* eventually gets the punters' attention and their background commentary drops off as a result. Bruford is clearly having a ball on *Thela Hun Ginjeet*, opting for double drumming that crunches all before it. *The Sheltering Sky*, though occasionally subject to conversational interference, is powerful with soaring runs from Fripp and squalling surges from Belew. Levin is on fire throughout *Neurotica* and Bruford knocks it out of the park for *Indiscipline*. A strong gig for the Crims that manages to take off despite the sonic limitations of the source recording.

24 SEPTEMBER 1982 – PALAIS DES SPORTS, DIJON

The quality of some gigs in the DGM archives present Alex Mundy with significant problems. Alex explains what he was up against with this particular concert: "I had transferred a 1/2" eight-track reel of this show. I had particular problem with the vocals but have managed to salvage them. What they had done was double up instruments on the eight tracks, so I had to make copies of some of the tracks and isolate the sound source and EQ each one to get the best out of each instrument. There were only two reels of tape, and *Waiting Man* cuts in more than halfway through, and the very end of a really good *Sheltering Sky* is missing. *Neal And Jack And Me* is incomplete, and the very end of *Heartbeat* is missing, but don't get too despondent about these problems, as I think I managed to get a really good mix in the end, and what is here is of good performance quality."

Alex is right. The band are on amazing form. Belew's solo on *Thela Hun Ginjeet* cooks up a storm of swirling layers, while Fripp's rhapsodic work on *The Sheltering Sky* sends shivers down places you didn't even know could shiver! The fact that track is missing the final theme doesn't detract or diminish from this rare moment. *Frame By Frame* also has a gorgeous pastoral variation by Fripp just ahead of the last verse which, albeit briefly, brings a different feel to the track. There are points during *Red* where the tempo teeters on the brink of a complete standstill as the drumming becomes extra spacious and abstracted, relying on Tony Levin to keep the pulse moving forward. Levin is also in a lyrical mood as he provides a lovely improv at the start of a wonderfully loose-limbed and fluid *Elephant Talk*.

Throughout the concert you'll hear little variations which will make your head turn or bring a smile to your face. Although the set is familiar, there's a sense that the band are having fun. While it's sad that there's a few incomplete tracks, and we suspect songs that are entirely missing (such as *Satori In Tangier* and *LTIA2*), there's still much to celebrate and enjoy.

29 SEPTEMBER 1982 – ALABAMAHALLE, MUNICH

Tight, complex, and startlingly ambitious, the gig represents what Rolling Stone's Chip Stern had in mind when he declared: "Crimson creates a new kind of electronic string music that achieves an orchestral density without resorting to ersatz art-rock bombast."

The gig was screened on German TV as part of a popular series featuring touring bands of the day, though quite how the wider TV audience responded to Crimson's brand of '80s gamelan-inspired direction isn't known.

1984

30 MAY 1984 – QUEEN ELIZABETH THEATRE, VANCOUVER

"Welcome to the start of the King Crimson 1984 tour of America. I hope you know some of these songs and note the discrepancies and applaud our bravery afterwards," says Belew. The band take a little time to bed down on this opening gig, ironing out a few wrinkles on the fly. A storming version of *Industry* with Belew at his pointillist, abstract best, coaxing all manner of elliptical sounds from his guitar and pedals. Belew's distorted voice in the verses of *Dig Me* continues the broodingly intense atmosphere. There's a sprightly yet thunderous *Sleepless* to savour although *Man With An Open Heart* has a heart-stopping moment as Belew realises he's using the wrong guitar and the song has to be restarted. Also of interest is a wild *Sartori In Tangier* and a rumbling *Discipline*.

The quality of the archive's audience recording isn't too shabby although close listening reveals there's something of an ongoing albeit enthusiastic commentary in the quieter sections.

8 JUNE 1984 – SAN DIEGO STATE UNIVERSITY

After a truly rhapsodic beginning from a clearly revved-up Fripp, Belew, Levin and Bruford add to a glowering improvisation which lifts the lid on an energetic show. While *LTIA3* doesn't always have the bite one hears in other shows, it functions as a superb loosening-up exercise, allowing the players room to focus and engage. The bootleg quality means that some of the nuances are blurred. Nevertheless Bruford's drumming throughout is full-blooded and bordering on the ecstatic. *Thela Hun Ginjeet* and *Indiscipline* stand out particularly – and he adds a real sparkle to the material taken from the just-released *Three Of A Perfect Pair* album.

"Are you warm, happy?" asks Belew of an upbeat crowd. "Me too!" It's true – his energy levels throughout the show are close to manic and, on pieces such as *Satori In Tangier* and *Sleepless*, threaten to go off the Richter scale completely – even more so on the sci-fi solo in *TOAPP*. Although there are occasional tuning problems (a result of poor monitor mixing), Crimson get up to take-off velocity around about the stark perspectives of *Industry*, with a sadly incomplete *LTIA2* blasting on all fronts. Sound quality is poor but you can still hear a band really going for it.

9 JUNE 1984 – IRVINE MEADOWS TERRACE, LAGUNA HILLS

There are times when this recording sounds more like a band interrupting a conversation but there are moments where the performance transcends the distraction. While everyone in the band thumps, plucks and pounds to heroic effect, it's Belew who gets the man-of-the-match award. The abrasive excesses of his guitar work on tracks such as *Industry* and *Dig Me* and even those machine-gone-mad fills on *Indiscipline* push this Crimson into harsher experimental territories than usually might be the case. Perhaps the highlight is their rendition of *Waiting Man* where the band fuse together to such an extent that the audience conversation falls silent. *Sleepless* roars at a demonic pace. However, given the unforgiving nature of the overall sound and the competition the band faces from a certain section of the audience, this one for the hardiest of hardcore KC enthusiasts only.

21 JUNE 1984 – EAGLES CLUB BALLROOM, MILWAUKEE

"Hello! How was dinner?" Belew wryly enquires after the barrage of *Entry Of The Crims* and an especially forceful *LTIA3* which occasionally sounded a little unsteady on this tour. This audience recording is a little ragged in places but not at all muddy, allowing us to get a sense of what went down in Wisconsin. "We have some more of that weird kind of stuff if you like it," adds Belew at the end of an especially gothic *Industry*, sounding more like a tour through a house of horror than a more traditional industrial setting. At the more conventional end of the repertoire *Waiting Man* possesses the sprightly energy that sounds like it was channelling Talking Heads' *I Zimbra*. "We have some other things to play from our very yellow third album," quips Belew before launching into *Man With An Open Heart*. "We made it folks, three albums. Amazing!" This last comment only hints at the internal politics and personal difficulties which would bring this incarnation of Crimson to a halt just 20 days later.

22 JUNE 1984 – POPLAR CREEK MUSIC THEATER, HOFFMAN ESTATES, ILLINOIS

Here's King Crimson in fine fettle near the halfway point of what would be their last American tour for 11 years. *Entry Of The Crims* is particularly robust. The sonic brutality of this piece evokes memories of *Beat*'s *Requiem*. Uncompromisingly fierce, it segues into a better-than-usual *LTIA3* (full of vim and vigour) which in turn gives way to a thrashingly savage *Thelma Hun Ginjeet*, with Tony Levin providing VFM entertainment. Fifteen minutes of pure Crim mayhem and an astonishingly bold start. Other aural highlights include a progtastic *Industry* (courtesy of a way-cool Bruford backbeat) and a frenzied *Indiscipline* in which Adrian, even more gregarious than usual, demonstrates his command of his instrument (including its attendant hands-free technology) and crowd control.

The set here is broadly the same as on the live album *Absent Lovers*, although this show boasts a really belting version of *The Sheltering Sky*, with Fripp hitting all kinds of sky-high inspirational octaves and whatnot. One possible reason for the lack of variation might be due to the fact that KC were by this stage in their career using a click track to keep strict tempo on several numbers.

The DGMLive recording was taken from two separate but incomplete bootlegs, stitched together by DGM engineer Alex "Stormy" Mundy, in order to recreate what the punters would have heard that night. What it lacks in sonic fidelity, it more than makes up for with tremendous atmosphere. One of the great KC take-no-prisoners shows.

26 JUNE 1984 – PIER 84, NEW YORK

"Thank you very much. Continuing on at this moment we'd like to do some more music from our very yellow record," says Adrian Belew straight after a powerful

Industry. It's possible that some in the audience with long memories might have been reminded of *Mars*, an earlier Crimson epic with a similarly dark and unforgiving feel.

Any such witless wondering is mown down by *Dig Me*, which veers between disturbing angularity and caustic experimentation through to a brightly-lit poppy swagger that embodies the excessive/accessible dichotomy referred to on *Three Of A Perfect Pair*'s cover art.

Tony's introduction to *Sartori In Tangier* clearly whets the appetite of an already lively audience. As Bruford and Belew indulge in some double drumming, Fripp's banshee squeal of a solo proves incendiary as does Belew's skydiving swoops and soaring skimming off the propulsive groove of *Waiting Man*.

This is a great-sounding audience recording and, with a truly barnstorming *Sleepless* taken at a rattling pace and an especially trippy and cosmic rendition of *The Sheltering Sky* hovering over the outdoor venue, the Crims are on astonishingly strong form.

29 JUNE 1984 – MANN MUSIC CENTER, PHILADELPHIA

"So you like that weird stuff?" asks Ade after an exceptional *Industry*. "Well here's some more," he declares before launching into *Dig Me*, arguably one of the most musically schizophrenic tracks King Crimson have ever recorded. In concert, those opposing factions – pop song colliding against atonal slabs of noise terror – seem even more stark and contradictory than they did in the studio. *Frame By Frame* has an almost laid-back quality belying the frenetic fretwork. After the bleeps, bloops and vworp noises from Bruford's Simmonds kit on *Indiscipline*, Fripp's solo is a real scorcher. Mind you, Belew steps up to the plate when it's time for his outing, proving that a little bit of competition clearly never does anyone any harm.

Although Tony's intro on *Sartori In Tangier* wanders into unexpected territory, he sets that trademark thump to provide the foundation for a fearsome series of runs from Fripp. Mister Stormy calls this a stomping performance and so it is. Sadly the source tape is incomplete – *Sleepless* and *LTIA2* are missing entirely, and we only have a fragment of what sounds like a promising *Elephant Talk*.

Eight gigs later, this line-up was no more.

1994

FRIPP BELEW LEVIN GUNN BRUFORD MASTELOTTO

28 SEPTEMBER 1994 – PRIX D'AMI, BUENOS AIRES

This is King Crimson's first performance in front of a crowd since they wowed the punters at Montreal's Le Spectrum (documented on *Absent Lovers*) more than a decade earlier. Tickets for what was essentially a dress rehearsal for invited guests and the South American press sold out in two hours flat.

You can hear the (easily forgiven) first-night nerves on tracks such as *VROOOM* and a slightly unsteady *Discipline*. A brisk *One Time* and an exceptional *Sleepless* show Adrian in fine voice, while the opening section of *B'Boom* has a hair-standing menacing edge. Elsewhere, *Funky Jam* makes the first of a short-lived series of appearances – there's a cutesy disco feel to the track which is appropriate considering that the venue used to be a premier dancing hotspot.

We're used to hearing *VROOOM VROOOM* taken at an energetic, sometimes breakneck, speed but here it's in something akin to slow motion replay. Overall, this is a performance where a somewhat tired Crimso leaps and sometimes makes it to the other side.

29 SEPTEMBER 1994 – PRIX D'AMI, BUENOS AIRES

A convincing King Crimson takes us into its confidence on its second night. Buoyant and self-assured, this gig has everything the previous evening lacked. Here, *Discipline* is indeed a vehicle for joy. On a fast-moving *Frame By Frame*, Belew has never sounded better and an irrepressible Bruford revels in his wild card percussionist role throughout. First aired during the *VROOOM* rehearsals the previous May, *Funky Jam* hops, skips and jumps across the boards. Honed and sharpened compared to its studio counterpart, it thumps along combining the feel of an instrumental *Elephant Talk* with the cyclical turn-over that was hardwired into the 80s Crim psyche. Fripp's high notes even evoke something of *Sunday All Over The World.*

30 SEPTEMBER 1994 – PRIX D'AMI, BUENOS AIRES

The energy levels are way up high in this last night prior to Crimso's transfer to the Broadway Theatre. Though *Funky Jam* is spread a bit thinly tonight, the up-tempo beat is in keeping the Prix d'Ami's disco reputation. The club had been packed to the rafters with journalists from all over South America, rock stars, actors, politicians – and the paying public. The crowd are really the co-stars here and as the gig progresses the intensity of this fiery performance mounts accordingly. Never mind heavy metal – this is more like an exploding junkyard of sound hurtling violently in your direction.

Fripp and Belew lock horns during a truly furious rendition of *The Talking Drum* and you've got to love the chanting crowd at the end of *LTIA2*. A stonking instrumental version of *People* is priceless with *Sleepless* and a reprised *Red* rounding off a grand Prix indeed!

6 OCTOBER 1994 – TEATRO BROADWAY, BUENOS AIRES

"Woah, what a night," says Belew at the end of the formal set just before embarking on *Heartbeat*. Crimson are clearly not quite up to boil on this occasion, providing the generous listener with the sound of a group still figuring out how it's all meant to fit together. Right from the off there are teething troubles which soon require root canal surgery as the night progresses through a combination of blindsided fingers and errant stompboxes going off script. *Frame By Frame* is curiously underpowered and ever so slightly lethargic as the Crimson crew get to grips with their onstage environment. *Discipline* isn't quite as together as you'd normally like but in these circumstances the interest lies in the recovery from the wrong turns and missed steps. The *B'Boom* and *THRAK* sections are where the band seems to find its feet although the vagaries of the soundboard mix relegate the storming guitar solo to something of a remote event on the distant horizon.

VROOOM VROOOM charges along nicely building momentum though it too suffers from a wobble or two. During *LTIA2* the extent of technical problems which have dogged tonight becomes evident as the piece teeters on the edge of falling apart entirely, saved only by some quick thinking from Gunn and a determined Belew.

7 OCTOBER 1994 – TEATRO BROADWAY, BUENOS AIRES

A mere seven days after King Crimson's formal return to active service and the band are really cutting the mustard, the rug and quite probably the very legs out from under the naysayers. Containing what is for this listener an arguably definitive live version of *Matte Kudasai*, the gig has real energy: *B'Boom* swings like the clappers while *THRAK* is downright down and dirt. Sounding comfortable and more in control, the Double Trio shred *Sex Sleep Eat Drink Dream* and fire off a cracking *Indiscipline* that shows Belew's mastery of comic timing while featuring a fearsome wigging out from the back three. The old and new elements have really started to gel. Don't you love it when a plan comes together?

8 OCTOBER 1994 – TEATRO BROADWAY, BUENOS AIRES: SECOND SHOW

Take a listen to *Frame By Frame*. You hear that? There's a real edge and urgency at work here. Those finely polished parts, well-oiled by years of use and familiarity, still twinkle and sparkle as they move through the sections. It's dazzling stuff and there's no wonder it gets a huge response from the crowd. That can-do vim and vigour isn't confined to that number either. *Sex Sleep Eat Drink Dream* is delivered with panache and *Red* skips along, positively roaring with rude health.

The middle section of *THRAK* moves at quite a pace with Belew's power drill routine smearing sounds over Fripp's rippling workout as Gunn applies spectral arcs that blaze across the stereo spectrum like a comet. There's no let-up in the intensity before they return to the end theme.

An error in foot control of the pedals lends the end freak-out of *Indiscipline* a rather surprising outcome that's almost worth the price of admission. "I do think it's good," laughs Belew off-mic at the end. This is as muscular a Crimson show as you could possibly want. Maybe even the best of this run?

10 OCTOBER 1994 – TEATRO DE LAS AMERICAS, CORDOBA

It's always interesting to hear a new track being unveiled for the first time. After

Sleepless, just audible over the cheers of the crowd, various Crims can be heard saying "Oh, it's the new one!" and other similar expressions of surprise and trepidation. They'd done a run-through of the song in the soundcheck. "I'm not sure how many of you speak English ... but for those who do this is the very first time we're going to play this song for anyone in the world. Wish us luck," says Ade as they go into their first proper public rendition of *People* in the encores. So eager are they to get on with it (Bruford can be heard yelling: "Just do it!") parts of the band start up before everyone is ready. The instrumental section is interesting with Bruford adding a sassy ride cymbal once Adrian's rather reflective and restrained solo is over. Amid the back-and-forth guitars there's clearly a lot of eye contact as players try to direct each other towards the finishing line. After they all hit the mark as required, coming to a dead stop, there's a palpable sense of relief.

12 OCTOBER 1994 – TEATRO MUNICIPAL COLISEO PODESTA, LA PLATA

It's probable that a couple of the opening numbers weren't captured on the board tapes as *Sex Sleep Eat Drink Dream* cuts in mid-track. Nevertheless, we still get a pretty good picture of what was going on. *THRAK* assumes an especially guttural rasp as it snips and clips away like a hedge-trimmer gone haywire. Initially carried by Bruford's incipiently funky beat before Mastelotto takes over the groove, the piece moves on as Gunn flies around the bass end of his instrument and the band sticks to the beat during the improv section. Out of the *Two Sticks* workout flies a hugely buoyant *Elephant Talk*. It's clear that the team are enjoying themselves and responding to encouragement. *Indiscipline* also blisters with a determined ferocity though comes momentarily unstuck being the "I repeat myself" verse, as though they were having so much fun they'd forgotten where they were. Nearly four minutes into *The Talking Drum* and there's a wonderful point of convergence for Fripp, Gunn and Belew, whose notes swirl and dance in breath-taking formation. It's moments like this that make being a Crimhead more than worthwhile. At the end of a barn-storming *LTIA2*, Bill Bruford can just be heard off-mic saying: "That was good!" He's not wrong.

14 OCTOBER 1994 – TEATRO BROADWAY, BUENOS AIRES

"Buenas noches," says Belew after the band have dispatched a flawless *Discipline*, a take-no-prisoners *VROOOM* and a knock-out *Frame By Frame*. You can hear various whoops and hoots from different parts of the stage as they prepare to blast off again with a truly ferocious *Sex Sleep Eat Drink Dream*. Oh, and *Red*. Whichever way you look at it, that's a turbocharged piledriver of a set. Understandably, they dial it down a bit with *One Time* but it offers only the briefest respite as *B'Boom* and *THRAK* raise the stakes once again. As in previous versions, the solo section sounds like a construction yard in full swing; busy and extremely cluttered with hardly any space at all for anyone to develop any lines deviating from the main thrust. That said, full marks for BB for playing the theme briefly on the marimba setting of his electronic kit. A good night indeed.

15 OCTOBER 1994 – TEATRO BROADWAY, BUENOS AIRES: FIRST SHOW

Twenty-five years on from these recordings, and the familiarity which Crimheads now have with *VROOOM*, it is perhaps easy to forget what a shock to the system the track was back in 1994. Placed here after the interlocking complexities of *Discipline*, there's a stark brutality to the piece as it bulldozes its way into the audience. Monumentally heavy in every regard, it leaves punters in no doubt that Crimson have arrived. Rumbling along, each downward repeat of the lines during the coda hammers the message home. If that piece is powerful then *VROOOM VROOOM* is lighter and quicker in tone and pace but no less heavy or shocking in its remorselessness. A classic bit of Crimson precision engineering proudly displayed in this first house.

There's a rather interesting version of *Walking On Air* which begins in the middle of the song rather than its usual introduction, propelled by Levin's undulating bass, with the other players eventually joining in and letting the piece gently amble along as an impromptu instrumental.

15 OCTOBER 1994 – TEATRO BROADWAY, BUENOS AIRES: SECOND SHOW

Imagine if, having played for well over an hour and a half, pulling no punches and giving it your all, you had to go back out on stage after only a quick breath of fresh air and perhaps a nippy wash and brush-up, and then do it all again in the same evening. Such was the demand from an ecstatic and profoundly enthusiastic South American audience, that's what Crimson had to do.

Nor was it the first such occasion in this run of gigs – they'd done the same at the show on 8 October. There are signs of tiredness here and there; Trey fluffs a harmony line in *VROOOM* and the guitarists drop the ball momentarily on the downbeat of *Indiscipline*. As an aside, can anyone work out Bruford's off-mic commentary in French as Belew recounts that "it took hours and hours"? A degree of playfulness can be discerned as Levin offers a bit of walking bass prior to *Heartbeat*, and Belew and others crack up as Fripp's fingers momentarily take in the brown zone on *Heartbeat*'s tender intro. Also of interest here is the appearance of *Coda: Marine 475* as a standalone encore leading straight into a rather pensive Soundscape.

16 OCTOBER 1994 – TEATRO BROADWAY, BUENOS AIRES

Never before have Crimheads had this kind of access to the development of the band as a live entity. Other incarnations have had to make to do with patchy audience boots, and in some cases even those are scant on the ground. We've heard the band move from tentative and sometimes faltering steps to a confidence that goes beyond the merely professional.

"Gracias. As this is unfortunately our last evening here we'd like to say thank you to our entire production team, to all the crew that we've had here who've worked with us. You don't see them but they're all over the place, on the stage, back there at the mixing board, at the lights, and we'd especially say thanks to all of you who've made this a very special beginning for the new King Crimson here in Argentina. Thank you!" announces Belew at the end of a terrific gig.

The next time the new King Crimson would take to a public stage would be seven months later in Austria – but first they were off to England and Real World Studios to record *THRAK*.

1995

1 MAY 1995 – KULTURHAUS, DORNBIRN

The first gig of any tour is always slightly fraught. Anything that can go wrong probably will. Gear will futz, fingers and feet will lie to their owners and the sound could well be unsound as the entire crew get to grips with the task of presenting nearly two hours of challenging music.

Understandably perhaps then, this version of *Discipline* is not an assertive statement but more a gentle easing in. A slow-burning version of *VROOOM* sounds more confident, especially on the remorselessly spiralling coda which, like *Frame By Frame* which follows, is not without the occasional wobble.

The band audibly settle in on *Dinosaur* and you can hear them really enjoying a high-rolling *Red* and the mutant-free-form jazz sextet reading of *THRAK*. *People* represents something of a "rock out" moment, which is no bad thing; Belew's splendidly squerning solo is especially tasty. Trey Gunn's spectral notes are a highlight of a driving version of *The Talking Drum*, and the band really get their collective teeth into *LTIA2*.

Overall verdict: a band in the process of arriving but not quite all at the same time.

3 MAY 1995 – TEATRO TENDA, FLORENCE

A wonderfully confident beginning with *VROOOM* a tad slower but not losing any energy. The benefits of this approach include Tony Levin's upright bowed bass on the coda having the space to chug up to the front of the sound. *Frame By Frame* is taken at a calmer pace so that the English guitarist doesn't have fingertips ablaze as a result of the double time phase shifts both during and at the end of the song. A perfect *One Time* and an astonishingly vibrant *Red* auger well for the rolling and tumbling of *B'Boom*; Bruford and Mastelotto really make this version come alive. During the improv section of *THRAK* Bruford executes some beautifully funky pockets but his buddies decline to lock in and freewheel above the beat. As Bill opts for his xylophone setting, Pat keeps the groove going. It's tight stuff throughout. *Indiscipline* is particularly incendiary and *Elephant Talk* dances with a real spring in its step. Though there are times when percussion showcase *Conundrum* dissipates the flow of the gig, *The Talking Drum* and *LTIA2* quickly get things back up to speed. A brilliant performance from start to finish.

4 MAY 1995 – TEATRO TONIOLO, MESTRE, VENICE

There are some nights when the energy flows and this gig is certainly one. The run from *VROOOM* to *Dinosaur* is possessed of such a glowering intensity that one wonders how the band can sustain such power. The answer is to dial things down a little with an elegant *One Time*. *B'Boom* and *THRAK* reconnect Crim to tumultuous forces, including Adrian's patented power-drill noise generator, Levin's prowling bass and a brief solo from Trey Gunn of the kind he would later throw out during ProjeKct 2. Within the space of only a few minutes, all kinds of musical landscapes are created and regenerated amid the ever-changing turbulence.

Bruford's encyclopaedic rhythmic interventions have him adding ride and rimshot work to the playout on *People* that that wouldn't be out of place on Miles Davis' *In A Silent Way*. Belew's sliding solo also adds to the magic and it's almost impossible not to see his undoubtedly grinning face while listening to this section.

Though *Discipline* was tried out during the soundcheck, the band decided to leave it off the setlist but we can enjoy its polar opposite *Indiscipline*, made all the more special by a sonic detonation that sees Adrian vainly attempting to rein in his laughter. The same cannot be said for another member of the band heard delivering a hearty belly laugh. An especially demonic solo from Fripp provides a hair-raising conclusion. Oh, and *LTIA2* will singe your eyebrows so make sure you're standing well back – the idiosyncratic mix reveals some zapping exchanges between Gunn and Fripp.

The audience deliver a deservedly rousing ovation, mirroring the applause sent in their direction by all six members of the band. And who's that very happy guitarist saying *Yo!* at the top of his voice?

3 JUNE 1995 – TOWN HALL, NEW YORK

A lithe and limber Crim begin a two-night run in the Big Apple. If you had to pick just one track from this concert then *VROOOM* might well be it. Bruford is on devastating form as he roves around the kit in his perspex prison like some pent-up animal. Levin is driving home the bass notes like they were six-inch nails and Fripp opens out a beguiling piano motif in the coda that suddenly transforms into the laser-beam sound of yore. *B'Boom* is taken at a sprightly lick which continues in a thrilling improvisation that for a while evokes the electrifying mutant jazz of *Beat*'s *Requiem*.

Commenting on the fact that this gig represented Crimson's first return to New York in ten years, Neil Strauss, writing for the *New York Times*, noted: "It was hard to believe that the band had lost little of its power, depth and flow in a decade apart."

4 JUNE 1995 – TOWN HALL, NEW YORK

Reviewing the second night for *Rolling Stone*, Steve Futterman wrote: "With solos and instrumental passages that stressed sonic experimentation over instrumental virtuosity,

King Crimson buried their image as purveyors of ice-cold fusionesque indulgences. Their music now has all the aural enchantment and commotion that marks adventurous pop in the '90s."

The gig takes a little while to find its level but once there, Crimson turn in another highly charged performance. Belew is a constantly moving presence darting between showman and demented technician as he coaxes and cajoles seriously deranged sounds from his guitar. But it's not all stunt FX with Belew as a beautifully moving performance on *One Time* makes abundantly clear.

As with the previous evening, the improvised section of *THRAK* moves along at a fair pace with some brutal barrelhouse piano runs. Another unexpected delight is the *Two Sticks* improvisation: Trey and Tony's differing styles dovetail into an area that certainly deserved greater exploration. *Indiscipline* has some of Fripp's wildest guitar outings to date which suggests he was an especially happy gigster that night.

1 OCTOBER 1995 – KANAGAWA KENMIN HALL, YOKOHAMA

The THRAK tour had taken Crimson to South and North America as well as selected destinations in Europe. Now it was Japan's turn. They'd visited there twice in the '80s and from the silence that opens the opening improv you could be forgiven for thinking they were overawed by the prospect. Not a bit of it. Once Bruford opens up with his xylophone, all manner of weird and wonderful sounds fill the air and don't let up for the next hour and a half.

It's a scorching start with *VROOOM VROOOM* and *Dinosaur* positively stomping along. During *Sex Sleep Eat Drink Dream*, Bruford and Mastelotto play with real imagination and the topsy-turvy rhythmic interplay continues through *People*. There's an urgency about the whole show, but during *Indiscipline* Adrian catches everyone off guard just after he wishes you were here to see it. The team make a pretty neat recovery, though. Afterwards, Bruford laughs: "We made it!"

2 OCTOBER 1995 – KOSEINENKIN KAIKAN, TOKYO

Crimson gigs are, of course, about the total experience but it's always interesting to focus in on the smaller moments. As the crowd applaud after *Indiscipline* and the end of the show proper, we can hear the Crims gathering in the centre of the stage. There's laughter, an obligatory *YO!* and the team being dazzled by stage lights rendering them virtually blind as they try to look out upon the ecstatic audience. With the rest leaving the stage as the three-drum set is put into place for *Prism*, we hear Bruford tell Mastelotto and Belew, "Nice and steady … not too fast," and off they go. It's Bruford who takes the first break, gently tinkering around the rig. As the audience cheer, Bill laughs to his bandmates: "I haven't done anything yet!" Of course he goes on to give the punters something to really cheer about.

3 OCTOBER 1995 – KOSEINENKIN KAIKAN, TOKYO

There are points here where Crimson take on a very different identity. When Fripp, Bruford and Mastelotto team up for *B'Boom*, Robert's swirling electronic washes and the galloping drums create a hybrid electronica that's highly intriguing. Fripp was no stranger to such textures, having worked with The Orb and Future Sound Of London and his own explorations with Radiophonics. Here, however, with the frantic interplay of drums it takes on a very different character and there's a sense that there was more in this direction to explore. The improvisation sections bookended by the crunching *THRAK* theme offer another facet of the Crimson beast. Brimming with a frenetic array of fierce, acerbic noises, staccato incursions and explosive runs, things are perhaps a little too dense and claustrophobic. Almost certainly what was intended!

5 OCTOBER 1995 – NAKANO SUN PLAZA, TOKYO

This show boasts a brand new stereo mix from the original multitracks by Alex "Stormy" Mundy as the board recording was missing from the archives – probably because this was one of the two shows filmed for the *Deja VROOOM* DVD. Only after some 17 minutes of hard-hat area rocking out with *VROOOM VROOOM*, *Frame By Frame* and *Dinosaur* do Crimson take the mood and tempo down with *One Time*. Eighteen minutes later, *Matte Kudasai* brings a touch of further calm after the storm of *Red*, *B'Boom* and *THRAK*. But those deliver the only real resource from the rest of the gig's intensity.

"We'd like to thank you for joining us back here in Tokyo. Feels great to be back here after 11 years. And we promise it won't be so long before we come back again," says Belew midway through the set, pausing to take the applause, and then adding, "In fact, we're back tomorrow."

After all the excitement, the extremes of dynamics and all that power, *Walking On Air* is a thing of exquisite, delicate beauty. It continues to fade and float long after the band have left the stage.

6 OCTOBER 1995 – NAKANO SUN PLAZA, TOKYO

The second of two shows filmed for the *Deja VROOOM* DVD. Trey Gunn once remarked that one of the challenges of the Double Trio was finding the space in which to operate especially when it came to tackling the '80s material. The unit was so tight, Gunn commented, that it was never going to be easy to find an appropriate part. With *Frame By Frame*, Gunn's work is located within the run of interlocking parts but is more easily heard playing the sign-off theme before the end. Similar embellishments are heard in the verses of *Matte Kudasai* and on *Three Of A Perfect Pair* – harmonic doubling on the main riff and a spotlight break entwines around Fripp's brief solo. Gunn's presence carries most of the melodic content against Levin's rhythmic undulations during the *Two Sticks* improv before *Elephant Talk*. When it comes to *Indiscipline*, it's every man for himself!

8 OCTOBER 1995 – SHIMIN KAIKAN, NAGOYA

In a live setting, it doesn't matter how many times you've rehearsed or played, the unexpected has a habit of joining you on the stage. *VROOOM* kicks along at a fair old lick but where the fairy fingers are supposed to be, we hear the sound of Fripp's feet failing to find the correct pedal. Smart recovery is the name of the game with Crimson and by the next time those magical digits are scheduled to appear they do so right on cue. Such is the nature of live performance – it can transport you to the heavens or become a brutal bear pit that constantly threatens to unseat you. As the piece tips into *Coda: Marine 475*, Levin's upright bass chugs like a fearsome engine building up steam as Gunn's touch guitar howls. It's a particularly good version. Also sounding good is the fierce improv in *THRAK*, a portion of which was edited into *Mother Hold The Candle Steady While I Shave The Chicken's Lip* from *THRaKaTTaK*.

9 OCTOBER 1995 – FESTIVAL HALL, OSAKA

What a way to get a gig under way – a dazzling improv followed by a superbly rolling, riotous *Thela Hun Ginjeet* and then into a glowering, towering *Red*. And how about a flawless *Frame By Frame*? Clearly a gig where the Crims are firing on all cylinders. Listen out for an almost funky improv in which Fripp turns in a stunning solo over a laid-back groove. After the return of the main theme the ending also benefits from a single sustained note, as though reluctant to let go of the mood. It's a classic Crim moment. You can hear lots of well-deserved whoops after a particularly muscular *Three Of A Perfect Pair* and the build in *The Talking Drum* is especially effective, with Gunn and Belew's snaking lines slithering over the increasingly busy groove as it climbs toward the resolution of *LTIA2*. All told, a hot gig indeed!

10 OCTOBER 1995 – HITOMI KINEN KODO, TOKYO

Listen out after the finish of a fearsome *Frame By Frame* – shouts of "*Yo!*" and a warble of approval can be heard emanating from somewhere between the two drummers. *VROOOM* features Bruford and Mastelotto constantly passing the baton of beat-keeping; Fripp and Belew swap lead lines; Levin and Gunn alternate melody and rhythm with Levin adding uber-texture on the upright. Fans of TLev will have a field day during *Neurotica* as the foibles of this particular soundboard mix put Tony right up front.

The keen listener will spot that a section of the improv in *THRAK* eventually found its way into *THRaKaTTaK*'s *Mother Hold The Candle Steady While I Shave The Chicken's Lip*.

12 OCTOBER 1995 – OMIYA SONIC CITY HALL, OMIYA

You might not think a day here or there would make too much difference, but tonight is a hotter show than the previous one. Perhaps the previous day spent resting and travelling recharged the collective batteries? Whatever the reason, you can feel the tension and energies of the opening numbers culminate in an especially aggressive *VROOOM VROOOM*. Something of that juice spills over into a particularly snappy *B'Boom* before bounding into an awesome *THRAK*. Busier than the improv from Tokyo, it's as though Bruford can't quite let go, opening up with some sprightly brushwork to dance around Adrian's recurring tinkling piano motif. This too was edited into *Mother Hold The Candle Steady While I Shave The Chicken's Lip* from *THRaKaTTak*. Here, however, we get to hear the full explosive sci-fi doodle-bug ending.

The change of pace necessitated by a somewhat doleful *Walking On Air* offers some respite though by *Sex Sleep Eat Drink Dream* it sounds like the roof is in danger of coming off. The overall speed of the evening gets the better of the band a little during *LTIA2* but I'm sure such critical nitpicking would get you a deserved cuff upside the head from any punter present on this night. This one's a hummer!

13 OCTOBER 1995 – SUN PLAZA HALL, SENDAI

There are more than a few bumps here, such as a bucking bronco *VROOOM* that occasionally threatens to unseat the players, especially during a fairly indeterminate "fairy fingers" section; and there's a hilarious moment after a cracking *Indiscipline* where some members' reading of the setlist is out of step with the others! Such entertaining false starts aside, it's a wholly confident *Frame By Frame* that takes up the slack encountered during the preceding *Red*, almost stealing the show. An unusually rhythmic improv section during *THRAK* is worthwhile exploring as RF's sharp lines hit the mark.

14 OCTOBER 1995 – KOSEINENKIN KAIKAN, TOKYO

"This is the end of our Japanese tour. We've been thrilled to be here, it's been a great time for all of us and I hope it has for all of you," says Adrian. "And we'd like to thank Mr Udo and his production company. They've done an excellent job. We'd also like to thank our crew that we brought with us – they've done an excellent job. And most of all, we'd like to thank you, the fans. Thank you very much." All told, the Japanese tour found Crimson in remarkably fine, consistent form as this spirited and energetic performance demonstrates. A smoking *LTIA2* brings the show to a fiery conclusion. Six days later, the band kicked off the next leg of their tour in Berkeley, their second American tour for 1995.

20 OCTOBER 1995 –ZELLERBACH AUDITORIUM, BERKELEY

The first night of Crimson's second stint in the USA is good but relatively cautious-sounding gig by the band's usual standards.

21 OCTOBER 1995 – MARIN CIVIC AUDITORIUM, SAN RAFAEL

An interestingly textured improv kicks open the second night of the tour. Like some demented waltz, Fripp's strings pan from one extreme to another in the stereo picture while Levin's upright bass growls and prowls around Belew's sustained notes and the combined percussion of Bruford and Mastelotto. After such an intriguing opening, *Thela Hun Ginjeet* is taken at a relaxed canter, while *Red*'s tempo is the equivalent of a stately procession. *VROOOM VROOOM* marks a rise in energy levels. There's an interesting rendition of the *THRAK* theme, with Fripp employing quite a different harmony, which appears to wrong-foot the other string players for a second or two. The rather dense improv contains some wrenching though fragmented soloing from Gunn and Fripp. Usually the band would return to the main theme as an outro to *THRAK* but here the cop car siren effect is ushered in and Belew and the rest of the band follow suit.

22 OCTOBER 1995 – HOUSE OF BLUES, LOS ANGELES

"Boy I miss this!" says Belew, clearly delighted to be playing in the more intimate surroundings of the House Of Blues. Perhaps energised by the sheer proximity of the audience, Crimson truly hit the ground running in this stomper of a set. *Frame By Frame* is a thrilling white-knuckle ride that at times teeters on the very edge of the abyss – which of course all adds to the excitement. *Sex Sleep Eat Drink Dream* is a corker in which Belew gets in a cheeky blues lick and Fripp plays an absolute blinder of a solo. *Elephant Talk* also receives a surprise makeover when Bruford kicks in a reprise at the song's intended conclusion, pulling the band along for a few bars. Clearly the Crims and the audience loved every minute. On Elephant Talk, eyewitness James B Erickson said: "My only request to RF is please release an 'Official Boot II' for this leg of the tour. And most selfishly for myself please release the House Of Blues entire show. It was truly a memorable occasion."

23 OCTOBER 1995 – SYMPHONY HALL, PHOENIX

"Warmed up? Ready to go? Well, all right!" says Belew to the crowd. His triggered voice on *Neurotica* contains both first and second verses running simultaneously after the band come out of *THRAK*. It's clearly a gaffe but it adds to the frenetic evocation of a busy New York teeming with exotic life. Crimson have a bit of a spring in their step, with *People* particularly edgy and rambunctious. Levin and Gunn's improv before *Elephant Talk* is a slowly unfurling piece as notes fade in and out, passing each other, in brief flares of brightness and intensity. There's the making of a rock-like stomp led by Levin across which Gunn opens up his uncompromising soloing. This listener wishes the rest of the band had come in behind that groove as it sounds like an idea waiting to be developed further. Levin caught the attention of concert eyewitness Bill Lantz who later observed on ET: "Noteworthy in *LTIA2* were Tony's basslines, especially toward the very end. He found a different groove and caught everyone's attention on stage. Listen for it."

25 OCTOBER 1995 – ABRAHAM CHAVEZ THEATRE, EL PASO

"Hola or even hello. Thank you for coming tonight and we hope you enjoy yourselves. One thing I would like to point out, if you are going to smoke that stuff please don't do it down here by the stage, OK? I'd like to be able to sing for the rest of the tour," says Belew. You can sympathise given that he has to sing *Frame By Frame*, *Dinosaur* and an especially plaintive *One Time* in a row. The singer does at least find some respite during a strong run at *VROOOM VROOOM* and the percussive counterweight of *B'Boom*. After the wryly syncopated chug of the improvised section of *THRAK*, the band emerge into the dazzling streets of *Neurotica*, once again with Belew's pre-recorded vocal sample doubling up and set to maximum gabble. The band shred the place apart with

Indiscipline's riotous tumult. "What you lack in size you've made up for in volume," says an appreciative Ade as they sprint toward the finishing line of *LTIA2*.

27 OCTOBER 1995 – PARAMOUNT THEATRE, DENVER

"Good evening and a fine evening it is since you're all here. One little announcement I'd like to make before we start. If you feel so inclined to smoke something, please go as far away from me as you can to do so. Otherwise, enjoy yourselves, have a great time. Buckle your seat belts, here we go." Thus speaks Captain Belew as Crimson takes off for a top-flight *Frame By Frame*. The improvisation in *THRAK* opens up into quite a special place. Eyewitness David Ewing thought so too, as he described the event on ET. "It was slow, brooding, dark, mysterious – the musicians were really listening to each other. Great stuff (which I'd love to hear them do more of). Fripp even played a trademark distorted, sustaining solo."

Aficionados of Clams Crimsonique are directed to *VROOOM*; some guitar tuning that isn't and a fascinating collision of bass notes on a downbeat lands the Stick players in places where they probably didn't expect to be. Good stuff here nevertheless!

29 OCTOBER 1995 – PIKES PEAK CENTER, COLORADO SPRINGS

A smooth-running show in which the band move from one piece to another with assurance and occasional swagger. *VROOOM VROOOM* opens up the extra energy as it has done on other gigs. There's a great improv in *THRAK* and the coda to *People* goes very widescreen indeed. One ET eyewitness Mark JX observed: "This was a different band than I had witnessed in the summer; looser, yet tighter are the only words that do them justice. They improvised and adapted effortlessly all the while grinning (with the exception of Robert, and – usually – Trey). Were mistakes made? Yes, but I would be hard-pressed to cite a specific example, as emotional impact and not perfection was the course for the night. (I say, 'If you want perfection, get the studio album!'). At one point, the music stopped, with just single spotlights on the performers. The silence must have lasted for 4–5 seconds (which is really a long time). The audience didn't know WHAT to do; Should we applaud? Should we wait? There were the usual ignorant '*21st Century*' heckles, then someone said, 'What, no applause?' Everyone clapped and the band burst into the next number."

31 OCTOBER 1995 – WILL ROGERS AUDITORIUM, FORT WORTH

"Good evening. Welcome to the very first show of this King Crimson here in Texas. We have some frightening stuff prepared for you, so hold on to your pumpkins," announces Belew at the start of the show. Belew had little idea just how frightening things would get on this Hallowe'en gig. Eyewitness Paul Ciminero explained: "At the end of the show the entire band stands out front and bows together … some moron threw something at the stage and hit Fripp in the head …" From a slightly different vantage point, Alan Edmonds: "I couldn't tell what it was; it appeared shaped like a small Frisbee but coloured red and white like a Coca-Cola can. The crowd groaned in shock and murmurs of 'there goes the encore' were heard throughout. Mr Fripp put his hand to his head and started looking around for the object. The band left the stage and the crowd started clapping and hollering again. For some reason, the band came back out and did three songs for the encore(s). One of them was the three-drum percussion number with Adrian, Bill and Pat. During this number, you could see Mr Fripp walking around in the back with his hand to his head. No word was mentioned about the incident with the thrown object."

1 NOVEMBER 1995 – MUSIC HALL, AUSTIN

Seemingly feeling none the worse after having been bopped on the bonce by a mystery object the previous evening in Fort Worth, Robert opens with a tasty Soundscape soon joined by the other members of the team. Notwithstanding the extra-curricular excursions of *THRAK*, it's a shame there aren't more of these improvisations in the Double Trio repertoire. "Buckle your seat belts," says Ade before counting off a galloping *Frame By Frame* that flies by the seat of its pants. A great soundboard mix with Pat and Bill's work bouncing off each other to great effect, and some of Trey's subtler shadings, often lost in the sonic melee, can be clearly discerned. A high-energy show.

2 NOVEMBER 1995 – MUSIC HALL, HOUSTON

"Everybody comfortable and ready to go?" asks Adrian after a piledriving *Thela Hun Ginjeet* and *Red*. *VROOOM VROOOM* is a ravaging beast while once again Bill and Pat whip up a terrific tornado on *B'Boom* before we head off into an intriguing *THRAK*. Here, after long sections where Ade, Trey and Fripp in particular do their best to strip the paint off the walls, the entire band adopts the now legendary KC "admirable restraint" mode. It's hard to know if the band is waiting for the leather-lunged punters to adopt similar circumspection or waiting to see who among them would blink first, but for the best part of a minute they fall entirely silent – before pounding back in with brutal force. The band evidently loved it: Fripp can be heard "*Yo*"-ing his appreciation while off-mic Ade laughs something about incorporating a certain John Cage into the piece. *Neurotica* has the edge over the previous evening's version though the wordplay required during *Sex Sleep Eat Drink Dream* gets the better of Ade in the second verse. The sound of King Crimson having fun.

5 NOVEMBER 1995 – HOUSE OF BLUES, NEW ORLEANS

With the ADAT tapes for KC's first night in New Orleans lost, we only have the second evening as a document of that stay-over. There are as many different perspectives as audience members. Here's two contrasting views. Keith Somers, who also caught the band later in the tour at Atlanta reckoned: "Although the New Orleans show was great, I couldn't help but feel that the band was just doing their 'job', you might say. Being in what is essentially a bar, the crowd was loud and irreverent. There wasn't much opportunity for the musicians to connect with the audience, just kick ass and hit the road." Ashley Morris saw the band perform both nights up close. "Being directly above Trey, we got to see exactly what he was doing. The first night, a lot of his work kind of escaped us. The second, we got to see and hear what he was doing much better. The 'swell' effects from his volume pedal were remarkable. Another benefit of our proximity was being able to actually hear Adrian strum his guitar when he was playing the string parts. It was odd to hear the faint twang, then the swell of the synths. Pat also had a very loud personal mix that second night."

7 NOVEMBER 1995 – SUNRISE THEATRE, SUNRISE, FLORIDA

A slightly different running order with the percussion piece opening rather than the circular improvisation. From there on, it's a high-octane gig where numbers such as *Three Of A Perfect Pair*, *Sex Sleep Eat Drink Dream* and *People* simmer and boil with an extra passion. There's something else going on inside *B'Boom* and *THRAK* as well. Against a slow steady groove, Levin's bass scuttles and gnaws at the beat; Gunn emerges with radiant solo lines between Fripp's soaring notes, before locking into stop-start games with Mastelotto that add depth and definition. It's arguably one of the most cohesive improvisations on the tour. Interestingly, the band then stop, giving way to a prolonged bout of silence that lasts an unprecedented two minutes! What might have caused this? Equipment problems? Catching a breather? Allowing the audience whoop and holler and let off a bit of steam? Who knows? When they re-enter with the closing *THRAK* theme, the energy is crackling and palpable, carrying over into a terrifically thunderous and clattering *LTIA2*.

8 NOVEMBER 1995 – MAHAFFEY THEATER, ST PETERSBURG

An excellent improvisation in *THRAK* – a portion of which made it on to the *THRaKaTTaK* album. Brutal, punishing and busy. There's an incredibly oppressive density to some of these sections and tonight's is a good one. Nice to hear *Two Sticks* transition into *Indiscipline* rather than the usual *Elephant Talk* and, after a barnstorming *LTIA2*, you can hear the various members of the band yo-ing and roaring to each other and the audience, clearly pleased. Just back from the gig at St. Petersburg, ET eyewitness tcona breathlessly posted: "I … must say that Crimson applied the LAW of MAXIMUM INTENSITY. The only soft part of the evening was during the playing of *Walking on Air* … They simply showed no quarter. It was intense from start to finish. They overwhelmed the theater with high-intensity playing and in the end left people shaken from an evening in the court of Crimson beast. This band is one of a kind. No one else can even come close." He's not wrong!

9 NOVEMBER 1995 – TUPPERWARE CENTER, ORLANDO

When the Crimson boys came to Orlando a certain drummer caught the eye and ear of ET eyewitness Ne13 who wrote: "Bill Bruford was simply the most amazing presence I have ever seen behind a drum kit. One thing I noticed about his drumming style – it's all in the wrist and lower arm for him (not unlike Dan Marino). The reason he gets off his attack with such speed is his ability to just flick those wrists with such power … Bill Bruford, my friend, is a devastating drummer whose equal I now know I have never seen. Put aside the telepathic communication with Mastelotto, put aside the demon snippets he constantly laid down in front of us. What truly astonished me was the way these two drummers would be building up greater and greater ferocity, each one's solos ebbing and flowing like the tide … the mind boggles, I tell you … air beats, double/triple/quadruple timing the beat, playing ahead and behind the beat, crunching the beat with Mastelotto right down on top of Levin's throbbing basslines, filling the space and yet leaving space for everyone … miraculoso …" Part of the improvisation in *THRAK* found its way into *This Night Wounds Time* on *THRaKaTTaK*.

11 NOVEMBER 1995 – ROXY THEATRE, ATLANTA

Having travelled up from Florida the day before, Crimson settled into the first of two nights at the Roxy. In front of 1,000 punters the band spiritedly played a well-drilled setlist. There are plenty of highlights, including Trey Gunn's work on *Three Of A Perfect Pair* and what is arguably one of the best *Two Sticks* improvs by Tony and Trey. Normally this track would lead into *Elephant Talk* but here again it turns into a thunderous *Indiscipline*. And speaking of *Elephant Talk*, they enjoyed playing it so much they decide to play it again – "Two for the price of one!" quips an excited Ade at the end. Other highpoints include a mercurial *THRAK* that covers a lot of ground and allows silence to come a-calling much like it did in Houston. A one-minute snippet from this improv was knitted into *The Slaughter Of The Innocents* from *THRAKaTTaK*.

12 NOVEMBER 1995 – ROXY THEATRE, ATLANTA

Though the previous evening had slightly more energy and zap overall, this is a solid show with plenty to write home about. Listen out for a seriously screwy *Neurotica*. Afterwards you can hear each member of the band laughing and commenting about what had just happened. Oh, and let's not forget a rather tasty Fripp stinger right at the end. Bruford and Mastelotto pull out the stops on *B'Boom*, while *THRAK* contains a truly malevolent improv in which Levin's bowed bass soars and swoops against Fripp's lines. *People* once again proves to be something of an unexpected highpoint with Tony giving it an uber-funk fingers workout and there's that majestic coda in which Adrian bends the plank almost to breaking point. The evening reaches a tumultuous conclusion with *The Talking Drum* and an eventful *LTIA2*, which occasionally goes off-road. But hey, let's face it – most Crimheads would prefer a bumpy ride to a smooth and polished one.

15 NOVEMBER 1995 – KIRBY PERFORMING ARTS CENTER, WILKES-BARRE

THRAK certainly caught the attention of a couple of eyewitnesses in the audience. MDA said: "Highlight of the show was definitely the *B'Boom*/*THRAK* section. The improvising and counter-play here was absolutely astounding. The middle section of *THRAK* was much different than the album version, much quieter and primal. Fripp's Soundscapes beforehand were also quite moving, as he used some cosmic sounds and even some vocal sounds. Someone else on ET also commented (I believe) on how when the band stopped during *THRAK*, they just picked back up in unison again without any noticeable cue. The same happened here. I didn't realise it until after it happened, but that amazed me."

Meanwhile Joe Mel had this take on the same piece. "It really slowed down to a quiet when the four string players started using different sounds. Tony played cello, Adrian seemed to be playing midi piano and then violin. Trey was doing guitar effects and also some other midi string work, I think. Robert may have been doing some sort of Soundscape. After about two minutes of this, Bill seemed to think it had gone on long enough and he started some percussion and gave Pat the eye. The two then began their own little jam on top of the group."

16 NOVEMBER 1995 – ROCHESTER AUDITORIUM CENTER, ROCHESTER
The setlist has been moved around a little more with the *Two Sticks* improv now dovetailing into *Neurotica* quite effectively with Belew picking up Trey's high note. There's a good *THRAK* improv, part of which found its way into *THRaKaTTaK Part II*. Though the show was not entirely to his liking, eyewitness Bruce acknowledged: "There was not a slack moment; even mediocre *THRAK* tracks like *People* contained vicious improvisations. Another six months of touring has gotten the band to the point that they inhabit the compositions … they stalk around inside them, kicking at the rafters, re-wiring the circuits, slamming all the doors and windows. Subtle refinements to the setlist have positioned every song to maximum effect. Absolutely *ripping* show. The low point of the show may have been the *Indiscipline* encore. Adrian rushed through the lyric; while this prevented the audience from stealing his thunder, it drained the tension from the piece. The instrumentals still shredded, though. At one point Fripp broke through the mix playing something so nasty I nearly wet myself."

17 NOVEMBER 1995 – PARAMOUNT THEATER, SPRINGFIELD
After seeing the Double Trio in Springfield, ET eyewitness Art Cohen wrote: "This could easily be the best version of King Crimson ever. This is the only band to flow effortlessly between every period of their existence. Consider this setlist fragment: *Frame By Frame*; *Red*; *Dinosaur*. This last song, of course, (explicitly) combines their earliest period (*Lizard*) with the present. The '80s band *played* some of the mid-70s material, but this band's *new* material is able to recall past eras as well (e.g., *THRAK*, *VROOOM*, *Dinosaur*). Strangely, this band's new material sounds the *least* like the '80s band, which makes the inclusion of more of those songs even more appealing, and (I think) emphasises their musical breadth." Fellow ET correspondent David Bronstein said: "Compared to the Boston show this past summer, I thought tonight's show was tighter, had better sound quality, and certainly 'rocked' much harder than the other show … Fripp, who stayed in the shadows in Boston, was much more visible (though never off his seat) and enthused. When the first set was over he shared a big grin with AB when they took their bows."

Eagle-eared listeners will notice that part of the improv in *THRAK* turned up on *THRaKaTTaK*'s *The Slaughter Of The Innocents*.

18 NOVEMBER 1995 – PALACE THEATER, NEW HAVEN

A different day and a different dynamic! Once again the setlist has been tweaked, putting *B'Boom* in prime position as curtain raiser with a strong, bustling improvisation not too long after in *THRAK*. Belew mentions the now-infamous Toast Bass – Levin's Music Man bass guitar destroyed in a fire, which would later grace the artwork of the *THRaKaTTaK* album – after a cracking *Neurotica* once again benefiting from its pairing with *Two Sticks*. "I imagine some of you will be among the 50 million viewers tomorrow night who will see the Beatles Anthology, and here for the first time, a brand new song called *Free As A Bird*, which has been a closely guarded secret throughout the industry, but as it happens, I have a demo tape of it with just John Lennon's voice and piano, and a lot of missing words. But I'll give you a world preview. You can say you heard it first here before the rest of the world." He then launches into what was then the still-unreleased Lennon ballad which would be remade by the surviving Beatles and ELO's Jeff Lynne. Fripp can be heard "yo"-ing encouragement after this interesting interlude in the Crimson setlist.

20 NOVEMBER 1995 – LONGACRE THEATRE, NEW YORK

The first in a five-night run in New York, and not surprisingly the Crim machine is pretty slick and well-oiled by now after an extensive North American tour. Opening with Belew's solo rendition of The Beatles' *Free As A Bird*, we move quickly into more regular Crimson territory. The gear shift seems to come in a frantic *Neurotica*, which seems appropriate given the setting and the subject matter despite the vocal trigger not being quite as synched as it might be. The improvisation in *THRAK* was later edited into *Fearless And Highly THRaKked* for the *THRaKaTTaK* album and it's formidable stuff indeed. Just in case you thought they'd peaked by the end of the gig, Fripp's circular solo over the coda makes for a truly hair-raising experience. Not a bad way to say hello to New York! Part of this concert was first released as KCCC 5/6.

21 NOVEMBER 1995 – LONGACRE THEATRE, NEW YORK

ET eyewitness Emory noted: "I attended the Tuesday night gig, first row mezzanine. Although I found the town hall gigs slightly fresher, some of the stuff done that evening was more interesting. Although the first couple of tunes were fairly rote, Levin and Bruford really started to get into it. At the beginning of *Thela Hun Ginjeet*, Bruford would not quit playing that intro, turning it into a fairly extended solo that seemed to amuse Belew quite a bit, who turned to look, waiting for a cue to start the rest of the tune. My brother the drummer went nuts: as a jazz drummer, Bruford is his idol. *THRAK* was amazing. When I first heard it on disc, I didn't really get it. But now, I feel it the ultimately expression of this 80s KC abstract-Stockhausenesque-rock-monster sound. It descended into a quietish improv section that seemed like a guided tour through purgatory or something. After it surged upward momentarily, it slunk back down. Soon afterward, Belew pulled it out into *Neurotica* by starting a low wail on his guitar that rose into the *Neurotica* siren. I don't know if they had ended this improv that way before, but they came in perfectly. Quite impressive." Part of this concert was first released as KCCC 5/6.

22 NOVEMBER 1995 – LONGACRE THEATRE, NEW YORK

"Thanks for coming out on this great Thanksgiving night. Are you psyched or what?" enquires Belew after a bulldozing *Red*. One member of the audience – ET eyewitness CV – certainly was. "The improvisation in the middle of *THRAK* was really wonderful. At one point, Adrian scratched his chin while making a scratching noise on the guitar at the same time. The place went nuts! … Adrian really hammed it up during *Indiscipline*. He messed up the words at one point, caught himself, and ran with it. During 'I repeat myself', he just kept going until he hit himself on the side of the head to stop it. At another break, he moved the whammy bar carefully, looked at it, admiring that it was 'just so'. Then he looked up, then looked back down at it some more, and moved it a fraction of an inch and made that sheepish grin that we all love. RF Laughed out loud at Adrian's antics at some points. Robert was really 'in the zone' tonight. The geezer really soloed his ass off tonight. I'm talking god-like brilliance, and I'm not exaggerating as some might. At some points, all of the Crims gave me cause to shake my head in disbelief. This was one of the best two or three shows I've ever seen." Part of this concert was first released as KCCC 5/6.

24 NOVEMBER 1995 – LONGACRE THEATRE, NEW YORK

There are moments in a King Crimson concert where the musical worlds are so much in contrast to each other that it's hard to imagine that it really is the same band. Take *One Time* and *VROOOM VROOOM*. During one, the listener is buoyed aloft into a blissful reverie, carried along a tranquil stream of strings and soundscapes as lyrics about romantic surrender float by. Then, a few scant seconds later, you're bruised and battered, pitched on the turbulent swell between bass and lead lines simultaneously ascending and descending. It's a bit like white water rapids, tossing the listener's attention from one side to another, as the twin waves of the Double Trio edge closer and closer threatening a deluge at any moment. Amid the tightness of the set, the improvisation in *THRAK* is spacious but rather speculative, and never quite takes hold. It's brought to an end by a bombastic orchestral trigger that acts as a kind of lets-get-out-of-here moment. You can hear Belew laugh ruefully at the conclusion of the track. Part of this concert was first released as KCCC 5/6.

25 NOVEMBER 1995 – LONGACRE THEATRE, NEW YORK

Back in 1995, Trey Gunn and Pat Mastelotto were still an unknown quantity for some folks, as Robert Parducci illustrated on ET. "I was a little surprised to finally see what Trey Gunn and Pat Mastelotto look like, since the other players are so familiar to me. A very energetic show from beginning to end. Everyone in the band seemed to be enjoying themselves, each in his own fashion …" Turning attention to the more established members of the troupe, Racheline Maltese noted: "Belew was less chatty than on Wednesday, but personable as always. He had a mishap with part of *Frame By Frame* that he tried to correct, but just couldn't, but otherwise was flawless. I really like *Frame By Frame* so it kinda bummed me out, but in a strange way it amused me too. Fripp is just too good. Perhaps it is his economy of motion that makes his speed and skill so much more astounding, I'm not sure, but there were several times where I just had to stare incredulously, jaw open, at his playing. I am, as per usual, extremely impressed." Part of this concert was first released as KCCC 5/6 and parts of the improvisation in *THRAK* were used in *This Night Wounds Time* and *THRaKaTTaK Part II* from the *THRaKaTTaK* album.

27 NOVEMBER 1995 – PALACE THEATRE, COLUMBUS

ET eyewitness Richard Karma wrote: "The Palace Theatre is a beautiful venue with great acoustics; ideally suited for Crimso … When *Red* was finished, my friend Greg turned to me and said, 'That was absolutely the best – it couldn't get any better than that.' When *VROOOM VROOOM* was over, I turned to Greg and replied 'You were saying something about *Red*?' When *THRAK* ended, I heard: 'That was absolutely the best – it couldn't get any better than that' and after *Sex Sleep Eat Drink Dream*, 'I'm ready to leave now – I don't think I can take anymore.' I agreed, but decided to keep my mouth shut. We stayed … None of which comes even close to describing the evening. Orgasmically, you had to be there. Especially when it lasts the better part of two hours. I have been attending concerts for almost 23 years, and Crimso concerts for the same period. I saw them tour *Larks' Tongues* in '73, *Starless* in '74 (the Pittsburgh show from *The Great Deceiver* boxed set, disc three), *Discipline* in '81, and *Three Of A Perfect Pair* in '84. Of the 187 different events I've seen (including Led Zeppelin, The Who, Genesis and so forth), I have never before felt justified in saying, 'That was the best show I've ever seen.' Until now."

Part of the improvisation in *THRAK* appears on *This Night Wounds Time* from *THRaKaTTaK*.

28 NOVEMBER 1995 – STATE THEATRE, DETROIT

Like many others seeing this tour, ET eyewitness Nick Bratton was especially impressed by Bill and Pat. "The opening tom duet by Bruford and Mastelotto was impressive. They were staring straight into each other's eyes, and I could see Bruford counting out the beat. The real coup de grace of the performance was when, in the middle of *THRAK*, everyone stopped except Adrian, who began playing a piano melody through his midi synth which sounded not too distant from *Fool On The Hill*. The resemblance was strikingly Beatles-esque, and when he began to sing, I realized that King Crimson was covering the 'new' Beatles song, *Free As A Bird*. It was hilarious … The final stunning blow came in the second encore, when Bruford, Mastelotto and Belew took the front of the stage and played a frenetic percussion improvisation on a rack of blocks and the two toms. Bruford's solo was sizzling, and later he and Pat really got down on one tom, Pat playing it with his drumsticks and Bill manipulating the sound by using his palms, fists, and fingers on the surface of the drum head. A truly astounding performance. The crowd was courteous for the most part. The token buffoons who invariably shouted 'Bruford!' during the improv could not match his endurance with their bellows. This was by far the best I have attended."

29 NOVEMBER 1995 – ROSEMONT THEATRE, CHICAGO

The final night of the American tour and a truly tired Crimson turned in a surprisingly sprightly performance. ET's very own Dan Kirkdorffer (future DGM webmaster) was there and shared his thoughts. "It was one highlight after another: *Thela*, *Red*, *Frame* … Belew was radiating his enjoyment right from the very start. It was clear that they were all enjoying playing tonight, and why not – this was their last show of the year. I sensed that this band was performing at such a level, I cannot imagine how they could improve even further. I'd love to think a future release will include something from this show – it was outstanding. The show continued into Fripp's Soundscapes, which were mesmerising. Fripp seemed to be barely doing anything, yet the hall was awash in sound. Soundscapes begat *B'Boom*, *B'Boom* begat *THRAK*, *THRAK* begat … magic! The *THRAK* improv section was at least twice as long as this summer. It seemed to continue for 10, maybe 15 minutes, and Fripp really let fly here … I admit I may not have the trained musician's ear, but I cannot recall hearing any mistakes, miscues, miseffects, or whatever. The band was truly running on all cylinders."

Part of the improvisation in *THRAK* was used in *This Night Wounds Time* and *THRaKaTTaK Part II* on the *THRaKaTTaK* album.

1996

28 MAY 1996 – LE KRAKATOA, BORDEAUX

An incomplete *Conundrum* gets the first gig of the Double Trio's final European tour under way. The band are in fine mettle as they plough through a classic setlist that touches upon almost every period of Crimso's long history. For the first time in 22 years, *21st Century Schizoid Man* is part of a KC concert, though it suffers from a few first-night jitters. Clearly the two drummers are enjoying themselves during *B'Boom*. The collective improv in *THRAK* is an object lesson in how to build up intensity from a standing-still position. Listen out for Fripp's neat signing-off solo at the end of a barnstorming *Neurotica* and the gorgeous Fripp/Gunn duet in the middle section of *Three Of A Perfect Pair*.

30 MAY 1996 – PALACIO DE CONGRESOS, MADRID

The first of two nights in Madrid and Crimson have already tightened up. The interweaving patterns of *Waiting Man* are spellbinding with lots of extra details and rhythms to relish. Belew's solo flows gorgeously over the constantly bubbling backdrop. If you'll forgive the pun, there's a particular driving version of *VROOOM VROOOM*. Although it veers uncomfortably near the edge of the road at some points in this rendition, it is undoubtedly one of the key Crimson signature tracks.

Air-raid siren arcs from Fripp announce the arrival of *THRAK* and the entry into what is an inconclusive but enjoyable improv. Though lacking the collective momentum of the previous concert, there's nevertheless some individual points of interest here.

31 MAY 1996 – PALACIO DE CONGRESOS, MADRID

One of the delights of a soundboard mix is that it occasionally gives you an up-close-and-personal ear-view of instruments that might otherwise go under-appreciated. Tonight it's the percussion and allsorts that threaten to take centre-stage during *The Talking Drum*. *LTIA2*, which had up until now been closing the sets, is a great next salvo. *Frame By Frame* gets a bit lost inside itself after the last verse and you can almost hear the anxious counting going on as various players attempt to get themselves back into the correct position. A cracking version regardless of the Russian roulette of spinning notes. Lovely to hear *The Sheltering Sky* again. The band had played it very occasionally during 1995. It's relative rarity makes it very special. Trey Gunn takes the first proper solo with beautifully transcendent results and Fripp's contribution is nothing short of sublime.

1 JUNE 1996 – AUDITORIO Y CONGRESOS, MURCIA

One of the highlights of this tour is listening to the speed of Ade's count-in for *Frame By Frame*. The resulting tempo is met with a heady mixture of excitement and sheer terror! This one's a bit of a smoker, to be sure. Although *One Time* was scheduled to be on the setlist after *Dinosaur* you can hear Belew making an on-the-fly alteration, urging the rest of the team to move on to *Red*. A good decision, it maintains a real sense of energy and momentum. Hurtling through *THRAK*, filled with ghostly sustained lines, distressed-sounding seagulls, rumbling percussion and gothic strings, an energetic *Waiting Man* and the raucous rough and tumble of *Indiscipline*, the pace finally slows down and gives way to the chilled climes of *The Sheltering Sky*. The remarkable energy generated in the first hour of this gig is quite spectacular even by Crimson's standards.

3 JUNE 1996 – AUDITORIUM MAURICE-RAVEL, LYON

"The only love affair I ever had was with music," said the great French composer whose name the venue commemorates. Appropriately enough, there's a bit of passion audibly present from both band and audience tonight especially after an indispensable *Indiscipline*. Earlier, *VROOOM VROOOM* really begins to find its feet with Tony Levin throwing the bass around with exceptional force and vigour. The introductory section of *B'Boom* languishes under swathes of disconsolate electronica before the real percussive fireworks start. The introductory *THRAK* theme gets a more impressionistic rendition. Levin, this time on upright bass, bows in a line or two from *LTIA* which finds echoes among the tinkling piano sounds and tapping xylophone notes. Gunn throws off some cleverly judged feedback lines which really push the piece into some intriguing encounters with Fripp. At the end, the band kick back to the main theme, this time with a scalpel-sharp edge. All this and arguably the best *Schizoid Man* of the tour to date.

4 JUNE 1996 – ROSENGARTEN-MUSANSAAL, MANNHEIM

Having been left out of the previous concert, *Walking On Air* is restored, providing something of a reflective mood early in the gig. But the swaying atmosphere is short-lived, as *Red* barges in to up the ante. *THRAK* is heavy on the discordant barrelhouse piano until Fripp hits the stomp box and Gunn hogs some of that particularly bright spotlight. Some cautious Bruford excursions tempt a couple of Crims to embellish the beat but they quickly fall away and for a few precious seconds silence falls. The appearance of *Schizoid Man* smack dab in the middle of the gig was sure to have taken a few folks by surprise but it works well and Bill's wacky electronic percussives prior to the soloing section turn a few heads. Belew's break-out is exhilarating and while Fripp's rejoinder is game enough, the two don't quite get to lock heads. *The Sheltering Sky* goes into intriguing harmonic territories after Trey's solo, making it even more special than usual. For a couple of minutes, Crimson seems to be drifting somewhere different, before Fripp steers the team back to the theme. A lovely highlight in a good gig.

5 JUNE 1996 – TEMPODROM, BERLIN

For the second of their eight concerts in Germany, the band take a couple of liberties with the standard set. Principally this involves *The Talking Drum* exploding into *Thela Hun Ginjeet* rather than *LTIA2*. Does it work? Well, expectation is a prison (as somebody once said) and Belew's soloing in the track is extraordinarily out there even by his note-bending standards. It's followed by a hurtling, churning *Neurotica*. *Red*, by comparison, sounds almost laid back. *THRAK*'s skittering brushwork whispers conspiratorially between rising strings, torrents of discordant piano, and waves of scorching bowed bass. The spell is broken when Mastelotto's thundering drums push the band into a few seconds of a bruising avant-rock punch-out. A particularly powerful *LTIA2*, *VROOOM* and *Coda: Marine 475* make a convincing conclusion to a show which has Belew shining brightly throughout.

7 JUNE 1996 – CONGRESS HALL, WARSAW

"Welcome to the No.1 King Crimson concert in Poland," says Belew just seconds after getting things under way with a growling solo during *LTIA2*. Jacek Czajka, writing on ET, wrote: "I think it was one of the most beautiful days of my life." Another punter, Marcin Gokieli, added: "Never believe in what people write as KC gig reviews. I do not think words can tell you anything about such a 'hot date'." Nevertheless Marcin continues: "The tune that came after *Waiting Man* was somewhat similar to *Neurotica*. I mean, the words were the same, and the middle part also. But nothing more." You kind of know what Marcin means. Over time the piece has undergone something of a transformation, evolving from its mutant jazz swing into something far more metallic. On the percussion front, *Prism* makes its debut on the setlist. For Ferenc Riesz, "*Red*, *Schizoid Man* and *The Sheltering Sky* were the finest moments of the show." *The Sheltering Sky* is indeed a highlight. Crimson are starting to hit their stride.

9 JUNE 1996 – TANZBRUNNEN, COLOGNE

Respected German guitarist and looper Michael Peters was at Cologne and shared his thoughts with Elephant Talk, saying: "I had not been too optimistic about this concert: Last year's KC Duesseldorf concert had been somewhat frustrating for me – although everything was perfect, I wasn't very thrilled for some reason. Now, reviews of the *THRaKaTTaK* tour said that there were no new pieces, so of course I expected something like last year's concert to happen more or less again. I actually thought, why bother going there at all only to see the same old stuff? Well, I went there anyway and I was thrilled to hear, yes, nothing but pieces that I already knew – but with an *amazing* amount of newness to them in arrangement and interpretation. All pieces had been worked on, not only the obvious classics like *Schizoid Man.* The pieces were arranged in a much more interesting way and played with even more vigour, virtuosity, preciseness and fun. (Sound and mix were also very good). The very same pieces that had left me (and many others), well, not very much impressed last year really blew my mind this time. Several times, I found myself crying at the sheer intensity of pieces I had never especially liked."

10 JUNE 1996 – ALTE OPER, FRANKFURT

A strong performance that sees the team ripping through the setlist with an almost absurd level of confidence. Yet it's always interesting that coming out of the heat of the main set, the improvised section of *THRAK* often comes across as somewhat tentative. Here, the established fragmentary nature of previous improvs pretty much keeps each musician in their separate corners, rather than having any of them tackle each other directly. A well-received run of *Schizoid Man*, *Waiting Man* and the adrenaline-infused *Neurotica* ensure the energy levels are high until a temporary pitstop under *The Sheltering Sky* provides a modicum of shade from the bright lights. Gunn's work here is stunning once again. *Elephant Talk* is dispatched with extreme vigour, while *Matte Kudasai*, which can suffer from being played a touch too briskly, makes a lovely swaying appearance.

11 JUNE 1996 – MEISTERSINGERHALLE, NURNBERG

Jan Kertzscher had been to a couple of other gigs on the German leg. On ET, he wrote: "The sound was much better this time than in Mannheim, at least on the balcony (interesting that when Adrian Belew's voice was far too high in the mix at the beginning of *Dinosaur* he gave a quick sign to the sound engineer at the right of the stage, who immediately fixed it). Especially good were *Larks' Tongues* with a good solo from Adrian Belew, *THRAK* featuring sounds like from a zoo on stage (my neighbour said 'I can't stand this', which is a good sign, isn't it?) and *Prism*, the drum trio Mastelotto-Bruford-Belew so committed even Pat Mastelotto loses one of his drumsticks."

I'd also add that the ferocious set-closer *Indiscipline*, with Belew's opening solo and Fripp's blasted, splintered chords, is worth your attention.

13 JUNE 1996 – WESTFALENPARK, DORTMUND

After a decent run-through the first five numbers, somehow Crimson shift gears, with *VROOOM VROOOM* particularly lethal. The delicate bells ushering in *B'Boom* give the punters time to catch their breath, but thereafter, Crimson really ramp up the excitement. *THRAK*'s improv is like something out of a demented horror movie with shock-and-awe percussion, creeping bass and pensive, sweeping strings. Even the appearance of a straightforward backbeat does little to dispel the ominous air. Fripp and Gunn's briefly intertwining duet is astonishingly powerful. After all that drama, *Schizoid Man* takes things to the next level, dominated by a louder-than-usual Fripp solo. Just these five tracks on their own provide a truly magnificent 25 minutes.

14 JUNE 1996 – STADTPARK, HAMBURG

Arguably one of the best pieces of music to get a Crimson gig settled down, this show's *Thela Hun Ginjeet* rattles along, full of fiery vim and brash dynamics. Quicker than you can shout "Wooh" in between the breaks near the end of *Schizoid Man* (and people really do), the team push on to a swaggering *Dinosaur* and an especially combative *Red*. There's a wonderfully serpentine improvisation in *THRAK* which eventually explodes into *Schizoid Man*. The transition took audience member Alex Brugger by surprise. "Unlike last Tuesday in Nuremberg *THRAK* was not played completely but the long (and once again superb) improvisation directly segued into *Schizoid Man*. I actually missed the end of *THRAK* – it's so bloody powerful, especially when you're in the first row." *Schizoid Man* itself is especially top-drawer. Highly recommended.

15 JUNE 1996 – STADTHALLE, CHEMNITZ

In his diary, Tony Levin seemed circumspect about this one and Presov: "Chemnitz in Germany, and Presov in Slovak Rep. were … well, the audiences were very enthusiastic – a pleasure to play for." Whatever the reasons for TLev's reticence, listening to the last show in Germany reveals something of a corker. There's a different kind of energy and attention in *One Time*. *VROOOM VROOOM* has a real edge and *B'Boom*, with its spectral soundscape opening, is one of the crispest of the tour. There's an excellent *THRAK* improv. Set in motion by Ade's *3OAPP*-style piano arpeggios, the team embark on a jazzy excursion that erupts into fiery interplay – Gunn's lead soloing is brief but makes its point with great eloquence. Gunn also provides some tasteful notes to *The Sheltering Sky*. Listen out at around the 3.30 mark when Fripp releases some ascending/descending arcs of spacey sound that he normally uses at the end of *THRAK*. Did he trigger the wrong patch on the pedalboard or was it intentional? Who cares. It's drop-dead gorgeous. *Schizoid Man* is nailed, pinning back the audience's ears and stunning them into silence in the breaks.

17 JUNE 1996 – PALACE OF CULTURE, PRAGUE

"Ahoy!" says Belew as the good ship Crim docks in Prague. The eccentricities of this soundboard mix puts the spotlight firmly on Tony's upright bass during the intro and outro of *THRAK*. During the improv Bill conjures a rhythm not unlike his beguiling solo on *The Drum Also Waltzes* from his collaboration with Patrick Moraz on the album *Flags*. With some strong contributions from Fripp, there's again a tentative feel to this section. Despite times where the energy levels sag, Miroslav Langer, describing his experience for ET, was more than happy. "There were really BIG ovations. People stood up, screaming, applauding to KC. They returned, played *Lark's Tongues In Aspic*, ovations again … I haven't seen so nice concert, so excited people … nothing could compare to it."

18 JUNE 1996 – AMPHITHEATRE, PRESOV

"Welcome to the first-ever King Crimson in Slovakia. We're very happy to be here – and a big hello to our Polish friends as well," says Belew working the sell-out concert like the pro he is. The improv in *THRAK* is propelled by a wonderful double-drum blast that serves as a fast-moving platform for sonic mayhem, with Gunn and Belew sneaking in soaring guitar work in just under blasts and booms. After the ballyhoo of *Schizoid Man*, *Waiting Man* has a real spring in its step with Bruford's marimba visiting some interesting variations. In *Elephant Talk*, Belew's solo really cuts through and Bruford's solo is cracking stuff on *Indiscipline*, although the song as a whole is taken at an uncannily speed as though hurrying to get to the end. That said, the final solos between Fripp and Belew shred!

19 JUNE 1996 – PETOFI CSARNOK, BUDAPEST

The start of this open-air gig was delayed for over an hour because of bad weather. Ferenc Riesz recalls: "Just before KC appeared on the stage, a beautiful rainbow appeared in the sky … They started with *The Talking Drum*. It was short, but featured an excellent Fripp solo! Then came *LTIA2*. It sounded like on *USA*! Especially, Levin's bassline was remarkable."

"Thanks for waiting in the rain. We appreciate it," says Belew after the scorching openers. If Crimson had sounded a little tired the previous evening, tonight they're firing on all cylinders. *B'Boom* borders on being one of the most percussive work-outs Bruford and Mastelotto have turned out so far, and *THRAK* has some especially acerbic interplay. The reappearance of *Three Of A Perfect Pair* is also welcome. An excellent gig.

21 JUNE 1996 – FIERA DI MILANO, MILAN

Crimson are really on fine form at this outdoor concert. From the very first note of *Thela Hun Ginjeet* you can tell that they're in command. Assertive renditions of *Red* and *Frame By Frame* whip along like there's no tomorrow. Little wonder Belew lets fly with a satisfied "yeah!" at the end of a flawless *Dinosaur*. After a sprightly *3OAPP*, it's the ambiguous bleeping and droning of *B'Boom* and the darkness of *THRAK*. A ray of sunshine is clearly needed and it comes with *Waiting Man* and *The Sheltering Sky*, on which Gunn's smooth solo lines are wonderfully lyrical and beautifully judged.

22 JUNE 1996 – ARENA ALPE ADRIA, LIGNANO

Not for the first time on this tour, rain almost stopped play at this outdoor concert. However, as Alessandro Bagno told ET readers: "The rain stopped graciously falling to welcome the appearance of KC. It was a really awesome view, the stage having an ominous cloudy sky for background, with strong gusts of wind." A good performance although later the weather moved in again, perhaps dampening the spirits of those present. The improv during *THRAK* contains some superb moments. After a busy rhythmic work-out, the piece coalesces into a steadily-building momentum akin to a military march with Fripp and Gunn's respective guitars howling and screaming.

One of the best of the tour. *Schizoid Man* is nailed although *Red* wobbles alarmingly toward the end. "It began to rain heavily and at a point Fripp just quit playing, trying to dry his hands, and the concert came to an end rather abruptly" says Mr Bagno. Tony Levin adds: "Really got soaked at the Lignano show … on the last encore, we abbreviated *Red* by visual cue as all our guitars got drenched."

24 JUNE 1996 – TENDA PARTENOPE, NAPLES

Indiscipline crops up earlier than usual, summoning up an early frenzied attack usually set aside for the end of a performance. Fripp's frantic chordal work-out on the last section shreds. No wonder we hear Bruford exclaiming "Wa-hey!" and "good one!". With *One Time* providing a brief pause, *VROOOM VROOOM* rocks out. Bruford says: "Wow what a set!" A barnstorming *Neurotica* throws us directly into the bubbling strangeness of electronica-crossed double-drumming of *B'Boom* and *THRAK*. On this occasion there's a steady backbeat with Robert dropping huge piano-FX doom chords, making it sound like very much like a new composition in the making. It catches the group in a spot of intense, but surprisingly melodic improvisation.

25 JUNE 1996 – CENTRALINO FORO ITALICO, ROME

The Crims are firing on all cylinders. After *Red*, *Frame By Frame* whooshes off like a greyhound out of a trap. How does Old Chuckles Fripp deal with it? Well let's just say it's a safe bet he blew the smoke off his fingertips at the end. *The Sheltering Sky* moves into a strange space set partly by Fripp's reinterpretation of the main theme which then leads into a serpentine solo from Gunn. The Bruford/Mastelotto partnership is given extra-sharp focus with a frankly jaw-dropping *B'Boom*. The band are clearly in the zone for a remarkable *THRAK* where the improvised section sounds like a tightly scripted collage mixing primeval rock and 12-tone serialism; it might be the best version ever. Oh, and *Schizoid Man* and *LTIA2* aren't too shabby either.

26 JUNE 1996 – TOWN CENTRE SQUARE, PISA

"Best show for me was the town centre in Pisa, with wonderful view and weather," wrote Tony Levin in his online diary. All of the Italian gigs had been outdoor and the weather had not been exactly kind. Tonight though, the Crims would remain dry for the duration. The improvised section leads off with fearsome columns of buzzsaw guitar lines and breaks out into a riotous flurry of Belew-driven soloing underpinned by another outbreak of Crimson on the march; relentless back-beat a la *Coda: Marine 475* with a dread, unstoppable menace that sends shivers down the spine. But Crimson isn't just about the darkness. Indeed, the run of tracks that includes *One Time*, *VROOOM VROOOM*, *Neurotica*, *B'Boom*, *THRAK*, *Waiting Man*, *Schizoid Man* and *The Sheltering Sky* is a remarkable 50 minutes that act as a demonstration of what makes Crimson special: energy, intensity and eclecticism – to borrow a phrase!

28 JUNE 1996 – PALAIS DES BRAUX-ARTS, BRUSSELS

"Friday night. How do you feel? All right? I know there's a lot of languages here so I'll just speak English," says our genial host. Of course the one language that everyone in the Centre for Fine Arts understands is music, and there's plenty of that tonight. This was Erik Matthysen's second Crimson concert and he told ET: "Even though no new material was played (except for drum solos and *THRaKaTTaK*) the set was quite different from last year (nine new songs out of 20 played). *Schizoid Man* was an absolute highlight. The band played it as if they wrote the song themselves, and yet remained true to the original version. It fitted amazingly well with the rest of the material. A definite killer."

A good show with a couple of interesting moments – *Dinosaur* gets slightly out of sync and *Elephant Talk* comes complete with a surprise reprise! One suspects that some members of the band were more surprised than some members of the audience.

29 JUNE 1996 – CONGRESGEBOUW, THE HAGUE

"Something you've waited a long time for," says Belew just before *21st Century Schizoid Man* and arguably one of his best solos on the song, the long opening notes a kind of echo of the original but suffused with his own irrepressible personality. When Fripp joins the fray he opts for an angular contrast, spiky runs and leaps. Eventually, the two guitarists lock together into a single sustained note that heralds the return to the intricacies of the final section. But it's definitely a gig of two halves. It's not until *Schizoid Man* that the band really seem to hit the mark. *The Sheltering Sky* gives Trey Gunn a centre-stage moment where he plays a gorgeous sinuous solo, gently undulating, as though blown by the wind. Belew's chordal work here is equally captivating, gently rising and falling, content to be adding to the reflective reverie. Flat-out rocking is the order of the day on *VROOOM VROOOM* and there's more metrical mayhem during *Sex Sleep Eat Drink Dream*. *Elephant Talk* is taken something of a gallop, while Fripp's solo in *Indiscipline* sounds like a fanfare for the horsemen of the apocalypse.

30 JUNE 1996 – SHEPHERDS BUSH EMPIRE, LONDON

"Wow. King Crimson with a moshpit. This is going to be a very special evening," says Belew observing the standing-room-only crowd crushed to the front of the stage at KC's first night in London. It's a gig brimming with atmosphere. Audience member Trevor Lever recalled: "I have seen KC around 20/25 times. The last time I was this close to the band was at the Marquee in London in 73/74. Being this close, and seeing the nods, winks, signs and appreciation the players showed to each other contributed immensely to a very enjoyable show. The only downside was the mix where I was standing. I could hear mostly Adrian and Tony, some Bill and Pat and hardly any Robert or Trey. However, the climax of the set for me was the *THRaKaTTaK* improvisation. Much more powerful and focused than anything on the *THRaKaTTaK* album. The rhythm section were really pushing things along at a pace, until a moment of beauty appeared as Tony and Adrian's improvisations worked closely around the same note as a focal point. Joined, eventually by Robert and Trey, the four then started playing very long, almost piercing notes, that slid past one another, but had a single tone at the centre. Very hard to explain, but an amazing sound. For me this was the highlight of a very enjoyable evening."

1 JULY 1996 – SHEPHERDS BUSH EMPIRE, LONDON

The gigs at Shepherds Bush Empire weren't just a pair of hot dates. They were a couple of scorchers. Although the band had been in town only a year before, the rather formal setting of the Royal Albert Hall had led to a slightly muted occasion. By contrast, the Empire was far more exciting. And who would have thought *Schizoid Man* would be knocking them dead a full 22 years after it had last been played? There's a storming *Three Of A Perfect Pair* (best live group version yet?) and the eerie *String Quartet* – a precursor to *Sus_Tayn_Z*? Am I the only who thinks it's a pity they didn't do more of that kind of thing? Elsewhere, *B'Boom* is a savage crowd-pleaser and *Frame By Frame* positively blows yer socks off, as Robert noted in his diary: "*Frame By Frame* is blasting away at an astonishing tempo. *FxF* was never written to be played at this speed. But in the fire of the moment, and in the context of the particular overall tempo of the unfolding performance, the front man hits the tempo that feels right; and the guitarist stage left is hung out to dry."

This concert was released as *The Collectable King Crimson Volume Three* (DGM5003).

26 AUGUST 1996 – MANN CENTER, PHILADELPHIA

With over 150 gigs under its collective belt this is the last live performance by the Double Trio. What we hear is a band undoubtedly tired and feeling the strains of an intensive and energy-consuming schedule. Bruford has remarked that his last show playing under the King Crimson banner was "played out with packs of ice, and through a fog of painkillers" thanks to a wrist injury. Being professionals they carry off a performance which probably doesn't count as one of their best but is lifted aloft by an enthusiastic and supportive crowd. They hurtle through the set like cross-country runners desperate to reach the finishing line. In what might well be the quickest version of *Indiscipline*, Belew delivers the words at breakneck speed, while the haste with which *LTIA2* is dispatched borders on the indecent.

This concert was first released as KCCC38 in 2008.

2000

FRIPP BELEW GUNN MASTELOTTO

19 MAY 2000 – 12th & PORTER, NASHVILLE

"Thanks for coming to the world premiere of most of the notes we know … and a few we don't," quips Belew after the Double Duo take to the stage for the first of four nights in Nashville before a European tour later that month. The gig also represents the debut of material from *The ConstruKction Of Light*. Of particular interest is the live rendition of *Heaven And Earth*. Having emerged out of the ProjeKct X experiment, the track was primarily the work of Pat Mastelotto and Trey Gunn, who favoured a more instrumental direction picking up on the exploratory work of the ProjeKcts. *FraKctured* is a nail-biting ride. It doesn't quite go according to plan but it's still enthralling. A good-natured if slightly tentative performance, as crinkles and rucks in the system are clearly still being ironed out.

20 MAY 2000 – 12th & PORTER, NASHVILLE

The second night at the 12th & Porter starts out well enough with Belew turning in a truly stunning guitar solo – arguably one of his very best – on *Oyster Soup* but after that things start to go off the rails. There'd been a hint that Robert's rig wasn't behaving as well as it might just ahead of the "spider-fingers" solo. At 5.10 into *FraKctured*, beneath a rolling tidal-wave of aberrant echo, the piece comes to a halt with Fripp announcing with a smile, "We'll be right back! Hold that moment … I'm going to power down and up again." Eyewitness Bill Colrus explained: "Robert's rig crashed during the piece … Adrian kidded that Robert stopped because his 'butt got tired' and an audience member shouted out 'take it from the top', at which time Robert politely declined, and picked it up in the middle …" Bill also makes an observation many more would go to share as the tour got under way. "Trey and Pat were excellent … They got sort of 'covered-up' during the *THRAK* tour, so it was great to HEAR every note they played …"

The instrumental jostle between Belew and Fripp during *Heaven And Earth* is altogether a more ballsier affair than the previous evening's outing.

21 MAY 2000 – 12th & PORTER, NASHVILLE: FIRST SHOW

Performing two sets in one night, you might think Crimson would conserve their energies early on but they decide to go for it. "I'm awfully sorry that shouldn't have happened," says an off-mic Fripp after starting *FraKctured* a touch too early. "That's OK Robert, we forgive you. Now play it right!" laughs Belew as the team go into the piece properly. The band have a greater confidence as this material gets under their fingertips. *Dinosaur* possesses some of the stomp and swagger it had when played by the Double Trio while *Cage* unexpectedly benefits from its loungecore-style treatment, providing some levity. Another beneficiary of this more assertive mood is *VROOOM* despite a touch-and-go moment. *Heaven And Earth* is worth the price of admission alone, despite the absence of the main riff from Trey, coalescing around sumptuous Soundscapes, rhapsodic runs from Belew and a yearning solo in the coda from Fripp.

21 MAY 2000 – 12th & PORTER, NASHVILLE: SECOND SHOW

"We've had a great run here in my hometown …" says Belew near the end of the last of four shows in just three days. Nashville resident Alan provided this description of the small venue for ET readers ahead of the gigs. "It is a wonderfully small club with plenty of tables and a small balcony. For anyone fortunate enough to catch any or all of the shows, you should be in for a real treat … there really is no bad seat in the house (especially if you nab a chair on the first row of the balcony)."

The running notes section of *FraKctured* is executed with the kind of conviction and authority only been hinted at on previous outings. As Gunn and Fripp double up on the ascending outro Belew can be heard whooping with delight. The lurching *Oyster Soup* provides Belew with an opportunity to serve up a wonderfully unhinged solo. There's all kinds of fun going on in there.

27 MAY 2000 – AMAGER BIO, COPENHAGEN

Just six days after their warm-up gigs, the Crims flew into Copenhagen to begin a substantial trek across Europe. It takes them a few numbers to get up to speed but by the time they get to *Oyster Soup* things are slowly starting to cook. Claus Poulsen was in the audience and wrote: "Robert didn't even look once at the audience during the concert. But I'm sure we meant something to him. Anyway, it seemed he enjoyed himself, smiling and watching Belew closely – a lot of communication between them in the front line. Same thing in the back line. Several among the audience were truly shocked at hearing Trey's bass sound and fast lines on the Warr. Pat was seriously trying to smash those goddam plastic pads (it seemed) – powerful. He's a very expressive player and you can watch his face how he's doing. Sometimes troubled during a tricky passage. Then he's angrily attacking the drum kit like a whirlwind. Then smiling sweetly during the highlights. Interesting orchestral/industrial stuff. More, please!"

Pat and Trey's *Heaven And Earth* forms the bulk of *Improv 1* containing some fine soloing from both Belew and Fripp.

28 MAY 2000 – AMAGER BIO, COPENHAGEN

It's clear the Crims are enjoying themselves; an unexpected percussive intervention on *Cage* has Belew guffawing in mid-song, providing him with an opportunity to comment on the beautiful rainbow he'd seen! An excerpt of *Improv 1* was used on the *Heavy ConstruKction* live album under the title *7 Teas*. The slow, smouldering nature of the improv lends an atmospheric dimension to the second night of the show. For connoisseurs of Clams Crimsonique, *VROOOM* will prove especially tasty!

30 MAY 2000 – MUSIKHALLE, HAMBURG

"So, how was the show in Hamburg?" wrote Fripp in his online diary. "The quick answer, probably from all the group, is no idea. The sound onstage was so bad, the entire performance was a fight to hang in: we played to the bounce-back from the hall. George Glossop had no fun at the mixing desk either. He found the sound "brittle" & if he pushed anything a tad, it became overpowering … Pat struggled heroically with equipment malfunction of a major order. The stage set-up put me slightly off-kilter with Adrian, so our eye contact was harder. A battery in my West 48th St guitar died; an Eventide programme failed to ignite. Et cetera. Another night in the life of working players."

Actually the gig wasn't too bad and in some respects holds together better than the Copenhagen shows. *FraKctured* is surprisingly sprightly despite the problems mentioned by Fripp, though *One Time* suffers from a touch of drift here and there. The improv has a slo-mo brooding feel as Belew stretches and drapes a strangulated series of notes across the rumble and roll of the rhythm buddies. All told, one of the more cohesive improvs from the European tour though one suspects that the band's misgivings about the gig prevented its inclusion on the *Heavy ConstruKction* set. *LTIA4* is one of the real highlights, being both incisive and swaggeringly monstrous. Never an easy thing to do but, against the odds, Crimso pull it off.

31 MAY 2000 – COLUMBIA, BERLIN

From the opening seconds it sounds like King Crimson have truly arrived. Powerful, confident and possessed of a driving momentum, this concert marks the best of the dates so far. Belew's soloing during *Oyster Soup* is scorching and the band really open up around him. Following some internal retooling of the piece in the soundcheck, *FraKctured* moves and grooves in a way it's not quite managed before. The improv begins in a subdued fashion before entering a turbo-charged P4-esque zone, enabling Fripp to step out of soundscape mode to briefly hurl a few laser beam bolts about the place. And *LTIA4* is about as good as you could want it to be.

2 JUNE 2000 – SERENADENHOF, NURNBERG

Judging by the missteps on the opening number it sounds as though the team are having monitor problems. Things settle down during *TCOL*, although *FraKctured*'s intro suffers from confusion between the guitarists. Tonight's improv inhabits the body of *Seizure* with Belew and Fripp trading a series of knock-out threatening blows. Bold and muscular, this is an exciting exploration and a highlight of the evening.

3 JUNE 2000 – LIEDERHALLE, STUTTGART

Crimson are up and running from the first note. Belew's soloing throughout the first half borders on manic. *ProzaKc Blues* has real swing and swagger and although *One Time* moves slightly out of kilter it nevertheless creates a spellbinding magic all its own. *FraKctured* is a savage blast particularly on the fast-running lines. Tonight's improv revisits *Seizure* with Belew once again delving into the his ganderbag of strangulated distortion and clanking chords. He doesn't have it all his own way as Fripp lets rip with a late surge of molten ferocity and the two are briefly locked in a surging, swirling duel before Fripp edges out in front. The doomy *Heavy ConstruKction* chords break down into a frenetic burst of fretwork. Despite the apparent chaos they all end at the same point. An edit of this piece was first released on the triple live album *Heavy ConstruKction*. At the end of *Oyster Soup* Fripp can be heard yelling encouraging noises to his colleagues. In his diary, he noted: "The venue tonight was a symphonic hall. Probably superb for an orchestra but utterly inappropriate for a rock group. So, technically, a very hard evening for the players onstage. But the audience were superb: enthusiastic and supportive. This revived my spirits after last night."

4 JUNE 2000 – CIRCUS KRONE, MUNICH

"Once again, a superb and supportive audience … The Circus Krone is a great venue for circuses, and a good atmospheric for groups. But not sound. All the same, we enjoyed playing," observed Robert. Trey Gunn agreed: "(The sound) wasn't as bad as last night in Stuttgart, but it was still pretty crappy. However, the audience really redeemed it, tonight." Belew responds particularly well to the crowd, showering them with power on a lethal *LTIA4*, delivering a great vocal on *Frying Pan* and shining on a convincing *Oyster Soup*. A wild soundboard mix lifts Gunn right up during *TCOL* with stabbing chord work that gives an insight into how these three guitarists worked so well together. "There were some very hot moments in the show tonight: *Seizure*; *Sex*; *Cage*; and *FraKctured* were real high points for me," offers Trey "*Heroes* was a complete limp … I don't know if the tempo was too slow, or if *Sex* was so hot just before it." Hmm. Answers on a postcard, please.

6 JUNE 2000 – MUSEUMSPLATZ, BONN

"A good, supportive audience … had a good-hearted group to play to them. But, as far as we could tell, probably not our best performance," said Robert at the time. But what does he know, eh? Several pieces from this gig would later turn up on the triple live album *Heavy ConstruKction*. With the band forced to use a borrowed PA, Trey observes that the opening sound felt limp and wimpy. The band compensated by playing some of the tunes faster. "I felt myself rushing ahead of the beat with every bar … Eventually we found our stride and the sound came together … The audience seemed generally pleased with having us there and we did three encores. *Thrush* was stunning with a spinning solo from RF and nice ending from myself. We did a new Projekct X improv in the middle of tonight's show and Adrian showed like a demon. Yes!"

7 JUNE 2000 – STADTHALLE, OFFENBACH

A strange beast of a concert that frequently bucks the riders. While *Oyster Soup* (complete with meat-grinding solo from ol' Chicken Fingers) and *Sex Sleep Eat Drink Dream* both have an alluring devil-may-care savagery, *FraKctured* sees KC tested and occasionally found wanting as fluffs and flubs take the piece into uncharted and possibly unwelcome territories. Robert observed "not our best performance", though that's not to say there aren't plenty of gems lurking in the rough patches. Following the improvisation the band seem to put things up a gear with a breathtaking *LTIA4* in which Belew is on devastating form. A sublime *Deception Of The Thrush* takes flight and, despite wobbling precariously in places, *VROOOM* rocks like there's no tomorrow. Trey reckoned: "The sound was fantastic and the band was hot." So one Crim says hot while the other says not. Fearless Crimhead, it's up to you to decide! Parts of the improv and *Cage* appeared on *Heavy ConstruKction*.

9 JUNE 2000 – ARENA, POZNAN

Disgruntled at having to play in a venue he expressly didn't want to play, RF is anything but a happy gigster and don't his mates know it! "For myself, it is certainly hard trying to play a gig when one of the guys really doesn't want to be there," says Trey. "I think, as a group, we played quite well … But it was definitely a case of going 'up a hill backwards' tonight." Not surprisingly, the band sound distracted in a couple of pieces. Nevertheless, there's plenty of good stuff. *Frying Pan* which, thanks to the eccentricities of the soundboard mix, sounds like it's being covered by Nirvana; *Improv I* (excerpted on *Heavy ConstruKction*) contains a terrific solo from Adrian who later in the set even whips off a snippet of *ITCOCK*, while an extremely playful *Improv II* provides the set-up for *Cage*; they even sound like they're having fun. Well, almost. "Adrian: What did you think of tonight? Robert: At the moment I'm radically re-evaluating my life as a working musician."

10 JUNE 2000 – ROMA, WARSAW

The improv appears to be the Crims mounting a search for *Seizure*. At 17 minutes plus and featuring a wayward *Tomorrow Never Knows*, it's a real treat. And how about that fired-up *FraKctured*? The heavy section is one of those moments where you kind of understand what's going on but haven't a clue how it's being done. For Trey Gunn, however, the real heat was elsewhere. "*Thrush* was fantastic. Robert wailed like a demon, and I had the most perfect feedback for my end solo. I have never experienced anything like this before. I could sustain forever. And for the very tail end, the feedback went into a perfect fifth. So, I sung out a parallel melody as if I were David Hykes. The audience was absolutely dead silent as the final note died away into infinity. Then the silence sustained itself for even longer. No applause, no nothing. Beautiful!" Krzysztof Ojczyk was at the gig and shared his impressions on ET. "I was extremely surprised that my favourite guitar solo in the last part of *Deception Of The Thrush* was performed by Trey, not by Robert Fripp. If Robert Fripp was ever anxious for his successor, now he should be sure that he has found him … First thought after end of the show: why didn't I buy ticket for the second gig in Warsaw?"

11 JUNE 2000 – ROMA, WARSAW

Is that the bassline to *Sailor's Tale* being played by Fripp on his phat-bass setting during the opening stages of tonight's improv? Well, close but no cigar. Gunn steps up to the mark and lets fly with some righteous shredding that recalls the glory days of P2 and P4. Then there's a deep-down and dirty duelling bass workout between Robert and Trey providing a bit of light relief before Ade joins in the fun with his customary abuse and misuse of the fretboard. Marcin Gokieli was at the previous night's gig and went back for a second helping. On ET, he wrote: "The character of the thing was a bit different: I think that during the first concert, it was Fripp who led the band, his solos and other work were the most stimulating. On the second one it was a bit different: first, Adrian played loads of fun stuff, mad parts in the most unexpected moments, etc. But THE STAR of the evening was Trey, who really blew everything away. During the improv he played a tremendous 'bass' duet with RF, and a killer 'guitar' solo after. Every note he played was extraordinary. He entered with strange motives in the most arranged songs (*FraKctured*, for example) and was really GREAT. Maybe he does that often, but I do think that he had one of the better nights of the tour."

13 JUNE 2000 – ARCHA THEATRE, PRAGUE

And it had all been going so well until *VROOOM*, as Donnon Murray explained to ET readers. "At the tune's end, Ade broke a string. The roadie came out to retrieve it and Ade went to switch guitars but Pat motioned him to come back behind the drums, which he did. Now this was great and they brought it to a rather dramatic finish but it was at this moment some boob who just doesn't get it decides to take a photo WITH FLASH. Duh. As I said, I was right in the eye of the storm and I was right there for Robert's reaction. Immediately his attention was drawn from looking on amused at Adrian playing drums with Pat and bringing *VROOOM* to a wonderful climax to this rude distraction. He got up, walked to centre-stage and asked that the house lights be brought up. He then asked the gentleman with the camera to surrender his camera to him. No response. He asked again. Still no response. He then walked back to the Lunar Module, put down his guitar and walked off stage. A seemingly disappointed and bewildered band followed soon after ... Of course by this point the rest of us without cameras were freaking out, the plug just having been pulled on one of the best Crimson shows we'd ever seen (OK, I'd ever seen). Apparently, the culprit was caught, though, because a few minutes later Fripp emerged from backstage holding up the confiscated film like a trophy for the crowd to see." The event is partially documented on the *Heavy ConstruKction* triple album. Despite the violation, this is an incredibly strong performance containing two outstanding improvs, a wonderfully fluid *Cage* and an extremely powerful *LTIA4*.

14 JUNE 2000 – HAUS AUENSEE, LEIPZIG

In its past Leipzig has been no stranger to battles of one kind or another and the night when Crimson came to play was no exception. Firstly, the venue presented some difficulties, and secondly Adrian Belew was coming down with a bug which would see the band having to cancel the next two gigs. Not that you can tell from this performance such are Belew's super-trouper tendencies on *TCOL* and *Oyster Soup*. The first improv follows the same format as the previous night; uber-phat Fripp basslines and Gunn going for the jugular with some especially jagged shredding – essentially revisiting ground covered by the ProjeKcts. The explosive gear-shift as Belew solos is both exciting and powerful, leading as it does into a furious and savage run up the fretboard by Fripp. After *One Time* (in which the hall's mains hum becomes the fifth onstage presence) they return to the improv, perhaps while Belew attends to some of his equipment trouble. Though short, it's a fast-moving, highly energetic P3-style excursion with Fripp taking the lead. The second section of *VROOOM* is a real highlight with the band sounding wonderfully loose and ferocious. As with *Dinosaur*, the parts only sound like guidelines rather than something to be slavishly copied.

20 JUNE 2000 – PIAZZA CIMA, CONEGLIANO VENETO

Heading in from Austria, the band arrived at Treviso for a day or so of R&R before this open-air gig attended (for a while anyway) by local dignitaries. Robert's diary noted: "Adrian felt the show was very good. I felt a hole at the centre that the music fell into, and then escaped us. By ProjeKct X (fourth piece) there was no platform from which to take a jump. Actually, a large hole had already appeared to provide the springboard."

That first improv has Robert and Trey in *Heavy ConstruKction* mode as Ade's solo winds and darts between thumping ersatz piano chords. The second improv offers a high-octane take on the *Seizure* riff featuring a fantastically soaring solo from Belew – which was used on *Heavy ConstruKction*. *Dinosaur* has Robert using a slightly different (mistaken?) setting, which produces an unusual harmony effect, and *One Time* becomes so delicate at some points as to almost disappear. Brown-moment-of-the-match award goes to Trey who comes adrift in the first fairy-fingers section of *VROOOM*. Happily his second pass goes by without incident. After a truly thundering *Oyster Soup*, Belew excels himself with a wildly squawking solo that rescues and redeems an *LTIA4* that is probably generously described as indeterminate. Overall an unusual concert which has the band veering dangerously between brutal belligerence and moments of alarming fragility.

21 JUNE 2000 – L'ANFITEATRO, GARDONE RIVIERA

There are some nights when the band are really in the zone and this is one of them. After the bulldozer opening of *Into The Frying Pan*, the way is cleared for *TCOL* to magically hang and hover above the ground. Trey Gunn's work here is outstanding, leading the way in the instrumental sections and then ducking out of view and digging deep in the verses. Gunn changes pace when they head into the first improv, delivering white-hot shards across Mastelotto's stately groove and Fripp's stalking bass FX. It's easy to overlook songs that have been in the setlist for a while but *Dinosaur* is in monstrous form, with a marvellously off-the-wall solo from the Dorset branch of the band. The second improv is based around *Seizure* and may well be a contender for the best of the tour. Fripp uses a slightly different pedal setting and really takes off, his running lines skipping over the undulating grooves. The handover to Belew pushes the drama to another level. This is an incredibly powerful improv as befits a truly powerful gig.

22 JUNE 2000 – CAMPO DELL'AMICIZIA LEGNANO, MILAN

"Hello! Beautiful night," says Belew after high-octane performances of *Frying Pan* and *TCOL*. They go into the first improv of the night with the slow-walk P3 vibe into which Robert sneaks a line from *Sunshine Of Your Love*. Marco Chrappan, attending his very first King Crimson concert, went on to make his very first post on ET about the experience. "I went with a friend of mine who only listened to *THRAK* sometimes. I was anxious about the concert and the other people too! The audience was really mixed, boys, girls, teenagers, husbands and their wives. One guy before the gig shouted 'He did not bring the cymbals too!', referring to the V-drum set ... The sound was just right speaking in terms of volume (I was in the rear section, I bought the cheap ticket, my greatest mistake!), the Warr guitar and the bass drum had a sharp attack but the rest sounded weak (the snares, the guitar and voice). Then came the first improvisation which I did not like much. They also played *Dinosaur*, *One Time*, *Cage*, *VROOOM* and still three tracks from *TCOL* – *FraKctured*, *The World's My Oyster Soup* and *Larks Part 4*, which they played smoothly ... Adrian played a great version of *Three Of A Perfect Pair*. The people gave him a standing ovation."

23 JUNE 2000 – CITTA DELLA MUSICA, ROME

"I sincerely wish we could play another three nights here in Rome," says Belew at the formal end of a set before adding off-mic, "to make up for all the mistakes we made tonight." Such self-critical analysis aside, this is a pretty hot gig and what a blistering improv P3 turn in; fast-moving, dramatic, searing off-the-wall soloing from Gunn and Fripp underpinned, pushed and otherwise heroically propelled by manic Mastelotto drums. This would have been worth the price of admission alone. Pedal problems with Adrian provide an interesting alternative ending to *Dinosaur* and as a result there's a short but sweet improv that sets up *One Time*. Such a shame then that such a great-sounding gig was marred by photography. On ET, Sergio Lombardi took up the story: "Everything was going fine, and the double duo KC incarnation had swept away any nostalgia for Bruford and Levin, when (after *LTIA4*) some fool flashes his camera in Fripp's eye. Very politely, RF goes to Ade's mic, saying: 'An announcement from the guitarist: no photos please!' As a royal retaliation against Rome, *FraKctured* is cut from the set (few noticed this, including us, having read Ade's tracksheet). The concert ends with a fantastic *VROOOM*. Encores: Adrian performs a lovely acoustic *TOAPP*, impressed by our enthusiastic reaction. Then Ade leaves and P3 enters the stage, playing a delicate, dreaming improvisation, including a jewel solo by Trey. When Ade joins the band, ready to play *ProzaKc Blues*, another genius (or the same?) flashes again his camera: Fripp leaves the stage without a blink, and an embarrassed Ade says desolately: 'I think Robert says goodnight.' Lights on, audience shocked. END."

25 JUNE 2000 – L'OLYMPIA, PARIS

"The Paris show, tonight, was a true winner," enthused Trey Gunn in his diary. "The audience gets a nine out of ten in my book. (Nobody gets a ten, so be happy Paris.) They were fantastic. They came purely to listen and receive. And that is a true treasure for a musician. The band also played very well. I couldn't say if it was our best-played show. But, overall it was great."

In the past, Gunn and Fripp have had diametrically opposing experiences of a show. So what did the Happy Gigster of Dorset make of it? "This audience was, for me, the best audience of the tour: supportive, considerate, sophisticated, responsive, engaged, active … In response to their support and demand, we gave a good performance. Not perfect, but when you take a shot, sometimes you miss. Somehow, that doesn't always matter and tonight it didn't."

This leg of the tour was producing some great results. The material from TCOL was bedded down and there was a real authority to the performance. Even the muffed notes in the frenzied section of *FraKctured* have the frisson of an on-the-ropes comeback.

A truly hot gig, which was extensively harvested for the *Heavy ConstruKction* live album. Highly recommended.

27 JUNE 2000 – ZELESTE, BARCELONA

It's a fact that Barcelona is one of the most exciting cities in Europe and it's also a fact that King Crimson is one the most exciting bands in concert. So, put these two incontrovertible facts together and we have a show with a real "Wow!" factor. This is King Crimson on take-no-prisoners mode at a sell-out gig in a city they last played 18 years before. Throughout, they play fast and loose: *Frying Pan* is raw and edgy; Pat unleashes the beast during *VROOOM* – refashioned here into a riotous collision between the V-Drum splashes and the front line. Belew is simply astonishing on *Oyster Soup*: a wild vocal followed up by an even wilder solo that bends and screeches its way into every corner of the hall. At the end you'll hear a "Yo" in a West Country accent by way of endorsement. A couple of minutes of the lengthy improv appeared on *Heavy ConstruKction*. It's a PM drum'n'bass spectacular and when Fripp layers in the *Seizure* chords something really begins to open up in the music. Listen out for Gunn's outrageous solo over Bobby Willcox's walking bass – no wonder he gets a round of applause. The version of *Sex Sleep Eat Drink Dream* here also appeared on *Heavy ConstruKction*.

28 JUNE 2000 – TEATRO KURSAAL, SAN SEBASTIAN

What a difference a day makes. Here the band sound looser and, in places, somewhat distracted. "We had constant small mistakes: pedals pressed when they shouldn't be, or not pressed when they should have been; a monitor man looking away as he was needed so notes got dropped; effect programmes out of sequence or dumped," Fripp wrote in his diary. Certainly the mistakes produced some interesting arisings; in *VROOOM* there's a head-on collision between Fripp and Belew resulting in a tumbling freefall of guitars which they manage to pull out of only at the last minute; *Oyster Soup* has an utterly wild ending and a tentative *FraKctured* vindicates Fripp's assessment that "the centre managed to escape us, for no easily apparent reason". Not everyone in the band agreed, of course. Belew felt it to be a solid performance and he is on especially fine form, turning in jaw-dropping solos on *Oyster Soup* and *LTIA4*. Ade also leads off on the improvisation which Fripp later declared to be "the feeblest improv of this tour". Don't believe a word of it. This is a good one, which you'll know as it was included (in a remixed form and retitled *Beautiful Rainbow*) on *Heavy ConstruKction*. An uneven show for sure but not without merit or appeal.

29 JUNE 2000 – RIVIERA, MADRID

As the European tour inched closer to its conclusion, Crimson delivered a tighter set. Even so, it's interesting to hear that *VROOOM* shares the same "phase shift" as Barcelona, only this time it seems the backline go out of phase with the front line. Was this a new arrangement being tried out or merely just a persistent brown moment brought about by dodgy monitoring? *Oyster Soup* is brilliantly out of kilter, rocking and rolling like a ship in a storm. Belew's guitar is playful, offering up a sensational solo and a hilarious mid-song plea for no pictures. Non-consensual photography and recording was a key factor in robbing this particular concert of one number in particular. As Fripp noted in his diary at the time "As *FraKctured* came closer in the set, I was thinking: there has been some re-equilibration; perhaps the photography has stopped. The centre is coming together. We'll do *FraKctured*. Then, flash. So, tonight no *FraKctured*."

Despite this setback there are a couple of strong improvisations, which appear in highly edited forms on *Heavy ConstruKction*. Listen out, too, for arguably the tour's strongest *Heroes*. Mastelotto blows off the doors at the back, moving the pulse of the tune to grind it out against the beat and the boys at the front, undaunted by Pat's rhythmic detonations, manfully keep swinging.

3 JULY 2000 – SHEPHERDS BUSH EMPIRE, LONDON

So here we are at the final date of Crimson's 2000's long, hard Euro-slog. Filmed by the Bootleg TV crew and included on the *Eyes Wide Open* DVD, the show doesn't always catch alight, even though the band work hard. Struggling with sound problems, it takes a little while for the team to warm up. The first improvisation has a tentative feel where the band individually dip their toes in the water from time to time but don't quite push the boat out. A sprightly trot through *Dinosaur* and a barnstorming *Oyster Soup* feel like the coming-together point, possibly accounting for a more successful improv, containing rare moments such as Adrian's staccato guitar jabs that he would later recycle for *Dangerous Curves*, the *Seizure* bass beat (complete with samples from *Easy Money*), a feisty Fripp blast and Ade's strangulated string-pulling. When combined together, they offer a compelling glimpse of the beast in action. *LTIA4* also has its fair share of thrills and spills with Fripp and Gunn's unison work being especially noteworthy. Belew's solo *Three Of A Perfect Pair* really gets the Empire crowd going, shining a well-deserved spotlight on this vintage number.

2 OCTOBER 2000 – TRIBUTE TO THE LOVE GENERATION, TOKYO

A very polite smattering of applause greets King Crimson on the first date in Japan. This play-in gig, in front of an invited audience, is the first time the team has played in public since London in July. Having had only one rehearsal the day before, a still-jetlagged band begins to acclimatise. "Good evening, fancy meeting you here. So this is what a club is like in Tokyo. Never played one before. Very interesting," says Adrian Belew as a guitar is tuned after a rousing *Thela Hun Ginjeet* and a very brisk *TCOL*. *FraKctured* whips along heroically with only minor diversions towards the end. Despite clearly being tired, Crimson pull off some impressive victories (how about that double time section in *Frame By Frame*'s coda!) in an honourable show.

3 OCTOBER 2000 – KANAGAWA KENMIN HALL, YOKAHAMA

The first night proper of King Crimson's fourth tour of Japan. Five numbers in and the band are sounding like they've arrived in body and in spirit. The blistering runs on *FraKctured* possess that jaw-dropping quality of being incredibly articulate while at the same time utterly brutal. It's a good stepping-off point as they begin to knit together a convincing show with *VROOOM* carpet-bombed throughout by Mastelotto's crunching snare. Mastelotto is at the forefront of the improvisation. As he drives forward a chunky beat that sounds as though it might drop into a *Seizure*-style groove, the rest of the team react with a degree of uncertainty. Fripp embarks on a lead sortie before dropping back to *Seizure*'s string sections, as Belew jams on a nagging chord. It's Gunn who takes the lead solo, all howls and ferocious flurries. There's a moment where the rhythm buddies are out on their own – it's hard to believe it's just two people at the centre of that particular storm. During *Interlude*, Belew goes into the "on soft grey mornings" section of *The Court Of The Crimson King*. Fripp, by now on phat midi bass mode, isn't having any of it. A decidedly odd moment.

4 OCTOBER 2000 – SHIBUYA KOKAIDO, TOKYO

King Crimson bulldoze their way a particularly barbarous *Red*. *Improv I* features Adrian on a waspish setting he would later refine for *Virtuous Circle*, the bass notes of which percolate through the rhythmic patterns. Fripp's lines take on an almost sinuous quality that eventually coalesces into a 13-second sustained note that carries over into the second, rockier excursion. In between *One Time* and *Dinosaur* a fleeting, seconds-long Belew-generated beat offers up an intriguing platform. Yet almost as soon as it arrives, it's gone. "Just thought I'd try that for a second," says the guitarist. There's a few clams but none so naked or apparent as on *LTIA4*. Here it's Ade's rig that fails to rise to the occasion rather than Ade himself, leaving Fripp the arduous task of trying to stay on the back of the beast alone. He stages a quick recovery in time for the fast running notes, executing a faultless run, by which time Ade's rig is back up to speed. At the time, Fripp noted: "The quality of our recoveries are only matched by the abandon which precipitates them." All in all, a very lively show!

5 OCTOBER 2000 – SHIBUYA KOKAIDO, TOKYO

No matter how many times it's performed, and almost no matter which part of the set its placed, *VROOOM* has the capacity to unseat those playing it. Be it the bass melody over the fairy fingers or the re-entry into the verses or the final section, and maybe all points in between, clams await unsuspecting players. Tonight's version gets all four players at some point in its duration. They get back on the horse with a stunning *Frame By Frame*. It's interesting to hear *Cage* deviate from the normal game plan, seemingly coming adrift until, after some paddling, Belew eventually guides it safely back to harbour. The improvs begin in a similarly ambiguous fashion, evoking the ProjeKcts with Gunn and Mastelotto making most of the running. As things settle into a loping, stomping groove, and the piece becomes considerably rockier, Belew offers some acerbic and assertive soloing. The curse of *VROOOM* returns to haunt a troubled *LTIA4*, which stutters and teeters during the early guitar off-set, steadily regaining its composure as it nears the fast-running lines. It's not the fall that kills you, they say, but hitting the ground. Thankfully Crimson stage a heroic recovery.

7 OCTOBER 2000 – SHIBUYA KOKAIDO, TOKYO

King Crimson are undertaking a matinee performance. *Frying Pan* finds Mastelotto moving the groove around in the first verse, enabling Trey Gunn's monster bass to be heard more clearly. Belew's solo at the end is a great example of how he coaxes some of the most extraordinary sounds from the fretboard. The improv is an interesting mix of bristling electronica, the sampled appearance of Jamie Muir and surging soloing from Fripp. Dropping into a modified *Seizure* groove, Belew trails notes on the high end while Fripp digs down deep. It's not as fluid as some of this tour's improvs but interesting nevertheless. Adrian's sounding a little hoarse on *One Time* but recovers nicely on the coda of *LTIA4* and on *Cage*, in which Fripp abandons the electric piano/vibes patch in favour of a tasty, very spacey solo. A very punchy *Oyster Soup*, with good soloing from the frontline guitarists, finishes off the set.

9 OCTOBER 2000 – NAGOYA-SHI KOKAIDO, NAGOYA

You don't hear Trey Gunn's bass so much as feel it during a barnstorming *Red*. Then there's the exceptionally nimble lines he devised for *TCOL*, which Tony Levin in a later incarnation of Crimson described as the hardest thing he'd ever had to play. Gunn is in very good form throughout. The fleet-fingered work during *LTIA4* – when he matches Fripp note for note in the turnaround on the fast-running lines and climb-out before the coda – is breathtaking. The improvs don't quite ever catch fire. There's a listless quality to them. Belew makes a valiant attempts to overcome his sore throat during his solo *Three Of A Perfect Pair*, and after the jokey throat-clearing before *Oyster Soup* seems relieved that this is going to be his last vocal for the night as his guitar solo mimics the wail of an ambulance. Not a bad gig by any stretch but somewhat subdued compared to the others in this run.

10 OCTOBER 2000 – FESTIVAL HALL, OSAKA

The curse of *VROOOM* strikes yet again as Robert's patch goes AWOL until just before the first fairy fingers section. The curse also alights momentarily on Trey, who includes a note that definitely wasn't included in the operating instructions. But this is just a minor wobble in an astonishingly good show containing one of the best renditions of *TCOL* you'll hear. And there's a strong workout through *Frying Pan*, an especially savage *FraKctured* and an ebullient *Oyster Soup* with a blistering solo from Belew. The first improv opens up into a mid-pace groove against which Belew paints with bright, luminous streaks which Fripp follows with some searing lines, ending in shimmering gongs and cymbals, swooping angelic voices and barbed bristling notes. This is made all the more impressive by the jump into a belligerent *LTIA4*. Sadly the opening of the ensuing improvisation is missing and we launch directly into the stomping *Virtuous Circle*-style improv filled with glittering electronica, percussion and doom-laden sorties from Fripp. The Crims more than make up for the previous night's under-par performance with this full-blooded, take-no-prisoners show.

11 OCTOBER 2000 – YUBIN CHOKIN HALL, FUKUOKA

Coming out of a skewed *Oyster Soup* the band go into an extended improv that swirls with glowering electronica, morphing clusters of light and shade and the rolling groove that provides the foundations for *Heaven And Earth*. Fripp's initial solo is cautious and investigatory before letting itself loose. The abrupt change to a thudding tempo heralds a sequence of growls and howls from Belew which the team build to a precipitous, over-the-cliff ending that hurtles into *LTIA4*. After that turbulence, in which Belew turns in a remarkable extended solo, the team wander off into Lynchian electric jolts, tinkling bells and what sounds like plant machinery on the attack. From genteel, whispered beginnings, *Deception Of The Thrush* develops into a complete monster, Fripp contributing what might be his most acerbic soloing to date on this piece. After the storm comes the calm with Trey Gunn's notes twinkling like stars in the firmament. It's a moment of gorgeous resolution.

13 OCTOBER 2000 – IZUMI T-21, SENDAI

An astonishing show. No if, ands or buts. When DGM engineer Alex "Stormy" Mundy heard the tape he declared: "This really is a great show. There is a great *VROOOM*, probably the best I have heard so far from this incarnation of Crim! Pat does a great job of playing all the drum parts on this piece. *Thrush* is very good, with a great solo from Robert!" Elsewhere it's just possible that we have the definitive version of *Seizure* – it's as though all the work of ProjeKct 4 and previous tours have been distilled into a near-perfect eight minutes. And if that wasn't enough there's a rather charming second bell-driven improv. If you ever needed to know why Adrian Belew is the mutt's nuts, then cop your listening gear around his solo on *Oyster Soup* where he not only takes a line for a walk, but swirls it around his head like a lasso. The resulting weird shapes and angular swipes are what make this track and a cracking *LTIA4* stand out.

15 OCTOBER 2000 – SUN PLAZA, TOKYO

The curse of *VROOOM* manifests again tonight, this time pointing firmly at the guitarist from Wimborne, who recalls: "In the first Fairy Fingers on F sharp, suddenly I found myself thinking 'this isn't sharp – it's natural'. So, I modulated down a semitone. Then, realising very quickly it was sharp, modulating back up again. But not quite quick enough. Meanwhile Trey was wondering whether to follow me down, as Adrian was looking at his fingerboard in puzzled disbelief, but decided to stay where he was. A sure sign the band is maturing: if one of the guys goes out on a limb, the other members are now inclined to smile and wave as it snaps beneath them." But why should the good punters of Tokyo's Sun Plaza care about this minor digression? After all they are served up spot-on renditions of *Thela Hun Ginjeet*, *Frame By Frame* and *TCOL* and what might be the most brutal, bulldozing *Oyster Soup* on this tour. And while the guitars come unstuck in time once or twice during *FraKctured*, it must be said that this is an energetic and engaged-sounding Crimso.

16 OCTOBER 2000 – SUN PLAZA, TOKYO

For the last show on this tour, the setlist is radically revamped. Opening with *LTIA4* requires everyone to be fully up to speed from the get-go. And they are. With Adrian's voice fully recovered, *ProzaKc Blues* returns after an absence of three shows. And again, the Crims mix it up, putting *FraKctured* in third rather later in the set. This is an absolute scorcher, with all four members firing on all cylinders. With the two big hitters dispatched so early in the set, there's a risk that things go off the boil. Not so. After the stomping mayhem of *Frying Pan*, the first improvisation is spacey and pensive, quite different to anything before. With its bells and delicate percussion, the second improv foreshadows *The Power To Believe*, with Ade's reverbed guitar creating a space we've not heard previously. After some ProjeKct-style vectoring they go into the precursor of *Virtuous Circle*. Also notable, for the first time on the tour, is *Sex Sleep Eat Drink Dream*. Three days later, the Crims kicked off a new US tour in San Francisco.

19 OCTOBER 2000 – FILLMORE, SAN FRANCISCO

Just two days after stepping off the stage in Tokyo, Crimson walk on to the boards at San Francisco's Fillmore to kick off a marathon autumn tour. With the first half presenting the bulk of *The ConstruKction Of Light*, the opening run hurtles along at some pace. Highlights include Belew's Dylanesque delivery of the vocal coda of *LTIA4*, and the especially savage fast-running lines of *FraKctured*. In the audience seeing Crimson for the first time was Aaron Deglanville. On Elephant Talk, he wrote: "It is immensely impressive to me in retrospect that KC began the first of their three SF shows (the very first show of the US tour, no less) with what may be the most difficult songs in their repertoire: *LTIA4*, *TCOL* and *FraKctured* were all played very early on – a ballsy if inadvisable choice. *LTIA4* began unevenly, plagued by intermittent timing errors until finding its feet about halfway through."

Though Aaron's not wrong, this is a pretty strong opening blast. The first improv in the second set morphs from spacey abstraction into stomping tearaway soloing from Fripp's fiery fretboard.

20 OCTOBER 2000 – FILLMORE, SAN FRANCISCO

The second improv finds the team focussing on a prototype *Virtuous Circle*, which would eventually become *The Power To Believe Part II*. ET eyewitness Adrian Cockcroft, at his first KC gig, said: "I thought the opening *Red* and *Thela* were much less interesting musically than the new tracks from *TCOL*, and *TCOL* itself and *FraKctured* were as amazing to watch as they are to listen to. A couple of pieces were unfamiliar to me. I was accompanied by two lady friends who didn't know KC music at all, and they were very impressed, both by the music as a whole and by the display of virtuosity."

When Belew steps out to do his solo spot he begins by again playing the middle section – "on soft grey mornings widows cry" – from *The Court Of The Crimson King*. As the crowd cheers, he cuts it short. "Just kidding!" he says as he then starts picking *Three Of A Perfect Pair*. What a tease!

21 OCTOBER 2000 – FILLMORE, SAN FRANCISCO

"Man, that's a mouthful," says Adrian after the band have charged through *The ConstruKction Of Light*. "That's a can full of words! Been here more than once?" he asks the crowd. "Yeah, so have I …" The last of a three-night run in San Francisco that had seen supportive cheers and applause on the first night, a peppering of photography in the second and the smell of herbal substances on all three. ET eyewitness Robert

Zeien wrote: "How amazing it is to watch them tackle *FraKctured* and *Larks IV* on stage and absolutely *nail* them. The improvs were what made the Saturday Fillmore show really come alive, though. When those pieces develop and take flight, Crimso transcends the limits of traditional musical performance. On this night the audience was willing to go right along with them. I also have to mention Ade's dramatic solo rendition of *I Left My Heart In San Francisco*, which opened the encore portion of the show. I've always thought of Ade as a good singer, but now I know that should he decide to move on from Crimso he could have a great career as a crooner …"

23 OCTOBER 2000 – HOUSE OF BLUES, LOS ANGELES

While acknowledging that the band didn't play very well on their first night at the House Of Blues, Trey Gunn declared it to be "a hot show. Very hot. Hot with energy that is … I have to scratch it up to the audience again. You little angels, you. What would we do without you?" The crowd can certainly be heard making their presence felt during a variable set of highs and lows. The improvs provide a glimpse of the electronica-based KC music of the ProjeKcts. Driven largely by Mastelotto's ingenious use of samples and on-the-fly editing, we can hear Belew's sarangi-style solo that would later be such a feature of *TPTB II*, as well as a scalding splash of twisted lines in the rhythmic second section. Clearly on something of a roll, he continues to shine on *Oyster Soup* with a superb break. Also there's a dreamy *Cage*, benefiting from some unexpected Fripp string-washes on the chorus. Elsewhere, *FraKctured* rips along like a bucking bronco with Fripp seemingly hanging on by the skin of his teeth. An incomplete *LTIA4* (the opening moments sadly cropped) also comes unstuck in places, and though they just about grab it back, Belew's vocals sound a touch stretched by the coda.

And what was Fripp's take? "I felt it was awful, but why? Did the setlist restrict the show's process? A continual series of small mistakes cumulatively unseated its unfolding. We recovered the flow to a degree during the encores – perhaps 90%, says Pat. David felt London was a better show, but suggests the bar is getting higher for what is accepted as a norm for this Crim."

24 OCTOBER 2000 – HOUSE OF BLUES, LOS ANGELES

The gremlins that stalked the previous evening take a hike here. With an authoritative *LTIA4* (including some gasp-inducing precision stops), a swaggering guest appearance from Hooter J. Johnson on *ProzaKc Blues* and a particularly strong *Frying Pan*, this is a strong set. Fripp thought the band were back on form: "Tuesday night was much more powerful than Monday with band and audience meeting and matching. This is the kind of performance I associate with King Crimson." Gunn wasn't entirely convinced, citing the improvs as somewhat problematic. "They just sucked the life out of the show. I think both Robert and Adrian heard practically nothing to play on these." The first tentatively touches upon the *TPTB* bell tones, while the second eventually finds solid ground on a rock-out *Seizure*. For Trey the show recovered to some extent after *Dinosaur* (here sadly missing the first few bars) going on to something of an emotional climax. "*Heroes* had something very powerful going on inside of it for me," reflected Gunn in his online diary. "I suppose it may just have been 'personal', but my heart began to tear apart inside of that piece. I suppose one of the things about a 'classic' piece is that something both 'universal' AND 'personal' can speak through it. For me this was one of those moments."

25 OCTOBER 2000 – 4TH & B, SAN DIEGO

A slightly unsteady *LTIA4* gets this gig under way, things only coming together several minutes in. "Good evening … so far," laughs Belew as they go into a straightforward *ProzaKc Blues*. Yet once again there's an equipment/monitoring problem that undermines the piece in mid-flight. The band recover by the time Belew's vocals come in, though there's a sense that they only just made it. Things aren't helped when, during *FraKctured*, the settings of Lunar Module are not where their pilot wanted them to be. The result is a fast metal section that consists of Gunn and Mastelotto belting along while Fripp's feet hit the pedalboard buttons as fast as fingers normally would in order to try and correct the course. He gets there, but only just. With Crimson it's not about the mistakes or the malfunctions but the recovery. On this, as elsewhere, they just about manage it. The first improv is fairly inconclusive. The second is a robust turn by the rhythm buddies with circumspect embellishments from Belew and Fripp. There was a degree of consensus among the Crims that this particular gig lacked energy.

27 OCTOBER 2000 – GOTHIC THEATRE, ENGLEWOOD

There's a fantastic moment in *LTIA4* just after Fripp and Gunn's scorching unison lines where you can momentarily hear the roar of approval from the folks in the Gothic a second before the whole band kicks back in. The track has a habit of pummelling listeners into the ground and then, with this section, whisking them aloft. ET eyewitness Kevin Rhoades wrote: "Pat and Trey exchanging mischievous glances, working as tightly together as Tony and Bill; Robert pleased throughout, grimacing only during the painfully fast passages of *FraKctured* and *Larks IV*, often amused by Adrian's antics; and irrepressible, ebullient Ade himself, having the time of his life bending, jabbing and thrashing his Stratocaster all over the place, grinning all the way. By the time they were playing *Red*, Pat was laughing with his mouth wide open from all the energy in the room, although he may have been reacting to the kooks doing whippets in the front row!" Whippets, the urban dictionary informs us, involves the inhalation of nitrous oxide found in refillable whipped cream canisters. Well.

28 OCTOBER 2000 – GOTHIC THEATRE, ENGLEWOOD

"Good evening. It's almost Hallowe'en – I've got my scary face on tonight!" says Belew after a *Thela Hun Ginjeet* that sounds like it's been recast as a thudding four-to-the floor headcrusher. The band sound a little subdued compared to the previous evening, though, with sections of *LTIA4* not quite gelling. Mind, that's not to say there aren't some memorable moments. Kevin Rhoades, who returned for the second night, said: "I thought the setlist and order of the songs worked a little better Saturday night than Friday night; *The ConstruKction Of Light* benefited tremendously by having strong songs before it. In fact, *TCOL* provided the highlight of the evening, when, after Trey and Pat's smoking, blistering introduction, there was a slight pause … then the guys onstage looked at each other … then they started laughing … then the audience started laughing … then Adrian ran to the back of the stage, grabbed something, ran back up to the microphone with his guitar, laughing, and said, 'It works a lot better when it's plugged in!' Cheers and laughter erupted everywhere. Adrian plugged in, Robert gestured with his hand over his head, indicating take it from the top, and Pat and Trey obliged by playing another peerless, fierce intro, after which the band executed the song fabulously."

30 OCTOBER 2000 – PARK WEST, CHICAGO

"Good evening. Almost Happy Hallowe'en," says Adrian a few numbers into the band's first night in Chicago. Thankfully there are no horror stories to speak of – at least none on stage. Offstage however, ET eyewitness Michael Flaherty reported that: "The band was extremely tight … perhaps too tight. The P3 set was ruined by a drunk yelling for *Starless* during Fripp's Soundscape … Fripp stopped playing and they moved to Trey's setpiece, which was a highlight. During the improv, there was nearly a fight by Trey's side of the stage … someone threatening a woman with a cane because she had asked him to be quiet so she could hear the band. In both cases, other members of the audience shut up the drunks, who were not representative of Monday's audience, but damage was done." Mercifully none of this is apparent on the archive recording and, for the record, the version of *Deception Of The Thrush* is a beauty.

31 OCTOBER 2000 – PARK WEST, CHICAGO

"Robert just said I'm suppurating," says an amused Adrian Belew ahead of his solo *Three Of A Perfect Pair*. "Does anybody know what that means? I'll give you ten bucks if you know what that means. Suppurating … well, whatever it is, that's what I'm doing right now." The gig, which Belew had earlier noted was attended by some members of the audience attired in fancy dress, coincided with Hallowe'en, which might account for both the fun and infernal elements which manifest during a spiffy gig. The transition from *VROOOM* to *Thela Hun Ginjeet* takes place at a lightning pace. After a playful *Dinosaur*, featuring Belew momentarily off-stride and a soaring middle instrumental section from Fripp, the levity is dialled down a little for a brimstone-tinged *LTIA4*, featuring one of Belew's best solos within this beast to date. The second improv covers quite a lot of ground before finally staking a claim in a particular groove, enabling Belew and Fripp to trade a series of escalating blows.

1 NOVEMBER 2000 – PARK WEST, CHICAGO

You can bet your bottom dollar that you will lose your blues listening to this show. It's worth spending some time with the first improv (*Seizure*), a wonderfully restrained but utterly uplifting *Deception Of The Thrush* and a fast-moving second improv.

Fripp referred to this as "the dangerous setlist" and he may have had a point. Michael Flaherty, who attended the first and third of the Chicago run, made clear to ET readers which night he preferred. "I feel like I have seen two different bands:

on Monday a band that is technically perfect, on Wednesday a band that takes risks, makes mistakes, and, unlike the Monday band, never offers a dull moment … On Wednesday everything was different. The audience was more responsive; the band was loose and adventurous. During the improvs Robert was more aggressive, as, I thought, was Pat. One reason for the improvement may have been the mixture of the set. P3 played about a half-hour into the night; on Monday all improv-oriented material was late in the set. This added more variety for performer and listener … They dropped all of the *THRAK* material from Monday, and for the first encore did *Cage* and *Sex Sleep Eat Drink Dream*. They dropped *Thela* and *Oyster* – fewer songs, more space. Maybe this had nothing to do with anything, but I thought it all worked a lot better."

2 NOVEMBER 2000 – MODJESKA THEATER, MILWAUKEE

"Oh sorry, my throat … Whose been smoking pot?" asks Adrian Belew after aborting the first couplet of *Three Of A Perfect Pair*. "Some of it got caught in my throat. OK, we'll try that again," and off he launches into another rendition of the song. Perhaps the smoky conditions encountered in Milwaukee and the effect upon Ade's voice were the cause of the encore being cancelled? However, this sounds like a keeper of a show. There's a vibrancy about much of this performance – the mid-set take-no-prisoners improv features some of Robert's most frenetic runs, which quite rightly draw cheers. It's one of those sets where even the older material sounds bright and fresh; the double-duo double-whammy of *Frame By Frame* and *Elephant Talk* hits hard. Elsewhere, *LTIA4* and *FraKctured* cast long and deep shadows, the latter sounding especially savage. The exhilarating rush that comes from Mastelotto's percussive punctuations as Gunn and Fripp wrangle those writhing notes is one of the reasons this group is so compelling.

4 NOVEMBER 2000 – ODEON, CLEVELAND

They say 13 can be unlucky for some but aside from a couple of Clams Crimsonique (especially in *VROOOM*), Crimson acquit themselves professionally on this their 13th gig of the tour. Some may disagree. Fripp thought the gig sucked, the band being "disjointed and untogether". To these ears, years after the event, this is not a bad show but not one that catches fire as much as one might hope.

8 NOVEMBER 2000 – 9:30 CLUB, WASHINGTON DC

A great little gig this one as the Crims really seem to be enjoying themselves. TJ Mathews observed: "All four band members smiled many times tonight at the 9:30." Eagle-eared listeners will notice that portions of *Thela Hun Ginjeet* sound rather stripped back. Jon Benfield, who was in the audience, explains: "Adrian breaks a string during his first solo. Robert laughed at Adrian as he missed his solo and frantically grabbed another guitar provided by the roadie … Fripp just played right through smiling the whole time." Of *Deception Of The Thrush*, Jon wrote: "Trey was amazing on this tune. Adrian came out to the alcoves above the balcony and waved at us! Trey put on a beautiful show for this one. Robert got up and gave him a standing ovation (we would have stood up had we been sitting!)"

8 NOVEMBER 2000 – 9.30 CLUB, WASHINGTON DC

The second night in DC took place in front of a much-reduced crowd with somewhere in the region of 500–600 punters. Not everyone was there to listen, as Robert noted in his diary. "Directly in front of me: two men talking (shouting) at the top of their voices in conversation. This is the archetypical Crimson fan scenario: having such a great time talking (shouting) about past Crimson glories that they are unavailable to the present, and miss Crimson unfolding right in front of them. During *Thrush* (second encore) finally I stopped and said: 'I feel I'm interrupting your conversation.' The man shouting looked embarrassed and fell quiet. His friend shouted: 'Interrupt us!'" Andrew Baxley shared the view on ET that: "The second night in DC was a much better show … Belew still had some guitar problems (most notably on *Dinosaur* and *Oyster Soup*) but they were less bothersome than the ones he had the night before."

10 NOVEMBER 2000 – PARAMOUNT THEATRE, ASBURY PARK

Opening with *LTIA4* is always risky. There's no opportunity to build up to one of the most demanding pieces in the KC repertoire – but the Crims are on the mark here. There's no part of the piece that is not astonishing – maybe the best of the tour? Who knows? But if you could bottle it, the word on the label would be: FEROCIOUS. "Fripp for President," yells a member of the audience after a flawless *TCOL*, prior to the musical manifesto of *Red*. Solid and steady it proves to be a big vote winner with the punters at the Paramount. There's so many details, both large and small, to admire in this gig. After *Dinosaur*, there's a wonderfully atmospheric interlude, lasting less than 30 seconds, from Fripp and Mastelotto setting up a plaintive *One Time*. It's an unexpected and beautiful gem. Ditto the gentle percolation between *Elephant Talk* and *Cage*. An interesting development during the first improv sounds like the beginnings of a new piece hovering in the wings. Although it doesn't quite arrive there's nevertheless a sense that something was trying to come through. A phenomenal gig.

12 NOVEMBER 2000 – SUPPER CLUB, NEW YORK

There's an uneven surging energy to this performance. Gear failure requires a *TCOL* reboot and Fripp encounters some finger flubs in *FraKctured*. "You enjoy it when we suffer for our art, don't you?" quips Belew. The improvs are short but muscular with Gunn issuing some fiery lines in the first section. The dead stop at around 1.56 is extraordinary and the subsequent vectoring has a thinking-out-loud vibe, as the team consider their next move. How do they get themselves out of the dead end? Switching to earth-shaking frequencies, Gunn's bass lines dig deep, scooping and swooping underneath Mastelotto's frantic turbo-charged clattering. Across the subsequent monster grooving the rhythm buddies establish Fripp and Belew trade a series of lines that spoil for a fight and maul at the air.

13 NOVEMBER 2000 – SUPPER CLUB, NEW YORK

The second night at the Supper Club is an interesting performance. There's a rough edginess to a lot of the music with band nerves also being tested by some (thankfully) brief equipment failure here and there. *LTIA4* is taken at quite a slow pace. The speed only serves to emphasise the lumbering, thudding content. The Mastelotto/ Gunn-led *Interlude* after *Frying Pan* has echoes of the ProjeKcts, creating a varied and ambiguous territory from which *FraKctured* cautiously emerges. This really flies by the seat of its pants with Ade's guitar occasionally missing out and Fripp's moto perpetuo becoming a tightrope walk that frequently teeters ominously over the abyss. The real drama, however, comes when it kicks into the distorted rock section and the furious finger-picking erupts into an uneven but totally thrilling flight. The venue erupts into spontaneous applause and shrieks of delight. At the end, the place goes bananas. A terrific improv around a drum'n'bass-style *Seizure* confirms the sky-high energy level and you can't help but smile at Ade's manful coping in a problem-plagued *Dinosaur* in which he breaks a string, urging the audience to fill in the vocals on his behalf while he tends to it. No wonder he laughs "We made it!" at the end. Fripp's verdict in his diary: "A more fun show for me. Once again, a very enthusiastic audience."

14 NOVEMBER 2000 – TOWN HALL, NEW YORK

Again, some of the surprises are found in the smaller moments. After *LTIA4* the band moves into an improvisation that, not for the first time, invokes and summons the spirit (and hints of the melody) of *The Power To Believe Part II*. The piece subsides and Robert brings in the moto perpetuo section of *FraKctured*. Was the decision to truncate the usual chiming introduction of the piece due to an equipment malfunction from Ade's rig? This seems likely as Ade is absent from the piece and the climb-out before the metal running lines is somewhat uneven as though Fripp were trying to compensate. Only on the last section does Ade seem back in the game. Writing to ET, Michael Russell astutely noted: "The level of musicianship in this band is stunning. I found that I did not miss any of the half-dozen past heroes of this band who have moved on, and who still remain dear in their own right. Instead, I was stuck at the degree to which the current unit functions as a whole. At this level of technical skill, it isn't Bill Bruford or Pat Mastelotto or John Wetton or Tony Levin or Trey Gunn playing a particular line in a particular piece, it is a collective person named King Crimson, whose appearances, sometimes a full decade apart, can be electrifying. In this sense, the continuity between where Crimson has been and where Crimson is going seems as natural as breathing."

16 NOVEMBER 2000 – THEATRE OF LIVING ARTS, PHILADELPHIA

Thela Hun Ginjeet immediately careers down a different road via a spacey interlude before coming back into focus for the chugging punchfest of *LTIA4*. This is a strong-sounding set with the band rocking hard throughout, though not without some off-piste moments. The first improv is an interesting melange of beat-boxy rhythms and handsonic bells melody smeared with vibrant day-glo guitar FX from which the moto perpetuo of *FraKctured* appears. And what a version! Just listen to Mastelotto and Gunn dig deep beneath Fripp's hurtling lines in the trio section – an astonishing feat of precision and power. After some gothic strings at the conclusion of *Frying Pan*, the second improv prowls and growls into place with some roaring elephantosity from

Trey Gunn. The second part thrums like some steam-belching industrial mechanism with Belew's squealing guitar constantly ducking and diving between the galloping beats. Pat's clearly having a wild time with some crazy samples in *Dinosaur*. And he's the star of *Frame By Frame*, beating out fascinating patterns during the verses every bit as beguiling as the phasing from the guitarists.

17 NOVEMBER 2000 – THEATRE OF LIVING ARTS, PHILADELPHIA

Lots of good humour abounds here with some real surprises. *Frying Pan* gives way to an undulating pattern of chugging beats with minimal notes arcing over the top. Ade laughs as they come to the end of the first improv after *ProzaKc Blues*, while the P3 team quickly fly in to whip things up, though this isn't one of their best. There's also a bonus improv to *Cage* which has a gravity the piece sometimes lacks. ET eyewitness Tim Forster recalled: "As they were about to play *Dinosaur*, Adrian inadvertently started an improv, which was to follow. Trey whispered 'We're doing *Dinosaur* …' Adrian said 'Whew, thanks for telling me!' and proceeded to play the opening swells of *Dino* … Between songs, someone yelled '*Easy Money*!' Robert paused (oh no!), then flung his hands in the air, casting an imaginary rope over an imaginary limb, tied this imaginary rope around his neck, pulled upwards and gave a mock choking sound (and a smile). Much laughter and applause!"

19 NOVEMBER 2000 – WEBSTER THEATER, HARTFORD

For reasons unknown this tape is truncated which means that *LTIA4*, *The ConstruKction Of Light* and *Frying Pan* are missing. It's a mystery so it seems that the somewhat spooky sci-fi interlude providing the backdrop to the beginning of this set is entirely appropriate. *FraKctured* is given an especially brutal reading. Gunn is on fiery form in the first improv, quickly handing the baton over to Fripp, whose dextrous digits rain down all kinds of mayhem! The insane tension is maintained throughout the second improv, stomping along at a slower tempo but no less furious. This is a show with lots of unexpected twists and turns.

20 NOVEMBER 2000 – BERKLEE PERFORMANCE CENTER, BOSTON

ET eyewitness Art Cohen thought this performance was "MASSIVE … much more coherent than Sunday night's in Hartford. The *VROOOM* and *Thela Hun Ginjeet* that opened the set were about as good as I could imagine any King Crimson music to be, and *LTIA4* was unbelievably heavy. Once again the band seemed to be having a lot of fun onstage. Adrian even said 'Good evening, I'm your host, Quincy Braintree' at one point(!!)." Meanwhile another eyewitness, Peter Shindler, put it this way: "These guys were like a high-energy punk band (even Fripp, in his own way), playing like their lives depended on it, and loving every second of it."

Pete's not wrong – this stuff absolutely cooks and one of the reasons is Mastelotto's propulsion. Shindler nails it when he observes: "Pat: The perfect drummer for this KC lineup. Not to disparage Bruford, but Pat's got a much better sense of groove, which is totally appropriate here. He rivalled Belew for sheer presence, and I think he generated enough energy on Monday night to power downtown Boston for a few weeks. He's playing the biggest drumset in the world, having augmented his V-drums with some acoustic drums and some random triggers here and there. The earlier comments comparing him to Animal from *The Muppet Show* are quite correct."

21 NOVEMBER 2000 – BERKLEE PERFORMANCE CENTER, BOSTON

Emerging out of a nebulous sample-driven interlude, this could well be the very best version of *FraKctured* of the tour. Not simply because all the parts are expertly executed but because the band, and Fripp in particular, seem to relax and grow into the piece. At the end with the sustained note, it definitely feels like something extraordinary has just taken place. The improvs on this tour are in a sense a collection of fraKctal showreels with different emphasis and contrasting configurations all displayed at breakneck speed. There's no smooth or cautious transitions here but rather a serious of abrupt handbrake turns into alternative grooves, atmospheres and musings. Not all of it works, of course, but there are always moments where the composite elements within the group as a whole become something else entirely – but blink and you might miss it. The improv tonight spills over into what was meant to be *Oyster Soup* but for nearly two minutes drifts off into something else entirely. There's always a fine line between what's formally composed and what comes out of the air. As Pat triggers the guitar sample that introduces *Oyster* but the track doesn't quite materialise, it's as though the improvisation process were reluctant to give itself up, coming back as it were to claim the track from whence it came. All things considered, a rather special concert.

23 NOVEMBER 2000 – LE MÉTROPOLIS, MONTREAL

It's the penultimate night of the tour and so you could forgive Crimson for being a little tired or lacklustre. Yet the performance is by turns jaunty and gutsy. A particularly good improv begins as usual with Trey spraying the napalm and ending up with a straight rock-out underpinned by Fripp's low register growls, Gunn's cyclical riffing and Belew wringing and strangling notes like there's no tomorrow. After a truly barnstorming *Elephant Talk*, Adrian comes out for *Three Of A Perfect Pair* but before he does he steps up to the microphone. "I don't really know this," he says as the crowd fall quiet. "I don't actually know this but I'll try it anyway" and begins playing and singing the first verse of *The Court Of The Crimson King*. The lyrics are subject to the vagaries of Belew's memory but regardless, it's a special moment not just in the setlist but the tour as a whole. When it comes to the chorus, the crowd take up the refrain with great enthusiasm. "You guys are beautiful!" Belew tells them. He's not wrong.

24 NOVEMBER 2000 – THE WAREHOUSE, TORONTO

At the end of a 40-date stint over two months, the Crims arrive in Toronto for their last gig of 2000. Though they're clearly tired and probably looking forward to a well-earned rest, opening with *LTIA4* ensures that the team hit the ground running. Despite the "shock and awe" nature of the piece, there's a playfulness that carries over into a fleet-fingered *TCOL*. Listen out for a brief unscheduled improv between *Frying Pan* and *FraKctured*. Beginning with the mournful string sequence from *Seizure*, things quickly vector off into impressionistic daubs and strange sonic events. Less than two minutes long, it's a nice, if slightly abstract, bonus. When Fripp starts playing the moto perpetuo that signals *FraKctured*, the gimlet-eyed focus snaps back with a vengeance and the band execute a blistering series of twist and turns. Gunn's baritone settings are well to the fore on this soundboard recording, enabling the listener to follow in detail the light and shade which the Warr guitarist brings to this extraordinary piece. The improv proper has a belligerent mood with Fripp's scrabbling sorties across the fretboard flying fast and loose across the pounding deliberation of the rhythm section. This was damned by the faint praise of the Toronto Globe And Mail whose correspondent noted: "It's a highly accomplished outfit, but one that seems to perform more for its own enjoyment than that of the audience." Adding that the band "managed to push the envelope too far, delving into pointless instrumental Sturm und Drang on numbers such as *Lark's Tongues in Aspic, Part IV* and [*TCOL*'s] title cut".

Four days later Fripp began a series of three Soundscape concerts in the Winter Garden of New York's World Financial Center.

2001

14 JUNE 2001 – 12TH & PORTER, NASHVILLE

"Be sure to name this bootleg *Warts And All*," quips a smiling Adrian Belew on the first of four evenings at a particularly hot and sweaty Nashville venue. Replete with cavernous digital reverb effects and a bright somewhat shiny mix that places every error and spontaneous exploration under an unforgiving spotlight, it's nevertheless a great gig. Highlights include a sensational off-the-leash solo from Belew on *Oyster Soup* and, at the end of a new piece called *Response To Stimuli*, indicating his bandmates, he announces: "That's the first time that anything's been sung on that one, even for these guys." The tune would eventually become better known as *Facts Of Life*. Other premieres include the old ProjeKcts favourite *Heavy ConstruKction* containing a nascent *Happy With What You Have To Be Happy With*. Describing it as "an honourable performance", Fripp added: "The audience were very generous and forgiving of the trainwrecks that appeared regularly, even in places never before known to Crim as likely to endanger forward motion. The band were well humoured, even light hearted."

15 JUNE 2001 – 12TH & PORTER, NASHVILLE

If you want to open a show in barnstorming style then *LTIA4* is the way to go. Another mix in which the reverb casts the guitars in a wash of sound as opposed to the customary dryness. Yet that echoing quality lends the track a truly epic feel. There's a drop in levels during the coda but after getting briefly acquainted with the details in the V-drum tom-tom department, everything rises back to something approaching normal. Crimson are stomping things flat right, left and centre, with a particularly deranged *Into The Frying Pan*. *FraKctured* briefly pauses as Robert makes an adjustment to an errant whammy bar. *Level Five*, while powerful, clearly hasn't bedded down yet though *Response To Stimuli (Facts Of Life)* has a fiery attitude that pushes onwards and upwards. While Fripp says that Clams Crimsonique was the only dish on the menu, the thrill and spills of a lively performance provide plenty of grand moments.

16 JUNE 2001 – 12TH & PORTER, NASHVILLE

The third night in Nashville finds the room again hot and sweaty. The early version of *Happy With What You Have To Be Happy With* finally finds its feet although the idea of bookending it with the *Heavy ConstruKction* theme is still something of an awkward fit. *Response To Stimuli/Facts Of Life* also has greater definition and sense of purpose. *FraKctured* is taken at a fearsome lick, providing a real white-knuckle ride, and arguably the real keeper for the night despite the odd metrical mishap here and there. After a comfortable *Dinosaur* and brisk trot through *Thela Hun Ginjeet*, *Virtuous Circle* makes its first appearance in this run. Revolving around a sinuous Gunn groove, various lines of enquiry are advanced by Belew and Fripp, the latter restricted to dreamy atmospherics while the former introduces some terse, jagged chords whose abrasive quality instills a sense of gnawing tension. *Level Five* also seems to have found its final shape. And yet Fripp notes in his diary: "Tonight's show lacked the integrity that characterised the performance yesterday."

17 JUNE 2001 – 12TH & PORTER, NASHVILLE

"Not only are we playing these shows for the pure pleasure of playing in front of you people tonight but we're also trying out brand new material in the hopes that some huge magnificent band like Tool will ask us to go on tour or something … and we can show 'em where it all came from," laughs Belew, tongue firmly in cheek. The fourth and final evening at 12th & Porter begins with an explosive *Level Five*. Adrian's high-octane guitar solo strips the paint off the walls and the tour-de-force continues with a fast-moving *TCOL*. Speed and fleet-fingered pace are features of a truncated *FraKctured* which bursts abruptly into life on the aggressive middle section instead of its usual fade in on the moto perpetuo. Belew quips that it was "close enough for … something". "Close enough" might also describe a slightly chaotic *VROOOM* and a good-natured *Dinosaur*. The material in development has a more pronounced focus before. Clearly, there was still work to be done but instrumentally the main structures are firmly in place.

10 AUGUST 2001 – COMMUNITY THEATER, BERKELEY

Crimson sound remarkably relaxed on the sixth of nine dates supporting Tool. Yet they retain a tight focus on a setlist designed to deliver the maximum impact. *Into The Frying Pan* rocks out thanks to a big backbeat from the Mastobeast and the acetylene blast of the twin guitars sound like they'd cut through sheet metal like butter. Could be the track of the gig! Once again it's Pat who stokes the engines on a devastatingly good *Level Five* whose precision detonations send shivers and shockwaves through the audience. Sadly the only downside is that Trey Gunn is often buried in the mix. Although he's often clearly audible (and on some tracks, such as *TCOL*, well to the fore), there are times when that gritty deep-down gut-punch bass lacks the oomph we're accustomed to. However, his solo on *Deception Of The Thrush* just keeps getting bigger and bigger, unfurling and unfolding one gorgeous chorus after another. Despite its "old dog" status, Belew manages to teach *Thela Hun Ginjeet* to perform a few new tricks during a more informal soloing section where his energy and invention are quite simply dazzling. And you've got to love the improvised Tinkerbell introduction to *Red*!

11 AUGUST 2001 – COMMUNITY THEATER, BERKELEY

What a fabulous start to King Crimson's seventh date supporting Tool! Pat's penchant for on-the-fly sampling and pressing his electronic-allsorts button make *Dangerous Curves* akin to an explosive hybrid of electronica and hard-edged rock. Extraneous non-specific noises swirl and snake around Adrian and Trey's steady pulse whilst Pat's clattering and Robert's soaring strings ramp up the excitement. "The next song we're about to play for you is so brand new it hasn't been recorded yet but it has been titled … Level Five," says Adrian ahead of a crushing beast of a version. It's the 19th time the piece had been played since June and there are moments when it sounds not quite fully tamed, threatening to slip off the leash. Threading his way through the titanic machinations of *LTIA4*, Belew pulls off a typically angular solo that nevertheless manages to delve into more reflective areas. It's a sprightly sprint out of the traps for *Frame By Frame* and you get a sense that Robert is hanging on by his fingertips. Add to this some gorgeously supple bass-end work from Gunn, and you've got a version of an old KC classic to sit up and take notice of.

15 AUGUST 2001 – STATE UNIVERSITY OPEN AIR THEATRE, SAN DIEGO

The last gig opening for Tool – part of a wider KC roadtrip which took in 21 concerts as the band tried and tested material for what would become *The Power To Believe* – catches Crimson on dazzling form. Transferred directly from the multi-track ADAT tapes, and mixed by Alex "Stormy" Mundy, the archive recording of this truncated set is a first-class introduction to King Crimson, which of course, for the many Tool fans in the audience, was exactly what it was. The swiping violence of *Level Five* would make even the most battle-weary KC vet stand back in wide-eyed admiration and this *Deception Of The Thrush* captures both sides to Crimson's musical personality, veering between the terrifying and the transcendent. The interlocking sections of *TCOL* are delivered with the kind of full-blooded passion that reminds us how tight a unit the Double Duo could be, while a knockout *LTIA4* has a savage reading of the fast lines from Fripp and a classic Belew solo at the end. A highly charged gig with a tight, uncompromising setlist in which even the older material sounds fresh. During the second portion of *Red*, the team are joined by Tool drummer Danny Carey, who slips behind Pat's kit and joins in. One word describes this gig: Essential.

9 NOVEMBER 2001 – 328 PERFORMANCE HALL, NASHVILLE

"A new Era of Terror emerges," wrote Trey Gunn and so it does. There's the first outing for the decidedly eclectic *EleKtriK*. Admirers of the Masto-beast will notice how he moves the groove into a looser, faux-jazz feel. Robert rocks out in the set-up during *Deception Of The Thrush* while Ade charms the pants off the home crowd during *ProzaKc Blues*. Hampered by monitoring problems, Trey also notes in his diary that despite the brown moments and stinkers "KC was good. I think". Spirited, even skittish, *Red* treads the fine line between stride and swagger. This version, along with *Thrush*, *Thela Hun Ginjeet*, *ProzaKc* and *EleKtriK*, first appeared on KCCC19.

10 NOVEMBER 2001 – 328 PERFORMANCE HALL, NASHVILLE

"*Curves* lured, *Level Five* slammed, *Thela* danced, *EleKtriK* shined and *Virtuous Circle* went somewhere wonderfully beautiful" says Trey of the second night in Nashville. Undoubtedly a hot gig for the band they certainly sound more confident; this version of *Dangerous Curves* delivers, especially if you like your electronica unleashed and unbound. Some missed cues and slippery notes all add to the drama during *Level Five* while *LTIA4* maintains the malevolent, crushing edge that it had acquired on the road. Belew's solo is jaw-droppingly expansive while those running lines written in '69 for *Schizoid Man* were clearly just getting the Great Roberto's fingers warmed up for this moment. Splendid! *Curves*, *Level Five*, *Virtuous Circle*, *Elephant Talk* and *LTIA4* first appeared on KCCC19.

14 NOVEMBER 2001 – THE WARFIELD THEATRE, SAN FRANCISCO

"One of the main reasons we subject you so often to our presence is so we can try out new trainwrecks on you, I mean new material," Belew wisecracks before *EleKtriK*. While there's a few wobbly moments in the ascending section in the middle, you'd have to be especially hard-hearted not to forgive Belew and Fripp a few indiscretions on what is otherwise a delightful light-touch version. It's interesting to hear a chugging guitar figure at the beginning of *Virtuous Circle* (*The Power To Believe II*) and some gorgeous harmonics and sensuous embellishments from Gunn. Beautiful shifting strings from Fripp and prominent percussion make this version rather special. *Level Five* is a rollercoaster ride that rattles and shakes alarmingly but which somehow gets to the other side and *LTIA4* simply pulverises. ET eyewitness Dave Gaither observed: "I am one of those folks who had my doubts about a Bruford/Levin-less King Crimson. At the show in San Francisco last Wednesday I was made to realise how wrong I was. The show was great. Pat played very well and his skills are not clouded by being in the shadows of Bill Bruford. They played a good selection of songs and, as I hoped, they played *Red*, one of my favourites. I am now a reformed fan and will try and see this line-up (or any other) with more of an open mind."

15 NOVEMBER 2001 – UNIVERSAL AMPHITHEATER, LOS ANGELES

Despite a slightly shaky opening, *The ConstruKction Of Light* gets this show off to a flying start although you can tell from the incredulous whoops from the band that they've only just made it. They more than make up for it with a truly ferocious *Into The Frying Pan*. Equipment problems appear to momentarily unseat *EleKtriK* as Ade's "Now that will make you sweat" comment afterwards indicates. *Level Five* reasserts the beast big time and *LTIA4* rages and roars to brilliant effect with Belew being especially potent.

16 NOVEMBER 2001 – WEB THEATRE, PHOENIX

Phoenix marks the start of an interesting, albeit brief, experiment for the setlist. Immediately after a pensive *Dangerous Curves*, the band hurtle into a piece that utilises the biting chords of *LTIA1* – the first time in over 27 years they'd been heard in concert. As Adrian solos the rest of the team coalesce around the growling slouch of *Level Five*. Used for only a few more gigs, it's an idea that never had the chance to be properly developed. *Frame By Frame* offers lots of intriguing details in Trey's work and Pat's constantly inventive percussion and is a true (if surprising) highlight. Belew pulls off a solo on *LTIA4* that's amazing even by his standards. The whoop you hear from Ade at the end lets you know how special it was. ET eyewitness John Moshier wrote: "Was I Impressed? Absolutely. Did I love the show? Probably not. I left feeling more drained than exhilarated. I was not disappointed. This is just very deep, heavy, disturbing stuff … I'm glad I went, and would go again, but I could never see these guys three nights in a row. It would probably do me in or send me to the asylum."

17 NOVEMBER 2001 – HOUSE OF BLUES, LAS VEGAS

Sadly this concert lacks the opening couple of numbers and indeed the opening bars of *TCOL*. That means there's no official record of the *LTIA1/Level Five* mini-epic this time. Yet there are other moments to relish. For example the middle section of *Thela Hun Ginjeet* presents us with an astonishing dogfight between Mastelotto and Belew who rumble, tumble and tangle, pushing and shoving around the sonic stage. It's an example of how exhilarating Crimson can be and in the moments where you least expect it. The segue into *Virtuous Circle* is quite beautiful, as is the momentary frisson between Fripp's dreamy solo and the Mastelotto-triggered Jamie Muir samples. A bruising *LTIA4* also provides plenty of moments which take you aback. Turbo-charged doesn't quite capture it really.

19 NOVEMBER 2001 – PARAMOUNT THEATRE, DENVER

Sometimes things don't go quite according to plan. This concert, which is missing *Dangerous Curves/LTIA1/Level Five Mini-Epic/TCOL*, as well as most of *Into The Frying Pan*, was also notable for a woman who insisted on dancing throughout the opening parts of the set. Her gyrations prompted Fripp to shuffle forwards to the microphone. "It's very rare that I come to the front but there was a lady in the front row who was dancing and I personally have no objection to this, and I appreciate that perhaps if I was sitting behind someone in front of me dancing I'd like them to sit. But … if we can find room for someone to dance at a King Crimson performance, I'd be really grateful." Posterity doesn't record what happened to the dancer but does record a fluffed intro to *EleKtriK* where Robert uses the patch for *TCOL*'s intro piano note. A laughing Belew requests a reboot and things get properly under way. Plagued by technical troubles, Belew bows out for a number as *Deception Of The Thrush* is moved up to the mid-way mark. The crew's efforts to sort out the gremlins, though sterling, aren't entirely successful and Crimso just about make it to the end, via an impressive *LTIA4* and *Virtuous Circle*. An eventful gig but not necessarily for the reasons you'd like!

21 NOVEMBER 2001 – GRAND BALLROOM, GRAND RIVER CENTER, MINNEAPOLIS

If the previous show captured an unsettled and ungainly Crimson, then this is an altogether more persuasive performance. ET eyewitness Darcianne Siefkes wrote: "Crimson really smoked. Any lingering questions about the ability of this 'double duo' to carry the torch were quickly snuffed out. The last time I saw Crimson (*THRAK* tour, double trio) the sound was thick and lush, but it was harder to distinguish the individual parts. My hat's off to Pat and Trey for stepping up to the plate and holding their own. Crimson is a new beast now. *Level Five* and *Dangerous Curves* are amazing new pieces. This four-piece band seems to be really coming into its own identity and a new Crimson is emerging once again. That's one of the things I like about Crimson is the ability to constantly challenge themselves and create new musical forms. On this, the seventh night of the tour, they seemed very at ease and confident with themselves."

23 NOVEMBER 2001 – BARRYMORE THEATRE, MADISON

One of the delights of *Dangerous Curves* is the way Mastelotto constantly seasons the percussion with sampled voices. If you listen carefully, you can hear Fripp's stage announcement at Denver about the dancing lady swirling in the mix. Having got off to a great start, we fly past the mini-epic of *LTIA 1/Level Five*, a wonderfully smooth *TCOL* and a terrific *Into The Frying Pan*. Tonight it sounds like they've got *EleKtriK* pretty much under their fingers. Listen out also for another tiny improv (or "vector" in ProjeKct-speak) as a little curtain-raising before *Thela Hun Ginjeet*. Short but very atmospheric. Belew is on top form during *ProzaKc Blues* and an especially potent *LTIA4*. When Crimson play with this kind of monstrous power it can be overwhelming.

24 NOVEMBER 2001 – CHICAGO THEATRE, CHICAGO

"I just signed my name on the wall upstairs right underneath Frank Sinatra. What a great place this is," says a clearly enthused Belew after a superb *Dangerous Curves* and *Into The Frying Pan*. Whenever Crimson play Chicago something magical seems to happen. Sadly for Adrian Belew, the magic of his vocal cords runs out about halfway through *Dinosaur*. He manfully continues but is clearly struggling. "I'm very sorry to say that the ghost of Frank Sinatra has taken my voice," he laughs. From there on in this becomes an instrumental-only concert. Even though Ade may have lost his voice, Crimson is a long way from losing its collective roar. A powerful *Virtuous Circle* and Belew's raggedly ascending guitar solo during *Level Five* are real triumphs.

25 NOVEMBER 2001 – THE PAGEANT, ST LOUIS

Showing no ill-effects from the previous night, Adrian ploughs into *Frying Pan* with his usual vim and vigour although vocal songs are kept down to a minimum, with *TCOL* and *Elephant Talk* the only others requiring singing. The major change (in deference to Ade's vocal cords perhaps?) is the reintroduction of *VROOOM* and *Coda: Marine 475*. Interesting to hear the truly beautiful but all-too brief Holst-like outro of *Virtuous Circle*, adding to the mystery and dreamy quality of the piece. Fripp burns the plank during the fast-running lines of *LTIA4*. From the pin-drop reverie of *Deception Of The Thrush* to the blasting dynamics of *Level Five* and *Red*, the last 20 minutes represent classic Crimson at its best.

26 NOVEMBER 2001 – THE MURAT EGYPTIAN ROOM, INDIANAPOLIS

Beginning with a truncated *Into The Frying Pan*, the Crims are in sharp form. *VROOOM* sounds a touch more steady than the previous evening, although during the coda Fripp's feet appear to fumble the patches. *Elephant Talk* becomes the only other vocal track as Adrian conserves his voice. *Virtuous Circle* is truly diaphanous with Gunn adding intricate detail around the top end of his Warr Guitar. Of course, he gets to drift off into the stratosphere during a beautiful *Deception Of The Thrush*. And when that cadence comes in toward the end even your goosebumps will have goosebumps! Gorgeous.

28 NOVEMBER 2001 – MADRID THEATRE, KANSAS CITY

KC in KC! The Madrid Theatre is noted for reputedly having received the patronage of notorious gangster Al Capone. With bullet-holes peppering the walls below stage, King Crimson unleash their own firepower in a real highpoint of the tour so far. *Virtuous Circle* becomes wonderfully elongated prior to RF's spectral appearance, with Trey repeating a single note, wafting in the draft of Mastelotto's ever-shifting percussion and allsorts. Pat recalls that "the stage sound was very strong from my seat … and the band seemed to be riding a wave … after Ade broke a string we altered the setlist on the fly and it seemed to have a great flow (shorter set/longer encores)". One eyewitness, Sydburnz, wrote: "One member of the audience was getting into the music so much, he reached up on to the stage and moved some of the equipment which in turn bumped one of the red spotlights right in front of Adrian. Adrian was going into this extensive guitar solo. I was surprised he didn't get thrown off. It took a long time for security to apprehend this dude. He was a big guy. One of the members of the audience tried to pull him away, but to no avail. Also, Robert Fripp didn't do much, but sit there with a content smile on his face watching the others perform while he played his riffs. His back was sorta turned to some of the audience. I felt sorry for them. He wasn't in the spotlight, and even when they took a bow, he was still in the dark."

29 NOVEMBER 2001 – PROMOWEST PAVILION, COLUMBUS

On this tour Crimson were sharing the stage with ex-Led Zep and fellow DGM recording artist John Paul Jones. Naturally, there were lots of folks there who'd never come across KC before. Here's one such eyewitness account of the Columbus show: "Throughout the entire performance, Robert Fripp never looked at the audience. He sat down on a stool set up to the left of Adrian Belew and never took his eyes off of his bandmates during the entire concert. I don't think he was being rude, or showing any contempt for the audience, he just seemed to concentrate on the music, leaving Mr Belew to interact with the crowd, which he did … All of the members of KC are excellent musicians. Sitting as close as I was I was able to see the expressions on their faces. The drummer concentrating on the quick and (to me) unpredictable starts and stops of the songs; Mr Fripp smiling momentarily when something tricky worked out well as the band took the audience on a sonic journey impossible to achieve with more mainstream acts. They were able to really set a unique mood and what I heard stayed with me for days after. Don't ask me about the setlist or anything like that, I haven't a clue. All in all, a concert unlike any other I have ever seen. I'm glad I hung around after Jonesy was through. It was well worth it."

30 NOVEMBER 2001 – CIVIC AUDITORIUM, LAKEWOOD

With *Dangerous Curves* and *Into The Frying Pan* back as the inseparable and, it must be said, unstoppable openers, Belew reflects for a moment on George Harrison, who had died the previous day. *EleKtriK* has a slightly woozy lilt in the picking sections but rocks with confidence, and *TCOL* bounces along with a real spring in its step. *Thela Hun Ginjeet* and *Elephant Talk* seem especially energised.

1 DECEMBER 2001 – MUSIC THEATRE, ROYAL OAK

An undeniably powerful concert. The band just charge ahead, unstoppable and assured without coming across as cocky or self-satisfied. For Mastelotto this was "a great gig – smiles beaming all night – Ade decided to go without a lyric sheet for *TCOL* and when he fumbled (was it was me? or Trey? or Ade?) Robert almost fell off his stool laughing". Of course there's room for some other wonderful moments where things go awry but in doing so, add another layer of drama to the proceedings. During *VROOOM* the guitars cascade worryingly out of sync with each other, eventually coming good by the first fairy-fingers section. It's a brilliant and endearing moment. As in the last few nights, *Virtuous Circle* contains a short but sweet handsonic duet between Belew and Mastelotto, but the real highlight of the gig is a ferocious *LTIA4*, a piece which has been consistently astonishing throughout the tour.

2 DECEMBER 2001 – PALACE THEATRE, GREENSBURG

Towards the end of the gig Ade engages in a little market research: "How many of you have never seen King Crimson until now?" A show of hands reveals that a lot of folks were new to the group, brought in by KC sharing the bill with John Paul Jones. Starting out with a *Dangerous Curves* that sounds like it was directed by David Lynch, Crimson take us on a guided tour of some familiar sights and one or two off the map. One of the fall-outs of soundboard recordings is the way the mix can be slightly out of kilter: *Into The Frying Pan* has a demented-sounding Belew living it large a touch too-close for comfort. Then again, who wants comfort at a Crimson gig? A rock solid *VROOOM* has the chandeliers shaking with Pat in particular crunching, stomping and swinging out on the coda. However the main highlight is the sequence that begins with *Virtuous Circle*, dances with the angels during *Deception Of The Thrush* and ends with a brutally rousing *Level Five*. After all that *Red* almost sounds like an anti-climax!

4 DECEMBER 2001 – UNIVERSITY AT BUFFALO

"No smoking, no video-taping, no photography, and no fun whatsoever," quips Belew. It's a solid gig, *VROOOM* being especially intense and parts of *Virtuous Circle* sounding like an outtake from Talk Talk's classic *Spirit Of Eden*.

Gunn was quoted in the pages of *Pitch* saying: "The language is more sophisticated. There's different shades, different chords, different rhythms and a broader emotional spectrum, which allows us to connect with the audience in infinitely different ways."

5 DECEMBER 2001 – MASSEY HALL, TORONTO

Massey Hall has been the scene of some remarkable Crimson gigs and this one is no exception. Despite feeling unwell (the result of a dodgy tuna sandwich backstage), Mastelotto drums up a storm. "I almost didn't get back for *Thrush* and must have been moving slow setting up for *L5* since Ade started it without me!"

6 DECEMBER 2001 – PLACE DE ARTS, MONTREAL

A change in the running order produces some glitches to the flow here; the changeover between *EleKtriK* and *Level Five* (here moved up earlier in the set) doesn't work as well as it should. Indeed it's a fair few bars before *Level Five* finally "arrives", suffering from drop-outs and fluffed lines. Of these new pieces eyewitness ET correspondent Antoine Caron observed: "It was really a thrill to hear these for the first time, without any expectations. I think it is safe to say that no other rock band requires so much patience and attention from the audience. Not too surprisingly, perhaps, the audience was relatively quiet, trying to digest the new stuff … *The ConstruKction Of Light* was played very well and picked up the pace. Then, another new piece (*Virtuous Circle*?). This one was magnificent, with a lush, exotic atmosphere. I must really commend Pat on his tasty use of samples and assorted sounds (including some from The Talking Drum!), as well as Ade's kalimba/synth sounds. A great way to evoke Crimson's long and magic past. I thought this was a turning point in the concert. The audience seemed more 'into it' and greeted *Lark's Tongues Part 4* with abandon. This one ROCKED so hard. The quality of the playing was unbelievable. Fripp zoomed though his 'impossible' section with such ease! Trey was a monster all the way and Adrian's solo was great. Quite a finish!"

8 DECEMBER 2001 – ORPHEUM THEATRE, BOSTON

Another venue with a long association with Crim-history and another ridiculously powerful gig. "Good evening and welcome to another hour and a half of risky listening. I'll be your host this evening. My name is Quincy Braintree," jokes Belew before *EleKtriK*. Ryan Tassone was 19 when he attended this, his first concert, and shared his observations on ET: "*ConstruKction Of Light* was the best live version I've ever heard. Ade seemingly sang without a list of words, never missed a lyric. Pat and Trey mixed it up awesomely during the 'pain, day, sky, beauty, etc.' bits. They really have a knack for adding rhythmic complexities and odd accents almost whimsically, as if challenging each other and the rest of the group … not to mention the audience.

Deception Of The Thrush was an encore piece. Ade was absent. The talking Warr was intriguing to watch … he's not just hitting random notes with the recording, there's a way he brings out particular lines. Spooky. Then, just as the grand slowdown began, and Trey was about to take his solo over Fripp's strings, we hear 'bzzzzzz …'. Trey mutes his strings with his hand, and Fripp hurriedly checks all his gear, before turning to Trey with a shrug. Like a ferret on steroids, some road crew guy comes scurrying out, adjusts a knob on Adrian's Strat, which was causing the feedback. Trey warmly applauds the roadie, and the audience gets a good laugh. I guess this time the *Thrush* deceived us all … well, Trey just began playing, and the spotlights churned around him like some fog. Truly a magical moment."

9 DECEMBER 2001 – PALACE THEATER, NEW HAVEN

Crimson cook up a potent stew that bubbles and boils here. As ever Belew excels. His vocals on *Thela Hun Ginjeet* sound like he's really revved up. Not just his vocals either. You can hear him shout "Take it boys!" when a string snaps and a swift change-over of guitars is required. For a few seconds, ProjeKct Three steps into the breach. Though no strings may have been snapped during its performance, one of the most arresting tracks of the gig comes from *Virtuous Circle*. As gorgeous as all the layers of guitars are, the ghostly appearance of Jamie Muir thanks to judicious sampling by Pat Mastelotto sends a shiver down the spine of this Crimhead. In fact Mastelotto shines throughout, adding extra musical allsorts in a way that perhaps makes him a Muir for the new millennium?

11 DECEMBER 2011 – TOWER THEATER, PHILADELPHIA

Subscribing to the old maxim "the show must go on", Belew trod the boards at Philadelphia with a sore tooth. ET eyewitness Tim Foster wrote: "At the end of the set someone threw a T-shirt up to Adrian (nice catch!). He looked at it, showed it to Fripp, who looked at it then scrunched his face as if to say 'Oh my …' He then took the shirt and placed it around his neck. After *Thrush*, Adrian came back on and explained to the audience that he had an abscessed tooth that it had been killing him all night. He offered $20 to anyone in the audience who would come backstage and punch him in the mouth. Upon asking if there were any takers, an exuberant Fripp could be seen madly waving his arm in the air. Belew turned to him and said, 'Not you, you already got a f-#%$-ing T-shirt!' Adrian went on to explain that the T-shirt said 'King F-%$#-ing Crimson', and had HIS picture on it (pointing to Fripp). Belew asked 'Why not a group shot?!'"

Tim thought the new material was "absolutely stunning. They continue to build off of ideas presented on *TCOL*, etc., and yet new ideas and textures are being introduced. This incarnation really seems to be hitting its stride and finding its own voice. It's a great shame that *EleKtriK* isn't on the *Level Five* CD (but you still need to pick it up anyway, it's tremendous). *LTIA4* and *Level Five* itself (let's not kid ourselves – *Larks' Tongues In Aspic, V*!) were breathtaking. *Deception Of The Thrush*: This has got to be my current fave – a bit of a new arrangement this time (during the first section), and a jaw-dropping solo from Trey."

Attending the same show, Jeff Sontag had a big "but" about the newer songs in the set. "Not that they were bad, but you've heard it all before, and more inspired, on the *TCOL* album … Is it time for KC to move on – maybe on to the direction some of the ProjeKcts (especially 2 and 3) took?"

Of course you can't please all of the people all of the time, something especially true when it comes to King Crimson fans.

12 DECEMBER 2001 – LISNER AUDITORIUM, WASHINGTON DC

If Belew was still feeling sore from his tooth problems of the previous evening then you'd never know it. *Level Five* is on killing form, even with a couple of dropped lines. There's a bit of rough and tumble during *VROOOM* and a blistering but short solo from Fripp. In order to compensate for trouble with Fripp's rig, there's a short improvisation, heavy on the dense atmospherics from Mastelotto with Belew adding some angular, note-bending squalls. Fripp rejoins the team for a frankly astonishing *LTIA4*.

13 DECEMBER 2001 – BEACON THEATRE, NEW YORK

"Man, I can just smell the testosterone in this room. At least I think that's what I can smell," wisecracks Belew when the band arrive in New York for the tour's penultimate gig. It's a confident Crimson on display here. Even so, there are a few bumps along the way. There's certainly some evidence of the band being a touch tired. ET correspondent Michael Russell wrote: "It's funny, but Crimson truly did seem to be a double duo last night: a fun duo (Pat and Adrian) and a serious duo (Trey and Robert). Pat reminded me of Bill Bruford in spirit: both of them just LOVE to play. Pat exuded the same sheer delight with bashing and crashing, though in terms of style, he's very much his own man. Adrian's broad grin on *Thela* and *LTIA4* was also quite winning. In spirit, Adrian and Pat were communicating a pleasure in the moment that helped make the link for me. Adrian's musical role was akin to his grin; he was repeatedly a Puckish, lighthearted foil for the stoic Fripp. Stoicism was truly the hallmark of the serious duo: both Robert and Trey wore 'Guitar Craft Face' for a good part of the evening. They were both very muddy in the mix at first, and frankly, I was straining to hear Robert at several points throughout the gig. That said, both are instrumental monsters and certainly lived up to their reputations last night. Trey's *Thrush* bit never fails to move me, and Robert's blistering *Part IV* was utterly magnificent. Robert's economy of movement at frenetic fairy fingers moments has always struck me as elegant. If he prefers to face the band more than the audience to facilitate that, then so be it."

14 DECEMBER 2001 – BEACON THEATRE, NEW YORK

"Welcome to the last night of our tour," says Adrian Belew a couple of numbers in. "We're going to kick it out!" And they do. The new material is still rather fluid in places – for example, the end picking section of *EleKtriK* gets a little sticky. That said, the occasional trap in the older repertoire manifests itself as on *The ConstruKction Of Light*, prompting Adrian to declare, "Forgive me, please forgive me. That's two New

York nights in a row that I've messed up those words. Remind me not to write so many words." Eyewitness Kelly Kincy, who had also been at the previous evening's gig, noted: "At one point during *Red*, Belew shouted 'Everybody dance!' and started springing about like mad on the stage. RF actually cracked up at this and a number of people started dancing."

2003

3 MARCH 2003 – THE BIRCHMERE, ALEXANDRIA

With Adrian Belew ill, the rest of the band decided that the show must go on. Thus, on the third night of the third month of the third year in the new millennium (that's a lot of threes!), the other three members – in their guise as ProjeKct 3 – took to the stage for an impromptu night of improvisations and stripped-back versions of the repertoire. Afterwards, Trey, Pat and Robert went back on to answer questions from the audience. Though the music and the Q&A were both officially recorded, when it came to compiling the Birchmere gig for release as part of the KCCC, the Q&A session was missing. We know Pat had a copy of the talk which he sampled and used in Crimson shows later in the tour. The master, however, had vamoosed. Following an announcement on the DGMLive news page, an audience recording of the Q&A was sent to us courtesy of the mighty Vargan.

4 MARCH 2003 – THE BIRCHMERE, ALEXANDRIA

This is the sound of a slightly unbalanced Crimson. Tonight, though, Adrian turned up. Though still clearly unwell, Belew nevertheless helps give a lively and eventful show. In his diary, Fripp comments: "The audience were supportive and generous, and the sound contained and tuned to the room; that is, not loud. Onstage, the sound was interesting. Very much a beginning again performance, with simple errors." Some of the errors Robert refers to can clearly be heard on *EleKtriK*, *Level Five* and *Facts Of Life*. Yet, as so often with Crimson, the potential threats are turned around and the acts of recovery add another frisson. Consequently, *Oyster Soup* is even more of a rollercoaster ride than usual, complete with an unexpected coda from Ol' Spider Fingers. *LTIA4* is an astonishing bulldozer in which Fripp's fast-running lines are delivered with accuracy and gusto while Pat ensures there's a rockier-than-usual punch to the piece.

10 MARCH 2003 – ALBERT ROUSSEAU THEATRE, QUEBEC CITY

What a belter! Although the setlist remains largely unchanged, there are some gigs with an extra-special vibe. Six days into the *The Power To Believe* tour, this concert is one of them. Despite a wobbly start to *The ConstruKction of Light* (sadly missing its opening bars), Crimson soon get to grips with the material. After a spirited *ProzaKc Blues*, *EleKtriK* suffers from a momentary lapse of steadiness but recuperates to become something monstrous and extremely powerful. Follow a stomping *Facts Of Life*, there are a few missteps as they go into *One Time*. While Adrian sounds like he's still getting over his flu-like cold, he provides heroic vocals and positively shines with his guitar solos on a storming *Level Five* and the rollercoaster *Oyster Soup*. Fripp's solo on *TPTB III* is nothing short of stellar, spiralling off into the stratosphere. On a kick-ass *Dangerous Curves* Pat swings like the clappers! The ensemble playing on *LTIA4* is devastating. Although it's easy to point to Belew's solo as a rare treat, here everyone shines: it's an astonishing example of how potent Crimson can be. Encore-wise an otherwise splendid *VROOOM* threatens to come apart near the end but is followed by a frankly riotous *Potato Pie*.

27 MARCH 2003 – LUTHER BURBANK CENTER FOR THE ARTS, SANTA ROSA

"If you don't mind, we'll try another one. I could use the practice!" says Adrian after a wobbly *Dinosaur*. The mid-section in particular counts as something of a classic Crimso clamfest. Then, a truly knockout *VROOOM* brings a solid enough performance to a close. There's something incredibly powerful about the run that runs from *TPTB II* to *LTIA4*. There are so many individual highlights: Adrian's strange, gritty sidewinding solo which opens *TPTB II*; Pat's frenetic in-flight sampling and shifting rhythms during *Dangerous Curves*; Fripp's ferocious runs on *LTIA4*. The only downside is that, just as the track moves into Adrian's solo spot, the recording is abruptly cut off! A great pity. In his diary, Fripp notes: "The negotiation of the space, between audience and performers, took about 70 minutes; then, there seemed to be some mutual accommodation; then, acceptance and applause; then, acknowledgement. Overall, a generous audience."

13 APRIL 2003 – HITOMI MEMORIAL HALL, TOKYO

After over 11 minutes of glorious Soundscaping, the sudden appearance of applause reminds us that (a) this is a King Crimson gig at which members of the audience are listening to Soundscapes (not always the case) and (b) this is a King Crimson gig and the rest of the band have just joined the 'scaping guitarist. The second night of the Japanese tour gets properly under way with a sprightly, incisive *Level Five*. After *One Time*, Adrian says: "It's wonderful to be back in Tokyo," which nets him a round of polite applause from the home crowd. "We all love it here. Can we move here?" A shuffling drum'n'bass vibe not normally heard on *EleKtriK* and an especially powerful *Facts Of Life* stomp the place flat. The group quickly go on to raise everything to blissful heights with the diaphanous waves of *The Power To Believe II*. Stunning.

20 APRIL 2003 – AICHI KOSEI NENKIN KAIKAN, NAGOYA

On the penultimate gig of their Japanese tour, KC sounds oddly poppy. *ProzaKc Blues* seems straighter than usual – with the end section sounding radio friendly. Ditto *Eyes Wide Open*, which has a more commercially polished sheen than other versions. There's an almost bemused silence at the end of the song with more than a hint of a question mark in Ade's "Thanks". *Level Five* delivers an early jolt and a rare outing for *Red* on this part of the tour has a bulldozer quality. "Not bad boys, not bad," says Belew after a fiery *Facts Of Life* in which Robert's revved-up solo scoops the hairs on the back of your neck to attention. *Dangerous Curves* retains its edgy menace with Pat pulling out the electronic mayhem. Fripp noted that the audience were "supportive and generous" while also observing some bumps in the performance. A solid and honourable gig.

8 JUNE 2003 – FINLANDIA HALL, HELSINKI

Five days into their European tour, the team played this sold-out gig. The careful listener will notice an extraneous sound or two at the very beginning of the Soundscape – a result of Fripp initially playing alongside what one eyewitness described as "the Elvis music" being played over the PA prior beforehand. Following an especially assertive *Level Five* and a flawless *TCOL*, *Facts Of Life* takes us into kick-ass territory. The intricate clockwork-toy percussives of *TPTB II* are especially spellbinding, with Ade's abrasive flourishes gliding over the top, and there's also a couple of interesting moments where Fripp departs from script in terms of voice-settings and notes toward the end of *EleKtriK*. The double-whammy of *Dangerous Curves* and *LTIA4* provides highlights from both Mastelotto and Belew. Sadly, the archive's board recording is incomplete with *Deception Of The Thrush*, *Oyster Soup*, *Elephant Talk* and *Red* missing. That said, Alex Mundy's description of the show as "nearly 80 minutes of stomp" is a fairly reliable summation.

20 JUNE 2003 – TEATRO SMERALDO, MILAN

A capacity crowd turned out in Milan and though Fripp performed a Soundscape before the main show his efforts were largely ignored by most of the audience. John Kimber was at the gig. "The Teatro Smeraldo was a magnificent setting for this concert – a very grand theatre. The soundscapes merged seamlessly into *The Power To Believe/Level Five*. The sound mix was fabulous and the band were punchy with Pat's drums sounding like cannons! They played most of *The Power To Believe* album and the emphasis was on the music of the new millennium."

It's interesting to hear how the band recovers from a slightly shaky *Level Five*, the guitars having come momentarily unstuck towards the final run-down. No such mishaps occur during *Facts of Life*, where Fripp tears chunks out of the plasterwork with the ferocity of his solo. Equally brutal is the bulldozing *LTIA4*, including a stunning, freefalling Belew solo. This concert was made available as KCCC39 in 2008.

21 JUNE 2003 – TEATRO CARLO FELICE, GENOVA

"It's been a bit of a strange evening," says Adrian Belew. What can he mean? Well, there are shaky moments and there's a slightly distracted quality to Crimson's overall performance, particularly through *EleKtriK*. Yet a minute later *The Power To Believe II* embarks on a sublime voyage that goes to bliss and back in a little over seven minutes; Fripp launches a solo that takes him off into inner space. Elsewhere, despite struggling with a back injury and the ongoing trauma of finding himself touring Europe (blimey how did that happen?), the guitarist turns in some vintage stuff: the superfast diddly-diddly bits (technical term) on *LTIA4* and a revved-up blaster on *Facts Of Life* are all deserving of further attention. Both a surprisingly brisk *Elephant Talk* with an interesting middle section and *Frame By Frame* positively glisten and sparkle.

5 JULY 2003 – TEATRO CERVANTES, MALAGA

Crim appeared to be in buoyant health in Europe but, as we all know, appearances can be deceptive. "Let me remind you one more time, please don't take a picture. Especially of him," says Adrian after a truly blazing *Level Five*. Fripp's aversion to flash photography had culminated in him repositioning his rig so that he was almost facing the band rather than the audience. Despite worries in his diary about the cumulative effect that all of this was having upon his playing and that of the group, Crimson still turn in a powerful performance. True, *VROOOM* is somewhat tentative but an astringent *Dinosaur*, a cavernous-sounding *The Power To Believe II* (complete with sampled thunder) and a glistening Gunn solo during *Deception Of The Thrush* provide plenty in way of compensation. Pretty much everything from *Happy* really cooks and in the case of *Dangerous Curves* seems to go beyond anything previously attempted to date. Whatever reservations RF might have had, one eyewitness reports that at the end of the evening "he went out from the darkness of the stage and applauded to everybody, to all the audience, as a farewell of a good performance, which is a not usual attitude on Mr Fripp, like you know very well".

13 JULY 2003 – MONTREAUX JAZZ FESTIVAL, MONTREAUX

With only one more date on this leg of the European tour to go, King Crimson wound up in the Miles Davis Hall at the Montreux Jazz Festival. In a weekend programme that included artists as diverse as Joe Jackson, Laurie Anderson and post-rock outfit Mogwai, Crimson served up something of a mixed show, starting off well enough with an incisive *Level Five* and a truly cutting *TCOL*. While preparing the show for download, Mister Stormy declared this version one of the best he's heard. But equipment problems momentarily dog *EleKtriK* and cause *Dinosaur* to teeter. In his diary, Fripp puts some of the blame down to the fact the show was being officially filmed by the festival. "An evening of clams, clunkers, recoveries – all on film." Perhaps the most spectacular of these can be heard during the coda of an otherwise superb *LTIA4*: following the drum roll and pause, both guitarists enter at exactly the same time but in positions on the fretboard not normally considered mutually compatible. With Adrian declaring to Robert that he considered this to be his worst performance in nine years of Crimsonising and Pat M diving off-stage at the end of a savage *Red* to remonstrate with a punter who shot off a load of flashes, this may well be one of the most controversial Crimson shows.

15 JULY 2003 – MILLENARIS CENTRE, BUDAPEST

There's a certain end-of-term aspect here – a rushing *Dinosaur*, a final flush in the cheeks of *Red* as it hits the finishing line. Humour plays its part as well when Belew quips to quell the photographers before a dazzling version of *The ConstruKction Of Light*. The Crimson machinery occasionally goes awry – *Level Five* has a minor disturbance but this doesn't spoil the overall thump and stomp; Belew's maniacal soloing in *LTIA4* is matched only by Fripp's ripping lines in one of the best renditions of the piece. The older material also has a spring in its step; Trey Gunn's animated delivery is a joy, while the soaring theme around the ten-minute mark of the introductory Soundscape is worth the price of admission on its own. All this and belly dancers too? Fripp noted:

"The Bright Idea For The Last Show Of The Tour appeared: two belly dancers. I saw the first come onstage, knew this was TBIFTLSOTT, and kept my focus close. Then, the second. I continued to keep my focus close. A good wheeze, presented and accepted in good humour." A stand-out gig without a doubt.

28 OCTOBER 2003 – HOUSE OF BLUES, ANAHEIM

The second night of the Double Duo's final tour is a little creaky. After a confident build during *Dangerous Curves*, *Level Five* falters badly. Crimson seem rattled. *ProzaKc Blues* is dogged by equipment troubles that take out some of Belew's FX but in doing so creates some interesting spaces within the piece, taken here at a fair old lick. Energy-wise, the set really takes off with *Facts Of Life*, including an absolutely scorching section from Fripp. *The Power To Believe* opens up a mood or feeling not too far removed from the kind of reverie which *The Sheltering Sky* would bring to the setlists of previous incarnations. An uneven gig largely due to equipment and tuning troubles but not without some presence and power. Fripp's take on the gig? "Crimson managed to discover new wrinkles where old wrinkles are well furrowed already, but with spirit and some strong playing. A generous, supportive audience. During the final encore, *Red*, a battery of flashes erupted. They were probably not aimed at me, but my show was killed stone dead. What a pity. After last night, performance seemed an option again."

8 NOVEMBER 2003 – PARK WEST, CHICAGO

"Old men ROCK!" shouts an enthusiastic member of the audience just before the band cut a rug through *TCOL*. Given the power of Mastelotto micro-managing the dynamics from the drumstool, our pal might just have a point. During a phenomenal *Level Five* Ade pulls off one of those mad scientist solos where notes do things they were surely never meant to do! This is the first of two nights at Park West – a venue which the Crims twice visited earlier in the year. Chicago and KC have always had a special relationship – Park West in particular. You get a sense of this bond when Ade introduces *ProzaKc Blues*. *Facts Of Life* is outstanding, taken at a punishing, almost punky, pace with *TPTB II* providing an ethereal but profoundly effective counterweight. Gunn's work is as incisive as ever and it's also interesting just how much Pat's percussion interludes here add an eclectic spice to the dynamics and flow of the gig, with *Happy* being especially effective. The pair also lend a wonderful swing and swagger to *LTIA4*. Minor mishaps aside (Ade experiences technical issues in *Dinosaur* and *One Time*), the band are generating an intense heat and firing on all cylinders.

14 NOVEMBER 2003 – ULSTER PERFORMING ARTS CENTER, KINGSTON

How best to describe the performance here? One word: savage. Taken from the FOH tapes recorded by Greg Dean and mixed with audience mics from multitrack ADATS by Alex Mundy, this is a powerful testament to the latitude and grasp of the Double Duo in the live arena. *Level Five* squashes all before it, packing in more musical weight and density into seven minutes than many groups manage over an entire career. A high-powered and potent *Facts Of Life* is compelling – Fripp's solo is a joy to behold as is Belew's rollercoaster solo on *LTIA4*. *EleKtriK* also has more bite than the album version despite the odd brown moment. Of course with Crimson it's not just a case of being big and clever. There's a spell-binding performance of *The Power To Believe II* in which the yearning of a lifetime is poured into those graceful notes. Despite a dodgy soundcheck, Fripp observes in his diary that the show ". . . began well and got better". With Tony Levin watching in the wings, Ade prophetically signed off with "Thank you you've been a great audience. See you ... probably never." Just four days later, Trey left the band.

16 NOVEMBER 2003 – TOAD'S PLACE, NEW HAVEN

You know it's been one hell of gig when Robert Fripp gets off his stool, wanders centre-stage and says: "It's exceptional nowadays that I step to a microphone and say 'good evening, hippies', but at the completion of this stage of King Crimson touring in America, perhaps something more is needed." At which point he holds up a bra that's been thrown onstage and proceeds to auction it with a KC trivia quiz! Yes, you read that right. A bra. And not just a bra. Balloons thrown on stage as well. Clearly the audience was having a great time, and the band as well. There's definitely something of an end-of-term atmosphere in the music as well. Perhaps it's the relief that weeks of touring is finally coming to an end? Or perhaps it's also awareness of another kind of finality?

Does the knowledge among band members that Trey Gunn is serving out his last days as a Crim impact and impinge on their musical responses? Does it lift their game slightly? Does it encourage each player to wring something other than music from the experience? Are mixed feelings and emotions employing a subtle pull or drag up the dynamics? Maybe it just comes down the fact that knowing that this line-up – together since 1999 – was about to split up, they decided to just flat-out enjoy themselves and savour the fun?